The Urbana Free Library

To renew materials call
217-367-4057

DATE DUE		
~~JAN 0 2 2009~~	~~FEB 2 4 2009~~	
~~MAR 0 3 2009~~	MAR 0 5 2013	

FOUNDED BY BURNS MANTLE

THE BEST PLAYS THEATER
YEARBOOK 2006–2007

JEFFREY ERIC JENKINS
Editor

○○○○○
○○○○○ THE BEST PLAYS
○○○○○ THEATER YEARBOOK
○○○○○
○○○○○

Editorial research and data compilation
for *The Best Plays Theater Yearbook 2006–2007*
has been partly underwritten by a generous grant from
the Harold and Mimi Steinberg Charitable Trust.

Carole A. Krumland, James D. Steinberg, Michael A. Steinberg,
Seth M. Weingarten, William D. Zabel
Directors

O O O O O O O O O O O O O O

THE BEST PLAYS
THEATER YEARBOOK
2006–2007

O O O O O O O O O O O O O O O

EDITED BY

JEFFREY ERIC JENKINS

Illustrated with production photographs

O O O O O

LIMELIGHT EDITIONS
AN IMPRINT OF HAL LEONARD CORPORATION
NEW YORK

Copyright © 2008 by Jeffrey Eric Jenkins

ISBN: 978-0-87910-352-1

ISSN: 1942-339X

Printed in the United States of America

Published in 2008 by
Limelight Editions
An Imprint of Hal Leonard Corporation
7777 West Bluemound Road
Milwaukee, WI 53213

Trade Book Division Editorial Offices
19 West 21st Street, New York, NY 10010
www.limelighteditions.com

INTRODUCTION

EVERY YEAR at this time we spend hundreds of hours checking thousands of names of plays, playwrights, actors, directors, designers, producers and technicians who make our nation's theater. Although it is, at times, an onerous task, it is also a source of unending inspiration to note the names of people who set their lives to the challenge of creating theater in this country. There are, of course, the well-known names of Broadway lore but we should never forget that most people who toil in professional theater in this country do it at some personal sacrifice. In these pages, we celebrate the work of thousands of theater artists throughout the United States. We begin by honoring playwrights in essays on the Best Plays in New York. But we continue by listing details of more than a thousand professional productions throughout the country—including essays on the Steinberg/ATCA New Play honorees from the previous calendar year.

Invariably there comes a moment when we feel as though these persons—these names—have become our friends. (Of course, many of these fine workers in theater are our friends in reality as well; and some are, as the saying goes, friends we've yet to meet.) As we assemble this compendious index, we wonder how many of these people know that their contributions to the larger body of work in United States theater have been recorded for posterity. Before you peruse the remarkable collection of essays from our terrific band of writers or dip into the Broadway and Off Broadway listings to recall the fascinating season of 2006–2007, take a few minutes with the index and see if you do not find yourself astonished by the effort expended to create theatrical work in this country during that year.

One of the more exciting projects of the 2006–07 season was the November 13, 2006, beginning of Suzan-Lori Parks's *365 Days/365 Plays*. For this project—which culminated November 12, 2007, long before this book appears but outside its purview—Parks has written a play a day for a year. The plays (most are just a few minutes in length) are then presented by a vast network of professional, academic and community theaters during the 365 Festival, which is produced by Bonnie Metzgar. It is a remarkable project that brings theater to communities and communities to theater, creating a new sense of possibility for theater in this country. We have listed some of the plays in this book: specifically, those performed at the 2007 Humana Festival of New American Plays in Louisville. Not included in our listing for the Public Theater are the 365 plays, which were read in two parts in 2006—August 17–18 and September 28–29—in anticipation of their impending publication. Participants in the readings included the playwright and her producer (serving as director), stage managers Stephanie Gatton and Taibi Magar, and a roster of some of the finest actors in this country: Rob Campbell, Reg E. Cathey, Kathleen Chalfant, Gail Grate, Peter Francis James, Ty Jones, David Patrick Kelly, Joan MacIntosh, S. Epatha Merkerson, Adina Porter, Michael Potts, Daphne Rubin-Vega, Ching Valdes-Aran. More information is available about the project at www.365days365plays.com.

II

ONCE THE VOTING is done for the Best Plays—by a group that includes our editorial board and selected members of the theatrical press, including a few academics—there is a temptation (a compulsion, perhaps) to find the thread that links these particluar works. Was there a "hip" factor? Possibly. Do these plays tell us something about the state of our culture, of our nation? We would certainly like to think so. Essentially, though, the Best Plays must reflect who we are at a particular moment; must allow us to preserve—as a second-draft of history—a sense of what it was to live in this time and to experience the most human(e) of all the forms of art.

After a season such as 2006–07, that ranged from an epic drama about the failure (or is it folly?) of utopian social ideals to a reconstructed German play from the Victorian-era about adolescents set to contemporary music it is seductive to think that perhaps Broadway audiences have grown more high-minded—or more fascinated with 19th century thought and culture. Those two works, *The Coast of Utopia* by Tom Stoppard and *Spring Awakening* by Steven Sater and Duncan Sheik, which between them received 60 percent of the Tony Awards given this season, are honored herein with essays by Charles Wright and Michael Feingold. Representing Stoppard's eighth Best Play and Sater and Sheik's first, these two pieces challenged audiences in divergent ways. Stoppard's *Coast*, which became the hot ticket of the season, demonstrated that the liberal social theories of the Russian aristocracy were empty-headed enterprises that failed to account for human nature's more base desires. At the other end of the sociopolitcal spectrum, *Spring Awakening* argued for a more open attitude toward those desires—particularly those of the sexual type.

Of the 10 plays this season, seven were written by first-time honorees of this series, always a sign that fresh writing continues to inspire us. In addition to Stoppard, returning honorees include the late August Wilson, whose final play *Radio Golf* marks his 10th (and sadly, final) appearance in this series. *Radio Golf* is an almost-comic elegy about the implications of endings and beginnings in a "blighted" Pittsburgh neighborhood and a fitting capstone to his 10-play cycle devoted to reclaiming the narrative of African-American culture. Christopher Rawson, the Pittsburgh theater critic who has functioned as Wilson's Boswell for the past two decades, offers his assessment of the final installment. Our final returning honoree this season is the always incisive Theresa Rebeck with her second Best Play, *The Scene.* Nominally concerned with those who claw their way to the top of our celebrity-obsessed culture without regard for who gets hurt along the way, Rebeck's play is also the hilariously painful study of a man who falls victim to one of these "culture vultures" (and to his own midlife crisis). Chicago theater critic Chris Jones, who wrote about Rebeck's collaboration with Alexandra Gersten-Vassilaros, *Omnium Gatherum,* for the 2003–04 edition, considers her latest Best Play.

There was an elegiac quality to several of the Best Plays that reflect tellingly where we, as a culture, are situated at the end of the 2006–07 season. In Christopher Shinn's *Dying City*, a gay New York actor tries to discover why his twin brother died in the Iraq War under mysterious, even suspicious circumstances. The actor looks to his brother's widow for answers, but she has none. As the tale unfolds, it becomes apparent that the boys' father—a Vietnam veteran—may be a source of what troubled the late soldier. The answers are not found in the play, but in the audience's consciousness about war and how its effects ripple through society in ways unknown. Charles Isherwood's essay examines the innovative ways in which Shinn moves through the characters's lives. This same haunted perspective also shadows Sarah Ruhl's *The Clean House* and Bruce Norris's *The Pain and the Itch.* In Ruhl's play, to which San Diego critic Anne Marie Welsh lends her analytic talents, characters seem almost to float through the scenes as one woman after another is dislodged from her reality by loss of love, the death of parents and the cruel twists of biological fate that plague the female gender. Despite these challenges, Ruhl's characters forge bonds between and among themselves that should serve as fitting reminders of what we all need to thrive in life: connection to others. It may be a simplistic observation—it certainly looks so on the page—but in an increasingly dislocated world of instant messaging and continuous stimulation, it is possible to forget that "connection" may mean something more than how fast one downloads data from the internet.

The Pain and the Itch is also concerned with dislocation and how the sins of the parents may be visited upon the children. But Norris's point of attack skewers a segment of upper-middle-class conspicuous consumers, whom essayist John Istel is happy to tweak as well, whose sense of entitlement may be familiar to anyone who has attempted to walk in a neighborhood where strollers the size of small automobiles clutter sidewalks as "mommy patrols" intimidate all who pass before them. Norris's characters are concerned only with maintaining their enhanced sense of identity and their privileged lifestyles—until they discover that their lives are as fragile and empty as the shell of a cracked egg.

Three other plays we honor in these pages embark upon visitations of the past as they attempt to unearth perspectives on the human condition. In David Harrower's *Blackbird*, a young woman who had sex with an older man many years earlier finds her former lover and confronts him. The added twist is that she was 12 years old when they had sex and he was in middle age. Has she come to wreak vengeance on this predator? He has served years in prison already. Is his debt to society paid? Is he still a danger? Harrower's taut examination of the nature of desire and taboo made it a compelling choice as a Best Play. Essayist David Cote locates Harrower's play in a modern literary tradition that may be unsettling to polite society. In *Frost/Nixon* by Peter Morgan, one of the most reviled characters of late-20th century American politics, Richard Nixon, took the stage opposite a widely known jetsetter and broadcast personality, David Frost. Set against the backdrop of negotiations for and taping of a series of interviews between Nixon and Frost, the play is most notable for the ways in which it captures the desperation of both men to attain a kind of redemption. Playing first in London and then on Broadway at a time when considerable political discourse centered on ranking the worst US presidents in history, the play made Nixon appear human, deeply flawed and only marginally aware of his shortcomings. While much of what appeared onstage was "true," it is worth noting that playwright Morgan is a dramatist, not a historian. In the play, each man attains some part of what he wanted to gain from the interviews—one audience member even said she could not believe that she found herself, in 2007, missing Richard Nixon's presidency. Elizabeth Drew, who had a recent book on Nixon in print at the time, rang alarm bells in *The Nation* over the distortions represented in the play. Los Angeles critic Charles McNulty finds Drew's references to the play as "propaganda" to be a "misreading" of Morgan's intentions. Ultimately, Morgan's play is a work of fiction and audiences would do well to keep that in mind—dramatic license is one that never requires renewal.

In *Passing Strange*, Stew and Heidi Rodewald collaborated with director Annie Dorsen to create a powerful, resonant picaresque in the form of a musical. A tale of an African-American's journey through the urban Los Angeles middle class and into the European artistic avant garde, *Passing Strange* is a story that anyone—regardless of race, class or ethnicity—who is (or has been) young should find truthful and deeply moving. Critic Alisa Solomon hopes (as do we) that it is not their last work for the theater.

In addition to the plays celebrated in these essays, we also hope that readers enjoy the volume's expanded statistics and index. Whenever possible we track all Broadway and Off Broadway revivals back to their original presentations in New York, around the country and abroad. In the case of William Shakespeare and others of his ilk, we employ George C.D. Odell's *Annals of the New York Stage*—which links with the *Best Plays Theater Yearbook* series to chronicle New York theater back to the 18th century. We also use the archives of *The New York Times* and other major publications as we attempt to locate plays in their original contexts.

With our colleagues in the American Theatre Critics Association, we also keep close tabs on new plays developing in theaters across the US. Through the Harold and Mimi Steinberg Charitable Trust, we recognize the honorees of the Steinberg/ATCA New Play Award and Citations. The Steinberg Charitable Trust, which has supported the *Best Plays Theater Yearbook* series since 2001, recently demonstrated its support of our mission by refocusing its commitment to our work. We extend our deepest thanks to the Trust and its board (William D. Zabel, Carole A. Krumland, James D. Steinberg, Michael A. Steinberg and Seth M. Weingarten) for making *Best Plays Theater Yearbook* a priority for their support.

Honorees for the 2007 Steinberg/ATCA New Play Award and Citations are Peter Sinn Nachtrieb's *Hunter Gatherers*, which won the Steinberg top prize ($25,000). Nachtrieb's play is discussed by Robert Hurwitt. The 2007 Steinberg/ATCA New Play Citations (along with $7,500 each) went to Jeff Daniels for *Guest Artist* (detailed here by Martin F. Kohn), and to Michael Hollinger for *Opus* (essay by George Hatza).

III

AS WE MOVE forward with the 88th volume of this chronicle of theater in the United States, we celebrate the beginning of a reinvigorated partnership with Limelight Editions, now under the management of the terrific publisher Michael Messina.

The collection of data for a volume such as this relies on the labors of many people. Our thanks to Paul Hardt for his efforts on the Cast Replacements and Touring Productions section, and to Garrett Eisler for his essay on Off Off Broadway theater. At a moment when we needed a keen observer of the burgeoning OOB scene, Eisler has provided a thorough and learned perspective. Rue E. Canvin, our retiring USA section editor, has worked on the *Best Plays* series in various capacities for more than 40 years. It is with deep gratitude that we wish her all of the best in the next phase of her admirable career. As we move forward, we welcome Sheryl Arluck and Jennifer Ashley Tepper to the ranks of our assistant editors for the Off Off Broadway and the USA sections. Jonathan Dodd, the longtime publisher of the *Best Plays* series, continues to provide important background information and good advice. In the absence of our dear friend and mentor, the late Henry Hewes, another friend and mentor, Robert Brustein, has generously agreed to accept the consulting editor position that Henry held until the end of his life—though I doubt anyone will ever consult as passionately (or frequently) as Henry.

We are also deeply indebted to all of the press representatives who assisted in the gathering of information for this volume, but we particularly acknowledge Adrian Bryan-Brown and Chris Boneau of Boneau/Bryan-Brown for their unflagging support of the series and its editors.

Thanks also are due to the members of the *Best Plays Theater Yearbook*'s editorial board, who give their imprimatur to our work by their presence on the masthead. We are grateful as well to those who have offered and provided extra support and assistance to this edition: Charles Wright, Christopher Rawson (Theater Hall of Fame Awards), Caldwell Titcomb (Elliot Norton Awards), David A. Rosenberg (Connecticut Critics' Circle Awards), Bill Hirschman (Steinberg/ATCA New Play Award and Citations), Edwin Wilson and Mimi Kilgore (Susan Smith Blackburn Prize) and Michael Kuchwara (New York Drama Critics' Circle Awards).

We especially note the ongoing joint efforts of the *Best Plays* editorial team and the research department of the League of American Theatres and Producers (renamed The Broadway League as we were preparing for press) over the past several years. First with Stephen Greer, later Neal Freeman and now with Jennifer Stewart, we have worked since 2002 to correct the records of the Internet Broadway Database (www.ibdb.com) as well as past errors made in the pages of *Best Plays*. Our thanks and compliments to our friends at the League for their cooperation in this long-term project of correcting the historical record.

We congratulate and thank all of the Best Plays honorees who made the 2006–07 season so invigorating to contemplate. David Harrower, Peter Morgan, Bruce Norris, Theresa Rebeck, Heidi Rodewald, Sarah Ruhl, Steven Sater, Duncan Sheik, Christopher Shinn, Stew, Tom Stoppard and August Wilson all enriched our lives during the season under review. The photographers who capture theatrical images on film and help keep those ephemeral moments alive for historical perspective are also due thanks for their generous contributions to the greater body of theatrical work. Building on our work from past years, we have included credits with each photograph and indexed the photographers' names for easier reference. Similarly, we continue offering biographical information about each of this volume's essayists and editors.

A personal note: In addition to serving as editor of this series, I teach full-time in the Drama Department at New York University's Tisch School of the Arts. Although I am blessed with superb students who inspire me to strive for excellence in my teaching, research, editing and writing, I also have the support and friendship of as fine a faculty of artists and scholars as I have had the honor to know. Each member of the faculty has provided the kind of encouragement one needs to keep in print an annual compendium of critical perspective and historical reference that runs more than 500 pages. Thanks to all of my colleagues for their advocacy, especially to the senior academic faculty: Awam Amkpa, Una Chaudhuri, Jan Cohen-Cruz, Laura Levine and Edward Ziter. For the season under review, I especially thank our department chair, Kevin Kuhlke, and our directors of theater studies, Robert Vorlicky and Carol Martin, for their continuing support of my work as a teacher, researcher and writer. Thanks also to Shayoni Mitra, my very capable teaching assistant during the season under review, for helping to make my work more manageable.

My wife, Vivian Cary Jenkins, continues to serve the theater and *Best Plays Theater Yearbook* as a tracker of what's happening in the New York theater. Despite facing challenges that would utterly stymie someone made of lesser stuff, she continues to contribute in ways large and small to the success of the series. Although I repeat these thanks each year, one thing remains true: It is largely through her consistent efforts that this series continues to appear.

JEFFREY ERIC JENKINS
NEW YORK

Contents

THE SEASON
ON AND OFF
BROADWAY

THE SEASON:
BROADWAY AND OFF BROADWAY

○ ○ ○ ○ ○ *By Jeffrey Eric Jenkins* ○ ○ ○ ○ ○

IN THIS SPACE last season, a question of the moment was whether the six
2006 Tony Awards received by the Broadway production of *The History
Boys* equaled or usurped *Death of a Salesman*'s longstanding record for
honors by a nonmusical play. The 2006–2007 season rendered that question
moot, however, with Lincoln Center Theater's epic production of *The Coast
of Utopia* by Tom Stoppard, which swept aside claims by both of the earlier
nonmusical plays when it received seven 2007 Tony Awards at the June 10
ceremony. (It was bound to happen after the Tonys doubled the number of
design categories, in 2005, so that plays do not compete against musicals
for design awards.) During typically eloquent remarks upon receiving his
honor for direction of *Coast*, Jack O'Brien said that he wanted to hear "no
more nonsense about the state of the American theater." After wrangling
more than three dozen actors who performed upwards of 70 roles, O'Brien
justly celebrated something that has been in decline—if not completely
extinct—in this country for decades: a system of repertory for plays and
performers. In a true repertory system, different plays are done on different
days with company members performing leading roles in one show,
supporting roles in another. In *Coast*'s three-play narrative arc, some of the
company performed the same characters throughout and some played several
distinct roles.

In an October 2006 piece for the *New York Times*, reporter Campbell
Robertson described the challenges that O'Brien and company faced:

> All of this is exponentially harder when you're talking about six and
> a half months of constant rehearsals[. . . .] Even harder when it's an
> ensemble piece, where the actor's name will appear somewhere in
> the crowd below the title. And harder still when it's at a not-for-profit
> theater, with its do-gooder pay scale.

Over the course of the production's six-month run, the company also
performed the entire trilogy in marathon days that began at 11 a.m. and

3

BROADWAY SEASON 2006–2007

Productions in a continuing run on May 31, 2007 in bold
Plays honored as Best Plays selections in italics
Best Plays from prior seasons are noted with a date in parentheses

NEW PLAYS (8)
Losing Louie
  (Manhattan Theatre Club)
The Little Dog Laughed
The Coast of Utopia
  (Lincoln Center Theater)
The Vertical Hour
Frost/Nixon
Coram Boy
Deuce
Radio Golf

NEW MUSICALS (11)
Martin Short: Fame Becomes Me
The Times They Are A-Changin'
Grey Gardens *(05–06)*
Dr. Seuss's How the Grinch
  Stole Christmas!
Mary Poppins
High Fidelity
Spring Awakening
Curtains
The Pirate Queen
Legally Blonde
LoveMusik (MTC)

PLAY REVIVALS (8)
Heartbreak House
  (Roundabout Theatre Company)
Butley (72–73)
Translations (80–81)
Journey's End *(28–29)*
Prelude to a Kiss 89-90
Talk Radio
A Moon for the Misbegotten *(56–57)*
Inherit the Wind *(54–55)*

MUSICAL REVIVALS (5)
A Chorus Line *(74–75)*
Les Misérables *(86–87)*
Company *(69–70)*
The Apple Tree (66–67) (RTC)
110 in the Shade (RTC)

SOLO PERFORMANCES (2)
Jay Johnson: The Two and Only
The Year of Magical Thinking

SPECIALTIES (1)
Kiki and Herb: Alive on Broadway

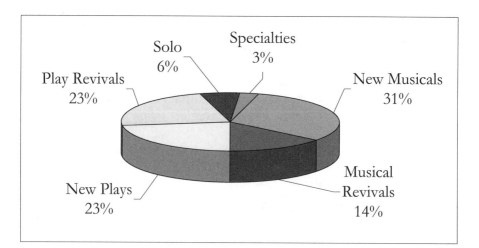

Specialties 3%
Solo 6%
Play Revivals 23%
New Musicals 31%
New Plays 23%
Musical Revivals 14%

ended approximately 12 hours later. One enthusiast who attended the marathon—more than once—proclaimed it a transformative experience at the theater and recruited others who had seen all three parts of the trilogy to join him for the superlative full-day performance. Beyond the marathon experience, however, *Coast of Utopia* was a thrilling theatrical event enhanced by the felicitous mix of O'Brien's steady hand at the helm, a committed band of versatile players and perhaps the best throughline of design conception seen on any stage. Even when Stoppard's text became dense with allusions requiring an advanced degree to fathom, there were always the emotional and visual contexts to lift the viewer ever higher. Due to the power of the designers' work, *Coast* swept the design awards for nonmusical plays. Co-scenic designer (with Scott Pask) Bob Crowley also received the design Tony for his (solo) scenery for the musical *Mary Poppins*. Crowley called the double awards "indecent" and "too generous" in his acceptance remarks. While Catherine Zuber designed the costumes for all three plays, the lighting designs of each were handled by three separate designers (Brian MacDevitt, Kenneth Posner and Natasha Katz). Stoppard's trilogy was treated as a single work for the purposes of the Tony Awards (and for *Best Plays*) and the playwright received his fourth Tony Award for best play. The other Tonys for *Coast* went to Billy Crudup (featured actor) and Jennifer Ehle (featured actress).

The big story of the 2007 Tony Awards, however, came at the end of the evening when *Spring Awakening*, a musical adaptation of Frank Wedekind's 1891 play about the tragic consequences of sexual repression, received the honor for best musical, bringing its total to eight awards received that night. As the stage filled with (literally) dozens of producers—it costs a lot of money to do a Broadway musical these days—the future of the musical theater seemed bright. It mattered little that Steven Sater (book) won a Tony for adapting an acknowledged classic play—let's not forget that both of Rodgers and Hammerstein's first big successes together were based on earlier plays—or that Duncan Sheik's winning music and orchestrations may have been a bit too "alternative rock" for some older listeners. (And so what if the musical had a scene that seemed uncomfortably close to date-rape? There are other fine musicals with equally dark thematics.) *Spring Awakening* captured that eternal internal struggle when we begin to define ourselves and to put away childish things—even as we are challenged by new feelings and changes to our bodies. The musical finally earned Michael Mayer a Tony Award for direction in addition to the choreography award for Bill T. Jones, the featured actor award for John Gallagher Jr. and the lighting design of a musical honor for Kevin Adams.

Though the youthful company of *Awakening* gyrated away with the most prizes, *Grey Gardens*, the lovely musical about the sad decline of two former society women (and Best Play for its 2005–06 Off Broadway run), managed to receive Tony Awards for costume design of a musical (William Ivey Long), best actress (Christine Ebersole) and best featured actress (Mary Louise Wilson). The big surprise of the evening, however, came when David Hyde Pierce—an actor of impeccable comic sensibility best known for his television role as the tightly wound brother of the title character on the comedy, *Frasier*—won the Tony Award for best actor in a musical. The only persons in Radio City Music Hall not astonished must have been the Lutz and Carr accountants who counted the ballots. Most of Broadway thought that Raúl Esparza's raw, powerful performance of Bobby in the revival of *Company* would surely win. But Hyde Pierce, whose Broadway credits extend back to 1982, carried the night with his tap-dancing, musical-theater-loving gumshoe in the Kander and Ebb musical about backstage murder, *Curtains*.

On the topic of surprises, Julie White, who received the Tony Award in the best actress in a play category for her work as an acerbic literary agent in Douglas Carter Beane's comedy *The Little Dog Laughed*, could not believe that she had been honored over such notables as Vanessa Redgrave and Angela Lansbury (not to mention Swoosie Kurtz and Eve Best). As Gordon Cox reported in *Variety*, White told the press backstage, "I heard that 'juh' sound, and I went, 'Nuh-uh!' [. . .] I didn't go to acting school, you know?" The other big prizes of the evening included a best play-revival trophy for the thunderously powerful World War I drama, *Journey's End*, a big hit in 1929 and a Best Play for the 1928–29 season. Unfortunately, the revival drew far less than 50 percent attendance throughout its critically acclaimed run—until it managed 67 percent in its final week, closing on the day of the Tony Awards. The new production of *Company* received the musical revival Tony, but it was a bittersweet win after its leading man's surprise loss.

Summer Doldrums?

LONG BEFORE 2007 Tony Award time, however, were the dog days of summer in the wake the 2006 Tony Awards, which is when our seasonal narrative truly begins. The *Best Plays* season for statistical purposes begins June 1 and ends the following May 31, which generally follows the contours of the Broadway season. Many shows manage to stay alive and pray for a Tony Award (or eight) in the hopes that an award will extend the life of a show. Indeed, one of the reasons that so many shows open in the weeks leading up to the Tony nominations is to minimize investors' exposure to supporting a long run until awards season. (And then there are those producers who spread their money around to several shows in order to maximize their chances of winning the Big Prize at season's end.)

By way of example, consider the summer of 2006, as our season commences. The 2006 Tony Awards were given June 11, by which time the previous season's revival of *The Odd Couple* with Nathan Lane and Matthew Broderick had ended its limited run just a week earlier (June 4; 249 performances). There is little question that the revival earned a profit given the draw of the stars when it opened. Even before it opened, *Odd Couple* projected a financial windfall for investors, and *Variety* declared it a hit in its June 2006 seasonal overview. As summer 2006 unfolded, however, another 13 shows—nearly half of all of the shows that closed during 2006–07—would close before Labor Day: *The Pajama Game* (June 17; 129 performances), *Three Days of Rain* (June 18; 70 performances), *The Threepenny Opera* (June 25; 77 performances), *Awake and Sing!* (June 25; 80 performances), *The Light in the Piazza* (July 2; 504 performances), *Doubt, a Parable* (July 2; 525 performances), *Shining City* (July 16; 80 performances), *Hot Feet* (July 23; 97 performances), *Bridge and Tunnel* (August 6; 213 performances), *Faith Healer* (August 13; 117 performances), *Dirty Rotten Scoundrels* (September 3; 627 performances), *Sweeney Todd* (September 3; 349 performances) and *The Lieutenant of Inishmore* (September 3; 142 performances).

This list of summer 2006 closings is somewhat unusual when compared with past seasons. It may mark a shift in the conventional wisdom on getting through the Tony Awards to make it to the post-Tony sales bounce—or it may be just an anomaly for this season. But it is difficult to find a cluster of shows among the summer 2006 closings, that were hanging on until after the Tony Awards. *Hot Feet* and *The Lieutenant of Inishmore* are probably the ones killed by summer's dog days. Three of the summer-closing shows—*Light in the Piazza, Doubt, a Parable* and *Dirty Rotten Scoundrels*—had run more than a year and been fairly successful. Several of the closing shows were slated only for limited runs and had to close, presumably for contractual reasons. *Three Days of Rain* averaged nearly 100 percent attendance in its 12-week limited run, which included three weeks of previews at 101 percent. *Faith Healer* ran in the upper 90 percentile—on a limited run as well—and Ian McDiarmid won the 2006 Tony Award for featured actor. *Pajama Game, Threepenny Opera, Awake and Sing!* and *Shining City* were all operated by nonprofit theaters—*Pajama Game* and *Awake and Sing!* both won Tony Awards as revivals.

To some extent, the nonprofits have changed the game on Broadway with three companies operating four Broadway theaters. Given the nonprofits' lower costs for union salaries and other operating expenses, they are able to recover expenses more quickly—and if they do not break even, there are no angry investors, only beaming supporters of art (theoretically). Gerald Schoenfeld, chairman of the Shubert Organization, is reportedly fond of saying, "There is no profit like nonprofit"—which infuriates some nonprofit theater leaders. Schoenfeld's point, of course, is that the playing field is not level. The advantage to nonprofit theaters, however, allows them to program such worthy plays as Brian Friel's *Translations* at Manhattan Theatre Club's Biltmore Theatre. Lincoln Center Theater's production of *The Coast of Utopia* could never have been funded as a for-profit enterprise; its only other production was at the subsidized National Theatre (UK) in London.

If there is a link to be found in the summer 2006 closings, it is among the nonmusical plays, which generally do not get long runs. The longest-running Broadway play is *Life With Father*, which closed in 1947 with 3,224 performances and is never likely to be equaled. Just behind it on the list is *Tobacco Road*, which closed in 1941 with 3,182 performances. They are the only plays among the 20 longest-running Broadway shows. The last blockbuster Broadway play was arguably the two-part *Angels in America*, which received the Pulitzer Prize, Tony Awards in 1993 and 1994, lost money on Broadway and played 584 performances between the two parts. (In fairness, it must be noted that *Angels*'s producers turned a profit during the national tour.)

Broadway Beginnings

IT WOULD BE the fifth month of the season before a new play opened on Broadway, when Manhattan Theatre Club presented *Losing Louie* (October 12; 52 performances), an Americanized version of a British play that opened in London under the title *Losing Louis* in 2005. A fairly conventional tale of familial dysfunction set in the 1960s and the present, *Louie* was not beloved by the critics. *Variety*'s David Rooney saw similarities to Alan Ayckbourn's and Richard Greenberg's work but ultimately found the comedy "hackneyed and toothless." *USA Today*'s Elysa Gardner was gentler, writing that the production offered "a thoroughly diverting couple of hours." Joe Dziemianowicz of the *Daily News* dismissed the piece as "big on sex and sex talk but short on laughs," with the *New York Times*'s Charles Isherwood calling it "dull-witted and vulgar." Linda Winer of Newsday referred to the piece as a "tired old sniggering sitcom" and a "snooze-button of a sentimental family comedy." Despite the critical drubbing, however, *Louie* managed the same number of performances as the aforementioned *Translations*—to which the critics were much kinder. And that is an advantage of having nonprofit theater presented on Broadway.

Although the season was nearly five months old when a new play finally appeared, Broadway got rolling in August with a pair of musical entertainments that were personality driven. The performance-art duo of "Kiki and Herb" (Justin Bond and Kenny Mellman) brought their parody of

---

Nonprofit theaters have changed the game on and Off Broadway.

---

an over-the-hill lounge act to Broadway for 27 performances beginning August 15. Titled *Kiki and Herb: Alive on Broadway*, the show featured the embittered "Kiki" getting drunk while doing songs and telling indiscreet stories as "Herb" provided backup on piano. Fans of the pair were enthralled to see them again, Ben Brantley from the *New York Times* among them, and noisily approved while more conventional Broadway theatergoers found their eyes glazing as dialogue once considered risqué or politically incorrect often landed with a thud. Gardner of *USA Today* got it just right when she wrote:

> In the first act, a few politically incorrect jokes didn't quite work—not because they were offensive, but because they weren't funny. But Bond delivered them with overwhelming panache. Later, some quips took on a whiff of preaching to the choir, as if to remind the faithful of the social conscience underlying Kiki and Herb's irreverent antics.

The show was nominated for a 2007 Tony Award in the category of special theatrical event, but ventriloquist Jay Johnson—the only other nominee—took the award for his show *Jay Johnson: The Two and Only*. Johnson's sweetly sentimental show, a transfer from a 2004 run Off Broadway at the Atlantic Theater Company, opened at the end of September and managed a run of 70 performances before closing in the same Helen Hayes Theatre where Kiki and Herb had their truncated run.

Two days after Kiki and Herb opened their show, comic actor Martin Short premiered *Martin Short: Fame Becomes Me* (making official a glut of eponymous shows at the season's start). Short's show was billed as a musical—with book, music and lyrics—and it included the stellar songwriting team of Marc Shaiman and Scott Wittman. The throughline of the show was a satire of celebrations of celebrity—including solo shows like Short's own. The production took a few well-publicized critical hits as it worked its way to New York and by the time it arrived knives had been carefully honed. Short himself, however, is such a charmer that critics could not bring themselves to unleash the venom reserved for, say, *Saturday Night Fever*. The *Times*'s Brantley wrote that Short was, "an appealing and immodestly modest (or is it modestly immodest?) performer, [who] arrives a little late at the table for such parody to feel very fresh." *Variety*'s Rooney essentially concurred writing, "there's a slight feeling of insubstantiality since the show never really abandons jokiness to expose the man behind the performer centerstage." Terry Teachout of the *Wall Street Journal* may have been the toughest when he wrote that it was a "toothless spoof of a tired subject." The show made it through the holidays before withdrawing January 7 after 165 performances.

By the opening of Jay Johnson's show September 28, we were nearly five months into the season and not much excitement was happening on the Main Stem—and Off Broadway was not much better. That was about to change, however, once October got underway with five openings. Once upon a time—before the proliferation of air conditioning—the Broadway season began after Labor Day: families were in their fall rhythms, children were in school, etc. These days, though, the season's true beginning seems to push farther away from Labor Day with each passing year. In October 2006, the new productions included three revivals, *Losing Louie* (see above) and Twyla Tharp's latest dance musical, *The Times They Are A-Changin'*, which was based on the music of Bob Dylan. Taking them in order of opening, October began with the revival of *A Chorus Line* (October 5; 273 performances as of May 31) in a slavish recreation of Michael Bennett's original production directed by Bennett collaborator Bob Avian. It was a perfectly acceptable production with the lovely Charlotte d'Amboise as Cassie, but it made some Broadway audiences wonder if they would ever see a rethinking of this great work. Of all of the versions seen in the past 25 years—Broadway, touring, regional—perhaps the most powerful was presented by Theatre-by-the-Sea in Matunuck, Rhode Island. Before readers snicker up their sleeves, they should know that the Matunuck version was directed by Tony Stevens who, with Michon Peacock, convinced Bennett to create the original workshop at the Public Theater. Stevens's version was darker and more poignant than any version likely to play in a first-class house, but someday it should. Lacking a reinvigoration—which Bennett himself almost surely would have done—the 2006–07 version was reviewed as if it were something of a museum piece. Rightly so.

Roundabout Theatre Company presented a fine production of George Bernard Shaw's *Heartbreak House* (October 11; 79 performances) with Philip Bosco, Swoosie Kurtz, Laila Robins, Byron Jennings and other noteworthy actors. While the World War I-era play itself was a timely reminder in 2006 that it is all-too-easy to concern ourselves with the mundane as larger issues begin to consume the world around us, critics could not seem to agree on the production's worth. Dziemianowicz of the *Daily News* found the production "enervating" with "listless direction," "torpid pacing" and "lackluster performances." Teachout at the *Wall Street Journal* agreed that the direction was "too-straightforward" but that Bosco and Kurtz gave "magnetic performances" and that the rest of the cast ranged "from perfectly acceptable to very fine." John Lahr of the *New Yorker* praised the "lively performances," but thought Shaw's comedy sank "under the weight of its own exposition."

As the month drew to a close, Nathan Lane did what stars of his stature rarely have the courage to attempt: something different. In a revival of Simon Gray's *Butley* (October 25; 94 performances), Lane shed his irrepressible comic persona for the more serious role that earned Alan Bates his first Tony Award in 1973. Bates, who played the role in London, on Broadway and in a film version, so indelibly stamped the work with his performance that it rarely has been revived—this was the first Broadway revival. A college professor of middle age, dying ambition and frustrated sexuality, Ben Butley drinks to numb the pain he feels over his failed marriage and the misery inflicted by his young male lover—who is also a colleague. The role cries for comic timing that can lacerate as it tickles. New York critics—who know a thing or two about lacerating wit, thank you very much—rejected the teasing (and increasingly dark) character arc created by Lane. The production that opened at the Booth Theatre this season had been staged in 2003 by Nicholas Martin at Boston's Huntington Theatre Company. For the 2003 version, the critics were kinder than 2006's New Yorkers with *Variety*'s Frank Rizzo calling the 2003 production "a triumph for Lane" who made "the demanding role look easy." *Times*man Bruce Weber visited Boston in 2003 and wrote of a possible transfer to Broadway, "Let's hope it happens." Ed Siegel of the *Boston Globe* wrote, "Lane makes the world of . . . Ben Butley shimmer with a kind of personal failure that turns the Huntington Theatre Company's revival into an ensemble success." When the show finally transferred in 2006, with a few cast changes, *Variety*'s Rooney had a different take from his colleague Rizzo: "*Butley* is shortchanged by an actor whose lead skill is being funny" and wished for Ralph Fiennes or Gabriel Byrne to essay the part. *Times*man Brantley simliarly demurred from his former colleague's assessment warning potential audiences that "if you were expecting a seamless, emotionally stirring marriage between a first-rate actor and a first-rate play, then *Butley* disappoints." Leave it to John Heilpern of the *New York Observer*, often a critical hatpin, to have the last words on the matter. Despite "one or two doubts" about Lane's performance, Heilpern called it an "excellent revival," praising Lane's performance as the "best he's ever given." And here's to the stars who stretch.

The final opening of October, *The Times They Are A-Changin'* (October 26; 28 performances), came to town with negative word-of-mouth (and lukewarm reviews) not unlike what director-choreographer Tharp experienced with the dance musical *Movin' Out* during its 2002 Chicago tryout. With West Coast reviewers using terms such as "half-baked conception" and "dancing takes a back seat" it seemed as though Tharp's work ethic of consistent improvement would be tested again. Employing a variety of numbers from Bob Dylan's music catalogue, Tharp constructed a circus-themed production that had an Oedipal love triangle at its center. Where *Movin' Out* had a narrative line that could be plucked from Billy Joel's work—essentially short stories set to music—Dylan's work is more poetic, fluid and resistant to narrative constructs. When it arrived on Broadway, the much-anticipated successor to the superb *Movin' Out* found itself nearly without defenders in the press and without much of an audience. As a piece of dance set to popular music, *Times* had a lyric beauty at certain moments that was breathtaking, but physical movement and the narrative had only a glancing relationship to one another. Tharp's product appeared to be the love child of the wonderfully bizarre (and much missed, in this corner) HBO television series *Carnivàle* and Wim Wenders's superb film *Wings of Desire* (*Der Himmel über Berlin*, 1987). Lacking the celebratory nature that bubbled through *Movin' Out* at times, the unrelieved darkness—and opaque narrative—of Tharp's *Times* insured its quick demise.

Onward to the Holidays

AS NOVEMBER BEGAN, so did a rush of eight Broadway openings—equaling the number of openings during the season to-date—which made it a busy month for habitual first-nighters. Five of the November openings were musicals undoubtedly hoping to get a sales bump from holiday theatergoers—though a couple of them, *Grey Gardens* and *Company* could hardly be placed in the category of typical holiday fare. When *Grey Gardens* opened (November 2; 241 performances as of May 31), Sara Gettelfinger had been replaced by Erin Davie as young "Little" Edie Beale and the show had been revised and tightened since its run at Playwrights Horizons in the previous season. It retained its charms, however, along with the haunting, heartbreaking performances of Christine Ebersole and Mary Louise Wilson in the central roles. A Best Play of 2005–06 for its Off Broadway production, see that volume for a fine essay by Michael Feingold. With the Broadway opening, it seemed as though Tony Awards might be in the offing for the creators and the performers. A few days later, *Dr. Seuss's How the Grinch Stole Christmas!* (November 8; 107 performances) made a bid for family audiences at the Hilton Theatre during a limited run scheduled to end in January, just after the holidays. Even attending without a child in tow, *Grinch* could be fun, but the production is limited by its holiday nature. The next night Jean Valjean and Javert locked horns for another stint of *Les Misérables* (November 9; 233 performances as of May 31) in a revival that followed the long-running original after a break of only 42 months. Four nights later, Julie White faced houses filled with laughing people—barely half-filled, actually, which was a shame—as she wisecracked her way to a Tony Award in Douglas Carter Beane's show-business-and-sexuality satire, *The Little Dog Laughed* (November 13; 112 performances). In the play, a closeted gay movie star weds the accidentally pregnant ex-girlfriend of his male lover. White's character, Diane, manages, massages and manipulates all of the possible hazards until everyone gets what he or she wants—except the male lover who does not want to be a hidden fixture in this strained arrangement. Family fare for the holidays, indeed.

Although *Mary Poppins*, the 2004 London musical hit, is fondly recalled by many baby boomers as a family film of their childhoods, the stage version was unsettling in comparison with the 1964 film. The London production caused a stir by forbidding children under three years of age and advertising the show as appropriate for children age seven and above. It may have been a bit of Disney and Cameron Mackintosh marketing savvy, but there was something darker and more ominous about the stage production. It was, however, 40 years later and some might suggest that children (and their parents) are more accustomed to a scary world. Brantley argued in the *Times*, however, that the Broadway version was altogether less frightening (and less powerful) than the West End production:

> Certainly a dark-clouded, Jungian air pervaded the *Mary Poppins* that opened nearly two years ago at the Prince Edward Theatre in London, where it continues to run. Its predominant palette when I

OFF BROADWAY SEASON 2006–2007

Productions in a continuing run on May 31, 2007 in bold
Productions honored as Best Plays selections in italics
Best Plays from prior seasons are noted with a date in parentheses

NEW PLAYS (36)
Nothing (Brits Off Broadway)
Some Girl(s) (MCC Theater)
Burleigh Grimes
The Water's Edge
 (Second Stage Theatre)
Satellites (Public Theater)
The House in Town
 (Lincoln Center Theater)
The Busy World Is Hushed
 (Playwrights Horizons)
Secrets
Pig Farm
 (Roundabout Theatre Company)
School of the Americas
 (Public/Labyrinth Theater)
Mr. Dooley's America (Irish Rep)
The Pain and the Itch (Playwrights)
Blue Door (Playwrights)
A Small, Melodramatic Story
 (Public/Labyrinth)
The Clean House (Lincoln Center)
Regrets Only
 (Manhattan Theatre Club)
Durango (Public)
The American Pilot (Manhattan)
Kaos (New York Theatre Workshop)
Murder Mystery Blues
 (59E59 Theaters)
The Scene (Second Stage)
Love in the Nick of Tyme
Frank's Home (Playwrights)
All That I Will Ever Be (NYTW)
The Last Word . . .
Sealed for Freshness
Howard Katz (Roundabout)
Dying City (Lincoln Center)
Bill W. and Dr. Bob
Jack Goes Boating (Labyrinth)
Our Leading Lady (Manhattan)
Some Men (Second Stage)

NEW PLAYS (*cont'd*)
Essential Self-Defense
 (Playwrights/Edge Theater)
Blackbird (Manhattan)
Memory (Brits Off Broadway)
Phallacy

PLAY REVIVALS (17)
Macbeth (Public)
*Mother Courage
 and Her Children (62–63)* (Public)
Seven Guitars (95–96) (Signature)
The Persians
 (National Theatre of Greece)
subUrbia (93–94) (Second Stage)
Peer Gynt (Peer Gynt Festival)
Waiting for Godot (55–56)
 (Skirball Center/Gate Theatre)
Suddenly Last Summer (Roundabout)
Room Service
The Voysey Inheritance
 (Atlantic Theater)
The Fever (New Group)
King Lear (Public)
King Hedley II (00–01) (Signature)
The Taming of the Shrew (BAM)
Twelfth Night (BAM)
Cymbeline (BAM)
Gaslight *(41–42)* as *Angel Street*
 (Irish Rep)

NEW MUSICALS (13)
[title of show]
Shout!
Evil Dead: The Musical
Mimi Le Duck
How to Save the World and Find
 True Love in 90 Minutes
Striking 12
Floyd and Clea Under
 the Western Sky (Playwrights)
That Time of the Year (York Theatre)

NEW MUSICALS (*cont'd*)
Gutenberg! The Musical!
In the Heights
Adrift in Macao (Primary Stages)
Edward Scissorhands (BAM)
Passing Strange (Public)

MUSICAL REVIVALS (5)
The Fantasticks
Annie (76–77)
The Yeoman of the Guard
  (G&S Players)
The Mikado (G&S Players)
The Rose of Persia (G&S Players)

SOLO (9)
A Jew†Grows†in†Brooklyn
Loose
No Child . . .
Wrecks (Public)

SOLO (*cont'd*)
25 Questions for a Jewish Mother
My Name Is Rachel Corrie
Emergence-See! (Public)
**My Mother's Italian, My Father's
  Jewish, and I'm in Therapy!**
All the Wrong Reasons (NYTW)

SPECIALTIES (9)
Amajuba: Like Doves We Rise
  (Culture Project)
¡El Conquistador! (NYTW)
An Oak Tree (Perry Street)
Follies (70–71) (Encores!)
Spalding Gray: Stories Left to Tell
My Fair Lady (Philharmonic)
Be
Face the Music (Encores!)
Stairway to Paradise (Encores!)

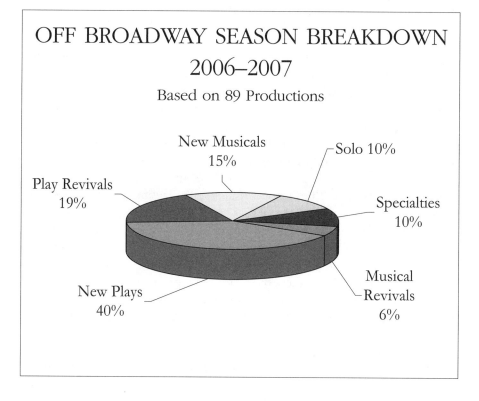

OFF BROADWAY SEASON BREAKDOWN
2006–2007
Based on 89 Productions

New Musicals 15%
Solo 10%
Play Revivals 19%
Specialties 10%
New Plays 40%
Musical Revivals 6%

saw it was gray. Then there was that notorious scene where the Banks children, Mary Poppins's charges, were sentenced to death by firing squad by their own toys. [. . .] The show's producers seem to have figured out that gray is not the favorite color of Americans. So cake-frosting pinks, greens, lilacs and yellows have, for the most part, pushed away sootier tones. As for those vengeful toys, well, they still get angry, but not homicidal. Nothing remains here to frighten anyone, except possibly diabetics.

Teachout at the *Wall Street Journal* had a different take, writing, "It's spectacular, and not even slightly boring, but anyone familiar with Walt Disney's 1964 film version of *Mary Poppins* is likely to come away asking what happened to the charm." There are probably several answers to Teachout's question including, "You grew up." *Mary Poppins* on Broadway was a perfectly acceptable family show sung and danced with great skill by Ashley Brown, as Mary, working with the original Bert from London, Gavin Lee.

As the end of November drew near, there were three openings in close succession after Thanksgiving. *The Coast of Utopia* opened *Part 1: Voyage* (November 27; 44 performances) to reviews that included terms such as "exhilarating," "genius" and "ravishing"—and that was just from *Times*man Brantley, the most powerful critic on the planet. (His colleague, Charles Isherwood, dissented from this perspective in February, two weeks before the third installment opened.) *Variety*'s Rooney was similarly inspired to use "impressive," "expert" and "ravishing." There were still problems noted by the critics with the exposition—some might argue that it is all exposition—but the theatrical achievement was breathtaking or if you prefer, ravishing. Two nights later, George Furth and Stephen Sondheim's *Company* opened (November 29; 210 performances as of May 31) in a John Doyle production that featured actors playing the instruments—which was the case in Doyle's production of *Sweeney Todd* in the 2005–06 season. The production had opened in March at Cincinnati Playhouse in the Park with *Variety*'s Chris Jones writing that it was "striking, revelatory and thoroughly compelling." The transfer to Broadway caused Jones's colleague Rooney to agree that Doyle had "spawned another arresting revival." Brantley chimed in that the "visually severe, aurally lush [. . .] musical of marriage and its discontents from 1970 is the chicest-looking production on Broadway." Dziemianowicz of the *Daily News* dissented, calling it a "suburban vanilla revue" hampered by Doyle's "lethargic direction." But the *Daily News* opinion was the minority report with the *Wall Street Journal*'s Teachout more typically proclaiming the production "intimate and intense" before concluding "this isn't your parents' *Company*—it's better." Whatever it was—and the word "electrifying" was suitable for at least one matinee—lethargic and vanilla it was not.

On the last day of the month, David Hare's exercise in political bafflegab, *The Vertical Hour* (November 30; 117 performances), opened to respectful reviews. In the play, which received its world premiere—an oddity on Broadway these days, though with *Deuce* and *The Year of Magical Thinking*, there were three this season—a pair of intellectuals clash over when it is appropriate to intervene in another country's affairs to relieve suffering or prevent acts of terrorism. Unlike his riveting, *Stuff Happens*, which was based on documented acts of recent history, *Vertical Hour* rambled on issues of theory and pragmatism. Making her Broadway debut, film star Julianne Moore took the brunt of criticism for her reserved performance while critics were fascinated by Bill Nighy's odd, rangy physicality—although some found his tics a distraction. Peter Marks of the *Washington Post* was not one of the distracted, calling Nighy's work "the kind of roguishly funny performance in which an audience loses itself." Marks also noted that Moore's character was "a bright, idealistic American of conflicting impulses and priorities" and that the actor opted to "play her a bit too introspectively, and so she never seems quite the woman of action [. . .] that Hare intends." What Hare intends, however, is never made fully clear as this muddled political argument spins into itself. In fairness to Hare, however, it must be noted that most critics laid the faults of the production at Moore's undoubtedly beautiful feet.

As the holidays crept closer, *High Fidelity* (December 7; 13 performances), a musical based on the 2000 film starring John Cusack and Jack Black, came and went—noisily—in 10 days on Broadway. (Is this a good time to discuss the overamplification of musicals? What's that? I'm sorry, I couldn't hear you.) *Spring Awakening* (December 10; 196 performances as of May 31) made its successful transfer to the Eugene O'Neill Theatre—though, again, its dark themes of troubled adolescence were hardly standard family fare for the holiday season. A Best Play of 2006–07, you may find Michael Feingold's essay on the musical later in this volume. Before *The Coast of Utopia*'s second part opened (December 21; 43 performances) to bring 2006 to a close, Roundabout Theatre Company revived *The Apple Tree* (December 14; 99 performances) at its Studio 54 theater. The deliciously funny Kristin Chenoweth received the kind of notices about which actors dream: "blindingly radiant," wrote Brantley; "funny, sexy, endearing and the best singer on Broadway," echoed Teachout. The 1966 musical was near its cultural-relevance expiration date when it first premiered, with its prefeminist attitudes toward women, men (and men and women). Chenoweth, however, with co-stars Brian d'Arcy James and Marc Kudisch managed a cartoonish quality that kept the laughs bright and bouncy for the limited run.

A New Year

WITH ONLY FIVE months remaining in the 2006–07 season there are still 16 new Broadway productions yet to open—and that number does not include the third part of *The Coast of Utopia*. Of these 16 remaining shows for this Broadway season, 14 will open in the last eight weeks of eligibility for Tony Award nominations. Once again, more than a third of the new Broadway productions in a given season open as close to the Tony Awards as possible. It is tempting to suggest that the season will soon be two months long, but as a percentage of total output per season the late Broadway entries this year account for 40 percent of the total—last season that number was 41 percent.

January is usually a slow month, but Manhattan Theatre Club presented a thoughtful revival of Brian Friel's *Translations* (January 25; 53 performances), which explored the intersections of language and love in a country where some colonizers (and some of the colonized) attempt to bridge the divide. The *Times*'s Isherwood wrote that "the play trades in a subtle glory, the kind that steals upon you furtively" and found the performances touching and beautiful. *Variety*'s Rooney cited the actors' "unfussy naturalness" noting that the ensemble had no weak link. Coming at a time when Americans were concerned about appearing as colonizers in the Middle East, the play—and its implicit tragedy—remained, as Gardner wrote in *USA Today*, "as haunting and relevant as ever." In February there were only two openings: the third part of *The Coast of Utopia* (February 18; 34 performances) and the stunning *Journey's End* (February 22; 113 performances as of May 31) at the Belasco Theatre.

The third part of *Coast*, subtitled *Salvage*, was greeted by the *Times*'s Brantley with the faint praise that it "rarely feels stodgy or overstuffed," even as he continued to celebrate the trilogy overall as "heavenly spectacle," if not a "major work of art." The praise was not universal, however, with Toby Zinman writing for the *Philadelphia Inquirer*, that it was a "melancholy and somewhat disappointing finale," adding "that's Russian history for you." *Variety*'s Rooney concurred, that *Salvage* was the "weakest of the three plays," even if the "overall achievement remains undiminished." A Best Play of 2006–07, Charles Wright's essay on Stoppard's entire trilogy appears in the next section of this volume.

Journey's End by R.C. Sherriff—a 1928–29 Best Play choice—was a huge success in its first Broadway run of 485 performances. At the time of that first Broadway run, there were four American touring companies also operating with success. Barely 10 years after the Great War, as it was then called, there was a wide-ranging interest in the experience of soldiers in mortal combat. (See the Plays Produced on Broadway section of this volume for more details on the play's origin.) The 2006–07 production was a brilliantly effective staging of the play, but after four years of Iraq War—with no end in sight—audiences could not be attracted. Perhaps if we do not see it, it does not exist. The production closed on the day it was honored with the 2007 Tony Award for best revival of a play.

March came in like a lamb with a revival of Craig Lucas's *Prelude to a Kiss* (March 8; 61 performances) by Roundabout Theatre Company. Under Daniel Sullivan's usual steady direction, the play seemed lost in the American Airlines Theatre. Starring veteran actor John Mahoney as an elderly man who swaps souls with a beautiful young woman (Annie Parisse) on her wedding day, there was an emotional distance throughout that made the production itself echo Rita's ambivalence about getting married. Alan Tudyk as the husband should have been a driving force behind the play's eventual solution, but every emotion, every nuance felt as if it were being held at arm's length. Things warmed considerably with the fiery Liev Schreiber as Barry Champlain in Eric Bogosian's *Talk Radio* (March 11; 93 performances as of May 31). Barry is a contrarian radio talk-show host, a provocateur determined to get his audience to think, but he is also on the brink of national success—if only he can control his rebellious urges. Schreiber kept the audience wondering if (or when) the big blow might come.

Awards Season Approaches

BEGINNING AS FAR back as 1985, Peter Stone, John Kander and Fred Ebb had talked of doing a musical that centered on a backstage murder mystery. Enid Nemy wrote in the *New York Times* theater column in October of that year that the team hoped to "have their as-yet-untitled musical finished by year-end. It's about a musical in trouble in Boston, and to make matters more complicated, the producer is murdered." The following September, Mel Gussow wrote in the same paper, "Listen closely and you will also hear the dancing feet of a musical called *Curtains, or Who Killed David Merrick?* by the *Woman of the Year* team of John Kander, Fred Ebb and Peter Stone." Along the way the project kept getting sidetracked by other commitments. After Stone's death in 2003, according to a July 2006 article in *Variety* by

Phil Gallo, Rupert Holmes was commissioned to rewrite Stone's script. After a reading of Holmes's script, producer Roger Berlind, got involved. The *Variety* article further detailed the changes: "Holmes moved the action to 1959 from the present day. Beyond that, Holmes says he retained characters, the plot and 'about 10 lines.'" It was while Holmes was working on the script that Ebb also died, forcing Holmes and Kander to collaborate in unexpected ways. When the musical finally opened at Center Theatre Group's Ahmanson Theatre in Los Angeles in 2006—more than 20 years after that first mention in the *Times*—Charles McNulty of the *Los Angeles Times* wrote that the "brilliantly directed production" did what musicals "rarely do anymore: entertain." Gallo concurred in *Variety*: "Word of mouth should make *Curtains* one of the toughest tickets to secure in Los Angeles" and lauded "David Hyde Pierce in a rich role, a stellar supporting cast and abundant laughs." After those notices, it was "Broadway, here we come." *Curtains* opened at the Al Hirschfeld Theatre (March 22; 81 performances as of May 31) and went on to secure Hyde Pierce's 2007 Tony Award. The final March opening featured Vanessa Redgrave as Joan Didion in *The Year of Magical Thinking* (March 29; 64 performances as of May 31) at the Booth Theatre. The solo performance piece traced the topic of Didion's book on the sudden death of her husband, John Gregory Dunne, as well as the subsequent illness and death of Didion and Dunne's daughter, Quintana.

The massive musical about a 16th-century Irish woman named Grace O'Malley, *The Pirate Queen* (April 5; 65 performances as of May 31), lumbered into the Hilton Theatre as the awards season drew near. Based on Morgan Llywelyn's novel *Grania: She-King of the Irish Seas*, the Alain Boublil, Claude-Michel Schönberg, Richard Maltby Jr. and John Dempsey musical told the romantic story of a seafaring woman who refused to be tied to conventional women's work and staked a claim to leadership of her people in a struggle with Elizabeth I. Directed by Chicago-based Frank Galati, whose résumé includes the Steppenwolf Theatre Company transfer to Broadway of *The Grapes of Wrath* (1990) and the Tony Award-winning musical *Ragtime* (1998), the show had a top-of-the-line creative team. Even after an initial run at the Cadillac Palace Theatre in Chicago and changes made by (and to) the creative team, there was no escaping unflattering comparisons to other Boublil and Schönberg works. It seemed as if the time for sweeping, romantic musicals had passed.

Kevin Spacey returned to New York with his third Broadway production of a Eugene O'Neill play, *A Moon for the Misbegotten* (April 9; 59 performances as of May 31). Spacey is that rare actor who has performed four classic roles on Broadway in addition to being a film star—though it was for his work on Neil Simon's *Lost in Yonkers* that he received his 1991 Tony Award. Before playing Jim Tyrone in *Moon* this season, he played a younger version of the character in O'Neill's *Long Day's Journey Into Night* in the 1986 production directed by Jonathan Miller and he played Theodore Hickman in the 1999 production of *The Iceman Cometh* directed by Howard Davies. (The fourth classic role was a 1982 performance of Osvald Alving opposite Liv Ullmann in Henrik Ibsen's *Ghosts*.) In the 2006–07 *Moon*, Spacey returned with Davies at the helm and offered an amusing, histrionic version of Tyrone. With the sylphlike Eve Best opposite him as Josie Hogan, Spacey (and his director) flew in the face of virtually everything O'Neill wrote or said about Josie. For the O'Neill aficionado, it was a mindbending experience that made the viewer think perhaps the playwright knew what he was talking about when it came to these two characters. There is a rough and rugged quality to Josie in the text that is, to some extent, a bluff exterior, but she needs a certain physical presence missing from the lovely Best. Spacey's performance was itself a kind of experiment: he appeared to be portraying Tyrone as if the character—based on O'Neill's brother, James Jr., a journeyman actor—were himself playing a theatrical role in an old-fashioned, pre-naturalistic style. As a result, Spacey at times appeared to float through his encounters with Josie and her father as if he were peddling a bill of goods, or as if he were O'Neill's Hickey, from *Iceman*, before that character killed his wife.

The final play revival of the season was Jerome Lawrence and Robert E. Lee's *Inherit the Wind* (April 12; 56 performances as of May 31) at the Lyceum Theatre. Starring Christopher Plummer and Brian Dennehy, the production made early April feel a bit like the 1950s again: both *Inherit* and *Moon* were Best Plays in the 1950s (see table on page 4 or the Plays Produced on Broadway section). Plummer and Dennehy were in fine fettle as the doppelgängers for Clarence Darrow and William Jennings Bryan in Lawrence and Lee's dramatization of the Scopes Monkey Trial of 1925. It was difficult to believe that the scientific and theological arguments made in the onstage courtroom at the Lyceum—arguments from 80 years ago—continue to be made today. In another year, *Inherit* might well have been a true contender for the play revival Tony Award, but it was another "issue play," about war (and its waste), that voters found most affecting.

With only a few weeks until the Tony Awards' nominations deadline, a flurry of seven shows opened in rapid succession beginning with Peter Morgan's *Frost/Nixon* (April 22; 45 performances as of May 31) at the Bernard B. Jacobs Theatre. Honored as a 2006–07 Best Play, an essay by Charles McNulty appears in the next section of this volume. Frank Langella's creation of disgraced former President Richard Nixon had been eagerly awaited after nearly six months at London's Donmar Warehouse and the West End's Gielgud Theatre. Langella did not disappoint, giving a nuanced, Tony Award-winning portrayal that made Nixon seem human, if flawed and more than a bit pathetic. Elizabeth Drew complained in the *Nation* that the play's perspective on Nixon was ahistorical, that some of the "facts" were incorrect and as a result the play sank to the level of propaganda. McNulty addresses these and other issues in his essay on the play. Yet another film became a Broadway musical with the premiere of *Legally Blonde* (April 29; 36 performances as of May 31), based on the 2001 Reese Witherspoon vehicle. Laura Bell Bundy brought bouncy life to the role of Elle Woods, a shallow, pampered California girl who excels—after the tiniest struggle—at Harvard Law School and finds true love along the way. *Variety*'s Rooney struck just the right chords when he wrote, "It may not be bulging with subtext or boast a score for the ages, but this pinksapoppin funhouse delivers exactly what it promises." *Times*man Brantley suggested, "Flossing between songs is recommended" because the show was a "nonstop sugar rush." *USA Today*'s Gardner was a bit more dour, calling *Legally Blonde*, "yet another self-consciously campy, intermittently clever wink-fest that flatters its audience's pop-culture awareness and populist impulses." Winer of *Newsday* noted the target audience for the show—girls between childhood and teen years known as "'tweens"—and seemed to answer Rooney's comment about subtext as she worried that the show reassured "America's 'tween girls that they can grow up to be a bimbo and a brain on Broadway today."

As April turned to May, theater became decidedly more serious with the opening of *Coram Boy* (May 2; 30 performances). The play is based on a juvenile novel about the tricks of fate that lead one—in this case a "Coram boy" or foundling—to become either privileged or deprived. Set in the mid-18th century, the story centered on the abuse of children by those who would sell them into servitude and those who "purchased" them. A popular holiday offering for two seasons at the National Theatre (UK), the play also featured an ending replete with Handel's "Hallelujah Chorus"—which seemed heavyhanded and borderline offensive to anyone not amused to stand, celebrate Jesus Christ and sing along. (Or maybe it was just a little trick to guarantee a standing ovation.) The final chorus, however, was perfectly in keeping with the production's unstinting, overheated melodrama. The New York critics were dismissive and the play departed before the season's end.

The next night a bit of musical-theater history was celebrated when *LoveMusik* (May 3; 32 performances as of May 31) opened under the direction of Harold Prince. The story of Kurt Weill and Lotte Lenya's long and torturous relationship, *LoveMusik* covered the 30-year period from their meeting until after his death. Starring Michael Cerveris and Donna Murphy, who were pitch-perfect in every sense, the production also highlighted Weill's relationship with the lusty (and crusty) Bertolt Brecht—David Pittu in a splendid turn. The songs, of course, featured music by Weill with lyrics by a variety of his collaborators, including Brecht, Maxwell Anderson, Ira Gershwin and others. Constructed from letters between Weill and Lenya, Alfred Uhry's book was gently dismissed—if there is such a thing—but the glory of the piece was to hear Murphy soar as Lenya.

As the Broadway season tumbled toward its conclusion, the brilliant Marian Seldes and the phenomenal Angela Lansbury joined forces to deliver Terrence McNally's play about a pair of elderly tennis players, *Deuce* (May 6; 29 performances as of May 31). Centered on a former doubles team, the story unearths all of the regrets and animosities of their past life together—which ended, as partnerships often do, with an aggrieved party. The play began life as a playlet performed for a theater benefit and evolved into a longer version. Some of the excitement was created by the return of Lansbury to a Broadway production after an absence of nearly 24 years, but the pairing with Seldes was particularly felicitous. As Isherwood wrote in the *Times*, "In my view if you have not seen Marian Seldes on a New York stage, you are not a true New Yorker." Although there is little in the way of dramatic conflict or action in the play, it was a marvel simply to sit in the theater and watch two grande dames work their magic.

There was an odd symmetry between the last two Broadway productions to open this season. August Wilson's final play, *Radio Golf* (May 8; 28 performances as of May 31), was chosen as a Best Play and an essay by Christopher Rawson follows in the next section of this volume. It has been sad to consider that there will be no more plays from one of our greatest, most poetic writers. In addition to the Broadway bow of *Radio Golf*, New Yorkers were treated to the Signature Theatre Company's productions of earlier work by Wilson. The Signature celebration had been planned before the playwright's illness, but was cancelled after Wilson's death when the family felt the need to reassess possible tributes. Less than a month later the decision was reversed, shows to be offered were shifted and Wilson's widow, Constanza Romero, was added as an associate artist.

The Off Broadway offerings were *Seven Guitars* (August 24; 53 performances) and *King Hedley II* (March 11; 49 performances). The Off Off Broadway production, *Two Trains Running* (December 3), directed by the excellent Wilson interpreter Lou Bellamy, did not rise to the number of performances per week required for the Plays Produced Off Broadway section of *Best Plays*. It was, however, a taut and intense production with exceptional performances by Chad L. Coleman, Frankie Faison, Arthur French, Ron Cephas Jones and the rest of the cast. The Signature celebration began in the summer with *Seven Guitars*, directed by Ruben Santiago-Hudson, who received a Tony Award for his acting in the play's 1996 Broadway production. In the first moments of the play, which ruminates on the nature of life and death, there was an immediate sense that all of Wilson's plays should be staged in the Signature's space. Beginning with a mournful, funereal tone, *Seven Guitars* conveyed the intimate emotional impact that Wilson's plays cannot attain in theaters that seat a thousand people. With the marvelous Stephen McKinley Henderson at the core of the play's ensemble, the production was a fitting start to a richly deserved tribute.

The final play of the Wilson celebration, *King Hedley II*, was less successful, although it would be hard to discern that from the New York reviews, which resembled "puff" journalism. Directed by Derrick Sanders, with Henderson again in a key role, *Hedley* is one of the two or three Wilson plays that have an unfinished feeling about them. In the 2001 Broadway production, director Marion McClinton and star Brian Stokes Mitchell seemed overmatched by material that retained a lugubrious, rambling rhythm despite the lead character's intense obsession with getting a fresh start in life—a theme that plays out in virtually all of Wilson's plays. It is one thing for a character to be forced to push against other characters in the world of the play, but when the play itself holds the character down, something has to give. A production at St. Paul's Penumbra Theatre Company in 2003—directed by the aforementioned Bellamy—featured an actor or two who might not have been up to the work and yet that version was gut-wrenchingly powerful in ways that neither New York production managed. It is also incumbent on young directors to research the periods about which Wilson was writing: behavior changed across the 20th century. Although the playwright's characters in 1985 Pittsburgh were dealing with contemporary issues such as drive-by shootings and drug-related crimes, people in the 1980s did not behave exactly as they do today. In the 2006–07 *King Hedley II*, it seemed as though the characters had just stepped in from the street and it made a difficult play more muddled than necessary.

Even as Wilson spent the final 25 or so years of his life working to reclaim the African-American narrative in a language and with a truth that he felt in his bones, the playwright also became—especially in his final decade—a lightning rod for his outspoken position on colorblind and nontraditional casting. As Wilson said in a 1996 speech to the Theatre Communications Group conference:

> To mount an all-black production of *Death of a Salesman* or any other play conceived for white actors as an investigation of the human condition through the specifics of white culture is to deny us our own humanity, our own history, and the need to make our own investigations from the cultural ground on which we stand as black Americans.

At the same conference, he also stated that any black actor—he specifically named Andre Braugher—performing an English king in Shakespeare was complicit in his own cultural erasure.

It was ironic, then, that the night after Wilson's gentle comedy on the mores (and cultural responsibilities) of African Americans in the 1990s opened on Broadway—the capstone to his 10-play cycle on the African-American experience—a musical revival of *110 in the Shade* (May 9; 26 performances as of May 31) made its bow at Roundabout Theatre Company's Studio 54. Audra McDonald, the superb singer and actor with four Tony Awards to her credit, played the crucial leading female role of Lizzie—the musical is based on N. Richard Nash's *The Rainmaker*—to unanimous critical approval. McDonald is African American, her father was played by John Cullum who is white, but she had a brother who was white and one who was not. The setting was Texas in 1936, but there were interracial relationships and no one seemed to notice. Do we no longer see color? Or is it merely wishful thinking? What would August Wilson say? Whatever the answers, directors probably should not pretend race does not exist—especially when the subject is Depression-era Texas. That said, the other challenge for the creators of *110 in the Shade* was to make the incredibly beautiful McDonald homely enough to blossom under the tutelage of Starbuck. Despite Wilson's reservations, there should be no doubt that McDonald can play any role, any time, and there will be no subversion or erasure—just pure virtuosity.

By the Numbers

AS WE COME to the end of our overview on the Broadway season, we should explore a few trends that arise by examining seasonal numbers published in *Variety* and gleaned from reports by the Broadway League, which changed its name from the League of American Theatres and Producers as we were preparing for press. The most significant number that jumps from the page is not the attendance total for the 2006–07 season, which was another record high of 12.3 million (an increase of 2.6 percent over the previous year). Ticket prices for musicals, arguably the bread-and-butter of the Broadway industry jumped an average of $5.13 this season to $77.28—an increase of 7 percent. This means that the average price of a ticket to a musical rose 13 percent over the past three years from $68.21. And it is even more unsettling that tickets for nonmusical plays rose by 16 percent over that same three-year period—though the average price for tickets to plays remains more than $13 less than those for musicals. Perhaps it is not so scary after all: attendance set a new record (12.3 million) and ticket prices overall (musicals and plays combined) increased only 6.2 percent. But a tipping point may come soon and Broadway producers, who increasingly rely on tourists, need to keep an eye on global economic health and the cost of travel. Besides equity traders on Wall Street, who out there is seeing a 6.2 percent annual rise in income?

The number of new Broadway productions was down by 4 this season. Despite an article by Robertson in the *New York Times* celebrating the wave of plays opening on Broadway in the spring season, play production actually declined from 2005–06 to 2006–07 (see the table and chart on page 4). New plays were steady this season—one could only argue that the new-play number rose this season if *The Coast of Utopia* were counted as three plays, which it was not—there were 8 new plays this year as there were last. One of the production declines on Broadway is in the play-revival category. The 2006–07 season saw a drop in play revivals from 11 in 2005–06 to 8 this year. New musicals were flat for our purposes because we did not count 2005–06's *Ring of Fire* as a musical last year but as a specialty. Broadway musical revivals increased this season from 3 to 5, solo performances declined from 4 to 2 and specialties were also cut in half to a single show. These last two statistics may be harbingers of good news if producers continue the trend toward plays and musicals, and away from solo and specialty shows.

Other good news, depending on how it is interpreted, might be found in the fact that 54 percent (19) of this season's productions survived to the end of the season. Most of those survivors, of course, opened in the final eight weeks of Tony Award eligibility. At the end of the prior season, the surviving shows equaled only 41 percent (16) of the total output. However one looks at it, though, the fact remains that many of those 2006–07 survivors will succumb to summer's siren call of "dim your lights and cut your losses."

Although there were 89 productions Off Broadway this season (see table and chart on pages 14 and 15), commercial theater production in those venues was significantly lower than last year. In raw numbers, there were 27 commercial and 62 nonprofit productions Off Broadway in 2006–07.

Last year those numbers were 42 and 46, respectively. Whereas nonprofit had a slight edge in its output during the 2005–06 season (52 to 48 percent commercial), this year the difference is 69.7 to 30.3 percent in favor of new nonprofit production. Within that model, though, it is worth noting that new-play production overall was down 12.1 percent in 2006–07 (36 new plays) while play revivals more than doubled to 17. New musicals also declined this season by almost 19 percent (13 new musicals this year). Musical revivals increased by 1, solo shows declined by 25 percent and specialties nearly doubled to 9 for the season. Clearly, the complaints Off Broadway producers have made about costs and recoupment have begun to slow development of new productions, with presenters opting for more revivals and fewer new works. Of the 89 new productions Off Broadway this season, only 10 were still running at the end of the season—and most of those were scheduled to close in summer 2007.

A final note about the numbers: a few years ago we realized that revivals of past Best Plays were another window into the adventurousness of programmers. This year 11 of the 35 Broadway shows were former Best Plays—that does not include four new ones honored in this volume. One of the things readers of the series should know is that for the first 80 years or so box-office success and critical approbation were keys to being honored by the series. These days we are less concerned with the box office of our honorees than we are with the quality of writing, how work connects on a human level and how it may reflect (or refract) society. In addition to the six Best Plays selected from the Off Broadway offerings in the 2006–07 season, eight former Best Plays are among the revivals, including the concert performances of *Follies* at Encores!

Off Broadway: Nonprofit Renaissance

NOW THAT OSKAR EUSTIS has had an opportunity to fully take the reins at the Public Theater, it is obvious that he has given that iconic theater an injection of energy that continues and enhances the work of his predecessor, George C. Wolfe. During the season under consideration, the Public continued its high-profile summer season at the Delacorte Theater in Central Park under its New York Shakespeare Festival banner in addition to keeping the beehive of theaters on Lafayette Street humming along. In *Macbeth* (June 28; 11 performances) Liev Schreiber and Jennifer Ehle—busy stage actors this season—offered a glimpse into the dark soul of naked ambition. Moisés Kaufman's rubble-strewn battlefield at the Delacorte provided a stark reminder not only of Macbeth's dilemma but of our own, in our own time. Teagle F. Bougere, a brilliant and underused actor, was a suitable Banquo. (When is this fine actor going to land his breakthrough role? Pay attention, casting directors.) The truly hot ticket at the Delacorte in summer 2006 was the production of Bertolt Brecht's *Mother Courage and Her Children* (August 21; 10 performances) with Meryl Streep, Kevin Kline and Austin Pendleton. Translated by Tony Kushner and staged by George C. Wolfe, this *Mother Courage* was part agitprop, part music hall, very funny and a bit too long. Streep worked her heart out onstage in a role that perhaps calls for a bit less passion, but it was her full-throated singing that surprised quite a few observers. Might she make her way back to Broadway in a musical? Kline made another appearance in a Public production this season when he essayed the title role of *King Lear* (March 7; 18 performances) as a sprightly, prematurely gray pomposity in the James Lapine production—with music by Stephen Sondheim and Michael Starobin. Kline as the old king meant there would be no difficulty in filling the theater with patrons, but the sticking point came in the conception of the main character (and the production). Lear is not a man trapped by his recollection of his innocent little girls—as Lapine seemed to conceive—unless in the case of this vital, youngish Lear there is an early onset of Alzheimer's disease. The character's tragic downfall is in his "unmaking" himself as a king; by doing so he opens a Pandora's Box of ill-nature that destroys his kingdom, civil society and, not coincidentally, his lineage.

Diana Son returned to the Public with *Satellites* (June 18; 17 performances) a comic drama about an interracial couple who pioneer a dicey Brooklyn neighborhood as they try to make a life amid the chaos of plaster dust and tensions among their friends. As directed by Michael Greif, Sandra Oh, Johanna Day, Ron Cephas Jones and Kevin Carroll kept the action—and anxiety—bubbling on an innovative set design by Mark Wendland. The Public continued its partnership with the Labyrinth Theater Company in productions of *School of the Americas* (July 6; 22 performances) by José Rivera and *A Small, Melodramatic Story* (October 24; 16 performances) by Stephen Belber. Later in the season, Labyrinth presented its own production *Jack Goes Boating* (March 18; 49 performances) by Bob Glaudini at the Public. The Labyrinth aesthetic is a clear one: hard-hitting, socially aware dramas about life at the margins of society. In *School*, co-artistic director John Ortiz portrayed the revolutionary Che Guevara in his final hours under the control of Bolivian and US authorities. *Melodramatic* turned on the lies we tell ourselves, the secrets our government keeps from us and our fear of what lies ahead. *Jack Goes Boating* featured both of the artistic directors, Ortiz and Philip Seymour Hoffman, in a production directed by Peter DuBois. With Daphne Rubin-Vega and Beth Cole in the female roles, the play explored the experience of a man who craves intimacy but is not sure how to get it (or what to do with it when he gets it). Hoffman subtly played the man with limited social skills in this fine piece of ensemble work. Another family at the margins of society, made an appearance in Julia Cho's *Durango* (November 20; 24 performances) when an Asian-American family found itself dispossessed of the American dream.

Finally, the Public (and Berkeley Repertory Theatre) commissioned a musical from Stew and Heidi Rodewald that became *Passing Strange* (May 14; 19 performances as of May 31). A 2006–07 Best Play based on its Off Broadway production, directed by Annie Dorsen, the musical is celebrated in an essay by Alisa Solomon in the next section of this volume. Suffice to say here that Stew's story of a young African-American maturing in a middle-class home in Los Angeles is one of the most visceral new musicals in many a day. Audience members need not be black, middle class, from California or have spent formative artistic years among the European avant garde to be moved by *Passing Strange*. All they needed, as was demonstrated in performance, was a pulse. And then, as the man says, "it's alright."

Playwrights Horizons and Manhattan Theatre Club kept their lights blazing with 10 Off Broadway productions between them. Neither company seemed to have thematics in mind other than trying to stage work that each organization felt passionate about presenting. Playwrights staged five new plays and a musical with MTC presenting four—though MTC also staged three productions on Broadway. Each company managed to get a Best Play on the 2006–07 roster: Bruce Norris's *The Pain and the Itch* (September 21; 30 performances) at Playwrights and an Americanized version of David Harrower's *Blackbird* (April 10; 60 performances as of May 31) at MTC.

As the season got underway Playwrights began with *The Busy World Is Hushed* (June 25; 17 performances) by Keith Bunin. A lovely play about the power of faith and love, *Busy World* featured Jill Clayburgh as an Episcopal priest whose estranged son finds love (and possibility) with the man who assists her theological writing. In *The Pain and the Itch*, a dysfunctional family—is there another kind?—finds itself trying to come to terms with its consumerist sense of entitlement as an encroaching immigrant population disturbs the family's comfort zone. John Istel discusses the scathing comedy of the piece in the section that follows. Tanya Barfield's *Blue Door* (October 8; 25 performances) sends an African-American man on an internal journey to face lingering issues regarding racial and cultural identity. Directed by Leigh Silverman, Reg E. Cathey provided the solid, central figure of a man who seeks not to be pigeon-holed for the color of his skin even as he finds there is more he needs to know about himself.

In *Floyd and Clea Under the Western Sky* (December 5; 16 performances) and *Frank's Home* (January 30; 24 performances), there was something of a Goodman Theatre festival at Playwrights around the holiday season. *Floyd and Clea* is a country-western musical by David Cale and Jonathan Kreisberg about an alcoholic singer of middle age and a sweet, young thing who is on the rise. Developed and first produced at the Goodman, *Floyd and Clea* has much in common with the themes of many country-western songs about life and heartache. Cale played Floyd and Mary Faber was the young woman who would remember him through all of her success. Cale and Faber made an unlikely pair that beguiled a fair number of critics. *Frank's Home* by Richard Nelson was essentially a transplanted production from Chicago, where it played a month earlier with the same cast and creative team. The Frank of the title is the great architect Frank Lloyd Wright (Peter Weller), who in 1923 spends time in California with his grown children, his mentor Louis Sullivan (Harris Yulin) and his girlfriend while working on a commission for a school. A school? This is a great genius, for heaven's sake. But that's what happens when genius has trouble relating to other human beings. Needless to say, perhaps, is that Wright bounced back from those dark days of 1923 with some of his greatest works over the next 45 or so years of life.

The final Playwrights entry this season was a collaboration with the innovative Edge Theater Company, founded by Carolyn Cantor and David Korins. *Essential Self-Defense* (March 28; 23 performances) is both a departure and somewhat familiar coming from playwright Adam Rapp—a frequent collaborator with Cantor and Korins. Following the Pulitzer Prize-finalist success of the darkly naturalistic *Red Light Winter*, a Best Play of 2005–06, *Essential* goes into quirky tangents that are implicitly (and explicitly) critical of American culture. Delivered by a goofy, alienated guy (played by Paul Sparks) who speaks in a monotone and works as a tackling dummy for a self-defense school, the cultural critique lingered only for a moment before it dispersed with audience laughter. Rapp's characters are given to saying things such as, "talent is a fallacy perpetuated by gym teachers and top-40 DJs." The dialogue is funny and incisive, but there is a sense that the playwright is using this play almost as a literary "palate cleanser" and that he does not want the play (or his goofball character's ideas) to be taken too seriously. Scene designer Korins helps him in that regard with cartoonish settings that are either mighty grim or far too cheerful. Cantor, who staged the production, kept the unruly script and company moving sensibly forward.

MTC got its fall season underway with Paul Rudnick's *Regrets Only* (November 19; 81 performances), a satirical look at the ways in which gays are overlooked in polite society—until they do something impolite. In *Regrets*, an elegant fashion designer (George Grizzard) is close friends with a rich Republican (Christine Baranski) whose husband and daughter are working on an antigay-marriage bill. The designer calls for a "day without gays" and the ensuing strike causes comic mayhem, giving Rudnick an excuse to traffic in all known stereotypes of gays. David Greig's *The American Pilot* (November 21; 47 performances) focuses on what happens when an American crashes in a Third World country beset by civil war. The coming culture clash—make that culture "crush"—is no less poignant for our knowing it will happen as surely as the sun will rise. Charles Busch's *Our Leading Lady* (March 20; 48 performances) centers on Laura Keene (Kate Mulgrew), a 19th century actor-manager who hopes to revive her flagging fortunes by inviting the President to see her current play: *Our American Cousin* at the Ford's Theatre in Washington, DC. The President attends, but the outcome is not as Keene had hoped when President Lincoln is assassinated during the show. Harrower's Best Play, *Blackbird*, caused many to say that he has just the right last name given the taut drama that evolves when a young woman (Alison Pill) confronts a man of middle age (Jeff Daniels) who had sex with her when she was 12 years old. Vacillating between anger and neediness, the young woman at times seems about to either kill him or kiss him. There are moments in the play in which almost no one in the audience seemed to moved or even breathe—and this was at MTC, where the audiences seem never to be quiet. David Cote's essay follows in the next section of this volume.

Women and Men

RELATIONSHIPS BETWEEN WOMEN and men were much on the minds of playwrights (and their nonprofit presenters) in the 2006–07 Off Broadway season. From MCC Theater, Second Stage Theatre, Lincoln Center Theater and back to the Public Theater, playwrights looked into the ways in which men and women relate, communicate, connect. What they showed did not make for a very pretty picture. In Neil LaBute's *Some Girl(s)* (June 8; 38 performances) at MCC Theater, a man who has used women badly and discarded them decides to make amends and travels to revisit his former conquests—meetings that do not end as he expects (or hopes) they might. LaBute's *Wrecks* (October 10; 42 performances) appeared at the Public in the fall with Ed Harris in the solo piece. Harris's character Edward Carr is in a room with a casket containing his dead wife, whom he loved very much. The piece is a confessional about their lives together that eventually reveals an Oedipal twist.

Second Stage Theatre had a Theresa Rebeck festival of sorts with two of the playwright's works receiving their New York premieres. *The Water's Edge* (June 15; 29 performances) featured the estimable Kate Burton as an embittered divorcee whose ex-husband returns with a new, younger woman and attempts to reclaim his place in the family he has abandoned. Scathingly funny, the story is reminiscent of Aeschylus's *Agamemnon* in that there is a dead daughter whose demise Burton's character blames on her ex-husband (Tony Goldwyn), an angry daughter in the Electra mold (Mamie Gummer), a son who might equal Orestes (Austin Lysy) and the sexy young woman (Katharine Powell) whose warnings go as unheeded as Cassandra's. There is even a (literal) bloodbath, though we only see the remnants. Rebeck writes terrific, snappy dialogue, knows how to tell a story and creates strong women characters. It's hard to know why the critics uniformly thought her bloodletting at the play's end was "illogical" and "inconsistent," unless none of them had ever been divorced—or in a relationship that soured badly. (Could there be lingering resentment over Rebeck's famously high-paying jobs in television? Do we want our playwrights poor?)

Rebeck's next foray at SST was a restaging of her satire that was the hit of the 2006 Humana Festival of New American Plays, *The Scene* (January 11; 33 performances). Although there are always dissenting opinions among the New York theater critics, *The Scene* received extremely good notices. There were rumors of a transfer to Broadway, where the play might have done well, but nothing came of them. The play's emphasis on the midlife crisis of a man living at the fringe of New York's cultural scene, when he feels as though he should be closer to its center, caused some of the most raucous, pained laughter from male New Yorkers of a certain age that one is ever likely to hear. Chris Jones's essay on this Best Play of 2006–07 appears in the next section of this volume.

Eric Bogosian's *subUrbia* (September 28; 37 performances) and Terrence McNally's *Some Men* (March 26; 32 performances), which also appeared at SST this season, do not truly fit under the "women and men" rubric of this section. In the case of the Bogosian revival, directed by his wife Jo Bonney, the 1994 play examines a group of arrested adolescents who have not quite acquired a taste for adulthood and remain stranded as they await the next thing. The fall 2006 production may have raised a question for many adults who work with young people in today's highly competitive culture: Are there any "aimless" kids left in the world? It seems today that every young person is programmed from birth to fill each day with achievement. McNally's *Some Men* has even less to do with intergender issues than Bogosian's play. A series of sketches set across 80 years, *Some Men* details the social and cultural strides made by gays over eight decades, ultimately suggesting what is left to be accomplished.

Lincoln Center Theater presented three plays in its Off Broadway theater that treated relationships between women and men in fascinating ways. The LCT summer season got underway with Richard Greenberg's *The House in Town* (June 19; 48 performances). Featuring Mark Harelik as a prosperous Jewish merchant and Jessica Hecht as his WASP wife, Greenberg and director Doug Hughes, examine the spoken and unspoken things that pass between a husband and wife. In the case of *House* these things happen against the backdrop of 1929 when people presumably did not communicate as "easily" as we do now. As the story unfolds, a marriage unravels because both husband and wife have secrets of which they are ashamed—and they misunderstand one another in every possible way. It is as if Greenberg is arguing that time passes—is passing—and if one is not right here, right now, one is surely lost. Sarah Ruhl's *The Clean House* (October 30; 88 performances) is a winner of several awards including the 2004 Susan Smith Blackburn Prize. Similar to other works by Ruhl, *Clean House* exists on an ethereal, magical plane where anything is possible. And yet, for all of its magical qualities, there is a broken heart at its core—the heart of a woman, any woman. The women in *Clean House* pursue their hearts' desires with wit, rue, hope and determination. For their effort, they get cancer, death, alienation, heartbreak; and yet they find ways to keep themselves moving forward. Anne Marie Welsh discusses her take on *Clean House*, a Best Play of 2006–07, in the next section of this volume. In Christopher Shinn's *Dying City* (March 4; 65 performances) an actor confronts the widow of his dead twin brother in a search for answers. Sometimes, he finds, there is no answer or, if there is, you may not want to hear it. A Best Play of 2006–07, Charles Isherwood discusses *Dying City* in his essay in the next section of this volume.

It would be unfair not to mention briefly the Atlantic Theater Company—which is generally listed in our Off Off Broadway section due to its number of performances per week. Atlantic's production of the Harley Granville Barker play, *The Voysey Inheritance* (December 6; 113 performances), as adapted by David Mamet, possessed a crispness of dialogue and yet captured perfectly the style of its 1905 setting. With a cast of 12 headed by Michael Stuhlbarg, Fritz Weaver, Peter Maloney and others, the revival was a sharp reminder that the dirty dealings of unethical speculators and financiers is nothing new. In fact, it had an odd kinship with other Mamet work such as *American Buffalo* and *Glengarry Glen Ross*. Director David Warren and designer Derek McLane managed to make the tiny stage at Atlantic feel exactly as though it were a sumptuous drawing room.

Roundabout Theatre Company presented three productions in its Laura Pels Theatre at the Harold and Miriam Steinberg Center for Theatre in the 2006–07 Off Broadway season. None of the productions seemed to have a thematic among them, but it is not required. Given the propensity for casting stars at the Roundabout, it was refreshing to see theater actors John Ellison Conlee, Denis O'Hare, Katie Finneran and Logan Marshall-Green in Greg Kotis's *Pig Farm* (June 27; 80 performances). A farce about a pig farmer polluting the environment and worrying that the Environmental Protection Agency will catch him dumping sewage, the play was directed with gusto by John Rando. Tennessee Williams's one-act play *Suddenly Last Summer* (November 15; 74 performances) featured radiant Blythe Danner opposite lovely Carla Gugino in a high-stakes battle for a central "truth" in their family. Patrick Marber's *Howard Katz* (March 1; 77 performances) starred Alfred Molina as a British talent agent in a midlife crisis, who also happens to be a Jew. As Katz, Molina is so thoroughly disliked he has nowhere to turn when his difficulties threaten to overtake him.

Art and Commerce

ALTHOUGH THESE ARE hard times for the commercial producer Off Broadway, eight of the 13 new musicals in those venues were commercial. Another, *Edward Scissorhands* (March 16; 19 performances) played at the nonprofit Brooklyn Academy of Music even though it looked as though it was financed by commercial producers. A couple of the commercial Off Broadway musicals will have future lives: just before this volume went to press, *[title of show]* (July 20; 84 performances) was preparing for a Broadway opening and *In the Heights* (February 8; 129 performances as of May 31) had received multiple Tony Awards at the 2008 ceremony—more about these in future volumes. Although we do not concern ourselves with subsequent seasons—we are, after all, creating a narrative of nearly 500 pages designed to help convey a sense of one particular year in theater—it seems reasonable to note that these "bootstrap" musicals have met with considerable success.

Elsewhere on the frontlines of commercial Off Broadway theater were the long-running solo shows *A Jew Grows in Brooklyn* (September 30; 339

performances as of May 31), *No Child . . .* (July 16; 297 performances as of May 31), *25 Questions for a Jewish Mother* (October 12; 178 performances) and *My Mother's Italian, My Father's Jewish, and I'm in Therapy!* (December 8; 197 performances as of May 31). These solo shows and the revival of *The Fantasticks* (August 23; 322 performances as of May 31) all demonstrate that it is possible to keep a show running Off Broadway if you keep expenses low and give audiences something to which they can relate. But are these shows good for the future of dramatic literature and, by extension, the theater itself? Will specialty, solo and revival productions come to dominate development in the commercial Off Broadway theater?

The guess here is that these productions will play a growing role in Off Broadway's short-term commercial future. Nonprofit theaters will surely continue to dominate when it comes to the development and presentation of new plays and musicals—and not just Off Broadway. Look for our future volumes to see how these concerns evolve.

THE BEST PLAYS
OF 2006–2007

2006–2007 Best Play

BLACKBIRD

By David Harrower

○ ○ ○ ○ ○

Essay by David Cote

UNA: How many other twelve-year old girls have you had sex with?

[. . .]

RAY: None.

UNA: Just me.

In that room.

SCOTTISH PLAYWRIGHT David Harrower's *Blackbird* was the most unconventional love story of the season. Anyone who has seen or read the wrenching, corrosive duet might stop at "love story" and question this essayist's morals. Harrower's 90-minute work concerns Ray, a 55-year-old middle-management type and Una, 27, a woman with whom he had an affair—15 years ago. That is, when she was 12 and he was 40. Ray spent several years in prison for molesting a minor. Nine years on, he changed his name, moved to a new town and found steady work. Una has tracked him down and their intense, real-time encounter in an office lunchroom constitutes the action. This is not your typical May-December romance.

Sensationalist though its premise is, *Blackbird* has highbrow antecedents. Ephebophilia drives the protagonists of *Lolita* and *Death in Venice* in which Humbert Humbert and Gustav von Aschenbach drape their panting pursuit of teens in aesthetic garlands. For Humbert, Lolita is a bewitching nymphet whom he cannot resist, while the Polish youth Tadzio casts a hypnotic spell over the dying Aschenbach. For both men, the pubescent girl or boy exerts a supernatural magic, like a myth of Ovidian transmutation.

Blackbird's Ray, however, is no silver-tongued aesthete, but a bland, corporate Everyman who "made the biggest [. . .] mistake of my life." Both a simple truth and a minimization of guilt, Ray's remorse is the first layer of a disturbing, maze-like drama about sexual attraction, power and the slippery nature of memory.

Cradle robber: Alison Pill and Jeff Daniels in Blackbird. *Photo: Joan Marcus*

BLACKBIRD'S SINGLE LOCATION is a drab canteen-cum-smoke room. In Manhattan Theatre Club's Stage I, scene designer Scott Pask created a supply-catalogue arrangement of plastic chairs, gray carpeting and a conference table, bleakly bathed in Paul Gallo's fluorescent lighting. More illumination trickled in from a frosted window in the upstage wall, beyond which we saw shadows of office workers passing through a corridor. For any poor soul who has labored in an office, this cheap, sunless environment was all too familiar. It was late in the workday; the floor and table were littered with sandwich wrappers, chips bags, soda bottles and the like.

Ray (Jeff Daniels) enters, his hand clamped around the twig-like arm of Una (Alison Pill), whom he briskly steers. He is dressed in standard business attire, dress shirt, tie, cell phone clipped to belt. She wears black pumps, a simple red-and-gold pattered dress, a dark scarf wound around her neck. He obviously wants to get them into this room, away from the eyes of his coworkers. She seems to be in a daze. They face each other across a small patch of space but—we'll soon learn—a vertiginous chasm of years. A spectator knowing nothing of the play might infer a fling gone bad, but would assume the affair happened recently. In a sense, it did: Lines spill out *in medias res:*

UNA: Shock.

RAY: Of course.

Yes.

Now

(*Pause.*)

UNA: And

RAY: Wait

(*Pause.*)

(*He goes to the closed door, opens it a small way.*)

Sensationalist as its premise is, *Blackbird* has highbrow antecedents.

Such economy of language: In seven words and three stage directions, Harrower establishes the dominant motifs—trauma, memory, power. Both are stunned, past events are flooding back, yet Ray's main concern is to create an exit. Is it her or himself he is protecting by the almost silly cracking open of the door? Who has power in this room? The language is not itself extraordinary, but we immediately grasp the playwright's strategy: Harrower seeks a fierce, staccato lyricism. The obvious debt is to Harold Pinter and his use of flatness and silence. The classic Pinter elements are there: two figures fight for dominance in an enclosed space, words used as weapons, some blunt, some scalpel-sharp. By stunting his characters' thoughts in fragments that sit precariously on the page, Harrower unlocks a jittery energy. As with a good painter, he exploits the negative space on his canvas.

UNA: But so what do you actually make here?

RAY: It's

Dentistry.

UNA: Because

RAY: Sometimes pharmaceutical.

UNA: The name on the front.

You can't tell.

[. . .]

Ray has tried to make himself as nondescript as the building he works in, to blend in and forget the "mistake" he made years before. He wanted to be invisible, as he now wants himself and Una to remain unseen, away from his coworkers.

> RAY: I don't have to listen.
>
> I don't have to say anything.
>
> So
>
> but a few minutes
>
> a couple of minutes and then you will have to go and
>
> because I will be needed back.

The flustered Ray demands to know what she wants. Una feels a draft through the cracked door, and wants to close it, but he insists that the door stay open. She gets up and closes the door.

Una saw Ray's picture in a trade magazine in a doctor's waiting room and drove seven hours to find him. He counters that he owes her nothing.

A threat? Alison Pill and Jeff Daniels in Blackbird. *Photo: Joan Marcus*

RAY: You don't have the right to my my my humiliation.

Where I work.

[. . .]

Walking in, asking for me

I've nothing to say to you.

I

You're a

some kind of ghost

[. . .]

She mournfully concurs:

UNA: I do feel like a ghost.

I do.

I feel like a ghost.

Everywhere I go.

[. . .]

This is a clever contrasting of Ray and Una's lives. He disappeared, changed his identity: He calls himself Peter and is seeing a woman. Una has stayed home in the town where she grew up, where she feels like a specter. In truth, both are shades of their former selves, corporeal to one another only in the shared secret of their past.

UP TO THIS POINT, the play has been quite tense, especially after Una explains that her father died six years ago and would have killed Ray if he had found him. Her eyes filling with tears, Una reaches into her handbag and Ray, along with us, assumes the worst: She's reaching for a gun. In a panic, Ray grabs the bag and rifles through it, finding a packet of tissues. "I was going to Kleenex you to death," Una says sardonically. He takes out a bottle of water. "And that's acid, not water," she tells him. The joke lightens the mood, and Una begins to draw information out of Ray. He changed his name to Peter Trowebridge, a fancy-sounding moniker that elicits a snigger from her. He is seeing a woman, who knows about his "mistake" and his time in prison. Of course, Una has little sympathy for the abuse Ray suffered in lockdown.

UNA: *I* did the sentence.

I did your sentence.

For fifteen years.

> I lost everything.
>
> I lost more than you ever did.
>
> I lost
>
> Because I never had
>
> had time to to to *begin*.

Una asks about photographs Ray took of her "Sitting on your sofa. / Lying down." He assures her they were burned, that he wouldn't, for example, put them on a website for delectation by genuine pedophiles: "Those people. / Those sick bastards," as he calls them. Perhaps disturbed by the notion that Ray incinerated her image or disgusted by his delusions, Una gets up to leave. But Ray wants her to stay, to plead his case. He is not a pedophile, he emphatically assures her. Una, he swears, was the only one. As quoted above, Ray admits he made the grossest error of his life, but he paid for it.

> RAY: Listen.
>
> I spent three years in hell.
>
> More.
>
> UNA: Yes.
>
> RAY: What they called me.
>
> Spat on, kicked.
>
> Shit, human shit thrown in my face.
>
> You know I wasn't one of them.

Harrower now eases us into a section of the play where Una and Ray reconstruct the past. Through speeches of increasing length, coherence and detail, Ray remembers the backyard barbeque to which Una's father invited him, where he met her. As evidence of him not being a child-molester, he points to the shorts he wore that day. They were tight, he says, and if he'd been aroused talking to a 12-year-old girl, there would have been a physical sign. Ray's reasoning—all at once tacky, pathetic and comical—provokes a derisive smile from Una, but Ray sticks by it. Further, he says that he read case studies about serial pedophiles, and he doesn't fit the profile.

Things then start getting complicated, as Ray alludes to Una's pursuit of him after their initial meeting at the barbeque. She wrote notes insulting his then-girlfriend and stuck them on his windshield. She got a Polaroid of him and, with her girlfriend, kissed his image. Una denies none of this. In fact, her tone seems to shift into something resembling wry nostalgia. She

Frayed nerves: Alison Pill and Jeff Daniels in
Blackbird. *Photo: Joan Marcus*

says she was stupid, too young and in love to know what was happening.
But Ray disagrees, saying that Una knew more about love than he did.

>RAY: [. . .] You couldn't wait to start menstruating.
>
>You told me that.
>
>You were sick of being treated like a child.
>
>The last thing you wanted was to be told you were a child.
>
>UNA: Jesus.
>
>RAY: You
>
>UNA: That's what children *say.*
>
>RAY: You weren't like other children.
>
>UNA: I was a girl.
>
>A virgin.
>
>An untouched body.
>
>[. . .]

The centerpiece of the play is a pair of speeches that Ray and Una deliver about the devastating final night of their affair. Ray rented a room at a bed-and-breakfast far from their town, and he drove her there. In the room, they had intercourse. During previous trysts, in a public park behind some bushes, Una alludes to fondling and possibly oral sex, but no intercourse. After sex in the rented room, she cried. They lay in each other's arms. Then Ray went out for a pack of cigarettes and never came back. In a long, devastating monologue that goes on in agonizing length and detail, Una relates the aching sense of loss and abandonment. She left the hotel room, wandering the streets to find Ray, attracting the curious attention of strangers. The desolation, the childlike terror that Harrower evokes is shattering.

Then it's Ray's turn to tell his side of the story. He didn't abandon her. He had a drink in the bar, to summon up courage and figure out a plan for their return on the ferry. When he returned to the bed-and-breakfast, Una had gone. Panicking, he backtracked to find her, but only aroused the locals' suspicions. Ray searched for her but, terrified of being caught, he drove away from the town. After hours of aimlessly driving around, he found a telephone booth by the side of the road and called the police.

TOWARD THE END of *Blackbird,* Harrower throws an escalating series of shocks. One is that Una refused to testify against Ray. Her parents and the police forcibly extracted DNA samples from her, providing evidence of Ray's sexual contact. We learn that Una is promiscuous, and has had dozen of lovers. She taunts his sagging, aged flesh and that of the woman he is dating—echoing her tactics of 15 years earlier—which prompts a burst of physical aggression from him. When the tussling subsides, they look at the garbage-strewn lunchroom, agree that it is disgusting and proceed to gleefully upend the trashcan, reveling in their childish, antisocial naughtiness. This excitement leads, inevitably, to a flash of erotic attraction between them. They kiss, he admits that he still masturbates to the memory of her, and they begin to undress each other hungrily. Ray pulls away. "I can't," he says. Una asks, with the innocence of a child, "Am I too old?"

At this key moment, Harrower throws a stomach-turning curveball. Someone calls out for "Peter" in the hallway. Una is confused, she retreats to a corner. The door opens and a young girl enters, goes to Ray and puts her arms around him. The girl sees Una and asks who she is. Una steers the child out of the room, saying that she is a friend of Peter's and they were just talking. Naturally, we think the worst: Ray remains a practicing pedophile and Una has met his latest victim. But Ray assures Una that the girl is the daughter of the woman he is dating.

The final lines of the play are desperately jagged. Una clings to Ray, begs him not to leave, says that the girl and her mother need to know. He throws her off, shouting, "Get the fuck off me," and leaves. She cries, "Ray," and runs after him. On this note of anguished, unresolved rawness, Harrower, true to his name, ends the drama. No closure, no justice, no take-away moral. We sit there, *Playbills* gnarled and damp, wondering if Ray is telling the truth, if Una will confront him and his current girlfriend, or even if they might resume their affair, this time as adults.

AND THEN THERE is another question: why *Blackbird?* In a March 2007 interview, Harrower explained that while working on the play he was listening to John Coltrane's version of the 1926 standard "Bye Bye Blackbird." According to the playwright, "[Coltrane] just improvised it for about fifteen minutes, and it felt like two people improvising, doing an extended kind of solo. After that, it came into my mind that, perhaps, [Ray] might have played the Beatles' 'White' album as he and [Una] were driving and he called her his blackbird." The jazz influence, instruments engaged in spirited interplay, then breaking out into extended solos, certainly can be seen in the structure of the play.

Harrower also explained that the theme of child abuse was secondary to his main preoccupation with memory. He expressed fascination with the psychic spectacle of two people jointly recreating the past. "I didn't want to write a pedophile drama," he explained. "It's been done before. What was more interesting to me was the reverberations of how people carry those experiences within them."

If there is a villain in this play, it is time. Time is out of joint, causing lovers to be born too far apart. Time, which can erode memory, muddle facts. As Harrower has done, let's put ourselves in Ray's place. You're at a party and you strike up a conversation with a young girl. She fascinates you with her premature wisdom and sensitivity. You are drawn with an intensity you haven't felt since your own youth. Embedded in all such asymmetrical relations there is a combination of power and nostalgia: A girl reaches forward to her future and the man stretches backwards for his past. A man sees a girl on the cusp of pubescence—*womanhood,* he substitutes in his mind. The very incompleteness of her sexuality arouses him; it complements his unfinished self.

THE MANHATTAN THEATRE CLUB production of *Blackbird* deviated from the British version in several respects. At its world premiere in the Edinburgh International Festival, then on London's West End, German director Peter Stein devised a wordless final scene in a parking garage where the couple's rage and lust were externalized in a frenzied, choreographed fight. Departing from the spare, hard-hitting naturalism of Harrower's script, Stein employed musical accompaniment in this epilogue, giving the sequence an expressionistic feel. Some critics felt the addition, which came after an elaborate scene change, was unnecessary.

This directorial emendation didn't scupper its shot at a prize. When the Laurence Olivier Awards were announced February 18, 2007, *Blackbird* beat Peter Morgan's *Frost/Nixon* and Tom Stoppard's *Rock 'n' Roll.* Harrower, 40, was draining a Guinness at his local pub in Glasgow when he heard the news. As he explained to Melena Ryzik of the *New York Times:* "I didn't want to go down there, put on a suit, get drunk, get the suit crumpled and fly back with nothing—with a headache."

New York director Joe Mantello avoided Stein's parking-garage gloss, but he and Harrower Americanized the play: "phone box" became "phone booth," "pub" became "bar" and place names were eliminated. In the MTC production, no residual "accent" could be detected in Mantello's superbly taut production. The easy cultural conversion highlighted the fact that life in the postindustrial West is strikingly uniform. We all eat the same junk food in the same wrappers and litter in the same ugly corporate boxes. Our cell phones are securely clipped to our belts and our coworkers float by frosted glass windows as efficient ghosts.

Daniels and Pill excelled in the hideously complex, emotionally draining roles. Daniels's affable manner would slide into paternalistic condescension and even menace. Ruffling his hand through his floppy blond hair, fidgeting and letting his broad shoulders slump in abashed resignation, Daniels conveyed an internally warring mensch. In film roles, Daniels has played his share of losers and damaged men, but Ray was a cut above, a man of tragic erotic impulses.

The lithe, moon-faced Pill was visually ideal as a girl trapped in a woman's body. Her thin frame was sexually alluring in an emaciated, woman-girl-model sort of way. Her performance was forthright and pellucid, but her vocal quality and line readings alternated between one-note shrillness and somewhat colorless passivity. The actress is luminous and undeniably talented, but at 21, she might have been a bit too young to hit all the shades of rage, loss and rue for Una.

And even if years pass before this disturbing, potentially offensive work is produced again, it remains a thrilling read. The questions that *Blackbird* raises rattle around the brain: What Ray and Una shared—was it love or abuse? If a girl loses her virginity before menarche, is she doomed to a limbo between childhood and adulthood? Is love always just an illusion, a lie we rehearse in the theater of our memory?

2006–2007 Best Play

THE CLEAN HOUSE

By Sarah Ruhl

○ ○ ○ ○ ○

Essay by Anne Marie Welsh

LANE: Virginia. I'm all grown up. I DO NOT WANT TO BE TAKEN CARE OF.

VIRGINIA: WHY NOT?

LANE: I don't want my sister to clean my house. I want a stranger to clean my house.

MORE PRECISELY, LANE wants Matilde, her live-in maid, to clean her house. Lane has just discovered, at the mid-point of Sarah Ruhl's piquant existential comedy, that her sister Virginia has been doing the cleaning: Virginia gets to satisfy her own compulsiveness and Matilde, whom Virginia has befriended, gets to keep her job. Matilde hates to clean because it makes her sad; she'd rather pursue her real passion—inventing the perfect joke. In this pivotal scene, Lane, a physician, also discovers that her husband Charles, an oncologist, has taken a lover, an older woman named Ana whose cancerous breast he recently removed. Lane fires Matilde. From this mélange of resolutely domestic, pop cultural premises, Ruhl has built one of the most acclaimed comedies of the last several years.

Set initially in the monochromatic living room of Lane and Charles, from this point on, *The Clean House* opens out into fantasy and the five characters are brought into a single orbit. The action widens and deepens its tonal, thematic and geographic reach—from suburban chic to sensual seaside to Alaskan wilderness—as if Ruhl's imagination were chafing against the artifice of a naturalism that would constrain it. As in Shakespeare's romances, memory here can conjure those loved and lost; forgiveness heals and grief can be transcended. Part of Ruhl's originality is this unfettered quality of imagination—too delicate to be called surreal, yet deftly mixing the mythic, the biblical and the commonplace. In Ruhl's worlds, the membrane between imagination and reality, tragedy and comedy, even life and death, is translucent and permeable. Memories of the beloved dead glide or dance across the stage; the barren bear fruit. Magically, four women

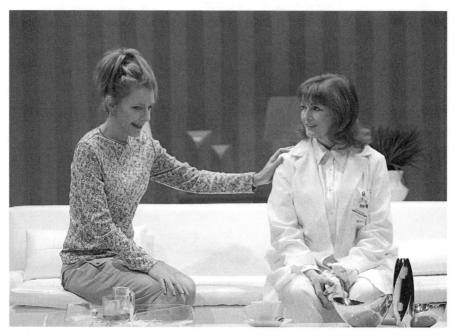

Sisterly touch: Jill Clayburgh and Blair Brown in The Clean House. *Photo: Joan Marcus*

at odds form a sisterhood of living-through-loss; Ana's survivors become a family of laughers-in-grief.

The McCarter Theatre Center in Princeton, New Jersey, commissioned the play as a one-act in 2000 and it was first heard as a reading at the Lark Play Development Center in November 2002. Mel Gussow reported in the *New York Times* that there was "general agreement that [Ruhl] should expand it to full length." Ruhl, a graduate of Paula Vogel's playwriting program at Brown University, said then she had been working on the script for eight months. She told Gussow, "one rewrite was as bad as the next." The reading at the Lark, she said, allowed her "to find the play's impulse again." Beginning with Bill Rauch's staging at Yale Repertory Theatre in September 2004, the full-length version of *The Clean House* had well-received productions at the Wilma Theater in Philadelphia, the Goodman Theatre in Chicago and South Coast Repertory in Costa Mesa, California, before its opening October 5, 2006, at Lincoln Center Theater's Mitzi E. Newhouse Theater. By the time of the New York run, Ruhl's play had been a Susan Smith Blackburn Prize winner and a finalist for the Pulitzer Prize in Drama. Just weeks before the *Clean House* opening at Lincoln Center, Ruhl herself was awarded a five-year, $500,000 MacArthur Foundation "genius" grant.

As in the production at Yale, the Lincoln Center production was directed by Rauch. The cast, however, was headlined by Broadway veterans Blair Brown, Jill Clayburgh, Concetta Tomei, John Dossett and Vanessa Aspillaga. The critical verdict in New York, as in previous cities, was strongly positive, led by *New York Times* critic Charles Isherwood who had praised the Yale production and also served on the Pulitzer jury that nominated Ruhl. Still, there were several high-profile naysayers: Robert Brustein in the *New Republic*, Michael Feingold in the *Village Voice* and Hilton Als in the *New Yorker*. For their out-of-hand dismissals, they cited the play's loose, nonlinear structure and characters verging on Latina stereotypes.

Ruhl's play announces its quirkiness from the start.

RUHL'S PLAY ANNOUNCES its quirkiness from the start. When the lights rise, Matilde (Aspillaga) addresses the audience. She's dressed in black. Her speech is animated; its brisk rhythms and her body language make plain that she is telling is a joke—a dirty joke. The hitch: It's in Portuguese. In the next scene, Lane addresses the audience. She's lean, elegant, dressed subtly in tailored neutrals, Matilde's opposite. Lane tells us that because the Brazilian maid she hired was too depressed to clean, she and her husband "had her medicated and She Still Wouldn't Clean. [. . .] I'm sorry. I did not go to medical school to clean my own house." A third woman arrives, Lane's doleful sister Virginia, and with her, another attitude toward housework. "People who give up the *privilege* of cleaning their own houses, they're insane people. If you do not clean, how do you know if you made any progress in life?"

This trio of women, their individual compulsions, conflicts and alliances, create the emotional dynamics of the first act. In its 14 scenes, each reveals her own disordered psyche in monologues and dialogues. Matilde tells us she is in mourning. What Lane reads as depression is unresolved grief over the death of her parents, "the funniest couple in Brazil." When her mother literally "died laughing" over her father's most remarkable joke, the man shot himself. Matilde was left not only an orphan, but also the funniest person in her family. Now her quest for the perfect joke keeps getting sidetracked by the housework she's been hired to do. Absurdly, given her job, she explains to Virginia:

MATILDE: I've never liked to clean. When I was a child I thought: if the floor is dirty, look at the ceiling. It is always clean.

[. . .]

I try not to think about cleaning when I am cleaning. I try to think of jokes. But sometimes the cleaning makes me mad. And then I am not in a funny mood. And *that* makes me sad.

Virginia and Matilde strike their bargain: Virginia will secretly clean Lane's house and Matilde will follow her comedian's dream of creating the perfect joke. As they fold laundry and putter about, class divisions get swept aside. Ruhl shows no interest in the kind of psychological and political issues raised by the maid's relationship to her female boss in Lisa Loomer's *Living Out*. Instead, Virginia and Matilde (and Matilde and Lane) get to know one another in a series of scenes that are vaudevillian in the timing of their give-and-take. With her "barren" husband and dashed dreams of being an archeologist, desperate Virginia finally acknowledges "I wanted something—big. I didn't know how to ask for it." She strangles even her laughter.

VIRGINIA: I don't like to laugh out loud.

MATILDE: Why?

Fast friends: Jill Clayburgh and Vanessa Aspillaga in The Clean House. *Photo: Joan Marcus*

VIRGINIA: I don't like my laugh. It's like a wheeze. Someone once told me that. Who was it—my husband?

Yet as the conversation continues, Virginia proves even funnier than Matilde. She doesn't tell jokes, but offers opinions—and in Jill Clayburgh's offhanded interpretation, she deadpanned her best lines: "My husband is like a well-placed couch. He takes up the right amount of space. [. . .] A man should be—functional. And well-chosen. Otherwise you're in trouble."

Housework is an antidote to Virginia's boredom and grief; humor serves as Matilda's anodyne. For Lane, who's also childless though she never mentions it, workaholic stress fills her life, displacing even her husband. When Virginia mentions that she hasn't seen Charles since Christmas, Lane answers: "He's been doing nine surgeries a day—we hardly see each other. I mean, of course we see each other, but, you know how it is." When Lane learns of Charles's infidelity—with an older woman he calls his soulmate or *bashert*—she's stunned. Her self-confidence has always centered on her competence:

LANE: I've never thought another woman was *my* equal. I'm the best doctor. I'm the smartest, the most well-loved by my patients. I'm athletic. I have poise. I've aged well. I can talk to *anyone* and be on an equal footing. How, I thought, could he even *look* at anyone else. It would be absurd.

She realizes she's been blind; yet she only half-sees when she decides Charles didn't want a doctor, he wanted a housewife.

Lane and Virginia's exchanges are fraught. Virginia, still jealous of Lane's career, envies her sister's marriage less than she once did. "When [Charles] and Lane first met," Virginia tells Matilde, "I thought: Lane gets the best of everything. A surgeon. With a specialty. He's—charismatic." She's revised that opinion, but the sisters' differences are encapsulated in a passing moment typical of the ways in which Ruhl complicates the comedy by turning up the dramatic heat. Lane tells Virginia:

LANE: I don't read magazines, Virginia. I go to work exhausted and I come home exhausted. That is how most of the people in this country function. At least people who have jobs.

Rauch guided Brown, as Lane, and Clayburgh to find the right beats in the charged moments specified in Ruhl's stage direction.

A pause.

For a moment,

Lane and Virginia experience

A primal moment during which they

Are seven and eight years old,

inside the mind, respectively.

They are mad.

Then they return quite naturally

To language, as adults do.

In the long scene that closes Act I, Charles and Ana at last appear. They are seen in dumb show, in the persons of the same actors (Dossett and Tomei) who have been playing Matilde's remembered parents. Lane describes her fantasy of the ritual lovemaking of Charles and Ana:

LANE: My husband undoes her gown.

He is very gentle.

He kisses her right breast.

He kisses the side of it.

He kisses the shadow.

He kisses her left torso,

He kisses the scar,

The one he made.

Matilde can also see Lane's fantasy, but she corrects the romantic musings of her boss. People only imagine that lovers are happy, she says, adding from knowledge of her parents' great love: "Love isn't clean like that. It's dirty. Like a good joke." Their conversation and the act end with the announcement that the real Charles and Ana are at Lane's door.

IN ACT II, RUHL explores Matilde's definition of love as Charles and Ana re-enact and explain their sudden overwhelming passion for one another. Ana's tale begins in her hatred of doctors for their brisk manners and self-importance. Yet with Charles, her heart leapt and walked out the door with him on her first visit. After the surgery, she felt he had "left his soul" inside her. Charles tells an equally compelling tale of falling in love with Ana all at once and loving her "to the point of invention." In a flashback, we watch her receive the cancer diagnosis and insist immediately that he "cut it off." With each bit of dialogue they fall further in love, with a conviction of their rightness that deposits them, naively and together, in Lane's living room where a tense little comedy of manners unfolds. Virginia serves coffee and Lane asks for "some hard alcohol in a glass with ice." Ana shares the story of her one previous passion decades ago and of her surprise when love

Laughing matter: John Dossett, Vanessa Aspillaga and Concetta Tomei in The Clean House. *Photo: Joan Marcus*

came to her again in the person of Charles. The lovers invoke a Jewish code that obliges persons to break off relations with their spouses when they find their true soulmate, their *bashert*. Lane can only sputter: "You're not Jewish," and later, in a comic moment: "And this is what you've come to tell me. That you're both innocent according to Jewish law."

Matilde cuts through the cold silence that ensues with a joke, in Portuguese; only Ana understands. Instead of leaving this mess unemployed, Matilde agrees to split her time 50-50 between the two houses: Lane and Ana both want her company, whether she cleans or not. She joins Charles and Ana for apple-picking, an activity Lane derides with her usual sardonic commentary:

> LANE: You must be insane! Apple picking! My god! I'm SORRY! But—apple picking? This is not a foreign film! We don't have an arrangement! You don't even *like* foreign films. [. . .]

Improbabilities mount. Ana's balcony by the sea is soon intercut with Lane's living room and scenes begin unfolding simultaneously in the two areas. Ana and Matilde, wearing hats and sunglasses, eat apples on the colorful balcony and toss the cores into Lane's living room, where she is weeping; Charles and Ana dance above, while Lane and Matilde play cards below. Charles and Ana play a game in which they try to read one another's minds, hoping they can stay mentally connected even if death separates them.

When Matilde describes the wild and volatile passions gripping Charles and Ana and brings news that the woman's cancer has recurred, Lane's control breaks. In a rage—first at Virginia's dirt fetish and then at herself—she rejects the very idea of a clean house. Virginia screams back that her sister has no compassion, and when Lane leaves, Virginia dirties the place in a cathartic orgy of piggery. Matilde brings further word. Charles has left Ana to quest for a Pacific yew tree that might cure her; the bark, Lane explains, is made into Taxol, a cancer-retarding drug. Virginia finds Charles's quest "beautiful," but Lane's common sense prevails:

> LANE: There is a woman dying, alone, while Charles chops down a
> fucking tree. How heroic.

With that, Lane begins to find within herself the real compassion Virginia said she lacked. While Lane examines Ana, we see Charles in the background ascending a snowy mountain looking for his tree as a great wind blows. In caring for Ana, the hyper-articulate Lane struggles to find words to say how she envies her radiance: "this—thing—sort of—glows off you—like a veil—in reverse—you're like anyone's soulmate—because you have that—thing." Lane learns the difference between love (which has besotted Charles, making him glow too) and admiration (which is what he and Lane felt for one another).

As Ana's condition worsens, the four women gather in Lane's living room. They eat chocolate ice cream Virginia has made. Lane forgives Ana and stays by her side like a guard dog while she sleeps. And when Ana can take the pain no longer, she asks Matilde to tell her the perfect joke so she can have a happy end. She wants to die laughing. And does. Lane closes her eyes and washes her body as any woman would, not as a doctor. The play comes full circle when Matilde imagines her dead parents again, awaiting her birth. She sings the lullaby her parents sang to make their newborn stop crying. Her own grief assuaged, she decides that heaven must be a "sea of untranslatable jokes. Only everyone is laughing."

GIVEN THE RANGE of its themes, the liebestod and lullaby with which it ends, the language of *The Clean House* is remarkably simple. One of Ruhl's favorite tropes is the aphorism. Virginia's hilarious riffs trade in such lines as "A husband should not be too beautiful. Or too good in bed." Matilde's wisdom centers on humor: "A good joke cleans your insides out"; or "A perfect joke is somewhere between an angel and a fart"; or most seriously, "A prayer cleans the air the way water cleans dirt." Charles's experience brings him to axiomatic wisdom too: "The difference between inspired medicine and uninspired medicine is love." Ana expresses her wish to die unmedicated at home in another epigram about maintaining control of her language. "As long as I live, I want to retain my own language," she says. "No extra hospital words." Thanks to Lane, Matilda and Virginia she achieves the fulfilling death she desires.

Seasonal imagery and Ruhl's use of color, both onstage and in the dialogue, rather than any overtly poetic language, gives the play its uncanny resonance. Matilde, Lane and Virginia are grieving and childless—with Virginia using the word "barren" to describe her husband and by implication, her marriage. Lane's house is as sterile as her husband's operating room and their marriage. Ana's presence, by contrast, is announced by her telltale underwear—sexy, shiny panties, a bold note in the otherwise neutral palette of Charles and Lane's laundry. Ironically, Ana's dying presence signals the return of the others to life: she brings multicolored apples into their lives and a long-lived fish. In describing the lovers' battles, Matilde conjures a smashed spice bottle, its contents covering Charles and Ana in yellow—curry, perhaps, or saffron. Even Matilde's sadness brings Virginia back into her busy sister's life; with her return, they come face to face with tensions and childhood conflicts.

Lane's forgiveness of Ana and her personal compassion may set her on a different path. As the play closes, we have no idea whether Charles and Lane's marriage will survive. Connection seems possible; for Ruhl's characters have learned mutual appreciation and tolerance. Yet these deeper currents are stirred without dulling the sparkling, essentially lighthearted spirit of the play.

Ruhl's play shares the nonlinear structure and cheerful absurdism of works by her mentor Vogel; she roams the world of literary archetypes as does playwright Charles L. Mee. Yet Ruhl's unsentimental and bracing voice is her own. She was 20 when her own father died of cancer. The persistence of love and grief after death, the power of memory, the possibility of antidotes to melancholy in humor, romance and familial love: all are recurring themes in *The Clean House*, in Ruhl's poignantly funny *Eurydice* (2003) and her whimsical satire, *Melancholy Play* (2002). Eventually wiser if still slightly daft, her characters find their way toward restored balance and new possibilities. Ruhl's writing jolts us awake not just with laughter, but with fresh insight.

2006–2007 Best Play

THE COAST OF UTOPIA

By Tom Stoppard

○ ○ ○ ○ ○

Essay by Charles Wright

HERZEN: This huge country, so vast it takes in fur-trappers, camel-herders, pearl-fishers . . . and yet not a single original philosopher, not one contribution to political discourse . . .

KETSCHER: Yes—one! The intelligentsia!

GRANOVSKY: What's that?

KETSCHER: It's the new word I was telling you about.

OGAREV: Well, it's a horrible word.

KETSCHER: I agree, but it's our own, Russia's debut in the lexicon.

HERZEN: What does it mean?

KETSCHER: It means us. A uniquely Russian phenomenon, the intellectual opposition considered as a social force.

—Shipwreck, **Act I**

NEVER MIND THAT Tom Stoppard's *The Coast of Utopia* is a very good play: that was clear enough in 2002 when Trevor Nunn staged the premiere at the National Theatre of Great Britain. In the UK, state-subsidized theaters such as the National and the Royal Shakespeare Company routinely undertake costly projects that aren't guaranteed crowd-pleasers. Such nonmusical productions, transported lock-stock-and-barrel across the Atlantic, have found favor in New York—*Nicholas Nickleby* springs to mind—but only after being successful in London. The economics of American theater, with its minimum of governmental subsidies, discourages that kind of risk and ambition in homegrown projects.

The Coast of Utopia concerns a group of 19th century Russian intellectuals—little known in the United States—who, in the playwright's view, delivered their country into the hands of totalitarianism. In choosing to mount this season's US debut of the trilogy, Lincoln Center Theater took a gamble on textual material that's extravagantly demanding in terms of production resources. The casting requirements—almost four dozen actors for more than 80 roles—were on a par with major motion pictures. The

Idling rich: Martha Plimpton, Ethan Hawke, Jennifer Ehle and Kellie Overbey in Voyage, *the first part of* The Coast of Utopia. *Photo: Paul Kolnik*

seven-and-a-half million dollar budget, admittedly modest in the film world, is gargantuan for a nonmusical at a nonprofit venue, which (due to artists' conflicting schedules) could play only a limited number of performances. With all of that money—provided by individual donors, seven private foundations, an investment bank and the National Endowment for the Arts—and with an impressive array of artists, designers and technicians, LCT managed to out-Herod Herod with a National Theatre scale extravaganza. What couldn't be predicted was the public's response which, surprisingly, occasioned an extension of the engagement and included a groundswell for the "marathons" in which all three plays could be seen in a single day.

Utopia became, in the words of the *New York Times* critic Charles Isherwood, a "cultural juggernaut and the season's indispensable ticket for those who consider[ed] themselves serious theatergoers." The first sign of this success was an uncharacteristic awareness of *Utopia* among ordinary New Yorkers who, though generally attuned to what is on movie screens, are nowadays largely indifferent to what is onstage. That this "awareness" was turning into something more significant was heralded by an item in the *Times* on January 26, 2007. *Utopia* had created such a market for Isaiah Berlin's *Russian Thinkers* (one of Stoppard's principal sources) that the publisher, Penguin, was hastening a reprint to supply the unforeseen demand:

> Before *Coast of Utopia* opened, *Russian Thinkers* sold about 36 copies a month in the whole country, placing it solidly in backlist territory. But late in November, customers began rushing to bookstores in search of the book, *Utopia* playbill in hand (or a November 24 clipping from the *New York Times* about suggested reading for the play).

With performances at the Vivian Beaumont packed throughout its run, *The Coast of Utopia* was swept into the *Zeitgeist* as no nonmusical production

Stoppard is occupied with themes that roiled post-Enlightenment Europe.

has been in the 15 years since Tony Kushner assessed the state of the nation with *Angels in America*.

Stoppard holds the record among living playwrights for New York "snob hits." He conquered Broadway 40 years ago with *Rosencrantz and Guildenstern Are Dead* (shortly after English critic Harold Hobson declared that play "the most important event in British professional theater" since the debut of Harold Pinter's *The Birthday Party*); and he has proved repeatedly that American audiences aren't intimidated by the exotic terrain where he sets his plays or by their sometimes arcane content. Despite the passage of time, Stoppard and his work retain an aura of the avant-garde. Gazing through the aura, though, one frequently glimpses elements in that work that are as conservative, even bourgeois, as Trollope. Though noted for sophisticated word play, literary references and disputatious dialogue, Stoppard is adept at drawing audiences into the worlds of his dramas, engaging viewers on an emotional, as well as intellectual, level.

In *Voyage, Shipwreck* and *Salvage*—the three parts of *Utopia*—Stoppard is occupied with intellectual themes that roiled post-Enlightenment Europe and inspired political experiments ostensibly aimed at improving the lot of humankind. The pieces are also an idiosyncratic memorial to Stoppard's relationship with philosopher Berlin, an authority on Russian intellectual history and a titanic figure in British cultural life during the second half of the 20th century. Berlin and Stoppard, both popular dinner guests in smart London society, were acquainted for a number of years; but the playwright recalls being "always tongue-tied in [the philosopher's] presence." Berlin urged Stoppard to visit him at his London flat, with an oblique warning that, unless Stoppard acted expeditiously, the opportunity might be lost. And, in November 1997, before the playwright had redeemed the offer of closer friendship, Berlin died at age 86. Yet the philosopher's influence fired the dramatist's imagination and the upshot, five years later, was *The Coast of Utopia*.

Stoppard's trilogy chronicles a group of friends (most of them classmates from Moscow University and all but one from the ranks of the Russian aristocracy or nobility), who rebel in various ways against their country's intellectual parochialism. These men are, in words of Edmund Wilson, members "of that unfortunate generation who [came] to manhood in Russia during the reign of Nicholas I." Before they were born, Napoleon's troops—invading Moscow in 1812 (the background of Tolstoy's *War and Peace*)—introduced Russia to ideas from Western Europe. Later, members

Russian thinkers: Billy Crudup and Brían F. O'Byrne in Voyage, *the first part of the* The Coast of Utopia. *Photo: Paul Kolnik*

of the Russian military, returning from their occupation of Paris, reinforced that foreign influence. Stoppard's principal characters have been impressed in early youth by the courage of the Decembrists, those Russian nobles who, upon the death of Alexander I in December 1825, staged a revolt against his successor, Nicholas I. The Decembrists protested their country's heritage of despotism and agitated for constitutional law, free speech and religious liberty. With the Decembrists squelched, press censorship in force and foreign travel largely forbidden, Russia was effectively sealed against further foreign influence.

> **BELINSKY: At the *Telescope*, we've got a manuscript that's been** going from hand to hand for years . . . [. . .] it's all about how backward Russia is compared with Europe . . . the *rest* of Europe, sorry . . . but the author could have pointed out that in the matter of the ownership of human beings we were years ahead of America . . .
> **—*Voyage*, Act I**

VOYAGE IS A CHEKHOVIAN comedy of hope and youthful idealism that contrasts rural Russia in the 1830s and '40s with the social and political ferment of Moscow and St. Petersburg during the same years. Pushkin's supremacy in Russian art is not yet on the wane; but foreign ideas in literature, politics and philosophy are beginning to conflict with what is traditional in Russian thinking. Stoppard places all of Act I on the Bakunin family's estate, far northwest of Moscow, between 1833 and 1841, then resets the clock at the beginning of Act II, recounting what occurs to the same characters when they're in urban precincts. Confusing as this dramaturgical strategy may sound, Stoppard's scenes are engaging; and they move trippingly, with the verbal pace of high comedy. In the LCT production, the fluidity of Stoppard's writing was accentuated—perhaps accelerated—by the designers' turntable, which occupied much of the Beaumont's thrust stage and seemed seldom to pause.

At the center of *Voyage* is Michael Bakunin (Ethan Hawke), scion of a family that owns 500 "souls" or serfs. His mother (Amy Irving) is notably harsh with household serfs, illustrating the rigidity, even brutality, of the Russian caste system. The son is an intellectual dragonfly, skimming the surface of Western philosophical fashion, from Kant to Schelling, Fichte and, ultimately, Hegel. The play portrays Bakunin's intense relationships with his siblings and his uneasy attempts to wean himself from a controlling father (Richard Easton). Bakunin is self-absorbed and manipulative. His freeloading ways are a source of humor in all three plays. The discontent that he stirs among his sisters—undermining the engagement of Liubov (Jennifer Ehle), urging Varenka (Martha Plimpton) to leave her marriage, opposing Alexandra's (Annie Purcell) flirtation with Belinsky, and smothering Tatiana (Kellie Overbey) with his jealous attentions—foreshadows the anarchism he will sow throughout Europe later in the trilogy. At the end of *Voyage*, the son escapes his father but only because the Tsar's government brings criminal proceedings against him, revoking his noble rank and leaving him no practical choice but European exile.

Bakunin founds a journal, the *Moscow Observer*, with literary critic Vissarion Belinsky (Billy Crudup), whom Bakunin's father derides as "the first middle-class intellectual in Russia." Focused and deeply thoughtful, Belinsky is a foil to the self-involved Bakunin. Belinsky transcends his patchy education to become a shrewd analyst of Russia's intellectual condition—especially, its shortcomings. Bakunin abandons the *Observer* to Belinsky's care, justifying his disloyalty by declaiming, "We haven't got the right to publish without a lot more study."

In *Voyage*, Stoppard introduces four other men who, as with Bakunin and Belinsky, are searching for philosophical moorings in a changing world: Nicholas Stankevich (David Harbour), brightest light of the University's Philosophical Circle; future novelist Ivan Turgenev (Jason Butler Harner); and childhood friends Nicholas Ogarev (Josh Hamilton), a poet, and Alexander Herzen (Brían F. O'Byrne), who have vowed to avenge their heroes, the Decembrists. Herzen, whom critic John Rockwell calls the "spiritual father of the Russian Revolution," will be the principal figure of the trilogy, though Stoppard doesn't introduce him until Act II and, for much of the period covered by *Voyage*, he is in exile, serving time for holding beliefs that are ostensibly subversive.

Although *Voyage* is set entirely in Russia, the principal characters have their eyes fixed on Europe, especially Germany, whose innovations in philosophy call to them tantalizingly. At *Voyage*'s conclusion, only Herzen, recently released from exile, is still in the homeland. The end of the first piece presages dark themes to come in the succeeding parts of the trilogy. News arrives that Stankevich, in Italy for his tuberculosis, has died of the ailment—as did Bakunin's sister Liubov previously—and that Pushkin has been killed in a duel. Onto the stage strolls the Ginger Cat—a figure plausible in the context of a fancy-dress ball in the play's penultimate scene, but primarily a bold thematic device to register the playwright's disdain for Hegelian notions of history as a systematic, irresistible process.

Marooned: Brían F. O'Byrne and Richard Easton in Shipwreck, *the second part of* The Coast of Utopia. *Photo: Paul Kolnik*

> **HERZEN: It's over with us Russians and the Western model.**
> [. . .] The West has nothing to teach us. It's sinking under its weight of precious cargo which it won't jettison—all those shackles for the mind.
>
> *—Shipwreck*, **Act II**

IF *VOYAGE* IS THE PROLOGUE of Stoppard's trilogy, *Shipwreck* is its core and, arguably, its heart. In *Shipwreck*, the playwright moves his chronicle to the Continent, which has preoccupied the Moscow classmates throughout *Voyage*. As the second part progresses from 1846 to 1852, the major characters approach middle age. By the end, they have reached ideological positions not only remote from where they started but disparate from one another. That disparity, if ever in doubt, becomes clear in the final part, *Salvage*.

In this middle play, Stoppard narrows his focus to the domestic lives of Herzen and his family circle, making their experiences his gauge for the feasibility of the Romantic era's utopianism. It is a drama of dampening hopes—both political and personal—that culminates in a family tragedy. The action captures Stoppard's view of how the intellectual innovations and political gestures of the *Shipwreck* years have affected subsequent decades of history. Throughout, however, the playwright steers clear of anything schematic: his characters are vivid and believable, with a sense of being contemporary as well as based in history. As a result, *Shipwreck* is darker and more psychologically complex than *Voyage*.

Herzen, age 34, has inherited a fortune but, for his beliefs, is forbidden to leave Russia. In the summer of 1846, he, Ogarev and Turgenev are biding time in country-house idleness, disputing about socialism, materialism, the immortality of the soul and the merits of various blends of coffee. To everyone's surprise, the government relents, issuing passports so that Herzen and family—wife Natalie (Jennifer Ehle), two little boys (Beckett Melville as Sasha and August Gladstone as Kolya), and an offstage daughter—may consult French doctors about Kolya, who is deaf. And so Herzen joins the westward "voyage" already begun by his classmates.

Cataclysmic events—the Revolution of 1789 and the student-inspired upheavals of 1832, for instance—have reshaped France. Herzen's arrival in Paris coincides with the moment when the "intelligentsia"—that newly

Women adrift: Amy Irving and Jennifer Ehle in Shipwreck, *the second part of* The Coast of Utopia. *Photo: Paul Kolnik*

recognized social category to which he and his friends belong—is galvanized by visions of utopian socialism. Marx and Engels are about to publish their *Communist Manifesto* and, in the year ahead, revolutions will erupt all over Europe—in Italy, Prussia and the Austrian empire, as well as in France. The Paris in which the political émigrés settle is the polestar of the Age of Revolution. "When the lid blows off this kettle," Herzen predicts, "it'll take the kitchen with it." From the comfort of a richly-appointed salon near the Arc de Triomphe (safe from the secret police and press censorship of their homeland), Herzen and his friends excitedly witness the pyrotechnics of 1848.

Those events extinguish Herzen's enthusiasm and his confidence in the inherent goodness of human beings. He despairs that political change cannot occur with the predictability and ease that he and his friends have anticipated. While Turgenev extols France as "the highest reach of civilization," Herzen focuses on the fact that nine million newly enfranchised Frenchmen have squandered their votes on "royalists, rentiers, lawyers . . . and a rump of socialists for the rest to kick." With a newly elected Assembly that's solidly monarchist, it has become clear that postrevolution power "is not to be shared with the ignoramuses who built the barricades." Those proletarians, ironically, are deemed "too poor to have a voice."

With mayhem outside his windows, Herzen intones a distinctly Stoppardian soliloquy, addressed to an imaginary representative of the French proletariat:

> HERZEN: What do you want? Bread? I'm afraid bread got left out of the theory. [. . .] We thought we had discovered that social progress was a science like everything else. The First Republic was to have been the embodiment of morality and justice as a rational enterprise. The result was, admittedly, a bitter blow. But now there's a completely new idea. History itself is the main character of the drama, and also its author. We are all in the story, which ends with universal bliss. [. . .] Your personal sacrifice, the sacrifice of countless others on History's slaughter-bench, all the apparent crimes and lunacies of the hour, which to you may seem irrational, are part of a much much bigger story which you probably aren't in the mood for—let's just say that this time, as luck would have it, you're the zig and they're the zag.

In Herzen's assessment, France is "the sleeping bride of revolution," aching "to be the kept woman of a bourgeois." Contemplating the incongruity of the Republic's practices and its founding ideals, Herzen reassesses the means of social change.

Still here: Josh Hamilton, Kat Peters, Brían F. O'Byrne, Martha Plimpton and Ethan Hawke in Salvage, *the third part of* The Coast of Utopia. *Photo: Paul Kolnik*

> HERZEN: Nobody's got the map. In the West, socialism may win next time, but it's not history's destination. Socialism, too, will reach its own extremes and absurdities, and once more Europe will burst at the seams. [. . .] It will be bloody, swift and unjust, and leave Europe like Bohemia after the Hussites. Are you sorry for civilization? I am sorry for it, too.

Purged of callow optimism, Herzen recalls the Ginger Cat—that weird figure from the last minutes of *Voyage*. In what amounts to Stoppard's assessment of modern history, Herzen recognizes the figure as an invidious specter from a dark fairy tale.

Shipwreck is also a domestic drama about love and the mutability of emotional attachment. With middle age approaching, Herzen and Natalie are no longer (in her words) "the intoxicated children we were when we eloped in the dead of night and I didn't even bring my hat." Their darkening relationship, which occupies much of *Shipwreck*, mirrors Alexander's discouragement with utopian socialism and, more significantly, his disillusion with the social and sexual innovations of the Romantic era.

Natalie, despite her intellectual pretensions, is far more concerned with personal entanglements than with the political events she is witnessing. While in Paris, she has imbibed ideas about sex, social hypocrisy and the status of women associated with that most influential woman of 19th century Europe, George Sand (1804–76). Obsessed with what she believes to be the primacy of a distinctly Romantic notion of "love," Natalie glories in various iterations of that emotion—physical and platonic, marital and adulterous, maternal and filial, heterosexual and Sapphic. She submits to an ecstatic fling with Natasha Tuchkov (Martha Plimpton), then plunges into an affair with Herzen's friend George Herwegh (David Harbour), a self-centered German poet living on the inherited wealth of his doormat wife Emma (Bianca Amato).

Intoxicated with Romantic excess, Natalie is a foolish, poignant figure. She rationalizes marital infidelity as the embodiment of a universal idea:

> NATALIE: I am pure before myself and before the world—I bear no reproach in the very depths of my heart—now you know.
>
> HERZEN: *(exasperated)* Now I know what?
>
> NATALIE: That I am yours, that I love you, that my affection for George is God-given—if he went away, I would sicken—if you went away, I would die! [. . .] Oh, how did this happen? How did this innocent world of my loving heart shatter to fragments?

Though Herzen blames Herwegh rather than Natalie, his discovery that both have betrayed him extinguishes his sanguinity about the novelties of modern European social thought.

In a comic interlude near the outset of Act II, Stoppard brings Natalie's Romantic cant about love into direct conflict with the blood-and-gristle perspective of Ogarev's estranged wife, Maria (Amy Irving). Exquisitely played by Irving (oily and earthy) and Ehle (measured but arch), the passage is an accelerando of one-upmanship. Reminiscent of the verbal fireworks in *Travesties* and *Jumpers*, it is the kind of audience-pleasing thing Stoppard does best.

Natalie pleads Ogarev's case for a divorce so he can marry her friend Natasha. Maria responds by ridiculing Natalie's notion of love as "a universal *idea*," and voicing a more pungent, less lofty assessment of human relations: "To arouse and satisfy desire is nature making its point about the sexes, everything else is convention." Maria dismisses her husband and his classmates as hopeless naifs, and mocks the lofty terms of Ogarev's courtship:

> MARIA: [. . .] We [. . .] talked twaddle at each other, and knew that this was love. We had no idea we were in fashion, that people who

> didn't know any better were falling in love quite adequately without
> dragging in the mind of the Universe as dreamt up by some German
> professor who left out the irritating details. [. . .]

Amid the melodramatic anguish of *Shipwreck*, the profoundly deaf Kolya and his cherished toy, a spinning top, emerge as symbols of Russia's intellectual and political struggle. At the play's beginning, it is clear that Kolya perceives thunder but uncertain what else gets through to him. "What do you think he thinks about?" wonders Natalie. "Can he have thoughts if he has no names to go with them?" Turgenev replies, "He's thinking muddiness . . . flowerness, yellowness, nice-smellingness, not-very-nice-tastingness . . . The names for things don't come first, words stagger after, hopelessly trying to become the sensation."

With the aid of European "learning specialists," Kolya begins scaling the barriers of his handicap. He is transformed by the attentions of an inspired teacher, offstage. By Act II, he reads lips and understands things to such an extent that, in Herzen's phrase, "you'd swear he was listening!" Throughout *Utopia*, Russia is awakening to the rumblings of modernity but, as Turgenev puts it, "words stagger after." The huge country must contend with a formidable barrier to understanding. For little Kolya, the impediment is physical; for Russia, it's a difference in geography and historical experience. Russia strains to grasp new ways, to fit them onto cultural structures that differ markedly from the West. Kolya is trying to form words without ever hearing; Russia struggles to speak in its own "voice."

The trilogy's second play concludes with the shipwreck of its title, an event with overwhelming consequences for Herzen and his family.

> HERZEN: [. . .] We lost Kolya. He was drowned at sea, my mother
> with him, and a young man who was teaching Kolya to speak. None
> of them was ever found. It finished my Natalie. She was expecting
> another baby, and when it came, she had no strength left. The baby
> died, too.

Herzen's journey has stripped him of his illusion that one can consciously mold, or even predict, the future.

> HERZEN: [. . .] Life's bounty is in its flow, later is too late. Where is
> the song when it's been sung? The dance when it's been danced? It's
> only we humans who want to own the future, too. We persuade
> ourselves that the universe is modestly employed in unfolding our
> destination. We note the haphazard chaos of history by the day, by
> the hour, but there is something wrong with the picture. Where is
> the unity, the meaning, of nature's highest creation? Surely those
> millions of little streams of accident and willfulness have their

correction in the vast underground river which, without a doubt, is carrying us to the place where we're expected! But there is no such place, that's why it's called utopia.

The concluding beats of *Shipwreck* include the most poignant—and thematically significant—moment of the trilogy:

HERZEN: The death of a child has no more meaning than the death of armies, of nations. Was the child happy while he lived? That is a proper question, the only question. If we can't arrange our own happiness, it's a conceit beyond vulgarity to arrange the happiness of those who come after us.

Last glance: Josh Hamilton and Martha Plimpton in Salvage, *the third part of* The Coast of Utopia. *Photo: Paul Kolnik*

HERZEN: History knocks at a thousand gates at every moment,
and the gatekeeper is chance.

—*Salvage*, Act II

SALVAGE—SET PRINCIPALLY IN London, between 1853 and 1868, with two final scenes in Switzerland—lends the trilogy a dying fall. Stoppard's finale contains the cinematic fluidity that marks the previous parts and is characteristic of his recent stage writing. Its vaudevillian turns and general frolicsomeness, however, bring to mind the playwright's early "entertainments," such as *The Real Inspector Hound* and *Dirty Linen*. In *Salvage*, Stoppard hops deftly in and out of his narrative arc to dramatize dreams and fantasies that lend texture to the portrait of Herzen and his circle.

Herzen is in London, among refugees from various political conflicts and collapsing cultures. He describes his fellow émigrés as "schemers, dreamers, monomaniacs" who constantly dispatch "agents with earth-shaking instructions to Marseille, Lisbon, Cologne" but can't afford to "get their shoes mended." After Ogarev and Natasha (now Madame Ogarev) arrive from Russia, the boyhood friends establish the Free Russian Press and publish a journal, *The Bell*, to disseminate literature that won't pass muster with the Tsar's censors. In time, the friendship among Herzen and the Ogarevs becomes an uneasy *ménage a trois*. Herzen and Natasha have three children together. As their domestic life becomes ever more fraught, Herzen and Ogarev gain greater stature in their homeland thanks to underground circulation there of *The Bell* and their courageous agitation for free speech, Polish independence and liberation of the Russian serfs.

At the trilogy's end, the six old friends have docked in radically different ports:

• Stankevich, the most intellectually promising among them, has succumbed to tuberculosis.

• Belinsky has also died of "consumption," after returning to the homeland to pursue, as a literary critic, his vision of a native Russian literature. "Our problem is feudalism and serfdom," he says, "What have these Western models got to do with us?"

• Turgenev, celebrated for *Fathers and Sons*, eschews anything doctrinaire and sympathizes—as a novelist should—with all viewpoints he chooses to contemplate.

• Bakunin, commanding and charismatic, will not fulfill his dream of leading a successful political revolt. With Russia still far from the revolutionary boiling point, he is destined for cameos in other countries' political movements, spreading the gospel of anarchism to receptive targets.

• Ogarev's capacities have been reduced by booze, neurosis, epilepsy and the distractions of the awkward home he has made with Natasha and Herzen. To the dismay of almost everyone, Ogarev has invited an English prostitute and her young son to join the eccentric domicile.

• Herzen is a lonely figure, unable to return to the homeland he loves or to imbue his children—assimilated as they are to the environs in which they've been raised—with Russian identity. He remains committed to constructive social change, but uncertain whether it will come from above or below.

> HERZEN: [. . .] We need wit and courage to make our way while our way is making us. But that is our dignity as human beings, and we rob ourselves if we pardon us by the absolution of historical necessity. [. . .]

Herzen and his peers are confronted with ideas, startling to them, of a new generation: nihilism, for instance, and the tenets of Marx. In Geneva, to which he retires, Herzen ruminates on the Ginger Cat who stepped so enticingly among the dancers at that St. Petersburg costume ball 25 years before. "What kind of beast is it," he asks, "this Ginger Cat with its insatiable appetite for human sacrifice? This Moloch who promises that everything will be beautiful after we're dead?" The question is rhetorical, but that doesn't alter the urgency of Herzen's response.

> HERZEN: [. . .] A distant end is not an end but a trap. The end we work for must be closer, the labourer's wage, the pleasure in the work done, the summer lightning of personal happiness . . . [. . .] We have to open men's eyes and not tear them out . . . and if we see differently, it's all right, we don't have to kill the myopic in our myopia . . . We have to bring what's good along with us. People won't forgive us. I imagine myself the future custodian of a broken statue, a blank wall, a desecrated grave, telling everyone who passes by, "Yes—yes, all this was destroyed by the revolution."

A RARE INSTANCE of repertory performance on Broadway, *The Coast of Utopia* was an opportunity to see first-rate actors, such as Ehle, Harbour and Irving undertake the physical and imaginative demands of multiple roles. Other actors—O'Byrne and Hawke, for example—developed one character at unaccustomed length. Under Jack O'Brien's direction, *Utopia* represented, more than anything else, real collaboration among theater crafts—stage director, designers (11 in total), composer, actors, stage technicians, musicians and playwright—yielding a quotient of enchantment unforeseeable from a mere tally of individual contributions.

In LCT's presentation, each play of the trilogy opened with a *coup de théâtre*, invented by O'Brien and his scenic designers, Bob Crowley and Scott Pask, that set a tone of grandeur and ambition—and established Herzen as central to the enterprise. As the house lights faded, wild surf and tolling bells were heard, then a reluctant piano and, moments later, in pitch darkness, bass, cello and, finally, higher strings. As grey-bluish light seeped across the stage, a roiling sea of China silk appeared behind the scrim. Out of the stormy void rose O'Byrne, as Herzen, clad in frock coat and seated on a spinning chair. Brooding, his eyes downcast, Herzen fondled something that—in *Salvage*—would be revealed as Kolya's lost glove, retrieved from the sea after the shipwreck. The melancholic intensity of actor, music and storm-tossed waters created an imposing, awe-inspiring effect. In diminishing light, O'Byrne and his chair were swallowed by the churning waves. Then, in *Voyage*, a spooky, ash-colored glow illuminated a tableau of people, seemingly scores of them, in Russian peasant costume. A large number of these "serfs" turned out to be mannequins (thoroughly realistic in appearance), but thirty-odd actors emerged from the tableau and marched downstage to initiate the play's principal action. Those shadowy figures haunted the entire action of *Voyage* and, metaphorically, all of Russia.

Throughout the New York run, critics, playgoers, and awards organizations debated whether *Utopia* is one play or three. Awards-granting organizations decided that it was a unit. In the LCT production, each play contained its own visual and aural surprises and O'Brien, quoted in the trade journal *Lighting and Sound America*, acknowledged that he and his designers viewed Stoppard's work as analogous to a symphony in three distinct movements. Mark Bennett's musical score—a cross between contemporary concert-hall fare and the most epic sort of movie music—enhanced the distinctive moods of each play while also tying the three together with recurrent themes.

With O'Brien making almost constant use of the turntable, the scenic designers kept stage properties to a minimum, relying on the lighting designers—Brian MacDevitt (*Voyage*), Kenneth Posner (*Shipwreck*) and Natasha Katz (*Salvage*)—to create appropriate atmospherics for the Beaumont's unusually deep stage. The glistening, reflective deck of the turntable gave the wide thrust a spare, clean appearance. Catherine Zuber's hundreds of period costumes brought color and variation to the scenes.

The simple look of the production was enhanced from time to time by astonishing images: in *Voyage*, the onion domes of St. Basil's Cathedral, apparently carved from ice and floating above the action; in *Shipwreck*, a view across Place de la Concorde, with lampposts leading to the distant Obelisk; two statues that broke apart in a battle scene. For the English section of *Salvage*, the stage was dressed with odds and ends, apparent junk (a cart, a spinet, a dilapidated chandelier), allusive of the prior plays and of aspects in the principal characters' odyssey, now nearing its conclusion. In contrast to the dour tones that pervade *Salvage*, the trilogy's final scene was as visually rich as anything in the first two plays. Set in Geneva, to which the members of the Herzen-Ogarev ménage (including Bakunin) have repaired, the sequence was played against a massive drop inspired by I.K. Aivazovsky's seascape *The Tenth Wave* (1850). By choosing this visual allusion, the scenic designers emphasized the notion that the aging émigrés are adrift in the turbulent drink of history.

UTOPIA RECEIVED A PREPONDERANCE of enthusiastic reviews (though some critics labeled it Grade B Stoppard), and the production played to capacity and near-capacity houses from October 2006 to May 2007. Its engagement was extended by nine weeks and instead of the three "marathons" originally scheduled, the company performed nine. The production collected a truckload of honors at awards time—its seven Tony Awards set a record for nonmusicals. On February 4 (two weeks before the premiere of *Salvage*), however, Charles Isherwood took issue in the Arts and Leisure section of the Sunday *New York Times* with most of the critical community (including his *Times* colleague Ben Brantley, who had found the production "exhilarating" and had lauded Stoppard's dialogue for "open[ing] into startling splendor like a peacock preening its tail"). Under the headline, "*Utopia* Is a Bore. There, I Said It." Isherwood dismissed the first two-thirds as a "stubbornly diffuse, inert and intractable slab of oral history, one that lacks either the driving force of a strong narrative or the emotional appeal of life drawn in sensitive, truthful detail."

Although no writer on a major publication trumpeted misgivings with similar glee, Isherwood was not a lone dissenting voice. Those who accused Stoppard of attempting to dramatize philosophical ideas were overlooking how vividly and intricately the playwright has drawn Herzen and the members of his circle—and how completely those characters were realized by the New York cast. Those who complained that Stoppard covers too much territory at insufficient depth were quibbling about the quicksilver nature of the playwright's mind and the hectic pace of his imagination. (Presumably Isherwood's characterization of *Utopia* as a theatrical equivalent of *CliffsNotes* was more braggadocio than critical assessment.) Such complaints, however, are not unfounded—especially as regards the first and last plays of the trilogy, which lack the heft, focus and emotional depth of *Shipwreck*. The playwright's dramatic concentration in the middle play, his enhanced attention there to the minutiae of character development and the way in which one scene builds upon another are what make *Shipwreck* superior to the other two. Viewed as a single, long work, *Utopia* has epic reach and sufficient variety (*pace* Isherwood) to hold the audience's attention. What cannot be denied is that, in *Salvage*, *Utopia* has an anemic final act.

The three parts of *Utopia* ran in repertory at a venue which theater historian Mary C. Henderson has described as the "playhouse [. . .] everyone loves to hate." Opened in 1965, the Vivian Beaumont was designed by architect Eero Saarinen and stage designer Jo Mielziner to house a permanent, rotating-repertory company. For two decades, its problematic configuration of backstage, playing space, and front-of-house baffled artists and technicians who worked there. (Joseph Papp derided the Beaumont repeatedly as "a disaster.") In the second half of the 1980s, however, director Jerry Zaks and scenic designer Tony Walton, working under LCT's first artistic director, Gregory Mosher, solved the Beaumont puzzle in a succession of crowd-pleasing productions and, in subsequent years, the house has enjoyed many artistic coups. The design and execution of *Utopia* surpassed—in scope and resourcefulness—all prior uses of this theater's facilities. New York's *Utopia* was a triumph of all components working together—text, performances, music, etc. But O'Brien and his design collaborators deserve special credit for making this American premiere—regardless of whether it is Grade A or Grade B Stoppard—the brightest months in the Beaumont's 42-year life.

2006–2007 Best Play

DYING CITY

By Christopher Shinn

○ ○ ○ ○ ○

Essay by Charles Isherwood

PETER: No one really talking.

KELLY: Mm. No one knew what to *say.*

PETER: About?

KELLY: Just—you know, the shock. Everyone was in shock.

CHRISTOPHER SHINN APPEARS to be in no great hurry to get somewhere, and that's good news for the American theater. A little more than 30 years old, Shinn already has more than a half-dozen solid plays behind him, and a sheaf of fine reviews. But unlike many playwrights who receive acclaim and attention for their initial efforts, Shinn has not skedaddled to television-land. He has continued, year after year, quietly to ply the playwright's trade, which in today's cultural environment increasingly resembles an artisanal craft more than a career that holds out the potential promise of fame and riches. Being a playwright in America in the 21st century requires an almost monastic devotion to the particular challenges and rewards of writing work to be performed live, in a particular place, with no effects more special than the artistry of stage acting, directing and design.

Even Broadway has not yet beckoned to Shinn, probably because his work's quiet humanism is at odds with the ethos that reigns in those precincts, where playwrights must dazzle with grabby meditations on history, culture or current affairs, or showy star vehicles. And yet Shinn's modest star continues to rise quietly above the sleepy theatrical landscape. His first play to be seen in New York, *Four,* was produced Off Off Broadway in 2001 on a shoestring budget, although after receiving strong reviews it later reappeared under the auspices of Manhattan Theatre Club. Later plays were produced at the Vineyard Theatre and Playwrights Horizons.

This past season, Lincoln Center Theater, one of the city's largest and most plushly funded nonprofit theaters, presented his new play, *Dying*

Damaged lives: Rebecca Brooksher and Pablo Schreiber in Dying City.
Photo: Joan Marcus

City, in its Off Broadway space, the Mitzi E. Newhouse Theater. The austere, effective production, directed by James Macdonald (who also directed the play's 2006 world premiere at the Royal Court Theatre in London), starred Pablo Schreiber and a talented actress essentially new to the New York stage, Rebecca Brooksher.

The new play ranks with *Where Do We Live* (2004)—Shinn's moving, oblique drama about the dislocated lives of young New Yorkers in the wake of the calamity of September 11, 2001—as his strongest work so far. Like the earlier play, *Dying City* takes a sidelong view of a momentous historic event, in this case the Iraq war. Shinn is neither a pedagogue nor a pedant, so the play is not an exercise in finger-wagging or a current affairs lecture. The live of its three characters—a soldier, his wife and his twin brother (Schreiber played both brothers)—are irrevocably altered by the fact of the American invasion, but *Dying City* is neither a political tract nor a simple dirge for the terrible human cost of war.

It explores in intimate, persuasively truthful detail the traumatic repercussion of the conflict on all three characters' lives, but it debunks the sound-bite storyline of loss that is retailed constantly in the news: young,

Shinn has mastered a skill too few young playwrights possess.

good-hearted kid with all his future before him and a loving new wife at home tragically and senselessly cut down in the prime of life. (True to the facts though such stories may be, they are irrefutably reductive.) *Dying City* adds haunting shadows to that familiar picture as it considers more complex questions.

How does upbringing and psychological history shape a soldier's behavior? How does the violent trauma of battle, in turn, feed or exacerbate his own pathologies? Can the psychic scars of a war veteran be passed on, as emotional DNA, to his offspring? Most of all the play questions, without answering, the idea that human personality—and, by extension, human behavior—can be easily mapped, diagrammed, understood. Peel the onion of a man's emotional makeup and you just keep finding more layers. The answer to a fundamental question—in this case did he take his own life, and if so, why?—only becomes more elusive. In Macdonald's exquisitely calibrated production, the stage itself was made a metaphor for the shiftng nature of perception and the elusiveness of fixed truth: the entire set turned slowly, almost undetectably, throughout the duration of the play, so the audience's view of the characters literally changed from moment to moment.

THE PLAY IS SET in the same New York apartment on two evenings separated by a year and a half and the gulf of a stark tragedy. It begins on the later evening, in July 2005, as Kelly, a woman in her late 20s, sorts through piles of books. An open cardboard box and the general disarray seem to signify an imminent move or at least a radical purge.

From the television comes the unmistakable sound of an episode of *Law and Order*. This detail is a knowing joke: the series is ubiquitous in the lives of urban dwellers between 20 and 40, like midcentury modern furniture. But it is also a subtle hint, to be taken up and explored later, that the play will involve some sleuthing, albeit without the satisfaction of a neatly wrapped-up case.

Kelly's work is interrupted by the arrival of Peter, also in his 20s and, as we will come to learn, the identical twin brother of Kelly's late husband, Craig. Among Shinn's gifts is a keen sense of the fractured cadences of

Seeking peace: Rebecca Brooksher in Dying City. *Photo: Joan Marcus*

contemporary American speech. His characters may be smart and comparatively sophisticated—as they are in *Dying City*—but their exchanges are full of clipped, half-started or half-finished sentences that leave much to subtext. We are immersed not in a neatly tailored, stagy simulacrum of life, but the lumpy, slack, unsatifyingly messy thing itself, with all its loose ends and unspoken meanings.

Despite the meticulous realism of his language, Shinn has also mastered a skill too few young playwrights possess: the ability to provide the audience with all the information it needs to engage with a play's characters without resorting to tidy exposition. As Kelly and Peter casually, awkwardly fumble through a getting-reacquainted conversation, various clues to the history that ties them together emerge naturally.

Peter's sudden arrival is unusually unnerving to Kelly:

> KELLY: [. . .] When they came to tell me about Craig, they just showed up—they just / show up, no warning, they don't call or—

It has been a year since Craig's funeral following his death in Iraq, and Kelly has avoided Peter's calls and e-mails. His need to see her has developed a sudden urgency since he suffered a small meltdown at work. An actor on the rise, he had been appearing in a production of *Long Day's Journey Into Night*. This particular evening he walked offstage after a colleague made a sniping, homophobic comment between scenes.

A celebrated line from that Eugene O'Neill play—Mary Tyrone's pained reflection that "the past is the present, it's the future too"—could almost serve as an epigraph for *Dying City*. For while Kelly, a therapist, is finally ready to move on, Peter is clearly locked in an internal dialogue with his brother and the mystery of his death. At the funeral, he reminds Kelly:

> PETER: [. . .] I felt that, underneath, that people kind of thought it wasn't an accident maybe, and that's why everyone was so quiet.

Craig died, it seems, from a self-inflicted wound that was deemed accidental, but as Peter's allusions to their upbringing suggest, there exists the possibility that something more disturbing occurred.

> PETER: [. . . E]veryone there knew that dad taught us, from the time we were little, how to shoot, how to handle weapons. [. . .]

Their father was a Vietnam war veteran whose violent outbursts had shadowed their childhood. These stresses led to an unusual intimacy that has left Peter feeling achingly bereft—and perhaps inspired his erratic behavior.

The state of Craig's mind as he prepared for another tour in Iraq is explored when the play moves back to an evening more than a year earlier. (The transition is effected with a simple theatrical trick: Peter walks offstage to answer a private phone call from his ex-boyfriend, and Schreiber walks back on in the guise of Craig.) Peter had been visiting, with his boyfriend Tim on that earlier occasion, and seems to have passed out in the bedroom. Kelly and Craig gingerly step around the subject of his imminent departure, and find their way into a mildly contentious argument about the efficacy of therapy, and the particular pathology of one of Peter's ex-boyfriends. Craig scoffs at a guy he calls "the psychopath"; Kelly patiently explains that "his personality was affected by the abuse he suffered." Later they argue about one of Kelly's patients, a man with a compulsive need to describe his brutish sexual conquests.

ALL OF THESE seemingly casual elements come to resonate with meaning when we return to the later evening and Peter presses Kelly on the issue of Craig's death. As the play shifts between the two evenings, the tensions in Kelly and Craig's marriage are further revealed as are the intimacies Craig shared with his brother about the futility of the Iraq mission. His war experience, it seems, brought into focus some dark impulses in his personality that, paradoxically, the adrenaline surge of combat may have served to assuage.

During a lull in the conversation, Peter comments on a small role he once played in a *Law and Order* episode, prompting Kelly to muse on the satisfactions of the series:

> KELLY: [. . .] I realized that all these shows, all the *Law and Orders* and all the ripoffs, have the same exact structure: someone dies, and a whole team of specialists springs up to figure out how to solve the mystery of the person's death.
>
> [. . .]
>
> Which I think is a fantasy people have—that they won't be forgotten. That their death won't just be accepted and mourned, but that an entire *community* will come together, all these special people—lawyers and scientists and forensics experts, judges, detectives—who are devoted, who will not stop until the mystery of the death is solved. And therefore symbolically reversed.

This is, of course, precisely what Peter—a one-man forensics expert, detective and a principal mourner—is hoping to do, with Kelly's help. The climactic piece of evidence in the case of the fallen soldier is Peter's revelation that he has a sheaf of e-mail printouts he had received from Craig while his

Happier times: Pablo Schreiber in Dying City. *Photo: Joan Marcus*

brother was on duty in Baghdad. One in particular he thinks Kelly should hear: he almost insists on reading it aloud to her.

> PETER: [. . .] It's clear to everyone now that we are not equipped to bring this country back to life. The city is dying and we are the ones killing it. Since the mission has no meaning, my men are making meaning for themselves. As you might expect the meaning they are making is perverse. I can't bear to tell you what I'm seeing. [. . .] But I do not blame my men. They were told they were heroes bringing freedom, and instead have been told to invade people's homes and take their freedom. They are ordered to protect themselves from

> violence by actively doing violence, which leads to more violence to protect themselves against: no sane person could survive these tasks. I have begun to wonder if I myself will recover from who I have become here, in just a few short months. But then in quieter moments I find myself thrown back into memories of who I was before and am faced with the realization that the horror I feel here is not . . . [. . . .]

Here Peter suddenly breaks off, and tells Kelly the next bit is irrelevant. But she insists on hearing it, and finally must take the page from Peter and read it herself:

> KELLY: [. . . T]he horror I feel here is not just a consequence of the war, but is horror of the core of me, of who I have always been. In fact I have felt more clear-headed here than ever before. I haven't felt the overwhelming need to sexually demean women that has haunted me my entire life[. . . .]

THE REVELATION, WHICH shocks and angers Kelly, hardly brings "closure" to the murky question of Craig's death. This pathology, perhaps bred into Craig by his violent-tempered father, as Peter suggests, does not supply an answer to anything—even to the cause of the fissures in Kelly and Craig's marriage. Life is a series of puzzles that, for the most part, go unsolved. Circumstances—being born into a damaged marriage, being shipped off to war—may shape psychology, but perhaps they merely reveal it.

In the play's final moments we witness the last, pained exchange between Kelly and Craig. The night before, Craig has confessed that he has fallen out of love with his wife, but in the morning Kelly tries to back away from such a painful resolution. "Listen," she says. "I think you were right. I think the stress is—I think it was a mistake to talk. I don't think this is really who we are—."

But Craig brushes her off, and heads back to combat. *Dying City* never strains to establish itself as a dramatic commentary on the futility of war. But if solving the riddle of "who we are" is central to making a meaningful life, Shinn's elliptical, moving play argues that one sad truth about the Iraq war (and indeed all war) is that it robs so many men and women of the chance to pursue the question. Often their lives are ended before they have had a chance really to ask it.

2006–2007 Best Play

FROST/NIXON

By Peter Morgan

○ ○ ○ ○ ○

Essay by Charles McNulty

NIXON: [. . .] They should tell anyone entering politics, "Forget intellect, conviction, or powers of argument, don't come near Capitol Hill unless you have a full head of hair, you don't perspire, and you don't need to shave twice a day."

WE ALWAYS KNEW he would end up on Broadway. Richard Nixon is, after all, the kind of complicated character historical dramatists lick their chops over—clumsy in his manner yet crafty in his machinations, blessed with a formidable intelligence yet fundamentally unable to connect the ethical dots, personally insecure (to the point of becoming a sweat-drenched caricature) yet professionally overreaching (to the point of becoming the public face of unscrupulous ambition). Nixon's ruthlessness, a blend of boldness and cowardice, was uniquely forged in the cracked furnace of a self that seemed to have as many glorious assets as it had egregious liabilities. It almost goes without saying that the American president whose name has become synonymous with scandal and coverup has a nature that's instructively contradictory: He contains not just multitudes but multiple object lessons.

While hardly inevitable, it makes perfect sense that Peter Morgan, the British screenwriter who has made a specialty of creating crackling dramas around modern-day British leaders (Tony Blair and Elizabeth II) and an infamous African tyrant (Idi Amin) would be the one to bring Tricky Dick to the Great White Way. In *Frost/Nixon*, Morgan continues to restore the faded luster of the history-play genre. In fact, he has given it new glamour, thanks in large part to Michael Grandage's sensational production, which began at the Donmar Warehouse in London before arriving on Broadway with Frank Langella's tour-de-force as Nixon—a role he will reprise in the Ron Howard film adaptation slated to be released in 2008.

What distinguishes Morgan's portraits of political figures at crisis points in their leadership from the vast slew of docudramas and biopics clamoring for attention on big and little screens is the circumscribed focus of his

Mano a mano: *Michael Sheen and Frank Langella in* Frost/Nixon. *Photo: Joan Marcus*

attention. Morgan has fully digested the Aristotlean principle laid out in the *Poetics* that poetry is "more philosophical and a higher thing than history: for poetry tends to express the universal, history the particular." Another way of putting this is that historical dramatists—the good ones, anyway—are not as concerned with meticulously reconstructing the past as they are with discovering its revelatory patterns. Documented details are drafted for interpretive purposes. A playwright's job, after all, is to give more than just the facts. Yet poetic license, of the kind that Shakespeare liberally exercised in deriving the plots for his history plays from Holinshed's *Chronicles*, is granted not willy-nilly but in the service of a large moral inquiry. (Not for nothing did the genre develop in Elizabethan England out of the medieval mystery plays in which biblical episodes were theatricalized to propound homiletic lessons.)

Of course the wisdom of the best historical dramas—Shakespeare's *King Henry IV* representing the high-water mark—tends to be more interrogative than prescriptive. Questions are posited rather than answered, and the scope of concern, while often dominated by a larger-than-life personality, extends beyond a single figure. Aristotle, still the best source of intellectual clarity when it comes to matters of dramatic form, contended that biography provides a playwright with an insufficiently taut organizing structure ("For infinitely various are the incidents in one man's life which cannot be reduced to unity"). Likewise, Morgan understands that his plays must be contained within a framework of ideas rather than anecdotes. The dramaturgy he has relied upon to do this typically involves the collision of two characters whose confrontation are in some way destiny changing.

In his screenplay for *The Queen* (2006), the action pivots on a series of tense tête-à-têtes between Queen Elizabeth and the newly elected Prime Minister Tony Blair after the tragic death of Princess Diana. Rather than recap the story in tabloid terms, Morgan transforms it into a rumination on media mastery and manipulation. Blair, the telegenic politician with the

Morgan understands that his plays must be contained within a framework of ideas.

silky, somewhat sophistic speech, dispenses an urgent tutorial to Her Royal Majesty on the necessity of giving the people what they think they need—in this case, a more outward expression of grief from their traditionally reserved monarch. Laggard in comparison to his slick example, she eventually is forced to conform to what she sees as the tactless etiquette of the age, offering a subdued version of the spectacle of public communication Blair has deftly and unstintingly employed to seize his political moment.

In *The Last King of Scotland* (2006), Morgan and Jeremy Brock's screenplay adaptation of a novel by Giles Foden, the saga of Amin's atrocity-ridden reign over Uganda was captured through Amin's relationship with an insouciant young Scottish physician. A carefree rebel against bourgeois expectation, the doctor finds himself at risk in the menacing African playground he has stumbled upon. The film provides a fascinating study in the lethal charisma of a military ruler whose monstrousness is harder to detect when you're in the full grip of his rousing self-belief—not to mention drinking his wine and bedding his woman. And in the television drama *The Deal* (2003), Morgan examines Tony Blair's rise to political prominence through his slippery behind-the-scenes dealings with Labor party rival and convenient Parliament ally Gordon Brown. Politics, as always, makes strange bedfellows, but a more sinister discernment, hinting at the duality of power and betrayal, is darkly gleaned.

IN *FROST/NIXON*, the antagonist is none other than David Frost (portrayed in dapper style by Michael Sheen), the British talk-show host who's desperate to regain lost stature by landing the interview "get" of his era: Nixon, post-impeachment. Bankrolling the project with his own money before sponsorship deals have been clinched, the smiling media bon vivant attempts to lure Nixon out of his Southern California seclusion—staking his solvent future on the prospect of renewed American stardom, Concorde frequent flier miles and a regular table at Sardi's.

The drama centers on the series of television interviews Frost conducted with the former president less than three years after he resigned in the aftermath of the Watergate scandal. Frost and his assembled team know that if the program is going to have any impact, Nixon is going to have to sound vaguely remorseful, if not say something out-and-out incriminating. The ensuing contest, then, pits Nixon's wily reticence against Frost's wily geniality.

It's a battle of wits, presided over by a narrator who can hardly be described as impartial. That historical personage is Jim Reston, the journalist who provided Frost with background research on Watergate and who, in Morgan's take on events, desperately wants to be part of the team that will

Perfectly clear: Frank Langella in Frost/Nixon.
Photo: Joan Marcus

elicit Nixon's long awaited apology to the nation. Justice is on his mind, yet his obsessive mania smacks a bit of vendetta, which might explain why the rhetoric he adopts, at least initially, grasps at classical tragedy:

> RESTON: Aeschylus and his Greek contemporaries believed that the gods begrudged human success, and would send a curse of "hubris" on a person at the height of their powers; a loss of sanity that would eventually bring about their downfall. Nowadays, we give the gods less credit. We prefer to call it self-destruction.

Reston's vehemence is unflagging as he introduces us to a few of the noteworthy players in his hot pursuit of an overreaching politician known for occasionally shooting himself in the foot. The dramatis personae include Hollywood agent Swifty Lazar (performed on Broadway by a comically galvanic Stephen Rowe), who extracts as much money as he can for Nixon to do the interviews, and John Birt, the producer of Frost's television show, who is astounded at the fortune that is being sunk into a project he is unsure will attract sponsors. And, of course, there's Frost himself:

> RESTON: [. . .] A man with no political convictions. Indeed, someone who had never voted in his life. But someone who had one big advantage over all of us. He understood television.

The character of Jack Brennan, Nixon's former chief of staff, provides additional narration from an opposing political perspective. He is less salient than Reston in the play's overa7ll scheme, but he reminds that Nixon was capable of engendering loyalty and compassion despite Reston's claim that is "impossible to feel anything close to sympathy" for him. With a gruff conservative's take on events, Brennan recalls the day Nixon left the White House after resigning from office:

> BRENNAN: [. . .] I'm a military man, but I don't mind telling you, watching from inside the helicopter, I wept at that moment. And wept for a good deal of the journey back to California. While 30,000 feet below us liberal America cheered. And gloated! The trendies. The hippies. The draft-dodgers and dilettantes. They had got rid of Richard Nixon. Their bogeyman. And who did they get in his place? Gerald Ford and Jimmy Carter.

The rat-tat-tat rhythm of the lines reflects Morgan's rapid fire pacing. There's a cinematic briskness to the proceedings, even when, once the taping begins, Frost finds himself stymied by Nixon's meandering solipsism, defensive crouch and double-talk. This accelerated speed might suggest superficiality, but it is really an offshoot of the work's structural tightness. The handling of subsidiary characters—for example, Caroline Cushing, the woman who becomes Frost's romantic companion after he pursues her during a flight to Los Angeles—can be too abrupt, turning real-life people into blurry dramatic accessories. But to his credit, Morgan leaves out what isn't germane to the underlying conflict between Nixon and Frost–a clash that has everything to do with the bank of 36 television monitors that stare out at us from set designer Christopher Oram's flexible recreation of Frost's studio. This locale, it should be stressed, is not just where the plot is centered; it is also the thematic heart of Morgan's vision.

FROST/NIXON is above all concerned with the connection between power and mass media. In show business and in politics, control over one's televised image is key, and the play's backstage perspective lets you see how cameras don't just capture reality but they falsify it as well. Nixon, who's not very personally adept in self-presentation, has had to learn the hard way how to use the medium to his advantage. He recounts to Frost his notorious meltdown in the 1960 debates with John F. Kennedy, where he disastrously let America see him sweat:

> NIXON: They say that moisture on my upper lip cost me the Presidency. That and the shadow from my beard. Of course—there's no actual correlation between perspiration and guilt. Nor between facial hair and duplicity. But television and the close-up—they create their own sets of meanings. So now they insist I bring my handkerchief and that I have my eyebrows trimmed.

Burned by the past, he's determined not to fall victim again to his inveterate awkwardness. A queer sort of sympathy develops for Nixon, who is bright enough to know what he needs to do in his war of wills against Frost on national television yet who nonetheless remains waylaid by a stubborn clumsiness and lack of charm. As Senator John Kerry's campaign managers know only too well, it is no easy task trying to turn a political stiff into a Cary Grant. Yet Nixon is too clever an operator not to use even this transparent weakness to his advantage. What little appeal he possesses stems from the pathos of not having much on his side beyond a sharp mind and purring manner of speech. Stripped of power, he evokes a faint (and somewhat perverse) sense of pity for the way he appears trapped in a lonely, reticent and shameful bubble.

Much of the credit for this should go to Langella, who revealed—magnified, really—the wounded psychology in the character's physical bearing. This was no Rich Little-style impersonation. It was an X-ray of a soul in purgatory. The sensitivity of the performance—which

Party boy: Michael Sheen and Sonya Walger in Frost/Nixon. *Photo: Joan Marcus*

Ben Brantley described in the *New York Times* as "one of those made-for-the-stage studies in controlled excess in which larger-than-life seems truer-to-life than merely life-size ever could"—didn't leave out physical quirks and tics that have achieved a kind of immortality in parody. There before us again were the hunched posture and the rumbling voice always in danger of retreating down his esophagus. Yet the portrait managed to eschew ridicule by appealing to our desire to understand Nixon as man rather than as a political piñata.

Not surprisingly, this humanizing of our 37th President raised hackles from commentators who fear history may be distorted in the process. Political journalist Elizabeth Drew, writing in *The Nation*, argued that the play "profoundly misleads as it entertains," transforming Nixon into a more companionable character than he was, giving only minimal context on an "out of control" presidency, and allowing the plot to hinge on an utter "contrivance."

That contrivance involves an imagined late-night drunken telephone call that Nixon makes to Frost the night before their final interview. In that exchange, Nixon appeals to Frost as a fellow outsider among the snobby elites. With a slight boozy slur, he says,

> NIXON: [. . .] That's our tragedy, isn't it, Mr. Frost? No matter how high we get, they still look down on us?

This moment, combined with Reston's 11th hour discover of documents that implicate Nixon's early knowledge of the coverup, supposedly sharpens Frost's attack the next day. The result leads to Nixon's sketchy admissions of wrongdoing and, more important, a close-up image of shrunken, defeated ex-President, which isn't how all commentators remember it. (The sense that these two men fought each other to a soporific draw might be closer to the truth.)

Drew argues that Morgan's freely dramatized handling "places commercial appeal over historical truth" and that it unintentionally gives support to Nixon defenders who "argue that his fate was undeserved." (The "smoking gun" that Reston finds wasn't even of interest to the Watergate prosecutors, she says, because they were "awash in far more incriminating evidence.") Drew's assessment that the play doesn't provide an adequate accounting—never mind prosecution—of an infamous record is correct. And there is certainly a danger that this sort of imaginative airbrushing might supplant rigorously documented truth. But to call the work "propaganda, perhaps inadvertent but effective and powerful nonetheless," seems a misreading of the work's intentions and effects.

Morgan may not be exposing the full array of Nixon's domestic crimes and foreign policy disasters, but he is not exactly letting him off the hook either. The drama, in fact, halts to a damning stop when Nixon remarks to Frost on the air, "I'm saying that when the President does it, that means it's not illegal." At the reviewed press performance, the audience erupted in laughter when these words passed from Langella's lips. But that was not an indication that their import was taken lightly. If anything, the tittering had a sardonic edge, which registered the contemporary resonance with our current president, George W. Bush and his Nixonian sidekick Dick Cheney. Morgan doesn't underscore the connection, but it is unmistakable—and one of the main reasons that the play seems so timely.

ONE SHOULD ALSO acknowledge that the kind of bright adult entertainments Morgan specializes in do not try to pass themselves off as the official record. Only the hopelessly naive would assume that the playwright is offering the truth, the whole truth and nothing but the truth, so help him God. Perhaps the danger of distortion will be greater with the film version, which will reach a wider audience and proceed more naturalistically than the play. But *Frost/Nixon* implicitly warns us against being too easily swayed by what we see on screens. Close-ups may have enormous power, but they are subject to all sorts of funny business. The hand controlling the camera is a liar, revealing what it wants to reveal and concealing what it wants to conceal. And Nixon and Frost are so evidently characterizations, which is to say invitations for world-class actors to make the roles their own.

Under Grandage's assured direction, that is exactly what Langella and Sheen managed to do. Langella offered a portrait of a once-powerful leader steeped so far in an inarticulate guilt that he can neither head back nor wade across, while Sheen gave us a bright, aging party boy who desperately does not want to be banished from the spotlight. Strange bedfellows, they mirror the fears and fantasies spurring each other on in a media-dominated landscape.

Morgan spells out his play's conclusions via Reston, who's never at a loss for a harangue. We are told that not only were the Nixon/Frost interviews "wildly successful" in terms of ratings, but that they managed to get

> RESTON: [. . . W]hat no investigative journalist, no State Prosecutor, nor Judiciary Committee, nor political enemy had managed to get—Richard Nixon's face, swollen and ravaged by loneliness, self-loathing and defeat—filling every television screen in the country.

Frost's secret: He understood "better than all of us" that there was little difference between "air-kissing politicians, actors and high fliers."

That may be overstating matters, but the media's ability to retouch reality—Morgan's specialty too, as it turns out—has undeniably become the ultimate power game.

2006–2007 Best Play

THE PAIN AND THE ITCH

By Bruce Norris

○ ○ ○ ○ ○

Essay by John Istel

CLAY: [. . .] And I hate to use the cliché, it sounds like such a cliché, but it's a *gift*, right? To be able to, with your kids, to recapture some of . . . our . . . *innocence*. Get some of that back. Reconnect with the innocence. Because if you *don't,* then, you know? Then it . . . it . . . it's *lost*. It *collapses*, like, like, like . . .

MR. HADID: Like a soufflé.

CAROL: (*to MR. HADID*) Ohhh, do you know the word soufflé?

A FTER THE LAUGHS and chuckles fade, and playwright Bruce Norris's satirical slings and arrows have found their targets with eerie accuracy, *The Pain and the Itch* turns out to be a very sad play. The lights rise on a well-appointed living room sofa on which a North African man is crying, surrounded by an American family of strangers; the lights' final fade occurs shortly after one of those Americans cries at the painful discovery that his kin are also strangers to him. In between crying jags, we're made aware of how the two characters' struggles for happiness—Hadid (Peter Jay Fernandez), an immigrant taxi driver; and Clay (Christopher Evan Welch), a feckless upper-middle-class house husband married to Kelly (Mia Barron), a high-powered corporate attorney—describe distinct visions of the American dream. By the end of the play, those dreams, like the soufflé of the epigraph, have collapsed.

The play is set in the living room and kitchen of a contemporary city house, not unlike those found in liberal enclaves across the country. It could be the Lincoln Park neighborhood in Chicago (near Steppenwolf Theatre, where the play debuted in 2005) or the Upper West Side of Manhattan (just uptown from Playwrights Horizons, where it was produced in September 2006). The stage directions in the performance script simply ask for "a very nice urban home. Expensive modern decor. Not homey."

The last two words hint at Norris's agenda. For all its modern conveniences and "tasteful neutral tones" (rendered by designer Dan

Beast within: Christopher Evan Welch and Mia Barron in The Pain and the Itch. *Photo: Joan Marcus*

Ostling), this "home" is purely aspirational. No matter how much it may resemble a fashionable spread in *House Beautiful* on the surface, something sinister lurks in the corners of these characters' lives. Norris makes this notion literal: within the first few minutes, in addition to the teary stranger on the couch, we learn that an intruder, probably a mysterious animal of the rodent variety, has been gnawing avocados left to ripen in Clay and Kelly's designer kitchen.

Clay's paranoia is particularly acute because he believes this unseen vermin may also be responsible for the strange and painful itch in and around the groin of his and Kelly's four-year-old daughter Kayla—hence the literal meaning of the play's title. We cannot help but suspect some form of sexual abuse, either from the father himself or someone else. Clay is the primary suspect because he is a stay-at-home dad and the sole caretaker of the children (they also have an infant, but within days of its birth Kelly returned to her law practice). Subsequent clues compound Clay's seeming guilt, especially when we learn about his extensive collection of pornographic videos that has become one of many issues in a marriage that seems as strained as the conversation they are having with the cab driver.

FOR ALL OF THE Halloween-like overtones in this situation, the participating action takes place around another most American holiday—Thanksgiving. The clan that gathers to celebrate includes Clay's perfect foil of an older brother, Cash (Reg Rogers), a plastic surgeon as politically conservative as Clay is politically correct. He has returned to his brother's house after a four-year absence. He's brought Kalina (Aya Cash), his 20-something Russian émigré girlfriend whose racist views and love of chain-store coffee make Kelly, Clay, and his mother Carol cringe. The latter, gloriously played both in Chicago and New York by Jayne Houdyshell, is the epitome of a ditzy

Norris's satirical target includes typical urban theater-subscribers.

matriarch, but with a twist: she is a former Socialist Worker's Party member now devoted to PBS documentaries when not teaching in an elementary school.

Norris satirizes the values and cultural mores of a segment of our society rarely ridiculed onstage: those socially progressive upper-middle-class professionals who are committed to recycling, consuming organic foodstuffs and reducing their carbon footprints. In other words, the playwright's target includes typical urban theater-subscribers. This is a comedy of manners mocking its audiences' own 21st century behavior with an energy and sting usually reserved for the vast middle of America. In fact, the liberal professional's propensity to mock ordinary folk is itself mocked, as when Kelly sneers about an experience at the John Wayne Airport in Orange County:

> KELLY: [. . .] And this Man opens his bag, and remember, I'm actually *conversing* with this person, opens his carry-on and it is filled, top to bottom, with *Bibles, American Flags*, and laminated pictures of our *president*.

> CAROL: Oh. Thank God, only two more years of that little *smirking* face.

> KELLY: And I'm thinking *how dare you*, you TGI Fridays customer. You TJ Maxx shopper with your iceberg lettuce and your ranch dressing and the right *to vote*. *How dare you*. I mean the *audacity*.

The playwright flings ripe tomatoes at this smug, well-to-do and sometimes patronizing family. Their obsession with politically correct speech, with the overparenting of children, and the need, as Clay expresses early on, to revel in that uniquely American intoxicant—innocence—is satirized and skewered.

The choice of holiday serves Norris well. He suggests that beneath our consumer culture's sometimes glib homilies about sharing bounty with different kith or kin lies the tacit acknowledgment that European colonists came, saw and conquered. The comfort and security of those gathered around that mythic Pilgrim table came at the expense of others in the form of lost land, disease, extinction. As the United States can be roughly divided into red and blue states, it also can be split between those who feel guilt about such matters—and try to assuage it—and those who embrace America's hegemony over the world as a divine right. Or, using the central metaphor of the play, there are those who are sensitive to America's moral "pain and itch" and then there are those who simply medicate.

Grandma's girl: Ada-Marie Gutierrez and Jayne Houdyshell in The Pain and the Itch. *Photo: Joan Marcus*

The play's literal "pain and itch" refers to Kayla's vaginal rash, described in blunt detail by her Uncle Cash, the plastic surgeon, who writes a prescription after examining her:

> CASH: So use this twice a day. [. . .] Just the ulcerated area around the outer part of the vulva. And around the anus, too, you know, if she starts scratching back there.

But the thematic "pain and the itch" is "liberal white guilt." In fact, older brother Cash explicitly states his loathing of liberal hypocrites:

> CASH: They think *oh no people are starving* and they can't *enjoy* how rich they are because they feel so *tacky*.
>
> [. . .]
>
> CASH: See, they *feel* bad because what they practice doesn't square with what they preach. Which makes them every bit as bad as the materialistic barbarians they despise!

Norris is adept at drawing dark comedy from his characters' strutting and fretting. The triumph of Norris's play is that sweeping themes tied to specific characters and actions unfold with the dramatic energy of a Feydeau farce—thanks, in part, to the expert direction of Anna D. Shapiro.

ESPECIALLY IN THE first act, the playwright's shrewd dramatic structure drives the comedy. Norris juggles not one but three mysteries onstage—the immigrant visitor, the invisible avocado-eating intruder and Kayla's horrific rash. The double plot unrolls in the present and the near past as the script moves back and forth between a snowy January evening and flashbacks of the fateful November gathering. We don't know why the family is describing their recent Thanksgiving to Mr. Hadid, for instance, but when the lights shift we're thrown back into a family maelstrom. Clay tries to catch the unseen rodent while arguing with his brother. Cash and Clay (named by their deceased father after Cassius Clay) are very different men and hold each other in varying states of contempt. They haven't seen each other for years until this holiday. While Carol and Kelly try to prepare the dinner, Kalina chases Kayla around the house as the little girl screams in frightened delight. Hadid, meanwhile, never completely leaves the set, serving as a ghostly presence.

The plot begins to boil when Kalina suggests she put makeup on Kayla to make her look "sexy." This gets Kelly upset enough to ask for Clay's intervention. The question of child abuse is raised, which the audience has been thinking all along regarding Kayla's rash. Clay cites statistics that show 1 out of 5 adults have experienced abuse. Carol counts the five adults and suggests its nonsense since no one among the adults present were abused. Kelly begs to differ. She insists she was abused not physically but psychically—by "neglect" and "sarcasm." Clay then suggests he was abused by his father. Carol dismisses that notion. "He was irritable, but I don't think abusive." Cash finds this all laughable.

Then, in her heavy Russian accent, Kalina coolly relates her story about being abused:

> KALINA: (*completely matter-of-fact*) [. . .] As little girl, when I was taken to the room and the soldiers, when they hold me down on the floor and they rape me over and over, when I was little girl? And then, after this, when having to have the bad abortion from doctor which makes it now so that I cannot ever have the children? And how I am now totally okay and everything despite these things? And when you think how you have family and big house and things and also the good job? I am saying maybe is good idea to put in perceptive.

Cash ignores the harrowing details and instead grows increasingly angry at his girlfriend's inability to pronounce "perspective": Kalina begins with "perceptive" and progresses to "per-skeptive" as her boyfriend's frustration increases. They start screaming at each other until Kalina throws her wine in his face and exits the room in a fury. At that moment, Clay swears he heard an animal in the house. He grabs a golf club and runs out into the backyard. Kayla tugs at her grandmother to change her diaper and Carol takes her offstage. Kalina reappears wearing her coat and leaves the house. For the first time, Cash and Kelly are alone onstage: their glares hint at an unusual animosity toward each other. Suddenly, we hear breaking glass and a security alarm blares. Everyone comes onstage but no one can stop the piercing sound—except the playwright. Norris cuts to the present with Hadid.

One of the common elements to these scenes is Hadid breaking one of the liberal WASP elite's strictest taboos: he asks about their money. In an early scene he wonders about the cost of Clay's shoes and we laugh at the squirming that ensues as the young father tries to dismiss the notion that he is fairly wealthy. In another, Hadid suggests he knows how to fix their table, which Clay must then awkwardly explain is "distressed" on purpose—it is meant to look like something that would cause a working-class man like Hadid to fetch sandpaper and shellac.

The third time we shift from Thanksgiving, just before the end of the first act, Hadid asks about their financial situation, specifically about the property taxes they pay. Clay loses his temper.

Innocence lost: Ada-Marie Gutierrez and Christopher Evan Welch in The Pain and the Itch. *Photo: Joan Marcus*

CLAY: I mean, the *property ta . . . who cares?* That's not the point, alright? This isn't about . . . where did we get the table or . . . how much were my . . . I mean, *come on*. Okay? Come on.

MR. HADID: I apologize.

[. . .]

CLAY: No. I'm only talking about advantages. Giving your child every possible advantage.

MR. HADID: Advantage over *my* child.

Hadid is calm and logical. Everyone is out to protect his own family at the expense of others, he maintains. Then the bomb: "And this is the reason you kill my wife," he concludes. As if this line wasn't a big enough explosion, Norris immediately cuts back to the past with the alarm sounding. As Kelly finds the key on top of the box and stops the alarm, Carol lifts Kayla's skirt to discover the rash. Cash, Kelly and Clay exchange quizzical looks and the first act ends.

THE SECOND ACT begins in the middle of a dour Thanksgiving meal. A couple of guests are missing: Cash has gone to search for Kalina who, in the meantime, wandered back to the house and passed out on the sofa with a sixpack of beer dangling from her hand. The tension at the table between Kelly and Clay is thicker than the gravy.   So, Carol dithers on about a PBS special while Clay complements his mom on the soy nuts in the salad.

Underneath, Clay is seething and Kelly wants to excuse herself from this "festival of regurgitation." When Cash returns to the house and tries to extricate Kalina, Kelly puts Kayla to bed and discovers an avocado with teeth marks in the girl's bedroom. The mysterious animal is now in the house.

As the tension escalates, Kelly admits she doesn't really love Clay any longer. In fact, she hasn't loved him for four years, since she first admitted at the time that she loved someone else. Although they worked through it, or so Clay thought, with the help of a $150-an-hour shrink, she's sick of supporting him and his porn collection. Clay is not only furious about being deceived into having two kids by someone who doesn't love him, but that he sacrificed his pet to her fear of disease while she was pregnant.

> KELLY: (*quietly*) Please, Clay. What do you possibly want me to say?
>
> CLAY: [. . .] *Possibly* you could say this: see, you *might* say, I'm the person who made Clay kill his cat. How would that feel? [. . .] I made him kill his cat so that I could have some babies, and now, I'm thinking maybe I'd like to go off and fuck someone else. [. . .]

That sends Kelly out of the room. Eventually, as the lights' cross fade brings us back to the present, the truth has become so clear that the family sits with a stranger and laughs about Clay's naivete: How could he not have known that the man Kelly had fallen for was Clay's Republican, toy-car-stealing brother? Not only that, but Cash had just started sleeping with Kalina before his fling with Kelly and had caught the venereal disease Kalina had received from being raped by the Russian soldiers. Cash then passed it to Kelly, who, pregnant with Kayla, infected her daughter. The first mystery solved. As they chuckle about this "absurd" course of events, Clay quietly begins weeping. All his hopes of a secure innocence is gone, his mini-Walden has been polluted. When his daughter (is she even his?) comes over to see what's the matter, he tells the child, "Leave me the fuck alone."

HADID'S PRESENCE ONSTAGE is then resolved in a harrowing monologue delivered with quiet intensity by Fernandez. His wife, who spoke little English, had been hired by Clay and Kelly as a housecleaner. There were suspicions that she had stolen bread, which Hadid confirmed. She could not ask for it because she did not know the words in English and, thinking no one would miss it, took it home for Hadid and their son. But when Kayla comes onstage and chases everyone around with a hypodermic needle she found in the back laundry room, Clay is convinced that the maid has willfully injected Kayla with something to give her the rash. Hadid explains that his wife was diabetic and was just about to eat when police burst into their apartment, handcuffed them and threw them into separate police cars—even as Hadid was screaming that his wife would die from diabetic shock if she did not eat.

> HADID: [. . .] Now I can no longer hold my temper. Now I shout at them. I say my wife must eat. [. . .] I cannot be calm. If only I could. But it is hard for me knowing that she has taken the injection and she now must eat and so I find that I cannot be calm.

Hadid tells the family that she went into a coma that night and died the next day. At last, it becomes clear that the family, while feigning concern, is only trying to get him to drop a lawsuit against them. They discover that if Kelly and Cash had been honest about their affair—and their STD—and told Clay the real cause of Kayla's rash, Hadid's wife would have been alive. That is a lot of pain to come from such an itch. The remaining mystery is that of the avocado-loving animal. Kayla resolves it when—as the lights fade on her— she goes to the bowl on the coffee table, takes an avocado and bites into it like an apple. The "innocent" child is the invisible monster in the well-furnished room.

Most Americans gladly embrace, as does Clay, a long tradition of "innocence"—or at worst, willful ignorance. The theme of the innocent American who awakens to his or her responsibility for the world's suffering is not a new one by any means—Rodgers and Hammerstein made a fortune setting it to music in classics such as *South Pacific*, where plucky Americans confront the "Other" and embrace it. Norris's message is less wide-eyed and optimistic. The intruder in our American home is neither the poor immigrant, nor a wild animal or bread-stealing worker. In *The Pain and the Itch*, Norris introduces us to the real outsider: human decency. Too many American citizens have become paranoid about personal and national security; they have locked themselves in their houses, isolated with their own fears. Norris raises an age-old conundrum. Who are truly imprisoned: those locked in, behind a gate, or those locked out? In the case of this play's family, their upper-class anxieties have turned them into their own "Other."

2006–2007 Best Play

PASSING STRANGE

By Stew and Heidi Rodewald

○ ○ ○ ○ ○

Essay by Alisa Solomon

NARRATOR: Every day I build a mask

Up to the task

But now there's no real me.

I cut clippings from my dreams

Then move them around

Til they look like me,

But there's no real me.

Call me a collage

Of spare parts found

In my mind's garage

Camouflage you see

Although my paste on eyes can see

Right through . . .

All of you.

But you can't see me . . .

DON'T CALL IT A rock musical. Stew, the co-creator and star of *Passing Strange*, considers that phrase "the most terrifying combination of words in the English language." For him and his collaborator, Heidi Rodewald, theater is an untrustworthy form—too polite and contained for a scruffy, irreverent rock band like theirs. In their public comments, at least, they described their venture into dramatic territory—through a commission from New York's Public Theater—as a treacherous journey in a foreign land. Actors, a plot, spectators seated in neat quiet rows: Wouldn't all those theatrical trappings pull the plug on the band's anarchic, acerbic energy? The duo couldn't imagine, Rodewald told a journalist, making music that would sound at home on Broadway. Meanwhile, in an online essay, Stew admonished potential audiences to "leave your fourth wall at home." A

Self awareness: Stew in Passing Strange. *Photo: Michal Daniel*

rock crowd, he noted, "acknowledges its *role* in the proceedings. It also drinks a lot of alcohol. Please feel free to follow suit."

Although patrons could not bring drinks to their seats at the Public (or at the Berkeley Repertory Theatre, which co-produced the play and presented the premiere), Stew and Rodewald needn't have worried. The production of *Passing Strange* made good use of standard dramatic conventions—telling the story of a middle-class, black male songwriter searching for selfhood and truth—while managing to maintain the immediacy of a rock gig. The fourth wall was blasted open a long, long time ago, even if Stew and Rodewald hadn't noticed—or more likely, even if their grungy troubadour credibility could be enhanced by suggesting that theater threatened to play a scolding superego to their rock 'n' roll id.

In fact, the songs Stew and Rodewald have been writing and performing together for the last decade are not just loud, antic outlets for sexual cravings and defiant urges, as the rock cliché might have it. They are also melodious, brainy and downright narrative. (That's why the Public, where the band had played in Joe's Pub, commissioned them in the first place. Along with the imaginative director Annie Dorsen, Stew and Rodewald developed the show at the Sundance Institute Theatre Lab.)

Rock's requisite spirit of rebellion lodges in an unusual, less obvious place in Stew's work: in the refusal to be categorized. For a black man in America, that means, first and foremost, racially. This repudiation is both aesthetic and political—and asserted with a hammy comic wink: Stew (his given name is Mark Stewart) named his band the Negro Problem and titled their first album, released in 1997, *Post Minstrel Syndrome*. Having grown up middle class in Los Angeles in the 1970s—as does *Passing Strange*'s autobiographically inspired protagonist—Stew claims the full range of influences that would be sloshing around in the head of anyone drenched

The humor—and angst—in Stew's songs come from skewering racial incongruity.

in American mass culture of the period. He heard just as much Glen Campbell as he did Earth, Wind and Fire, and you can recognize both strains in his playful, perceptive songs about bad affairs, post-spat reconciliations, daily drudgery or drug rehab. Stew's lyrics can quip like Cole Porter's; his harmonies can turn as treacly as the Carpenters. He can also do a mean James Brown—as a quick musical joke in *Passing Strange* reveals—or charge into full-throated gospel.

MUCH OF THE humor—and the angst—expressed in Stew's songs comes from his skewering the idea of racial incongruities. In one sweet-sounding ditty called "Black Men Ski," which is not in *Passing Strange*, Stew sings:

> STEW: [. . .] Chinese guys can jump real high
>
> And Germans cook soul food.
>
> White boys rap
>
> And hippies nap their dreads up
>
> To look rude.
>
> Jazz is now suburban,
>
> It's Marsalisally clean.
>
> And now we've got Viagra
>
> Everyone's a sex machine.
>
> So black men ski. [. . .]

In this same way, *Passing Strange* frankly confronts the limits and merits of racial and class identity. This theme—along with sharp, driving songs—is what lifts the show above the trope of its core narrative: an artist-as-a-young-man *Bildungsroman*. The show follows Youth, Stew's alter ego, on a quest for artistic fulfillment, taking him from Los Angeles's middle-class comforts and conventions to free-for-all Amsterdam, to radical Berlin and finally back home. Youth sets out to find himself even though his mother's friends admonish, "You better leave that kinda crap to whitey!" Stew's twist on the well-worn story is that Youth must disentangle the "self" he is trying to find—and give voice—from notions of "blackness" that feel to him arbitrary and meaningful, externally imposed and as integral as his own skin.

Such an unsentimental and forthright—and also humorous—take on race and class remains rare in the American theater, though the country could certainly use more honest and complex discussion of the topic. To cite just a proximate example: *Passing Strange* opened in New York shortly after a public outcry forced CBS and MSNBC to suspend radio "shock-jock" Don Imus after he referred to the Rutgers University women's basketball team as a bunch of "nappy-headed hos." Offensive as the remark was, the scandal it produced not only isolated that single statement from a constant barrage of racist and sexist speech on the airwaves, but also disconnected

Spiritual revival: Chad Goodridge, Daniel Breaker and Stew in Passing Strange. *Photo: Michal Daniel*

it from a long history of government policy based on that very stereotype of black women as sexually incontinent.

For all of the ink and airtime spent on the Imus affair—and there was a lot of it—very little actually advanced the national conversation on race, gender and class. Class was a major factor in the Imus situation—the protests repeatedly emphasized that the women so slurred were admirable college students. Their coach, Vivian Stringer, told the press at the time, "They are young ladies of class, distinction, they are articulate, they are brilliant, they are gifted." Indeed, they are. But a troubling implication hovers over these defenses—and over the defense of the use of such language in rap music that soon joined them: that it is fine to use these terms for black women who do not make it to college. Imus apologized. But nothing changed.

THE THEATER, WHICH itself remains largely racially segregated, cannot be expected to correct such persistent and corrosive problems. But sometimes it can open them for inspection. Stew's approach is as audacious as it is ambitious. And not everyone appreciates his sardonic humor. (The NAACP objected to the name of his band some years back. Stew did not change it.) Nonetheless, *Passing Strange* provided an extraordinary opportunity for thinking hard—and laughing hard—about the intertwining strictures of race and class, and the cautious pieties with which we typically discuss them, or, more likely, avoid discussing them.

In this respect, the production's unusual use of four black actors to play the roles of everyone Youth encounters—whether African American or white European characters—is a refreshing reminder of the nonrealistic theater's capacity to push the imagination beyond literal reflections on race.

Alongside this ensemble, plus Youth (the winning Daniel Breaker) and his mother (Eisa Davis), Stew presents himself as Narrator, sometimes singing from behind a lectern, sometimes striding downstage with his guitar bouncing against his belly. Of middle age and pear shape, sporting a fuzzy goatee between puffy jowls and beneath bald pate, Stew doesn't exactly look like a rock star. But he holds the stage like one. His punkish I-dare-you glare peers over the top of forbidding black-rimmed glasses, and is balanced by a seductive, even soothing, baritone. Singing almost non-stop through the two-and-a-half-hour show, by turns Stew croons with suave assurance, bellows with bluesy angst and rocks with abandon.

Presented on a three-quarter thrust stage that pitches the actors almost into the front rows, *Passing Strange* keeps the band central as well. The musicians dominate the space for the opening number—a peppy rock 'n' roll prologue—and then partially sink into the floor. From their separate, shallow pits—drummer upstage center, keyboard player stage-right and bassist (Rodewald) stage-left—the band pokes into the dramatic proceedings, assuring that the show remains as much a rock concert as a play with music.

In the prologue, Narrator sings:

> NARRATOR: Now since it's my job ah'ma set the scene
>
> In a big two story black middle class dream
>
> With all the mod cons, the manicured lawns
>
> Some savings bonds
>
> A Boy and his Mom
>
> Talkin' mid '70s south central LA
>
> A colored paradise where the palm trees sway
>
> But this promised land wasn't delivering the goods [. . .]
>
> Even in this best of all possible hoods.

Youth is the innocent Candide in this scenario, dressed in a cherry-red T-shirt that matches the hue of Narrator's silky button-down. He is 14 as the story begins, refusing to accompany his mom to church. The show's themes are set in motion in this domestic squabble over what Youth, a budding Buddhist, regards—and the band sings about—as the "Baptist fashion show." In running commentary on the scene—and in a hilarious introduction to the show's upending of black stereotypes—Narrator notes how Mother's speech takes on a "Negro dialect mask" as she gets agitated, shifting from lines like "It's such a beautiful Sunday morning. Sunrise was like the slow unveiling of a masterpiece" to "Jump outta dat bed n come a churchin wit me!" Once at church, Youth awakens to a new kind of religion: music.

> NARRATOR: [. . .] All then the chilly church pews got suddenly warm
>
> And the notes of the music began to swarm.

The preacher engages in a blues-influenced call and response, building to the song "Freight Train." The musical excitement causes Youth to announce the epiphany he experiences:

> YOUTH: [. . .] church ain't nothin' but rock and roll . . .
>
> (MOTHER slaps YOUTH)

Siren song: Rebecca Naomi Jones and Stew in Passing Strange. *Photo: Michal Daniel*

[. . .]

MOTHER: Don't you know the difference between the sacred and
the profane?

YOUTH: I can't hear the difference.

PERSUADED BY THE participation of his high school's "teenage goddess,"
Youth accedes to his mother's suggestion that he join the church choir, and
there, along with rock 'n' roll, Youth finds its constant companions: sex and
drugs. Youth's fumbling advances provide Narrator another opportunity for
satirizing bourgeois projections of "blackness." As Youth loses his
virginity—panting on a darkened stage—the teen goddess prattles about
her fantasy of the house they will live in some day with "Malcolm X
commemorative plaques lining the walls of our airy, peach colored breakfast
nook." As for drugs, Youth soon bonds with the choir director, Franklin, a
closeted gay man who takes him on drives in his VW bug and turns him on
not only to marijuana, but also to Puccini and the allures of Europe. And to
the high cost of compromise.

These lessons lead Youth to dump Franklin and the choir in order to
pursue "the real" with his friends by writing their own songs. Their garage

punk band, the Scaryotypes, is rotten, even by punk's low standards. (Stew's band offers a noisy joke of a sample.) But the tuneless lyrics bite:

> YOUTH: 1-2-3-4 1-2-3-4
>
> I'm at war with Negro mores
>
> I'm at war with ghetto norms
>
> My mother stands in doorways
>
> Beggin' me to conform
>
> Be a good football-playin' snazzy-dressin' brother
>
> So the sisters won't be able to tell me from the others . . .
>
> Yeah I'm the sole brother
>
> Up in this motherfucker.

As Youth's friends edge into conventional lives, he continues his quest for "the real" by moving to Europe, parting from Mother in a caricature of an Antonioni movie: headscarf, sunglasses, overwrought dialogue. Narrator sings of what Youth hopes to discover there:

> NARRATOR: Naked girls at breakfast tables
>
> Talking Hegel and Camus. [. . .]
>
> And men dressed up in Gauloise smoke
>
> Quote Marx right back at you.

More or less, that is what Youth finds as, "He sits in a cafe like Baldwin in the day." Though Youth is trying to escape a constricting idea of racial belonging, he constantly figures himself within the terms of African-American history, going so far as to imagine his escape from the black bourgeoisie as a "trip / Out the slave holder's grip."

In one of the most poignant scenes, Youth is greeted at an Amsterdam cafe with astonishing hospitality. It is startling enough that hashish is on the menu. More surprising, a woman working there offers him the recently vacated room of a housemate. That Youth is not feared or merely tolerated with anxious politeness signals that he has, indeed, left Los Angeles far behind—and prompts a lovely, lyrical song with the simple refrain: "She gave him these / Her keys." (Not that some stereotypes don't follow him. "So, do you play jazz?" "Do you play duh blues?" some Dutch fellows ask upon meeting him. "Do you live in a fuckin' windmill?" Youth replies. "Do you wear clog shoes?")

One stereotype Youth is eager to embrace is that of the freewheeling bohemian, and Amsterdam amply delivers that romance (despite one roommate who regards artmaking as labor like any other.) It also liberates him from a mild self-loathing for his own body. In an amusing cha-cha, Youth and two roommates sing "We Just Had Sex":

> MARIANNA: We just had sex
>
> There's nothing sleazy 'bout
>
> A natural reflex
>
> It's nice and easy
>
> No need to crane your necks
>
> It's all cool breezy, baby
>
> What's a little bedroom traffic?
>
> Evening News is pornographic!

But soon, Youth finds his creativity dulled by how easy life has become and he unceremoniously splits from his lover and heads for Berlin. There he falls in with a group of postpunk anarchist performers who are staging a riot the day he arrives. These tough radicals school him in a new aesthetic: spurning the myth of inner truth and celebrating the surface. And he is exposed to a new drug: cocaine. When they ridicule his pop love-songs as insufficiently revolutionary, he wins their approval by claiming the very role he left America to avoid. "Do you know what it's like to be the object of oppression living under police occupation in the ghetto?" he asks them rhetorically. Narrator rolls his eyes, saying, "Uh, nobody in this play knows what it's like to hustle for dimes on the mean streets of south central."

In no time, Youth is performing to great acclaim as "Mr. Middle Passage," parodying a vaudevillian "coon show" and answering audience questions about how to cook fried chicken. It doesn't take long for his radical roommates to catch on that his ghetto claims are all shtick. But they, too, get busted for lack of authenticity when Youth learns that these anticapitalist, convention-crushing atheists all plan to visit their families for Christmas, a gesture he has refused his mother for years. Are they all just playacting?

Alone in Berlin and full of self-pity, Youth, along with Narrator, sings the plaintive, pivotal song: "Every day I build a mask / Up to the task / Now there's no real me."

Youth recovers himself, though, when he returns to Los Angeles. He has been called back for his mother's funeral. Given the show's trite trajectory, it ends on what is perhaps an inevitably banal note. Now that Youth has learned that he has been playing a series of roles and disavowing genuine attachments, he can see that, "Home was a song inside me all along."

IT IS NOT ONLY in the pat ending, though, that one wishes Stew's dramaturgy might display as much irony as his song lyrics. Given the band's presence, the straightforward, episodic nature of the plot and its central, selfish hero need not leave the piece so lacking in productive tension. "Linear narrative is the religion of the opiated!" proclaims one of the Berlin cabaret militants. He has a point.

For much of the show, Youth is a passive figure, a man in a tornado of desires that sets him down one place, then another. He is doubly passive because he is narrated: Stew often sings about him rather than Youth speaking and acting for himself. When these two figures contradict each other or clash a bit, the show gives off its brightest nonmusical sparks.

Meanwhile, the characters Youth encounters do not travel with him, so they disappear as he moves on, having served their functions. That Youth treats people as mere furniture in his life makes him not wholly likeable, which lends the show some emotional texture. It would be heightened if Narrator offered as much distanced commentary on Youth's self-serving gender politics as he does on his relationship to race.

There is one thrilling moment in *Passing Strange* that suggests the possible effect of such multilayered action. In the Berlin scene, Narrator introduces a character named Desi (with whom Youth will later have an affair that he also will abandon) and she interrupts him. "A woman can speak for herself," she chides. The puncturing of Narrator's authority, the stage-taking assertion of someone other than Youth, the challenge to the established dramatic convention—all of these move the scene into a fresh theatrical and thematic register. And then, to seal the sisterly deal, Rodewald pipes up from her pit: "Yeah, that's right."

A big promise of future possibilities lies in that disruption of Stew's all-controlling centrality to the story and the telling of it. After closing at the Public, the band went back on the road, playing the critically acclaimed, modest gigs on which it survives, rejecting the megahit machinery of a big corporate label for a sustainable life of work with integrity. I, for one, hope the team returns to the theater to make something new, offering their great musical gifts to a more multivocal and complex invention. Whatever rocking, musical creation they come up with next, for sure it will not be a rock musical.

2006–2007 Best Play

RADIO GOLF

By August Wilson

○ ○ ○ ○ ○

Essay by Christopher Rawson

> HARMOND (*pointing to the ceiling*): See those marks. It's all hand tooled. That's the only way you get pattern detail like that. That tin ceiling's worth some money.
>
> MAME: Then take it down and sell it. At least put some new paint on it. I wouldn't want to do business here.

THE FINAL INSTALLMENT in August Wilson's epic Pittsburgh Cycle, *Radio Golf*, features something new: the black middle class. In the previous nine dramas chronicling the decade-by-decade 20th-century tragedy and triumph of African Americans, the middle class was glimpsed only in embryo (Caesar in *Gem of the Ocean*, Avery in *The Piano Lesson*) or askance (West in *Two Trains Running*). In *Radio Golf*, ambition has led to financial success for Roosevelt Hicks, who is happy to let the white man use him if there is money to be made. But in Harmond Wilks, a handsome lawyer, real-estate dealer, urban developer and incipient politician, we meet the established middle class, complete with inherited position and an Ivy League education.

You can hear the class distinction even in chitchat with his wife, Mame, a rising public relations star and striver. No one has spoken this way in an August Wilson play:

> MAME: Harmond, don't forget we're going to Marcie and Jim's tonight. Six o'clock.
>
> HARMOND: Remind me to take Jim one of those Cohibas I got in Costa Rica. I haven't smoked any of them yet.
>
> MAME: I hope for you it stays warm out tonight. Marcie's not going to let you stink up her house either.

Nor has anyone sung pop songs such as "Blue Skies." Harmond, his wife and friend revel in their broad horizons. But in joining the American bourgeoisie, Wilson suggests they risk losing their souls.

In posing difficult questions about the relationships of commerce to spirit, individual to group and past to future, *Radio Golf* ends the Pittsburgh

Power couple: Tonya Pinkins and Harry Lennix in Radio Golf. *Photo: Carol Rosegg*

Cycle by pointing ahead. Wilson, who died in 2005 after completing a second revision of the script, concluded the cycle by dumping the past century's hopes and frustrations right in the laps of this middle class, which he implicitly indicts for not doing enough to lead the black community out of economic and cultural stagnation.

IT IS 1997. The pressed tin ceiling is in the new office of Bedford Hills Redevelopment on Centre Avenue, in the same Hill District of Pittsburgh where all but one of the cycle's plays are set. Everything is fresh and optimistic as Harmond and Roosevelt plan their lucrative redevelopment scheme, a 180-apartment high-rise with an urban mall that will include the usual national chain stores. But on the Hill, any development raises the specter of past spasms of destructive "urban renewal," characterized in sardonic Hill folklore as "Negro removal." (It is a motif in *Two Trains Running* and *Jitney*, the plays set in 1969 and 1977.) In *Radio Golf*, the beleaguered community, which once achieved fame through such jazz greats as Art Blakey, Errol Garner and Ahmad Jamal—and now, as in cosmic compensation, in the Pittsburgh Cycle—is still under attack.

Even small details show how thinly middle-class modernity lies atop an angry past. Harmond's response to that pressed-tin ceiling suggests he appreciates history, but possibly more as decoration or nostalgia than for its hard truths. It is a more positive sign that he insists the development's health center be named not for a corporation but for a historic pioneer, Sarah Degree. But he is also enough in love with economic value (and with Mame) to justify the ceiling in monetary terms—and for Mame, that's really what counts. In this tentative, seemingly incidental way, the play begins its struggle for Harmond's soul, which is to say, the soul of his class and community.

No one has spoken this way in an August Wilson play.

But is it a community? "The Hill District's dead," says Mame, who wants Harmond to leave it behind in his campaign for mayor. But the Broadway production—celebrating continuity by using the same Cort Theatre where Wilson's first Broadway entry, *Ma Rainey's Black Bottom*, opened in 1984—put that community's heritage front and center. The cycle's previous plays and the history of the Hill (real and mythic) were vividly present in the David Gallo's set, which launched the play with a couple of emotional haymakers.

First was the show curtain, a panorama of Hill storefronts in the style of Romare Bearden, the artist who was a powerful influence on Wilson and had his own Pittsburgh history. The curtain—a dark, brooding reminder of history and art—contained allusions to other plays in the cycle. When it rose on the arena of conflict, a functional office appeared: work tables, folding chairs, boxes, files, maps and posters. But standing mute on either side was Gallo's other emotional coup—to the left, a derelict barber shop; to the right, a dusty, abandoned diner; above, empty, shattered floors. Barber shop and diner were the lively communal spaces of the once-vibrant Hill. Now they stood as ghosts of a community that once nurtured in spite of adversity. In the conflict between that communal past and the competitive present, those dark rooms, as loud with mute testimony as unopened chambers in an ancient funeral mound, spoke for discarded heritage.

But this is now, or at least 1997. In Roosevelt's view, community has been replaced by the individual. The play's title derives from his discovery of a pointedly individual game that historically has been the preserve of the white middle class:

ROOSEVELT: [. . . When] I hit my first golf ball I asked myself where
have I been? How'd I miss this? I couldn't believe it. I felt free. Truly
free. For the first time. [. . .] I felt like the world was open to me. [. . .]

This paean to the glories of golf might seem to be progress. But in the
context of the long struggle for black civic and economic rights, "truly free"
is ironic: is golf really a measure of black freedom? It isn't long before we
realize that for Roosevelt, what this freedom really means is access to the
country club and the backroom deal:

ROOSEVELT: [. . .] I'm at the table! There was a time they didn't let
any blacks at the table. You opened the door. You shined the shoes.
You served the drinks. And they went in the room and made the
deal. I'm in the room! Them motherfuckers who bought and traded
the railroads . . . how do you think they did it? This is business. This
is the way it's done in America. [. . .]

As a newly minted Mellon Bank vice president, Roosevelt thinks he's gained
access to capitalism's inner sanctum. He even considers trading up for a
new wife. But while he is going to do well for himself, he has really just
become a black front man for white money.

Narrative reclaimed: John Earl Jelks and Anthony Chisholm in Radio Golf. *Photo: Carol
Rosegg*

EVERYTHING SEEMS ON TRACK with the redevelopment scheme and Harmond's political ambitions until the appearance of Sterling Johnson, Old Joe Barlow and Aunt Ester's house at 1839 Wylie Avenue, which was there all along. This is the ramshackle old mansion whose past is connected to the Hill's historic soul. Although Wilson's Hill is very real—and in fact *Radio Golf* reads as a commentary on a real Pittsburgh development struggle that arose, in 2006, after the play was written—the mansion is fictitious: the address refers to the 1839 revolt on the slave ship Amistad. In Wilson's *Gem of the Ocean, Two Trains Running* and *King Hedley II*, it was the home of Aunt Ester, last in a line of spiritual healers reaching back to 1619, when the first African slaves were brought to Virginia. The various Esters (Aunts Ester, anc-estor) were repositories of centuries of trial and tribulation, wisdom and solace, but the last in the line apparently died in 1985 in *King Hedley II*.

That is the problem. Aunt Ester's absence signals the loss of cultural tradition and spiritual life. The urgent dramatic question—as with the piano in Wilson's *The Piano Lesson*—is who owns the house? Who owns the legacy of black oppression and achievement? Who makes decisions for the black community? But Harmond doesn't even seem to have heard of Aunt Ester. When he discovers it is her house he has to tear down, he does not fully realize the cost. Sterling does. He is the same man who 28 years earlier was the young central character in Wilson's *Two Trains Running*, pursuing the waitress and studying "black is beautiful." He had served time for robbing a bank. As he explains in *Radio Golf*:

> STERLING: [. . .] I just wanted to know what it was like to have some money. Seem like everybody else had some. I said let me get me some. So I robbed that bank. I had some money. It didn't make me any smarter. It didn't make me any better than anyone else. You can't do nothing with money but spend it. After that you back where you started from. Then what you gonna do? I found out I was looking for something that you couldn't spend. [. . .]

Sterling found that peace by going to Aunt Ester for spiritual advice. Here, we learn she told him to carry tools, not weapons, and he became a self-reliant handyman, at peace with present and past.

In *Radio Golf*, Sterling appears as Harmond's contemporary, with memories of their being together at St. Richard's School (where Wilson attended). As a result, Sterling's age does not dovetail perfectly with his prior appearance in *Two Trains Running*, a reminder that in the Pittsburgh Cycle, each play stands alone. But his early history and philosophy make him the perfect adversary for Roosevelt. He has street smarts, as when he needles Harmond: "White crimes, white lawyer, country-club jail. Black crimes, black lawyer, Western State Penitentiary." But he also has a firm moral compass: "You ain't got to study up on right and wrong."

In this conflict, although Wilson knows which man is right, he performs the Shakespearean balancing act of giving each a compelling statement in the play's electric, final showdown:

> STERLING: You know what you are? It took me a while to figure it out. You a Negro. White people will get confused and call you a nigger but they don't know like I know. I know the truth of it. I'm a nigger. Negroes are the worst thing in God's creation. Niggers got style. Negroes got blindyitis. A dog knows it's a dog. A cat knows it's a cat. But a Negro don't know he's a Negro. He thinks he's a white man. It's Negroes like you who hold us back.
>
> ROOSEVELT: Who's "us"? Roosevelt Hicks is not part of any "us." It's not my fault if your daddy's in jail, your mama's on drugs, your little sister's pregnant and the kids don't have any food 'cause the welfare cut off the money. Roosevelt Hicks got money. Roosevelt Hicks got a job because Roosevelt Hicks wanted one. You niggers kill me blaming somebody else for your troubles.

AS HE DID with Caesar in *Gem*, Wilson gives Roosevelt his due. But the crux of the issue is right there: Roosevelt refuses to be part of any "us" except for one defined by success. He's a classic capitalist. Sterling calls Harmond to something better—and Harmond gradually responds. As his historical sensitivities are raised, he finally goes to explore Aunt Ester's house.

> HARMOND: You should feel the woodwork. If you run your hand slow over some of the wood you can make out these carvings. There's faces. Lines making letters. An old language[. . . .] The air in the house smells sweet like a new day.

Harmond changes as he recovers the past, guided by Old Joe, who speaks in garbled, emblematic ways of deeper values. Thrillingly, but not until the end of the second scene in Act II, Harmond and Old Joe discover they're related. Old Joe is the son of the last Aunt Ester, whom we met in 1904 as Black Mary in *Gem of the Ocean*, and Harmond is the grandson of her older half-brother, the ambitious and callous Caesar Wilks. As hard as he was, Caesar and then his son, who passed their real estate firm on to Harmond, regularly paid the taxes on 1839 Wylie—the tribute that even a Caesar can pay to the spirit.

Wilson makes the conflicts between past and present, commerce and spirit both messy and personal. But isn't the past always personal? Harmond,

Blood money? Anthony Chisholm and Harry Lennix in Radio Golf. *Photo: Carol Rosegg*

who hopes to bridge the gulf between black and white, is forced to choose. There is a moment when he thinks he can resolve the conflict by incorporating Aunt Ester's house into a new design. Indeed, preservation would make commercial sense as a way to humanize a high-rise monstrosity. But the deal is too patched together with city, federal and corporate financing to allow for humane amendment, making it a microcosm of black community development within a dominantly white economy.

IT IS HARD to imagine a more personable Harmond than Harry Lennix, who played the role on Broadway this season. Calm, self-possessed, handling phones, files and the language of civics with practiced ease, he really listened: you would vote for him in a second. If anything, Harmond is perhaps too perfect: if Wilson had lived to do more polishing, he might have added complexity. There is an interesting area of further exploration in Harmond's suppressed antagonism toward his father—a potent theme throughout the cycle—and in his acceptance of Old Joe as substitute father. But Lennix let us see the growing vulnerability that leaves him irresolutely stranded between Roosevelt and Sterling in the climactic, insult-spitting battle of the class war.

The spiritual heart of the play rests in Old Joe, a delicious variant on the crackpot prophet, played by Pittsburgh Cycle veteran Anthony Chisholm with rich idiosyncrasy. Old Joe always strikes out on tangents that lead straight to important truths. The reunion between him and Harmond is the emotional heart of the play. John Earl Jelks was a stalwart Sterling and James A. Williams a dynamic Roosevelt. The underwritten Mame is the least of the roles, but simply by lending her considerable presence, Tonya Pinkins gave it significance.

To director Kenny Leon and Wilson's longtime assistant and dramaturg, Todd Kreidler, fell the delicate task of taking the playwright's final revisions—completed after the script was frozen for the 2005 Center Theatre Group production in Los Angeles—and incorporating them for five more regional theater productions leading up to Broadway. The Los Angeles script was published in the November 2005 issue of *American Theatre*. The final revision, however, as performed on Broadway, was considerably changed. In this version, the first scene of Act II is moved into Act I, significant speeches are expanded or combined and even small details are improved. Taken together, the changes move the play more quickly and sharpen its conflicts.

THE AUGUST WILSON CENTURY begins in *Gem of the Ocean* with an insistent knock on the door at 1839 Wylie Avenue. It ends with a passionate confrontation outside that same door. The ending is not dark: *Radio Golf* is one of the five plays—half of the cycle—that end with gestures of defiance. As Roosevelt plans to go ahead with the demolition, which Harmond has tried to stop, Sterling plans a community paint party to frustrate the bulldozers. He paints his face: "I learned that from Cochise," he tells Roosevelt. "We on the battlefield now."

Alone in his office, abandoned by his wife and at war with his friend, Harmond decides to join Sterling's demonstration. But first—not in the text, but in the Broadway production, and cited in a footnote—he paints his face with the same warrior stripes, picks up a brush and marches out. He is leaving to join the August Wilson army—the cadre of those who know that you can move forward only in tune with the past. He has discovered himself, bringing the suffering, wisdom and energy of his forebears to the ongoing struggle.

The final exit in *Radio Golf* is not just Harmond's return to his roots or our farewell to the 10-play cycle, but also the playwright's farewell. He knew *Radio Golf* was the end of the cycle, but as he revised, he knew it was his own end, too, so he indulged himself. All of the plays are filled with allusions to people, places and events of the Hill, and of Wilson's life, but here he goes further, seeding the text with dates of private significance. These details are also part of the history he celebrates.

By having Harmond join the struggle—perhaps a lost cause, but still the right cause—Wilson rededicates himself. We recall that he considered himself a warrior, hardened in the Black Power movement of the 1970s. In Pittsburgh, the struggle found urgency in the specific ways that a creative and resilient community had its heart crushed. As *Radio Golf* ends, we do not know whether Aunt Ester's house will be saved. Is the juggernaut of commerce unstoppable?

Maybe. Wilson's last substantial interview, two months before his death, was with fellow Pulitzer Prize-winning playwright Suzan-Lori Parks for *American Theatre*. (Fittingly, Parks provides a characteristically energetic foreword to the published *Radio Golf*.) To her, Wilson spoke of the "slickness" of redevelopment schemes "simply to entice middle-class people to move back to the Hill." He believed such schemes deny the nourishment of the Hill's spiritual, artistic legacy. And he was not optimistic. After the end of the play, he said, "I think the bulldozer might come and the police [. . .] that's usually the way it goes." But he also said that his "idea behind the play" was that in the 21st century, "we can go forward together." Symbolically, he told Parks, "1839 will always be standing, as part of our repository of wisdom and knowledge that we as an African people have collected."

2006–2007 Best Play

THE SCENE

By Theresa Rebeck

○ ○ ○ ○ ○

Essay by Chris Jones

CHARLIE: [. . .] You look like that, you screw like a bunny, and you have no soul! Maybe that's why I wanted you so bad, you're the sea that I swim in. Everything I used to think that I wanted, art, meaning, some connection to the divine spirit of creativity, and it just, turned into nothing! Because why—because the ego—which was never the dream to begin with—just collapsed under the contempt—because that's what it is—contempt for the self, in this—this narcissism—this collapse. Is it?

CLEA: I do not know what you are fucking talking about.

CHARLIE: That's because you're the end product! You're what we are. You never had a dream. You don't know what you want. You just want to be part of the scene. [. . .]

POOR CHARLIE. He is a perfectly decent Off Broadway actor with ample artistic education, a serviceable early career and a serious belief in the potential of the performing arts to make the world a more humane and tolerable place. Like most people who work in the American theater, he likes to think it is really not about the money. But like a lot of overly educated theatrical foot-soldiers—actors, playwrights, dramaturgs, theater critics—Charlie is also condemned to oscillate around The Scene. It is a parallel universe of stimulant-fueled parties in Chelsea lofts that can lead to stupid (but endlessly lucrative) television pilots and Hollywood development deals.

As with many earnest theater people, he is close enough to that über-seductive, bicoastal sea to feel some of its warm ripples, even as he knows he cannot fully bathe in its scented waters. And the older Charlie has become, the more foolish his own artistic ideals have started to seem. He long ago realized that rich and beautiful people like this young hottie Clea are not smarter; they are, in fact, dumber. They just make more expedient choices—and, in The Scene, youth is always more marketable than experience.

House husbandry: Patricia Heaton, Christopher Evan Welch and Tony Shalhoub in The Scene. *Photo: Joan Marcus*

Poor Charlie. A lot of us know how he feels as he prowls bitterly through Midtown:

> CHARLIE: [. . .] Have you been to Times Square, lately? You look up and they're everywhere. Movie stars. TV stars. Underwear models. Those crazy rap people nobody understands, they're everywhere. Three and four stories tall, hovering over everything, like gods. Laughing. All of them, laughing at us. [. . .]

To a large extent, Charlie's midlife crisis—that all-too-common loss of artistic faith in a cruel world—is the main theme of Theresa Rebeck's widely admired four-character drama, *The Scene*. Incisive and caustic, Rebeck's work is a wholly recognizable satire of the struggles that face creative New Yorkers. The play confronts, in a darkly funny manner, the ugly truth of being an aging arts lover in a youth-obsessed culture that is invested in cheap, glamorous trivia.

As most of us in similar situations well know, any attempt to rectify this condition can easily bring about greater disaster—nothing is worse than an off-the-boil, middle-age man trying to simmer again. Rebeck's Charlie, though, fails to see that. Once he has sex with a young she-devil, he falls as fast and as far as Dr. Faustus.

CHARLIE FIRST ENCOUNTERS Clea at a friend's party. She's a vacant—but gorgeous—20-something seductress recently arrived in New York without knowledge or interest in art but with a rapacious desire to land in the middle of The Scene. At first Charlie finds her pathetic:

> CLEA: [. . . I]t's just so surreal, the lights and the water, it's like unbelievable. I love this loft! Do you know the guy who lives here? He must be incredible. Because I have just no idea, I came with a friend, who knows, like, everybody and I know she told me it was

---

Nothing is worse that a middle-age man trying to simmer again.

> somebody in the fashion industry who I just so had never heard of, my bad. 'Cause he's like, what, like clearly so talented, this place is so beautiful. The water, the air. It's just so surreal.
>
> CHARLIE: How is that surreal?
>
> CLEA: What?
>
> CHARLIE: The air and the water, you said that before, that you found it surreal. How is air and water surreal?
>
> CLEA: Oh you know, it's—just—wow! You know.

But even as Charlie and his best friend Lewis are laughing at Clea's youthful inanity that night, they are also checking out her body. We also learn that Clea has briefly worked with Stella, Charlie's wife and soulmate. Stella is a hard-working television booker who despises the dirtying hypocrisies of the business. Unsurprisingly, she didn't think much of shallow, callow Clea. Without knowing she was describing his wife, Clea tells Charlie that working for Stella was like working for a "Nazi Priestess."

Later that night at home, Charlie complains about Clea to Stella. But we already know that Charlie is too stupid—or sexually blind—to see that Clea is an enemy who prefers to work behind enemy lines. Even as he denies it to the wife with whom he plans to adopt a baby in coming weeks, Charlie gets hooked fast into a toxic combination of hatred and desire. Meanwhile, Stella—who has a better sense of the balance between artistic integrity and the necessary self-promotion required of anyone who works in the entertainment business—tells Charlie he should put aside his pride and lunch with Nick, an arrogant old schoolmate who is developing a television show.

Charlie hates the idea.

> STELLA: [. . .] You're a wonderful actor, Charlie, come on, you have to fight for yourself.
>
> CHARLIE: Talking to Nick at a party is not going to get him to give me a part on his pilot!
>
> STELLA: Well, if you don't talk to him he's certainly not going to give you a part, I can guarantee you—
>
> CHARLIE: Oh yeah he really is desperate to have people he knew in a previous life suck up to him at parties—
>
> STELLA: (*firm*) People like that, Charlie. These people, these T.V. people like it when you suck up—they like it—
>
> CHARLIE: Oh. That's why I should do it—
>
> STELLA: You should do it because you need a fucking job.

Charlie sucks up the humiliation and has the lunch, which humiliates him further. But directly afterwards, he runs into Clea again—at the home

Feelin' lucky: Anna Camp and Christopher Evan Welch in The Scene. *Photo: Joan Marcus*

of his best friend, Lewis, with whom she is on a date. In fact, he interrupts Clea and Lewis, just as Lewis is about to get lucky. Charlie doesn't notice, at first. He is too busy raging about the evils of television, Nick and all he represents:

> CHARLIE: [. . .] These are the fucking end times. The entire fucking culture has devolved to such a point that what we WANT, what we DESIRE isn't love or passion or sex or money, it's MEANINGLESSNESS. And that's what I'm supposed to sell myself for. Time to sell it, my heart, my soul, my common sense, my hope, my dreams, my pride, anything that means anything at all to my little pre-conscious, sub-conscious self, all of it goes on the auction block for what? That's what I want to know. What am I supposed to get? To give up everything? What do I get? [. . .]

Clea finds Charlie's idealistic neediness appealing and she dumps Lewis. By the next scene, Charlie and Clea are having sweaty sex in Charlie's marital apartment. Unfortunately for Charlie, his wife walks in on them, *in flagrante delicto*. It is an agonizing theatrical moment on many different levels.

ONCE THE AUDIENCE gets over its *Schadenfreude*, it sees that Stella is furious at her weak husband and the young seductress who has invaded her living room:

> STELLA: You know, I will hurt you. I will find some sort of weapon, there's got to be something somewhere, a knife or a vase, anything really is starting to look good, and I will hurt you and we will all end up in the *Daily News*. I promise you, I am not kidding. You need to get out of my house, right now. RIGHT NOW.

> CLEA: Look at you, you don't even get it yet! You're just acting like a man, threatening violence and oh you're in charge of everything, why don't you just start waving your highlighters and screaming Heil Hitler? If you knew how to keep him, you would've. Look at him! He's just like totally silent around you. He's nobody with you. Let me tell you something, he isn't like that with me. With me, he's a lion, roaming the earth. With me, he's a god!

Charlie falls for the ennobling rhetoric and chooses Clea over his wife. He leaves the apartment and the marriage.

In the next scene, which is set some days later, Stella is taking comfort with Lewis, the couple's best friend. Aside from her horrors at being dumped, Stella is also mortified that the breakdown of her marriage now will make it impossible for her to adopt the baby from China, as she and Charlie had been planning. The agency, of course, had approved the adoption to a man and woman, not a woman alone.

Lewis quickly reveals that he has always been in love with Stella and that, in the apparent absence of her husband, he is ready to take his place.

As the play crosscuts to Clea's place, we see the hot fling between her and Charlie quickly dissolving. The melancholy Charlie—drowning his guilt in vodka—becomes less and less attractive to his party-loving girlfriend with no interest in the malaises of the self-doubting in middle-age. Charlie has no money—his ex-wife canceled his credit cards—and he is consumed by jealousy. Clea, it seems, has met Nick, the television executive who was the source of Charlie's humiliation and, in some way, the cause of his current crisis. Clea likes Nick—the two are very much alike. Slowly but surely, Charlie sees the horror of his mistake. Clea kicks him out.

The final scene comes full circle at another party in the same apartment where the play began. It is four months later. Charlie runs into his ex-wife. Homeless and broken, he tries to borrow money from her. But she is now with Lewis, who has indeed taken Charlie's place. The two are off to China soon to pick up the baby. Stella, who has almost moved beyond her hapless ex-husband, asks him why he left.

> STELLA: [. . .] We had a good life. We had ups and downs. We had something real.
>
> CHARLIE: (*snapping*) I DON'T WANT ANYTHING REAL. [. . .] Why should I want to be real? Fuck reality. I want to be a god.

As Stella exits, Clea appears. She has now become Nick's personal assistant—a position that, Charlie rightly surmises, doubtless required several sexual behaviors to procure. Clea makes no apology for that: she dispensed similar sexual favors to Charlie, didn't she? All she has done is ditch a loser and find a winner.

In the play's main *coup de théâtre*, Charlie then physically attacks Clea—strangling her until her body goes limp. We think that he has killed her. There is a very tense pause. But then she starts coughing. Charlie is startled and resigned:

> CHARLIE: I should have known I can't kill you! You're some sort of new life form that can't be killed. A creature straight out of science fiction, that's where we live now. The fucking end times.

THE SCENE HAD its premiere in April 2006 at Actors Theatre of Louisville's Humana Festival of New American Plays. Most visiting critics deemed 2006

Before the fall: Tony Shalhoub and Anna Camp in The Scene. *Photo: Joan Marcus*

to be an unusually weak year in Louisville—the product of a prestigious but 30-year-old festival of new plays approaching, as with Charlie, the onset of middle-age and something of a self-evident crisis of purpose.

Without too much of a stretch that spring, one could see in Rebeck's play, which premiered under the skilled direction of Rebecca Bayla Taichman, an apt if unintended metaphor for the apparent malaise in Louisville. Here was a self-aware play about how the epicenter of culture (which, in theater terms, once meant the Humana Festival) is constantly shifting, if only to grow ever younger in orientation.

Actors Theatre was the first regional theater to import tastemakers from theater, film and television and ply them with bourbon. To a large extent, it created a hipster market for the new American play—only then to find itself struggling to appease an increasingly critical crowd very much of its own creation.

For newspaper critics, Clea could also take on other guises. To many, she may have appeared as a "blogger" in tight clothes.

To its great credit (and unlike most of the lions of the old media), Actors Theatre of Louisville has always been willing to take its critical lumps and exhibited a sense of humor about its own place in the theatrical milieu. *The Scene* wasn't the first Louisville play to poke fun at the theater's low status in big-bucks entertainment circles—Jane Martin's *Anton in Show Business* (2000) did much the same thing.

The company's work has frequently succeeded during the festival, but most of the 2006 entries at Humana were roundly criticized—except for *The Scene*. Rebeck's standout was the hit of the festival and widely regarded as worthy of an immediate Off Broadway production. And that is exactly what happened.

The Scene re-opened at New York's Second Stage Theatre the following January in a production also under Taichman's direction. Anna Camp, the glamorous, high-energy young actress who made such a splash in Louisville as the ameliorating blonde seductress who knocks Charlie off his hinges, went to New York along with the show, which received generally favorable reviews.

But in a weirdly apt example of the play's imagined power structure coming true, the authentic, earthy Louisville cast of Stephen Barker Turner, Carla Harting and David Wilson Barnes did not appear in the New York production. Their places were taken by better-known thespians. Such is the business.

In the lead role, Turner was replaced by Tony Shalhoub (best known as multiple Emmy Award-winning star of the television series *Monk*). Harting was replaced by Patricia Heaton—an Emmy winner herself for the longrunning sitcom, *Everybody Loves Raymond*). Barnes's role was taken by Christopher Evan Welch, a young character actor who is well known in New York. Not only did Camp—the youngest and least experienced member of the cast—go to New York with the show, she received a lot of notice thereafter. Agents circled, and Camp booked a television pilot with James Brolin. Most assuredly, this was a career-making role.

Given their shared director and mostly unchanged script, the productions were similar. But with its move to the north and east, the production acquired a more aggressive set of elbows. In New York, the show was faster and more caustic. In most ways, the Off Broadway version was a better, funnier, nastier and more invasive show, but one missed the pain that was on clearer display in Louisville. Much of that pain was demonstrated by the middle-age woman. As Rebeck has shown several times before, she has a rich-but-brutal understanding of how male sexual weakness causes half of the human species to jettison its natural allies and prostrate itself in the jaws of the enemy.

The Scene seems mostly about the cheapening of culture—and how worthwhile artistic endeavor invariably finds itself at the bottom of the new hierarchy topped by Britney Spears and Paris Hilton. But the playwright also makes clear that the reason the media gets away with the profitable pabulum they inflict on the American public is that it has figured out how to tease men with sex. Even men who claim to have more serious things on their minds.

Stella's belief and investment in Charlie are destroyed by his inability to avoid a blonde in a little black dress. If the middle-age crises of the cultural man are marginalization and spiritual impotence, then the middle-age cultural woman has to deal with all of that *and* the devastating disloyalty of her partner. As *The Scene* amply articulates, Charlie can rationalize his adultery in terms of self-actualization. But one always suspects that in the playwright's mind, screwing around is screwing around.

Rebeck's play surely is well served by the playwright's demonstrable ambivalence towards her leading character. Badly behaved men are familiar to fans of the work of David Mamet or Neil LaBute, but their works tend to be at least partly informed by a boys-will-be-boys gestalt. After all, middle-age men understand the neuroses of their kind.

By contrast, *The Scene* laments the cheap and the ignorant in American entertainment, and those who create it. But Rebeck saves most of her hyperarticulate commentary for men who discard their long-suffering partners to dally with such women—and then wonder why they are forced into an even worse kind of hell.

2006–2007 Best Play

SPRING AWAKENING

By Steven Sater and Duncan Sheik

○ ○ ○ ○ ○

Essay by Michael Feingold

MELCHIOR: [. . .] But I know

There's so much more to find—

Just in looking through myself, and not at them.

[. . .]

On I go,

To wonder and to learning—

Name the stars and know their dark returning. [. . .]

SOME PLAYS, LIKE SOME flowers, are perennials; others must wait for exactly the right time to bloom. The German playwright Frank Wedekind (1864–1918) wrote *Frühlingserwachen* in 1891. It has been translated, read and staged numerous times in America. But only after a century's worth of changes in our social climate did it really arrive, on Broadway and in the theatergoing public's consciousness. And then not in its original form but streamlined and modernized—though thankfully not updated—in Steven Sater and Duncan Sheik's new musical version.

The long wait has many explanations. Controversial when first published, Wedekind's masterpiece immediately ran up against a wall of stage censorship, first in his native Germany and then all across Europe. The Germans didn't see it onstage till the most influential director-producer of his time, Max Reinhardt, maneuvered it past the censors, with a few deletions, in 1906. Even after that, the United States, ironically, was one of the few places where the play could be both published and produced. Even productions here, however, tended to be small-scale and in out-of-the-way places, mostly at universities; they also tending not to attract wide attention, probably the main reason the original play has provoked few censorship incidents over here. (There have been one or two, however: In the early 1990s, a small but enterprising resident theater out West elected to close a production voluntarily, rather than provoke right-wing censorship attempts during a bitterly contested local election.)

The bitch: John Gallagher Jr. and Stephen Spinella in Spring Awakening. Photo: Joan Marcus

The play has had few notable New York productions: Its large cast tended to rule out Off Broadway, while Broadway producers found the touchy subject matter—teenage sexuality—too "risky" to be good box office. Sater and Sheik had their own struggles with the remnants of this attitude; more than one producer toyed with the musical version and then backed off before Atlantic Theater Company finally took the plunge in the summer of 2006. Another reason for the lack of commercial interest in New York may have been the British government censorship of the stage, which prevented London from seeing the play anywhere except in small private-club stagings for members only. There was no complete public production of the play in England until after the Lord Chamberlain's function as censor of plays was finally abolished in 1968, the only complete public production of the play in England was performed in German, by a guest company from Bremen.

What makes Wedekind's play exciting now, and makes it such good material for musical theater, has much to do with what kept it from European stages in its early years. You might ascribe it, in part, to the "American-ness" of his sensibility. Though born in Germany, the playwright was technically an American: His father, a radical physician, had become a US citizen while practicing in San Francisco; the son, born after the father's return to Germany, was christened Benjamin Franklin Wedekind. Similar to the famous statesman, scientific experimenter and amorist for whom he was named, young Frank grew to be inquisitive, inventive, a flamboyant personality and a born nonconformist, fascinated all his life by the varieties of human sexual experience.

Wedekind's view of adolescent springtime is anything but sentimental.

WEDEKIND FIRST MADE his reputation as a performer and songwriter in the cabarets that developed, in the late 19th century, in the big cities of Imperial Germany and Austria. These were places where those who cared to venture could escape, for a few hours, the stuffy respectability of a straitlaced and strictly regulated society. Cabaret artists, including Wedekind, constantly ran afoul of the multitude of laws restricting obscenity, blasphemy and "dangerous" political speech. On one occasion, Wedekind himself was arrested and spent time in jail for a song satirizing the Kaiser; in more than one of his plays, he chronicled, tragically or satirically, the disasters wrought by repression and censorship. (The prologue to *Pandora's Box*, the second half of his best-known work, the giant dramatic diptych *Lulu*, is a discussion of censorship and free speech set in a bookstore, while one of his short plays, literally titled *Censorship* [*Die Zensur*], takes place in the censor's office itself.)

In a gesture of compassionate irony, Wedekind's dramatic study of teenage sexuality takes its title—literally *Spring's Awakening* or "The Awakening of Spring"—from a then-popular piece of sentimental salon music. His view of the springtime that awakens when pubescent glands start to stir is, of course, anything but sentimental. His characters come in what might be described as three layers, as in geological strata: First come the adolescents themselves, all near the same age and members of the same stultifying community. They are treated in three-dimensional depth, given dramatic chances—many of which the musical translates into song—to express their deep inner passions and inevitable confusions. Next come the parents, who are depicted naturalistically but in sketchier form, not caricatures but pencil drawings rather than fully painted portraits.

Last are the authority figures, who cast a shadow over the parents' lives and dominate, sometimes with fatal results, those of the children. These are caricatures: In addition to his cabaret work, Wedekind was a founder of the satirical magazine *Simplizissimus*, noted for its cartoons. In his play, he gives these petty tyrants—schoolteachers, pastors, bureaucrats—absurd names like Sonnenstich ("sunstroke") and Fliegentod ("flyswatter"); the director of the reform school to which Melchior is sent late in the play (who does not appear in the musical version) is named Dr. Procrustes. The unkind names suggest the limited tolerance Wedekind has for these self-important placeholders, whom he depicts with contempt.

For the parents, in contrast, the original play often conveys a degree of sympathy: Though some worse cases are mentioned by their children—mentions that the musical has heightened in one or two lyrics—the parents we see are mostly not monsters but ordinary people in a state of terrible emotional conflict, not knowing how to raise their children because they themselves have not been raised well; not knowing how to tell the

First bloom: Gideon Glick and Jonathan B. Wright in Spring Awakening. *Photo: Joan Marcus*

truth because they have been taught so systematically to lie or to euphemize where serious matters are concerned.

Take the first scene, for instance, preceded in the musical by a plaintive cry in song from Wendla Bergmann, who will become its tragic heroine—a pubescent girl desperate to know more about life as she feels herself growing into adult womanhood. But in the dialogue that follows, which closely echos Wedekind's original, Wendla's mother, noticing that the girl is "in bloom," insists that Wendla alter her clothing to suit her age, but still declines to be truthful with her about the facts of life:

> FRAU BERGMANN: [. . .] Just imagine, Wendla, last night the stork finally visited your sister. Brought her another little baby girl.
>
> [. . .]
>
> WENDLA: Mama, don't be cross—don't be. But I'm an aunt for the second time now, and I still have no idea how it happens.
>
> (*FRAU BERGMANN looks stricken*)
>
> WENDLA: (*cont'd*) Mama, please. I'm ashamed to even ask. But then, who can I ask but you?
>
> FRAU BERGMANN: Wendla, child, you cannot imagine that I could—
>
> WENDLA: But you cannot imagine I still believe in the stork.
>
> FRAU BERGMANN: I honestly don't know what I've done to deserve this kind of talk. And on a day like today! Go, child, put your clothes on.
>
> WENDLA: And if I run out, now, and ask Gregor—? Our chimney sweep . . .?
>
> (*A beat*)
>
> FRAU BERGMANN: Very well, I'll tell you everything. But not today. Tomorrow. Or the day after.

Such parents are torn between their own good impulses and a misguided notion of social duty or propriety, which, especially when they are prodded by the authorities to whom they look for guidance, inevitably backfires. As in many of Wedekind's plays, the tendency toward unquestioning obedience, so deeply bred into German cultural patterns, is a particular target. Not surprisingly, the Nazis—whose totalitarian control of German life was achieved to a large extent by exploiting this willingness to obey—banned all of Wedekind's plays, and viewed this one with particular loathing.

WITH AN ECONOMY of structure that is the musical's second most arresting feature, Sater and Sheik reduce the elaborate, grotesque adult world of Wedekind's original to two people, one male and one female, who stand in for all the parents and all the authority figures alike. While this tends to oversimplify the complex and nuanced interactions Wedekind has painted, the streamlining enables the musical to place its focus on the adolescents without any distraction. That tightening of focus strongly supports the writers' first brilliant stroke—one that, in Michael Mayer's production, makes the story literally jump to vivid life in the theater: the dynamic tension between song and dialogue.

This tension is graphically physicalized, for when the driving rock beat of Sheik's score begins, and Bill T. Jones's choreography (based on colloquial, everyday movement) hurtles the young cast headlong into the musical numbers, the disjunction is nearly palpable. The dialogue, whether the kids are speaking among themselves or quailing before their adult masters, is for the most part carried on in the noncommittal, unrevealing tone that kids and adults employ to keep the other generation out of their private affairs. Even when rich with subtext, speech here is flat information; song is life—a division of labor ideal for a work of musical theater. And the power of song belongs to the kids, to the uninformed young, searching for their way through life, all the while knowing that their young bodies tell them a truth very different from the official truth promulgated by their parents and other adults.

That inner bodily truth can bring maddening frustration, as when the boys sing of the sexual urge they have to keep secret:

> BOYS: It's the bitch of living
>
> With nothing but your hand.
>
> The bitch of living
>
> As someone you can't stand . . .

Or it may breed terror, as when Martha and Ilse sing, in "The Dark I Know Well," about the fathers who abuse them and coerce them into silence:

> MARTHA: [. . .] So, I leave, wantin' just to hide.
>
> Knowin' deep inside,
>
> You are comin' to me.
>
> You are comin' to me . . .
>
> [. . .]
>
> ILSE: I don't scream. Though I know it's wrong.
>
> I just play along.
>
> I lie there and breathe.
>
> Lie there and breathe . . . [. . .]

In the dark: John Gallagher Jr., Jonathan Groff and Lea Michele in the Atlantic Theater Company production of Spring Awakening. *Photo: Monique Carboni*

Led by their inner truth—by what Sater calls, in one striking song title, "The Word of Your Body"—the youngsters stumble toward adulthood as best they can without factual guidelines. The action follows them as they come to various degrees of misfortune, and cope with it in varying ways. Determined Ilse runs away from her abusive father, to lead a promiscuous life, among the local Bohemian artists—which, the musical suggests, is not much of an improvement. The less rebellious Martha stays home, allowing her father to continue his abuse, likely to lead ultimately to deeper trauma. Hanschen sets out on the wandering, clandestine path of homosexuals in the era before gay rights (an era whose laws and attitudes still linger in many parts of the US). Georg writhes in agonized frustration over the unattainable erotic charms of his piano teacher.

]EACH OF THE THREE principal characters, as in Wedekind's original, goes through a more sustained odyssey of torments: Wendla, starting as a naive child, arrives at a sexual encounter with Melchior that contains elements of sadomasochism and rape; she becomes pregnant, without ever wholly realizing what she's done, and ultimately dies at the hands of a back-alley abortionist. Moritz, his mind dizzied by sexual fantasies that are further aroused when helpful Melchior puts the facts of life in writing for him, flunks out of school. Humiliated by his unyielding father, Moritz contemplates running away and ultimately commits suicide. (It is also made clear that Moritz's academic failure is partly the result of a self-fulfilling prophecy on his teachers' part.)

Melchior, the intelligent and comparatively levelheaded son of parents who are comparatively understanding and liberal, finds himself trapped on two fronts: To the adult world, he is the criminal who has disrupted Moritz's mind by passing him "pornography." Sent to reform school on the authorities' advice, despite his parents' misgivings, he escapes its sordid atmosphere when he hears about Wendla's death. Now an active criminal in the eyes of the law, he returns home to learn that both Wendla and Moritz are dead. A perpetual outsider in the larger society, he must also face the inner responsibility of having been instrumental in the loss of the two friends who meant most to him.

Yet Melchior is not the hero of a tragedy. Wedekind, perhaps feeling overly protective of his hero's fate, invented an allegorical figure, a "Man in a Mask," who convinces Melchior, in the original play's final scene, to choose life, under whatever circumstances, rather than following Moritz into death. The musical understandably omits this rather abstract, proto-Expressionistic finale: Men in masks carry different meanings today than they did in Wedekind's time. As the musical's Melchior, in the graveyard, mourns the deaths of Wendla and Moritz, the ghost of Moritz rises, as in the play, to tempt Melchior, too, toward suicide, only in this version with song:

> MORITZ: Those you've known,
> And lost, still walk behind you . . .
> [. . .]
> All alone,
> They linger till they find you . . .
> [. . .]
> Without them,
> The world grows dark around you—
> And nothing is the same until you know that they have
> found you.

Melchior, desolate and deeply moved, prepares to slash his own throat with a razor but stops when Wendla appears to offer a contrasting view:

WENDLA: Those you've pained

May carry that still with them . . .

[. . .]

All the same,

They whisper: "All forgiven."

Still, your heart says:

The shadows bring the starlight,

And everything you've ever been is still there in the

dark night.

The dueling ideas bring Melchior to a precarious but hopeful balance as he takes over the song:

MELCHIOR: I'll walk now with them.

I'll call on their names,

And I'll see their

thoughts are known.

[. . .]

They walk with my heart—

I'll never let them go. [. . .]

Granting Melchior the melancholy hope of this song, the musical closes with its entire cast flooding back onstage—flooding his memory, in effect, with the recollection of his classmates thronging around him, singing a song of youth and fertility, of spring burgeoning into summer. The effect is optimistic, but the audience is left to ponder what will become of Melchior, what choices he will make, how much he can do against the obstacles that already beset his adolescence. In intellectual resource, in daring and in honesty, he represents the best that can be hoped from the young. The disturbing question that *Spring Awakening* leaves as we exit—our bloodstreams throbbing to Sheik's forceful rhythms—is how Melchior's efforts to build a new life will be marred by the one that has brought him this far. As in the original, the musical ends by offering hope; it makes an explicit point of not offering any guarantees. As the lines of its final song point out:

ILSE: And all shall fade

The flowers of spring,

The world and all the sorrow

At the heart of everything [. . .]

No spring, no summer, no amount of hope can alter that fatal fact.

PLAYS PRODUCED IN
NEW YORK

PLAYS PRODUCED ON BROADWAY

○ ○ ○ ○ ○

FIGURES IN PARENTHESES following a play's title give the number of performances from the press-opening date. These figures do not include previews or extra nonprofit performances. In the case of a transfer, the prior run is noted but not added to the figure in parentheses.

Plays marked with an asterisk (*) were still in a projected run June 1, 2007. Their number of performances is figured through May 31, 2007.

In a listing of a show's numbers—dances, sketches, musical scenes, etc.—the titles of songs are identified wherever possible by their appearance in quotation marks (").

HOLDOVERS FROM PREVIOUS SEASONS

BROADWAY SHOWS THAT were running on June 1, 2006 are listed below. More detailed information about them appears in previous *Best Plays* volumes of the years in which they opened. Important cast changes since opening night are recorded in the Cast Replacements section in this volume.

*The Phantom of the Opera (8,065). Musical with book by Richard Stilgoe and Andrew Lloyd Webber; music by Andrew Lloyd Webber; lyrics by Charles Hart; additional lyrics by Richard Stilgoe; adapted from the novel by Gaston Leroux. Opened January 26, 1988.

*Beauty and the Beast (5,393). Musical with book by Linda Woolverton; music by Alan Menken; lyrics by Howard Ashman and Tim Rice. Opened April 18, 1994.

*Rent (4,612). Transfer from Off Broadway of the musical with book, music and lyrics by Jonathan Larson. Opened Off Off Broadway January 26, 1996 and Off Broadway February 13, 1996 where it played 56 performances through March 31, 1996; transferred to Broadway April 29, 1996.

*Chicago (4,390). Revival of the musical based on the play by Maurine Dallas Watkins; book by Fred Ebb and Bob Fosse; music by John Kander; lyrics by Fred Ebb; original production directed and choreographed by Bob Fosse. Opened November 14, 1996.

*The Lion King (3,974). Musical adapted from the screenplay by Irene Mecchi, Jonathan Roberts and Linda Woolverton; book by Roger Allers and Irene Mecchi; music by Elton John; lyrics by Tim Rice; additional music and lyrics by Lebo M, Mark Mancina, Jay Rifkin, Julie Taymor and Hans Zimmer. Opened November 13, 1997.

The Producers (2,502). Musical with book by Mel Brooks and Thomas Meehan; music and lyrics by Mel Brooks. Opened April 19, 2001. (Closed April 22, 2007)

*Mamma Mia! (2,337). Musical with book by Catherine Johnson; music and lyrics by Benny Andersson and Björn Ulvaeus, some songs with Stig Anderson. Opened October 18, 2001.

*Hairspray (1,996). Musical with book by Mark O'Donnell and Thomas Meehan; music by Marc Shaiman; lyrics by Marc Shaiman and Scott Wittman; based on the film by John Waters. Opened August 15, 2002.

*Avenue Q (1,599). Transfer from Off Off Broadway of the musical with book by Jeff Whitty; music and lyrics by Robert Lopez and Jeff Marx. Opened July 31, 2003.

*Wicked (1,496). Musical with book by Winnie Holzman; music and lyrics by Stephen Schwartz; based on a novel by Gregory Maguire. Opened October 30, 2003.

Dirty Rotten Scoundrels (627). Musical with book by Jeffrey Lane; music and lyrics by David Yazbek; based on the film by Dale Launer, Stanley Shapiro and Paul Henning. Opened March 3, 2005. (Closed September 3, 2006)

*Spamalot (920). Musical with book and lyrics by Eric Idle; music by John Du Prez and Mr. Idle; based on the motion picture *Monty Python and the Holy Grail.* Opened March 17, 2005.

Doubt, a Parable (525). Transfer from Off Broadway of the play by John Patrick Shanley. Opened March 31, 2005. (Closed July 2, 2006)

Lincoln Center Theater production of **The Light in the Piazza** (504). Musical with book by Craig Lucas; music and lyrics by Adam Guettel; based on the novella by Elizabeth Spencer. Opened April 18, 2005. (Closed July 2, 2006)

*The 25th Annual Putnam County Spelling Bee (867). Transfer from Off Broadway of the musical with book by Rachel Sheinkin; music and lyrics by William Finn; conceived by Rebecca Feldman; additional material by Jay Reiss. Opened May 2, 2005.

The Odd Couple (249). Revival of the play by Neil Simon. Opened October 27, 2005. (Closed June 4, 2006)

Sweeney Todd, the Demon Barber of Fleet Street (349). Revival of the musical with book by Hugh Wheeler; music and lyrics by Stephen Sondheim; from an adaptation by Christopher Bond. Opened November 3, 2005. (Closed September 3, 2006)

*Jersey Boys: The Story of Frankie Valli and the Four Seasons (653). Musical with book by Marshall Brickman and Rick Elice; music by Bob Gaudio; lyrics by Bob Crewe. Opened November 6, 2005.

*The Color Purple (623). Musical with book by Marsha Norman; music and lyrics by Brenda Russell, Allee Willis, Stephen Bray; adapted from the novel by Alice Walker and the Warner Bros./Amblin Entertainment film. Opened December 1, 2005.

Bridge and Tunnel (213). Solo performance piece by Sarah Jones. Opened January 26, 2006. (Closed August 6, 2006)

Roundabout Theatre Company production of **The Pajama Game** (129). Revival of the musical with book by George Abbott and Richard Bissell; music and lyrics by Richard Adler and Jerry Ross; based on Mr. Bissell's novel *7½ Cents*; book revisions by Peter Ackerman. Opened February 23, 2006. (Closed June 17, 2006)

Lincoln Center Theater production of **Awake and Sing!** (80). Revival of the play by Clifford Odets. Opened April 17, 2006. (Closed June 25, 2006)

Three Days of Rain (70). Revival of the play by Richard Greenberg. Opened April 19, 2006. (Closed June 18, 2006)

Roundabout Theatre Company production of **The Threepenny Opera** (77). Revival of the musical with book and lyrics by Bertolt Brecht; music by Kurt Weill; translation by Wallace Shawn; based on Elisabeth Hauptmann's German translation of John Gay's *The Beggar's Opera*. Opened April 20, 2006. (Closed June 25, 2006)

The History Boys (185). By Alan Bennett. Opened April 23, 2006. (Closed October 1, 2006)

The Wedding Singer (285). Musical with book by Chad Beguelin and Tim Herlihy; music by Matthew Sklar; lyrics by Mr. Beguelin; based on the New Line Cinema film by Tim Herlihy. Opened April 27, 2006. (Closed December 31, 2006)

Hot Feet (97). Musical with book by Heru Ptah; music and lyrics by Maurice White. Opened April 30, 2006. (Closed July 23, 2006)

*****The Drowsy Chaperone** (452). Musical with book by Bob Martin and Don McKellar; music and lyrics by Lisa Lambert and Greg Morrison. Opened May 1, 2006.

The Lieutenant of Inishmore (142). Transfer from Off Broadway of the play by Martin McDonagh. May 3, 2006. (Closed September 3, 2006)

Faith Healer (117). Revival of the play by Brian Friel. Opened May 4, 2006. (Closed August 13, 2006)

Manhattan Theatre Club production of **Shining City** (80). By Conor McPherson. Opened May 9, 2006. (Closed July 16, 2006)

*****Tarzan** (441). Musical with book by David Henry Hwang; music and lyrics by Phil Collins; based on *Tarzan of the Apes* by Edgar Rice Burroughs and the Disney film *Tarzan*. Opened May 10, 2006.

PLAYS PRODUCED JUNE 1, 2006–MAY 31, 2007

Kiki and Herb: Alive on Broadway (27). Musical revue by Justin Bond and Kenny Mellman. Produced by David J. Foster, Jared Geller, Ruth Hendel, Jonathan Reinis, Inc., Billy Zavelson, Jamie Cesa, Anne Strickland Squadron, Jennifer Manocherian, in association with Gary Allen and Melvin Honowitz, at the Helen Hayes Theatre. Opened August 15, 2006. (Closed September 10, 2006)

Kiki .... Justin Bond   Herb .... Kenny Mellman

Directed by Messrs. Bond and Mellman; scenery, Scott Pask; costumes, Marc Happel; lighting, Jeff Croiter; sound, Brett Jarvis; production stage manager, Peter Hanson; press, The Karpel Group, Bridget Klapinski, Billy Zavelson.

Presented in two parts.

Performance of a lounge-singer act that satirizes the form.

Martin Short: Fame Becomes Me (165). Musical with book by Martin Short and Daniel Goldfarb; music by Marc Shaiman; lyrics by Scott Wittman and Marc Shaiman; additional material by Alan Zweibel. Produced by Base Entertainment, Harbor Entertainment, Roy Furman, Jeffrey Sine, in association with Lisa Lapan and Terry E. Schnuck, at the Bernard B. Jacobs Theatre. Opened August 17, 2006. (Closed January 7, 2007)

Performed by Martin Short, Brooks Ashmanskas, Mary Birdsong, Nicole Parker, Marc Shaiman, Capathia Jenkins and special guests.

Orchestra: Charlie Alterman conductor, keyboard; Craig Baldwin associate conductor, keyboard; Dick Sarpola bass, electric bass; Eddie Salkin tenor sax, alto sax, clarinet, flute; Dave Trigg trumpet, piccolo trumpet, flugelhorn; Mike Christianson trombone, bass trombone; Mr. Shaiman piano; Ed Shea percussion; Rich Mercurio drums.

Understudies: Jill Abramovitz, Charlie Alterman, Aisha deHaas, Edward Staudenmayer.

Directed by Mr. Wittman; choreography, Christopher Gattelli; scenery, Scott Pask; costumes, Jess Goldstein; lighting, Chris Lee; sound, Peter Hylenski; wigs and hair, Charles LaPointe; orchestrations, Larry Blank; music direction, Mr. Alterman; music coordination, John Miller; executive producers, Joanna Hagan and Bernie Brillstein; associate producer, Brown-Pinto Productions; casting, Telsey and Company; production stage manager, Bess Marie Glorioso; press, Barlow-Hartman, Michael Hartman, John Barlow, Dennis Crowley, Ryan Ratelle.

Presented without intermission.

Satirical celebration of Mr. Short's career and celebrity that is based on fact and fancy. First presentation of record was given at San Francisco's Curran Theatre (5/9–5/21/2006) before runs at Toronto's Canon Theatre and Chicago's LaSalle Bank Theatre on the way to Broadway.

MUSICAL NUMBERS

"Another Curtain Goes Up" .... Nicole, Brooks, Capathia, Marc
"All I Ask" .... Martin
"Three Gorgeous Kids" .... Martin
"Babies" .... Nicole, Martin, Brooks, Mary
"The Farmer's Daughter" .... Mary
"Sittin' on the Fence" .... Martin, Mary
"Don't Wanna Be Me" .... Martin
"Ba-Ba-Ba-Bu-Duh Broadway!" .... Mary, Nicole, Brooks
"Hello Boy!" .... Martin
"Step Brother de Jesus" .... Martin, Mary, Nicole, Brooks
"Married to Marty" .... Nicole
"The Triangle Song" .... Martin
"Sniff, Sniff" .... Martin, Mary, Nicole, Brooks
"Twelve Step Pappy" .... Martin
"Would Ya Like to Star in Our Show?" .... Brooks, Nicole, Mary
"I Came Just as Soon as I Heard" .... Martin
"The Lights Have Dimmed on Broadway" .... Nicole, Mary
"Michael's Song" .... Brooks
"Heaven, Heaven" .... Mary, Nicole, Brooks, Marc
"Stop the Show" .... Capathia, Mary, Nicole, Brooks, Martin
"All I Ask" (Reprise) .... Martin
"Another Curtain Comes Down" .... Nicole, Mary, Brooks, Capathia, Marc, Martin
"Glass Half Full" .... Martin

Jay Johnson: The Two and Only (70). Transfer from Off Broadway of the solo performance piece by Jay Johnson. Produced by Roger Alan Gindi, Stewart F. Lane and Bonnie Comley, Dan Whitten, Herbert Goldsmith Productions, Ken Grossman, Bob and Rhonda Silver, Michael A. Jenkins, Dallas Summer Musicals, Inc., Wetrock Entertainment at the Helen Hayes Theatre. Opened September 28, 2006. (Closed November 26, 2006)

Performed by Mr. Johnson.

Directed by Murphy Cross and Paul Kreppel; scenery, Beowulf Boritt; lighting, Clifton Taylor; sound, David Gotwald; music, Michael Andreas; associate producer, Jamie deRoy; production stage manager, Lori Ann Zepp; press, O and M Company, Rick Miramontez, Richard Hillman.

Presented without intermission.

Ventriloquist who achieved fame on the television program *Soap* recounts his fascination with his art form. First presentation of record was given Off Broadway at Atlantic Theater Company

(5/13–8/15/2004; 110 performances). The production received received a Tony Award for special theatrical event.

*A Chorus Line (273). Revival of the musical with book by James Kirkwood and Nicholas Dante; music by Marvin Hamlisch; lyrics by Edward Kleban. Produced by Vienna Waits Productions at the Gerald Schoenfeld Theatre. Opened October 5, 2006.

Bobby	Ken Alan	Lois	Nadine Isenegger
Don	Brad Anderson	Richie	James T. Lane
Tricia	Michelle Aravena	Vicki	Pamela Fabello
Roy	David Baum	Mark	Paul McGill
Zach	Michael Berresse	Judy	Heather Parcells
Tom	Mike Cannon	Greg	Michael Paternostro
Butch	E. Clayton Cornelious	Bebe	Alisan Porter
Diana	Natalie Cortez	Mike	Jeffrey Schecter
Cassie	Charlotte d'Amboise	Connie	Yuka Takara
Maggie	Mara Davi	Paul	Jason Tam
Val	Jessica Lee Goldyn	Frank	Grant Turner
Sheila	Deidre Goodwin	Kristine	Chryssie Whitehead
Larry	Tyler Hanes	Al	Tony Yazbeck

Orchestra: Patrick Vaccariello conductor; Jim Laev associate conductor, keyboard 2; Maggie Torre assistant conductor, keyboard 3; Bill Sloat bass; Ted Nash woodwind 1; Lino Gomez woodwind 2; David Young woodwind 3; Jacqueline Henderson woodwind 4; John Chudoba trumpet 1; Trevor Neumann trumpet 2; Scott Wendholt trumpet 3; Michael Seltzer trombone 1; Ben Herrington trombone 2; Jack Schatz bass trombone; Greg Anthony keyboard 1; Dan McMillan percussion; Brian Brake drums.

Understudies: Mr. Yazbeck—David Baum, Mike Cannon; Ms. Porter—Michelle Aravena, Lyndy Franklin; Mr. Alan—David Baum, Tyler Hanes; Ms. d'Amboise—Jessica Lee Goldyn, Nadine Isenegger; Ms. Takara—Michelle Aravena, Lyndy Franklin; Ms. Cortez—Michelle Aravena, Jessica

Cassie's turn: Charlotte d'Amboise in A Chorus Line. *Photo: Paul Kolnik*

Breaking dawn: Philip Bosco and Swoosie Kurtz in Heartbreak House. *Photo: Joan Marcus*

Lea Patty; Mr. Anderson—E. Clayton Cornelious, Grant Turner; Mr. Paternostro—David Baum, Grant Turner; Ms. Parcells—Pamela Fabello, Jessica Lea Patty; Ms. Whitehead—Pamela Fabello, Lyndy Franklin; Mr. Hanes—E. Clayton Cornelious, Grant Turner; Ms. Davi—Michelle Aravena, Lyndy Franklin; Mr. McGill—Mike Cannon, Joey Dudding; Mr. Schecter—David Baum, Mike Cannon; Mr. Tam—E. Clayton Cornelious, Joey Dudding; Mr. Lane—Mike Cannon, E. Clayton Cornelious; Ms. Goodwin—Pamela Fabello, Jessica Lea Patty; Ms. Goldyn—Pamela Fabello, Nadine Isenegger; Mr. Berresse—Tyler Hanes, Grant Turner.

Swings: Joey Dudding, Lyndy Franklin, Jessica Lea Patty.

Directed by Bob Avian; choreography, Mr. Avian and Baayork Lee; scenery, Robin Wagner; costumes, Theoni V. Aldredge; lighting, Tharon Musser and Natasha Katz; sound, Acme Sound Partners; orchestrations, Jonathan Tunick, Bill Byers and Hershy Kay; music direction and supervision, Mr. Vaccariello; vocal arrangements, Don Pippin; music coordination, Michael Keller; casting, Jay Binder Casting; production stage manager, William Joseph Barnes; press, Barlow-Hartman, John Barlow, Michael Hartman, Wayne Wolfe, Andrew Snyder.

Time: 1975. Place: A Broadway theater. Presented without intermission.

Dancers bare themselves emotionally in an audition for a Broadway show. A 1974–75 *Best Plays* choice, the first presentation of record was given at the Public Theater (4/15–7/13/1975; 101 performances). Through a quirk of recordkeeping, the previous editor counted Public Theater performances from the first public viewing and not from the press date (5/21/1975). It is now our policy to count performances from the press date. The first Broadway production opened at the Shubert Theatre (7/25/1975–4/28/1990; 6,137 performances). At the 1976 Tony Awards, *A Chorus Line* was honored in nine categories: musical, book, score, actress, featured actor, featured actress, lighting, choreography and direction. It also received the 1976 Pulitzer Prize in Drama and a special Tony Award in 1984 when it became the longest-running musical in history. Since surpassed on the long-run list by *The Phantom of the Opera* (8,065), *Cats* (7,485) and *Les Misérables* (6,680), the original production of *A Chorus Line* (6,137) remains the longest-running American musical in Broadway history. The 2006–07 production was the first Broadway revival.

MUSICAL NUMBERS

"I Hope I Get It" .... Company
"I Can Do That" .... Mike
"And" .... Bobby, Richie, Val, Judy
"At the Ballet" .... Sheila, Bebe, Maggie
"Sing!" .... Kristine, Al
"Hello Twelve, Hello Thirteen, Hello Love" .... Company
"Nothing" .... Diana
"Dance: Ten; Looks: Three" .... Val
"The Music and the Mirror" .... Cassie
"One" .... Company
"The Tap Combination" .... Company
"What I Did for Love" .... Diana, Company
"One" (Reprise) .... Company

Roundabout Theatre Company production **Heartbreak House** (79). Revival of the play by George Bernard Shaw. Todd Haimes artistic director, Harold Wolpert managing director, Julia C. Levy executive director, at the American Airlines Theatre. Opened October 11, 2006. (Closed December 17, 2006)

Ellie Dunn	Lily Rabe	Mazzini Dunn	John Christopher Jones
Nurse Guinnes	Jenny Sterlin	Hector Hushabye	Byron Jennings
Captain Shotover	Philip Bosco	Boss Mangan	Bill Camp
Ariadne Utterword	Laila Robins	Randall Utterword	Gareth Saxe
Hesione Hushabye	Swoosie Kurtz		

Understudies: Messrs. Jennings, Camp, Saxe—Tony Carlin; Messrs. Bosco, Jones—Doug Stender; Mses. Rabe, Robins—Angela Pierce; Mses. Kurtz, Sterlin—Robin Moseley.

Directed by Robin Lefevre; scenery, John Lee Beatty; costumes, Jane Greenwood; lighting, Peter Kaczorowski; sound and music, John Gromada; wigs and hair, Tom Watson; casting, Jim Carnahan and Mele Nagler; production stage manager, Leslie C. Lyter; press, Boneau/Bryan-Brown, Adrian Bryan-Brown, Matt Polk, Jessica Johnson.

Time: A fine evening in September 1914. Place: Sussex. Presented in two parts.

Amid the cultural echoes of the "guns of August," an eccentric family in decline begins to face the encroaching modern world. First presentation of record was given by the Theatre Guild at the Garrick Theatre in New York (11/10/1920–2/26/1921; 125 performances). The 2006–07 production was the fourth Broadway revival.

Manhattan Theatre Club production of **Losing Louie** (53). By Simon Mendes da Costa. Lynne Meadow artistic director, Barry Grove executive producer, at the Biltmore Theatre. Opened October 12, 2006. (Closed November 26, 2006)

Reggie Ellis	Matthew Arkin	Sheila Ellis	Michele Pawk
Louie Ellis	Scott Cohen	Bobbie Ellis	Rebecca Creskoff
Tony Ellis	Mark Linn-Baker	Bella Holland	Jama Williamson
Elizabeth Ellis	Patricia Kalember		

Understudies: Messrs. Cohen, Linn-Baker, Arkin—John Bolger; Mses. Williamson, Creskoff—Julie Lauren; Mses. Pawk, Kalember—Charlotte Maier.

Directed by Jerry Zaks; scenery, John Lee Beatty; costumes, William Ivey Long; lighting, Paul Gallo; sound, Dan Moses Schreier; casting, Nancy Piccione and David Caparelliotis; production stage manager, Barclay Stiff; press, Boneau/Bryan-Brown, Chris Boneau, Jim Byk, Aaron Meier, Heath Schwartz.

Time: Early 1960s and the present. Place: Pound Ridge, NY. Presented in two parts.

The past influences and overshadows the present as rivalrous brothers gather to bury their father in this dark comedy. First presentation of record was given under the title *Losing Louis* at Hampstead Theatre in London (1/20–2/19/2005) before a transfer to the West End's Trafalgar Studios (2/23–6/25/2005).

Butley (94). Revival of the play by Simon Gray. Produced by Elizabeth Ireland McCann, Stephanie P. McClelland, Chase Mishkin, Eric Falkenstein, Debra Black, Barbara Manocherian, Larry Hirschhorn, Barbara Freitag, Jeffrey Sine, Frederick Zollo, Joey Parnes, in association with Huntington Theatre Company (Nicholas Martin artistic director, Michael Maso managing director), at the Booth Theatre. Opened October 25, 2006. (Closed January 14, 2007)

Ben Butley .... Nathan Lane
Joseph Keyston .... Julian Ovenden
Miss Heasman .... Jessica Stone
Edna Shaft .... Dana Ivey
Anne Butley .... Pamela Gray

Reg Nuttall .... Darren Pettie
Mr. Gardner .... Roderick Hill
Students .... Marguerite Stimpson,
                                                    Chad Hoeppner

Understudies: Mr. Lane—John Leonard Thompson; Messrs. Pettie, Ovenden—Anthony Crane; Ms. Stone—Marguerite Stimpson; Mses. Ivey, Gray—Gloria Biegler; Messrs. Ovenden, Hill—Chad Hoeppner.

Directed by Nicholas Martin; scenery, Alexander Dodge; costumes, Ann Roth; lighting, David Weiner; sound, John Gromada; wigs and hair, David Brian Brown; associate producer Tommy Damaio; casting, Jay Binder, Jack Bowdan; production stage manager, Michael McGoff; press, Boneau/Bryan-Brown, Chris Boneau, Jackie Green, Matt Ross.

Time: 1971. Place: An office in a college of London University. Presented in two parts.

A college professor struggles with his demons as he attempts to balance work and love, succeeding at neither. A 1972–73 *Best Plays* choice, the original Broadway production opened at the Morosco Theatre (10/31/1972–2/24/1973; 135 performances). Alan Bates was honored with a 1973 Tony Award for his performance of the title role. First presentation of record was given under the direction of Harold Pinter at the Criterion Theatre in London (7/14/1971). The 2006–07 production, which first played at Boston's Huntington Theatre Company (10/29–12/7/2003) was the first Broadway revival.

Say goodbye: Pamela Gray and Nathan Lane in Butley. *Photo: Joan Marcus*

The Times They Are A-Changin' (28). Musical by Twyla Tharp; music and lyrics by Bob Dylan. Produced by James L. Nederlander, Hal Luftig, Warren Trepp, Debra Black, East of Doheny, Rick Steiner, Mayerson Bell Staton Group, Terry Allen Kramer, Patrick Catullo, Jon B. Platt, Roland Sturm at the Brooks Atkinson Theatre. Opened October 26, 2006. (Closed November 19, 2006)

Coyote .... Michael Arden	Cleo .... Lisa Brescia
Captain Ahrab .... Thom Sesma	

Ensemble: Lisa Gajda, Neil Haskell, Jason McDole, Charlie Neshyba-Hodges, Jonathan Nosan, John Selya, Ron Todorowski.

Orchestra: Henry Aronson conductor, keyboard, accordion, percussion; John "JJ" Jackson guitar, banjo, dobro, harmonica; Dave MacNab guitar, banjo; Paul Ossola electric bass, upright bass; Brian Doherty drums, percussion.

Standbys: Mr. Arden—Jason Wooten, Mr. Sesma—John Herrera, Ms. Brescia—Katie Klaus.

Swings: Alexander Brady, Alaine Kashian, Keith Kühl, Marty Lawson, Joseph Putignano, Cary Tedder.

Directed and choreographed by Ms. Tharp; scenery and costumes, Santo Loquasto; lighting, Donald Holder; sound, Peter Hylenski; orchestrations, Michael Dansicker and Bob Dylan; music arrangement, adaptation and supervision, Michael Dansicker; music direction, Mr. Aronson; music coordination, Howard Joines; associate producers, Jesse Huot, Ginger Montel, Rhoda Mayerson; casting, Jay Binder, Jack Bowdan, Megan Larche; production stage manager, Arthur Gaffin; press, Shaffer-Coyle Public Relations, Bill Coyle, Jeremy Shaffer, Adriana Douzos.

Time and place: Sometime between awake and asleep. Presented without intermission.

A fantasia, set to the iconic music of Bob Dylan, that centers on a love triangle among a circus owner, his son and the woman they both love. First presentation of record was given at the Old Globe in San Diego (2/9–3/19/2006).

*****Grey Gardens** (241). Transfer from Off Broadway of the musical with book by Doug Wright; music by Scott Frankel; lyrics by Michael Korie; based on the film *Grey Gardens* by David Maysles, Albert Maysles, Ellen Hovde, Muffie Meyer and Susan Froemke. Produced by East of Doheny, Staunch Entertainment, Randall L. Wreghitt, Morton Swinsky, Michael Alden, Edwin W. Schloss, in association with Playwrights Horizons, at the Walter Kerr Theatre. Opened November 2, 2006.

Prologue (1973)		
Edith Bouvier Beale .... Mary Louise Wilson	Edith Bouvier Beale .... Christine Ebersole	
"Little" Edie Beale .... Christine Ebersole	Joseph P. Kennedy Jr. .... Matt Cavenaugh	
	J.V. "Major" Bouvier .... John McMartin	

Act I (1941)		Act II (1973)	
Young "Little" Edie Beale .... Erin Davie		Edith Bouvier Beale .... Mary Louise Wilson	
Jacqueline "Jackie" Bouvier .... Sarah Hyland		"Little" Edie Beale .... Christine Ebersole	
Lee Bouvier .... Kelsey Fowler		Brooks, Jr. .... Michael Potts	
Brooks, Sr. .... Michael Potts		Jerry .... Matt Cavenaugh	
George Gould Strong .... Bob Stillman		Norman Vincent Peale .... John McMartin	

Orchestra: Lawrence Yurman conductor; Paul Staroba associate conductor, keyboard; Eric DeGioia violin; Anik Oulianine cello; Ken Hitchcock, Todd Groves reeds; Daniel Urness trumpet, flugelhorn; Patrick Pridemore, French horn; Brian Cassier acoustic bass; Tim McLafferty percussion, drums.

Standbys: Ms. Ebersole—Maureen Moore; Ms. Wilson—Dale Soules; Mses. Hyland, Fowler—Abigail Ferenczy; Mr. McMartin—Donald Grody; Mr. Potts—Michael W. Howell; Ms. Davie—Megan Lewis; Messrs. Cavenaugh, Stillman—Asa Somers.

Directed by Michael Greif; scenery, Allen Moyer; costumes, William Ivey Long; lighting, Peter Kaczorowski; sound, Brian Ronan; projections, Wendall K. Harrington; wigs and hair, Paul Huntley; orchestrations, Bruce Coughlin; music direction, Mr.Yurman; music coordination, John Miller; executive producer, Beth Williams; casting, Telsey and Company; production stage manager, Judith Schoenfeld; press, The Publicity Office, Marc Thibodeau, Bob Fennell, Michael S. Borowski.

Lives unraveled: Matt Cavenaugh, Mary Louise Wilson and Christine Ebersole in Grey Gardens. *Photo: Joan Marcus*

Time: 1941; 1973. Place: Grey Gardens, East Hampton, New York. Presented in two parts.

Musical based on the imagined early life of a pair of former society dames and the reality of their later lives as depicted in a cult-hit documentary film. A 2005–06 *Best Plays* choice, the first presentation of record was given Off Broadway at Playwrights Horizons (3/7–4/30/2006; 63 performances).

PROLOGUE (1973)

"The Girl Who Has Everything" .... Edith, Edie

ACT I (1941)

"The Girl Who Has Everything" .... Edie, Jackie, Lee
"The Five-Fifteen" .... Edith, Gould, Jackie, Lee, Brooks
"Mother, Darling" .... Edie, Edith, Gould
"Goin' Places" .... Joe, Edie
"Marry Well" .... Major Bouvier, Brooks, Jackie, Lee, Edie
"Hominy Grits" .... Edith, Gould, Jackie, Lee
"Peas in a Pod" .... Edie, Edith
"Drift Away" .... Gould, Edith
"The Five-Fifteen" (Reprise) .... Edith
"Daddy's Girl" .... Edie
"The Telegram" .... Edie
"Will You" .... Edith

ACT II (1973)

"The Revolutionary Costume for Today" .... Edie
"The Cake I Had" .... Edith
"Entering Grey Gardens" .... Company
"The House We Live in" .... Edie, Company
"Jerry Likes My Corn" .... Edith, Edie

"Around the World" .... Edie
"Will You?" (Reprise) .... Edith, Edie
"Choose to Be Happy" .... Norman Vincent Peale, Company
"Around the World" (Reprise) .... Edie
"Another Winter in a Summer Town" .... Edie, Edith
"The Girl Who Has Everything" (Reprise) .... Edith, Edie

Dr. Seuss's How the Grinch Stole Christmas! (107). Musical with book and lyrics by Timothy Mason; music by Mel Marvin; additional music by Albert Hague; additional lyrics by Theodor Seuss Geisel (Dr. Seuss); based on the book *How the Grinch Stole Christmas* by Dr. Seuss. Produced by Running Subway, EMI Music Publishing, Michael Speyer and Bernie Abrams with Allen Spivak, Janet Pailet, Spark Productions, Maximum Entertainment, Jonathan Reinis, in association with Target, at the Hilton Theatre. Opened November 8, 2006. (January 7, 2007)

Old Max .... John Cullum	Annie Who .... Heather Tepe, Caitlin Belcik
Cindy Lou Who .... Nicole Bocchi, Caroline London	Danny Who .... Eamon Foley, James Du Chateau
JP Who .... Price Waldman	Betty-Lou Who .... Brynn Williams, Libbie Jacobson
Mama Who .... Kaitlin Hopkins	Young Max .... Rusty Ross
Grandpa Seth Who .... Michael McCormick	The Grinch .... Patrick Page
Grandma Who .... Jan Neuberger	
Boo Who............................... Malcolm Morano, Aaron D. Conley	

Citizens of Whoville: Janet Dickinson, André Garner, Josephine Rose Roberts, William Ryall, Pearl Sun, Jeff Skowron.

Little Whos: Antonio D'Amato, Danielle Freid, Jess Le Protto, Katie Micha, Nikki Rose, Corwin Tuggles, Kelley Rock Wiese, Jahaan Amin, Kevin Csolak, Brianna Gentilella, Sky Jarrett, Daniel Manche, Jillian Mueller, Molly J. Ryan.

Orchestra: Joshua Rosenblum conductor; Sue Anschutz associate conductor, keyboard; Mark Mitchell assistant conductor, keyboard; Steven Kenyon, Robert DeBellis, Terrence Cook, John Winder woodwinds; Christian Jaudes, Philip Granger, Wayne J. du Maine trumpet; Wayne Goodman, Robert Fournier trombone; Louis Bruno bass; Dave Roth percussion; Greg Landes drums.

Standby: Mr. Cullum—Martin Van Treuren.

Understudies: Messrs. Page and Cullum—William Ryall; Mr. Ross—André Garner; Messrs. Waldman, McCormick—Jeff Skowron; Ms. Hopkins—Pearl Sun; Ms. Neuberger—Janet Dickinson; Mses. Bocchi, London—Katie Micha, Molly J. Ryan; Messrs. Morano, Conley—Antonio D'Amato, Daniel Manche; Mses. Tepe, Belcik—Nikki Rose, Jillian Mueller; Messrs. Foley, Du Chateau—Jess Le Protto, Kevin Csolak; Mses. Williams, Jacobson—Danielle Freid, Jahaan Amin.

Swings: Kurt Kelly, Amy Griffin, Rafael Luis Tillis, Lawson Young.

Directed by Matt August; choreography, John DeLuca and Bob Richard; scenery, John Lee Beatty; costumes, Robert Morgan; lighting, Pat Collins; sound, Acme Sound Partners; special effects, Gregory Meeh; wigs and hair, Thomas Augustine; orchestrations, Michael Starobin; vocal arrangements and music direction; Mr. Rosenblum; dance arrangements, David Krane; music coordination, Seymour Red Press; executive producer, James Sanna; associate producers, Audrey Geisel, Mr. Rosenblum; casting, Telsey and Company; production stage manager, Michael Brunner; press, Alison Brod Public Relations, Alison Brod, Robin Edlow, Jodi Simms Hassan.

Time: Christmas. Place: Whoville. Presented without intermission.

Musical based on the popular children's book about the true gifts of Christmas. First presentation of record was given in a production created and directed by Jack O'Brien at the Old Globe in San Diego (1998).

MUSICAL NUMBERS

"Who Likes Christmas?" .... Whoville Citizens
"I Hate Christmas Eve" .... Grinch, Young Max, Who Family
"Whatchama Who" .... Grinch, Little Whos

"Welcome, Christmas" ....Whoville Citizens
                          (Albert Hague and Dr. Seuss)
"I Hate Christmas Eve" (Reprise) .... Grinch
"Once in a Year" .... JP Who, Mama Who, Grandma Who,
                          Grandpa Seth Who, Whoville Citizens, Little Whos
"One of a Kind" .... Grinch
"Now's the Time" ....JP Who, Mama Who, Grandma Who, Grandpa Seth Who
"You're a Mean One, Mr. Grinch" .... Old Max, Young Max, Grinch
                          (Albert Hague and Dr. Seuss)
"Santa for a Day" .... Cindy Lou Who, Grinch
"You're a Mean One, Mr. Grinch" (Reprise) .... Old Max
                          (Albert Hague and Dr. Seuss)
"Who Likes Christmas?" (Reprise) ....Whoville Citizens
"One of a Kind" (Reprise) .... Young Max, Grinch, Cindy Lou Who
"Welcome, Christmas" (Reprise) ....Whoville Citizens
                          (Albert Hague and Dr. Seuss)
"Finale" .... Grinch, Cindy Lou Who, Whos Everywhere
"Who Likes Christmas?" .... Whos Everywhere, Grinch

*Les Misérables (233). Revival of the musical with book by Alain Boublil and Claude-Michel Schöenberg; music by Mr. Schöenberg; lyrics by Herbert Kretzmer; based on the novel by Victor Hugo; French text by Mr. Boublil and Jean-Marc Natel; additional material by James Fenton; adapted by John Caird and Trevor Nunn. Produced by Cameron Mackintosh at the Broadhurst Theatre. Opened November 9, 2006.

Jean Valjean .... Alexander Gemignani	Madame Thénardier .... Jenny Galloway
Javert .... Norm Lewis	Young Eponine .... Carly Rose Sonenclar,
Farmer .... Doug Kreeger	Tess Adams,
Innkeeper .... Drew Sarich	Kylie Liya Goldstein
Innkeeper's Wife .... Karen Elliot	Old Beggar Woman .... Karen Elliott
Laborer .... JD Goldblatt	Madeleine .... Nikki Renée Daniels
Bishop of Digne .... James Chip Leonard	Gavroche .... Brian D'Addario,
Constables .... Nehal Joshi,	Jacob Levine,
Jeff Kready	Austyn Myers
Foreman .... Robert Hunt	Eponine .... Celia Keenan-Bolger
Fantine .... Daphne Rubin-Vega	Cosette .... Ali Ewoldt
Factory Girl .... Haviland Stillwell	Major Domo .... Justin Bohon
Sailors .... Justin Bohon,	Montparnasse .... JD Goldblatt
Victor Hawks, Nehal Joshi	Babet .... Jeff Kready
Pimp .... JD Goldblatt	Brujon .... Victor Hawks
Madame .... Kate Chapman	Claquesous .... James Chip Leonard
Old Woman .... Karen Elliott	Enjolras .... Aaron Lazar
Crone .... Marya Grandy	Marius .... Adam Jacobs
Bamatabois .... Daniel Bogart	Combeferre .... Daniel Bogart
Fauchelevant .... Jeff Kready	Feuilly .... Blake Ginther
Champmathieu .... Robert Hunt	Courfeyrac .... Robert Hunt
Young Cosette .... Kylie Liya Goldstein,	Joly .... Justin Bohon
Tess Adams,	Grantaire .... Drew Sarich
Carly Rose Sonenclar	Lesgles .... Nehal Joshi
Thénardier .... Gary Beach	Jean Prouvaire .... Doug Kreeger

Workers: Becca Ayers, Daniel Bogart, Justin Bohon, Kate Chapman, Nikki Renée Daniels, Karen Elliot, Marya Grandy, Blake Ginther, JD Goldblatt, Victor Hawks, Nehal Joshi, Jeff Kready, Doug Kreeger, James Chip Leonard, Megan McGinnis, Drew Sarich, Idara Victor.

Whores: Becca Ayers, Nikki Renée Daniels, Ali Ewoldt, Celia Keenan-Bolger, Megan McGinnis, Haviland Stillwell, Idara Victor.

Orchestra: Kevin Stites conductor; Paul Raiman, associate conductor, keyboard; Annbritt duChateau assistant conductor, keyboard; Martin Agee violin; Debra Shufelt-Dine viola; Clay C.

Ruede cello; Dave Phillips bass; Jonathan Levine clarinet, bass clarinet, tenor recorder; Bob Bush flute, piccolo, alto flute; alto recorder; Laura Wallis, oboe, English horn; Tim Schadt trumpet, flugelhorn; Brad Gemeinhardt, Sara Cyrus, Michael Atkinson, French horn; Chris Olness, bass trombone, tuba; Charles Descarfino mallets, timpani, percussion.

Understudies: Mr. Gemignani—Victor Hawks, Jeff Kready; Mr. Lewis—Robert Hunt, Drew Sarich; Mr. Beach—James Chip Leonard; Ms. Galloway—Karen Elliott; Ms. Rubin-Vega—Nikki Renée Daniels, Haviland Stillwell; Ms. Ewoldt—Idara Victor; Mr. Jacobs—Daniel Bogart, Doug Kreeger; Ms. Keenan-Bolger—Megan McGinnis, Marissa McGowan; Mr. Lazar—Drew Sarich.

Swings: Matt Clemens, Marissa McGowan, Q. Smith, Stephen Trafton.

Directed by Messrs. Caird and Nunn; scenery, John Napier; costumes, Andreane Neofitou; lighting, David Hersey; sound, Jon Weston, Andrew Bruce, Autograph; orchestrations, Christopher Jahnke, Stephen Metcalfe and John Cameron; music supervision, Stephen Brooker; music direction, Mr. Stites; music coordination, John Miller; wigs and hair, Tom Watson; executive producers, Nicholas Allott, Matthew Dalco, Fred Hanson; casting, Tara Rubin Casting; production stage manager, Michael J. Passaro; press, The Publicity Office, Marc Thibodeau, Bob Fennell, Michael S. Borowski, Candi Adams.

Time: Early 19th century. Place: France. Presented in two parts.

A 1986–87 *Best Plays* choice, the original Broadway production opened at the Broadway Theatre (3/12/1987–10/14/1990) before moving to the Imperial Theatre (10/17/1990–5/18/2003; 6,680 total performances). At the 1987 Tony Awards, the original Broadway production was honored in eight categories: musical, book, score, featured actor, featured actress, scenery, lighting and direction. First presentation of record in English was given at London's Barbican Theatre—with Patti LuPone as Fantine—under the aegis of the Royal Shakespeare Company (10/8/1985) before transferring to the West End's Palace Theatre (12/4/1985). The London production later moved to the Queen's Theatre (4/3/2004), where it continues at this writing. The 2006–07 production was the first Broadway revival.

ACT I

Prologue: 1815, Digne

"Prologue" .... Company
"Soliloquy" ....Jean Valjean

Prologue: 1823, Montreuil-sur-Mer

"At the End of the Day" .... Unemployed, Factory Workers
"I Dreamed a Dream" .... Fantine
"Lovely Ladies" .... Ladies, Clients
"Who Am I?" ....Jean Valjean
"Come to Me" ....Fantine, Jean Valjean
"Castle on a Cloud" .... Young Cosette

1823, Montfermeil

"Master of the House" .... Thénardier, Madame Thénardier, Customers
"Thénardier Waltz" .... Thénardier, Madame Thénardier, Jean Valjean

1832, Paris

"Look Down" .... Gavroche, Beggars
"Stars" .... Javert
"Red and Black" .... Enjolras, Marius, Students
"Do You Hear the People Sing" .... Enjolras, Students, Citizens
"In My Life" .... Cosette, Jean Valjean, Marius, Eponine
"A Heart Full of Love" .... Cosette, Marius, Eponine
"One Day More" .... Company

ACT II

"On My Own" .... Eponine
"A Little Fall of Rain" ....Eponine, Marius
"Drink with Me to Days Gone By" .... Grantaire, Students, Women
"Bring Him Home" ....Jean Valjean
"Dog Eats Dog" .... Thénardier
"Soliloquy" (Javert's Suicide) ....Javert
"Empty Chairs at Empty Tables" .... Marius

Power demon: Julie White in The Little Dog Laughed. *Photo: Carol Rosegg*

"Wedding Chorale" .... Guests
"Beggars at the Feast" .... Thénardier, Madame Thénardier
"Finale" .... Company

The Little Dog Laughed (112). Transfer from Off Broadway of the play by Douglas Carter Beane. Produced by Roy Gabay, Susan Dietz, Morris Berchard, Steve Bozeman, Ted Snowdon, Jerry Frankel, Doug Nevin, Jennifer Manocherian, Ina Meibach, in association with Second Stage Theatre (Carole Rothman artistic director, Ellen Richard, executive director), at the Cort Theatre. Opened November 13, 2006. (Closed February 18, 2007)

Diane .... Julie White   Alex .... Johnny Galecki
Mitchell .... Tom Everett Scott   Ellen .... Ari Graynor
    Understudies: Messrs. Scott, Galecki—Brian Henderson; Mses. White, Graynor—Dana Slamp.
    Directed by Scott Ellis; scenery, Allen Moyer; costumes, Jeff Mahshie; lighting, Donald Holder; music, Lewis Flinn; casting, Mele Nagler; production stage manager, Linda Marvel; press, Richard Kornberg and Associates, Tom D'Ambrosio, Don Summa.
    Time: The present. Place: New York and Hollywood. Presented in two parts.
    First presentation of record was given at Off Broadway's Second Stage Theatre (1/9–2/26/2006; 56 performances). Show business comedy about a male movie star attempting to cloak his homosexuality in a sudden marriage and baby. A truncated version titled *He Meaning Him* was given as part of the Downtown Plays festival under the auspices of the Drama Dept. (10/21–31/2004). Ms. White received the 2007 Tony Award for best actress in a play.

*Mary Poppins (225). Musical with book by Julian Fellowes; music and lyrics by Richard M. Sherman and Robert B. Sherman; additional music and lyrics by George Stiles and Anthony Drewe; based on the stories of P.L. Travers and the film by Walt

Disney Productions. Produced by Disney Theatrical Productions (Thomas Schumacher) and Cameron Mackintosh at the New Amsterdam Theatre. Opened November 16, 2006.

Bert .... Gavin Lee	Neleus .... Brian Letendre
George Banks .... Daniel Jenkins	Queen Victoria .... Ruth Gottschall
Winifred Banks .... Rebecca Luker	Bank Chairman .... Michael McCarty
Jane Banks .... Katherine Leigh Doherty,	Miss Smythe .... Ruth Gottschall
Kathryn Faughnan,	Von Hussler .... Sean McCourt
Delaney Moro	Northbrook .... Matt Loehr
Michael Banks .... Matthew Gumley,	Bird Woman .... Cass Morgan
Henry Hodges,	Mrs. Corry .... Janelle Anne Robinson
Alexander Scheitinger	Fannie .... Vasthy E. Mompoint
Katie Nanna .... Megan Osterhaus	Annie .... Megan Osterhaus
Policeman .... James Hindman	Valentine .... Tyler Maynard
Miss Lark .... Ann Arvia	William .... Eric B. Anthony
Admiral Boom .... Michael McCarty	Mr. Punch .... James Hindman
Mrs. Brill .... Jane Carr	Glamorous Doll .... Catherine Walker
Robertson Ay .... Mark Price	Jack-in-A-Box .... Sean McCourt
Mary Poppins .... Ashley Brown	Miss Andrew .... Ruth Gottschall
Park Keeper .... Nick Corley	

Ensemble: Eric B. Anthony, Ann Arvia, Kristin Carbone, Nick Corley, Case Dillard, Ruth Gottschall, James Hindman, Brian Letendre, Matt Loehr, Michelle Lookadoo, Tony Mansker, Tyler Maynard, Michael McCarty, Sean McCourt, Vasthy E. Mompoint, Jesse Nager, Kathleen Nanni, Megan Osterhaus, Dominic Roberts, Janelle Anne Robinson, Shekitra Starke, Catherine Walker, Kevin Samual Yee.

Orchestra: Brad Haak conductor; Kristen Blodgette associate conductor, keyboard 2; Stephanie Cummins cello; Nate Brown guitar, banjo, e-bow; Peter Donovan bass; Paul Garment clarinet; Alexandra Knoll oboe, English horn; Brian Miller flute; John Sheppard, Louis Hanzlik trumpet; Russell Rizner, Lawrence DiBello horns; Marc Donatelle trombone, euphonium; Randy Andos bass trombone, tuba; Milton Granger piano; Daniel Haskins percussion; Dave Ratajczak drums.

Lucky sweep-stakes: Ashley Brown, Katherine Leigh Doherty, Alexander Scheitinger and Gavin Lee in Mary Poppins. *Photo: Joan Marcus*

Understudies: Ms. Brown—Kristin Carbone, Megan Osterhaus, Catherine Walker; Mr. Lee—Eric B. Anthony, Matt Loehr; Mr. Jenkins—James Hindman, Sean McCourt; Ms. Luker—Kristin Carbone, Megan Osterhaus; Ms. Carr—Ann Arvia, Pam Bradley; Mr. Price—Tyler Maynard, Dominic Roberts; Ms. Morgan—Ann Arvia, Stephanie Kurtzuba; Ms. Gottschall—Ann Arvia, Stephanie Kurtzuba; Mr. McCarty—James Hindman, Sean McCourt; Ms. Robinson—Stephanie Kurtzuba, Megan Osterhaus; Ms. Osterhaus—Stephanie Kurtzuba, Pam Bradley; Ms. Arvia—Pam Bradley, Stephanie Kurtzuba; Mr. Letendre—Kevin Samual Yee, Brian Collier; Mr. McCourt—Nicolas Dromard, Rommy Sandhu; Mr. Loehr—Nicolas Dromard, James Hindman; Mr. Hindman—Sean McCourt, Tony Mansker; Mr. Corley—James Hindman, Tony Mansker; Mr. Anthony—Brian Collier, Nicolas Dromard; Mr. Maynard—Brian Collier, Nicolas Dromard; Ms. Walker—Suzanne Hylenski, Stephanie Kurtzuba.

Swings: Pam Bradley, Brian Collier, Nicolas Dromard, Suzanne Hylenski, Stephanie Kurtzuba, Rommy Sandhu.

Directed by Richard Eyre and Matthew Bourne; choreography, Mr. Bourne and Stephen Mear; scenery and costumes, Bob Crowley; lighting, Howard Harrison; sound, Steven Canyon Kennedy; orchestrations, William David Brohn; music supervision, David Caddick; dance and vocal arrangements, George Stiles; music direction, Mr. Haak; associate producer, James Thane; casting, Tara Rubin Casting; production stage manager, Tom Capps; press, Boneau/Bryan-Brown, Chris Boneau, Jackie Green, Aaron Meier, Matt Polk, Matt Ross.

Time: Turn of the 20th century. Place: Somewhere in London. Presented in two parts.

A magical nanny helps a family to become closer. Based on the 1964 Walt Disney film, the first presentation of record was given at London's Prince Edward Theatre (12/15/2004–1/12/2008) after a run at the Hippodrome in Bristol (9/18–11/6/2004).

ACT I

"Chim Chim Cher-ee" .... Bert
"Cherry Tree Lane" (Part 1) .... George and Winifred Banks, Jane,
Michael, Mrs. Brill, Robertson Ay
"The Perfect Nanny" .... Jane, Michael
"Cherry Tree Lane" (Part 2) .... George and Winifred Banks, Jane,
Michael, Mrs. Brill, Robertson Ay
"Practically Perfect" .... Mary Poppins, Jane, Michael
"Jolly Holiday" .... Bert, Mary Poppins, Jane, Michael, Neleus, Statues
"Cherry Tree Lane" (Reprise),
   "Being Mrs. Banks,"
   "Jolly Holiday" (Reprise) .... George, Winifred, Jane, Michael
"A Spoonful of Sugar" .... Mary Poppins, Jane, Michael, Robertson Ay, Winifred
"Precision and Order" .... Bank Chairman, Bank Clerks
"A Man Has Dreams" .... George Banks
"Feed the Birds" .... Bird Woman, Mary Poppins
"Supercalifragilisticexpialidocious" .... Mary Poppins, Mrs. Corry, Bert,
Jane, Michael, Fannie, Annie, Customers
"Temper, Temper" .... Valentine, William, Mr. Punch, Glamorous Doll, Toys
"Chim Chim Cher-ee" (Reprise) .... Bert, Mary Poppins

ACT II

"Cherry Tree Lane" (Reprise) .... Mrs. Brill, Michael, Jane,
Winifred, Robertson Ay, George
"Brimstone and Treacle" (Part 1) .... Miss Andrew
"Let's Go Fly a Kite" .... Bert, Park Keeper, Jane, Michael
"Cherry Tree Lane" (Reprise),
   "Being Mrs. Banks" (Reprise) .... George, Winifred
"Brimstone and Treacle" (Part 2) .... Mary Poppins, Miss Andrew
"Practically Perfect" (Reprise) .... Jane, Michael, Mary Poppins
"Chim Chim Cher-ee" (Reprise) .... Bert
"Step in Time" .... Bert, Mary Poppins, Jane, Michael, Sweeps
"A Man Has Dreams,"
   "A Spoonful of Sugar" (Reprise) .... George, Bert

"Anything Can Happen" ....Jane, Michael, Mary Poppins, Company
"A Spoonful of Sugar" (Reprise) ....Mary Poppins
"A Shooting Star" .... Orchestra

Lincoln Center Theater production of **The Coast of Utopia, Part One: Voyage** (44). By Tom Stoppard. André Bishop artistic director, Bernard Gersten executive producer, at the Vivian Beaumont Theater. Opened November 27, 2006. (May 12, 2007)

Alexander Bakunin .... Richard Easton	Vissarion Belinsky .... Billy Crudup
Varvara .... Amy Irving	Ivan Turgenev .... Jason Butler Harner
Liubov ....Jennifer Ehle	Alexander Herzen .... Brían F. O'Byrne
Varenka .... Martha Plimpton	Nicholas Ogarev ....Josh Hamilton
Tatiana .... Kellie Overbey	Nicholas Sazonov .... Aaron Krohn
Alexandra .... Annie Purcell	Nicholas Ketscher .... Baylen Thomas
Miss Chamberlain .... Bianca Amato	Nicholas Polevoy .... David Pittu
Baron Renne .... Andrew McGinn	Mrs. Beyer .... Patricia Conolly
Semyon ....David Manis	Natalie Beyer .... Mia Barron
Masha .... Felicity LaFortune	Peter Chaadaev .... David Cromwell
Michael Bakunin .... Ethan Hawke	Stepan Shevyrev .... Robert Stanton
Dyakov ....Anthony Cochrane	Katya ....Jennifer Lyon
Nicholas Stankevich .... David Harbour	Pushkin; Cat .... Adam Dannheisser

Ensemble: Larry Bull, Denis Butkus, Michael Carlsen, Amanda Leigh Cobb, William Connell, Matt Dickson, Scott Parkinson, Erika Rolfsrud, Brian Sgambati, Eric Sheffer Stevens, David Christopher Wells.

Musicians: Marshall Coid violin; Alissa Smith viola; Bruce Wang cello; Kevin Kuhn balalaika, mandolin; Josh Camp accordion; Dan Lipton piano.

Understudies: Ms. Lyon—Bianca Amato; Mr. Dannheisser—Larry Bull; Mses. Barron, Overbey, Purcell—Amanda Leigh Cobb; Messrs. Manis, Pittu, Stanton—Anthony Cochrane; Mr.

Russian mirror: Jennifer Ehle, Kellie Overbey, Amy Irving, Felicity LaFortune, Richard Easton, David Manis and Ethan Hawke in The Coast of Utopia, Part One: Voyage. *Photo: Paul Kolnik*

Hawke—Adam Dannheisser; Mr. Cochrane—Aaron Krohn; Mses. Amato, Conolly, Irving—Felicity LaFortune; Ms. LaFortune—Jennifer Lyon; Mr. Hamilton—Andrew McGinn; Messrs. Cromwell, Easton, McGinn—David Manis; Messrs. Crudup, Krohn—Scott Parkinson; Mses. Ehle, Plimpton—Erika Rolfsrud; Mr. O'Byrne—Eric Sheffer Stevens; Mr. Harner—Baylen Thomas; Messrs. Harbour, Thomas—David Christopher Wells.

Directed by Jack O'Brien; scenery, Bob Crowley and Scott Pask; costumes, Catherine Zuber; lighting, Brian MacDevitt; sound and music, Mark Bennett; music direction, Mr. Bennett and Dan Lipton; dramaturgy, Anne Cattaneo; casting, Daniel Swee; production stage manager, Robert Bennett; press, Philip Rinaldi, Barbara Carroll.

Time: The 1830s and 1840s. Place: Premukhino, the Bakunin estate 150 miles northwest of Moscow; Moscow; St. Petersburg. Presented in two parts.

Part One of the playwright's sweeping epic on revolutionary ideology among the Russian ruling class. Openings, closings and creative teams for the other parts may be found below in December and February listings. First presentation of record was given in the Olivier Theatre at the National Theatre (UK) (8/3–11/23/2002). A 2006–07 *Best Plays* choice (see essay by Charles Wright in this volume). The three plays were treated as a single entity, receiving seven 2007 Tony Awards—a record for nonmusical drama—in the categories of new play (Mr. Stoppard; Lincoln Center Theater), featured actor (Mr. Crudup), featured actress (Ms. Ehle), scenic design (Mr. Crowley and Mr. Pask), costume design (Ms. Zuber), lighting design (Mr. MacDevitt, for Part One; Kenneth Posner, for Part Two; Natasha Katz, for Part Three) and director (Mr. O'Brien).

*Company (210). Revival of the musical with book by George Furth; music and lyrics by Stephen Sondheim. Produced by Marc Routh, Richard Frankel, Thomas Viertel, Steven Baruch, Ambassador Theater Group, Tulchin/Bartner Productions, Darren Bagert, in association with Cincinnati Playhouse in the Park (Edward Stern producing artistic director, Buzz Ward executive director), at the Ethel Barrymore Theatre. Opened November 29, 2006.

Robert .... Raúl Esparza	Sarah .... Kristin Huffman
(percussion)	*(flute, alto sax, piccolo)*
Joanne .... Barbara Walsh	Susan .... Amy Justman
(orchestra bells, percussion)	*(piano, keyboard, orchestra bells)*
Harry .... Keith Buterbaugh	Amy ....Jane Pfitsch
(trumpet, trombone)	*(French horn, trumpet, flute)*
Peter .... Matt Castle	Jenny .... Leenya Rideout
(piano, keyboard, double bass)	*(viola, guitar, double bass)*
Paul................................. Robert Cunningham	David .... Fred Rose
(trumpet; drums)	*(cello, alto sax, tenor sax)*
Marta .... Angel Desai	Larry .... Bruce Sabath
(keyboard, violin, alto sax)	*(clarinet, drums)*
Kathy .... Kelly Jeanne Grant	April .... Elizabeth Stanley
(flute, alto sax)	*(oboe, tuba, alto sax)*

Standbys: Mr. Esparza—Fred Rose; Mses. Huffman, Walsh—Renée Bang Allen (flute alto sax, tenor sax, orchestra bells, percussion); Messrs. Cunningham, Rose—Brandon Ellis (cello, drums, double bass, guitar); Messrs. Buterbaugh, Sabath, Cunningham—David Garry (trumpet, trombone, clarinet, drums, alto sax, tenor sax); Mr. Castle—Jason Ostrowski (piano, keyboard, double bass); Mses. Pfitsch, Justman, Rideout—Jessica Wright (flute, violin); Mses. Desai, Grant, Stanley—Katrina Yaukey (alto sax, flute, oboe, tuba, trumpet).

Direction and choreography by John Doyle; scenery, David Gallo; costumes, Ann Hould-Ward; lighting, Thomas C. Hase; sound, Andrew Keister; wigs and hair, David H. Lawrence; orchestrations and music supervision, Mary Mitchell Campbell; casting, Telsey and Company; production stage manager, Gary Mickelson; press, Barlow-Hartman, John Barlow, Michael Hartman, Leslie Baden.

Presented in two parts.

A New York bachelor observes the many ways his married friends cope with life, love and domestic arrangements. A 1969–70 *Best Plays* choice, the original Broadway production opened

Got company? Raúl Esparza (center) with the cast of Company. *Photo: Paul Kolnik*

at the Alvin Theatre (4/26/1970–1/1/1972; 705 performances). First presentation of record was given at the Shubert Theatre in Boston (3/24–4/11/1970). The original production—an adaptation of a three-character comedy by Mr. Furth previously optioned as a straight play for a March 1969 Broadway debut with Kim Stanley—had some difficulty keeping its Robert: Anthony Perkins departed to direct Bruce Jay Friedman's *Steambath* Off Broadway and was replaced by Dean Jones, who withdrew a few weeks after opening due to hepatitis and exhaustion. Successful on its opening, the production was re-reviewed with Larry Kert, who eventually received a 1971 Tony nomination. At the 1971 Tony Awards, the original production was honored in the categories of musical (Harold Prince), book (Mr. Furth), score (Mr. Sondheim), lyrics (Mr. Sondheim), scenery (Boris Aronson) and direction (Mr. Prince). The 2006–07 production, which received the 2007 Tony Award for best musical revival, was first presented at Cincinnati Playhouse in the Park (3/17–4/14/2006). It was the third Broadway revival, excluding a concert version in April 1993.

ACT I

"Company" .... Robert, Company
"The Little Things You Do Together" .... Joanne and Company
"Sorry-Grateful" ....Harry, David, Larry
"You Could Drive a Person Crazy" .... April, Kathy, Marta
"Have I Got a Girl for You" .... Larry, Peter, Paul, David, Harry
"Someone Is Waiting" .... Robert
"Another Hundred People" .... Marta
"Getting Married Today" .... Amy, Paul, Sarah, Company
"Marry Me a Little" .... Robert

ACT II

"Side by Side by Side" .... Robert, Company
"What Would We Do Without You?" .... Robert, Company
"Poor Baby" .... Sarah, Jenny, Susan, Amy, Joanne
"Barcelona" ....Robert, April
"The Ladies Who Lunch" ....Joanne
"Being Alive" .... Robert

The Vertical Hour (117). By David Hare. Produced by Scott Rudin, Robert Fox, Neal Street Productions, Roger Berlind, Debra Black, The Shubert Organization at the Music Box. Opened November 30, 2006. (Closed March 11, 2007)

Oliver Lucas	Bill Nighy	Philip Lucas	Andrew Scott
Nadia Blye	Julianne Moore	Terri Scholes	Rutina Wesley
Dennis Dutton	Dan Bittner		

Standbys: Ms. Moore—Jennifer Roszell; Messrs. Bittner, Scott—Matthew Humphreys; Mr. Nighy—Steven Crossley; Ms. Wesley—Crystal Noelle.

Directed by Sam Mendes; scenery, Scott Pask; costumes, Ann Roth; lighting, Brian MacDevitt; sound, Christopher Cronin; casting, Daniel Swee; production stage manager, James Harker; press, Barlow-Hartman, John Barlow, Michael Hartman, Dennis Crowley, Ryan Ratelle.

Time: The present. Place: Yale University and in Wales. Presented in two parts.

Characters with opposing political views clash over appropriate international remedies to threats of terrorism and human suffering.

High Fidelity (13). Musical with book by David Lindsay-Abaire; music by Tom Kitt; lyrics by Amanda Green; based on the novel by Nick Hornby and the Touchstone Pictures film. Produced by Jeffrey Seller, Kevin McCollum, Robyn Goodman, Live Nation, Roy Miller, Dan Markley, Ruth Hendel, Danzansky Partners, Jam Theatricals at the Imperial Theatre. Opened December 7, 2006. (Closed December 17, 2006)

Rob	Will Chase	Anna; Alison	Kirsten Wyatt
Hipster; Roadie	Andrew C. Call	Penny; Singer	Anne Warren
Futon Guy	Justin Brill	Charlie; Marie LaSalle	Emily Swallow
Mohawk Guy; Neil Young	Matt Caplan	Sarah	Caren Lyn Manuel
Dick	Christian Anderson	Liz; Jackie	Rachel Stern
Barry	Jay Klaitz	T.M.P.M.I.T.W.; Bruce	Jon Patrick Walker
Laura	Jenn Colella	Ian; Middle-Aged Guy	Jeb Brown

Orchestra: Adam Ben-David conductor, piano, harmonica; Matt Gallagher associate conductor, organ, keyboard; Antoine Silverman violin; Peter Sachon cello; Randy Landau bass; Dan Willis reeds; Bud Burridge trumpet; Kenny Brescia guitar; Michael Aarons guitar, sitar, banjo, mandolin; Damien Bassman drums, percussion.

Understudies: Mr. Chase—Matt Caplan, Jon Patrick Walker; Ms. Colella—Caren Lyn Manuel, Betsy Morgan, Emily Swallow, Anne Warren; Mr. Anderson—Justin Brill, Paul Castree; Mr. Klaitz—Andrew C. Call, Matt Caplan; Mr. Brown—George Merrick, Tom Plotkin; Ms. Stern—Caren Lyn Manuel, Betsy Morgan, J.B. Wing; Ms. Swallow—Caren Lyn Manuel, Betsy Morgan, J.B. Wing; Ms. Wyatt—Betsy Morgan, J.B. Wing; Mr. Walker—Andrew C. Call, Tom Plotkin.

Swings: Paul Castree, George Merrick, Betsy Morgan, Tom Plotkin, J.B. Wing.

Directed by Walter Bobbie; choreography, Christopher Gattelli; scenery, Anna Louizos; costumes, Theresa Squire; lighting, Ken Billington; sound, Acme Sound Partners; orchestrations, Tom Kitt and Alex Lacamoire; music supervision, Mr. Lacamoire; vocal arrangements, Stephen Oremus; music direction, Mr. Ben-David; music coordination, Michael Keller; associate producers, Sonny Everett and Mariano Tolentino Jr.; casting, Telsey and Company; production stage manager, Steven Beckler; press, Sam Rudy Media Relations, Dale R. Heller, Robert Lasko.

Time: The present. Place: A remote neighborhood in Brooklyn. Presented in two parts.

A young man suffers from serial-relationship difficulties, a passion for rock music on vinyl records and a touch of arrested adolescence in a musical adaptation of the 2000 film. First presentation of record was given at Boston's Colonial Theatre (10/5–10/22/2006) before its Broadway bow.

ACT I

"The Last Real Record Store on Earth"	Rob, Pale Young Men, Dick, Barry
"Desert Island Top Five Break-Ups"	Rob, Top-Five Girls
"It's No Problem"	Dick
"She Goes"	Liz, Rob
"Ian's Here"	Ian, Laura

"Number Five With a Bullet" .... Laura, Top-Five Girls
"Ready to Settle" .... Marie, Back-Up Singer
"Terrible Things" .... Marie
"The Last Real Record Store" (Reprise) .... Barry, Dick, Rob, Pale Young Men
"Nine Percent Chance" .... Rob, Barry, Dick, Pale Young Men

ACT II

"I Slept With Someone" .... Rob, Laura
"Exit Sign" .... Neil
"Cryin' in the Rain" .... Rob, Top-Five Girls
"Conflict Resolution" .... Rob, Dick, Barry, Pale Young Men, Company
"Goodbye and Good Luck" .... Bruce, Rob
"It's No Problem" (Reprise) .... Dick, Anna
"Ian's Prayer" .... Ian
"Laura, Laura" .... Rob
"Saturday Night Girl" .... The Skids
"Turn the World off (and Turn You On)" .... Barry, T.M.P.M.I.T.W.,
Klepto Boy. Rob, Laura, Liz, Company

*Spring Awakening (196). Transfer from Off Off Broadway of the musical with book
and lyrics by Steven Sater, music by Duncan Sheik; based on the play by Frank Wedekind.
Produced by Ira Pittelman, Tom Hulce, Jeffrey Richards, Jerry Frankel, Atlantic Theater
Company (Neil Pepe artistic director, Andrew D. Hamingson managing director), Jeffrey
Sine, Freddy DeMann, Max Cooper, Morton Swinsky, Cindy and Jay Gutterman, Joe
McGinnis, Judith Ann Abrams, ZenDog Productions, CarJac Productions, Aron Bergson
Productions, Jennifer Manocherian, Ted Snowdon, Harold Thau, Terry Schnuck, Cold
Spring Productions, Amanda Dubois, Elizabeth Eynon Wetherell, Jennifer Maloney,
Tamara Tunie, Joe Cilibrasi, StyleFour Productions, at the Eugene O'Neill Theatre.
Opened December 10, 2006.

Wendla	Lea Michele	Otto	Brian Charles Johnson
Adult Women	Christine Estabrook	Hanschen	Jonathan B. Wright
Martha	Lilli Cooper	Ernst	Gideon Glick
Ilse	Lauren Pritchard	Georg	Skylar Astin
Anna	Phoebe Strole	Moritz	John Gallagher Jr.
Thea	Remy Zaken	Melchior	Jonathan Groff
Adult Men	Stephen Spinella		

Ensemble: Gerard Canonico, Jennifer Damiano, Robert Hager, Krysta Rodriguez.

Orchestra: Kimberly Grigsby conductor, keyboard; Trey Files associate conductor, drums;
Oliver Manchon violin, guitar; Hiroko Taguchi violin; Benjamin Kalb cello; Thad deBrock guitar;
George Farmer bass.

Understudies: Mr. Groff—Robert Hager, Jonathan B. Wright; Mr. Gallagher—Gerard Canonico,
Brian Charles Johnson; Mr. Astin—Gerard Canonico, Robert Hager, Brian Charles Johnson; Messrs.
Wright, Johnson, Glick—Gerard Canonico, Robert Hager; Mr. Spinella—Rob Devaney; Ms.
Michele—Krysta Rodriguez, Phoebe Strole; Ms. Pritchard—Krysta Rodriguez, Phoebe Strole, Mses.
Strole, Cooper, Zaken—Jennifer Damiano, Krysta Rodriguez; Ms. Estabrook—Frances
Mercanti-Anthony.

Swings: Rob Devaney, Frances Mercanti-Anthony.

Directed by Michael Mayer; choreography, Bill T. Jones; scenery, Christine Jones; costumes,
Susan Hilferty; lighting, Kevin Adams; sound, Brian Ronan; orchestrations, Mr. Sheik; vocal
arrangements, AnnMarie Milazzo; additional arrangement, Simon Hale; music direction, Ms. Grigsby;
music coordination, Michael Keller; fight direction, J. David Brimmer; associate producers, Joan
Cullman Productions, Patricia Flicker Addiss; casting, Jim Carnahan, Carrie Gardner; production
stage manager, Heather Cousens; press, Jeffrey Richards Associates, Irene Gandy, Christopher
Hanley, Michael Dressel, Hannah Oberman-Breindel, JC Cassis.

Time: 1890s. Place: A provincial German town. Presented in two parts.

Not forgotten: John Gallagher Jr., Jonathan Groff and Lea Michele in Spring Awakening.
Photo: Joan Marcus

Musical based on Mr. Wedekind's controversial 1891 play about dawning sexuality among a group of adolescents in a repressed society. A 2006–07 *Best Plays* choice (see essay by Michael Feingold in this volume). First presentation of record was given Off Off Broadway at Atlantic Theater Company (6/15–8/5/2006; 54 performances).

ACT I

"Mama Who Bore Me" .... Wendla
"Mama Who Bore Me" (Reprise) .... Girls
"All That's Known" .... Melchior
"The Bitch of Living" .... Moritz, Boys
"My Junk" .... Girls, Boys
"Touch Me" .... Boys, Girls
"The Word of Your Body" .... Wendla, Melchior
"The Dark I Know Well" .... Martha, Ilse, Boys
"And Then There Were None" .... Moritz, Boys
"The Mirror-Blue Night" .... Melchior, Boys
"I Believe" .... Boys, Girls

ACT II

"The Guilty Ones" .... Wendla, Melchior, Boys, Girls
"Don't Do Sadness" .... Moritz
"Blue Wind" .... Ilse
"Left Behind" .... Melchior
"Totally Fucked" .... Melchior, Company
"The Word of Your Body" (Reprise) .... Hanschen, Ernst, Boys, Girls
"Whispering" .... Wendla
"Those You've Known" .... Moritz, Wendla, Melchior
"The Song of Purple Summer" .... Company

Roundabout Theatre Company production of **The Apple Tree** (99). Revival of the musical with book, music and lyrics by Jerry Bock and Sheldon Harnick; additional material by Jerome Coopersmith; based on stories by Mark Twain, Frank R. Stockton and Jules Feiffer. Todd Haimes artistic director, Harold Wolpert managing director, Julia C. Levy executive director, at Studio 54. Opened December 14, 2006. (Closed March 11, 2007)

"The Diary of Adam and Eve" (Mark Twain)

Adam .... Brian d'Arcy James
Eve .... Kristin Chenoweth
Snake .... Marc Kudisch

"The Lady or the Tiger?" (Frank R. Stockton)

Balladeer .... Marc Kudisch
King Arik .... Walter Charles
Princess Barbára .... Kristin Chenoweth
Prisoner .... Mike McGowan
Tiger .... Sean Palmer
Prisoner's Bride .... Sarah Jane Everman
Nadjira .... Lorin Latarro
Captain Sanjar .... Brian d'Arcy James
Guards .... Mike McGowan, Dennis Stowe

King Arik's Court: Meggie Cansler, Julie Connors, Sarah Jane Everman, Justin Keyes, Lorin Latarro, Mike McGowan, Sean Palmer, Dennis Stowe.

"Passionella. A Romance of the '60s." (Jules Feiffer)

Narrator .... Marc Kudisch
Ella; Passionella .... Kristin Chenoweth
Mr. Fallible; Producer .... Walter Charles
Newsboy .... Justin Keyes
Director .... Dennis Stowe
Film Critic .... Julie Connors
Stage Hand .... Mike McGowan
Flip; Prince; Charming ..... Brian d'Arcy James

Ensemble: Meggie Cansler, Julie Connors, Sarah Jane Everman, Justin Keyes, Lorin Latarro, Mike McGowan, Sean Palmer, Dennis Stowe.

Sweet temptation: Kristin Chenoweth and Marc Kudisch in The Apple Tree. *Photo: Joan Marcus*

Orchestra: Rob Fisher conductor; Sam Davis associate conductor, keyboard; Marilyn Reynolds, Sylvia D'Avanzo violin; David Blinn viola; Roger Shell cello; John Beal bass; James Ercole, Sean Frank, Mark Thrasher woodwinds; Dominic Derasse, Charles Porter trumpet; Clint Sharman trombone; Roger Wendt, French horn; Paul Pizzuti drums, percussion; Susan Jolles harp.

Understudies: Ms. Chenowith—Sarah Jane Everman, Messrs. James, Charles—Mike McGowan, Mr. Kudisch—Sean Palmer.

Swings: Jennifer Taylor Farrell, Eric Santagata.

Directed by Gary Griffin; choreography, Andy Blankenbuehler; scenery, John Lee Beatty; costumes, Jess Goldstein; lighting, Donald Holder; sound, Dan Moses Schreier; wigs and hair, Charles LaPointe; orchestrations, Jonathan Tunick; vocal orchestrations and music direction, Mr. Fisher; music coordination, Seymour Red Press; dramaturgy, Jerry Patch; casting, Jim Carnahan; production stage manager; Peter Hanson; press; Boneau/Bryan-Brown, Adrian Bryan-Brown, Matt Polk, Jessica Johnson.

Time: Saturday, June 1; a long time ago; then. Place: Eden; a semi-barbaric kingdom; here. Presented in two parts.

Musical based on humorous stories regarding human creation, the choices we are forced to make and the consequences of those choices. A 1966–67 *Best Plays* choice, the first presentation of record at Broadway's Shubert Theatre (10/18/1966–11/25/1967; 463 performances). Barbara Harris was honored at the 1967 Tony Awards in the category of best actress in a musical. The 2006–07 production was the first Broadway revival.

ACT I (THE DIARY OF ADAM AND EVE)

"Eden Prelude"	Orchestra
"Here in Eden"	Eve
"Feelings"	Eve
"Eve"	Adam
"Friends"	Eve
"The Apple Tree (Forbidden Fruit)"	Snake
"Beautiful, Beautiful World"	Adam
"It's a Fish"	Adam
"Go to Sleep Whatever You Are"	Eve
"What Makes Me Love Him"	Eve

ACT II (THE LADY OR THE TIGER?)

"The Lady or the Tiger Prelude"	Orchestra
"I'll Tell You a Truth"	Balladeer
"Make Way"	King Arik, Court
"Forbidden Love (In Gaul)"	Princess Barbára, Sanjar
"The Apple Tree" (Reprise)	Balladeer
"I've Got What You Want"	Princess Barbára
"Tiger, Tiger"	Princess Barbára
"Make Way" (Reprise)	King's Court
"Which Door"	Sanjar, Princess Barbára, King Arik, Court
"I'll Tell You a Truth" (Reprise)	Balladeer

ACT III (PASSIONELLA: A ROMANCE OF THE '60S)

"Passionella Mini-Overture"	Orchestra
"Oh, to Be a Movie Star"	Ella
"Gorgeous"	Passionella
"(Who, Who, Who, Who,) Who Is She?"	Company
"Wealth"	Passionella
"You Are Not Real"	Flip, Company
"George L."	Ella, George

Lincoln Center Theater production of **The Coast of Utopia, Part Two: Shipwreck** (43). By Tom Stoppard. André Bishop artistic director, Bernard Gersten executive producer, at the Vivian Beaumont Theater. Opened December 21, 2006. (Closed May 12, 2007)

Best times: Jason Butler Harner, Billy Crudup, Jennifer Ehle, August Gladstone, Beckett Melville and Patricia Conolly in The Coast of Utopia, Part Two: Shipwreck. *Photo: Paul Kolnik*

Alexander Herzen .... Brían F. O'Byrne
Natalie Herzen .... Jennifer Ehle
Sasha Herzen .... Beckett Melville
Kolya Herzen .... August Gladstone
Nurse .... Mia Barron
Nicholas Ogarev .... Josh Hamilton
Ivan Turgenev .... Jason Butler Harner
Timothy Granovsky .... Andrew McGinn
Nicholas Ketscher .... Baylen Thomas
Konstantin Aksakov .... Scott Parkinson
Policeman .... David Manis
Vissarion Belinsky .... Billy Crudup
Madame Haag .... Patricia Conolly
Jean-Marie .... David Cromwell
George Herwegh .... David Harbour

Emma Herwegh .... Bianca Amato
Shop Boy .... Tolan Aman
Nicholas Sazonov .... Aaron Krohn
Michael Bakunin .... Ethan Hawke
Marianne
  on the Barricades .... Felicity LaFortune
Karl Marx .... Adam Dannheisser
Natasha Tuchkov .... Martha Plimpton
Benoit .... David Pittu
Beggar .... Scott Parkinson
Maria Ogarev .... Amy Irving
Franz Otto .... Robert Stanton
Leonty Ibayev .... Richard Easton
Rocca .... David Pittu
Rosa .... Felicity LaFortune

Ensemble: Larry Bull, Denis Butkus, Michael Carlsen, Anthony Cochrane, Amanda Leigh Cobb, William Connell, Michael D'Addario, Matt Dickson, Jennifer Lyon, Kellie Overbey, Annie Purcell, Erika Rolfsrud, Brian Sgambati, Maximillian Sherer, Eric Sheffer Stevens, David Christopher Wells.

Musicians: Jake Schwartz guitar; Andrew Sterman clarinet, flute; Sarah Schram oboe; Dominic Derasse trumpet; Dan Lipton piano.

Understudies: Ms. Plimpton—Mia Barron; Messrs. Dannheisser, Cromwell—Larry Bull; Messrs. Pittu, Easton—Anthony Cochrane; Ms. LaFortune—Amanda Leigh Cobb; Messrs. Melville, Gladstone—Michael D'Addario; Messrs. Parkinson, Hawke—Adam Dannheisser; Mr. Manis—Aaron Krohn; Mses. Connolly, Irving—Felicity LaFortune; Ms. Barron—Jennifer Lyon; Mr. Stanton—David Manis; Messrs. Hamilton, Krohn, Parkinson—Andrew McGinn; Mr. Crudup—Scott Parkinson; Mses. Ehle, Amato—Erika Rolfsrud; Mr. O'Byrne—Eric Sheffer Stevens, Mr. Harner—Baylen Thomas; Messrs. McGinn, Thomas, Harbour—David Christopher Wells; Mr. Aman—Beckett Melville.

Directed by Jack O'Brien; scenery, Bob Crowley and Scott Pask; costumes, Catherine Zuber; lighting, Kenneth Posner; sound and music, Mark Bennett; music direction, Mr. Bennett and Dan Lipton; dramaturgy, Anne Cattaneo; casting, Daniel Swee; production stage manager, Robert Bennett; press, Philip Rinaldi, Barbara Carroll.

Time: The 1840s and 1850s. Place: Salons, apartments and gardens in Russia, Germany and France. Presented in two parts.

Part Two of the playwright's sweeping epic on revolutionary ideology among the Russian ruling class. Openings, closings and creative teams for the other parts may be found above in November and below in February listings. First presentation of record was given in the Olivier Theatre at the National Theatre (UK) (8/3–11/23/2002). A 2006–07 *Best Plays* choice (see essay by Charles Wright in this volume). The three plays were treated as a single entity, receiving seven 2007 Tony Awards—a record for nonmusical drama—in the categories of new play (Mr. Stoppard; Lincoln Center Theater), featured actor (Mr. Crudup), featured actress (Ms. Ehle), scenic design (Mr. Crowley and Mr. Pask), costume design (Ms. Zuber), lighting design (Brian MacDevitt, for Part One; Mr. Posner, for Part Two; Natasha Katz, for Part Three) and director (Mr. O'Brien).

Manhattan Theatre Club production of **Translations** (53). Revival of the play by Brian Friel. Lynne Meadow artistic director, Barry Grove executive producer, in association with McCarter Theatre Center (Emily Mann artistic director, Jeffrey Woodward managing director), at the Biltmore Theatre. Opened January 25, 2007. (Closed March 11, 2007)

Manus	David Costabile	Bridget	Geraldine Hughes
Sarah	Morgan Hallett	Hugh	Niall Buggy
Jimmy Jack	Dermot Crowley	Owen	Alan Cox
Maire	Susan Lynch	Captain Lancey	Graeme Malcolm
Doalty	Michael Fitzgerald	Lieutenant Yolland	Chandler Williams

Culture clash: Chandler Williams, Michael Fitzgerald, Morgan Hallett, Geraldine Hughes, Susan Lynch and Alan Cox in Translations. *Photo: Joan Marcus*

Wrecked ideals: Brían F. O'Byrne (seated, center right) and company in The Coast of Utopia, Part Three: Salvage. *Photo: Paul Kolnik*

Understudies: Messrs. Costabile, Fitzgerald, Cox, Williams—Jeremy Bobb; Mses. Hallett, Lynch, Hughes—Diane Landers; Messrs. Crowley, Buggy, Malcolm—Kenneth Tigar.

Directed by Garry Hynes; scenery and costumes, Francis O'Connor; lighting, Davy Cunningham; sound, John Leonard; music; Sam Jackson; casting, Laura Stanczyk, Nancy Piccione, David Caparelliotis; production stage manager, Richard Costabile; press, Boneau/Bryan-Brown, Chris Boneau, Jim Byk, Aaron Meier, Heath Schwartz, Christine Olver.

Time: August 1833. Place: A hedge school in Baile Beag/Ballybeg, County Donegal, Ireland. Presented in two parts.

The struggle between British colonizers and the colonized Irish erupts when divergent languages (and love) cannot bridge a cultural divide. First presentation of record was given under the aegis of Mr. Friel and Stephen Rea's Field Day Theatre Company at Guild Hall, Derry, Northern Ireland (9/23/1980) before runs at the 1980 Dublin Theatre Festival and London's Hampstead Theatre (5/12/1981). A 1980–81 *Best Plays* choice, the first US production of record, featuring Barnard Hughes, Daniel Gerroll and Valerie Mahaffey, was presented Off Broadway by Manhattan Theatre Club (4/7–5/17/1981; 48 performances). First Broadway presentation of record was given at the Plymouth Theatre (3/19–4/9/1995; 25 performances).

Lincoln Center Theater production of **The Coast of Utopia, Part Three: Salvage** (34). By Tom Stoppard. André Bishop artistic director, Bernard Gersten executive producer, at the Vivian Beaumont Theater. Opened February 18, 2006. (Closed May 13, 2007)

Alexander Herzen	Brían F. O'Byrne	Malwida von Meysenbug	Jennifer Ehle
Sasha	Matt Dickson	Mrs. Blainey	Patricia Conolly
Sasha, as a child	Evan Daves	Rose	Mia Barron
Tata	Annie Purcell	English Servants	Tolan Aman,
Tata, as a child	Kat Peters		Amanda Leigh Cobb,
Olga	Amanda Leigh Cobb		Matt Dickson,
Olga, as a child	Kat Peters		Brian Sgambati
Olga, as a young child	Vivien Kells	Count Stanislaw Worcell	Richard Easton
Maria Fomm	Felicity LaFortune	Arnold Ruge	David Cromwell

Gottfried Kinkel	David Manis	Nicholas Ogarev	Josh Hamilton
Joanna Kinkel	Bianca Amato	Natasha Ogarev	Martha Plimpton
Karl Marx	Adam Dannheisser	Ivan Turgenev	Jason Butler Harner
Ernest Jones	Robert Stanton	Mary Sutherland	Kellie Overbey
Emily Jones	Jennifer Lyon	Henry	Tolan Aman
Giuseppe Mazzini	Brian Sgambati	Nicholas Chernyshevsky	Andrew McGinn
Louis Blanc	David Pittu	Doctor	David Harbour
Alexandre Ledru-Rollin	Larry Bull	Perotkin	David Christopher Wells
Alphonse de Ville	Baylen Thomas	Semlov	Brian Sgambati
Lajos Kossuth	Anthony Cochrane	Lt. Korf	Denis Butkus
Teresa Kossuth	Erika Rolfsrud	Vetoshnikov	David Pittu
Captain Peks	Denis Butkus	Sleptsov	Scott Parkinson
Zenkowicz	David Cromwell	Waiter	Eric Sheffer Stevens
Tchorzewski	Michael Carlsen	Teresina	Mia Barron
Czerniecki	Aaron Krohn	Liza	Kat Peters
Polish Émigré	Denis Butkus	Ensemble	William Connell,
Michael Bakunin	Ethan Hawke		Beckett Melville, Sophie Rudin

Musicians: Aaron Krohn guitar; Dan Lipton piano.

Understudies: Ms. Barron—Bianca Amato; Mr. Daves—Tolan Aman; Mses. Purcell, Plimpton—Mia Barron; Mr. Dannheiser—Larry Bull; Messrs. Dickson, Cochrane—Denis Butkus; Messrs. Sgambati, Butkus, Parkinson—Michael Carlsen; Ms. Lyon—Amanda Leigh Cobb; Messrs. Easton, Cromwell—Anthony Cochrane; Mr. Hawke—Adam Dannheisser; Mr. Butkus—Matt Dickson; Messrs. McGinn, Harbour—Aaron Krohn; Ms. Conolly—Felicity LaFortune; Mses. LaFortune, Barron—Jennifer Lyon; Messrs. Manis, Hamilton—Andrew McGinn; Mr. Aman—Beckett Melville; Mr. Cromwell—Scott Parkinson; Ms. Amato—Annie Purcell; Mses. Cobb, Ehle, Overbey—Erika Rolfsrud; Mses. Peters, Kells—Sophie Rudin; Mr. Stevens—Brian Sgambati; Messrs. O'Byrne, Wells, Sgambati—Eric Sheffer Stevens; Messrs. Stanton, Bull, Harner—Baylen Thomas; Messrs. Krohn, Pittu, Thomas—David Christopher Wells.

Directed by Jack O'Brien; scenery, Bob Crowley and Scott Pask; costumes, Catherine Zuber; lighting, Natasha Katz; sound and music, Mark Bennett; music direction, Mr. Bennett and Dan Lipton; dramaturgy, Anne Cattaneo; casting, Daniel Swee; production stage manager, Robert Bennett; press, Philip Rinaldi, Barbara Carroll.

Time: 1853–66. Place: England and Geneva. Presented in two parts.

Part Three of the playwright's sweeping epic on revolutionary ideology among the Russian ruling class. Openings, closings and creative teams for the other parts may be found above in November and December listings. First presentation of record was given in the Olivier Theatre at the National Theatre (UK) (8/3–11/23/2002). A 2006–07 *Best Plays* choice (see essay by Charles Wright in this volume). The three plays were treated as a single entity, receiving seven 2007 Tony Awards—a record for nonmusical drama—in the categories of new play (Mr. Stoppard; Lincoln Center Theater), featured actor (Mr. Crudup), featured actress (Ms. Ehle), scenic design (Mr. Crowley and Mr. Pask), costume design (Ms. Zuber), lighting design (Brian MacDevitt, for Part One; Kenneth Posner, for Part Two; Ms. Katz, for Part Three) and director (Mr. O'Brien).

*Journey's End (113). Revival of the play by R.C. Sherriff. Produced by Boyett Ostar Productions, Stephanie P. McClelland, Bill Rollnick, James D'Orta, Philip Geier at the Belasco Theatre. Opened February 22, 2007.

Capt. Hardy	John Curless	Pvt. Brown	John Behlmann
Lt. Osborne	Boyd Gaines	Lt. Hibbert	Justin Blanchard
Pvt. Mason	Jefferson Mays	Sgt. Major	John Curless
Lt. Raleigh	Stark Sands	Colonel	Richard Poe
Capt. Stanhope	Hugh Dancy	German Soldier	Kieran Campion
Lt. Trotter	John Ahlin	Lance Cpl. Broughton	Nick Berg Barnes

Understudies: Messrs. Dancy, Campion, Barnes—John Behlmann; Mr. Gaines—Richard Poe; Messrs. Mays, Poe—John Curless; Messrs. Sands, Blanchard, Behlmann, Barnes—Kieran Campion; Messrs. Curless, Ahlin—Nick Berg Barnes.

Directed by David Grindley; scenery and costumes, Jonathan Fensom; lighting, Jason Taylor; sound, Gregory Clarke; casting, Jay Binder, Jack Bowdan; production stage manager, Arthur Gaffin; press, The Pete Sanders Group, Pete Sanders, Glenna Freedman.

Time: March 1918. Place: A dugout in the British trenches near St. Quentin, France. Presented in two parts.

The horrors of war and the humanity of the men who fight for each other and die with one another. First presentation of record was given by London's Stage Society (12/9/1928), with Laurence Olivier as Capt. Stanhope and Maurice Evans as Lt. Raleigh, before a transfer to the West End's Savoy Theatre (1/21/1929)—Mr. Olivier was the sole cast member not retained in the move. A 1928–29 *Best Plays* choice, the original Broadway production opened at Henry Miller's Theatre (3/22/1929–5/17/1930; 485 performances). While the original Broadway production ran, there were four American touring companies operating. Prior to the 2006–07 revival, there was another short-lived revival at Broadway's Empire Theatre (9/18–9/30/1939; 15 performances). The 2006–07 production, first presented at London's Comedy, Playhouse and Duke of York's Theatres (1/21/2004–2/18/2005), was honored at the 2007 Tony Awards for best play-revival.

Roundabout Theatre Company production of **Prelude to a Kiss** (61). Revival of the play by Craig Lucas. Todd Haimes artistic director, Harold Wolpert managing director, Julia C. Levy executive director, at the American Airlines Theatre. Opened March 8, 2007. (Closed April 29, 2007)

Old Man	John Mahoney	Dr. Boyle	James Rebhorn
Peter	Alan Tudyk	Mrs. Boyle	Robin Bartlett
Rita	Annie Parisse	Minister	MacIntyre Dixon
Taylor	Matthew Rauch	Uncle Fred	John Rothman
Tom; Jamaican Waiter	Francois Battiste	Aunt Dorothy; Leah	Marceline Hugot

Stop kiss: John Mahoney, Annie Parisse and Alan Tudyk in Prelude to a Kiss. *Photo: Joan Marcus*

Ensemble: Brandon J. Dirden, Susan Pellegrino, Karen Walsh.

Understudies: Messrs. Battiste, Rauch, Dixon—Brandon J. Dirden; Messrs. Mahoney, Rothman—MacIntyre Dixon; Mses. Hugot, Bartlett—Susan Pellegrino; Mr. Tudyk—Matthew Rauch; Mr. Rebhorn—John Rothman; Ms. Parisse—Karen Walsh.

Directed by Daniel Sullivan; scenery, Santo Loquasto; costumes, Jane Greenwood; lighting, Donald Holder; sound and music, John Gromada; wigs and hair, Tom Watson; casting, Jim Carnahan, Mele Nagler; production stage manager, Leslie C. Lyter; press, Boneau/Bryan-Brown, Adrian Bryan-Brown, Matt Polk, Jessica Johnson.

Time: The present. Place: New York City. Presented in two parts.

A bride undergoes a frightening transformation after she is kissed by an elderly man at her wedding. A 1989–90 *Best Plays* choice, the first presentation of record was given Off Broadway by Circle Repertory Company (3/14–4/19/1990; 33 performances) with a cast that included Alec Baldwin, Mary-Louise Parker, Barnard Hughes, John Dossett, Debra Monk and Larry Bryggman. Mr. Baldwin was replaced Off Broadway by Timothy Hutton (4/12/1990) after an 11-day hiatus. The production closed one week later and transferred to Broadway's Helen Hayes Theatre (5/1/1990–5/19/1991; 440 performances). The 2006–07 production was the first Broadway revival.

*Talk Radio (93). Revival of the play by Eric Bogosian; created for the stage with Tad Savinar. Produced by Jeffrey Richards, Jerry Frankel, Jam Theatricals, Francis Finlay, Ronald Frankel, James Fuld Jr., Steve Green, Judith Hansen, Patty Ann Lacerte, James Riley, Mary Lu Roffe, Morton Swinsky, Sheldon Stein, Terri and Timothy Childs, StyleFour Productions, Irving Welzer, Herb Blodgett, at the Longacre Theatre. Opened March 11, 2007.

Sid Greenberg	Adam Sietz	Barry Champlain	Liev Schreiber
Bernie	Cornell Womack	Dan Woodruff	Peter Hermann
Spike	Kit Williamson	Jordan Grant	Christy Pusz
Stu Noonan	Michael Laurence	Kent	Sebastian Stan
Linda MacArthur	Stephanie March	Dr. Susan Fleming	Barbara Rosenblat
Vince Farber	Marc Thompson	Rachael	Christine Pedi

Callers' Voices: Christine Pedi, Christy Pusz, Barbara Rosenblat, Adam Sietz, Marc Thompson, Cornell Womack.

Standby: Mr. Schreiber—Michael Laurence.

Understudies: Mr. Hermann—Michael Laurence, Lee Sellars; Mr. Laurence—Lee Sellars, Cornell Womack; Mses. March, Pedi—Christy Pusz; Mr. Stan—Kit Williamson; Mr. Williamson—Lee Sellars; Messrs. Sietz, Womack, Thompson—Oliver Vaquer; Ms. Rosenblat—Christine Pedi; Male Callers—Adam Sietz, Marc Thompson, Oliver Vaquer, Cornell Womack; Female Callers—Christine Pedi, Christy Pusz, Barbara Rosenblat.

Directed by Robert Falls; scenery, Mark Wendland; costumes, Laura Bauer; lighting, Christopher Akerlind; sound, Richard Woodbury; casting, Telsey and Company; production stage manager, Jane Grey; press, Jeffrey Richards Associates, Irene Gandy, Mark Barber, Matt Greenstein, Nicole Lee, Elon Rutberg.

Time: Spring 1987. Place: Studio B, WTLK radio in Cleveland. Presented without intermission. First New York presentation of record was given Off Broadway in the Public Theater's Martinson Hall (5/28–11/29/1987; 210 performances). First presentation of record was given in 1985 at the Portland Center for the Visual Arts. The 2006–07 production was the first Broadway production. It was, however, considered a revival due to its substantial earlier run Off Broadway.

*Curtains (81). Musical with book by Rupert Holmes and Peter Stone; music by John Kander; lyrics by Fred Ebb, Mr. Kander and Mr. Holmes. Produced by Roger Berlind, Roger Horchow, Daryl Roth, Jane Bergère, Ted Hartley, Center Theatre Group, at the Al Hirschfeld Theatre. Opened March 22, 2007.

Jessica Cranshaw	Patty Goble	Bambi Bernét	Megan Sikora
Randy Dexter	Jim Newman	Bobby Pepper	Noah Racey
Niki Harris	Jill Paice	Johnny Harmon	Michael X. Martin

Showstopper: Debra Monk and company in Curtains. *Photo: Joan Marcus*

Georgia Hendricks .... Karen Ziemba	Daryl Grady .... John Bolton
Aaron Fox .... Jason Danieley	Sasha Iljinsky .... David Loud
Carmen Bernstein .... Debra Monk	Marjorie Cook .... Paula Leggett Chase
Oscar Shapiro .... Michael McCormick	Arlene Barruca .... Nili Bassman
Christopher Belling .... Edward Hibbert	Roy Stetson .... Kevin Bernard
Lt. Frank Cioffi .... David Hyde Pierce	Brick Hawvermale .... Ward Billeisen
Mona Page .... Mary Ann Lamb	Jan Setler .... Jennifer Dunne
Harv Fremont .... Matt Farnsworth	Connie Subbotin .... Patty Goble
Roberta Wooster .... Darcie Roberts	Peg Prentice .... Brittany Marcin
Sidney Bernstein .... Ernie Sabella	Ronnie Driscoll .... Joe Aaron Reid
Detective O'Farrell .... Kevin Bernard	Russ Cochran .... Christopher Spaulding

Orchestra: David Loud conductor; Steven Kenyon flute, piccolo, clarinet, alto sax; Al Hunt oboe, English horn, clarinet, tenor sax; Owen Kotler clarinet, alto sax, soprano sax; Mark Thrasher bassoon, bass clarinet, baritone sax, flute, clarinet; R.J. Kelley, French horn 1; Angela Cordell, French horn 2; Don Downs trumpet 1; Matt Peterson trumpet 2; Charles Gordon trombone 1; Jennifer Wharton bass trombone, tuba; Greg Utzig acoustic guitar, electric guitar, banjo, classical guitar; Robert Renino acoustic bass; Sam Davis associate music director, piano, synthesizer; Greg Landes percussion; Bruce Doctor drums.

Understudies: Messrs. Hyde Pierce, Hibbert—Kevin Bernard; Ms. Paice—Nili Bassman, Allison Spratt; Ms. Sikora—Ashley Amber, Jennifer Dunne; Mr. Danieley—Kevin Bernard, Matt Farnsworth; Mr. Bolton—Matt Farnsworth, Michael X. Martin; Ms. Monk—Paula Leggett Chase, Patty Goble; Messrs. McCormick, Sabella—Michael X. Martin, Jerome Vivona; Mr. Martin—Jim Newman, Jerome Vivona; Mr. Racey—Ward Billeisen, David Eggers, Jim Newman; Mses. Ziemba, Goble—Paula Leggett Chase, Darcie Roberts.

Swings: Ashley Amber, David Eggers, J. Austin Eyer, Allison Spratt, Jerome Vivona.

Directed by Scott Ellis; choreography, Rob Ashford; scenery, Anna Louizos; costumes, William Ivey Long; lighting, Peter Kaczorowski; sound, Brian Ronan; flying, Paul Rubin; wigs and hair,

Annus horribilis: *Vanessa Redgrave in* The Year of Magical Thinking. *Photo: Joan Marcus*

Paul Huntley; fight direction, Rick Sordelet; orchestrations, William David Brohn; vocal orchestrations and music direction, Mr. Loud; music coordination, John Monaco; associate producers, Barbara and Peter Fodor; casting, Jim Carnahan; production stage manager, Beverley Randolph; press, Boneau/Bryan-Brown, Chris Boneau, Jim Byk, Juliana Hannett, Matt Ross.

Time: 1959. Place: The Colonial Theatre, Boston. Presented in two parts.

When the hated leading lady of *Robbin' Hood!* is murdered as the show prepares for Broadway, everyone has a motive—including the theater critic. First presentation of record was given under the aegis of Center Theatre Group in Los Angeles at the Ahmanson Theatre (8/9–9/10/2006). At the 2007 Tony Awards, Mr. Hyde Pierce was honored for best actor in a musical.

ACT I

"Wide Open Spaces"	Randy, Niki, Jessica, Bobby, Ensemble
"What Kind of Man?"	Carmen, Oscar, Aaron, Georgia
"Thinking of Him"	Georgia, Aaron, Bobby
"The Woman's Dead"	Company
"Show People"	Carmen, Cioffi, Company
"Coffee Shop Nights"	Cioffi
"In the Same Boat 1"	Georgia, Niki, Bambi
"I Miss the Music"	Aaron
"Thataway!"	Georgia, Bobby, Ensemble

ACT II

"He Did It"	Company
"In the Same Boat 2"	Bobby, Randy, Harv
"It's a Business"	Carmen, Stagehands
"Kansasland"	Randy, Niki, Harv, Bobby, Bambi, Ensemble
"Thinking of Him" / "I Miss the Music" (Reprise)	Aaron, Georgia

"A Tough Act to Follow" .... Cioffi, Niki, Ensemble
"In the Same Boat 3" .... Company
"A Tough Act to Follow" (Reprise) .... Company

*The Year of Magical Thinking (64). Solo performance piece by Joan Didion; based on her memoir. Produced by Scott Rudin, Roger Berlind, Debra Black, Daryl Roth, The Shubert Organization at the Booth Theatre. Opened March 29, 2007.

Joan Didion .... Vanessa Redgrave

> Standby: Ms. Redgrave—Maureen Anderman.

> Directed by David Hare; scenery, Bob Crowley; costumes, Ann Roth; lighting, Jean Kalman; sound, Paul Arditti; executive producers, Stuart Thompson, John Barlow; production stage manager, Karen Armstrong; press, Boneau/Bryan-Brown, Chris Boneau, Steven Padla, Heath Schwartz.

> Presented without intermission.

> Monologue on the coping process undergone by Ms. Didion after the deaths of her husband, John Gregory Dunne, and her daughter, Quintana Dunne Michael.

*The Pirate Queen (65). Musical with book by Alain Boublil, Claude-Michel Schönberg, Richard Maltby Jr.; music by Mr. Schönberg; lyrics by Messrs. Boublil, Maltby Jr. and John Dempsey; based on the novel *Grania: She-King of the Irish Seas* by Morgan Llywelyn. Produced by Riverdream (Moya Doherty, John McColgan) at the Hilton Theatre. Opened April 5, 2007.

Grace O'Malley .... Stephanie J. Block	Donal O'Flaherty .... Marcus Chait
Tiernan .... Hadley Fraser	Chieftain O'Flaherty .... Joseph Mahowald
Dubhdara .... Jeff McCarthy	Majella .... Brooke Elliott
Evleen .... Áine Uí Cheallaigh	Eoin .... Christopher Grey Misa,
Elizabeth I .... Linda Balgord	Steven Barath
Sir Richard Bingham .... William Youmans	

> Ensemble: Nick Adams, Richard Todd Adams, Caitlin Allen, Sean Beglan, Jerad Bortz, Troy Edward Bowles, Grady McLeod Bowman, Alexis Ann Carra, Noelle Curran, Bobbie Ann Dunn, Brooke Elliott, Christopher Garbrecht, Eric Hatch, Cristin J. Hubbard, David Koch, Timothy Kochka, Jamie LaVerdiere, Joseph Mahowald, Tokiko Masuda, Padraic Moyles, Brian O'Brien, Kyle James O'Connor, Michael James Scott, Greg Stone, Katie Erin Tomlinson, Daniel Torres, Jennifer Waiser, Briana Yacavone.

> Orchestra: Julian Kelly conductor; Joshua Rosenblum assistant conductor, keyboard 2; Liz Knowles fiddle, violin; Kenneth Edge soprano sax, clarinet; Jeff Nelson horn; Steve Roberts guitars, banjo; Michael Pearce electric bass; Kieran O'Hare, Uilleann pipes, whistles; Brian Connor keyboard I; Dave Roth percussion; Frank Pagano drums, bodhran; Kirsten Agresta harp, Gaelic harp.

> Standby: Ms. Block—Kathy Voytko.

> Understudies: Ms. Block—Katie Erin Tomlinson; Mr. Fraser—Jamie LaVerdiere, Greg Stone, Daniel Torres; Ms. Balgord—Kimilee Bryant, Cristin J. Hubbard; Mr. Chait—Richard Todd Adams, Daniel Torres; Mr. Youmans—Richard Todd Adams, Joseph Mahowald; Mr. McCarthy—Christopher Garbrecht, Joseph Mahowald; Ms. Cheallaigh—Brooke Elliott, Cristin J. Hubbard; Ms. Elliott—Kimilee Bryant, Cristin J. Hubbard; Mr. Mahowald—Don Brewer, Brian O'Brien, Jeff Williams.

> Swings: Timothy W. Bish, Rachel Bress, Don Brewer, Kimilee Bryant.

> Directed by Frank Galati; choreography, Graciela Daniele, Carol Leavy Joyce, Mark Dendy; scenery, Eugene Lee; costumes, Martin Pakledinaz; lighting, Kenneth Posner; sound, Jonathan Deans; special effects, Gregory Meeh; flying, Paul Rubin; wigs and hair, Paul Huntley; fight direction; J. Steven White; orchestrations, vocal arrangments, music supervision and direction, Mr. Kelly, music coordination, Sam Lutfiyya; executive producers, Edgar Dobie, Ronan Smith; associate producer; Dancap Productions, Inc.; casting, Tara Rubin Casting; production stage manager, C. Randall White; press, Boneau/Bryan-Brown, Adrian Bryan-Brown, Matt Polk, Adriana Douzos, Jessica Johnson.

Time: Late 16th century. Place: Ireland and England. Presented in two parts.

Musical tale of a seafaring Irish woman who stakes a claim to leadership among her people and struggles against the forces of another formidable female, Elizabeth I. First presentation of record was given at the Cadillac Palace Theatre in Chicago (10/29/2006).

ACT I

Prologue .... Grace, Tiernan
Scene 1: "The Pirate Queen" .... Dubhdara, Tiernan, Grace,
Evleen, Oarsmen, Company
"Woman" .... Grace
Scene 2: "The Storm" .... Company
"My Grace" .... Dubhdara, Grace
Scene 3: "Here on This Night" .... Grace, Tiernan, Crew
Scene 4: "The First Battle" .... Grace, Tiernan,
Dubhdara, Company
Scene 5: "The Waking of the Queen" .... Elizabeth, Ladies-in-Waiting
"Rah-Rah, Tip-Top" .... Elizabeth, Bingham,
Lords, Ladies-in-Waiting
Scene 6: "The Choice Is Mine" .... Grace, Dubhdara, Chieftain,
Tiernan, Donal, Company
"The Bride's Song" .... Grace, Evleen, Women
Scene 7: "Boys'll Be Boys" .... Donal, Mates, Barmaids
Scene 8: "The Wedding" .... Grace, Tiernan, Donal, Dubhdara,
Chieftain, Evleen, Company
Scene 9: "I'll Be There" .... Tiernan
Scene 10: "Boys'll Be Boys" (Reprise) .... Donal, Mates, Grace, Chieftain
Scene 11: "Trouble at Rockfleet" .... Grace, Tiernan, Donal,
Bingham, Company
Scene 12: "A Day Beyond Belclare" .... Grace, Tiernan, Donal, Company
Scene 13: "Go Serve Your Queen" .... Elizabeth, Bingham
Scene 14: "Dubhdara's Farewell" .... Dubhdara, Grace
"Sail to the Stars" .... Grace, Tiernan, Donal,
Evleen, Company

ACT II

Entr'Acte
Scene 1: "It's a Boy" .... Grace, Tiernan, Donal,
Evleen, Majella, Sailors
Scene 2: "Enemy at Port Side" .... Grace, Tiernan, Donal,
Evleen, Majella, Sailors
"I Dismiss You" .... Grace, Donal, Sailors
Scene 3: "If I Said I Loved You" .... Tiernan, Grace
Scene 4: "The Role of the Queen" .... Elizabeth, Bingham,
Lords, Ladies-in-Waiting
Scene 5: "The Christening" .... Evleen, Grace,
Tiernan, Company
"Let a Father Stand by His Son" .... Donal, Grace, Bingham,
Tiernan, Evleen, Company
Scene 6: "Surrender" .... Bingham, Tiernan,
Elizabeth, Company
Scene 7: "She Who Has All" .... Elizabeth, Grace
Scene 8: "Lament" .... Grace, Majella, Eoin, Company
Scene 9: "The Sea of Life" .... Grace, Company
Scene 10: "Terra Marique Potens" .... Elizabeth, Grace, Bingham
"Woman to Woman" .... Elizabeth, Grace
"Behind the Screen" .... Company
"Grace's Exit" .... Elizabeth, Grace,
Bingham, Company
Scene 11: "Finale" .... Grace, Tiernan, Company

Before the fall: Eve Best and Kevin Spacey in A Moon for the Misbegotten. *Photo: Simon Annand*

*A Moon for the Misbegotten (59). Revival of the play by Eugene O'Neill. Produced by Elliot Martin, Max Cooper, Ben Sprecher, Nica Burns, Max Weitzenhoffer, The Old Vic, Spring Sirkin, Wendy Federman, Louise Forlenza, Ian Osborne, Thomas Steven Perakos, James L. Nederlander, at the Brooks Atkinson Theatre. Opened April 9, 2007.

Josie Hogan	Eve Best	Jim Tyrone	Kevin Spacey
Mike Hogan	Eugene O'Hare	T. Stedman Harder	Billy Carter
Phil Hogan	Colm Meaney		

Understudies: Ms. Best—Kati Brazda; Mr. Meaney—Billy Carter; Messrs. O'Hare, Carter—Nick Westrate.

Directed by Howard Davies; scenery, Bob Crowley; costumes, Lynette Mauro; lighting, Mark Henderson; sound, Christopher Shutt; music, Dominic Muldowney; casting, Maggie Lunn, Stuart Howard Associates; production stage manager, Bruce A. Hoover; press, Barlow-Hartman, John Barlow, Michael Hartman, Dennis Crowley, Michelle Bergmann.

Time: September 1923. Place: A farm in Connecticut. Presented in two parts.

An tortured drunk carries dark secrets to a raw farm woman whom he teases and cajoles. A 1956–57 *Best Plays* choice, the original Broadway production opened at the Bijou Theatre (5/2–6/29/1957; 68 performances) with Franchot Tone, Wendy Hiller and Cyril Cusack. Including the 2006–07 production, there have been four Broadway revivals of the play. First presentation of record was given under the aegis of the Theatre Guild at the Hartman Theatre in Columbus, Ohio, before stops in Cleveland, Pittsburgh, Detroit and St. Louis (2/20–3/29/1947). The play shocked audiences in Pittsburgh and was briefly closed by censors in Detroit until minor changes to the script were made; it would be 10 years before the play made its Broadway bow.

*Inherit the Wind (56). Revival of the play by Jerome Lawrence and Robert E. Lee. Produced by Boyett Ostar Productions, The Shubert Organization, Lawrence Horowitz, Jon Avnet, Ralph Guild, Roy Furman, Debra Black, Daryl Roth, Bill Rollnick, Nancy Ellison Rollnick, Stephanie P. McClelland, at the Lyceum Theatre. Opened April 12, 2007.

Howard	Conor Donovan	Rachel	Maggie Lacey
Melinda	Amanda Sprecher	Mr. Meeker	Scott Sowers

Bert Cates	Benjamin Walker	E.K. Hornbeck	Denis O'Hare
Mr. Goodfellow	Henry Stram	Monkey Man	Kevin C. Loomis
Mrs. Krebs	Charlotte Maier	Matthew Harrison Brady	Brian Dennehy
Rev. Jeremiah Brown	Byron Jennings	Mrs. Brady	Beth Fowler
Sillers	Andrew Weems	Mayor	Jeff Steitzer
Dunlap	Jay Patterson	Judge	Terry Beaver
Bannister	Bill Buell	Tom Davenport	Jordan Lage
Mrs. Loomis	Anne Bowles	Photographer	Randall Newsome
Mrs. Blair	Pippa Pearthree	Henry Drummond	Christopher Plummer
Vendor	Bill Christ	Reuters Reporter;	
Elijah	Raynor Scheine	Esterbrook	Erik Steele
Timmy	Matthew Nardozzi		

Gospel Quartet: Carson Church, Katie Klaus, Mary Kate Law, David M. Lutken.

Townspeople: Anne Bowles, Steve Brady, Bill Christ, Kit Flanagan, Sherman Howard, Philip LeStrange, Kevin C. Loomis, Charlotte Maier, Matthew Nardozzi, Randall Newsome, Jay Patterson, Pippa Pearthree, Erik Steele, Andrew Weems.

Understudies: Mr. Plummer—Sherman Howard; Mr. Dennehy—Jeff Steitzer; Mr. O'Hare—Jordan Lage; Ms. Lacey—Anne Bowles; Messrs. Sowers, Steele—Kevin C. Loomis; Messrs. Walker, Newsome—Erik Steele; Messrs. Stram, Jennings—Bill Christ; Mses. Pearthree, Fowler, Maier—Kit Flanagan; Messrs. Weems, Patterson, Scheine—Steve Brady; Messrs. Buell, Steitzer, Beaver—Philip LeStrange; Mr. Loomis—Sherman Howard; Mr. Donovan, Ms. Sprecher—Matthew Nardozzi.

Directed by Doug Hughes; scenery and costumes, Santo Loquasto; lighting, Brian MacDevitt; sound and music; David Van Tieghem; wigs and hair, Paul Huntley; associate producer, Judith Resnick; casting, Jay Binder, Jack Bowdan; production stage manager, Michael Brunner; press, Boneau/Bryan-Brown, Adrian Bryan-Brown, Jackie Green, Danielle Crinnion.

Time: Summer, not too long ago. Place: A small town. Presented in two parts.

Cultural icons: Christopher Plummer and Brian Dennehy in Inherit the Wind. *Photo: Joan Marcus*

Bated breath: Remy Auberjonois, Michael Sheen, Armand Schultz and Stephen Kunken in Frost/Nixon. *Photo: Joan Marcus*

Two titans of American culture engage in a battle pitting religious faith against scientific inquiry in an echo of the "Scopes Monkey Trial" of 1925. A 1954–55 *Best Plays* choice, the original Broadway production opened at the National Theatre (4/21/1955–6/22/1957; 806 performances). Due to its late opening in spring 1955, *Inherit the Wind* received consideration for the 1956 Tony Awards, where it received honors for actor in a play (Paul Muni), featured actor in a play (Ed Begley) and scenery (Peter Larkin). The 2006–07 production was the second Broadway revival. First presentation of record was given by Margo Jones at Dallas's Theatre '55 (1/10/1955).

Frost/Nixon (45). By Peter Morgan. Produced by Arielle Tepper Madover, Matthew Byam Shaw, Robert Fox, Act Productions, David Binder, Debra Black, Annette Niemtzow, Harlene Freezer, The Weinstein Company, in association with Donmar Warehouse (Michael Grandage artistic director, Lucy Davies executive producer), at the Bernard B. Jacobs Theatre. Opened April 22, 2007.

Richard Nixon .... Frank Langella
Jim Reston .... Stephen Kunken
David Frost .... Michael Sheen
Jack Brennan .... Corey Johnson
Evonne Goolagong .... Shira Gregory
John Birt .... Remy Auberjonois
Manolo Sanchez .... Triney Sandoval

Swifty Lazar;
  Mike Wallace .... Stephen Rowe
Caroline Cushing .... Sonya Walger
Bob Zelnick .... Armand Schultz
Ensemble .... Dennis Cockrum,
                                         Antony Hagopian,
                                         Roxanna Hope

Understudies: Mr. Langella—Bob Ari; Mr. Sheen—Remy Auberjonois; Messrs. Rowe, Schultz, Sandoval—Dennis Cockrum; Messrs. Auberjonois, Johnson, Sandoval—Antony Hagopian; Mses. Gregory, Walger—Roxanna Hope, Mr. Kunken—Triney Sandoval.

Directed by Michael Grandage; scenery and costumes, Christopher Oram; lighting, Neil Austin; sound and music, Adam Cork; video, Jon Driscoll; wigs and hair, Richard Mawbey; casting,

Daniel Swee; production stage manager, Rick Steiger; press, Boneau/Bryan-Brown, Adrian Bryan-Brown, Steven Padla, Heath Schwartz.

Time: The 1974–77. Place: Washington, Sydney, London, Southern California, New York, Baltimore. Presented without intermission.

A disgraced ex-president attempts to profit politically (and financially) when facing an interviewer who is believed to lack intellectual heft. First presentation of record was given at London's Donmar Warehouse (8/21–10/7/2006) before a run at the West End's Gielgud Theatre (11/16/2006–2/3/2007). A 2006–07 *Best Plays* choice (see essay by Charles McNulty in this volume).

*Legally Blonde (36). Musical with book by Heather Hach; music and lyrics by Laurence O'Keefe and Nell Benjamin; based on the novel by Amanda Brown and the MGM film. Produced by Hal Luftig, Fox Theatricals (Kristin Caskey, Mike Isaacson), Dori Berinstein, James L. Nederlander, Independent Presenters Network, Roy Furman, Amanda Lipitz, Broadway Asia, Barbara Whitman, FWPM Group, Hendel/Wiesenfeld, Goldberg/Binder, Stern/Meyer, Lane/Comley, Bartner-Jenkins/Nocciolino, Warren Trepp, in association with MGM On Stage, Darcie Denkert and Dean Stolber, at the Palace Theatre. Opened April 29, 2007.

Elle Woods .... Laura Bell Bundy	Shandi;
Warner Huntington III .... Richard H. Blake	Brooke Wyndham .... Nikki Snelson
Vivienne Kensington .... Kate Shindle	Kate; Chutney .... Kate Wetherhead
Emmett Forrest .... Christian Borle	Leilani .... Becky Gulsvig
Professor Callahan .... Michael Rupert	Cece .... Michelle Kittrell
Paulette .... Orfeh	Kristine .... April Berry
Serena .... Leslie Kritzer	Gabby .... Beth Curry
Margot .... Annaleigh Ashford	Veronica; Enid .... Natalie Joy Johnson
Pilar .... DeQuina Moore	Judge .... Amber Efé

School daze: Laura Bell Bundy and Christian Borle in Legally Blonde. *Photo: Paul Kolnik*

Mom; Whitney .... Gaelen Gilliland
Grandmaster Chad;
  Dewey; Kyle .... Andy Karl
Dad; Winthrop .... Kevin Pariseau
Carlos .... Matthew Risch

Padamadan; Nikos .... Manuel Herrera
Aaron; Guard .... Noah Weisberg
Bruiser .... Chico
Rufus .... Chloe

Ensemble: April Berry, Paul Canaan, Beth Curry, Amber Efé, Gaelen Gilliland, Jason Gillman, Becky Gulsvig, Manuel Herrera, Natalie Joy Johnson, Andy Karl, Nick Kenkel, Michelle Kittrell, Kevin Pariseau, Matthew Risch, Jason Patrick Sands, Noah Weisberg, Kate Wetherhead.

Orchestra: James Sampliner conductor, keyboard 1; Jason DeBord associate conductor, keyboard; Antoine Silverman concertmaster; Jonathan Dinklage viola; Peter Sachon, cello; Mark Vanderpoel bass; Vincent DellaRocca reed 1; Dan Willis reed 2; Chad Smith reed 3; Dave Trigg lead trumpet; Bud Burridge trumpet; Keith O'Quinn trombone; Roger Wendt, French horn; John Putnam, Kenny Brescia guitar; Matt Gallagher keyboard; Pablo Rieppi percussion, Greg Joseph drums.

Understudies: Ms. Bundy—Annaleigh Ashford, Becky Gulsvig; Mr. Borle—Andy Karl, Noah Weisberg; Mr. Rupert—Andy Karl, Kevin Pariseau; Orfeh—Amber Efé, Gaelen Gilliland; Mr. Blake—Jason Gillman, Matthew Risch; Ms. Shindle—Tracy Jai Edwards, Gaelen Gilliland; Ms. Snelson—Beth Curry, Michelle Kittrell.

Swings: Lindsay Nicole Chambers, Tracy Jai Edwards, Rusty Mowery, Rod Harrelson.

Directed and choreographed by Jerry Mitchell; scenery, David Rockwell; costumes, Gregg Barnes; lighting, Kenneth Posner and Paul Miller; sound, Acme Sound Partners; wigs and hair, David Brian Brown; orchestrations, Christopher Jahnke; arrangements, Mr. O'Keefe and Mr. Sampliner; music direction, Mr. Sampliner; music coordination, Michael Keller; associate producers, PMC Productions, Yasuhiro Kawana, Andrew Asnes, Adam Zotovich; casting, Telsey and Company; production stage manager, Bonnie L. Becker; press, Barlow-Hartman, Michael Hartman, John Barlow, Carol Fineman, Kevin Robak.

Time: The present. Place: Delta Nu sorority in Southern California; Harvard Law School in Cambridge. Presented in two parts.

Musical tale of a shallow, consumerist young woman who evolves into a clever law student. Based largely on the successful 2001 film starring Reese Witherspoon. First presentation of record was given at San Francisco's Golden Gate Theatre (2/6/2007).

ACT I

Scene 1: UCLA Delta Nu Sorority House; Mall; Elle's Door
  "Omigod You Guys" .... Margot, Serena, Pilar, Delta Nus,
                                                                                                    Elle, Shopgirl, Manager
Scene 2: Restaurant
  "Serious" .... Warner, Ellie
Scene 3: Delta Nu Sorority House; Golf Course; Harvard Law School Admissions Office
  "Daughter of Delta Nu" .... Margot, Serena, Pilar, Kate, Delta Nus
  "What You Want" .... Elle, Margot, Serena, Pilar, Kate,
                                                                                Mom, Dad, Grandmaster Chad, Winthrop,
                                                                                Pforzheimer, Lowell, Delta Nus, Company
Scene 4: Harvard Yard
  "The Harvard Variations" .... Emmett, Aaron, Enid,
                                                                                        Padamadan, Harvard Students
Scene 5: Callahan's Classroom
  "Blood in the Water" .... Callahan, Company
Scene 6: Harvard Yard
  "Positive" .... Elle, Margot, Serena, Pilar, Greek Chorus
Scene 7: The Hair Affair
  "Ireland" .... Paulette
  "Ireland" (Reprise) .... Paulette
Scene 8: Harvard Party
  "Serious" (Reprise) .... Elle, Warner

Scene 9: Harvard Yard; Elle's Room; Callahan's Classroom
"Chip on My Shoulder" ....Emmett, Elle, Greek Chorus, Company
Scene 10: Dewey's Trailer
Scene 11: Harvard Hallway
"So Much Better" .... Elle, Greek Chorus, Company

ACT II

Scene 1: Conference Room of Hearne, Fox, Zyskowski and Callahan; Women's Prison
"Whipped Into Shape" .... Brooke, Callahan, Company
Scene 2: Hansen-Harkness Department Store
"Take It Like a Man" ....Elle, Emmett, Salespersons
Scene 3: The Hair Affair
"Bend and Snap" .... Elle, Paulette, Serena, Margot, Pilar, Salonfolk
Scene 4: Courtroom
"There! Right There!" .... Elle, Callahan, Emmett, Brooke,
Vivienne, Warner, Enid, Judge,
Nikos, Carlos, Company
Scene 5: Callahan's Office; Elle's Door
"Legally Blonde" .... Elle, Emmett
Scene 6: The Hair Affair
"Legally Blonde Remix" .... Vivienne, Enid, Elle, Company
Scene 7: Courtroom; Bathroom of the Wyndham Mansion
"Omigod You Guys" (Reprise) .... Elle, Company
Scene 8: Harvard Law Graduation
"Find My Way"; "Finale" .... Elle, Paulette, Company

Coram Boy (30). By Helen Edmundson; adapted from the novel by Jamila Gavin. Produced by Boyett Ostar Productions, The Shubert Organization, Roy Furman, Lawrence Horowitz, Stephanie P. McClelland, Debra Black, Daryl Roth, Eric Falkenstein, Ralph Guild, Elan McAllister, Allan S. Gordon, in association with Jamie deRoy, Jam Theatricals, CPI Entertainment, Harriet Leve, Ron Nicynski, Laurence Braun, Bill Rollnick, Nancy Ellison Rollnick, the National Theatre (UK), at the Imperial Theatre. Opened May 2, 2007. (Closed May 27, 2007)

Act I (1742)

Meshak Gardiner .... Brad Fleischer	Lady Ashbrook .... Christina Rouner
Angel .... Ivy Vahanian	Isobel Ashbrook .... Karron Graves
Dr. Smith .... Quentin Maré	Mrs. Milcote .... Kathleen McNenny
Young Thomas Ledbury .... Charlotte Parry	Melissa .... Ivy Vahanian
Young Alexander Ashbrook .... Xanthe Elbrick	Edward Ashbrook .... Laura Heisler
Otis Gardiner .... Bill Camp	Alice Ashbrook .... Cristin Milioti
Mrs. Lynch .... Jan Maxwell	Lord Ashbrook ...... David Andrew Macdonald
Miss Price .... Angela Lin	Adult Alexander Ashbrook ...... Wayne Wilcox
Mr. Claymore .... Tom Riis Farrell	

Act II (1750)

Mrs. Hendry .... Jacqueline Antaramian	Molly ....Jolly Abraham
Philip Gaddarn .... Bill Camp	Handel .... Quentin Maré
Toby .... Uzo Aduba	Adult Thomas Ledbury .... Dashiell Eaves
Aaron .... Xanthe Elbrick	

Choir: Philip Anderson, John Arbo, Sean Attebury, Renée Brna, Charlotte Cohn, Sean Cullen, Katie Geissinger, Zachary James, Tinashe Kajese, bj Karpen, Katherine Keyes, Evangelia Kingsley, Eric William Morris, Daniel Neer, Nina Negri, Mark Rehnstrom, Martin Solá, Samantha Soule, Alison Weller, Gregory Wright.

Orchestra: Constantine Kitsopoulos conductor, keyboard; Chip Prince associate conductor, keyboard; Dale Stuckenbruck, Elizabeth Lim-Dutton violin; Maxine Roach viola; Deborah Assael cello; Judith Sugarman bass.

Understudies: Messrs. Fleischer, Eaves, Wilcox—Eric William Morris, Mses. Vahanian, Graves, Milioti—Samantha Soule, Mses. Parry, Elbrick, Heisler—Renée Brna; Messrs. Camp, Macdonald, Farrell, Maré—Sean Cullen; Mses. Maxwell, Rouner, Antaramian, McNenny—Alison Weller; Mses. Lin, Aduba, Abraham—Tinashe Kajese.

Directed by Melly Still; scenery and costumes, Ti Green and Ms. Still; lighting, Paule Constable and Ed McCarthy; sound, Christopher Shutt and Acme Sound Partners; music, Adrian Sutton; wigs and hair, David H. Lawrence; fight direction, Thomas Schall; additional arrangements, Derek Barnes; music direction, Mr. Kitsopoulos; music coordination, John Miller; casting, Stanczyk/Cherpakov Casting; production stage manager, Kim Vernace; press, Boneau/Bryan-Brown, Adrian Bryan-Brown, Joe Perrotta, Ian Bjorklund.

Time: 1742; 1750. Place: England. Presented in two parts.

A Dickensian tale, based on a 2000 juvenile novel, of impoverished foundlings who struggle to survive amid the oppression of 18th century aristocratic wealth and privilege. First presentation of record was given at the National Theatre's Olivier (11/15/2005–2/4/2006, in repertory). It returned to the same theater for another holiday engagement the following season (11/29/06–2/22/07) before its debut on Broadway.

*Manhattan Theatre Club production of **LoveMusik** (32). Musical with book by Alfred Uhry; music by Kurt Weill; lyrics by Maxwell Anderson, Bertolt Brecht, Howard Dietz, Roger Fernay, Ira Gershwin, Oscar Hammerstein II, Langston Hughes, Alan Jay Lerner, Maurice Magre, Ogden Nash, Elmer Rice, Mr. Weill; based on the letters of Mr. Weill and Lotte Lenya. Lynne Meadow artistic director, Barry Grove executive producer, in association with Marty Bell, Aldo Scrofani, Boyett Ostar Productions, Tracy Aron, Roger Berlind, Debra Black, Chase Mishkin, Ted Snowdon, at the Biltmore Theatre. Opened May 3, 2007.

Kurt Weill	Michael Cerveris	Bertolt Brecht	David Pittu
Lotte Lenya	Donna Murphy	George Davis	John Scherer

Love boat: Michael Cerveris and Donna Murphy in LoveMusik. *Photo: Carol Rosegg*

Magistrate; Judge	Herndon Lackey	Interviewer	Erik Liberman
Court Secretary	Rachel Ulanet	Otto	Graham Rowat
Brecht's Women	Judith Blazer,	Tilly Losch	Judith Blazer
	Ann Morrison,	Photographer	Ann Morrison
	Rachel Ulanet	Allen Lake	Graham Rowat
Auditioners	Herndon Lackey,	Handyman	Erik Liberman
	Rachel Ulanet		

Orchestra: Nicholas Archer conductor, piano; Stan Tucker associate conductor; Katherine Livolsi-Landau, Suzy Perelman, violin; David Blinn viola; Mairi Dorman cello; Jeffrey Cooper bass, James Ercole, John Winder woodwinds; Christian Jaudes trumpet; Billy Miller drums, percussion.

Understudies: Messrs. Cerveris, Pittu—Edwin Cahill; Mr. Pittu—Erik Liberman; Ms. Murphy—Ann Morrison; Mr. Scherer—Graham Rowat.

Swings: Edwin Cahill, Jessica Wright.

Directed by Harold Prince; choreography, Patricia Birch; scenery, Beowulf Boritt; costumes, Judith Dolan; lighting, Howell Binkley; sound, Duncan Robert Edwards; wigs and hair, Paul Huntley; orchestrations, Jonathan Tunick; additional vocal arrangements, Milton Granger; music supervision, Kristen Blodgette; music coordination, Seymour Red Press; casting, Mark Simon; production stage manager, Joshua Halperin; press, Boneau/Bryan-Brown, Chris Boneau, Jim Byk, Aaron Meier, Heath Schwartz, Christine Olver.

Time: 1924–54. Place Europe and the US. Presented in two parts.

The complex relationship of Kurt Weill and Lotte Lenya—replete with betrayals caused and experienced by two great artists of the stage—demonstrated through his songs and her performance of them.

ACT I (EUROPE)

Author of lyrics in parentheses below song titles.

"Speak Low" .... Weill, Lenya
(Ogden Nash)

"Nana's Lied" .... Woman on Stairs
(Bertolt Brecht)

"Kiddush" .... Weill's Family
(Kurt Weill)

"Song of the Rhineland" .... Lenya's Family
(Ira Gershwin)

"Klops Lied" (Meatball Song) .... Weill
(Kurt Weill)

"Berlin Im Licht" .... Lenya
(Kurt Weill)

"Wooden Wedding" .... Weill, Lenya, Magistrate, Court Secretary
(Ogden Nash)

"Tango Ballad" .... Brecht, Brecht's Women
(Bertolt Brecht)

"Alabama Song" .... Auditioners, Lenya
(Bertolt Brecht)

"Girl of the Moment" .... Company
(Ira Gershwin)

"Moritat" .... Brecht, Lenya, Otto, Company
(Bertolt Brecht)

"Schickelgruber" .... Weill, Brecht
(Howard Dietz)

"Come to Paris" .... Company
(Ira Gershwin)

"I Don't Love You" .... Weill, Lenya
(Maurice Magre)

"Lust" .... Lenya
(Kurt Weill)

"Wouldn't You Like to Be on Broadway?" .... Weill, Lenya
                (Langston Hughes and Elmer Rice)
"Alabama Song" (Reprise) .... Lenya, Weill, Brecht, Company
                (Bertolt Brecht)

ACT II (AMERICA)

"How Can You Tell An American?" .... Company
                (Maxwell Anderson)
"Very, Very, Very" .... Weill
                (Ogden Nash)
"It's Never Too Late to Mendelssohn" .... Weill, Lenya, Stenographer, Judge
                (Ira Gershwin)
"Surabaya Johnny" .... Lenya
                (Bertolt Brecht)
"Youkali" .... Brecht, Brecht's Women
                (Roger Fernay)
"Buddy on the Night Shift" .... Allen
                (Oscar Hammerstein II)
"That's Him" .... Weill
                (Ogden Nash)
"Hosannah Rockefeller" .... Brecht, Brecht's Women
                (Bertolt Brecht)
"I Don't Love You" (Reprise) .... Lenya, Weill
                (Maurice Magre)
"The Illusion Wedding Show" .... Davis, Company
                (Alan Jay Lerner)
"It Was Never You" .... Weill
                (Maxwell Anderson)
"Bird of Passage" .... Company
                (Maxwell Anderson)
"September Song" .... Lenya, Davis
                (Maxwell Anderson)

*Deuce (29). By Terrence McNally. Produced by Scott Rudin, Stuart Thompson, Maberry Theatricals, The Shubert Organization, Roger Berlind, Debra Black, Bob Boyett, Susan Dietz, Daryl Roth at the Music Box. Opened May 6, 2007.

An Admirer .... Michael Mulheren   Ryan Becker .... Brian Haley
Midge Barker .... Marian Seldes   Kelly Short ....Joanna P. Adler
Leona Mullen .... Angela Lansbury

Standbys: Ms. Seldes—Jennifer Harmon; Ms. Lansbury—Diane Kagan; Ms. Adler—Linda Marie Larson, Messrs. Haley, Mulheren—Robert Emmet Lunney.

Directed by Michael Blakemore; scenery, Peter J. Davison; costumes, Ann Roth; lighting, Mark Henderson; sound, Paul Charlier; projections, Sven Ortel; casting, Telsey and Company; production stage manager, Steven Beckler; press, Boneau/Bryan-Brown, Chris Boneau, Jim Byk, Danielle Crinnion.

Time: The recent past. Place: The US Open. Presented without intermission.

Former tennis stars, who were doubles partners, reunite to watch a prominent tennis match while reviewing past glory and ignominy. First presentation of record was given in an earlier, briefer version at a benefit for MCC Theater in February 2006 with Ms. Seldes and Zoe Caldwell.

*Radio Golf (28). By August Wilson. Produced by Jujamcyn Theaters, Margo Lion, Jeffrey Richards, Jerry Frankel, Tamara Tunie, Wendell Pierce, Fran Kirmser, Bunting Management Group, Georgia Frontiere, Open Pictures, Lauren Doll, Steven Greil, The AW Group, Wonder City, Inc., Townsend Teague, in association with Jack Viertel and Gordon Davidson, at the Cort Theatre. Opened May 8, 2007.

Pair of aces: Marian Seldes and Angela Lansbury in Deuce. *Photo: Joan Marcus*

Mame Wilks .... Tonya Pinkins
Harmond Wilks .... Harry Lennix
Roosevelt Hicks .... James A. Williams
Sterling Johnson .... John Earl Jelks
Elder Joseph Barlow .... Anthony Chisholm

Standbys; Ms. Pinkins—Rosalyn Coleman; Messrs. Lennix and Williams—Billy Eugene Jones; Messrs. Chisholm and Jelks—Cedric Young.

Directed by Kenny Leon; scenery, David Gallo; costumes, Susan Hilferty; lighting, Donald Holder; music, Dan Moses Schreier; executive producer, Nicole Kastrinos; dramaturg, Todd Kreidler; casting, Stanczyk/Cherpakov Casting; production stage manager, Narda E. Alcorn; press, Barlow-Hartman, John Barlow, Michael Hartman, Dennis Crowley, Michelle Bergmann.

Time: 1997. Place: The Hill District in Pittsburgh, Pennsylvania. Presented in two parts.

An African-American politician faces his cultural and familial past as he looks forward to the future in Mr. Wilson's final play of the Pittsburgh Cycle. First presentation of record was given at Yale Repertory Theatre in New Haven (4/28–5/14/2005). A later version ran at the Center Theatre Group's Mark Taper Forum (8/10–9/18/2005). Final revisions were made by the playwright not long before his death October 2, 2005. A 2006–07 *Best Plays* choice (see essay by Christopher Rawson in this volume).

*Roundabout Theatre Company production **110 in the Shade** (26). Revival of the musical with book by N. Richard Nash; music by Harvey Schmidt; lyrics by Tom Jones; based on a play by N. Richard Nash. Todd Haimes artistic director, Harold Wolpert managing director, Julia C. Levy executive director, at Studio 54. Opened May 9, 2007.

File .... Christopher Innvar
H.C. Curry .... John Cullum
Noah Curry .... Chris Butler
Jim Curry .... Bobby Steggert

Lizzie Curry .... Audra McDonald
Snookie .... Carla Duren
Starbuck .... Steve Kazee
Little Girl .... Valisia Lekae Little
Clarence .... Darius Nichols
Odetta Clark .... Colleen Fitzpatrick
Vivian Lorraine Taylor .... Valisia Lekae Little

Clarence J. Taylor .... Darius Nichols
Curt McGlaughlin .... Devin Richards
Reverend Clark .... Michael Scott
Cody Bridger .... Will Swenson
Lily Ann Beasley .... Elisa Van Duyne
Katheryn Brawner .... Betsy Wolfe

Orchestra: Paul Gemignani conductor; Mark Mitchell associate conductor, keyboard; Sylvia D'Avanzo, Sean Carney violin; Joseph Gottesman viola; Roger Shell cello; John Beal bass; Rick Heckman, Eric Weidman, Don McGeen woodwinds; Susan Rotholz flute, piccolo; Dominic Derasse, Mike Ponella trumpet; Bruce Eidem trombone; Paul Pizzuti drums, percussion; Jennifer Hoult harp.

Understudies: Ms. McDonald—Colleen Fitzpatrick; Mr. Kazee—Will Swenson; Messrs. Cullum, Innvar—Michael Scott; Mr. Butler—Devin Richards; Mr. Steggert—Darius Nichols; Ms. Duren—Valisia Lekae Little.

Swings: Matt Wall, Mamie Parris.

Directed by Lonny Price; choreography, Dan Knechtges; scenery and costumes, Santo Loquasto; lighting, Christopher Akerlind; sound, Dan Moses Schreier; wigs and hair, Tom Watson; orchestrations, Jonathan Tunick; dance music arrangments, David Krane; music direction, Mr. Gemignani; fight direction, Rick Sordelet; casting, Jim Carnahan; production stage manager, Peter Hanson; press, Boneau/Bryan-Brown, Adrian Bryan-Brown, Matt Polk, Jessica Johnson.

Musical vamp: Audra McDonald and John Cullum in 110 in the Shade. *Photo: Joan Marcus*

Time: July 4, 1936. Place: The Texas panhandle. Presented in two parts.

A Texas spinster finds her emotions awakened by a traveling confidence man in this adaptation of Mr. Nash's *The Rainmaker*. First Broadway presentation of record of *110 in the Shade* was given at the Broadhurst Theatre (10/24/1963–8/9/1964; 330 performances). The 2006–07 production was the first Broadway revival. The underlying play had its first Broadway presentation of record at the Cort Theatre (10/28/1954–2/12/1955; 125 performances). Roundabout Theatre Company also presented the only Broadway revival of *The Rainmaker* at the Brooks Atkinson Theatre (11/11/1999–1/23/2000; 74 performances).

ACT I

Scene 1: Outside on the Prairie
"Another Hot Day" .... File, Townspeople
Scene 2: The Curry Ranch
"Lizzie's Comin' Home" .... H.C., Noah, Jimmy
"Love, Don't Turn Away" .... Lizzie
Scene 3: File's Office
"Poker Polka" .... File, H.C., Noah, Jimmy
Scene 4: The Picnic Grounds
"The Hungry Men" .... Lizzie, Townspeople
"The Rain Song" .... Starbuck, Townspeople
"You're Not Fooling Me" .... Starbuck, Lizzie
"Cinderella" .... Little Girl
"Raunchy" .... Lizzie
"A Man and a Woman .... File, Lizzie
"Old Maid" .... Lizzie

ACT II

Scene 1: Outside at twilight
"Evenin' Star" .... Starbuck
Scene 2: Picnic Area
"Everything Beautiful" .... Lzzie, Townspeople
Scene 3: Near Starbuck's Wagon
"Melisande" .... Starbuck
"Simple Little Things" .... Lizzie
Sene 4: Picnic Area
"Little Red Hat" .... Jimmy, Snookie
Scene 5: Starbuck's Lean-to
"Is It Really Me?" .... Lizzie
Scene 6: Picnic Area
"Wonderful Music" .... Starbuck, File, Lizzie
"The Rain Song" (Reprise) .... Townspeople

PLAYS PRODUCED OFF BROADWAY
○ ○ ○ ○ ○

FOR THE PURPOSES of *Best Plays* listing, the term "Off Broadway" signifies a show that opened for general audiences in a Manhattan theater seating 499 or fewer and 1) employed an Equity cast, 2) planned a regular schedule of eight performances per week in an open-ended run (seven per week for solo shows and some other exceptions) and 3) offered itself to public comment by critics after a designated opening performance.

Figures in parentheses following a play's title give the number of performances from the press-opening date. These numbers do not include previews or extra nonprofit performances. Performance interruptions for cast changes and other breaks have been taken into account. Performance numbers are figured in consultation with press representatives and company managements.

Plays marked with an asterisk (*) were still in a projected run on June 1, 2007. The number of performances is figured from press opening through May 31, 2007.

In a listing of a show's numbers—dances, sketches, musical scenes, etc.—the titles of songs are identified wherever possible by their appearance in quotation marks (").

HOLDOVERS FROM PREVIOUS SEASONS

OFF BROADWAY SHOWS that were running on June 1, 2006 are listed below. More detailed information about them appears in previous *Best Plays* volumes of appropriate date. Important cast changes since opening night are recorded in the Cast Replacements section in this volume.

*Perfect Crime (8,191). By Warren Manzi. Opened October 16, 1987.

*Blue Man Group (Tubes) (8,241). Performance piece by and with Blue Man Group. Opened November 17, 1991.

*Stomp (5,579). Percussion performance piece created by Luke Cresswell and Steve McNicholas. Opened February 27, 1994.

*I Love You, You're Perfect, Now Change (4,517). Musical revue with book and lyrics by Joe DiPietro; music by Jimmy Roberts. Opened August 1, 1996.

*Naked Boys Singing! (2,554). Musical revue conceived by Robert Schrock; written by various authors. Opened July 22, 1999.

Slava's Snowshow (1,004). By Slava Polunin. Opened September 8, 2004. (Closed January 14, 2007)

Jewtopia (1,052). By Bryan Fogel and Sam Wolfson. Opened October 21, 2004. (Closed April 29, 2007)

Forbidden Broadway: Special Victims Unit (816). Musical revue by Gerard Alessandrini. Opened December 16, 2004. Production hiatus May 29–June 24, 2005 and March 27, 2006 through the end of the 2005–06 season. Re-opened June 9, 2006. (Closed April 15, 2007)

*Altar Boyz (939). Transfer from Off Off Broadway of the musical with book by Kevin Del Aguila; music and lyrics by Gary Adler and Michael Patrick Walker; conceived by Marc Kessler and Ken Davenport. Opened March 1, 2005.

Drumstruck (607). By Warren Lieberman and Kathy-Jo Ross. Opened June 16, 2005. (Closed November 12, 2006)

Red Light Winter (158). By Adam Rapp. Opened February 9, 2006. (Closed June 25, 2006)

Manhattan Theatre Club production of **Defiance** (112). By John Patrick Shanley. Opened February 28, 2006. (Closed June 4, 2006)

Jacques Brel Is Alive and Well and Living in Paris (384). Revival of the musical revue with book and English lyrics by Eric Blau and Mort Shuman; music and lyrics by Jacques Brel. Opened March 27, 2006. (Closed February 25, 2007)

Sandra Bernhard: Everything Bad and Beautiful (97). Solo performance piece by Ms. Bernhard. Opened April 5, 2006. (Closed July 9, 2006)

Tryst (76). By Karoline Leach. Opened April 6, 2006. (Closed June 11, 2006)

The Public Theater production of **Stuff Happens** (86). By David Hare. Opened April 13, 2006. (Closed June 25, 2006)

All Dolled Up (40). By Bobby Spillane. Opened May 7, 2006. (Closed June 11, 2006)

Annulla (19). Revival of the solo performance piece by Emily Mann. Opened May 14, 2006. (Closed June 11, 2006)

New York Theatre Workshop presentation of the **United States Theatre Project** production of **columbinus** (24). By Stephen Karam and PJ Paparelli; additional material by Josh Barrett, Sean McNall, Karl Miller, Michael Milligan, Will Rogers. Opened May 22, 2006. (Closed June 11, 2006)

PLAYS PRODUCED JUNE 1, 2006–MAY 31, 2007

Nothing (30). By Henry Green; adapted by Andrea Hart. Produced by Brits Off Broadway, Sophie Ward and Simon Dutton, in association with Nothing Productions, at 59E59 Theaters. Opened June 7, 2006. (Closed July 2, 2006)

John Pomfret	Simon Dutton	Liz Jennings	Andrea Hart
Mary Pomfret	Candida Benson	Richard Abbot	Derwent Watson
Jane Wetherby	Sophie Ward	Gaspard	Tristram Wymark
Philip Wetherby	Pete Ashmore		

Directed by Robert David MacDonald and Philip Prowse; scenery, Mr. Prowse; costumes, Jane Hamilton; lighting, Gerry Jenkinson; production stage manager, Jenny Deady; press, Karen Greco Entertainment.

Presented in two parts.

Mischievous upper-class parents of tedious children torment their offspring in wicked fashion. First presentation of record was given in Glasgow at the Citizen's Theatre (11/27–12/20/2003).

*A Jew Grows in Brooklyn (339). Transfer from Off Off Broadway of the solo performance piece by Jake Ehrenreich. Produced by Dana Matthow, Philip Roger Roy and Second Generation Productions at the Lamb's Theatre. Opened June 7, 2006. (Closed September 17, 2006) Production hiatus due to permanent closing of theater on September 30, 2006. Re-opened October 11, 2006 at 37 Arts.

Performed by Mr. Ehrenreich.

Directed by John Huberth; scenery, Joseph Egan; costumes, Lisa Ehrenreich; lighting, Anjeanette Stokes; sound, David Ferdinand; music direction, Elysa Sunshine; press, Keith Sherman and Associates, Brett Oberman.

Presented in two parts.

A tale of pursuing a career in entertainment while growing up Jewish with immigrant parents in Brooklyn's postwar era. First presentation of record was given Off Off Broadway at American Theatre of Actors (4/10–5/28/2006).

MCC Theater production of **Some Girl(s)** (38). By Neil LaBute. Robert LuPone, Bernard Telsey, William Cantler artistic directors, John G. Schultz executive director, in association with the Lucille Lortel Theatre Foundation, at the Lucille Lortel Theatre. Opened June 8, 2006. (Closed July 8, 2006)

Guy	Eric McCormack	Lindsay	Fran Drescher
Sam	Brooke Smith	Bobbi	Maura Tierney
Tyler	Judy Reyes		

Directed by Jo Bonney; scenery, Neil Patel; costumes, Mimi O'Donnell; lighting, David Weiner; sound, Robert Kaplowitz; casting, Telsey and Company; production stage manager, Kevin Bertolucci; press, O and M Co., Rick Miramontez, Jon Dimond.

Presented without intermission.

A man who uses women for his own gratification, and quickly discards them, attempts to make amends. First presentation of record was given at the West End's Gielgud Theatre (5/12–8/13/2005; 96 performances) with David Schwimmer in the central role.

Burleigh Grimes (39). By Roger Kirby. Produced by Lewis Productions, in association with J. Murray Logan and Judith Ann Abrams Productions, Craig L. Burr, Claire and Robert Chamine, Robert L. Chapman Jr., Harold Edgar, Geoffrey R. Hoguet, Robert D. Kissin, Mary Ann and Don La Guardia at New World Stages. Opened June 13, 2006. (Closed July 16, 2006)

The Wife	Nancy Anderson	Elizabeth Bigley	Wendie Malick
Hap	Jason Antoon	Burleigh Grimes	Mark Moses
George Radbourn	James Badge Dale	Grace Redding	Ashley Williams
Buck	John Lavelle		

Musicians: Jack Petruzzelli guitar, drums, keyboard; Stephen Ullrich guitar, bass; Dean Sharenow, David Berger drums.

Understudies: Ms. Malick—Nancy Anderson; Mses. Williams, Anderson—Kelly Sullivan; Messrs. Moses, Dale, Antoon, Lavelle—Doug Wert.

Directed by David Warren; choreography, Andy Blankenbuehler; scenery, James Youmans; costumes, Gregory Gale; lighting, Jeff Croiter; sound, Peter Fitzgerald; music, David Yazbek; projections, Michael Clark; music direction, Mr. Sharenow; casting, Jamie Fox and Kristin Lewis; production stage manager, Jane Pole; press, Shaffer-Coyle Public Relations, Jeremy Shaffer.

Presented in two parts.

Greed is not only good, it is the key to adrenaline rushes—the attainment of power and corruptions of the spirit—that makes sex pale in comparison. First presentation of record was given in London at the Bridewell Theatre (6/3–7/3/2004).

Second Stage Theatre production of **The Water's Edge** (29). By Theresa Rebeck. Carole Rothman artistic director, Ellen Richard interim executive director. Opened June 15, 2006. (Closed July 9, 2006)

Helen	Kate Burton	Nate	Austin Lysy
Richard	Tony Goldwyn	Lucy	Katharine Powell
Erica	Mamie Gummer		

Directed by Will Frears; scenery, Alexander Dodge; costumes, Junghyun Georgia Lee; lighting, Frances Aronson; sound, Vincent Olivieri; music, Michael Friedman; casting, Tara Rubin Casting; production stage manager, Roy Harris; press, Richard Kornberg and Associates, Tom D'Ambrosio, Don Summa, Carrie Friedman.

Time: The present. Place: A family house on a body of water. Presented in two parts.

A man returns to his abandoned family with a new woman at his side in a tale that echoes Agamemnon's return from Troy. First presentation of record was given at the Williamstown Theatre Festival on the Nikos Stage (6/23–7/4/2004).

The Public Theater production of **Satellites** (17). By Diana Son. Oskar Eustis artistic director, Mara Manus executive director, at Martinson Hall. Opened June 18, 2006. (Closed July 2, 2006)

Miles	Kevin Carroll	Nina	Sandra Oh
Kit	Johanna Day	Eric	Clarke Thorell
Reggie	Ron Cephas Jones	Walter	Ron Brice
Mrs. Chae	Satya Lee		

Directed by Michael Greif; scenery, Mark Wendland; costumes, Miranda Hoffman; lighting, Kenneth Posner; sound, Walter Trarbach and Tony Smolenski IV; music, Michael Friedman; casting, Jordan Thaler, Heidi Griffiths; production stage manager, Martha Donaldson; press, Arlene R. Kriv.

Welcome wagon? Ron Cephas Jones, Sandra Oh and Kevin Carroll in Satellites. *Photo: Michal Daniel*

Faith and hope: Jill Clayburgh and Hamish Linklater in The Busy World Is Hushed. *Photo: Joan Marcus*

Time: The present. Place: A gentrifying neighborhood in Brooklyn. Presented without intermission.

An interracial couple struggle to hold their nascent family together amid financial crisis, extrafamilial stress and plaster dust.

Lincoln Center Theater production of **The House in Town** (48). By Richard Greenberg. André Bishop artistic director, Bernard Gersten executive producer, at the Mitzi E. Newhouse Theater. Opened June 19, 2006. (Closed June 30, 2006)

Sam Hammer .... Mark Harelik	Christopher Valence .... Dan Bittner
Con Eliot .... Armand Schultz	Hammers' Maid .... Barbara McCulloh
Jean Eliot .... Becky Ann Baker	Hammers' Footman .... Matt Dickson
Amy Hammer .... Jessica Hecht	

Understudies: Mr. Bittner—Matt Dickson; Messrs. Harelik, Schultz, Dickson—R. Ward Duffy; Mses. Hecht, McCulloh—Susan Knight; Ms. Baker—Barbara McCulloh.

Directed by Doug Hughes; scenery, John Lee Beatty; costumes, Catherine Zuber; lighting, Brian MacDevitt; sound and music, David Van Tieghem; casting, Daniel Swee; stage manager, James FitzSimmons; press, Philip Rinaldi, Barbara Carroll.

Time: Early in 1929. Place: A townhouse on Millionaire's Row, New York City. Presented without intermission.

In the months before the Wall Street crash of 1929, a prosperous Jewish merchant and his WASP wife skim the surface of midlife together before issues of health and fidelity rise from the depths.

Loose (30). Solo performance piece by Tommy Tiernan. Produced by WestBeth Entertainment at the Actors Playhouse. Opened June 20, 2006. (Closed July 29, 2006)

Performed by Mr. Tiernan.

Press, The Karpel Group.

Presented without intermission.

Irish comedian returns to New York with his particular brand of storytelling. His earlier piece, *Cracked*, played New York in 2004.

Playwrights Horizons production of **The Busy World Is Hushed** (17). By Keith Bunin. Tim Sanford artistic director, Leslie Marcus managing director, William Russo general manager, at the Mainstage Theater. Opened June 25, 2006. (Closed July 9, 2006)

Brandt .... Hamish Linklater   Thomas .... Luke MacFarlane
Hannah .... Jill Clayburgh

Directed by Mark Brokaw; scenery, Allen Moyer; costumes, Michael Krass; lighting, Mary Louise Geiger; sound and music, Lewis Flinn; casting, Alaine Alldaffer, James Calleri; production stage manager, David Sugarman; press, The Publicity Office, Bob Fennell, Marc Thibodeau, Michael S. Borowski, Candi Adams.

Time: The present. Place: The library of an apartment on West 122nd Street, New York City. Presented in two parts.

An Episcopal priest struggles with her writing and her son struggles with his faith until a man comes into their lives bringing hope and love. First presentation of record was given as a reading by New York Stage and Film at Vassar College (6/17–19/2005) before readings at the Ojai Playwrights Conference in California (8/13/2005) and Madison Repertory Theatre in Wisconsin (9/22/2005).

Secrets (41). By Gerald Zipper. Produced by John Chatterton, in association with La Muse Venale, at the Theatre at St. Luke's. Opened June 25, 2006. (Closed July 30, 2006)

G-man: John Ellison Conlee and Denis O'Hare in Pig Farm. *Photo: Joan Marcus*

Performed by Mark Hamlet, Darren Lougee, Lissa Moira, Alyce Mayors, Tom Sminkey, Elena Zazanis.

Directed by Ted Mornel; press, David Gersten and Associates.

Time: 1985. Place: Upper West Side, New York City. Presented in two parts.

Three couples of middle age vent frustrations bottled for far too long.

Roundabout Theatre Company production of **Pig Farm** (80). By Greg Kotis. Todd Haimes artistic director, Harold Wolpert managing director, Julia C. Levy executive director, at the Laura Pels Theatre in the Harold and Miriam Steinberg Center for Theatre. Opened June 27, 2006. (Closed September 3, 2006)

Tom	John Ellison Conlee	Tina	Katie Finneran
Tim	Logan Marshall-Green	Teddy	Denis O'Hare

Understudies: Messrs. Conlee, O'Hare—Bill Coelius; Mr. Marshall-Green—Nicholas Heck; Ms. Finneran—Jennifer Regan.

Directed by John Rando; scenery, Scott Pask; costumes, Gregory Gale; lighting, Brian MacDevitt; sound and music, John Gromada; hair, Josh Marquette; fight direction, Steve Rankin; casting, Mele Nagler; production stage manager, Pat Sosnow; press, Boneau/Bryan-Brown, Matt Polk, Jessica Johnson.

Time: The present. Place: A farm. Presented in two parts.

In this farce, a farmer panics when the Environmental Protection Agency wants to know where his pigs' waste is going. Developed in collaboration with the Old Globe in San Diego, where it played with a different creative team (9/28–10/29/2006).

The Public Theater production of **Macbeth** (11). Revival of the play by William Shakespeare. Oskar Eustis artistic director, Mara Manus executive director, at the Delacorte Theater. Opened June 28, 2006. (Closed July 9, 2006)

Weird Sister 1	Joan MacIntosh	Porter	Lynn Cohen
Weird Sister 2	Ching Valdes-Aran	Macduff	Sterling K. Brown
Weird Sister 3	Lynn Cohen	Donalbain	Sanjit De Silva
Duncan	Herb Foster	Seyton	Graeme Malcolm
Malcolm	Jacob Fishel	Murderer 1	Andrew McGinn
Bloody Sergeant	Pedro Pascal	Murderer 2	Pedro Pascal
Lennox	Mark L. Montgomery	Lady Macduff	Florencia Lozano
Ross	Philip Goodwin	Boy	Tolan Aman
Macbeth	Liev Schreiber	Servant	Clancy O'Connor
Banquo	Teagle F. Bougere	Doctor	Herb Foster
Angus	Andrew McGinn	Gentlewoman	Joan MacIntosh
Lady Macbeth	Jennifer Ehle	Messenger	Lucas Near-Verbrugghe
Messenger	Stephanie Fieger	Messenger	Seth Duerr
Fleance	Amefika El-Amin		

Ensemble: Seth Duerr, Amefika El-Amin, Stephanie Fieger, Hollie Hunt, Michael Markham, Lucas Near-Verbrugghe, Clancy O'Connor.

Understudies: Mr. Fishel—Sanjit De Silva; Messrs. Brown, Malcolm—Seth Duerr; Mr. Bougere—Amefika El-Amin; Meses. Ehle, Valdes-Aran—Stephanie Fieger; Mses. MacIntosh, Lozano, Cohen—Hollie Hunt; Mr. Montgomery—Michael Markham; Mr. Foster—Andrew McGinn; Mr. Schreiber—Mark L. Montgomery; Messrs. Goodwin, McGinn, El-Amin—Lucas Near-Verbrugghe; Messrs. Aman, De Silva, Pascal—Clancy O'Connor.

Directed by Moisés Kaufman; scenery, Derek McLane; costumes, Michael Krass; lighting, David Lander; sound, Acme Sound Partners; fight direction, Rick Sordelet; music, Peter Golub; associate producers, Peter DuBois, Mandy Hackett; casting, Jordan Thaler, Heidi Griffiths; dramaturg, Robert Blacker; production stage manager, K.E. Armstrong; press, Arlene R. Kriv.

Time: The 1930s. Place: Scotland and England. Presented in two parts.

A Scottish thane and his lady wife are seized by a power madness that leads murder and ruin. First presentation of record was given at the Globe Theatre (4/20/1611) with Richard Burbage in

Deed done: Jennifer Ehle and Liev Schreiber in Macbeth. *Photo: Michal Daniel*

the title role. It is believed, however, to have been given earlier at Hampton Court (8/7/1606). First presentation of record in this country was given at the John Street Theatre (3/3/1768) with Lewis Hallam II in the title role. In May 1849, there were three competing productions in New York, two of which—with the Englishman William Charles Macready and the American Edwin Forrest in the title roles—helped to spark the deadly Astor Place Riots (5/7–10/1849).

The Public Theater presentation of the **Labyrinth Theater Company** production of **School of the Americas** (22). By José Rivera. Oskar Eustis artistic director, Mara Manus executive director, at LuEsther Hall. Opened July 6, 2006. (Closed July 23, 2006)

Lucila Cortes	Karina Arroyave	Che	John Ortiz
First Ranger	Raúl Castillo	Lt. Feliz Ramos	Felix Solis
Second Ranger	Nathan Lebron	Julia Cortes	Patricia Velasquez

Directed by Mark Wing-Davey; scenery, Andromache Chalfant; costumes, Mimi O'Donnell; lighting, David Weiner; sound, Robert Kaplowitz; fight direction, Qui Nguyen; production stage manager, Damon W. Arrington; press, Arlene R. Kriv.

Time: October 7–9, 1967. Place: La Higuera, Bolivia. Presented in two parts.

A famed revolutionary encounters a woman of substance and good sense during his detention by the Bolivian and American governments. Part of a series of collaborations between the Public Theater and the Labyrinth Theater Company (Philip Seymour Hoffman and John Ortiz artistic directors, Steve Asher executive director).

[title of show] (84). Transfer from Off Off Broadway of the musical with book by Hunter Bell; music and lyrics by Jeff Bowen. Produced by Kevin McCollum, Laura Camien and Vineyard Theatre (Douglas Aibel artistic director, Jennifer Garvey-Blackwell executive director), at the Vineyard Theatre. Opened July 20, 2006. (Closed October 1, 2006)

Hunter	Hunter Bell	Heidi	Heidi Blickenstaff
Susan	Susan Blackwell	Jeff	Jeff Bowen

Directed and choreographed by Michael Berresse; scenery, Neil Patel; costumes, Chase Tyler; lighting, Ken Billington and Jason Kantrowitz; sound, Acme Sound Partners; music direction and arrangements, Larry Pressgrove; production stage manager, Martha Donaldson; press, Sam Rudy Media Relations, Sam Rudy, Bob Lasko, Dale Heller.

Time: [time]. Place: [place]. Presented without intermission.

Metamusical about what it takes to write, cast and stage a low-budget musical on a tight deadline. First presentation of record was given at the New York Musical Theatre Festival (9/13–10/3/2004).

MUSICAL NUMBERS

"Untitled Opening Number" .... Company
"Two Nobodies in New York" .... Jeff, Hunter
"An Original Musical" .... Hunter, Jeff
"Monkeys and Playbills" .... Company
"Part of It All" .... Hunter, Jeff
"I Am Playing Me" .... Heidi
"What Kind of Girl Is She?" .... Heidi, Susan
"Die Vampire, Die!" .... Susan, Company
"Filling Out the Form" .... Company
"September Song" (Festival Medley) .... Company
"Secondary Characters" .... Susan, Heidi
"Montage" / "Photo Shoot" .... Company
"A Way Back to Then" .... Heidi
"Nine People's Favorite Thing" .... Company

Last hours: John Ortiz and Patricia Velasquez in School of the Americas. *Photo: Michal Daniel*

Mod squad: Denise Summerford, Erin Crosby, Marie-France Arcilla, Erica Schroeder, Julie Dingman Evans in Shout! *Photo: Joan Marcus*

*No Child . . . (297). Transfer from Off Off Broadway of the solo performance piece by Nilaja Sun. Produced by Scott Morfee, Tom Wirtshafter and Epic Theatre Center. Opened July 16, 2006.

Performed by Ms. Sun.

Directed by Hal Brooks; scenery, Narelle Sissons; costumes, Jessica Gaffney; lighting, Mark Barton; sound, Ron Russell; production stage manager, Tom Taylor; press, O and M Co.

Presented without intermission.

A teacher enacts the characters she experienced while teaching drama at Malcolm X high School in the Bronx. Transferred after a run at the Beckett Theatre (5/10–6/18/2006).

The Culture Project production of **Amajuba: Like Doves We Rise** (32). By Yael Farber. Allan Buchman artistic director. Opened July 25, 2006. (Closed August 20, 2006)

Performed by Tshallo Chokwe, Roelf Matlala, Bongeka Mpongwana, Phillip "Tipo" Tindisa, Jabulile Tshabalala.

Directed by Ms. Farber; lighting, Tim Boyd and Garin Marschall; press, O and M Co.

Presented without intermission.

Six performers tell of their lives in apartheid South Africa in story and song. First presentation of record was given in Mafikeng, South Africa (12/2000) before touring to London and Australia.

Shout! (157). Musical revue by Phillip George and David Lowenstein; additional material by Peter Charles Morris. Produced by Victoria Lang and Pier Paolo Piccoli, in association with Patricia Melanson, Pat Addiss and Robin Gurin, at the Julia Miles Theater. Opened July 27, 2006. (Closed December 10, 2006)

Blue Girl .... Marie-France Arcilla

Yellow Girl .... Erin Crosby

Orange Girl .... Julie Dingman Evans

Green Girl .... Erica Schroeder

Red Girl .... Casey Clark

Gwendolyn Holmes .... Carole Shelley

Musicians: Bradley Vieth conductor, keyboard; Christopher Stephens keyboard; Joe Brady percussion.

Directed by Mr. George; choreography, Mr. Lowenstein; scenery, David Gallo; costumes, Phillip Heckman; lighting, Jason Lyons; sound, Tony Meola; orchestrations, arrangements, music direction, Mr. Vieth; production stage manager, Jana Llynn; press, Boneau/Bryan-Brown, Chris Boneau, Jackie Green, Heath Schwartz.

Presented in two parts.

Musical revue of 1960s hits performed by an all-female cast. First presentation of record was given at Jermyn Street Theatre in London (7/2001).

Irish Repertory Theatre production of **Mr. Dooley's America** (25). By Philip Dunne and Martin Blaine; based on the newspaper articles of Finley Peter Dunne. Charlotte Moore artistic director, Ciarán O'Reilly producting director.Opened August 20, 2006. (Closed September 10, 2006)

Finley Peter Dunne;

Mr. Hennessy .... Des Keogh

Mr. Dooley .... Vincent Dowling

Directed by Charlotte Moore; scenery, Charles Corcoran; costumes, Linda Fisher; lighting, Renee Molina; production stage managers, Elis C. Arroyo and Pamela Brusoski; press, Shirley Herz Associates, Shirley Herz, Daniel Demello.

Presented in two parts.

Fictional Irish bartender who was a favorite of early 20th century newspaper readers shares his thoughts on American culture and political trends. First presentation of record was given at Boston's Huntington Theatre Company (5/1–5/1991) after a 1990 run at Mr. Dowling's Miniature Theatre of Chester, Massachusetts—with William Ivey Long as the scene design supervisor. The company is now known as the Chester Theatre Company.

The Public Theater production of **Mother Courage and Her Children** (10). Revival of the play by Bertolt Brecht; translated by Tony Kushner. Oskar Eustis artistic director, Mara Manus executive director, at the Delacorte Theater. Opened August 21, 2006. (Closed September 3, 2006)

Army Recruiter .... Glenn Fleshler

Sergeant .... George Kmeck

Mother Courage .... Meryl Streep

Eilif .... Frederick Weller

Swiss Cheese .... Geoffrey Arend

Kattrin .... Alexandria Wailes

Cook .... Kevin Kline

General .... Larry Marshall

Chaplain .... Austin Pendleton

General's Servant .... Michael Izquierdo

Quartermaster .... Max Maker

Yvette .... Jenifer Lewis

Soldier (Eyepatch) .... Michael Izquierdo

Sergeant .... Waleed F. Zuaiter

Colonel .... Raul Aranas

Clerk .... Paco Lozano

Young Soldier;

Lieutenant .... Ato Essandoh

Older Soldier .... Raul Aranas

Soldier (Fur Coat) .... Max Baker

Looting Soldier .... Sean Phillips

Injured Farmer's Wife .... Jade Wu

Injured Farmer .... Raul Aranas

Regimental Secretary .... Waleed F. Zuaiter

Singing Soldier .... Michael Markham

Soldier (Guitar) .... Paco Lozano

Young Man (Mattress);

First Soldier .... Jack Noseworthy

Old Woman .... Colleen Fitzpatrick

Yvette's Manservant .... Eugene Jones

Soldier .... Glenn Fleshler

Mother .... Colleen Fitzpatrick

Daughter .... Brittany Underwood

Farmer .... Larry Marshall

Farmer's Wife .... Jade Wu

Young Man (Violin);

Farmer's Son .... Silvestre Rasuk

Ensemble: Michael Izquierdo, Eugene Jones, Paco Lozano, Michael Markham, Sean Phillips, Matthew Bondy, Joachim Boyle, Robert Michael Bray, Richard Busser, Nixon Cesar, Jackie Chung,

Foreplay? Meryl Streep and Kevin Kline in Mother Courage and Her Children. *Photo: Michal Daniel*

Charlie Hudson III, Jarde Jacobs, Chris Keogh, Evan Lubeck, Francis Mateo, M. Nana Mensah, Serena Merriman, Corydon Merritt, Brian Morvant, Eric Murdoch, Michael Pafunda, Michelle Pruett, J. Enrique Rivas, Tim Rock, Raushanah Simmons, Joseph Sousa, Dawen Wang, Lloyd Watts, Christopher Zorker.

Musicians: Chris Fenwick conductor, keyboard; Todd Groves woodwinds; Christian Jaudes trumpet; Charles Gordon trombone; Melissa Kacalanos hurdy gurdy; Patrick Glynn acoustic bass, tuba; Carlos Valdes, Larry Spivak percussion.

Understudies: Mr. Kmeck—Ato Essandoh; Mses. Streep, Wu—Colleen Fitzpatrick; Mr. Kline—Glenn Fleshler; Mr. Arend—Michael Izquierdo; Mr. Lozano—Eugene Jones; Mr. Fleshler—Paco Lozano; Messrs. Weller, Marshall—Michael Markham; Mr. Aranas—Jack Noseworthy; Mr. Essandoh—Sean Phillips; Mr. Noseworthy—Silvestre Rasuk; Ms. Wailes—Brittany Underwood; Mr. Pendleton—Waleed F. Zuaiter; Ms. Lewis—Jade Wu.

Directed by George C. Wolfe; scenery, Riccardo Hernandez; costumes, Marina Draghici; lighting, Paul Gallo; sound, Acme Sound Partners; projections, Batwin and Robin Productions; flying, Foy; music, Jeanine Tesori; orchestrations, Bruce Coughlin; music direction, Kimberly Grigsby; music coordinator, Seymour Red Press; fight direction, Thomas Schall; associate producers, Peter DuBois, Heidi Griffiths, Mandy Hackett; casting, Jordan Thaler, Heidi Griffiths; production stage manager, Rick Steiger; press, Arlene R. Kriv.

Time: 1624–36, amid the Thirty Years War. Place: Sweden; Poland; Germany. Presented in two parts.

A woman prizes what she can sell above all other relationships and loses her children as the story unfolds. First presentation of record was given in Zurich (4/19/1941). A 1962–63 *Best Plays* choice, the original Broadway production opened at the Martin Beck Theatre (3/28/1963–5/11/1963; 52 performances) with Anne Bancroft under the direction of Jerome Robbins. First US presentation of record was given by the Actor's Workshop of San Francisco at the Marines Memorial Theatre (1/17/1956) in a production directed by Herbert Blau and starring Beatrice Manley.

*The Fantasticks (322). Revival of the musical with book by Tom Jones; music by Harvey Schmidt; lyrics by Mr. Jones; based on *Les Romanesques* by Edmond Rostand. Produced by Steven Baruch, Marc Routh, Richard Frankel, Thomas Viertel at the Snapple Theatre Center. Opened August 23, 2006.

Narrator (El Gallo)	Burke Moses	Girl's Father (Bellomy)	Martin Vidnovic
Boy (Matt)	Santino Fontana	Old Actor (Henry)	Thomas Bruce
Girl (Luisa)	Sara Jean Ford	Man Who Dies (Mortimer)	Robert R. Oliver
Boy's Father (Hucklebee)	Leo Burmester	Mute	Douglas Ullman Jr.

Musicians: Dorothy Martin piano, Erin Hill harp.

Understudies: Messrs. Vidnovic, Bruce, Burmester; Oliver—John Deyle; Messrs. Moses, Burmester, Vidnovic—Paul Jackel; Ms. Ford, Mr. Ullman Jr.—Betsy Morgan.

Directed by Mr. Jones and Word Baker; choreography, Janet Watson; scenery and costumes, Ed Wittstein; lighting, Mary Jo Dondlinger; sound, Domonic Sack; music direction, Dorothy Martin; casting, Telsey and Company; production stage manager, Gregory R. Covert; press, Barlow-Hartman, John Barlow, Michael Hartman.

Presented in two parts.

Young lovers, their meddling fathers and a handsome stranger engage a story as old as the cycle of life. First Off Broadway presentation of record was given in New York at the Sullivan Street Playhouse (5/3/1960–1/13/2002; 17,162 performances) with Jerry Orbach in the role of El Gallo. First presentation of record was given by the Barnard Summer Theatre in the Minor Latham Playhouse (8/4–8/1959). The actor named "Thomas Bruce" in the 2006–07 production was Mr. Jones.

ACT I

"Overture" .... Company
"Try to Remember" .... Narrator
"Much More" .... Girl
"Metaphor" .... Boy, Girl
"Never Say No .... Fathers
"It Depends on What You Pay" .... Narrator, Fathers
"Soon It's Gonna Rain" .... Boy, Girl
"Abduction Ballet .... Company
"Happy Ending .... Company

ACT II

"This Plum Is Too Ripe" .... Boy, Girl, Fathers
"I Can See It" .... Boy, Narrator
"Plant a Radish" .... Fathers
"Round and Round" .... Narrator, Girl, Company

Signature Theatre Company production of **Seven Guitars** (53). Revival of the play by August Wilson. James Houghton founding artistic director, Kathryn M. Lipuma executive director. Opened August 24, 2006. (Closed October 15, 2006)

Louise	Brenda Pressley	Hedley	Charles Weldon
Red	Stephen McKinley Henderson	Floyd	Lance Reddick
Canewell	Kevin Carroll	Ruby	Cassandra Freeman
Vera	Roslyn Ruff		

Directed by Ruben Santiago-Hudson; choreography, Ken Roberson; scenery, Richard Hoover; costumes, Karen Perry; lighting, Jane Cox; sound, Darron L. West; music and music direction, Bill Sims Jr.; fight direction, Rick Sordelet; casting, Telsey and Company; associate artists, Todd Kreidler, Constanza Romero; production stage manager, John M. Atherlay; press, The Publicity Office, Bob Fennell, Candi Adams, Marc Thibodeau, Michael S. Borowski.

Time: 1948. Place: The backyard of a house in Pittsburgh. Presented in two parts.

A musician in the 1940s attempts to right the wrongs of the past and start his life afresh. A 1995–96 *Best Plays* choice, the original Broadway production opened at the Walter Kerr Theatre

(3/28–9/8/1996; 188 performances). For that production, Mr. Santiago-Hudson received the 1996 Tony Award in the category of featured actor in a play. First presentation of record was in a reading at the Eugene O'Neill Theater Center in Connecticut (7/15–16/1994). First production of record was given at the Goodman Theatre in Chicago (1/23–2/25/1995).

National Theatre of Greece presentation of **The Persians** (6). Revival of the play by Aeschylus; translated by Nikoletta Frindzila; English translation by Yannis Papadakis. Nikos Kourkoulos artistic director, at City Center. Opened September 16, 2006. (Closed September 20, 2006)

Atossa .... Lydia Koniordou   Xerxes .... Christos Loulis
Darius .... Yannis Kranas

Messengers: Sampson Fytros, Yorgos Gallos, Dimitris Kanellos, Phaidon Kastris, Panagiotis Klinis, Apostolis Pelakanos, Takis Sakellariou, Yorgos Stamos.

Ensemble: Chrysanthi Avloniti, Yorgos Dousis, Manolis Dragatsis, Yorgos Frindzilas, Alexandros Kalpakidis, Stephanos Kosmidis, Yannis Kotsifas, Katerina Liontaki, Vassilis Margetis, Elena Marsidou, Dimitris Mosxonas, Dinos Pontikopoulos, Takis Sakellariou, Vassilis Spiropoulos, Elena Topalidou, Yorgis Tsampourakis, Vassilis Zaifidis.

Musicians: Takis Farazis, Stephanos Logothetis, Stephanos Tortopoglou, Nikos Xinos.

Directed by Ms. Koniordou; choreography, Apostolia Papadamaki; scenery and costumes, Lili Kendaka; lighting, Lefteris Pavlopoulos; music, Takis Farazis; press, Richard Kornberg and Associates, Richard Kornberg, Laura Kaplow-Goldman.

Time: 480 BCE. Place: Susa, in Persia.

Characters recount the ill-advised invasion of Greece by Persian forces who were defeated at Salamis, where the playwright was a member of the winning army. First presentation of record was in 472 BCE.

Walking wounded: Christopher Evan Welch, Jayne Houdyshell, Ada-Marie L. Gutierrez (child), Mia Barron and Aya Cash in The Pain and the Itch. *Photo: Joan Marcus*

Playwrights Horizons production of **The Pain and the Itch** (30). By Bruce Norris. Tim Sanford artistic director, Leslie Marcus managing director, William Russo general manager, at the Mainstage Theater. Opened September 21, 2006. (Closed October 15, 2006)

Mr. Hadid .... Peter Jay Fernandez	Kalina .... Aya Cash
Clay .... Christopher Evan Welch	Cash .... Reg Rogers
Kelly .... Mia Barron	Carol .... Jayne Houdyshell
Kayla .... Ada-Marie L. Gutierrez,	
Vivien Kells	

Directed by Anna D. Shapiro; scenery, Dan Ostling; costumes, Jennifer von Mayrhauser; lighting, Donald Holder; sound, Rob Milburn and Michael Bodeen; casting, Alaine Alldaffer; production stage manager, Susie Cordon; press, The Publicity Office, Bob Fennell, Marc Thibodeau, Michael S. Borowski, Candi Adams.

A family's dysfunction manifests itself in rash behavior and infections of the skin. Presented in two parts. First presentation of record was given by Chicago's Steppenwolf Theatre Company (7/10–8/28/2005). A 2006–07 *Best Plays* choice (see essay by John Istel in this volume).

Second Stage Theatre production of **subUrbia** (37). Revival of the play by Eric Bogosian. Carole Rothman artistic director, Ellen Richard executive director. Opened September 28, 2006. (Closed October 29, 2006)

Pakeeza Chaudry .... Diksha Basu	Jeff Gallagher .... Daniel Eric Gold
Erica Gerson .... Jessica Capshaw	Sooze .... Gaby Hoffmann
Buff Macleod .... Kieran Culkin	Nazeer Chaudry .... Manu Narayan
Neil "Pony" Moynihan .... Michael Esper	Tim Mitchum .... Peter Scanavino
Bee-Bee Douglas .... Halley Feiffer	

Directed by Jo Bonney; scenery, Richard Hoover; costumes, Mimi O'Donnell; lighting, David Weiner; music, Mr. Bogosian, Michael Esper; sound, Robert Kaplowitz; fight direction, Rick Sordelet; production stage manager, Wendy Ouellette; press, Richard Kornberg and Associates, Tom D'Ambrosio.

Time: The present. Place: A suburb. Presented in two parts.

Stranded between adolescence and adulthood, a group of young people aimlessly seek the next thing. A 1993–94 *Best Plays* choice, the first presentation of record was given Off Broadway by Lincoln Center Theater in the Mitzi E. Newhouse Theater (5/22–9/28/1994; 113 performances).

New York Theatre Workshop production of **¡El Conquistador!** (22). Transfer from Off Off Broadway of the performance piece by Thaddeus Phillips, Tatiana Mallarino and Victor Mallarino. James C. Nicola artistic director, Lynn Moffat managing director. Opened October 3, 2006. (Closed October 22, 2006)

Polonio .... Thaddeus Phillips

Video ensemble: Cristina Campuzano, Luis Fernando Hoyos, Helena Mallarino, Tatiana Mallarino, Victor Mallarino, Antonio Sanint.

Directed by Ms. Mallarino; scenery, Mr. Phillips; lighting, Jeff Sugg; sound, Jamie McElhinney; video, Austin Switser; production stage manager, Rachel Zack; press, Richard Kornberg and Associates, Richard Kornberg, Don Summa.

Presented without intermission.

A multimedia piece employing film, theater and history to tell a tale of international domestic drama. First presentation of record was given at the 2005 Philadelphia Live Arts Festival.

Peer Gynt Festival of Gudbrandsdalen production of **Peer Gynt** (3). Revival of the play by Henrik Ibsen. Eli Blakstad administrative director, at the Delacorte Theater. Opened October 5, 2006. (Closed October 7, 2006)

Peer Gynt .... Svein Sturla Hungnes

Ensemble: Nina Moen, Kari Simonsen, Linda Ovrebo, Mari Maurstad, Stein Gronli, Rune Reksten, Karoline Kruger, Camilla Granlien.

Directed by Mr. Hungnes; costumes, Ingrid Nylander, Mr. Hungnes; lighting, Jeff Nellis; sound, David Meschter; music, Edvard Grieg; film, Arne Rostad; music direction, Timothy Myers; music arrangements, Atie Halstensen; production stage manager, C. Townsend Olcott II.

Presented in two parts.

Dramatic concert based on Mr. Ibsen's allegorical tale of a man whose soul is filled with wanderlust. The production has been part of an annual event in scenic Gudbrandsdalen, Norway, since 1967—though the first such event was held in 1928. Written in 1867, *Peer Gynt*'s first presentation of record was given at Christiania Theater in Oslo (2/24/1876) with music composed by Mr. Grieg. First New York presentation of record of the play was given as a recital in Norwegian by Ole Bang at the Manhattan Theatre (1/12/1905). First presentation of record in English was given at the Grand Opera House in Chicago (10/29–12/1/1906) with Richard Mansfield in the title role. First presentation of record on Broadway was given at the New Amsterdam Theatre (2/25–3/23/1907; 22 performances). Despite declining health due to a two-year battle with cancer, Mr. Mansfield performed the long piece twice a day on Wednesdays and Saturdays. He died several months later at his New London, Connecticut home (8/30/1907).

Playwrights Horizons production of **Blue Door** (25). By Tanya Barfield. Tim Sanford artistic director, Leslie Marcus managing director, William Russo general manager, at the Mainstage Theater. Opened October 8, 2006. (Closed October 29, 2006)

Lewis .... Reg E. Cathey   Simon; others .... André Holland

Directed by Leigh Silverman; scenery, Narelle Sissons; costumes, Toni-Leslie James; lighting, Mary Louise Geiger; sound, Ken Travis; music, Daryl Waters; production stage manager, Amy McCraney; press, The Publicity Office, Bob Fennell, Marc Thibodeau, Michael S. Borowski, Candi Adams.

Presented without intermission.

An African-American man struggles to control his sense of identity—racial and otherwise—as he confronts representations from his cultural and familial past. First presentation of record was given by South Coast Repertory, Costa Mesa, California, on its Julianne Argyros Stage (4/28–5/14/2006).

The Public Theater production of **Wrecks** (42). Solo performance piece by Neil LaBute. Oskar Eustis artistic director, Mara Manus executive director, at the Anspacher Theater. Opened October 10, 2006. (Closed November 19, 2006)

Edward Carr .... Ed Harris

Directed by Mr. LaBute; scenery and costumes, Klara Zieglerova; lighting, Christopher Akerlind; sound, Robert Kaplowitz; associate producers, Peter DuBois, Mandy Hackett; production stage managers, Cole Bonenberger, Mary Michele Miner; press, Arlene R. Kriv.

Presented without intermission.

A car salesman unburdens his private grief while pacing near the casket of his wife of 30 years. First presentation of record was given at Everyman Palace Theatre in Cork, Ireland (11/23–12/3/2005).

25 Questions for a Jewish Mother (178). Transfer from Off Off Broadway of the solo performance piece by Kate Moira Ryan and Judy Gold. Produced by Ars Nova and StyleFour Productions/Off Broadway Booking at Theatre at St. Luke's. Opened October 12, 2006. (Closed March 18, 2007)

Performed by Ms. Gold.

Directed by Karen Kohlhaas; scenery, Louisa Thompson; lighting, Jennifer Tipton; sound, Jorge Muelle; production stage manager, Damon W. Arrington; press, The Publicity Office, Bob Fennell, Marc Thibodeau, Michael S. Borowski, Candi Adams.

Presented without intermission.

Autobiographical performance based on Ms. Gold's experiences as a Jewish (lesbian) mother and interviews conducted with Jewish women throughout the United States. First presentation of record was given at Off Off Broadway's Ars Nova (1/25–3/19/2006; 40 performances). An earlier version was presented under the title *G–d Doesn't Pay Rent Here* at Seattle's Empty Space Theatre (6/5–30/2002). See the 2002–2003 edition of *Best Plays Theater Yearbook* for more information.

My Name Is Rachel Corrie (71). Solo performance piece by Katharine Viner and Alan Rickman; based on the writings of Rachel Corrie. Produced by Dena Hammerstein, Pam Pariseau for James Hammerstein Productions, in association with the Royal Court Theatre, at the Minetta Lane Theatre. Opened October 15, 2006. (Closed December 17, 2006)

Rachel Corrie .... Megan Dodds   Rachel Corrie (mat.) .... Bree Elrod

Directed by Mr. Rickman; scenery and costumes, Hildegard Bechtler; lighting, Johanna Town; sound and video, Emma Laxton; associate producer, John O'Boyle; casting, David Caparelliotis; production stage manager, Renée Rimland; press, Barlow-Hartman, Michael Hartman, John Barlow, Carol Fineman, Leslie Baden.

Presented without intermission.

A young American woman's passionate feelings on justice in the Mideast as adapted from her diaries and e-mail after her tragic death. First presentation of record was given in London at the Royal Court Upstairs Theatre (4/14–30/2005) before a later engagement on the theater's mainstage (10/11–29/2005). The 2006–07 Off Broadway production had been scheduled for presentation in the prior season by New York Theatre Workshop (3/22/2006). The company postponed the production due to concerns about its political content, creating an intense controversy over perceived censorship. The Royal Court production moved instead to the West End's Playhouse Theatre (3/28–5/21/2006) before a run at the Edinburgh Festival's Pleasance Courtyard (8/3–28/2006).

The Public Theater production of **Emergence-See!** (26). Solo performance piece by Daniel Beaty. Oskar Eustis artistic director, Mara Manus executive director, at LuEsther Hall. Opened October 22, 2006. (Closed November 19, 2006)

Performed by Mr. Beaty.

Directed by Kenny Leon; scenery, Beowulf Boritt; costumes, Reggie Ray; lighting, Michael Chybowski; sound, Drew Levy and Tony Smolenski IV; music, Will Calhoun, Dan Moses Schreier; associate producers, Peter DuBois and Mandy Hackett; casting, Jordan Thaler; production stage manager, Barbara Reo; press, Arlene R. Kriv.

Presented without intermission.

A ghostly slave ship rises near the Statue of Liberty in New York harbor, giving an African-American performer many perspectives from which to view "freedom." First presentation of record was given by the Urban Theatre Arts Festival at Chashama (7/17–8/10/2003; 17 performances).

The Public Theater presentation of the **Labyrinth Theater Company** production of **A Small, Melodramatic Story** (16). By Stephen Belber. Oskar Eustis artistic director, Mara Manus executive director, at the Shiva Theater. Opened October 24, 2006. (Closed November 5, 2006)

Cleo .... Carlo Alban   Keith .... Lee Sellars
O .... Quincy Tyler Bernstine   Perry .... Isiah Whitlock Jr.

Directed by Lucie Tiberghien; scenery, Takeshi Kata; costumes, Mimi O'Donnell; lighting, Matthew Richards; sound, Elizabeth Rhodes; production stage manager, Paige Van Den Burg; press, Arlene R. Kriv.

Presented without intermission.

First presentation of record was given in a reading during the "District Views" series at Arena Stage in Washington, DC (3/22–24/2002). Further developed at the Eugene O'Neill Theater Center

Reflection: Quincy Tyler Bernstine in A Small, Melodramatic Story. *Photo: Monique Carboni*

in Connecticut, it was also given a public airing there (7/4–5/2003). The 2006–07 production is part of a series of collaborations between the Public Theater and the Labyrinth Theater Company (Philip Seymour Hoffman and John Ortiz artistic directors, Steve Asher executive director).

Skirball Center for the Performing Arts presentation of the **Gate Theatre Dublin** production of **Waiting for Godot** (5). By Samuel Beckett. L. Jay Oliva executive producer, Wiley Hausam executive director, at the Jack H. Skirball Center for the Performing Arts. Opened October 24, 2006. (Closed October 28, 2006)

Estragon	Johnny Murphy	Pozzo	Alan Stanford
Vladimir	Barry McGovern	A Boy	Devin O'Shea-Farren
Lucky	Stephen Brennan		

Directed by Walter D. Asmus; scenery and costumes, Louis le Brocquy; lighting, Rupert Murray; production stage manager, R. Michael Blanco.

Presented in two parts.

Two men await destiny unaware that they have met it. First presentation of record was given as excerpts on French radio under the title *En attendant Godot* (2/1952). The play had at that point awaited production for slightly more than three years. The first *En attendant Godot* production of record was given under the direction of Roger Blin at Théâtre de Babylone in Paris (1/5/1953). First presentation of record in this country was given in South Florida at the Coconut Grove Playhouse (1/3–14/1956) with Tom Ewell and Bert Lahr under the direction of Alan Schneider. After a puzzled Florida reception, the Broadway bow was cancelled and most of the company was fired. Mr. Lahr was retained and joined by E.G. Marshall, Alvin Epstein and Kurt Kaszner with Herbert Berghof at the helm. Audiences and critics remained nonplused, though mindful of the successful runs in London, Dublin and other European capitals. A 1955–56 *Best Plays* choice, the original Broadway production opened at the John Golden Theatre (4/19–6/9/1956; 59 performances). The production was revived the next season at the Ethel Barrymore Theatre by the same producer and director team with an African-American cast that included Geoffrey Holder, Earle Hyman, Rex Ingram and Mantan Moreland (1/21–26/1957; 6 performances).

Lincoln Center Theater production of **The Clean House** (88). By Sarah Ruhl. André Bishop artistic director, Bernard Gersten executive producer, at the Mitzi E. Newhouse Theater. Opened October 30, 2006. Production hiatus December 18, 2006–January 1, 2007. (Closed January 28, 2007)

Matilde	Vanessa Aspillaga	Matilde's Father; Charles	John Dossett
Lane	Blair Brown	Matilde's Mother; Ana	Concetta Tomei
Virginia	Jill Clayburgh		

Understudies: Ms. Aspillaga—Nicole Shalhoub; Mr. Dossett—Peter Samuel; Mses. Brown, Clayburgh—Maureen Mueller; Ms. Tomei—Marilyn Dodds Frank.

Directed by Bill Rauch; choreography, Sabrina Peck; scenery, Christopher Acebo; costumes, Shigeru Yaji; lighting, James F. Ingalls; sound and music, Andre Pluess; casting, Daniel Swee; production stage manager, Roy Harris; press, Philip Rinaldi, Barbara Carroll.

Time: The present. Place: A house not far from the city, not far from the sea. Presented in two parts.

Mature women struggle to adjust to the petty (and large) indignities of life in this comedy. The playwright received the 29th Susan Smith Blackburn Prize in 2004 for the best play written in English by a woman. First presentation of record was given at the Yale Repertory Theatre in New Haven (9/23/2004). A 2006–07 *Best Plays* choice (see essay by Anne Marie Welsh in this volume).

Rapprochement: Concetta Tomei and Blair Brown in The Clean House. *Photo: Joan Marcus*

Evil Dead: The Musical (126). Musical with book and lyrics by George Reinblatt; music by Frank Cipolla, Christopher Bond, Melissa Morris and Mr. Reinblatt; additional music by Mr. Bond; additional lyrics by Rob Daleman. Produced by Jenkay LLC, Jeffrey Latimer Entertainment, Just For Laughs Live, Jay H. Harris, Bruce Hills, Evi Regev, Gilbert Rozon, at New World Stages. Opened November 1, 2006. (Closed February 17, 2007)

Linda	Jennifer Byrne	Ash	Ryan Ward
Cheryl	Jenna Coker	Scott; Spirit	Brandon Wardell
Shelly; Annie	Renee Klapmeyer	Fake Shemp	Ryan Williams
Ed; Moose	Tom Walker	Jake	Darryl Winslow

Orchestra: Daniel Feyer conductor, keyboard; Jake Schwartz guitar, banjo; Brad Carbone percussion, drums.

Directed by Mr. Bond and Hinton Battle; choreography, Mr. Battle; scenery, David Gallo; costumes, Cynthia Nordstrom; lighting, Jason Lyons; sound, Peter Fitzgerald and Kevin Lacy; orchestrations and arrangements, Eric Svejcar; music coordination, Frank Cipolla; fight direction, B.H. Barry; casting, Arnold J. Mungioli; production stage manager, Jane Pole; press, The Karpel Group.

Presented in two parts.

Musical parody of Sam Raimi's contributions to the zombie genre of film. First presentation of record was given under the title *Evil Dead 1 and 2: The Musical* at the Tranzac Club in Toronto (8/14–23/2003) with a return engagement (10/16–11/1/2003). The piece continued to develop at Toronto's Bathurst Street Theatre (6/22–26/2004; 7 performances) before a run at Montreal's Cabaret du Plateau during the Just for Laughs Festival (7/8–25/2004).

ACT I

"Cabin in the Woods"	Ash, Linda, Scott, Shelly, Cheryl
"Housewares Employee"	Ash, Linda
"It Won't Let Us Leave"	Cheryl
"Look Who's Evil Now"	Cheryl, Shelly
"What the . . .?"	Ash, Scott, Cheryl
"Join Us"	Cheryl, Moose, House Spirits
"Good Old Reliable Jake"	Jake, Annie, Ed
"Housewares Employee" (Reprise)	Ash, Linda
"I'm Not a Killer"	Ash

ACT II

"I'm Not a Killer" (Reprise)	Ash, Ed
"Bit-Part Demon"	Ed
"All the Men in My Life"	Annie, Ash, Jake
"Ode to an Accidental Stabbing"	Jake, Annie, Cheryl
"Do the Necronomicon"	Canadian Demons
"It's Time"	Company
"You Blew That Bitch Away"	Company

Perry Street Theatre Company production of **An Oak Tree** (73). By Tim Crouch. David Elliott and Martin Platt directors, in association with Rosalie Beer, A.J. Epstein, Richard Jordan Productions, at the Barrow Street Theatre. Opened November 4, 2006. (Closed January 14, 2007)

Hypnotist	Tim Crouch	Father	Special Guest

Directed by Mr. Crouch, Karl James and A. Smith; scenery, Narelle Sissons; lighting, Mr. Epstein; sound and music, Peter Gill; production stage manager, Richard A. Hodge; press, Springer Associates Public Relations, Gary Springer, Joe Trentacosta.

Presented without intermission.

Mr. Crouch coaxes an unscripted performance from a guest artist portraying a grief-stricken "father" whose daughter was killed in an auto accident by Mr. Crouch's character. Special guests included F. Murray Abraham, Joan Allen, Laurie Anderson, Mary Bacon, Jeremy Bieler, Reed Birney, Steve Blanchard, Mark Blankenship, Walter Bobbie, Charles Busch, Kelly Calabrese, Michael Cerveris, Kathleen Chalfant, Christopher Cook, Michael Countryman, Michael Cullen, Peter Dinklage, Tovah Feldshuh, Katie Finneran, Hunter Foster, Rachel Fowler, Alison Fraser, Randy Harrison, Leslie Hendrix, Wendy Vanden Heuvel, Judith Ivey, Richard Kind, Amy Landecker, Brian Logan, Carolyn McCormick, Frances McDormand, Mike Myers, Alexandra Neil, Tim Blake Nelson, Austin Pendleton, David Hyde Pierce, Maryann Plunkett, Laila Robbins, Lucas Caleb Rooney, John Shuman, Kristen Sieh, Pearl Sun, Lili Taylor, Maura Tierney, Tamara Tunie, James Urbaniak, Peter Van Wagner, Maja Wampuszyc. First presentation of record was given at the Traverse Theatre during the Edinburgh Festival (8/4–28/2005).

Mimi Le Duck (30). Musical with book and lyrics by Diana Hansen-Young; music by Brian Feinstein. Produced by Mango Hill Productions and Aruba Productions, in association with Marie Costanza and Paul Beattie, at New World Stages. Opened November 6, 2006. (Closed December 3, 2006)

Miriam	Annie Golden	Claude	Robert DuSold
Peter	Marcus Neville	Madame Vallet	Eartha Kitt
Ernest Hemingway	Allen Fitzpatrick	Ziggy	Tom Aldredge
Gypsy	Ken Jennings	Clay	Candy Buckley

Directed by Thomas Caruso; choreography, Matt West; scenery, John Arnone; costumes, Ann Hould-Ward; lighting, David Lander; sound, Tony Smolenski IV and Walter Trarbach; orchestrations and music direction, Chris Fenwick; production stage manager, Charles M. Turner III.

Presented in two parts.

A duck painter moves to Paris in order to become a "real" artist. First presentation of record was given at the Adirondack Theatre Festival in Glens Falls, New York, (7/21–31/2004) before opening at the Players Theatre during the New York International Fringe Festival (8/13/2004).

ACT I

"Ketchum, Idaho"	Ketchum Choir, Miriam
"Gray"	Miriam
"Paris Is a City"	Gypsy
"22 Rue Danou"	House
"A Thousand Hands"	Hemingway
"Why Not?"	Claude, Ancestors
"It's All About"	Vallet, Miriam
"Empty or Full"	Ziggy, Miriam
"Everything Changes"	Vallet
"There Are Times in Life"	Clay, Miriam
"Don't Ask"	Clay
"Get Outta Here Peter"	Miriam, Peter
"Is There Room?"	Miriam, Peter

ACT II

"The Green Flash"	Hemingway
"My Mother Always Said"	Miriam
"The Only Time We Have Is Now"	Ziggy
"Cozy Dreams Come True"	Peter, Claude, Gypsy
"Paris Is a City" (Reprise)	Gypsy
"Peter's Reprise"	Peter
"All Things New"	Vallet
'The Garden Is Green"	Miriam
"There is Room"	Miriam, Peter, House

How to Save the World and Find True Love in 90 Minutes (57). Musical with book and lyrics by Jonathan Karp; music by Seth Weinstein. Produced by Lawrence Anderson and the Singing Comedians at New World Stages. Opened November 12, 2006. (Closed December 31, 2007)

Miles Muldoon ....Michael McEachran   Violet Zipper ....Nicole Ruth Snelson
Julie Lemmon ....Anika Larsen

Ensemble: Stephen Bienskie, Natalie Joy Johnson, Kevin Smith Kirkwood.

Orchestra: Mr. Weinstein conductor; Jonah Speidel keyboard; James Bettincourt bass; Greg Germann drums.

Directed and choreographed by Christopher Gattelli; scenery, Beowulf Boritt; costumes; David Murin; lighting, Jeff Croiter; sound, Peter Hylenski; orchestrations and arrangements, Messrs. Weinstein and Speidel; music direction, Mr. Weinstein; press, The Karpel Group.

Presented without intermission.

A man hit by a flying melon develops telepathic powers and an understanding of true love. First presentation of record was given at the Lucille Lortel Theatre during the New York International Fringe Festival (8/25–29/2004; 5 performances).

MUSICAL NUMBERS

"Only the Paranoid Survive" .... Miles, Greeks
"Love or Fear" ....Julie, Miles
"1 Want What You Want" .... Miles, Violet, Greeks
"The Melon Ballet" .... Company
"Julie's Prayer" ....Julie, Greeks
"The Voices in My Head" .... Miles, Greeks
"Violet's Confession" .... Violet
"Love Is Violet" ....Julie, Yogi
"Yoga Class" .... Yogi, Julie, Miles, Students
"I Want to Know You" .... Miles, Violet
"Read My Mind" ....Greeks
"It's Over" .... Company
"When the Music Played" ....Julie
"We Can Save the World and Find True Love" .... He, Violet
"Save the People" .... Miles, Greeks
"Oh, God 'T' Read My Mind" .... Company

Striking 12 (61). Musical with book and lyrics by Rachel Sheinkin, Brendan Milburn and Valerie Vigoda; music by Mr. Milburn and Ms. Vigoda. Produced by Nancy Nagel Gibbs and Greg Schaffert at the Daryl Roth Theatre. Opened November 12, 2006. (Closed December 31, 2006)

Party Host; others ....Gene Lewin   Sad Light Seller; others ....Valerie Vigoda
Man ....Brendan Milburn

Musicians: Ms. Vigoda electric guitar; Mr. Milburn keyboard; Mr. Lewin drums.

Directed by Ted Sperling; scenery, David Korins; costumes, Jennifer Caprio; lighting, Michael Gilliam; sound, Robert J. Killenberger; production stage manager, Kim Vernace.

Presented without intermission.

Anti-holiday holiday musical underpinned by themes from Hans Christian Andersen's "The Little Match Girl." First presentation of record was given at the Prince Music Theater in Philadelphia (11–12/2002). It was later chosen, under the title *Striking 12: The GrooveLily Holiday Show*, to participate in a National Alliance for Musical Theatre showcase (10/3–4/2004). *Striking 12* was later presented at Ars Nova (12/3–23/2005; 17 performances).

MUSICAL NUMBERS

"Snow Song"	"Can't Go Home"
"Last Day of the Year"	"Wonderful"
"Resolution"	"Give the Drummer Some"
"The Sales Pitch"	"Picture This"
"Red and Green (And I'm Feeling Blue)"	"Caution to the Wind"
"Matches for Sale"	"Screwed-Up People Make Great Art"
"Say What?"	"It's Not All Right"
"Hey La La" / "Fine Fine Fine"	"Wonderful" (Reprise)

"Picture This" / "Snow Song" (Reprise)   "Closing"

Roundabout Theatre Company production of **Suddenly Last Summer** (74). Revival of the play by Tennessee Williams. Todd Haimes artistic director, Harold Wolpert managing director, Julia C. Levy executive director, at the Laura Pels Theatre in the Harold and Miriam Steinberg Center for Theatre. Opened November 15, 2006. Closed January 20, 2007.

Mrs. Venable .... Blythe Danner	George Holly .... Wayne Wilcox
Dr. Cukrowicz .... Gale Harold	Catharine Holly .... Carla Gugino
Miss Foxhill .... Karen Walsh	Sister Felicity .... Sandra Shipley
Mrs. Holly .... Becky Ann Baker	

Directed by Mark Brokaw; scenery and costumes, Santo Loquasto; lighting, David Weiner; sound, Peter Golub and Ryan Powers; music, Mr. Golub; wigs and hair, Tom Watson; fight direction, Rick Sordelet; production stage manager, James FitzSimmons; press, Boneau/Bryan-Brown, Adrian Bryan-Brown.

Presented without intermission.

A Southern woman struggles to reveal the truth about her dead cousin as the woman's aunt conspires to keep the memory of her son pure. First presentation of record was given Off Broadway at the York Playhouse (1/7–7/13/1958) paired with another one-act, *Something Unspoken*, under the general title of *Garden District*. The first Broadway production of *Garden District* was presented in and under the aegis of Circle in the Square (10/10–11/5/1995; 31 performances).

Temptress: Blythe Danner and Gale Harold in Suddenly Last Summer. *Photo: Joan Marcus*

Fast friends: George Grizzard and Christine Baranski in Regrets Only. *Photo: Joan Marcus*

Manhattan Theatre Club production of **Regrets Only** (81). By Paul Rudnick. Lynne Meadow artistic director, Barry Grove executive producer, at City Center Stage I. Opened November 19, 2006. (Closed January 28, 2007)

Tibby McCullough	Christine Baranski	Marietta Claypoole	Siân Phillips
Spencer McCullough	Diane Davis	Jack McCullough	David Rasche
Hank Hadley	George Grizzard	Myra Kesselman	Jackie Hoffman

Understudies: Ms. Baranski—Kit Flanagan; Ms. Davis—Sofia Jean Gomez; Messrs. Grizzard, Rasche—Terry Layman; Mses. Phillips, Testa, Hoffman—Patricia O'Connell.

Directed by Christopher Ashley; scenery, Michael Yeargan; costumes, William Ivey Long; lighting, Natasha Katz; sound, John Gromada; casting, Nancy Piccione, David Caparelliotis; production stage manager, Martha Donaldson; press, Boneau/Bryan-Brown, Chris Boneau, Jim Byk, Aaron Meier, Heath Schwartz.

Republican lawyers from New York's upper crust alienate a gay friend when they support an anti-gay-marriage bill, which triggers a day-without-gays strike. Mary Testa temporarily replaced Ms. Hoffman during the run (12/10/2006–1/7/2007).

The Public Theater production of **Durango** (24). By Julia Cho. Oskar Eustis artistic director, Mara Manus executive director, in association with the Long Wharf Theatre (Gordon Edelstein artistic director, Joan Channick managing director), at Martinson Hall. Opened November 20, 2006. (Closed December 10, 2007)

Isaac Lee	James Yaegashi	Jimmy Lee	Jon Norman Schneider
Boo-Seng Lee	James Saito	Red Angel; Bob	Jay Sullivan
Jerry; Ned	Ross Bickel		

Directed by Chay Yew; scenery, Dan Ostling; costumes, Linda Cho; lighting, Paul Whitaker; sound and music, Fabian Obispo; songs, Ms. Cho; associate producers, Peter DuBois, Mandy Hackett; casting, Jordan Thaler, Heidi Griffiths; production stage manager, Buzz Cohen; press, Arlene R. Kriv.

Time: The near present. Place: The Southwest. Presented without intermission.

An Asian-American immigrant family trying to thrive in the United States takes a road trip after the father finds himself suddenly unemployed. First presentation of record was given at the Long Wharf Theatre in New Haven, Connecticut (9/13–10/15/2006).

Manhattan Theatre Club production of **The American Pilot** (47). By David Greig. Lynne Meadow artistic director, Barry Grove executive producer, at City Center Stage II. Opened November 21, 2006. (Closed December 31, 2006)

Translator	Geoffrey Arend	Farmer	Ron Domingo
Evie	Anjali Bhimani	American Pilot	Aaron Staton
Soldier 1	Brian Bielawski	Sarah	Rita Wolf
Trader	Yusef Bulos	Captain	Waleed F. Zuaiter
Soldier 2	Josh Casaubon		

Understudies: Mses. Bhimani, Wolf—Aadya Bedi; Mr. Staton—Brian Bielawski; Messrs. Arend, Bulos, Bielawski, Casaubon—Arian Moayed; Messrs. Domingo, Zuaiter, Bielawski, Casaubon—Thom Rivera.

Directed by Lynne Meadow; scenery, Derek McLane; costumes, Ilona Somogyi; lighting, Christopher Akerlind; sound, Obadiah Eaves; fight direction, J. David Brimmer; casting, Nancy Piccione, David Caparelliotis; press, Boneau/Bryan-Brown, Chris Boneau, Jim Byk, Aaron Meier, Heath Schwartz.

Time: The present. Place: A remote valley in a country mired in war. Presented in two parts.

Lost in translation: Anjali Bhimani, Waleed F. Zuaiter, Ron Domingo, Geoffrey Arend and Aaron Staton in The American Pilot. *Photo: Carol Rosegg*

An American pilot becomes a pawn to local leaders when he crashes in a foreign country, which leads to a show of superpower force. First presentation of record was given by the Royal Shakespeare Company at the Other Place in Stratford-upon-Avon (5/5–7/9/2005). The RSC later presented it at London's Soho Theatre (3/28–4/8/2006) during the New Work Festival.

Room Service (158). Transfer from Off Off Broadway of the play by John Murray and Allen Boretz. Produced by Peccadillo Theater Company, in association with Jonathan Reinis Productions, Jeffrey Sine and the StoryLine Project, at Soho Playhouse. Opened November 28, 2006. (Closed April 8, 2007)

Harry Binion .... Fred Berman	Christine Marlowe .... Kim Rachelle Harris
Joseph Gribble .... Dale Carman	Faker Englund .... Robert O'Gorman
Dr. Glass .... Jerry Coyle	Sasha Smirnoff;
Gregory Wagner .... Sterling Coyne	Sen. Blake .... Louis Michael Sacco
Gordon Miller .... David Edwards	Simon Jenkins .... Raymond Thorne
Leo Davis .... Scott Evans	Timothy Hogarth;
Hilda Manney .... Blythe Gruda	Messenger .... Dennis Wit

Directed by Dan Wackerman; scenery, Chris Jones; costumes, Gail Cooper-Hecht; lighting, Jeffrey E. Salzberg; stage manager, Scott Earley.

Time: The 1930s. Place: A hotel in the Theater District. Presented in two parts.

A theater producer under increasing pressure faces eviction as he comically struggles to keep his company together. First presentation of record was given in Baltimore (05/10/1937). The original Broadway production opened at the Cort Theatre (05/19/1937–07/16/1938; 500 performances). Burns Mantle chose Victor Wolfson's comedy *Excursion* over *Room Service* for *The Best Plays of 1936–37*, citing the former's "greater surprise" and "a majority of virtues looked

Unlikely pair: David Cale and Mary Faber in Floyd and Clea Under the Western Sky. *Photo: Joan Marcus*

for in a popular success." The public disagreed, keeping *Room Service* in business for 484 more performances than *Excursion*. The 2006–07 production transferred to Off Broadway after a run at the Bank Street Theatre (7/06–8/05/06).

New York Theatre Workshop production of **Kaos** (31). By Martha Clarke; adapted by Frank Pugliese; dramaturgy by Giovanni Papotto; based on the stories of Luigi Pirandello and the film *Kaos* by the Taviani Brothers. James C. Nicola artistic director, Lynn Moffat managing director. Opened December 4, 2006. (Closed December 31, 2006)

Performed by Felix Blaska, Sophie Bortolussi, George de la Pena, Daria Deflorian, Vito Di Bella, Lorenzo Iacona, Jim Iorio, Gabrielle Malone, Matthew Mohr, Rocco Sisto, Christina Spina, Rebecca Wender, Robert Wersinger, Julia Wilkins.

Musicians: Irving Grossman, John T. La Barbara, Richard Sosinsky.

Directed and choreographed by Ms. Clarke; scenery, Scott Pask; costumes, Donna Zakowska; lighting, Christopher Akerlind; projections, Tal Yarden; music direction, Jill Jaffe, Mr. La Barbera; production stage manager, Anita Ross; press, Richard Kornberg and Associates, Richard Kornberg, Don Summa.

Time: Turn of the 20th century. Place: A Sicilian hamlet. Presented without intermission.

Parts of four stories by Mr. Pirandello, featured in the 1984 film *Kaos*, which demonstrate the hardscrabble lives of people set against an unforgiving landscape. Performed in Italian with English subtitles.

Playwrights Horizons production of **Floyd and Clea Under the Western Sky** (16). Musical with book and lyrics by David Cale; music by Jonathan Kreisberg and Mr. Cale. Tim Sanford artistic director, Leslie Marcus managing director, William Russo general manager, at the Mainstage Theater. Opened December 5, 2006. (Closed December 17, 2006)

Floyd .... David Cale   Clea .... Mary Faber

Musicians: Dylan Schiavone guitar, piano; Jimmy Heffernan dobro, pedal steel; Brad Russell acoustic, electric bass; Bill Campbell drums, percussion.

Directed by Joe Calarco; scenery, David Korins; costumes, Anne Kennedy; lighting, Chris Lee; sound, Ken Travis; music direction and orchestrations, Mr. Kreisberg; casting, Alaine Alldaffer; production stage manager, Emily N. Wells; press, The Publicity Office, Bob Fennell, Marc Thibodeau, Michael S. Borowski, Candi Adams.

Time: Five years ago; the present. Place: Texas; Montana; Los Angeles. Presented without intermission.

Intergenerational, unconditional love and country music join forces to enhance the lives of two persons. First presentation of record was given by the Goodman Theatre in Chicago during its New Stages Series (1/21/2004) before further development at Hartford Stage's Brand: New Festival in Connecticut (10/29/2004). The world premiere production was given at the Goodman (4/19/2005).

ACT I

Scene 1: Five years ago. A club in Lubbock, Texas
    "burnt angel at aol.com" .... Floyd
    "One Foot in the Real World" .... Floyd
Scene 2: Three years later. Night. Great Falls, Montana.
Scene 3: A few days later.
    "I Dread the Night" .... Floyd
    "Greedy" .... Clea
Scene 4: A Great Falls diner.
Scene 5: A high school gym.
    "Safety Net" .... Floyd
Scene 6: The next day.
Scene 7: Two weeks later. A high school gym.

"I'll Be Your Secret" .... Clea
Scene 8: Back at the Studebaker.
Scene 9: Days later.
"Can't I Stay Awhile?" .... Floyd
Scene 10: One month later. A motel room.
"Linger Awhile" .... Floyd
"Help's on the Way" .... Clea
Scene 11: The following evening.
"White Cowboy Hat" .... Floyd
Scene 12: Two days later. Back at the Studebaker.

ACT II
Scene 1: The present. An AA meeting in Austin, Texas. Locations in Los Angeles.
"A Simple Life" .... Floyd
"White Cowboy Hat" (Reprise) .... Clea
"Would You Give a Damn?" .... Clea
Scene 2: Floyd's house in Austin.
Scene 3: A club in Austin.
"Left Hook" .... Floyd, Clea
"(We're in It for) the Long Haul" .... Floyd, Clea

Atlantic Theater Company production of **The Voysey Inheritance** (113). By Harley Granville Barker; adapted by David Mamet. Neil Pepe artistic director, Andrew D. Hamingson managing director, at the Atlantic Theater Company. Opened December 6, 2006. (Closed March 25, 2007)

Edward Voysey	Michael Stuhlbarg	Maj. Booth Voysey	C.J. Wilson
Alice Maitland	Samantha Soule	Rev. Evan Colpus	Geddeth Smith
Mrs. Voysey	Judith Roberts	Ethel Voysey	Katharine Powell
George Booth	Peter Maloney	Honor Voysey	Rachel Black
Mr. Voysey	Fritz Weaver	Trenchard Voysey	Christopher Duva
Mr. Peacey	Steven Goldstein	Hugh Voysey	Todd Weeks

Directed by David Warren; scenery, Derek McLane; costumes, Gregory Gale; lighting, Jeff Croiter; sound, Fitz Patton; music direction, David Chase; casting, Telsey and Company; production stage manager, Freda Farrell; press, Boneau/Bryan-Brown, Chris Boneau, Joe Perrotta.

Time: 1905. Place: The Voysey house in England. Presented in two parts.

A family of financiers with an impeccable reputation discovers something amiss among its investments. First presentation of record was given at London's Court Theatre (11/7–24/1905; 6 performances). First presentation of record in this country was given as a radio program for the Theatre Guild of the Air on WRC in Washington, DC, (11/12/1950) with Douglas Fairbanks Jr. and Angela Lansbury. First theatrical presentation of record in this country was given Off Off Broadway by the Mint Theater Company (6/14/1999–7/3/1999; 20 performances). First presentation of record of Mr. Mamet's adaptation was given by the American Conservatory Theater, in association with the Kansas City Repertory Theatre, at San Francisco's Geary Theater (3/23–4/17/2005).

59E59 Theaters presentation of **Murder Mystery Blues** (27). By Janey Clarke; based on a series of *New Yorker* short stories by Woody Allen; music by Warren Wills; lyrics by Ms. Clarke. Elysabeth Kleinhans artistic director, Peter Tear executive producer. Opened December 7, 2006. (Closed December 31, 2006)

Performed by Stephanie Dodd, Mary Fahl, Jeff Ganz, Alex Haven, Michael Murray, Andromeda Turre.

Directed by Ms. Clarke; scenery and lighting, Maruti Evans; costumes, Michael Bevins; music direction, Mr. Wills; press, Karen Greco Entertainment, Lauren Pokras.

Presented in two parts.

A familiar *dramatis personae* of neurotics and knockouts inhabit a noirish world infused by jazz music. First presentation of record was given in London's Warehouse Theatre (12/9/2005–2/19/2006).

Model of rectitude: Samantha Soule and Michael Stuhlbarg in The Voysey Inheritance. *Photo: Monique Carboni*

The York Theatre Company production of **That Time of the Year** (22). Musical revue with book and lyrics by Laurence Holzman and Felicia Needleman; music by Sanford Mark Cohen, Nicholas Levin, Donald Oliver, Kyle Rosen, Brad Ross, Mark Wherry, Wendy Wilf. James Morgan producing artistic director, in association with Whiskey Down Productions, at Theatre at St. Peters. Opened December 7, 2006. (Closed December 24, 2006)

Performed by Bridget Beirne, Kerri Jill Garbis, Erin Maguire, Jonathan Rayson, Nick Verina.

Musicians: Mort Silver reeds; Annie Pasqua piano; Chris Pagano percussion.

Directed and choreographed by Annette Jolles; scenery, James Morgan; costumes, Terese Wadden; lighting, Chris Robinson; orchestrations and music direction, Ms. Pasqua; casting, Norman Meranus; production stage manager, Scott Dela Cruz; press, David Gersten and Associates.

Presented in two parts.

Holiday revue that celebrates all aspects of the season.

ACT I

"That Time of the Year"	Company
"Angelo Rosenbaum"	Jonathan
"Stay Home Tonight"	Kerri
"Rock 'n' Roll Hanukkah"	Nick, Jonathan
"Little Colored Lights"	Erin
"God Only Knows"	Robert
"Country Christmas"	Bridget
"That Time of the Year" (Reprise)	Kerri
"People With Obligations"	Company
"You're the Reason Why"	Jonathan

"Mama's Latkes" .... Kerri
"Husbands' Blues" .... Nick, Jonathan
"That Time of the Year" (Reprise) .... Erin
"Welcome" .... Bridget
"Judah Maccabee" .... Company

ACT II

"Calypso Christmas" .... Kerri, Company
"They All Come Home" .... Erin
"Time for a Spin" .... Nick
"Underneath the Mistletoe" .... Bridget, Jonathan
"Wong Ho's China Garden" .... Kerri, Nick
"Christmastime" .... Bridget, Kerri, Erin
"That Time of the Year" (Reprise) .... Kerri, Erin, Bridget
"Candles in the Window" .... Jonathan
"It's Everywhere" .... Erin, Men
"Holiday Lament (The Fruitcake Song)" .... Kerri, Erin, Bridget
"Miracles Can Happen" .... Company
"That Time of the Year" .... Company
"What Are We Gonna Do?" .... Company
"That Time of the Year" (Reprise) .... Company

Annie (28). Revival of the musical with book by Thomas Meehan; music by Charles Strouse; lyrics by Martin Charnin; based on "Little Orphan Annie" created by Harold Gray. Produced by Networks Presentations, Rodger Hess and TC Theatrical at Theater at Madison Square Garden. Opened December 8, 2006. (Closed December 30, 2006)

Molly	Anastasia Korbal	Oliver Warbucks	Conrad John Schuck
Pepper	Madison Zavitz	Star-to-Be	Monica L. Patton
Duffy	Amanda Balon	Rooster Hannigan	Scott Willis
July	Nickayla Tucker	Lily St. Regis	Ashley Puckett Gonzales
Tessie	Brandy Panfili	Bert Healy	Christopher Vettel
Kate	Gabi Carrubba	Fred McCracken	Allen Kendall
Annie	Marissa O'Donnell	Jimmy Johnson	Richard Costa
Miss Hannigan	Kathie Lee Gifford	Sound Effects Man	Harry Turpin
Bundles McCloskey	Aaron Kaburick	Ronnie Boylan	Natalie Backman
Apple Seller	Richard Costa	Connie Boylan	Kelly Lynn Cosme
Dog Catcher	Harry Turpin	Bonnie Boylan	Liz Power
Sandy	Lola	Oxydent Producer	Katherine Pecevich
Lt. Ward	Allen Kendall	Kaltenborn's Voice	Archie T. Tridmorten
Sophie	Katherine Pecevich	FDR	Allan Baker
Grace Farrell	Elizabeth Broadhurst	Ickes	Harry Turpin
Drake	David Chernault	Howe	Allen Kendall
Mrs. Pugh	Katherine Pecevich	Hull	Christopher Vettel
Cecille	Natalie Backman	Perkins	Katherine Pecevich
Annette	Kelly Lynn Cosme	Morgenthau	Richard Costa
Mrs. Greer	Liz Power	Justice Brandeis	Aaron Kaburick

Ensemble: Natalie Backman, David Chernault, Kelly Lynn Cosme, Richard Costa, Antoinette DiPietropolo, Brian Michael Hoffman, Aaron Kaburick, Allen Kendall, Billy Kimmel, Monica L. Patton, Katherine Pecevich, Liz Power, Harry Turpin, Christopher Vettel.

Orchestra: Kelly Ann Lambert conductor; Karen Dryer assistant conductor, keyboard; John Trombetta trumpet; Tom Bradford drums.

Understudies: Mr. Schuck—David Chernault, Christopher Vettel; Ms. Gifford—Alene Robertson, Katherine Pecevich, Julie Cardia; Ms. O'Donnell—Gabi Carrubba; Ms. Broadhurst—Liz Power, Natalie Backman; Mr. Baker—Christopher Vettel, Billy Kimmel; Mr. Willis—Richard Costa, Harry Turpin; Ms. Gonzales—Kelly Lynn Cosme; Mr. Kaburick—Brian Michael Hoffman; Messrs. Chernault, Vettel—Allen Kendall, Aaron Kaburick; Ms. Korbal—Amanda Balon; Ms. Patton—Natalie Backman; Lola—Buster, Mikey.

Swings: Julie Cardia, Billy Kimmel, Antoinette DiPietropolo.

Directed by Mr. Charnin; choreography, Peter Gennaro and Liza Gennaro; scenery, Ming Cho Lee; costumes, Theoni V. Aldredge and Jimm Halliday; lighting, Ken Billington; sound, Peter Hylenski; orchestrations, music direction and music supervision, Keith Levenson; music coordination, John Mezzio; hair, Bernie Ardia; executive producer, Kary M. Walker; casting, Patricia Pearce Gentry, Bob Cline; production stage manager, Molly Meg Legal; press, TMG–The Marketing Group.

Time: December 1933. Place: New York City; Washington, DC. Presented in two parts.

An underprivileged orphan changes the lives of everyone around her and looks forward to a brighter tomorrow. First presentation of record was given at Goodspeed Opera House in Connecticut (8/10/1976). A 1976–77 *Best Plays* choice, the original Broadway production opened at the Alvin (now Neil Simon) Theatre and moved three times in its maiden voyage on the Main Stem to the ANTA Playhouse (now named for August Wilson), Eugene O'Neill and Uris (now Gershwin) Theatres (4/21/1977–1/2/1983; 2,377 performances). At the 1977 Tony Awards, *Annie* received honors in the categories of musical (producers Lewis Allen, Mike Nichols, Irwin Meyer, Stephen R. Friedman), book, score, actress (Dorothy Loudon), scenery (David Mitchell), costumes (Theoni V. Aldredge) and choreography (Peter Gennaro). There has been one Broadway revival at the Martin Beck (now Al Hirschfeld) Theatre (3/26–10/19/1997; 239 performances).

ACT I

December 11–19, 1933
Scene 1: The New York Municipal Orphanage (Girls Annex), St. Mark's Place
"Maybe" .... Annie
"It's the Hard-Knock Life" Annie, Orphans
"It's the Hard-Knock Life" (Reprise) .... Orphans
Scene 2: Lower Broadway
"Tomorrow" .... Annie
Scene 3: Hooverville Under the Brooklyn Bridge
"We'd Like to Thank You Herbert Hoover" .... Annie, Hooverville-ites
Scene 4: Hannigan's Office at the Orphanage
"Little Girls" .... Miss Hannigan
"Little Girls" (Reprise) .... Miss Hannigan
Scene 5: The Warbucks Mansion at Fifth Avenue and 82nd Street
"I Think I'm Gonna Like It Here" .... Grace, Annie, Drake,
Cecille, Annette, Mrs. Pugh,
Mrs. Greer, Servants
Scene 6: From Fifth Avenue to Times Square
"NYC" .... Warbucks, Grace, Annie,
Star to Be, New Yorkers
Scene 7: Hannigan's Office at the Orphanage
"Easy Street" .... Miss Hannigan, Rooster, Lily
Scene 8: Warbucks's Study
"You Won't Be an Orphan for Long" .... Grace, Drake, Mrs. Pugh, Cecille,
Annette, Servants, Warbucks
"Maybe" (Reprise) .... Annie

ACT II

December 21–25, 1933
Scene 1: NBC Radio Studio at 30 Rockefeller Center
"You're Never Fully Dressed Without a Smile" .... Bert Healy, Boylan Sisters,
Hour of Smiles Family
Scene 2: Sewing Room at the Orphanage
"You're Never Fully Dressed Without a Smile" (Reprise) .... Orphans
"Easy Street" (Reprise) .... Miss Hannigan, Rooster, Lily
Scene 3: Washington: The White House
"Tomorrow" (Reprise) .... Annie, FDR, Warbucks, Cabinet
Scene 4: Gallery at the Warbucks Mansion
"Something Was Missing" .... Warbucks

Scene 5: East Ballroom of the Warbucks Mansion
"Annie" .... Grace, Drake, Staff
"I Don't Need Anything but You" .... Warbucks, Annie
"Maybe" (Reprise) ....Annie
"A New Deal for Christmas" .... Annie, Warbucks, Grace,
FDR, Orphans, Staff

*My Mother's Italian, My Father's Jewish, and I'm in Therapy! (197). Solo performance piece by Steve Solomon. Produced by Rodger Hess, Abby Koffler and Howard Rapp at the Little Shubert Theatre. Opened December 8, 2006.

Performed by Mr. Solomon.

Directed by John Bowab; scenery, Ray Klausen; lighting, Brian Nason; sound, Carl Casella; production stage manager, Patricia Keefer-Davis; press, Keith Sherman and Associates.

Presented without intermission.

Mr. Solomon describes his attempts to synthesize the elements of his ethnic heritage and family dysfunction in comedic fashion. After 165 performances at the Little Shubert Theatre, production transferred to the Westside Theatre Downstairs (5/4/2007). First presentation of record was given at the Leventhal-Sidman Jewish Community Center in Newton, Massachusetts (10/23–24/2004; 2 performances).

New York Gilbert and Sullivan Players production of **The Yeoman of the Guard** (3). Revival of the operetta with book by W.S. Gilbert; music by Arthur Sullivan. Albert Bergeret artistic director, at City Center. Opened January 5, 2007. (Closed January 13, 2007)

Sir Richard Cholmondely .... Keith Jurosko	First Yeoman .... Daniel Lockwood
Colonel .... David Root	Second Yeoman .... Alexander Elisa
Sergeant Meryll .... Richard Alan Holmes	Elsie Maynard .... Laurelyn Watson Chase
Leonard Meryll .... David Chase	Phoebe Meryll .... Erika Person
Jack Point .... Stephen Quint	Dame Carruthers .... Angela Smith
Wilfred Shadbolt .... David Wannen	Kate .... Meredith Borden
Headsman .... Lucian Russell	

Ensemble: Kimberly Deana Bennett, Ted Bouton, Susan Case, Michael Connolly, Donata Cucinotta, Louis Dall'Ava, Alena Gerst Dailey, Dianna Dollman, Shana Farr, Michael Galante, Katie Hall, Alan Hill, Lynelle Johnson, Michael Levesque, David Macaluso, James Mills, Lance Olds, Lauren Pastorek, Monique Pelletier, Fausto Pineda, Paul Sigrist, Lauren Wenegrat, William Whitefield.

Understudies: Mr. Chase—Fausto Pineda; Mr. Quint—David Macaluso; Mr. Wannen—Lance Olds; Ms. Chase—Shana Farr; Ms. Smith—Dianna Dollman.

Directed by Albert Bergeret; choreography, Janis Ansley-Ungar; scenery, Richard Manfredi and Albere; costumes, Jan Holland and Gail J. Wofford; lighting, Sally Small, music direction, Mr. Bergeret; production stage manager, David Sigafoose; press, Cromarty and Company, Peter Cromarty.

Time: 16th century. Place: Tower Green. Presented in two parts.

Deception and a thwarted execution lead to a series of confusions until all can be set right. First presentation of record was given at the Savoy Theatre in London (10/3/1888).

ACT I

"When Maiden Loves, She Sits and Sighs" ....Phoebe
"Tower Warders, Under Orders" .... People, Yeomen, 1st, 2nd Yeoman
"When Our Gallant Norman Foes" .... Dame Carruthers, Yeomen
"Alas! I Wander to and Fro" .... Phoebe, Leonard, Meryll
"Is Life a Boon?" .... Fairfax
"Here's a Man of Jollity" .... People, Elsie, Jack Point
"I Have a Song to Sing, O!" .... Elsie, Point
"How Say You, Maiden, Will You Wed" .... Elsie, Point, Lieutenant

"I've Jibe and Joke" .... Jack Point
"Tis Done! I Am a Bride!" .... Elsie
"Were I Thy Bride" .... Phoebe
"Oh, Sergeant Meryll, Is It True" .... Company

ACT II

"Night Has Spread Her Pall Once More" .... People, Yeomen, Dame Carruthers
"Oh! A Private Buffoon is a Light-Hearted Loon" .... Jack Point
"Hereupon We're Both Agreed" .... Point, Wilfred
"Free From His Fetters Grim" .... Fairfax
"Strange Adventure!" .... Kate, Dame, Point, Sergeant
"Hark! What Was That Sir?" .... Company
"A Man Who Would Woo a Fair Maid" .... Fairfax, Elsie, Phoebe
"When a Wooer Goes a-Wooing" .... Elsie, Phoebe, Fairfax, Point
"Rapture, Rapture!" .... Dame Carruthers, Sergeant Meryll
"Comes The Pretty Young Bride" .... Company

New York Gilbert and Sullivan Players production of **The Mikado** (6). Revival of the operetta with book by W.S. Gilbert; music by Arthur Sullivan. Albert Bergeret artistic director, at City Center. Opened January 6, 2007. (Closed January 14, 2007)

The Mikado	Keith Jurosko	Yum-Yum	Jennifer Piacenti,
Nanki-Poo	Michael Scott Harris,		Elizabeth Hillebrand
	Daniel Lockwood	Pitti-Sing	Melissa Attebury
Ko-Ko	Stephen Quint,	Peep-Bo	Robin Bartunek,
	David Macaluso		Lauren Wenegrat
Pooh-Bah	Louis Dall'Ava	Katisha	Dianna Dollman
Pish-Tush	Edward Prostak		

Ensemble: David Auxier, Kimberly Deana Bennett, Susan Case, Derrick Cobey, Michael Connolly, Michael Galante, Robert Garner, Alena Gerst Dailey, Kathleen Glauber Tarello, Alan Hill, Morgan James, Lynelle Johnson, Jenny Millsap, Chris-Ian Sanchez, Rebecca O'Sullivan, Erika Person, Paul Sigrist, Angela Smith, David Wannen, William Whitefield.

Understudies: Mr. Prostak—Robert Garner; Ms. Attebury—Erika Person; Mr. Dall'Ava—David Auxier; Ms. Dollman—Angela Smith.

Swings: Michael Levesque, Lauren Wenegrat.

Directed by Albert Bergeret; scenery, Albere; costumes, Gail J. Wofford and Kayko Nakamura; lighting, Sally Small; music direction, Mr. Bergeret and Jeffrey Kresky; production stage manager, David Sigafoose; press, Cromarty and Company, Peter Cromarty.

Place: A Japanese Garden. Presented in two parts.

Star-crossed love and mistaken identity played in a fantasy Japan. First presentation of record was given at the Savoy Theatre in London (3/14/1885).

ACT I

"If You Want to Know Who We Are" .... Nanki-Poo, Men
"A Wand'ring Minstrel I" .... Nanki-Poo, Men
"Our Great Mikado, Virtuous Man" .... Pish-Tush, Men
"Young Man, Despair" .... Pooh-Bah, Nanki-Poo, Pish-Tush
"And Have I Journeyed for a Month" .... Nanki-Poo, Pooh-Bah
"Behold the Lord High Executioner" .... Ko-Ko, Men
"As Some Day It May Happen" .... Ko-Ko, Men
"Comes a Train of Little Ladies" .... Girls
"Three Little Maids From School Are We" .... Yum-Yum, Peep-Bo,
Pitti-Sing, Girls
"So Please You, Sir, We Much Regret" .... Yum-Yum, Peep-Bo,
Pitti-Sing, Pooh-Bah, Girls
"Were You Not to Ko-Ko Plighted" .... Yum-Yum, Nanki-Poo
"I Am so Proud" Pooh-Bah, Ko-Ko, Pish-Tush
"With Aspect Stern and Gloomy Stride" .... Company

ACT II

"Braid the Raven Hair" .... Pitti-Sing, Girls
"The Sun, Whose Rays Are all Ablaze" .... Yum-Yum
"Brightly Dawns Our Wedding Day" .... Yum-Yum, Pitti-Sing,
Nanki-Poo, Pish-Tush
"Here's a How-de-do!" .... Yum-Yum, Nanki-Poo, Ko-Ko
"Mi-ya Sa-ma" .... Mikado, Katisha, Girls, Men
"A More Humane Mikado" .... Mikado, Girls, Men
"The Criminal Cried as He Dropped Him Down" .... Ko-Ko, Pitti-Sing,
Pooh-Bah, Girls, Men
"See How the Fates Their Gifts Allot" .... Mikado, Pitti-Sing, Pooh-Bah,
Ko-Ko, Katisha
"The Flowers That Bloom in the Spring" .... Nanki-Poo, Ko-Ko, Yum-Yum,
Pitti-Sing, Pooh-Bah
"Alone, and Yet Alive!" .... Katisha
"Willow, Tit-Willow" .... Ko-Ko
"There Is Beauty in the Bellow of the Blast" .... Katisha, Ko-Ko
"For He's Gone and Married Yum-Yum" .... Company

New York Gilbert and Sullivan Players production of **The Rose of Persia** (1). Revival of the operetta with book by Basil Hood; music by Arthur Sullivan. Albert Bergeret artistic director, at City Center. Opened January 11, 2007. (Closed January 11, 2007)

Sultan Mahmoud .... David Wannen	Heart's Desire .... Kimberly Deana Bennett
Hassan .... Richard Alan Holmes	Honey-of-Life .... Megan Loomis
Yussuf .... Michael Scott Harris	Dancing Sunbeam .... Angela Smith
Abdallah .... Edward Prostak	Blush-of-Morning .... Meredith Borden
Grand Vizier .... David Auxier	Wives of Hassan
Physician-in-Chief .... Paul Sigrist	Oasis-in-the-Desert .... Lauren Pastorek
Royal Executioner .... Louis Dall'Ava	Moon-on-the-Waters ...... Rebecca O'Sullivan
Royal Guard Soldier .... Ted Bouton	Song-of-Nightingales ...... Alena Gerst Dailey
Sultana .... Laurelyn Watson Chase	Whisper-of-West-Wind .... Jenny Millsap
Sultana's Favorite Slaves	
Scent-of-Lilies .... Carol Ambrogio	

Ensemble: Michael Connolly, Michael Galante, Alena Gerst Dailey, Katie Hall, Alan Hill, Michael Levesque, Daniel Lockwood, David Macaluso, Jenny Millsap, Lance Olds, Rebecca O'Sullivan, Monique Pelletier, Jennifer Piacenti, Lauren Wenegrat.

Directed by Albert Bergeret; choreography, Janis Ansley-Ungar; scenery, Albere; costumes, Gail J. Wofford and Louis Dall'Ava; lighting, Sally Small; music direction, Mr. Bergeret; production stage manager, David Sigafoose; press, Cromarty and Company, Peter Cromarty

Place: Hassan's House; Sultan's Palace. Presented in two parts.

Love conquers all and a reprieve is granted when a sultan spares a boy's life after many complications. First presentation of record was given at the Savoy Theatre in London (11/29/1899).

ACT I

"As We Lie in Languor Lazy" .... Chorus of Wives
"I'm Abul Hassan" .... Hassan, Chorus of Wives
"When Islam First Arose" .... Abdallah, Chorus of Wives
"O Life Has Put Into My Hand" .... Sunbeam
"Five And Twenty Widows–If a Sudden Stroke of Fate" .... Blush, Sunbeam, Abdallah
"If You Ask Me to Advise You" .... Rose, Scent, Heart
"Neath My Lattice Through the Night" .... Rose
"Tramps and Scamps and Halt and Blind" .... Mendicants, Wives, Hassan
"When My Father Sent Me to Ispahan" .... Hassan, Company
"Peace Be Upon This House–I Care Not if the Cup I Hold" .... Yussuf, Company
"Musical Maidens Are We–Dance and Song" .... Rose, Scent, Heart, Honey, Hassan
"We Have Come to Invade" .... Abdallah, Hassan

"The Sultan's Executioner .... Rose, Scent, Heart, Honey,
Sunbeam, Hassan, Yussuf, Abdallah
"I'm the Sultan's Vigilant Vizier" .... Sultan, Grand Vizier, Physician, Executioner
"O Luckless Hour" Company

ACT II

"Oh, What Is Love" .... Heart, Yussuf
"If You or I Should Tell the Truth" .... Scent, Honey, Heart, Yussuf
"From Morning Prayer the Sultan of Persia Comes" .... Grand Vizier, Physician,
Executioner, Company
"Let a Satirist Enumerate a Catalogue" .... Sultan, Chorus
"In the Heart of My Hearts I've Always Known" .... Sunbeam, Blush, Honey,
Oasis, Physician, Vizier, Sultan
"Suppose–I Say, Suppose" .... Rose, Sultan
"Laughing Low, on Toe-Tip" .... Hassan, Vizier, Physician,
Executioner, Compnay
"It's a Busy, Busy, Busy, Busy Day for Thee" .... Scent, Heart, Yussuf,
Hassan, Executioner, Company
"Our Tale Is Told" .... Yussuf
"What Does It Mean" .... Blush, Sunbeam, Yussuf, Royal Guard
"It Has Reached Me a Lady Named Hubbard" .... Scent, Honey, Heart, Sunbeam,
Yussuf, Hassan, Abdallah
"Hassan, the Sultan With His Court" .... Company
"There Was–Once a Small Street Arab" .... Hassan, Company
"A Bridal March the Funeral Dirge Becomes" .... Company

Midlife crisis: Tony Shalhoub and Patricia Heaton in The Scene. *Photo: Joan Marcus*

Second Stage Theatre production of **The Scene** (33). By Theresa Rebeck. Carole Rothman artistic director, Ellen Richard executive director. Opened January 11, 2007. (Closed February 11, 2007)

Clea	Anna Camp	Charlie	Tony Shalhoub
Stella	Patricia Heaton	Lewis	Christopher Evan Welch

Directed by Rebecca Bayla Taichman; scenery, Derek McLane; costumes, Jeff Mahshie; lighting, Natasha Katz; sound, Martin Desjardins; casting, Tara Rubin Casting; production stage manager, Kelly Hance; press, Barlow-Hartman, Michael Hartman, Tom D'Ambrosio, Ryan Ratelle.

Time: The present. Place: New York. Presented in two parts.

A New York actor who is married to a successful television professional finds himself on the receiving end of an attractive young woman's attention. First presentation of record was given at the 2006 Humana Festival of New American Plays in Louisville, Kentucky (3/14–4/8/2006). A 2006–07 *Best Plays* choice (see essay by Chris Jones in this volume).

Love in the Nick of Tyme (8). By David E. Talbert. Produced by Mr. Talbert and Morris Chestnut at the Beacon Theatre. Opened January 16, 2007. (Closed January 21, 2007)

Marcelles Wynters	Morris Chestnut	Elgin	Byron "Blu" Mitchell
Tyme Prentice	Terry Dexter	Geralyn	Christi Dickerson
Dee-Dee	Ellia English	Lauren	Lyn Talbert
Dashon	Avant	Man Wynters	Jerrell Roberts
Portia	Trenyce Cobbins	Non-Stop	Michael Anthony Scott
Harvey	Andre Pitre	Narrator	C.O.C.O. Brown

Directed by Mr. Talbert; scenery, Gary Wissman; lighting, Michael Gilliam; music, Robert Johnson Jr.; songs, Vivian Green; music direction, Mr. Johnson and Lo Key; arrangements, Rob Lewis; production stage manager, Anthony Kennibrew.

Time: The present. Place: A beauty salon. Presented in two parts.

Urban-themed tale of love, loss, redemption and African-American community.

Gutenberg! The Musical! (126). Transfer from Off Off Broadway of the musical by Scott Brown and Anthony King. Produced by Trevor Brown, Ron Kastner, Terry Allen Kramer, Joseph Smith, in association with Upright Citizens Brigade Theatre, at the Actors' Playhouse. Opened January 21, 2007. (Closed May 6, 2007)

Bud Davenport	Christopher Fitzgerald	Doug Simon	Jeremy Shamos

Musician: T.O. Sterrett piano

Understudy: Messrs. Fitzgerald, Shamos—Ryan Karels.

Directed by Alex Timbers; costumes, Emily Rebholz; lighting, Tyler Micoleau; arrangements and music direction, Mr. Sterrett; production stage manager, Wesley Apfel; press, Shaffer-Coyle Public Relations, Bill Coyle, Jeremy Shaffer.

Presented in two parts.

Metatheatrical musical about the making of a musical that centers on the inventor of the printing press. First presentation of record was given at Upright Citizens Brigade Theatre in New York (11/22/2003). After further development at Upright Citizens during the 2005 New York Musical Theatre Festival (9/24–10/1/2005), it was presented in London at the Jermyn Street Theatre (1/6–28/2006). *Gutenberg! The Musical!* continued its journey in expanded form at the Sage Theater during the 2006 New York Musical Theatre Festival (9/22–30/2006; 6 performances). Prior to the Off Broadway stand there was a limited run Off Off Broadway at 59E59 Theaters (12/3–31/2006; 33 performances).

ACT I

"Prologue"	Doctor, Friend of Gutenberg, Gutenberg
"Schlimmer!"	Woman, Gutenberg, Daughter,
	Another Woman, Beef Fat Trimmer,
	Drunk 1, Drunk 2, Bootblack, Anti-Semite

"I Can't Read" .... Helvetica
"Haunted German Wood" .... Monk, Young Monk
"The Press" .... Gutenberg, Old Black Narrator,
Helvetica, Company
"I Can't Read" (Reprise) .... Young Monk
"Biscuits" .... Young Monk, Bootblack
"What's The Word" .... Woman, Beef Fat Trimmer, Another Woman,
Friend of Gutenberg, Monk
"Stop the Press" .... Monk, Helvetica
"Tomorrow Is Tonight" .... Gutenberg, Monk, Helvetica

ACT II

"Second Prologue" .... Daughter, Bootblack
"Words, Words, Words" .... Gutenberg, Drunk 1, Drunk 2,
Helvetica, Company
"Monk With Me" .... Monk, Gutenberg
"Go to Hell" .... Helvetica, Company
"Festival!" .... Company
"Finale" .... Company

The New Group production of **The Fever** (40). Solo performance piece by Wallace Shawn. Scott Elliott artistic director, Geoffrey Rich executive director, at the Acorn Theatre. Opened January 29, 2007. (Closed March 9, 2007)

The Traveler .... Mr. Shawn

Directed by Scott Elliott; scenery, Derek McLane; costumes, Eric Becker; lighting, Jennifer Tipton; sound, Bruce Odland; production stage manager, Valerie A. Peterson; press, The Karpel Group.

Presented without intermission.

Sitting in a comfortable chair, a narrator describes peculiar happenings in a foreign country and the dawning consciousness of his privileged position in the world. First presentations were given in living rooms throughout New York City for gatherings of a dozen or so people in 1990 for 50 or more performances. First presentation of record was given at the Public Theater's Shiva Theater (11/28–12/1/1990; 4 performances). It then played at the Royal Court Upstairs, in association with the National Theatre (UK) (1/8–12/1991), before a tour of Liverpool, Sheffield, Salisbury, Hemel Hempstead, Warwick, Mold, Leicester and Harlow. The tour finished at the National Cottesloe (2/8–9/1991). On his return, Mr. Shawn performed the piece at Second Stage Theatre (3/3/1991), returned to the Public Theater (3/4–10/1991; 7 performances), Lincoln Center Theater (3/11–17/1991; 7 performances), La MaMa E.T.C. (3/21–31/1991; 12 performances), and a return to Lincoln Center Theater (4/2–21/1991; 18 performances). In acknowledgement of his privileged status, Mr. Shawn reportedly donated his salary back to the presenting companies in New York. After these runs, other performers began doing the piece.

Playwrights Horizons production of **Frank's Home** (24). By Richard Nelson. Tim Sanford artistic director, Leslie Marcus managing director, William Russo general manager, in association with the Goodman Theatre (Robert Falls artistic director, Roche Schulfer executive director), at the Mainstage Theater. Opened January 30, 2007. (Closed February 18, 2007)

Frank Lloyd Wright	Peter Weller	Louis Sullivan	Harris Yulin
Catherine	Maggie Siff	Miriam Noel	Mary Beth Fisher
Helen Girvin	Holley Fain	Lloyd	Jay Whittaker
William	Jeremy Strong	Kenneth	Chris Henry Coffey

Directed by Robert Falls; scenery, Thomas Lynch; costumes, Susan Hilferty; lighting, Michael Philippi; sound and music, Richard Woodbury; casting, Alaine Alldaffer; production stage manager, Barclay Stiff; press, The Publicity Office, Bob Fennell, Marc Thibodeau, Michael S. Borowski, Candi Adams.

Legends confer: Mary Beth Fisher, Peter Weller, Harris Yulin and Maggie Siff in Frank's
Home. *Photo: Michael Brosilow*

Time: 1923. Place: Los Angeles. Presented without intermission.

In a midcareer crisis, a great architect encounters the indignities inflicted by family and friends.
First presentation of record was given at the Goodman Theatre in Chicago (11/25–12/23/2006).

New York Theatre Workshop production of **All That I Will Ever Be** (39). By Alan
Ball. James C. Nicola artistic director, Lynn Moffat managing director. Opened February
6, 2007. (Closed March 11, 2007)

White Guy; Others .... Patch Darragh	Omar .... Peter Macdissi
Cynthia; Beth .... Kandiss Edmundson	Raymond .... David Margulies
Dwight .... Austin Lysy	Chuck Bennett; Phil .... Victor Slezak

Directed by Jo Bonney; scenery, Neil Patel; costumes, Emilio Sosa; lighting, David Lander;
sound, Darron L. West; fight direction, J. Steven White; casting, Jack Doulin; production stage
manager, Larry K. Ash; press, Richard Kornberg and Associates, Richard Kornberg, Don Summa.

Time: The present. Place: Los Angeles. Presented in two parts.

The intersections of race, culture, class, sex and identity set against the backdrop of
contemporary Los Angeles. First presentation of record was a reading given at Dartmouth College
(8/20/2005) during New York Theatre Workshop's Works-in-Progress series.

*In the Heights (129). Musical with book by Quiara Alegría Hudes; music and lyrics
by Lin-Manuel Miranda. Produced by Kevin McCollum, Jeffrey Seller, Jill Furman at 37
Arts. Opened February 8, 2007.

Graffiti Pete .... Seth Stewart	Carla .... Janet Dacal
Usnavi .... Lin-Manuel Miranda	Daniela .... Andrea Burns
Piragua Guy .... Eliseo Roman	Kevin .... John Herrera
Abuela Claudia .... Olga Merediz	Camila .... Priscilla Lopez

Sonny	Robin De Jesus	Nina	Mandy Gonzalez
Benny	Christopher Jackson	Bolero Singer	Doreen Montalvo
Vanessa	Karen Olivo		

Ensemble: Rosie Lani Fiedelman, Asmeret Ghebremichael, Joshua Henry, Nina Lafarga, Doreen Montalvo, Eliseo Roman, Jon Rua, Luis Salgado, Rickey Tripp.

Orchestra: Alex Lacamoire conductor, keyboard; Manny Moreira guitar; Irio O'Farrill bass; David Richards woodwinds; Raul Agraz trumpet; Doug Hinrichs percussion; Andres Patrick Forero percussion; drums.

Understudies: Mr. Miranda—Michael Balderrama, Shaun Taylor-Corbett; Ms. Merediz—Michelle Rios, Doreen Montalvo; Ms. Gonzalez—Nina Lafarga; Mr. Jackson—Joshua Henry, Rickey Tripp; Mr. Herrera—Eliseo Roman; Ms. Lopez—Doreen Montalvo, Michelle Rios; Ms. Olivo—Janet Dacal, Asmeret Ghebremichael; Mr. De Jesus—Jon Rua, Shaun Taylor-Corbett; Ms. Burns—Doreen Montalvo, Michelle Rios; Ms. Dacal—Asmeret Ghebremichael; Mr. Stewart—Michael Balderrama, Jon Rua, Rickey Tripp; Mr. Roman—Michael Balderrama, Shaun Taylor-Corbett.

Swings: Michael Balderrama, Stephanie Klemons, Shaun Taylor-Corbett.

Directed by Thomas Kail; choreography, Andy Blankenbuehler; scenery, Anna Louizos; costumes, Paul Tazewell; lighting, Jason Lyons; sound, Acme Sound Partners; orchestrations and arrangements, Mr. Lacamoire and Bill Sherman; music direction, Mr. Lacamoire; music coordination, Michael Keller; casting, Telsey and Company; production stage manager, J. Phillip Bassett; press, Barlow-Hartman, Michael Hartman, John Barlow, Matt Stapleton, Wayne Wolfe.

Time: Fourth of July weekend. Place: Washington Heights in New York City. Presented in two parts.

A New York bodega owner celebrates his Latino roots as he and his neighbors pursue their American dreams. First presentation of record was in a reading at the Eugene O'Neill Theater Center in Connecticut (7/23–31/2005).

Art v. commerce: Christopher Jackson, Seth Stewart, Lin-Manuel Miranda and Robin De Jesus in In the Heights. *Photo: Joan Marcus*

ACT I

"In the Heights" .... Usnavi, Company
"Breathe" .... Nina
"Benny's Dispatch" .... Benny, Nina
"It Won't Be Long Now" .... Vanessa, Usnavi, Sonny
"Plan B" .... Kevin, Camila, Nina
"Inútil" ("Useless") .... Kevin
"No Me Diga" .... Daniela, Carla, Vanessa, Nina
"96,000" .... Usnavi, Benny, Sonny, Vanessa,
Daniela, Carla, Company
"Paciencia Y Fe" ("Patience and Faith") .... Abuela Claudia, Company
"When You're Home" .... Nina, Benny, Company
"Piragua" .... Piragua Guy
"Siempre" ("Always") .... Camila, Bolero Singer
"The Club" / "Fireworks" .... Company

ACT II

"Sunrise" .... Nina, Benny, Company
"Hundreds of Stories" .... Abuela Claudia, Usnavi
"Carnaval del Barrio" .... Daniela, Company
"Atención" .... Kevin
"Alabanza" .... Usnavi, Nina, Company
"Everything I Know" .... Nina
"Hear Me Out" .... Benny
"Goodbye" .... Usnavi, Vanessa
"Finale" .... Usnavi, Company

The Last Word . . . (37). By Oren Safdie. Produced by Les Gutman and Elizabeth Cockrell, in association with Friendly Fire and Lynn Shaw Productions, at Theatre at St. Clement's. Opened February 8, 2007. (Closed March 11, 2007)

Henry Grunwald .... Daniel J. Travanti   Len Artz .... Adam Green

Directed by Alex Lippard; scenery, Michael V. Moore; costumes, Kirche Leigh Zeile; lighting, Lucas Benjaminh Krech; sound, Gabe Wood; production stage manager, Marci Skolnick.

Presented without intermission.

A retired advertising man, an escapee from the Nazis who aspires to become a playwright, employs a young man to provide administrative assistance. First presentation of record was given by Malibu Stage Company in California (7/9–7/31/2005; 14 performances).

New York City Center Encores! presentation of **Follies** (6). Concert version of the musical with book by James Goldman; music and lyrics by Stephen Sondheim. Jack Viertel artistic director, at City Center. Opened February 8, 2007. Closed February 12, 2007.

Sally Durant Plummer .... Victoria Clark	Carlotta Campion .... Christine Baranski
Young Sally .... Katie Klaus	Phyllis Rogers Stone .... Donna Murphy
Emily Whitman .... Anne Rogers	Benjamin Stone .... Victor Garber
Theodore Whitman .... Robert E. Fitch	Young Phyllis .... Jenny Powers
Dee Dee West .... Dorothy Stanley	Young Ben .... Colin Donnell
Sandra Cranes .... Diane J. Findlay	Buddy Plummer .... Michael McGrath
Heidi Schiller .... Lucine Amara	Young Buddy .... Curtis Holbrook
Young Heidi .... Leena Chopra	Dimitri Weismann .... Philip Bosco
Hattie Walker .... Mimi Hines	Young Emily .... Denise Payne
Solange LaFitte .... Yvonne Constant	Young Theodore .... Barrett Martin
Roscoe .... Arthur Rubin	Young Solange .... Shannon Marie O'Bryan
Max Deems .... Gerry Vichi	Young Hattie .... Cameron Adams
Stella Deems .... Joanne Worley	Young Stella .... Ashlee Fife

Young Sandra .... Jenifer Foote
Young Carlotta .... Jennifer Mathie
Young Dee Dee .... Natalie King Smith
Kevin .... Clyde Alves

"Buddy's Folly" Girls
Margie .... Kristen Beth Williams
Sally .... Emily Fletcher

Ensemble: Cameron Adams, Clyde Alves, Ashlee Fife, Andrew Fitch, Emily Fletcher, Jenifer Foote, Ben Hartley, Natalie King Smith, Brian J. Marcum, Barrett Martin, Jennifer Mathie, Shannon Marie O'Bryan, Denise Payne, Matt Wall, J.D. Webster, Kristen Beth Williams.

Orchestra: The *Encores!* Orchestra.

Directed and choreographed by Casey Nicholaw; scenery, John Lee Beatty; costumes, William Ivey Long and Gregg Barnes; lighting, Ken Billington; sound, Tom Morse; orchestrations, Jonathan Tunick; music direction, Eric Stern; music coordination, Seymour Red Press; casting, Jay Binder; production stage manager, Karen Moore; press, Helene Davis Public Relations.

Time: 1971. Place: Weismann Theatre, New York. Presented in two parts.

The closing of a decrepit theater occasions a reunion of showgirls who formerly trod its boards and who now consider the choices made in their lives. First presentation of record was given as a Broadway tryout at Boston's Colonial Theatre (2/20–3/20/1971). A 1970–71 *Best Plays* choice, the original Broadway production opened at the Winter Garden Theatre (4/4/1971–7/1/1972; 522 performances). At the 1972 Tony Awards, the musical was honored in seven categories: score (Mr. Sondheim), actress (Alexis Smith), scenery (Boris Aronson), costumes (Florence Klotz), lighting (Tharon Musser), choreography (Michael Bennett) and direction (Harold Prince and Mr. Bennett). Earlier known as *The Girls Upstairs*, it had been originally slated for Broadway production in fall 1967 under the aegis of David Merrick and Leland Hayward before passing into the hands of producer Stuart Ostrow for a scheduled 1970 debut. After Mr. Ostrow dropped the production a few weeks before the planned opening, Mr. Prince joined as producer and co-director for what became the 1971 original production of *Follies*.

MUSICAL NUMBERS

"Beautiful Girls" .... Roscoe, Company
"Don't Look at Me" .... Sally, Benjamin
"Waiting for the Girls Upstairs" .... Buddy, Benjamin, Phyllis,
Sally, Young Buddy, Young Ben,
Young Phyllis, Young Sally
"Rain on the Roof" .... Emily, Theodore
"Ah, Paris!" .... Solange
"Broadway Baby" .... Hattie
"The Road You Didn't Take" .... Benjamin
"Bolero D'Amour" .... Emily, Theodore,
Young Emily, Young Theodore
"In Buddy's Eyes" .... Sally
"Who's That Woman?" .... Stella, Women
"I'm Still Here" .... Carlotta
"Too Many Mornings" .... Sally, Benjamin
"The Right Girl" .... Michael McGrath
"One More Kiss" .... Heidi, Young Heidi
"Could I Leave You?" .... Phyllis

LOVELAND

The Folly of Love
  "Loveland" .... Company
The Folly of Youth
  "You're Gonna Love Tomorrow" .... Young Ben, Young Phyllis
  "Love Will See Us Through" .... Young Buddy, Young Sally
Buddy's Folly
  "The God-Why-Don't-You-Love-Me Blues" .... Buddy, Margie, Sally
Sally's Folly
  "Losing My Mind" .... Sally
Phyllis's Folly
  "The Story of Lucy and Jessie" .... Phyllis, Men

Ben's Folly
"Live, Laugh, Love" .... Benjamin, Company

Primary Stages production of **Adrift in Macao** (24). Musical with book and lyrics by Christopher Durang; music by Peter Melnick. Casey Childs founder and executive producer, Andrew Leynse artistic director, Elliot Fox managing director, in association with Ina Meibach, Susan Dietz, Jennifer Manocherian, Barbara Manocherian, at 59E59 Theaters. Opened February 13, 2007. (Closed March 4, 2007)

Rick Shaw .... Will Swenson	Lureena .... Rachel De Benedet
Tempura .... Orville Mendoza	Trenchcoat Chorus
Corinna .... Michele Ragusa	(Joe, Daisy) .... Jonathan Rayson,
Mitch .... Alan Campbell	Elisa Van Duyne

Directed by Sheryl Kaller; choreography, Christopher Gattelli; scenery, Thomas Lynch; costumes, Willa Kim; lighting, Jeff Croiter; sound, Peter Fitzgerald; orchestrations, Michael Starobin; music direction, Fred Lassen; music coordination, Howard Joines; casting, Mark Simon; associate producer, Jamie deRoy; production stage manager, Emily N. Wells; press, O and M Co., Rick Miramontez, Philip Carrubba.

Time: 1952. Place: Macao, China. Presented without intermission.

Musical parody on film noir replete with stereotypical characters from what was once known as "the Orient." First presentation of record was given as a reading by New York Stage and Film at Vassar College (7/10–20/2002) after an airing in the York Theatre Company's Developmental Reading Series. Its first production of record was given by Philadelphia Theatre Company (10/26–11/20/2005).

MUSICAL NUMBERS

"In a Foreign City" .... Lureena
"Grumpy Mood" .... Mitch
"Tempura's Song" .... Tempura, Mitch
"Mister McGuffin" .... Tempura, Corinna, Joe, Daisy
"Pretty Moon Over Macao" .... Lureena
"Mambo Malaysian" .... Corinna
"Sparks" .... Lureena, Mitch
"Mitch's Story" .... Mitch, Corinna, Lureena
"Adrift in Macao" .... Lureena, Corinna, Mitch, Tempura
"So Long" .... Lureena
"The Chase" .... Mitch, Company
"Revelation" .... Tempura
"Ticky Ticky Tock" .... Lureena, Corinna, Trenchcoat Chorus

Sealed for Freshness (75). By Doug Stone. Produced by Cannon Entertainment Group, in association with Fresh Ice Productions, at New World Stages. Opened February 24, 2007. (Closed April 29, 2007)

Bonnie Kapica .... Jennifer Dorr White	Tracy Ann McClain .... Kate Vandevender
Richard Kapica .... Brian Dykstra	Sinclair Benevente ....................J.J. Van Name
Jean Pawlicki .... Nancy Hornback	Diane Whettlaufer .... Patricia Dalen

Directed by Mr. Stone; scenery, Rob Odorisio; costumes, Rob Bevenger; lighting, Traci Klainer; sound, Ken Hypes; production stage manager, Elizabeth Grunewald.

Time: 1968. Place: The Midwest. Presented in two parts.

Midwestern housewives unpack their darker selves at a 1960s Tupperware party.

Roundabout Theatre Company production of **Howard Katz** (77). By Patrick Marber. Todd Haimes artistic director, Harold Wolpert managing director, Julia C. Levy executive director, at the Laura Pels Theatre in the Harold and Miriam Steinberg Center for Theatre. Opened March 1, 2007. (Closed May 6, 2007)

Howard's end? Euan Morton and Alfred Molina in Howard Katz. *Photo: Joan Marcus*

Robin	Euan Morton	Jo	Alvin Epstein
Howard Katz	Alfred Molina	Ollie	Patrick Henney
Bern	Max Baker	Ellie	Elizabeth Franz
Nat	Charlotte Parry	Jess	Jessica Hecht
Norm	Edward Hajj		

Understudies: Ms. Franz—Nancy Franklin; Mses. Parry, Hecht—Natalie Gold; Mr. Epstein—Stan Lachow; Mr. Hajj—Thom Rivera; Mr. Henney—Noah Ruff; Messrs. Baker, Morton—Mark Saturno.

Standby: Mr. Molina—Nick Wyman.

Directed by Doug Hughes; scenery, Scott Pask; costumes, Catherine Zuber; lighting, Christopher Akerlind; sound and music, David Van Tieghem; fight direction, Rick Sordelet; casting, Mele Nagler; production stage manager, James FitzSimmons; press, Boneau/Bryan-Brown, Adrian Bryan-Brown, Matt Polk, Jessica Johnson.

Time: The present and the past. Place: London. Presented without intermission.

A Jewish talent agent in London finds midlife empty and attempts to take arms against a sea of troubles—but does not end them. First presentation of record was given by the National Theatre (UK) in the Cottesloe Theatre (6/13–10/6/2001).

Lincoln Center Theater production of **Dying City** (65). By Christopher Shinn. André Bishop artistic director, Bernard Gersten executive producer, in the Mitzi E. Newhouse Theater. Opened March 4, 2007. (Closed April 29, 2007)

Kelly	Rebecca Brooksher	Peter; Craig	Pablo Schreiber

Understudies: Ms. Brooksher—Dana Powers Acheson; Mr. Schreiber—Greg Keller.

Directed by James Macdonald; scenery and costumes, Anthony Ward; lighting, Pat Collins; sound, Aural Fixation; casting, Daniel Swee; press, Philip Rinaldi, Barbara Carroll.

Time: July 2005; February 2004. Place: New York City. Presented without intermission.

Grave secrets: Rebecca Brooksher and Pablo Schreiber in Dying City. *Photo: Joan Marcus*

The surviving twin brother of a soldier who died in Iraq—under suspicious circumstances—confronts his sister-in-law in his search for answers. First presentation of record was given in London at the Royal Court Theatre (5/12–6/10/2006). A 2006–07 *Best Plays* choice (see essay by Charles Isherwood in this volume).

*Bill W. and Dr. Bob (99). By Stephen Bergman and Janet Surrey. Produced by Bradford S. Lovette, Michael and Judith Weinberg, Evelyn Freed, Milton D. McKenzie, in association with New Repertory Theatre, at New World Stages. Opened March 5, 2007.

Bill Wilson	Robert Krakovski	Anne Smith	Kathleen Doyle
Dr. Bob Smith	Patrick Husted	Woman	Deanna Dunmyer
Lois Wilson	Rachel Harker	Man	Marc Carver

Understudies: Mses. Harker, Dunmyer—Katherine Leask; Messrs. Krakovski, Carver—Paul Niebanck; Messrs. Husted, Carver—Ted Pejovich; Mses. Doyle, Dunmyer—Kay Walbye.

Directed by Rick Lombardo; scenery, Anita Fuchs; costumes, Jane Alois Stein; lighting, Daniel Meeker; sound, Mr. Lombardo; music, Ray Kennedy; fight direction, Ted Hewlett; production stage manager, Cheryl Olszowka; press, Sam Rudy Media Relations, Dale Heller.

Time: 1930s. Place: Ohio. Presented in two parts.

Two out-of-control drinkers find their ways to sobriety through the creation of Alcoholics Anonymous. First presentation of record was given by Emerson Stage at Emerson Majestic Theatre (6/22–7/3/1994) with Mr. Bergman writing under the pseudonym Samuel Shem. A revised version premiered at New Repertory Theatre in Watertown, Massachusetts (3/5–26/2006).

*Spalding Gray: Stories Left to Tell (99). By Kathleen Russo and Lucy Sexton; adapted from the writing of Spalding Gray. Produced by Eric Falkenstein and Michael Alden, in association with Naked Angels (Jenny Gersten artistic director), at the Minetta Lane Theatre. Opened March 6, 2007.

Love	Kathleen Chalfant	Family	Frank Wood
Adventure	Hazelle Goodman	Career	Fisher Stevens
Journals	Ain Gordon		

Directed by Ms. Sexton; scenery, David Korins; costumes, Michael Krass; lighting, Ben Stanton; sound and music, Fitz Patton; projections, Leah Gelpe; associate producers, Judith Ann Abrams, Jamie deRoy, Morton Swinsky; production stage manager, Matthew Silver; press, The Publicity Office, Bob Fennell, Marc Thibodeau, Michael S. Borowski, Candi Adams.

Presented without intermission.

Tribute to the monologist who took his own life in 2004. Replacement players during the run (through May 31, 2007) included Lisa Kron, Bruce Vilanch, Valerie Smaldone, Dylan Walsh, Charles Busch, Anthony Rapp, Richard Kind, Estelle Parsons, Josh Lucas and Rachel Dratch. First presentation of record was given under the title *Leftover Stories to Tell* at Off Off Broadway's Performance Space 122 (5/31–6/4/2006; 5 performances) before a stand at Los Angeles's Freud Playhouse (6/14–18/2006; 5 performances). The West Coast version featured Teri Garr, Tony Shalhoub, Roger Guenveur Smith, Brooke Adams and Loudon Wainwright, among others.

The Public Theater production of **King Lear** (18). Revival of the play by William Shakespeare. Oskar Eustis artistic director, Mara Manus executive director, at the Anspacher Theater. Opened March 7, 2007. (Closed March 25, 2007)

Kent	Michael Cerveris	Regan	Laura Odeh
Gloucester	Larry Bryggman	Albany	Michael Rudko
Edmund	Logan Marshall-Green	Cornwall	Daniel Pearce
Lear	Kevin Kline	Burgundy	Joaquin Torres
Goneril	Angela Pierce	France	Piter Marek
Cordelia	Kristen Bush	Edgar	Brian Avers

Take that! Kristen Bush, Laura Odeh, Daniel Pearce, Kevin Kline, Michael Rudko and Angela Pierce in King Lear. *Photo: Michal Daniel*

Oswald .... Timothy D. Stickney	Young Goneril .... Paris Rose Yates
Fool .... Philip Goodwin	Young Regan .... Nicole Bocchi
Curan .... Joaquin Torres	Young Cordelia .... Talicia Martins
Old Man .... Philip Goodwin	

Ensemble: Piter Marek, Ryan McCarthy, Joaquin Torres.

Musicians: Henry Aronson conductor, keyboard; David Wechsler reeds; Ray Grappone, Larry Spivak percussion.

Directed by James Lapine; scenery, Heidi Ettinger; costumes, Jess Goldstein; lighting, David Lander; sound, Dan Moses Schreier and Phillip Scott Peglow; music, Stephen Sondheim and Michael Starobin; music direction, Mr. Aronson; fight direction, Rick Sordelet; associate producers, Peter DuBois, Mandy Hackett; casting, Jordan Thaler, Heidi Griffiths; production stage manager, James Latus; press, Arlene R. Kriv.

Presented in two parts.

An aged king disrupts all of civilized society when he injudiciously divides his kingdom and sets in motion grave events. First presentation of record at the court of James I (12/26/1606). First presentation of record in this country at New York's Theatre in Nassau Street (1/14/1754) was influenced by Nahum Tate's 1681 adaptation of *King Lear*. First US presentation of the Shakespeare version was given by William Charles Macready at the Park Theatre (9/27/1844).

New York Philharmonic presentation of **My Fair Lady** (4). Concert version of the musical with book and lyrics by Alan Jay Lerner; music by Frederick Loewe; adapted by David Ives. Loren Maazel music director, at Avery Fisher Hall. Opened March 7, 2007. (Closed March 10, 2007)

Eliza Doolittle .... Kelli O'Hara	Jamie .... Michael J. Farina
Freddy Eynsford-Hill .... Philippe Castagner	Alfred P. Doolittle .... Brian Dennehy
Colonel Pickering .... Charles Kimbrough	Mrs. Pearce .... Meg Bussert
Henry Higgins .... Kelsey Grammer	Mrs. Higgins .... Marni Nixon
Harry .... Joe Grifasi	Zoltan Karpathy .... Tim Jerome

Directed by James Brennan; choreography, Peggy Hickey; scenery, Ray Klausen; costumes, Gail Baldoni; lighting, Ken Billington; sound, Peter Fitzgerald; orchestrations, Robert Russell Bennett and Philip J. Lang; dance music arrangements, Trude Rittman; conductor, Rob Fisher; executive producer, Matias Tarnopolsky; producer, Thomas Z. Shepard; production stage manager, Peter Hanson.

Time: 1912. Place: In and around London. Presented in two parts.

A 1955–56 *Best Plays* choice, the original Broadway production opened at the Mark Hellinger Theatre (3/15/1956–9/29/1962; 2,717 performances) with Julie Andrews and Rex Harrison. At the 1957 Tony Awards, the production was honored in the categories of musical (Messrs. Lerner and Loewe, producer Herman Levin), actor (Mr. Harrison), scenery (Oliver Smith), costumes (Cecil Beaton), conductor and music director (Fritz Allers) and direction (Moss Hart). There have been three Broadway revivals.

Musical numbers included: "Why Can't the English?," "Wouldn't It Be Loverly?," "With a Little Bit of Luck," "Just You Wait," "The Rain in Spain," "I Could Have Danced All Night," "On the Street Where You Live," "Show Me," "Get Me to the Church on Time," "Without You," "I've Grown Accustomed to Her Face."

Signature Theatre Company production of **King Hedley II** (49). By August Wilson. James Houghton founding artistic director; Kathryn M. Lipuma executive director. Opened March 11, 2007. (Closed April 22, 2007)

Stool Pigeon .... Lou Myers	Mister .... Curtis McClarin
King .... Russell Hornsby	Tonya .... Cherise Boothe
Ruby .... Lynda Gravatt	Elmore .... Stephen McKinley Henderson

Directed by Derrick Sanders; scenery, David Gallo; costumes, Reggie Ray; lighting, Thom Weaver; sound, Jill BC DuBoff; fight direction, Rick Sordelet; casting, Telsey and Company; associate artists, Todd Kreidler, Constanza Romero; production stage manager, Winnie Y. Lok; press, The Publicity Office, Bob Fennell, Marc Thibodeau, Michael S. Borowski, Candi Adams.

Time: 1985. Place: A backyard in Pittsburgh's Hill District. Presented in two parts.

The eighth installment in Wilson's ten-play cycle about 20th-century African-American life focuses on the destruction of black men by white society and other black men. A 2000–01 *Best Plays* choice, the first presentation of record was given by the Pittsburgh Public Theater at the O'Reilly Theater (12/15/1999–1/16/2000). The original Broadway production opened at the Virginia Theatre (5/1–7/1/2001; 72 performances). The Virginia was renamed the August Wilson Theatre two weeks after the playwright's death in 2005.

*Be (91). By Eylon Nuphar and Boaz Berman. Produced by Marc Routh, Thomas Viertel, Steven Baruch, Roy Ofer, Mayumana, Annette Niemtzow and Pamela Cooper at the Union Square Theatre. Opened March 13, 2007.

Performed by Sharon Ben Naim, Mr. Berman, Alba Bonal Garcia, Eva Boucherite Martin, Vicente De Andres, Silvia Garcias De Ves, Michael Feigenbaum, Ido Kagan, Yael Mahler, Taly Minkov, Reut Rotem, Ido Stadler, Aka Jean Claude Thiemele, Hila Yaffe.

Directed by Ms. Nuphar and Mr. Berman; scenery, Nizan Refaeli; costumes, Neta Haker; lighting, Eyal Tavori and Roy Milo; sound, Amir Schorr; press, Shaffer-Coyle Public Relations, Jeremy Shaffer, Bill Coyle.

Presented without intermission.

Performance piece with music, dance and percussion that relies on attractive performers and unusual instruments to make its nonlinear theatrical journey.

Brooklyn Academy of Music presentation of a **New Adventures, Martin McCallum and Marc Platt** production of **Edward Scissorhands** (19). By Matthew Bourne, with Caroline Thompson; based on the 20th Century Fox film by Ms. Thompson and Tim Burton. Alan H. Fishman chairman of the board, Karen Brooks Hopkins president, Joseph V. Melillo executive producer, at the Howard Gilman Opera House. Opened March 16, 2006. (Closed March 31, 2006)

Edward Scissorhands	Sam Archer	Bill Boggs	Scott Ambler
Kim Boggs	Kerry Biggin	Jim Upton	James Leece
Peg Boggs	Madelaine Brennan	Joyce Monroe	Michela Meazza

Directed and choreographed by Mr. Bourne; scenery and costumes, Lez Brotherston; lighting, Howard Harrison; sound, Paul Groothuis.

Presented in two parts.

Dance musical adaptation of a film about a lonely boy whose sharp-pointed hands are lethal weapons. First presentation of record was given at the Theatre Royal in Plymouth, England, (11/14–19/2005) before a run at London's Sadler's Wells (11/30/2005–2/6/2006).

Brooklyn Academy of Music presentation of the **Watermill Theatre**, **Old Vic** and **Propeller** production of **The Taming of the Shrew** (10). Revival of the play by William Shakespeare; adapted by Edward Hall and Roger Warren. Alan H. Fishman chairman of the board; Karen Brooks Hopkins president; Joseph V. Melillo executive producer, at the Harvey Theater. Opened March 17, 2007. (Closed April 1, 2007)

Christopher Sly;		Bianca	Jon Trenchard
Petruchio	Dugald Bruce-Lockhart	Gremio; Vincentio	Chris Myles
Lucentio	Tam Williams	Hortensio	Jack Tarlton
Tranio	Tony Bell	Grumio; Pedant	Jason Baughan
Biondello	Alasdair Craig	Curtis	Joe Flynn
Baptista	Bob Barrett	Tailor; Widow	Dominic Tighe
Katherine	Simon Scardifield		

Directed by Mr. Hall; scenery and costumes, Michael Pavelka; lighting, Mark Howland and Ben Ormerod; music by Propeller; stage manager, R. Michael Blanco.

Presented in two parts.

An overbearing woman and her male equal struggle for superiority in their relationship. Although the play is believed to be an early work of Mr. Shakespeare's, the 1631 quarto suggests that it was performed at the Globe and Blackfriars, which the King's Men controlled after August 1608. The play's first presentation of record was given at the court of Charles I in 1633. First presentation of record in this country was given in New York at the John Street Theatre (1/8/1768) in an adaptation by David Garrick titled *Catharine and Petruchio*. The 2006–07 production was presented in repertory with *Twelfth Night* (see below).

Brooklyn Academy of Music presentation of the **Watermill Theatre**, **Old Vic** and **Propeller** production of **Twelfth Night** (10). Revival of the play by William Shakespeare; adapted by Edward Hall and Roger Warren. Alan H. Fishman chairman of the board; Karen Brooks Hopkins president; Joseph V. Melillo executive producer, at the Harvey Theater. Opened March 17, 2007. (Closed April 1, 2007)

Feste .... Tony Bell	Olivia .... Dugald Bruce-Lockhart
Orsino .... Jack Tarlton	Malvolio .... Bob Barrett
Curio; Priest .... Jon Trenchard	Sir Toby Belch .... Jason Baughan
Viola; Cesario .... Tam Williams	Maria .... Chris Myles
Sebastian ....Joe Flynn	Sir Andrew Aguecheek .... Simon Scardifield
Ship Captain .... Dominic Tighe	Antonio .... Alasdair Craig

Directed by Mr. Hall; scenery and costumes, Michael Pavelka; lighting, Ben Ormerod; music by Propeller; stage manager, R. Michael Blanco.

Presented in two parts.

Comedy about the mysteries of sexual attraction. First presentation of record at the Middle Temple, London (2/2/1602). First New York presentation of record at the Park Theatre (6/11/1804). The 2006–07 production was presented in repertory with *The Taming of the Shrew* (see above).

Smokin': Beth Cole, Philip Seymour Hoffman, John Ortiz and Daphne Rubin-Vega in Jack Goes Boating. *Photo: Monique Carboni*

Drama queen: Maxwell Caulfield, Kate Mulgrew and Ann Duquesnay in Our Leading Lady. *Photo: Joan Marcus*

Labyrinth Theater Company production of **Jack Goes Boating** (49). By Bob Glaudini. Philip Seymour Hoffman and John Ortiz artistic directors, Steve Asher executive director, at Martinson Hall. Opened March 18, 2007. (Closed April 29, 2007)

Connie .... Beth Cole
Clyde .... John Ortiz
Jack .... Philip Seymour Hoffman
Lucy .... Daphne Rubin-Vega

Understudies: Mses. Cole, Rubin-Vega—Maggie Bofill; Mr. Ortiz—Felix Solis; Mr. Hoffman—Sidney Williams.

Directed by Peter DuBois; scenery, David Korins; costumes, Mimi O'Donnell; lighting, Japhy Weideman; sound and music, David Van Tieghem; production stage manager, Damon W. Arrington; press, Boneau/Bryan-Brown, Adrian Bryan-Brown, Juliana Hannett, Matt Ross.

Time: The present. Place: New York City. Presented in two parts.

A man who possesses limited social skills finds a woman who seems willing to overlook his shortcomings.

Manhattan Theatre Club production of **Our Leading Lady** (48). By Charles Busch. Lynne Meadow artistic director, Barry Grove executive director, at City Center Stage II. Opened March 20, 2007. (Closed April 29, 2007)

Laura Keene .... Kate Mulgrew
W.J. Ferguson .... Billy Wheelan
Harry Hawk .... Maxwell Caulfield
Madame Wu-Chan .... Ann Duquesnay
Gavin De Chamblay .... Reed Birney
Clementine Smith .... Amy Rutberg
Verbena De Chamblay .... Kristine Nielsen
Major Hopwood .... J.R. Horne
Maude Bentley .... Barbara Bryne

Understudies: Ms. Duquesnay—Joy Lynn Matthews; Mses. Bryne, Nielson—Robin Moseley; Ms. Mulgrew—Rita Rehn; Messrs. Birney, Caulfield, Horne—James Riordan; Mr. Wheelan—Paul David Story.

Directed by Lynne Meadow; scenery, Santo Loquasto; costumes, Jane Greenwood; lighting, Brian MacDevitt; sound, Scott Lehrer; fight direction, J. David Brimmer; wigs, Tom Watson; casting,

Nancy Piccione, David Caparelliotis; production stage manager, Donald Fried; press; Boneau/Bryan-Brown, Chris Boneau, Jim Byk, Aaron Meier, Heath Schwartz, Christine Olver.

Time: April 1865. Place: In and around Ford's Theatre in Washington, D.C. Presented in two parts.

Laura Keene, famed actor and theater manager in the 19th century, hopes President Lincoln will visit her show and provide her career with a much-needed boost.

Second Stage Theatre production of **Some Men** (32). By Terrence McNally. Carole Rothman artistic director, Ellen Richard executive director. Opened March 26, 2007. (Closed April 22, 2007)

Performed by Don Amendolia, Kelly AuCoin, Romain Frugé, David Greenspan, Jesse Hooker, Michael McElroy, Pedro Pascal, Randy Redd, Frederick Weller.

Directed by Trip Cullman; scenery, Mark Wendland; costumes, Linda Cho; lighting, Kevin Adams; sound, John Gromada; production stage manager, Lori Ann Zepp; press, Tom D'Ambrosio.

Presented in two parts.

A cavalcade of contemporary gay life set to music. First presentation of record was given at Philadelphia Theatre Company (5/17–6/11/2006) after development at the Sundance Theatre Lab (11/2004).

The boys: David Greenspan, Don Amendolia, Frederick Weller and Pedro Pascal in Some Men. *Photo: Joan Marcus*

Playwrights Horizons presentation of the **Edge Theater Company** production of **Essential Self-Defense** (23). By Adam Rapp. Tim Sanford artistic director, Leslie Marcus managing director, William Russo general manager, at the Peter Jay Sharp Theater. Opened March 28, 2007. (Closed April 15, 2007)

Sorrell	Cheryl Lynn Bowers	Sadie	Heather Goldenhersh
Chuck the Barber	Guy Boyd	Todd; others	Lucas Papaelias
Isaak Glinka	Michael Chernus	Bob Beard	Ray Rizzo
Klieg the Butcher	Joel Marsh Garland	Yul	Paul Sparks

Directed by Carolyn Cantor; scenery, David Korins; costumes, Miranda Hoffman; lighting, Ben Stanton; sound, Eric Shim; music and lyrics; Messrs. Rizzo, Rapp and Papaelias; arrangements, Mr. Rizzo; wigs and hair, Erin Kennedy Lunsford; fight direction, Joseph Travers; casting, Alaine Alldaffer; production stage manager, Charles M. Turner III; press, The Publicity Office, Marc Thibodeau, Michael S. Borowski, Candi Adams.

Time: The present. Place: Bloggs, USA. Presented in two parts.

A collection of misfits discover various types of comfort in the company of one another. First presentation of record was given as a workshop by the Cape Cod Theatre Project in Falmouth, Massachusetts (7/6–8/2006). The 2006–07 production was presented in association with Edge Theater Company (Carolyn Cantor artistic director, David Korins producer, Ted Rounsaville general manager).

New York City Center Encores! presentation of **Face the Music** (5). Concert version of the musical with book by Moss Hart; music and lyrics by Irving Berlin; adapted by David Ives. Jack Viertel artistic director, at City Center. Opened March 29, 2007. Closed April 1, 2007.

Myrtle Meshbesher	Judy Kaye	Pickles Crouse	Mylinda Hull
Hal Reisman	Walter Bobbie	Joe Malarkey	Eddie Korbich
Martin Meshbesher	Lee Wilkof	Streetwalker	Felicia Finley
Pat Mason	Jeffry Denman	Rodney St. Clair	Chris Hoch
Kit Baker	Meredith Patterson	O'Rourke	Timothy Shew

Ensemble: Christine Arand, Heather Ayers, Sara Brians, Rachel Coloff, Rick Crom, Susan Derry, Jack Doyle, Jerold Goldstein, Todd A. Horman, Justin Keyes, Cara Kjellman, Robyn Kramer, Todd Lattimore, Mike Masters, Brent McBeth, Shannon Marie O'Bryan, Wes Pope, Eric Santagata, Jacqueline Thompson, Kevin Vortmann, J.D. Webster, Anna Aimee White, Kristen Beth Williams.

Orchestra: The *Encores!* Orchestra.

Directed by John Rando; choreography, Randy Skinner; scenery, John Lee Beatty; costumes, Toni-Leslie James; lighting, Clifton Taylor; sound, Scott Lehrer; original orchestrations, Robert Russell Bennett, Maurice De Packh, Frank Tours; music direction, Rob Fisher; music coordination, Seymour Red Press; casting, Jay Binder, Jack Bowdan; production stage manager, Rolt Smith; press, Helene Davis Public Relations.

Presented in two parts.

Crooked cops dabble in show business as investors, leading to all sorts of antic behavior. First presentation of record was given at Broadway's New Amsterdam Theatre (2/17–7/9/1932; 165 performances). There has been one Broadway revival, which opened at the 44th Street Theatre six months after the closing of the original production (1/31–2/25/1933; 31 performances).

ACT I
Asterisk (*) indicates archival songs restored for this concert version.

"Overture"	Orchestra
"Lunching at the Automat"	Company
"Let's Have Another Cup of Coffee"	Kit, Pat
"Let's Have Another Cup of Coffee" (Reprise)	Kit, Pat
"The Police of New York"*	O'Rourke, Martin, Policemen
"Reisman's Doing a Show"	Joe, Pickles, Street Walker, Company
"Torch Song"	Street Walker
"You Must Be Born With It"	Joe, Pickles, Company

"Castles in Spain (on a Roof in Manhattan)" .... Kit, Pat
"Crinoline Days" .... Street Walker, Kit, Women
"My Beautiful Rhinestone Girl" .... Rodney, Women
"Soft Lights and Sweet Music" .... Kit, Pat
"The Police of New York"* .... Policemen
"If You Believe"* .... Myrtle, Company

ACT II

"Entr'acte" .... Orchestra
"Well, of All the Rotten Shows" .... Company
"I Say It's Spinach (and the Hell With It)" .... Kit, Pat, Company
"How Can I Change My Luck?"* .... Hal, Men
"A Toast to Prohibition" .... Myrtle, Martin, Rodney, Men
"The Nudist Colony" .... Street Walker, Kit, Company
"I Don't Want To Be Married (I Just Want to Be Friends)" .... Joe, Pickles
"Manhattan Madness" .... Pat, Company
"The Investigation" .... Company

*Manhattan Theatre Club production of **Blackbird** (60). By David Harrower. Lynne
Meadow artistic director, Barry Grove executive producer, in association with Michael
Edwards and Carole Winter, at City Center Stage I. Opened April 10, 2007.

Ray .... Jeff Daniels   Una .... Alison Pill
    Understudies: Ms. Pill—Stephanie Janssen; Mr. Daniels—John Ottavino.
    Directed by Joe Mantello; scenery, Scott Pask; costumes, Laura Bauer; lighting, Paul Gallo;
sound, Darron L. West; fight direction, J. David Brimmer; casting, Nancy Piccione, David
Caparelliotis; production stage manager, Jill Cordle; press, Boneau/Bryan-Brown, Chris Boneau,
Jim Byk, Aaron Meier, Heath Schwartz, Christine Olver.
    Presented without intermission.
    A young woman confronts a man of middle age with whom she had sex at the tender age of
12. First presentation of record was given during the Edinburgh Festival at the King's Theatre in
Edinburgh (8/15–24/2005) before a West End run at the Albery Theatre (2/13–5/13/2006). A
2006–07 *Best Plays* choice (see essay by David Cote in this volume).

New York Theatre Workshop production of **All the Wrong Reasons** (24). Solo
performance piece by John Fugelsang. James C. Nicola artistic director, Lynn Moffat
managing director. Opened April 15, 2007. (Closed May 6, 2007)
    Performed by Mr. Fugelsang.
    Directed by Pam MacKinnon; scenery and costumes, Kaye Voyce; lighting, Mark Barton; sound,
Jeremy J. Lee; stage manager, Odessa Spruill; press, Richard Kornberg and Associates, Don Summa.
    Presented without intermission.
    Topical bits and pieces of comedy woven into a thread of personal narrative.

Brooklyn Academy of Music presentation of a **Cheek by Jowl** production of
Cymbeline (12). Revival of the play by William Shakespeare. Alan H. Fishman chairman
of the board, Karen Brooks Hopkins president, Joseph V. Melillo executive producer,
at the Harvey Theater. Opened May 2, 2007. (Closed May 12, 2007)

Queen .... Gwendoline Christie   Cymbeline .... David Collings
Posthumus; Cloten .... Tom Hiddleston   Pisanio .... Richard Cant
Imogen .... Jodie McNee   Iachimo .... Guy Flanagan
    Ensemble: Laurence Spellman, Jake Harders, Lola Peploe, Ryan Ellsworth, John Macmillan,
Daniel Percival, Mark Holgate, David Caves.
    Directed by Declan Donnellan; scenery, Nick Ormerod; lighting, Judith Greenwood; sound,
Ross Chatfield; music, Catherine Jayes; production stage manager, R. Michael Blanco; press,
Sandy Sawotka, Fatima Kafele, Tamara McCaw, Christina Norris.

Presented in two parts.

Romance that demonstrates humanity's reliance on happenstance (with a bit of help from the great beyond). Earliest known performance was at the Globe Theatre in 1611. The first New York presentation of record was 12/28/1767 by the American Company (David Douglass played Iachimo, Lewis Hallam II played Posthumus) at the John Street Theatre.

Memory (22). By Jonathan Lichtenstein. Produced by Brits Off Broadway at 59E59 Theaters. Opened May 10, 2007. (Closed May 27, 2007)

Chris; Director .... Christian McKay	Huw; Bashar .... Ifan Huw Dafydd
Viv; Eva .... Vivien Parry	Dan; Felix .... Daniel Hawksford
Lee; Peter .... Lee Haven-Jones	Simon; Aron .... Simon Nehan
Olly; Isaac .... Oliver Ryan	

Directed by Terry Hands; scenery, Martyn Bainbridge; lighting, Mr. Hands; sound, Matthew Williams; production stage managers, Caryl Carson and Jim Davis; press, Karen Greco Entertainment.

Presented without intermission.

Backstage story of a play-within-a-play linking elements of the Holocaust with the current struggle between Israelis and Palestinians. First presentation of record was given at Clwyd Theatr Cymru in Mold, North Wales (11/4–25/2006).

New York City Center Encores! presentation of **Stairway to Paradise** (6). Musical revue with sketches, music and lyrics by Nora Bayes, Irving Berlin, Eubie Blake, Henry Blossom, Elisse Boyd, Bob Cole, Betty Comden, B.G. DeSylva, Howard Dietz, Jimmy Durante, Leo Edwards, Dorothy Fields, George Gershwin, Ira Gershwin, Jay Gorney, Murray Grand, Adolph Green, E.Y. Harburg, Lorenz Hart, Victor Herbert, J.W. Johnson, Jerome Kern, Jean Kerr, Walter Kerr, Duke Leonard, Jimmy McHugh, Blanche Merrill, Ed G. Nelson, Jack Norworth, Harry Pease, Andy Razaf, Richard Rodgers, Harold Rome, Arthur Schwartz, Paul Gerard Smith, Jule Styne, P.G. Wodehouse. Jack Viertel artistic director, at City Center. Opened May 10, 2007. (Closed May 14, 2007)

Performed by Kristin Chenoweth, Kevin Chamberlin, Christopher Fitzgerald, Jenn Gambatese, Michael Gruber, Shonn Wiley, J. Mark McVey, Holly Cruikshank, Kendrick Jones, Capathia Jenkins, Ruthie Henshall, Timothy J. Alex, Robin Campbell, Erin Crouch, Susan Derry, Lianne Marie Dobbs, Emily Fletcher, Bob Gaynor, Laura Griffith, Dale Hensley, Renee Klapmeyer, Barrett Martin, Sean McKnight, James Patterson, Eric Santagata, Kira Schmidt, Dennis Stowe, Sarrah Strimel, Kevin Vortmann, J.D. Webster, Teal Wicks.

Orchestra: The *Encores!* Orchestra.

Directed by Jerry Zaks; choreography, Warren Carlyle; scenery, John Lee Beatty; costumes, William Ivey Long; lighting, Paul Gallo; sound, Tom Morse; orchestrations, Jonathan Tunick; arrangements and music direction, Rob Berman; music coordination, Seymour Red Press; casting, Jay Binder, Jack Bowdan; production stage manager, Rolt Smith; press, Helene Davis Public Relations.

Presented in two parts.

Musical numbers: "The Land Where the Good Songs Go" (1917), "Everything in America Is Ragtime" (1915), "The Maiden With the Dreamy Eyes" (1901), "If I Were on the Stage (Kiss Me Again)" (1917), "Oh! How I Hate to Get Up in the Morning" (1918), "The Yellow Peril" (1924), "Pack Up Your Sins and Go to the Devil" (1922) "Manhattan" / "Mountain Greenery" (1925, 1926), "I Guess I Have to Change My Plan" (1929), "Memories of You" (1930), "I Know Darn Well I Can Do Without Broadway" (1929), "Get Yourself a Geisha" (1935), "Doin' the New Low-Down" (1928), "My Handy Man Ain't Handy No More" (1930), "I'll Build a Stairway to Paradise" (1922), "Brother Can You Spare a Dime?" (1932), "Dancing in the Dark" (1931), "F.D.R. Jones" (1938), "Supper Time" (1944), "The Land Where the Good Songs Go" (Reprise), "Sing Me a Song With Social Significance" (1937), "Josephine Please No Lean on the Bell" (1945), "Rhode Island Is Famous for You" (1948), "Triplets" (1932), "Gorilla Girl" (1949), "This Is the Army, Mr. Jones" (1942), "I Left My Heart at the Stage Door Canteen" (1942), "Ev'ry Time We Say Goodbye" (1944),

"Goin' Home Train" (1951), "Call Me Mister" (1951), "Guess Who I Saw Today" (1952), "Catch Our Act at the Met" (1951).

*The Public Theater presentation of **Passing Strange** (19). Musical with book and lyrics by Stew; music by Stew and Heidi Rodewald. Oskar Eustis artistic director, Mara Manus executive director, in association with Berkeley Repertory Theatre (Tony Taccone artistic director, Susan Medak managing director), at the Anspacher Theater. Opened May 14, 2007.

Edwina; others .... de'Adre Aziza	Hugo; others .... Chad Goodridge
Youth .... Daniel Breaker	Sherry; others .... Rebecca Naomi Jones
Mother .... Eisa Davis	Narrator .... Stew
Franklin; others .... Colman Domingo	

Musicians: Jon Spurney keyboard, guitar; Marc Doten keyboard; Ms. Rodewald bass, vocals; Christian Cassan drums.

Directed by Annie Dorsen; choreography, Karole Armitage; scenery, David Korins; costumes, Elizabeth Hope Clancy; lighting, Kevin Adams; sound, Tony Smolenski IV; music direction, Ms. Rodewald; music supervision, Mr. Spurney; associate producers, Bill Bragin, Peter DuBois and Mandy Hackett; production stage manager, Cynthia Cahill; press, Arlene R. Kriv.

Presented in two parts.

An African-American musician from Los Angeles accumulates a wide range of experience as he matures in Europe. First presentation of record was given at Berkeley Repertory Theatre (10/19–12/3/2006) after development, with collaborator Ms. Dorsen, at the Sundance Theatre Lab (7/2005). A 2006–07 *Best Plays* choice (see essay by Alisa Solomon in this volume).

Wound worker: Stew and Rebecca Naomi Jones in Passing Strange. *Photo: Michal Daniel*

*Irish Repertory Theatre production of **Gaslight** (17). By Patrick Hamilton. Charlotte Moore artistic director, Ciarán O'Reilly producing director. Opened May 17, 2007.

Rough	Brian Murray	Jack Manningham	David Staller
Elizabeth	Patricia O'Connell	Police Officers	April Ann Kline,
Bella Manningham	Laura Odeh		Jon Levenson
Nancy	Laoisa Sexton		

Directed by Charlotte Moore; scenery, James Morgan; costumes, Martha Hally; lighting, Brian Nason; sound, Zachary Williamson; music, Mark Hartman; fight direction, Rick Sordelet; stage manager, Christine Lemme; press, Shirley Herz Associates, Daniel Demello.

Time: Victorian era. Place: London Presented in two parts.

Psychological thriller in which a husband attempts to drive his wife mad by playing mental tricks on her. First presentation of record was given under the title *Gas Light* at London's Richmond Theatre (12/5/1938). First presentation of record in this country was given at the Spa Theatre in Saratoga Springs, New York (8/22/1939) before a run the following week at the Casino Theatre in Newport, Rhode Island. After various artists and producers expressed interest in a Broadway mounting, including Norman Bel Geddes at one point, there was a summer-theater appearance at the Mount Washington Casino in Baltimore (8/7/1941). The play underwent title changes—first *Five Chelsea Lane*, later *Angel Street*—as producer Shepard Traube made revisions to the third act before a three-year Broadway stand at the John Golden and the Bijou Theatres (12/5/1941–12/30/1944; 1,295 performances). Alexander H. Cohen joined as a producer during the rehearsal period. In its *Angel Street* form, the play was a 1941–42 *Best Plays* choice.

*Phallacy (16). By Carl Djerassi. Produced by Redshift Productions at the Cherry Lane Theatre. Opened May 18, 2007.

Regina Leitner-Opfermann	Lisa Harrow	Rex Stolzfuss	Simon Jones
High School Student's Voice	CJ Laroche	Otto Ellenbogen	Vince Nappo
Emma Finger	Carrie Heitman		

Directed by Elena Araoz; scenery, Susan Zeeman Rogers; costumes, Victoria Tzykun; lighting, Justin Townsend; sound, Arielle Edwards; casting, Redshift Productions, Jack Doulin; production stage manager, Libby Steiner; press, Springer Associates Public Relations, Gary Springer, Joe Trentacosta, D'Arcy Drollinger, Shane Marshall Brown, Jennifer Blum.

Time: The recent past; 1572. Place: Vienna; Luxembourg. Presented in two parts.

A scientist insists upon proving that a statue is a Renaissance copy, not a Roman original, which causes an art historian great distress. First presentation of record was given at London's New End Theatre (4/15–5/14/2005) before a run at the King's Head Theatre (5/18–6/19/2005).

CAST REPLACEMENTS
AND TOURING COMPANIES

○ ○ ○ ○ ○

Compiled by Paul Hardt

THE FOLLOWING IS a list of the major cast replacements of record in productions that opened during the current and in previous seasons, and other New York shows that were on a first-class tour in 2006–2007.

The name of each major role is listed in *italics* beneath the title of the play in the first column. In the second column directly opposite appears the name of the actor who created the role in the original New York production (whose opening date appears in *italics* at the top of the column). Indented immediately beneath the original actor's name are the names of subsequent New York replacements—with the date of replacement when available.

The third column gives information about first-class touring companies. When there is more than one roadshow company, #1, #2, etc., appear before the name of the performer who created the role in each company (and the city and date of each company's first performance appears in *italics* at the top of the column). Subsequent replacements are also listed beneath names in the same manner as the New York companies, with dates when available.

ALTAR BOYZ

	New York 3/1/05	*Chicago 6/10/06*
Matthew	Scott Porter	Matthew Buckner
	James Royce Edwards 2/9/06	
	John Celaya 4/3/06	
	Kyle Dean Massey	
	Matthew Buckner	
Mark	Tyler Maynard	Ryan J. Ratliff
	Danny Calvert 7/12/05	
	Tyler Maynard 1/9/06	
	Zach Hannah	
	Ryan J. Ratliff	
Luke	Andy Karl	Jesse JP Johnson
	James Royce Edwards	
	Andrew C. Call 2/9/06	
	Landon Beard	
Abraham	David Josefsberg	Nick Blaemire
	Dennis Moench	Ryan Strand

	Eric Schneider	
	Ryan Strand	
Juan	Ryan Duncan	Jay Garcia
	Nick Sanchez	
	Clyde Alves	
	Ryan Duncan 5/1/06	
	Shaun Taylor Corbett 7/3/06	
	Jay Garcia	

AVENUE Q

New York 7/31/03

Princeton; Rod	John Tartaglia
	Barrett Foa 2/1/05
	Howie Michael Smith 7/3/06
Brian	Jordan Gelber
	Evan Harrington
Kate Monster; Lucy	Stephanie D'Abruzzo
	Mary Faber 12/26/05
	Kelli Sawyer 10/30/06
	Mary Faber
Nicky; Trekkie	Rick Lyon
	Christian Anderson 7/5/05
	Rick Lyon 5/2/06
	Robert McClure 10/30/06
	David Benoit
Christmas Eve	Ann Harada
	Ann Sanders 10/26/04
	Ann Harada 1/25/05
	Ann Sanders
Gary Coleman	Natalie Venetia Belcon
	Haneefah Wood

BEAUTY AND THE BEAST

New York 4/18/94

Beast	Terrence Mann
	Jeff McCarthy
	Chuck Wagner
	James Barbour
	Steve Blanchard
	Jeff McCarthy 2/17/04
	Steve Blanchard 4/13/04
Belle	Susan Egan
	Sarah Uriarte Berry
	Christianne Tisdale
	Kerry Butler
	Deborah Gibson
	Kim Huber
	Toni Braxton
	Andrea McArdle
	Sarah Litzsinger
	Jamie-Lynn Sigler
	Sarah Litzsinger 2/11/03

Megan McGinnis 4/15/03
Christy Carlson Romano 2/17/04
Brooke Tansley 9/14/04
Ashley Brown 9/20/05
Sarah Litzsinger 5/30/06
Sarah Uriarte Berry 9/19/06
Deborah Lew 12/26/06
Anneliese van der Pol 4/3/07

Lefou

Kenny Raskin
Harrison Beal
Jamie Torcellini
Jeffrey Schecter
Jay Brian Winnick 11/12/99
Gerard McIsaac
Brad Aspel
Steve Lavner
Aldrin Gonzalez

Gaston

Burke Moses
Marc Kudisch
Steve Blanchard
Patrick Ryan Sullivan
Christopher Sieber
Chris Hoch 12/10/02
Grant Norman
Donny Osmond 9/19/06
Stephen R. Buntrock 12/26/06
Chris Hoch
Donny Osmond

Maurice

Tom Bosley
MacIntyre Dixon
Tom Bosley
Kurt Knudson
Timothy Jerome
JB Adams 11/12/99
Jamie Ross

Cogsworth

Heath Lamberts
Peter Bartlett
Robert Gibby Brand
John Christopher Jones
Jeff Brooks 11/12/99
Christopher Duva
Jonathan Freeman 11/26/06

Lumiere

Gary Beach
Lee Roy Reams
Patrick Quinn
Gary Beach
Meshach Taylor
Patrick Page
Paul Schoeffler
Patrick Page
Bryan Batt
Rob Lorey 5/7/02
David DeVries
Peter Flynn
Jacob Young 5/9/05
John Tartaglia 11/21/06

Babette	Stacey Logan
	Pamela Winslow
	Leslie Castay
	Pam Klinger
	Louisa Kendrick
	Pam Klinger
	Meredith Inglesby
Mrs. Potts	Beth Fowler
	Cass Morgan
	Beth Fowler
	Barbara Marineau 11/12/99
	Beth Fowler
	Cass Morgan
	Alma Cuervo 2/17/04
	Jeanne Lehman 11/10/05

THE BIG VOICE: GOD OR MERMAN?

New York 11/30/06
Closed 5/13/07

Steve	Steve Schalchlin
	Carl Danielsen 3/11/07
Jim	Jim Brochu
	Dale Radunz 3/11/07

CHICAGO

New York 11/14/96

Roxie Hart	Ann Reinking
	Marilu Henner
	Karen Ziemba
	Belle Calaway
	Charlotte d'Amboise
	Sandy Duncan 8/12/99
	Belle Calaway 1/18/00
	Charlotte d'Amboise 3/24/00
	Belle Calaway
	Nana Visitor
	Petra Nielsen 10/8/01
	Nana Visitor 11/19/01
	Belle Calaway 1/13/02
	Denise Van Outen 3/18/02
	Belle Calaway 4/22/02
	Amy Spanger 8/6/02
	Belle Calaway
	Tracy Shayne 4/15/03
	Melanie Griffith 7/11/03
	Charlotte d'Amboise 10/7/03
	Bianca Marroquin 12/15/03
	Gretchen Mol 1/5/04
	Charlotte d'Amboise 3/1/04
	Tracy Shayne
	Charlotte d'Amboise
	Brooke Shields 9/5/05
	Robin Givens
	Tracy Shayne

	Charlotte d'Amboise
	Rita Wilson 6/12/06
	Bianca Marroquin
	Bebe Neuwirth 12/31/06
	Bianca Marroquin 4/23/07
Velma Kelly	Bebe Neuwirth
	Nancy Hess
	Ute Lemper
	Bebe Neuwirth
	Ruthie Henshall 5/25/99
	Mamie Duncan-Gibbs 10/26/99
	Bebe Neuwirth 1/18/00
	Donna Marie Asbury 3/23/00
	Sharon Lawrence 4/11/00
	Vicki Lewis
	Jasmine Guy
	Bebe Neuwirth
	Donna Marie Asbury
	Deidre Goodwin
	Vicki Lewis
	Deidre Goodwin 6/29/01
	Anna Montanaro 7/9/01
	Deidre Goodwin 9/14/01
	Donna Marie Asbury
	Roxane Carrasco 1/13/02
	Deidre Goodwin 3/18/02
	Stephanie Pope
	Roxane Carrasco
	Caroline O'Connor 11/8/02
	Brenda Braxton 3/3/03
	Deidre Goodwin 6/24/03
	Reva Rice 10/7/03
	Brenda Braxton 1/1/04
	Pia Dowes 4/8/04
	Brenda Braxton 5/16/04
	Terra C. MacLeod 7/27/04
	Donna Marie Asbury 2/14/05
	Brenda Braxton 2/21/05
	Luba Mason 6/28/05
	Brenda Braxton
	Robin Givens
	Brenda Braxton
	Amra-Faye Wright
	Brenda Braxton 4/17/06
Billy Flynn	James Naughton
	Gregory Jbara
	Hinton Battle
	Alan Thicke
	Michael Berresse
	Brent Barrett
	Robert Urich 1/11/00
	Clarke Peters 2/1/00
	Brent Barrett 2/15/00
	Chuck Cooper
	Brent Barrett 7/2/01
	Chuck Cooper 8/27/01
	George Hamilton 11/12/01

Eric Jordan Young 1/18/02
Ron Raines 3/26/02
George Hamilton 5/21/02
Michael C. Hall 8/8/02
Destan Owens
Taye Diggs
Billy Zane 11/8/02
Kevin Richardson 1/20/03
Clarke Peters
Gregory Harrison
Brent Barrett 6/2/03
Patrick Swayze 12/15/03
James Naughton 1/5/04
Norm Lewis 2/2/04
Christopher Sieber 3/23/04
Tom Wopat 5/16/04
Christopher Sieber 6/17/04
Marti Pellow 8/3/04
Wayne Brady 9/7/04
Tom Wopat 12/7/04
Brent Barrett 1/4/05
Christopher McDonald 7/1/05
Huey Lewis 11/18/05
John O'Hurley 1/16/06
Obba Babatunde 4/17/06
Usher 8/22/06
Christopher McDonald 10/15/06
Huey Lewis 11/20/06
Philip Casnoff 1/12/06
Joey Lawrence 5/4/07

Amos Hart   Joel Grey
Ernie Sabella
Tom McGowan
P.J. Benjamin
Ernie Sabella 11/23/99
P.J. Benjamin
Tom McGowan
P.J. Benjamin
Raymond Bokhour 7/30/01
P.J. Benjamin 8/13/01
Rob Bartlett
P.J. Benjamin 3/3/03
Raymond Bokhour
P.J. Benjamin
Raymond Bokhour
Kevin Chamberlin 6/12/06
Rob Bartlett

Matron   Marcia Lewis
Roz Ryan
Marcia Lewis
Roz Ryan
Marcia Lewis
Roz Ryan
Marcia Lewis
Jennifer Holliday 6/18/01
Marcia Lewis 8/27/01
Roz Ryan 11/16/01

Michele Pawk 1/14/02
Alix Korey 3/4/02
B.J. Crosby 3/3/03
Angie Stone 4/15/03
Camille Saviola 6/10/03
Debbie Gravitte 12/15/03
Roz Ryan 3/15/04
Carol Woods
Roz Ryan
Anne L. Nathan 9/13/04
Carol Woods 1/31/05
Anne L. Nathan 2/21/05
Mary Testa
Carol Woods
Debra Monk 9/5/06
Lillias White 1/31/07
Roz Ryan

Mary Sunshine   D. Sabella
J. Loeffelholz
R. Bean
A. Saunders
J. Maldonado
R. Bean
A. Saunders 1/2/02
R. Bean 1/14/02
M. Agnes
D. Sabella 3/24/03
R. Bean 5/17/04
R. Lowe

THE COLOR PURPLE

	New York 12/1/05	Chicago 4/17/07
Celie	LaChanze Jeannette I. Bayardelle 11/7/06 Fantasia Barrino 4/10/07	Jeannette I. Bayardelle
Shug Avery	Elisabeth Withers-Mendes	Michelle Williams
Master	Kingsley Leggs	Rufus Bonds Jr.
Sophia	Felicia P. Fields NaTasha Yvette Williams 1/30/07	Felicia P. Fields
Nettie	Renee Elise Goldsberry Darlesia Cearcy 1/17/07	LaToya London
Harpo	Brandon Victor Dixon	Stu James
Old Man	Lou Meyers Larry Marshall	Adam Wade

DIRTY ROTTEN SCOUNDRELS

	New York 4/3/05 Closed 9/3/06	Seattle 8/04/06
Lawrence Jameson	John Lithgow Jonathan Price 1/17/05 Keith Carradine 7/21/06	Tom Hewitt
Freddy Benson	Norbert Leo Butz	Norbert Leo Butz

	Brian d'Arcy James 7/21/06	Timothy Gulan DB Bonds
Christine Colgate	Sherie René Scott Rachel York Sherie René Scott	Laura Marie Duncan
Muriel Eubanks	Joanna Gleason Lucie Arnaz	Hollis Resnik
Jolene Oakes	Sara Gettelfinger Mylinda Hull 1/17/06 Sara Gettelfinger	Jenifer Foote Paige Pardy
André Thibault	Gregory Jbara Richard Kind	Drew McVety Joe Cassidy

DOUBT

	New York 3/31/05 *Closed 7/2/06*	*Los Angeles 9/22/06* *Closed 05/20/07*
Sister Aloysius	Cherry Jones Eileen Atkins 1/17/06	Cherry Jones
Father Flynn	Brían F. O'Byrne Ron Eldard 1/11/06	Chris McGarry
Mrs. Muller	Adriane Lenox	Adriane Lenox Caroline Stefanie Clay
Sister James	Heather Goldenhersh Jena Malone 1/11/06	Lisa Joyce

THE DROWSY CHAPERONE

	New York 5/1/06
Janet Van De Graff	Sutton Foster Janine LaManna 4/17/07
Man in Chair	Bob Martin Jonathan Crombie 3/20/07 John Glover 4/17/07
Mrs. Tottendale	Georgia Engel Jo Anne Worley 4/17/07
Underling	Edward Hibbert Peter Bartlett 1/16/07
George	Eddie Korbich Patrick Wetzel 5/22/07
Feldzieg	Lenny Wolpe Gerry Vichi 6/5/07
The Drowsy Chaperone	Beth Leavel
Aldopho	Danny Burstein
Robert Martin	Troy Britton Johnson

THE FANTASTICKS

| | *New York 8/23/06* |
| *Matt* | Santino Fontana |

	Douglas Ullman Jr. Anthony Fedorov 5/1/07
Luisa	Sara Jean Ford Julie Craig Betsy Morgan Whitney Bashor
El Gallo	Burke Moses
Hucklebee	Leo Burmester John Deyle
Bellomy	Martin Vidnovic
Henry	Thomas Bruce (Tom Jones)
Mortimer	Robert R. Oliver
Mute	Douglas Ullman Jr. Nick Spanger

GUTENBERG! THE MUSICAL!

New York 1/16/07
Closed 5/6/07

Doug Simon	Jeremy Shamos Darren Goldstein 4/10/07
Bud Davenport	Christopher Fitzgerald David Turner 2/13/07

HAIRSPRAY

New York 8/15/02

Tracy Turnblad	Marissa Jaret Winokur Kathy Brier 8/12/03 Carly Jibson 5/4/04 Marissa Jaret Winokur 6/8/05 Shannon Durig
Edna Turnblad	Harvey Fierstein Michael McKean 5/4/04 Bruce Vilanch John Pinette 9/6/05 Blake Hammond Paul C. Vogt 1/30/07
Wilbur Turnblad	Dick Latessa Peter Scolari Todd Susman Stephen DeRosa 9/6/05 Jere Burns
Amber Von Tussle	Laura Bell Bundy Tracy Jai Edwards 7/14/03 Jordan Ballard Becky Gulsvig Brynn O'Malley
Velma Von Tussle	Linda Hart Barbara Walsh 7/14/03 Leah Hocking Liz Larsen

	Leah Hocking 3/13/06
	Isabel Keating 6/6/06
Link Larkin	Matthew Morrison
	Richard H. Blake 1/13/04
	Andrew Rannells
	Ashley Parker Angel 1/19/06
Motormouth Maybelle	Mary Bond Davis
	Darlene Love
Seaweed	Corey Reynolds
	Chester Gregory II 7/14/03
	Tevin Campbell 12/13/05
Penny Pingleton	Kerry Butler
	Jennifer Gambatese 6/15/04
	Brooke Tansley 4/11/04
	Jennifer Gambatese 6/15/04
	Tracy Miller
	Diana DeGarmo 2/7/06
	Haylie Duff 7/18/06
	Diana DeGarmo
	Alexa Vega 2/13/07
	Niki Scalera
Corny Collins	Clarke Thorell
	Jonathan Dokuchitz 1/13/04
Little Inez	Danelle Eugenia Wilson
	Aja Maria Johnson 7/19/03
	Nia Imani Soyemi

HOT FEET

New York 4/30/06
Closed 7/23/06

Kalimba	Vivian Nixon
Mom	Ann Duquesnay
Victor	Keith David
	Mel Johnson Jr.
Naomi	Wynonna Smith
Louie	Allen Hidalgo
Anthony	Michael Balderrama

I LOVE YOU, YOU'RE PERFECT, NOW CHANGE

New York 8/1/96

Man #1	Jordan Leeds
	Danny Burstein 10/1/96
	Adam Grupper 8/22/97
	Gary Imhoff 2/9/98
	Adam Grupper 4/1/98
	Jordan Leeds 3/17/99
	Bob Walton 10/27/00
	Jordan Leeds 1/30/01
	Darrin Baker 1/29/02
	Danny Burstein 4/12/02

Jordan Leeds 6/3/02
Will Erat 12/20/05
Ron Bohmer 3/20/06
Will Erat
Jim Stanek

Man #2   Robert Roznowski
Kevin Pariseau 5/25/98
Adam Hunter 4/20/01
Sean Arbuckle 9/23/02
Frank Baiocchi 2/17/03
Colin Stokes 10/10/03
Jamie LaVerdiere
Adam Arian
Brian McElroy 1/29/07

Woman #1   Jennifer Simard
Erin Leigh Peck 5/25/98
Kelly Anne Clark 1/10/00
Andrea Chamberlain 3/13/00
Lori Hammel 11/4/00
Andrea Chamberlain 1/29/01
Amanda Watkins 8/24/01
Karyn Quackenbush 1/2/02
Marissa Burgoyne 8/9/02
Andrea Chamberlain 12/17/02
Karyn Quackenbush 2/17/03
Sandy Rustin 6/13/03
Andrea Chamberlain 11/19/04
Jordan Ballard
Jodie Langel
Courtney Balan 12/8/06

Woman #2   Melissa Weil
Cheryl Stern 2/16/98
Mylinda Hull 9/17/00
Melissa Weil 2/9/01
Evy O'Rourke 3/13/01
Marylee Graffeo 6/11/01
Cheryl Stern 1/18/02
Marylee Graffeo 3/11/02
Janet Metz 4/26/02
Anne Bobby 12/17/02
Janet Metz 3/3/03
Anne Bobby 5/23/05

JACQUES BREL IS ALIVE AND WELL AND LIVING IN PARIS

New York 3/27/06
Closed 2/25/07

Robert Cuccioli

Gay Marshall

Natascia Diaz
Jayne Patterson 1/9/07

Rodney Hicks
Drew Sarich 7/7/06
Jim Stanek 10/9/06
Constantine Maroulis 1/9/07

JERSEY BOYS

	New York 11/6/05	#1 San Francisco 12/1/06 #2 San Francisco 5/4/07
Frankie Valli	John Lloyd Young	#1 Jarrod Spector #2 Christopher Kale Jones
Tommy DeVito	Christian Hoff	#1 Deven May #2 Jeremy Kushnier
Bob Gaudio	Daniel Reichard	#1 Erich Bergen #2 Drew Gehling
Nick Massi	J. Robert Spencer	#1 Michael Ingersoll Steve Gouveia #2 Michael Ingersoll

LES MISÉRABLES

	New York 11/9/06
Jean Valjean	Alexander Gemignani
Inspector Javert	Norm Lewis Ben Davis 4/24/07 Drew Sarich (alt.)
Fantine	Daphne Rubin-Vega Lea Salonga 3/6/07
Marius	Adam Jacobs
Cosette	Ali Ewoldt
Eponine	Celia Keenan-Bolger Mandy Bruno 4/24/07
Madame Thernardier	Jenny Galloway Ann Harada 4/24/07
Thernardier	Gary Beach
Enjolras	Aaron Lazar Max von Essen 4/24/07

THE LIGHT IN THE PIAZZA

	New York 4/18/05 Closed 7/02/06	San Francisco 8/01/06
Margaret Johnson	Victoria Clark	Christina Andreas
Clara Johnson	Kelli O'Hara Katie Rose Clarke	Elena Shaddow Katie Rose Clarke
Fabrizio Naccarelli	Matthew Morrison	David Burnham
Signora Naccarelli	Patti Cohenour	Diane Sutherland Evangelia Kingsley Diana DiMarzio 3/27/07
Franca Naccarelli	Sarah Uriarte Berry	Laura Griffith Wendi Bergamini
Giuseppe Naccarelli	Michael Berresse	Jonathan Hammond
Signor Naccarelli	Mark Harelik Chris Sarandon 9/13/05	David Ledingham
Roy Johnson	Beau Gravitte	Brian Sutherland

THE LION KING

	New York 11/13/97	#1 Gazelle Company
		#2 Cheetah Company
Rafiki	Tsidii Le Loka	#1 Futhi Mhlongo
	Thuli Dumakude 11/11/98	Phindile Mkhize
	Sheila Gibbs	#2 Thandazile A. Soni
	Nomvula Dlamini	Gugwana Dlamini
	Tshidi Manye	
Mufasa	Samuel E. Wright	#1 Alton Fitzgerald White
	Alton Fitzgerald White	Thomas Corey Robinson
	Nathaniel Stampley	L. Steven Taylor
		Dionne Randolph
		#2 Rufus Bonds Jr.
		Nathaniel Stampley
		Geno Segers
Sarabi	Gina Breedlove	#1 Jean Michelle Grier
	Meena T. Jahi 8/4/98	Lashanda Reese-Fletcher
	Denise Marie Williams	#2 Marvette Williams
	Meena T. Jahi	
	Robyn Payne	
	Jean Michelle Grier	
Zazu	Geoff Hoyle	#1 Jeffrey Binder
	Bill Bowers 10/21/98	Mark Cameron Pow
	Robert Dorfman	#2 Derek Hasenstab
	Tony Freeman	Timothy McGeever
	Adam Stein	Michael Dean Morgan
	Jeffrey Binder	
Scar	John Vickery	#1 Patrick Page
	Tom Hewitt 10/21/98	Dan Donohue
		Timothy Carter
	Derek Smith	#2 Larry Yando
	Patrick Page	Kevin Gray
	Derek Smith	
	Patrick Page	
Banzai	Stanley Wayne Mathis	#1 James Brown-Orleans
	Keith Bennett 9/30/98	Randy Donaldson
	Leonard Joseph	#2 Melvin Abston
	Curtiss I'Cook	Rudy Roberson
	Rodrick Covington	
	Benjamin Sterling Cannon	
	James Brown-Orleans	
Shenzi	Tracy Nicole Chapman	#1 Jacquelyn Renae Hodges
	Vanessa S. Jones	Kimberly Hebert Gregory
	Lana Gordon	Jayne Trinette
	Marlayna Sims	#2 Shaullanda Lacombe
	Bonita J. Hamilton	Danielle Lee Greaves
		Jacquelyn Renae Hodges
Ed	Kevin Cahoon	#1 Wayne Pyle
	Jeff Skowron 10/21/98	Michael Nathanson
	Jeff Gurner	#2 Brian Sills
	Timothy Gulan	Robbie Swift
	Thom Christopher Warren	
	Enrique Segura	
Timon	Max Casella	#1 John Plumpis

	Danny Rutigliano 6/16/98	Mark Shunock
	John E. Brady	#2 Benjamin Clost
	Danny Rutigliano	Adam Hunter
		Damian Baldet
		John Gardiner
Pumbaa	Tom Alan Robbins	#1 Ben Lipitz
		#2 Bob Amaral
		Phil Fiorini
		Bob Amaral
Simba	Jason Raize	#1 Alan Mingo Jr.
	Christopher Jackson	S.J. Hannah
	Josh Tower	Dashaun Young
		#2 Brandon Victor Dixon
		Brandon Louis
		Wallace Smith
		Clifton Oliver
Nala	Heather Headley	#1 Kissy Simmons
	Mary Randle 7/7/98	Lisa Nicole Wilkerson
	Heather Headley 12/8/98	Adrienne Muller
	Bashirrah Creswell	Chauntee Schuler
	Sharon L. Young	Erica Ash
	Renée Elise Goldsberry	#2 Adia Ginneh Dobbins
	Kissy Simmons	Ta'rea Campbell

MAMMA MIA!

	New York 10/18/01	*#1 US Tour*
		#2 Las Vegas
Donna Sheridan	Louise Pitre	#1 Dee Hoty
	Dee Hoty 10/22/03	Laurie Wells
	Carolee Carmello 10/20/04	Mary Jayne Raleigh
	Michele Pawk 10/19/05	#2 Tina Walsh
	Corinne Melancon	Jacqueline Holland
	Leah Hocking	Carol Linnea Johnson
	Carolee Carmello	
Sophie Sheridan	Tina Maddigan	#1 Chilina Kennedy
	Jenny Fellner 10/22/03	Carrie Manolakos
	Sara Kramer 10/20/04	Vicki Noon
	Carey Anderson 10/19/05	#2 Jill Paice
		Suzie Jacobsen Balser
		Kelly Anise Daniells
		Libby Winters
Tanya	Karen Mason	#1 Cynthia Sophiea
	Jeanine Morick	Lisa Mandel
	Tamara Bernier	Christine Sherrill
	Judy McLane 10/20/04	#2 Karole Foreman
		Reyna Von Vett
		Vicki Van Tassel
Rosie	Judy Kaye	#1 Rosalyn Rahn Kerins
	Harriett D. Foy	Laura Ware
	Liz McCartney 10/20/04	Allison Briner
	Olga Merediz 10/19/2005	#2 Jennifer Perry
	Gina Ferrall	Kristine Zbornik
		Robin Baxter

Sky	Joe Machota Aaron Staton Andy Kelso 10/19/05	#1 P.J. Griffith Corey Greenan Timothy Ware #2 Victor Wallace Patrick Sarb
Sam Carmichael	David W. Keeley John Hillner David W. Keeley John Hillner Daniel McDonald 10/20/04 John Dossett 10/19/05 David McDonald	#1 Gary Lynch Sean Allan Krill #2 Nick Cokas Lewis Cleale Rick Negron Rob Sutton
Harry Bright	Dean Nolen Richard Binsley Michael Winther David Beach 10/20/04 Michael Mastro	#1 Michael DeVries Ian Simpson #2 Michael Piontek Andy Taylor T. Scott Cunningham
Bill Austin	Ken Marks Adam LeFevre Mark L. Montgomery Pearce Bunting	#1 Craig Bennett Milo Shandel #2 Mark Leydorf Patrick Gallo Jefferson Slinkard Ron McClary

MARTIN SHORT: FAME BECOMES ME

New York 8/17/06
Closed 1/7/07

Himself	Martin Short
Comedy All Star	Brooks Ashmanskas
Comedy All Star	Capathia Jenkins
Comedy All Star	Mary Birdsong
Comedy All Star	Nicole Parker Donna Vivino 10/3/06 Nicole Parker 12/26/06
Comedy All Star	Marc Shaiman

THE ODD COUPLE

New York 10/28/05
Closed 6/4/06

Oscar Madison	Nathan Lane
Felix Unger	Matthew Broderick
Roy	Peter Frechette
Vinnie	Lee Wilkof
Murray	Brad Garrett Mike Starr 1/3/07
Speed	Rob Bartlett
Cecily Pigeon	Jessica Stone
Gwendolyn Pigeon	Olivia d'Abo

THE PHANTOM OF THE OPERA

New York 1/26/88

#1 National Tour
#2 Las Vegas (95 minutes)

The Phantom	Michael Crawford	#1 Franc D'Ambrosio
	Thomas James O'Leary	Brad Little
	Hugh Panaro 2/1/99	Ted Keegan
	Howard McGillin 8/23/99	Brad Little
	Brad Little	Ted Keegan
	Howard McGillin	Brad Little
	Hugh Panaro 4/14/03	Gary Mauer
	Howard McGillin 12/22/03	John Cudia
	Hugh Panaro 1/5/04	#2 Brent Barrett (alt.)
	Howard McGillin	#2 Anthony Crivello (alt.)
	Gary Mauer	
	Howard McGillin	
Christine Daaé	Sarah Brightman	#1 Tracy Shane
	Sandra Joseph 1/29/98	Kimilee Bryant
	Adrienne McEwan 8/2/99	Amy Jo Arrington
	Sarah Pfisterer 1/17/00	Rebecca Pitcher
	Sandra Joseph 10/30/00	Kathy Voytko
	Sarah Pfisterer 8/6/01	Julie Hanson
	Elizabeth Southard 3/25/02	Rebecca Pitcher
	Lisa Vroman 4/22/02	Lisa Vroman
	Sandra Joseph 6/10/03	Rebecca Pitcher
		Marie Danvers
		Jennifer Hope Wills
		Marni Raab
		#2 Sierra Boggess (alt.)
		#2 Elizabeth Loyacano (alt.)
		Kristi Holden
Christine Daaé (alt.)	Patti Cohenour	#1 Tamra Hayden
	Adrienne McEwan	Marie Danvers
	Sarah Pfisterer	Megan Starr-Levitt
	Adrienne McEwan	Marni Raab
	Lisa Vroman 10/30/00	Elizabeth Southard
	Adrienne McEwan 7/9/01	Sarah Lawrence
	Julie Hanson 9/20/03	
	Elizabeth Loyacano 12/8/07	
Raoul	Steve Barton	#1 Ciaran Sheehan
	Gary Mauer 4/19/99	Jason Pebworth 1/29/97
	Jim Weitzer 4/23/01	Jim Weitzer
	Michael Shawn Lewis 11/2/01	Jason Pebworth 7/22/98
	John Cudia 4/7/03	Richard Todd Adams 3/31/99
	Jim Weitzer 10/3/03	Jim Weitzer 1/12/00
	John Cudia 12/21/03	John Cudia
	Tim Martin Gleason 5/27/05	Tim Martin Gleason
	Michael Shawn Lewis	Jim Weitzer
		Adam Monley
		Michael Gillis
		Greg Mills
		#2 Tim Martin Gleason

THE PRODUCERS

New York 4/19/01
Closed 4/22/07

Las Vegas 2/9/07

Max Bialystock	Nathan Lane	Brad Oscar
	Henry Goodman 3/19/02	
	Brad Oscar 4/16/02	
	Lewis J. Stadlen	
	Fred Applegate 10/7/03	
	Nathan Lane 12/31/03	
	Brad Oscar 4/6/04	
	Richard Kind 1/11/05	
	Brad Oscar	
	John Treacy Egan 10/25/05	
	Tony Danza 12/19/07	
	John Treacy Egan	
Leo Bloom	Matthew Broderick	Larry Raben
	Steven Weber 3/19/02	
	Roger Bart 12/17/02	
	Don Stephenson 5/20/03	
	Matthew Broderick 12/31/03	
	Roger Bart 4/6/04	
	Hunter Foster 6/13/04	
	Alan Ruck 1/11/05	
	Hunter Foster	
	Roger Bart 5/15/06	
	Hunter Foster 1/23/07	
Ulla	Cady Huffman	Leigh Zimmerman
	Sarah Cornell 8/5/03	
	Angie L. Schworer 11/4/03	
Roger De Bris	Gary Beach	David Hasselhoff
	John Treacy Egan	Lee Roy Reams 5/7/07
	Gary Beach 10/7/03	
	Jonathan Freeman 8/31/04	
	Gary Beach 9/6/05	
	Lee Roy Reams	
Carmen Ghia	Roger Bart	Rich Affanato
	Sam Harris 7/2/02	
	Brad Musgrove 12/17/02	
	Brooks Ashmanskas 8/31/04	
	Jai Rodriguez 11/1/05	
	Brad Musgrove	
Franz Liebkind	Brad Oscar	Fred Applegate
	John Treacy Egan	Bill Nolte 5/7/07
	Peter Samuel	
	John Treacy Egan	
	Bill Nolte	

RENT

New York 4/29/96

Roger Davis	Adam Pascal
	Norbert Leo Butz
	Richard H. Blake (alt.)
	Manley Pope 6/1/02
	Sebastian Arcelus 12/30/02
	Ryan Link 9/8/03
	Jeremy Kushnier 11/14/03
	Carey Shields 1/18/05
	Will Chase 12/26/05
	Tim Howar 1/30/06

Mark Cohen	Anthony Rapp
	Jim Poulos
	Trey Ellett 5/15/00
	Matt Caplan 6/1/02
	Joey Fatone 8/5/02
	Matt Caplan 12/23/02
	Drew Lachey 9/10/04
	Matt Caplan 3/14/04
	Christopher J. Hanke 8/5/06
Tom Collins	Jesse L. Martin
	Michael McElroy
	Rufus Bonds Jr. 9/7/99
	Alan Mingo Jr. 4/10/00
	Mark Leroy Jackson 1/15/01
	Mark Richard Ford 2/3/02
	Destan Owens 8/16/04
	Mark Richard Ford 12/20/04
	Destan Owens
	Troy Horne 11/27/06
Benjamin Coffin III	Taye Diggs
	Jacques C. Smith
	Stu James 3/13/00
	D'Monroe
	Stu James 11/29/04
	D'Monroe
Joanne Jefferson	Fredi Walker
	Gwen Stewart
	Alia León
	Kenna J. Ramsey
	Danielle Lee Greaves 10/4/99
	Natalie Venetia Belcon 10/2/00
	Myiia Watson-Davis 6/1/02
	Merle Dandridge 10/28/02
	Kenna J. Ramsey 3/3/03
	Merle Dandridge
	Nicole Lewis
	Kenna J. Ramsey 11/29/05
	Tonya Dixon 11/13/06
Angel Schunard	Wilson Jermaine Heredia
	Wilson Cruz
	Shaun Earl
	Jose Llana
	Jai Rodriguez
	Andy Señor 1/31/00
	Jai Rodriguez 3/10/02
	Andy Señor 2/17/03
	Jai Rodriguez 7/05/04
	Andy Señor 7/19/04
	Jai Rodriguez 8/2/04
	Justin Johnson 8/16/04
	Andy Señor 3/15/04
	Justin Johnson
Mimi Marquez	Daphne Rubin-Vega
	Marcy Harriell 4/5/97
	Krysten Cummings
	Maya Days

Loraine Velez 2/28/00
Karmine Alers 6/1/02
Krystal L. Washington 5/15/03
Melanie Brown 4/19/04
Krystal L. Washington 8/23/04
Jamie Lee Kirchner
Antonique Smith 3/6/07
Tamyra Gray 5/29/07

Maureen Johnson

Idina Menzel
Sherie René Scott
Kristen Lee Kelly
Tamara Podemski
Cristina Fadale 10/4/99
Maggie Benjamin 6/1/02
Cristina Fadale 10/28/02
Maggie Benjamin
Melanie Brown
Maggie Benjamin 4/19/04
Kelly Karbacz 7/19/04
Maggie Benjamin
Ava Gaudet
Maggie Benjamin 10/5/06
Nicolette Hart 1/8/07

SPAMALOT

	New York 3/17/05	*#1 Boston 3/7/06* *#2 Las Vegas 3/31/07 (90 minutes)*
King Arthur	Tim Curry John Bolton 7/22/05 Tim Curry 8/9/05 Simon Russell Beale 12/20/05 Harry Groener 4/25/06 Jonathan Hadary 10/31/06	#1 Michael Siberry #2 John O'Hurley
Lady of the Lake	Sara Ramirez Lauren Kennedy 12/20/05 Marin Mazzie 10/31/06	#1 Pia C. Glenn 　Esther Stilwell #2 Nikki Crawford
Sir Dennis Galahad	Christopher Sieber Lewis Cleale 7/5/06	#1 Bradley Dean 　Anthony Holds #2 Edward Staudenmayer
Sir Robin	David Hyde Pierce Martin Moran 4/4/06	#1 David Turner 　David Petkoff #2 Harry Bouvy
Sir Lancelot	Hank Azaria Alan Tudyk 8/6/05 Hank Azaria 12/2/05 Steve Kazee 4/4/06 Chris Hoch 10/3/06 Richard Holmes	#1 Richard Holmes #2 J. Anthony Crane
Patsy	Michael McGrath David Hibbard Michael McGrath	#1 Jeff Dumas #2 Justin Brill
Sir Bedevere	Steve Rosen Jeffrey Kuhn	#1 Christopher Gurr #2 Randal Keith

Prince Herbert	Christian Borle	#1 Tom Deckman
	Tom Deckman	Christopher Sutton
		#2 Steven Strafford

TARZAN

New York 5/10/06

Tarzan	Josh Strickland
Jane	Jenn Gambatese
Kerchak	Shuler Hensley
	Robert Evan 3/28/07
Kala	Merle Dandridge
Terk	Chester Gregory II

THE 25TH ANNUAL PUTNAM COUNTY SPELLING BEE

	New York 5/2/05	*Baltimore 9/19/06*
William Barfee	Dan Fogler	Eric Peterson
	Josh Gad 1/31/06	Dan Fogler 5/24/07
	Jared Gertner 1/30/07	
Marcy Park	Deborah S. Craig	Katie Boren
	Greta Lee 4/17/07	Deborah S. Craig 5/24/07
Leaf Coneybear	Jesse Tyler Ferguson	Michael Zahler
	Barrett Foa 6/25/06	Jesse Tyler Ferguson 5/24/07
	Stanley Bahorek 4/17/07	
Rona Lisa Peretti	Lisa Howard	Jennifer Simard
	Jennifer Simard 4/17/07	Sally Wilfert 4/11/07
		Lisa Howard 5/24/07
Olive Ostrovsky	Celia Keenan-Bolger	Lauren Worsham
	Jessica-Snow Wilson 9/19/06	Celia Keenan-Bolger 5/24/07
	Jenni Barber 4/17/07	
Mitch Mahoney	Derrick Baskin	Alan H. Green
	James Monroe Inglehart 4/17/07	Derrick Baskin 5/24/07
		Alan H. Green
Chip Tolentino	Jose Llana	Miguel Cervantes
	Aaron J. Albano 4/17/07	Jose Llana 5/24/07
Douglas Panch	Jay Reiss	James Kall
	Greg Stuhr 10/25/06	Jay Reiss 5/24/07
	Moe Rocca 4/17/07	
Logainne S.	Sarah Saltzberg	Sarah Stiles
	Sara Inbar 4/17/07	Sarah Saltzberg 5/24/07

THE WEDDING SINGER

New York 4/27/06
Closed 12/31/06

Robbie Hart	Stephen Lynch
Julia Sullivan	Laura Benanti
	Tina Maddigan 8/16/06
	Laura Benanti 10/3/06
Sammy	Matthew Saldivar
	Constantine Maroulis 9/8/06

George	Kevin Cahoon
Linda	Felicia Finley
Glen Guglie	Richard H. Blake
Holly	Amy Spanger
Rosie	Rita Gardner

WICKED

	New York 10/30/03	*#1 Toronto 3/9/05* *#2 Chicago 7/13/05* *#3 Los Angeles 2/21/07*

Glinda	Kristin Chenoweth
	Jennifer Laura Thompson 7/20/04
	Megan Hilty 5/31/04
	Kate Reinders 5/30/05
	Kendra Kassebaum
		#1 Kendra Kassebaum
		    Megan Hilty
		    Christina DeCicco
		#2 Kate Reinders
		    Stacie Morgain Lewis '
		    Erin Mackey
		#3 Megan Hilty

Elphaba	Idina Menzel
	Eden Espinosa 6/15/04
	Idina Menzel 7/6/04
	Shoshana Bean 1/11/05
	Eden Espinosa 1/10/06
	Ana Gasteyer 10/10/06
	Julia Murney 1/9/07
		#1 Stephanie J. Block
		    Julia Murney 3/8/06
		    Victoria Matlock
		    Shoshana Bean 9/6/06
		    Victoria Matlock
		#2 Ana Gasteyer
		    Kristy Cates 1/24/05
		    Dee Roscioli
		#3 Eden Espinosa

Wizard of Oz	Joel Grey
	George Hearn 7/20/04
	Ben Vereen 5/31/05
	David Garrison 4/4/06
		#1 David Garrison
		    P.J. Benjamin 3/8/06
		#2 Gene Weygandt
		    Peter Kevoian
		#3 John Rubinstein

Madame Morrible	Carole Shelley
	Rue McClanahan 5/31/05
	Carol Kane
	Jayne Houdyshell
		#1 Carol Kane
		    Carole Shelley
		    Alma Cuervo
		    Barbara Tirrell
		#2 Rondi Reed
		    Carole Shelley
		    Barbara Robertson
		#3 Carol Kane

Fiyero	Norbert Leo Butz 12/21/04
	Taye Diggs 1/18/05
	Norbert Leo Butz 1/20/05
	Joey McIntyre 7/20/04
	David Ayers 1/11/05
	Derrick Williams 1/10/06
	Sebastian Arcelus 1/9/07
		#1 Derrick Williams
		    Sebastian Arcelus 3/8/06
		    Clifton Hall
		#2 Derrick Williams
		#3 Kristoffer Cusick

Boq	Christopher Fitzgerald
	Randy Harrison 6/22/04
	Christopher Fitzgerald 7/27/04
	Robb Sapp 1/4/05
	Jeffrey Kuhn 1/11/05
	Robb Sapp
	Logan Lipton 8/8/06
		#1 Logan Lipton
		    Kirk McDonald
		#2 Telly Leung
		    Adam Flemming
		#3 Adam Wylie

Dr. Dillamond	William Youmans	#1 Timothy Britten Parker
	Sean McCourt	K. Todd Freeman
	Steven Skybell	Tom Flynn
		#2 Steven Skybell
		Timothy Britten Parker
		K. Todd Freeman
		#3 Timothy Britten Parker
Nessarose	Michelle Federer	#1 Jenna Leigh Green
	Cristy Candler 1/10/06	Jennifer Waldman 3/8/06
	Jenna Leigh Green 3/14/06	Deedee Magno Hall
	Cristy Candler	#2 Heidi Kettenring
		Summer Naomi Smart
		#3 Jenna Leigh Green

FIRST-CLASS NATIONAL TOURS

ALL SHOOK UP

Milwaukee 9/12/06
Closed 7/1/07

Chad	Joe Mandragona
Natalie	Jenny Fellner
Miss Susan	Susan Anton
Sherrif Earl	David Benoit
Jim Haller	Wally Dunn
Mayor Hyde	Beth Glover
Lorraine	Valisia Lekae Little
	Tracee Beazer
Dennis	Dennis Moench
Dean Hyde	Brian Sears
	James Royce Edwards
Sylvia	NaTasha Yvette Williams
	Jannie Jones

ANNIE

Seattle 8/21/05

Annie	Marissa O'Donnell
Miss Hannigan	Alene Robertson
	Victoria Oscar
	Alene Robertson
	Kathie Lee Gifford
	Alene Robertson
Daddy Warbucks	Conrad John Schuck
Rooster Hannigan	Scott Willis
Lily St. Regis	Mackenzie Phillips
	Julie Cardia
	Ashley Puckett Gonzales
FDR	Allan Baker
Sandy	Lola

BROOKLYN

St. Paul 6/11/06
  Closed 8/13/06

Brooklyn	Diana DeGarmo
Paradice	Melba Moore
Street Singer	Cleavant Derricks
Faith	Julie Reiber
Taylor Collins	Lee Morgan

CAMELOT

San Jose 1/30/07

King Arthur	Michael York
Guenevere	Rachel York
Lancelot	James Barbour
Mordred	Shannon Stoeke

LITTLE WOMEN

San Diego 9/2/05

Jo March	Kate Fisher
Marmee March	Maureen McGovern
Meg March	Renee Brna
Amy March	Gwen Hollander
Beth March	Autumn Hurlbert
Aunt March	Louisa Flaningam
	Neva Rae Powers
Laurie	Stephen Patterson

ON GOLDEN POND

St Paul 8/22/06
  Closed 3/4/07

Norman Thayer	Tom Bosley
Ethel Thayer	Michael Learned
Chelsea Thayer	Kate Levy
Bill Ray	Evan Pappas
	Brian Russell
Billy Ray	Shadoe Brandt
Charlie	Craig Bockhorn

PIPPIN

West Point 10/7/06
  Closed 1/15/07

Pippin	Joshua Park
Leading Player	Andre Ward

Berthe	Barbara Marineau
Catherine	Teal Wicks
Charlemagne	Mickey Dolenz
Fastrada	Shannon Lewis
Lewis	James Royce Edwards
Theo	Jason Blaine

SWEET CHARITY

San Diego 9/12/06

Charity Hope Valentine	Molly Ringwald
Oscar Lindquist	Guy Adkins
Vittorio Vidal	Aaron Ramey Steve Wilson 11/17/06

Helene	Kisha Howard
	    Francesca Harper
	    Kisha Howard

Nickie	Amanda Watkins Bridget Berger
Herman	Richard Ruiz

TWELVE ANGRY MEN

New Haven 9/19/06

Juror #1	George Wendt
Juror #2	Todd Cerveris
Juror #3	Randle Mell
Juror #4	Jeffrey Hayenga
Juror #5	Jim Saltouros
Juror #6	Charles Borland
Juror #7	Mark Morettini
Juror #8	Richard Thomas
Juror #9	Alan Mandell
Juror #10	Julian Gamble
Juror #11	David Lively
Juror #12	T. Scott Cunningham
Guard	Patrick New

THE SEASON OFF
OFF BROADWAY

THE SEASON OFF OFF BROADWAY

○ ○ ○ ○ ○ *By Garrett Eisler* ○ ○ ○ ○ ○

A S THE 2006–2007 season came to a close, hundreds of Off Off Broadway veterans gathered April 29, 2007, at John Jay College to remember Curt Dempster, artistic director of Ensemble Studio Theatre, who died in January at the age of 71. Dempster had founded EST in 1972 and run it ever since. Over those three decades he had premiered, it was estimated, over 6,000 new plays, most of them one-acts for EST's famous Marathon evenings, where new writers might share a bill with eminent names such as David Mamet, Wendy Wasserstein and John Patrick Shanley (all of whom had early work done at EST). Run as practically a one-man show out of a small West 52nd Street space, EST is a quintessential OOB operation, fueled by much idealism, little income and a small but loyal community of artists and audiences. That Dempster's death was discovered to have been a suicide made it all the sadder for those who knew him, and especially eerie for those who looked to EST as one of the last remnants of the spirit of the original OOB movement of the 1960s and 1970s. Thanks to a determined board and supportive sponsors, EST lives on. On the last day of the season, May 31, the annual Marathon brought together new one-acts by writers established (Neil LaBute, Israel Horovitz) and developing (Julia Cho, Daniel Reitz).

Theater companies come and go, of course, and those that survive more than a few years in the volatile landscape of OOB show exceptional resolve and resourcefulness. In the forefront of the new avant-garde companies was Les Freres Corbusier, which mixes high intellect, mock earnestness and unabashed silliness. Its 2004 *A Very Merry Unauthorized Children's Scientology Pageant* (a musical bio of L. Ron Hubbard sung by a cast of preteens) was revived at New York Theatre Workshop's annex space for a brief holiday run as an OOB antidote to the obligatory *Christmas Carol* of establishment theaters. But for a new undertaking director Alex Timbers and producer Aaron Lemon-Strauss turned to a an evangelical minister. The *Hell House* pageant marketed by Pastor Keenan Roberts, of Colorado's New Destiny Christian Center, aims at scaring youths away from the sins of modern culture by showing gruesome morality tales of abortions,

AIDS and school shootings. But to Les Freres Corbusier it promised a provocative and confrontational evening for jaded OOB denizens. The company converted St. Ann's Warehouse in Brooklyn into the *Hell House* gallery of horrors. Patrons bought tickets not for seats but for "tours," offered two or three times nightly, that walked them through a progression of scenes until all were asked (true to the *Hell House* "script") to sign a pledge professing their faithfulness to Jesus, followed by a "celebratory hoedown" with church fair-type refreshments. Many New Yorkers declined to sign the pledge, but Les Freres's conceit was to play the material absolutely straight—as demanded by the pastor in granting rights—and exploit the tensions between red- and blue-state America in these religiously polarized times. The ironies were not lost on enthusiastic critics. *Time Out New York*'s David Cote pronounced, in appropriately mock-King James English: "Mightily doth it resist ironic temptation, but thou mayest as well bid the wind be still or the desert to yield Evian."

New Plays and New Writing

THE PLAYWRIGHTS' COLLECTIVE 13P saw its stock rise this season due less to its one official opening—Kate Ryan's *Mark Smith*—than to the flourishing of some of its thirteen members, who banded together to avoid the "development hell" of readings and workshops young writers often receive in lieu of full productions. Not only have the economic risks and star-driven marketing of Broadway banished much new writing from the Rialto, but even the Off Broadway community of nonprofit theaters—with older, conservative subscribers and tendency to favor the established—are increasingly perceived as gated communities to new writers. 13P's goal of presenting fully staged, albeit small, mountings of at least one member play a year began to pay dividends when Anne Washburn's *The Internationalist*—its first venture in 2004—was presented by Vineyard Theatre in November 2006.

The aura of the company as the new "elect" of playwrights under 40 was further enhanced by other members' successes around town. Sheila Callaghan's *Dead City* (produced by New Georges in a multimedia staging at the 3LD Art and Technology Center in the financial district) applied themes and motifs from James Joyce's *Ulysees* to post-September 11 New York. Young Jean Lee had two prominent premieres, which she directed, each drawing from a different aspect of her past. In *Songs of the Dragons Flying to Heaven*, presented at HERE Arts Center in September, she humorously exploited Asian stereotypes to give voice to her own conflicted

Korean-American heritage. *Church*, which opened at Performance Space 122 in April, drew from her experience attending an evangelical congregation in the Pacific Northwest. While a self-professed atheist, Lee used the frame of a service not to mock religion, but, as she told the *Village Voice* "to target myself and my own demographic." As in *Hell House*, *Church* used the format of a service to confront New Yorkers with their own spiritual complacency by staging the rituals of devout belief. In recognition of her work this season Lee was awarded a playwriting grant at the Obie Awards.

Will a real estate crisis change "Off Off Broadway" into "Off Manhattan"?

It was a good year OOB for new plays and new writers in general. The biggest individual breakthrough was that of Adam Bock, Obie winner for *The Thugs*—which helped secure Off Broadway premieres for him next season at Manhattan Theatre Club and Playwrights Horizons. Produced by Soho Rep—where it easily extended two weeks past its initial short run—*The Thugs* displayed Bock's gift for finding the absurd in the mundane. Set in a drab paralegal office, where three-per-desk temps highlight generic documents, it resembled an episode of the barbed sitcom *The Office* filtered through Pinter's comedy of menace. The title figures are never seen, only alluded to when bodies pile on the floors. Deliberately static and elusive, Bock's writing is alternately funny and frightening without bowing to standard conventions of exposition and narrative. Under the expert direction of Anne Kauffman (another Obie honoree), the production featured an eerily average workplace design by David Korins with a creepy soundscape by Robert Kaplowitz and Jeremy J. Lee.

Playwright Thomas Bradshaw had a prolific year OOB with three race-themed works that divided critics but solidified his reputation for flouting cultural taboos. A 2005 play, *Strom Thurmond Is Not a Racist*—about the segregationist senator's secret black daughter—was revived at the Brick in Brooklyn on a double bill with *Cleansed*, in which a biracial teenage girl's self-hatred leads her to join the Ku Klux Klan. More controversial was Bradshaw's *Purity* (at P.S. 122) about a black college-professor so desperate to assimilate that he persecutes newly arrived faculty in his African-American studies department for too much racial pride. In the most controversial scene, the professor bonds with a white colleague on a sex-tourism binge during which they graphically rape a 9-year-old Ecuadorean girl. Reviews were decidedly mixed, dividing those who were outraged from those who championed the provocative nature of Bradshaw's work.

Another new playwright arrived just as the season ended in May with New Georges's production of *God's Ear* by Jenny Schwartz. The play had already accumulated buzz on the nonprofit reading circuit due to its inventive dialogue of nonsense-poetry—but no Off Broadway theater would commit to it. Strong word of mouth, though, helped fill the East 13th Street Theatre for the entire four-week run. Using as a framework the story of a married couple facing the death of a young son, Schwartz and her characters spiral into aphasic loops of language that explore complex emotional swings from grief to betrayal. Director Anne Kauffman assembled a skilled cast—featuring Gibson Frazier, Christina Kirk and Annie McNamara—that was adept at navigating Schwartz's twisted verse. Songs by Obie-winning composer-lyricist Michael Friedman added to the playful appeal.

The most prominent OOB solo show took the form of a political lecture. *My Trip to Al-Qaeda* was a 75-minute condensation by journalist Lawrence Wright of his Pulitzer Prize-winning book, *The Looming Tower: Al-Qaeda and the Road to 9/11*. Enlisting Gregory Mosher as director, Allan Buchman presented it for a six-week run at his Culture Project—which was forced by a rent increase to leave its prime Bleecker Street venue for the former Manhattan Ensemble Theater on Mercer Street. As the press release acknowledged, Wright was following "in Al Gore's footsteps" by making performance art out of a slide show and a book tour. Buchman, though, told the *New York Times* that he welcomes figures from politics and journalism to his politically-themed company: "We're finding that people are coming to us who feel that their stories will be more effective if they can climb off the op-ed page." In his review, the *Times*'s Charles Isherwood judged Wright's acting sometimes "awkward" but noted "it hardly matters [since] his subject is so absorbing that presentation is almost incidental." Two months after ending his run OOB in April, Wright revived the show for two encore performances at Town Hall before launching a national tour.

Since the New York International Fringe Festival launched in the summer of 1997, such smorgasbords of new work have only multiplied OOB. This season saw more than 10 self-described "festivals." At the 2006 Fringe Festival, among the more acclaimed titles of the 200-plus offered were Alexander Poe's *I Am Tom Cruise*, Ashlin Halfnight's *Diving Normal*, Michael Perlman's solo show *Flying on the Wing*, and Charlie Schulman and Michael Roberts's musical tribute to a flatulent footnote from French cabaret history, *The Fartiste*. Two Fringe shows received interest for Off Broadway transfers: Steven Banks's clown act, *Billy the Mime*, and the anticorporate musical-satire *Walmartopia*. But the impact of the Fringe increasingly seems overshadowed by the plethora of other summer slates of new work, such as the Midtown International Theatre Festival, New York Musical Theatre Festival; avant-garde outposts Clubbed Thumb, Ice Factory, Soho Think Tank and Incubator; and the more commercial and well-connected Summer Play Festival. This season the Culture Project added an Impact Festival of new political plays, featuring premieres by Eve Ensler, Elizabeth Swados and many others. The Brick in Brooklyn affirmed its place on the map with the ironically titled Sellout Festival. Although the company claimed to be compromising its integrity "as fast as we can," what followed in the programming was hardly standard commercial fare, with such titles as *Die Hard—The Puppet Musical* and *The Kung Fu Importance of Being Earnest*. But in its mix of appropriated pop-culture artifacts with avant-garde performance traditions, the festival typified an evolving OOB sensibility.

Alongside the newer writers, some experienced artists returned to the OOB community as well. Richard Foreman made his annual appearance at his Ontological Theater with *Wake Up Mr. Sleepy! Your Unconscious Mind Is Dead!* With his 50th play Foreman hardly rested on his laurels, continuing an exploration of recorded video that began with the previous year's *Zomboid* and ventured into the growing field of theater blogging—an increasingly essential communication medium for the OOB scene—by keeping an online journal of his rehearsal process. Another veteran of the New York theater, A.R. Gurney, seems an unlikely OOB playwright these days, having made his name as a bourgeois favorite of 1980s Off Broadway. While enjoying an OOB success uptown at Primary Stages this season with *Indian Blood*—a fond autobiographical remembrance of his privileged youth in Buffalo—Gurney also returned to the smaller Flea Theater to air more political work. In the self-referential and metatheatrical *Post Mortem*, Gurney imagines himself as a banned writer in a future US theocracy, where an intrepid drama teacher discovers his lost plays. Meanwhile, the ubiquitous Charles L. Mee—one of the most popular and influential dramatists among today's theater artists—offered more of his trademark textual collages of recycled classics. Mee's *Orestes 2.0* played at HERE Arts Center; Resonance Theatre Ensemble paired his comedy *The Mail Order Bride* with the classic that inspired it: Molière's *The Imaginary Invalid*; and *Gone*, at 59E59, collected meditations on loss from everyone from Proust to Kelly Clarkson.

After the Broadway and Pulitzer Prize-winning success of *Topdog/Underdog* Suzan-Lori Parks marked a return to fringe theater with a vengeance. After writing a short play every day for a year, she unveiled the final result—365 Days/365 Plays—in "real time" over the course of a year. Parks licensed the scripts to companies around the country for free in exchange for charging no admission (the "year" began November 13, 2006 and was to end November 12 of the following season). The playwright also co-produced the immense undertaking, which entailed setting up sixteen separate "regional hubs" in different cities. In New York, the project got underway in November at the Public with an hourlong bill of the first seven playlets directed by Michael Greif, with an ensemble cast including Reg E. Cathey and Joan Mackintosh. Afterward the dramatic torch passed from company to company, including 65 OOB ensembles—ranging from Atlantic Theater Company to Brooklyn's Robot Vs. Dinosaur. The project's website declared: "One of the goals of 365 Festival is to reveal community where it already exists—a thriving, worldwide theater community—in theaters both grand and modest, in schoolrooms, storefronts, nursing homes and alleyways."

Revivals and Classics

ANOTHER FORMER MAINSTAY of OOB, the Jean Cocteau Repertory—a contemporary of EST—lost its founders, its theater and its name. After the departure several years ago of founding director Eve Adamson and actors Elise Stone, Craig Smith and Harris Berlinsky, the company continued (in name) at the Bouwerie Lane Theater for a few more seasons. An unusual merger toward the end of the 2005–2006 season with two other troupes—Catskill Mountain Foundation and New Orleans's Ego Po—did little to improve the Cocteau's fortunes. Early in 2007, Catskill's Ari Edelson took over sole leadership, renamed the company the Exchange, moved it to Theatre Row and shifted the mission from the Cocteau's diet of classics to exclusively new works. Performing two new British plays—Anthony Neilson's *Realism* and Lisa McGee's *Jump!*—at the uptown Theatre Row complex, the eccentric spirit of Cocteau Rep, steeped in the intellectualism of a bygone Greenwich Village bohemia, was clearly long gone. The Bouwerie Lane, its rent doubled, sits empty; Adamson died in October 2006. Former Cocteau actors Stone and Smith have continued to carry the torch with the Phoenix Theatre Ensemble, mounting this season a characteristic repertory of classics in the winter (Jean Anouilh's *Antigone*, *The Lesson* and *The Painting* by Eugene Ionesco and other works) and an adaptation of Tennyson's *Maud—The Madness* in the spring.

In dedicating nearly each of its seasons to work by a single living American author, the Signature Theatre Company has provided an invaluable annual retrospective of many of our national treasures in playwriting. That August Wilson died in late 2005, after the schedule of three of his works was announced but before it could begin made this season particularly poignant. But perhaps Wilson's absence from the scene allowed his interpreters here to shine in their own contributions to what are already becoming modern classics. Directing the first entry, *Seven Guitars* was actor Ruben Santiago-Hudson, who won a Tony Award for his supporting performance in the 1996 Broadway premiere. Under his guidance, it was Roslyn Ruff, though, as the steely wife of the doomed hero, who won the most accolades, including an Obie Award for performance. Another Obie Award went to director Lou Bellamy of the Penumbra Theatre Company in St. Paul, Minnesota (one of the country's leading African-American theater companies) for his direction of the next production, *Two Trains Running*, featuring a cast nearly universally praised for its cohesiveness and sensitivity. Signature's *King Hedley II* made a case for a play that was not well regarded in the 2001 original. Here Russell Hornsby took the title role, embodying the impotent rage that fuels some of Wilson's self-destructive African-American male heroes. Other standout performances across the three productions were Arthur French, a Lortel Award winner for *Two Trains*, and Stephen McKinley Henderson, who played in both *Seven Guitars* and *Hedley*. Both of these productions competed against each other for the Lortel Award for best revival—*Two Trains* was the winner.

As if following the Signature's example, other, smaller companies mounted ambitious single-author festivals as well this season. In March, the Michael Chekhov Company planned to present 45 plays by Sam Shepard over two seasons. (A notable, but unrelated Shepard revival in October was *The Tooth of Crime*, reuniting actor Ray Wise and director George Ferencz at La MaMa, where they performed a famous staging of the play in 1983.) And the Storm Theatre began an ongoing Karol Wojtyla Festival, staging early dramatic efforts by the young Polish theologian who would later become Pope John Paul II.

Director Edward Einhorn managed the feat of coordinating productions of all the plays of Václav Havel, in honor of the playwright-president's 70th birthday. The 16 full productions, plus ancillary readings and forums, included six US premieres and were presented at various companies, schools, and even apartments around town. Havel himself—in residence at Columbia University for the fall semester—made a point of dropping by each production in person. In a concurrent and moving tribute in December, the *Village Voice* hosted a special ceremony to finally bestow upon Havel his three Obie citations (ranging from 1968 to 1984) that communist Czechoslovakia never let him collect. As the *Voice* dryly noted in reporting the occasion: "He is the only head of state ever to have received an Obie Award."

For Harley Granville Barker, it was something of a renaissance on the New York stage. In addition to Atlantic Theater Company's Off Broadway staging of *The Voysey Inheritance* (adapted by David Mamet), the Mint Theater offered an uncut revival of Granville Barker's *The Madras House* (1909), a daunting comedy about the turn-of-the-century fashion industry, marital politics and even the rise of Islam. It was nearly an all-Edwardian season for the Mint, which continues to succeed with opulent period pieces despite its small budget and claustrophobic stage. *Madras House* was preceded in the season's order by St. John Ervine's *John Ferguson* (1919) and followed by St. John Hankin's *The Return of the Prodigal* (1905). It says a lot about the Mint's idiosyncratic tastes that no other theater in town is likely to produce one, let alone two titles by two authors with the first name of St. John.

Mint's first season offering in June—Rachel Crothers's *Susan and God*, a 1937–1938 Best Play—was one of many popular OOB stagings this year to champion specifically American neglected plays. Crothers's 1937 drama about the use of religious righteousness and self-help gurus to mask domestic unhappiness was a timely reminder of a prolific female voice in early 20th century US theater. Metropolitan Playhouse (which specializes in the forgotten 19th century American repertoire) mounted Dion Boucicault's 1859 antislavery melodrama *The Octoroon*, usually considered unperformable today due to its dated racial depictions. Producer-director Alex Roe and a strong ensemble cast managed to sensitively depict the trade in human lives and offer a sense of Boucicault's vital theatricality—even if the big "sensation" scenes were cramped by the company's postage-stamp stage.

Peccadillo Theater Company and Keen Company have also laid claim in recent years to America's theatrical past. The former scored a big success this season with the 1937 comedy *Room Service*, proving there is life after the Marx Brothers for the original John Murray-Allen Boretz script. Reviewers and audiences alike reveled in director Dan Wackerman's clipped pacing. Enthusiasm generated during its run at the Bank Street Theatre encouraged Peccadillo to consider a transfer to Off Broadway. Keen, meanwhile, mounted two mid-century dramas: *Tea and Sympathy*, Robert Anderson's 1953 tale of closet homosexuality in a boarding school, and an adaptation of Thornton Wilder's novel *Theophilus North*.

Pearl Theatre Company began its season with the type of classical repertory they have presented for over twenty years, this time *Arms and the Man* and *The School for Wives*. As reception of those productions attested, however, the Pearl's aspirations often seem beyond the means of its acting company and earthbound direction. But when the company broke with precedent in the spring to present three American rarities, the actors seemed to bloom with more modern material. With Lillian Hellman's *Toys in the Attic*, William Saroyan's *The Cave Dwellers*, and S.N. Behrman's *Biography*, the Pearl received consistently good reviews. Directed by guest artist Austin Pendleton, *Toys* proved the most satisfying in achieving a combination of narrative flow and naturalistic performances. Among the acting company, Sean McNall shone brightest across the three productions in such roles as Hellman's charming conman, Saroyan's quixotic Russian bear-tamer, and Behrman's angry, young journalist.

Transport Group has pursued a dual mission of producing old plays and new musicals. But with the current season of *All the Way Home* (Tad Mosel's adaptation of James Agee's *A Death in the Family*) and William Inge's *The Dark at the Top of the Stairs*, the company and its founding director, Jack Cummings III, emerged as a successful interpreter of mid-century American family drama. Both productions were praised for seamlessly blending naturalistic acting with poetically suggestive designs and for unusually strong performances given by child actors in key roles. In the Inge play, Michael Feingold argued, Cummings gave "an elegantly spare, contemporary feel to a work that in other hands might have seemed heavy and archaic." Such praise from the *Village Voice* led to a special Obie grant for Transport and to a performance award for Donna Lynne Champlin's performance as the mother in *The Dark at the Top of the Stairs*.

From the vantage point of 2006–07, the origins of OOB itself now qualify as theater history, especially to the younger generation. One of the most vibrant, and just plain ambitious, site-specific works of recent years was the Peculiar Works Project's time-traveling "walking tours" of great moments in OOB. In September, *West Village Fragments* offered recreations by actors of excerpts from such famous titles as *The Madness of Lady Bright* and *Dionysus in 69* at or near their original sites. (Where the original theater was not accessible—or no longer existed, as with Caffe Cino—the performance was set on the street outside.) The companion piece, *East Village Fragments*, followed in June and similarly celebrated the heyday of venues such as La MaMa Experimental Theatre Club and St. Mark's Church, early works by Sam Shepard and Charles Ludlam and groundbreaking 1960s plays such as *America Hurrah* and *Hair*.

New Yorkers were also treated to a revival of a seminal protest piece: The Living Theatre's production of *The Brig* (1963) by Kenneth Brown. Founded by Judith Malina and Julian Beck, the company's nomadic existence in performance spaces around the world was prodded to some extent by the troupe's frequent encounters with legal authorities over tax issues and performance spaces. Now housed in a new space in the gentrified Lower East Side, Malina and a new generation of performer-activists have continued the work she and Beck started more than 50 years ago—including street theater pieces to protest the war in Iraq. The revival of *The Brig* provoked debate over its lasting power. Charles Isherwood in the *Times*, while paying respect to the play's historical importance, felt that its shock techniques were dated, particularly in light of imagery from Abu Ghraib in Iraq. Playwright Brown himself responded to Isherwood in a letter to the *Village Voice* arguing, "Failure to recognize the current importance of the play is a frightening affirmation of the fallacy that history is irrelevant."

As far as more "classical" classics were concerned, perhaps the most ambitious undertaking was Theatre for a New Audience's provocative rotating repertory of Shakespeare's *The Merchant of Venice* and Christopher Marlowe's *The Jew of Malta*. (Rounding out a season devoted to anti-Semitism and the "exploration of the other" was Neil Bartlett's dark adaptation of *Oliver Twist*, starring Ned Eisenberg as Fagin.) F. Murray Abraham, who starred as both Shylock and Barabas, told *American Theatre* that the joint productions invited controversy and aimed "to portray the stereotypes as vividly and flamboyantly and outrageously as possible—to show people how ridiculous they are." Different directors were hired to contrast the styles of the two texts: Darko Tresnjak, known for precise physicality and elegant staging, took on *Merchant*; David Herskovits, the irreverent iconoclast behind the Target Margin Theatre, was matched with the more problematic *Malta*. Critics preferred Tresnjak's sleek modernization replete with cell phones and laptops—three of which replaced Portia's famous three caskets. Herskovitz's more mocking approach to the potentially anti-Semitic Marlowe play was received with considerably less enthusiasm. As for Abraham's performance(s), Isherwood praised his Shylock as, "the more unsettling of the two figures . . . making him a little more sinister than sympathetic, sinning as much as sinned against." While *Merchant* remained more popular among critics and audiences alike, many still appreciated the effects of the double-bill as conceived.

Other Shakespeare highlights of the season included *King Lear* as played by the venerable Alvin Epstein in a small chamber production at La

MaMa by Boston's Actors' Shakespeare Company. Terry Teachout in the *Wall Street Journal* considered it "the best *King Lear* I've ever seen onstage." Classical Theatre of Harlem offered its own *Lear* with Andre De Shields, and having achieved this career milestone of a role, both De Shields and Epstein were honored with lifetime achievement Obie Awards at season's end. Another standout classical performance was Michael Cumpsty's *Richard II*, his second in what is becoming an annual visitation to Classic Stage Company to collaborate with artistic director Brian Kulick on major Shakespearean roles.

Beyond Shakespeare, CSC also offered a rare staging of Aeschylus's *Prometheus Bound* by the Aquila Theatre Company. But less traditional Hellenic adaptations sparked greater interest. John Epperson—aka the cabaret drag performer Lypsinka—rewrote Attic tragedy as camp in *My Deah*, which explored the comic possibilities of the Medea story. Nancy Opel won an Obie Award for her delightfully over-the-top performance as the spoofed murderous matriarch. David Herskovits's Target Margin offered an evening of two adaptations of nondramatic classical texts: the *Symposium* became *Dinner Party*, staged in almost improvisational fashion by the company, finding hip contemporary idioms for Plato's discourses on love; and actor David Greenspan returned to the very roots of Western drama with his "performance" of Aristotle's *Poetics*, entitled *The Argument*.

One of the most original reinterpretations of a modern classic text was offered by the Classical Theatre of Harlem—honored with a Lortel Award this season for its body of work—whose *Waiting for Godot* drew on the imagery of post-Hurricane Katrina New Orleans. Wading in a stage full of water, Wendell Pierce's Didi and J. Kyle Manzay's Gogo at one point scrawled Godot's name on a nearby rooftop, as a moving and recognizable cry for rescue. Brian Parks in the *Village Voice* praised the bold re-imagining as a fitting, if irreverent tribute for the author's centenary year: "Director Christopher McElroen and designer Troy Hourie's production is not for purists. Or for Beckett himself, who was famously resistant to reconceptions of his plays. Their loss."

International Festivals

THE LINCOLN CENTER Festival and Brooklyn Academy of Music contributed to the OOB scene by exposing New Yorkers to major work from international artists. The summer highlight of the Lincoln Center Festival was *DruidSynge*: six works by John Millington Synge in a daylong marathon directed by Garry Hynes's Druid Theatre of Galway. While the tireless energy of the ensemble acting and the chance to see such rarities as the unfinished *Deirdre of the Sorrows* made it worthwhile, the density of Synge's texts—especially to American ears—and the lack of a strong uniting concept for the plays detracted. Brooklyn Academy of Music continues to dub its fall season the Next Wave Festival, even though programming relies heavily on established European artists rather than the evolving avant-garde championed at Next Wave's outset in the 1980s. Still, many were grateful for two modernized Ibsen stagings that marked the centenary of the playwright's death with shocking reminders of his relevance: Thomas Ostermeier's *Hedda Gabler* from Berlin's Schaubühne and Eirik Stubo's *The Wild Duck* from the National Theatre of Norway. Declan Donnellan's all-male *Twelfth Night*—with a Russian cast—was also part of the Next Wave Festival. Donnellan's company, Cheek by Jowl, also presented a spring production of *Cymbeline* (which, as with Edward Hall's Propeller productions of Shakespeare lie within the rubric of Off Broadway for *Best Plays*'s purposes). As popular and sometime daring as these stagings may be, the dominance of Shakespeare and Ibsen marked a growing trend toward conservative programming for BAM's expanding subscriber base.

By 2007, the world of OOB seemed caught between two historical forces. No longer can artists survive on the grants and cheap rents that enabled the flourishing of experimental and anticommercial performance in the late 1960s. Yet with costs and risks rising for high-end production as well, the dream of moving up to Broadway and national recognition can seem ever more remote.

The one major exception to this trend in 2006–07 is illustrative. *Spring Awakening*, Duncan Sheik and Steven Sater's Wedekind-inspired rock musical—honored in this volume as a Best Play—went from a small opening at the Atlantic in June 2006 to a Tony Award for best musical one year later. Yet this show, directed by a Broadway veteran and developed in Broadway-level workshops over years, was hardly typical OOB fare, and only settled at the Atlantic after other companies passed on it. Compare this to the two-actor comedy *Gutenberg! The Musical!*, a hit of the 2005 New York Musical Theatre Festival. *Gutenberg* moved to a commercial Off Broadway house where it enjoyed a five-month run at the Actor's Playhouse in the West Village.

After *Gutenberg* closed May 6, the Actors Playhouse shuttered permanently in August, going the way of many longtime Off Broadway spaces in recent years. Without these midsize theaters, most OOB shows have nowhere left to transfer without losing their intimacy. *Spring Awakening* may fill the 1,108-seat Eugene O'Neill Theatre, but few OOB dramas—even a *Thugs* or a *God's Ear*—could survive such a move.

And so the wall between OOB and Broadway—and between OOB and Off—seems less permeable than ever, leaving us with separate subcultures of theater with separate audiences in danger of losing the kind of cross-pollination that has driven so much great theater in the past.

PLAYS PRODUCED OFF OFF BROADWAY
AND ADDITIONAL NYC PRESENTATIONS
○ ○ ○ ○ ○
Compiled by Vivian Cary Jenkins and Sheryl Arluck

BELOW IS A broad sampling of 2006–07 Off Off Broadway productions in New York. There is no definitive "Off Off Broadway" area or qualification. To try to define or regiment it would be untrue to its fluid, often exploratory purpose. This listing of hundreds of works produced by scores of OOB groups is as inclusive as reliable sources and space allow. This section pertains to professional theater in New York that is covered by neither Broadway nor full Off Broadway contracts.

The more active and established producing groups are identified in **bold face type**, in alphabetical order, with artistic policies and the names of company leaders given whenever possible. Each group's 2006–07 schedule, with emphasis on new plays, is listed with play titles in CAPITAL LETTERS. Often these are works-in-progress with changing scripts, casts and directors, sometimes without an engagement of record (but an opening or early performance date is included when available).

Many of these Off Off Broadway groups have long since outgrown a merely experimental status and offer programs that are the equal—and in many cases the superior—of anything in the New York theater. These listings include special contractual arrangements such as the showcase code, letters of agreement (allowing for longer runs and higher admission prices than usual) and, closer to the edge of commercial theater, so-called "mini-contracts." Certain productions of companies below may be found in the Plays Produced Off Broadway section when performances per week or size of venue indicate such a shift. Available data has been compiled from press representatives, company managers and publications of record.

A large selection of developing groups and other shows that made appearances Off Off Broadway during the season under review appears under the "Miscellaneous" heading at the end of this listing. Festival listings include samples of the schedules offered and are sometimes limited to the title and author of the work listed to allow for the inclusion of more works.

Atlantic Theater Company. Produces new plays and reinterpretations of classics that reflect today's society. Neil Pepe artistic director, Andrew D. Hamingson managing director.

Atlantic's season of "love": Jonathan Groff and Lea Michele in Spring Awakening *(top); Jeff Binder, Jordan Gelber, Kate Blumberg and Peter Benson in* Birth and After Birth *(middle); Michelle Federer and Remy Auberjonois in* Anon. *(bottom). Photos: Monique Carboni*

SPRING AWAKENING. Musical with book and lyrics by Steven Sater; music by Duncan Sheik. June 15, 2006. Directed by Michael Mayer; choreography, Bill T. Jones; scenery, Christine Jones; costumes, Susan Hilferty; lighting, Kevin Adams; sound, Brian Ronan; music direction, Kimberly Grigsby; fight direction; J. David Brimmer; stage manager, Heather Cousens. With Skylar Astin, Lilli Cooper, John Gallagher Jr., Gideon Glick, Jonathan Groff, Brian Charles Johnson, Mary McCann, Lea Michele, Lauren Pritchard, Phoebe Strole, Frank Wood, Jonathan B. Wright, Remy Zaken. A 2006–07 Best Play (see essay by Michael Feingold in this volume.)

BIRTH AND AFTER BIRTH. By Tina Howe. October 3, 2006. Directed by Christian Parker; scenery, Takeshi Kata; costumes, Bobby Frederick Tilley II; lighting, Josh Bradford; sound, Obadiah Eaves; stage manager, Matthew Silver. With Peter Benson, Jeff Binder, Kate Blumberg, Jordan Gelber, Maggie Kiley.

STAGE 2.
ANON. By Kate Robin. January 31, 2007. Directed by Melissa Kievman; scenery, Chris Muller; costumes, Anne Kenney; lighting, Tyler Micoleau; sound, Eric Shim; stage manager, Adam Ganderson. With Remy Auberjonois, Michelle Federer, Caroline Aaron, Bill Buell, Kate Nowlin, Shannon Burkett, Anna Foss Wilson, Jenny Maguire, Dana Eskelson, Katy Grenfell, Danielle Skraastad, Linda Marie Larson, Susan Blackwell, Saidah Arrika Ekulona.

Brooklyn Academy of Music Next Wave Festival. Since 1983, this annual festival has presented hundreds of cutting-edge events, including dozens of world premieres. Featuring leading international artists, it is one of the world's largest contemporary performing arts festivals. Alan H. Fishman chairman of the board; Karen Brooks Hopkins president; Joseph V. Melillo executive producer.

THE END OF CINEMATICS. By Mikel Rouse. October 4, 2006. Directed by Mr. Rouse; scenery, Thomas Kamm; costumes, Anne Kenney; lighting, Hideaki Tsutsui; sound, Christopher Thomas Ericson; video, Jeff Sugg.

MYCENAEAN. By Carl Hancock Rux; based on Jean Racine's *Phaedre*. October 10, 2006. Directed by Mr. Rux; scenery, Efren Delgadillo and Alison Heimstead; costumes, Toni-Leslie James; lighting and sound, Pablo N. Molina; mask, Ms. Heimstead; video, Jaco van Schalkwyk and Mr. Molina; dramaturgy, Morgan Jenness; stage manager, Ginger Castleberry. With Mr. Rux, Helga Davis, Patrice Johnson, Tony Torn, David Barlow, Ana Perea, Darius Mannino, Celia Gorman, Christalyn Wright, Marcelle Lashley, Niles Ford, Paz Tanjuaquio, Kelly Bartnik.

NINE HILLS ONE VALLEY. By Ratan Thiyam. October 11, 2006. With Chorus Repertory Theatre of Manipur, India.

THE WILD DUCK. By Henrik Ibsen; adapted by Eirik Stubo and Ole Skjelbred; performed in Norwegian, with English surtitle translatation by Judith Messick and Katherine Hansen. October 25, 2006. Directed by Mr. Stubo; scenery and costumes, Kari Gravklev; lighting, Ellen Ruge; dramaturgy, Olav Torbjorn Skare; stage manager, Kine Sorboe. With Petronella Barker, Eindride Eidsvold, Gard Eidsvold, Kim Haugen, Birgitte Larsen, Kai Remlov, Fridtjov Saheim, Agot Sendstad, Bjorn Skagestad. Presented in association with the National Theatre of Norway.

TWELFTH NIGHT. Revival of the play by William Shakespeare. November 7, 2006. Directed by Declan Donnellan; choreography, Jane Gibson; scenery, Nick Ormerod; costumes, Natalia Vedeneeva; lighting, Judith Greenwood; stage manager, Olga Vasilevskaya. With Andrey Kuzichev, Vladimir Vdovichenkov, Dmitry Shcherbina, Alexey Dadanov, Sergey Mukhin, Mikhail Zhigalov, Vsevolod Boldin, Yury Makeev, Mikhail Dementiev, Alexander Feklistov, Dmitry Dyuzhev, Igor Yasulovich, Ilia Ilyin. Presented in association with Chekhov International Theatre Festival.

LE TEMPÊTE (THE TEMPEST). Revival of the play by William Shakespeare; translated into French by Normand Chaurette. November 15, 2006. Directed by Michael Lemieux, Victor Pilon and Denise Guilbault; scenery, Anick La Bissonnière; costumes, Michel Robidas; lighting, Alain Lortie; music, Michel Smith. With Denis Bernard, Manon Brunelle, Éveline

Gélanas, Pierre Etienne Rouillard, Éric Bernier, Vincent Bilodeau, Pierre Curzi, Jacques Girard, Patrice Robitaille, Robert Toupin. Presented in association with 4D Art.

HEDDA GABLER. By Henrik Ibsen; translated by Hinrich Schmidt-Henkel. November 28, 2006. Directed by Thomas Ostermeier; scenery, Jan Pappelbaum; costumes, Nina Wetzel; lighting, Erich Schneider; video, Sebastien Dupouey; music, Malte Beckenbach; dramaturgy, Marius von Mayenburg. With Annedore Bauer, Lars Eidinger, Jorg Hartmann, Kay Bartholomaus Schulze, Katharina Schuttler, Lore Stefanek. Presented in association with Schaubuhne am Lehniner Platz, Berlin.

STILL LIFE WITH COMMENTATOR: AN ORATORIO. By Vijay Iyer and Michael C. Ladd. December 6, 2006. Directed by Ibrahim Quraishi; scenery, Robert Pyzocha; lighting, Stephen Arnold; video, Prashant Bhargava. With Pamela Z.

Classic Stage Company. Reinventing and revitalizing the classics for contemporary audiences. Brian Kulick artistic director, Jessica R. Jenen executive director.

RICHARD II. Revival of the play by William Shakespeare. September 17, 2006. Directed by Brian Kulick; scenery, Tom Gleeson; costumes, Oana Botez-Ban; lighting, Brian H. Scott; sound, Jorge Muelle; stage manager, Robyn Henry. With Craig Baldwin, Michael Cumpsty, Bernarda de Paula, Jon De Vries, David Greenspan, Doan Ly, George Morfogen, Ellen Parker, Jesse Pennington, Graham Winton.

A SPANISH PLAY. By Yasmina Reza; translated by David Ives. January 10, 2007. Directed by John Turturro; scenery, Riccardo Hernandez; costumes, Donna Zakowska; lighting, Christopher Akerlind. With Zoe Caldwell, Katherine Borowitz, Linda Emond, Denis O'Hare, Larry Pine.

PROMETHEUS BOUND. By Aeschylus; translated by James Kerr. March 21, 2007. Directed by Mr. Kerr; scenery and costumes, Paul Willis; lighting, Mark Jonathan; sound, Christopher Shutt; music, Dan Lipton; stage manager, Rebecca Goldstein-Glaze. With Therese Barbato, George Bartenieff, Michael Dixon, Autumn Dornfeld, Erin Krakow, Julie McNiven, Susannah Millonzi, Sipiwe Moyo, David Oyelowo. Presented in association with Aquila Theatre Company.

Drama Dept. A collective of theater artists who create new works and revive neglected classics. Douglas Carter Beane artistic director, Michael S. Rosenberg executive director.

THE CARTELLS: A PRIME TIME SOAP . . . LIVE. By Douglas Carter Beane. October 16–November 6, 2006. EPISODE 1: "The Eye of the Needle." October 16, 2006. EPISODE 2: "Far Above Rubies." October 23, 2006. EPISODE 3: "Perish With the Sword." October 30, 2006. EPISODE 4: "Cast a Stone." November 6, 2006.Directed by Carl Andress; scenery, B.T. Whitehill; costumes, Jeriana Hochberg; lighting, Kirk Bookman and Julie Seitel; sound and music, Lewis Flinn; fight direction, Rick Sordelet; stage manager, Don Myers. With Vanessa Aspillaga, Elizabeth Berkley, Keith Davis, Peter Frechette, Joanna Gleason, Julie Halston, Jason Butler Harner, Peter Hermann, Cady Huffman, Brian d'Arcy James, Alan O'Brien, Pedro Pascal, David Rakoff, Kristen Schaal, Joey Slotnick. Presented in association with Comix.

Ensemble Studio Theatre. Membership organization of playwrights, actors, directors and designers dedicated to supporting individual theater artists and developing new works. Stages more than 300 projects each season, ranging from readings to fully mounted productions. Curt Dempster and William Carden artistic directors.

Schedule included:

MARATHON 2006 (SERIES B). June 1–19, 2006.

THE 100 MOST BEAUTIFUL NAMES OF TODD. By Julia Cho. Directed by Jamie Richards. With Alison Bartlett, William Jackson Harper, Diana Ruppe.

BONE CHINA. By David Mamet. Directed by Curt Dempster. With Victor Slezak, Marcia Jean Kurtz.

INTERMISSION. By Will Eno. Directed by Michael Sexton. With Autumn Dornfeld, Jayne Houdyshell, JJ Kandel, Brian Murray.

ON THE SPORADIC. By James Ryan. Directed by Charles Richter. With Jordan Gelber, Ean Sheehy, Greta Muller.

MARATHON 2006 (SERIES C). June 13–25, 2006.

DOMINICA: THE FAT, UGLY 'HO. By Stephen Adly Guirgis. Directed by Adam Rapp. With Carlo Alban, Liza Colón-Zayas, Dominic Cloon.

THE NIGHT THAT ROGER WENT TO VISIT THE PARENTS OF HIS OLD HIGH SCHOOL GIRLFRIEND. By Ann Marie Healy. Directed by Andrew McCarthy. With Jack Carpenter, Patricia Kalember, Daniel Gerroll.

DETAIL. By Michael Louis Wells. Directed by Lou Jacob. With John Leonard Thompson, Dana Powers Acheson.

LILA ON THE WALL. By Edward Allan Baker. Directed by Kevin Confoy. With Julie Leedes, Will Janowitz.

THE BUS TO BUENOS AIRES. Musical by Curtis Moore and Thomas Mizer. Directed by Carlos Armesto. With Sebastian La Cause, Jennie Eisenhower.

ABSENCE OF MAGIC. By Eric Davis and Sue Morrison. July 5, 2006. Directed by Ms. Morrison. With Mr. Davis.

PROJECT 35. November 10–December 18, 2006.

MASTERBUILDER JOHNSON. By Romulus Linney. BICOASTAL. By Adam Forgash. MASSACRE (SING TO YOUR CHILDREN). By Jose Rivera. EXISTING PRIVILEGE. By James DeMarse. THE CHIMES. By Kevin Christopher Snipes. THE MISSIONARY POSITION. By Keith Reddin. HEMINGWAY. By Laurence Luckinbill. THE COFFEE TREES. By Arthur Giron. MAY DAY. By Conrad Bromberg. HOME FIRES BURNING. By Chris Caraso. FANNY. By Julie Leedes. TBD. By Marti Evans Charles. THREE KNOCKS. By Annie Baker. ESCAPE VELOCITY. By James Ryan. FOOTPRINTS IN THE SNOW. By Jeanne Dorsey. LOONS. By Rob Ackerman. YUMEE AND JACK. By Bill Bozzone. THE TILTED HOUSE. By Susan Haar. BOB. By Anton Dudley. THE SEQUENCE. By Paul Mullin. FAST BLOOD. By Judy Tate. FREE GIFT INSIDE. By Edward Allan Baker. DYING IN BOULDER. By Linda Faigao-Hall. MY BEFORE AND AFTER. By Michael Louis Wells. ALL THROUGH THE NIGHT. By Shirley Lauro. CAT.HER.IN.E. By Amy Staats. OWNERS. By Edith Freni. PA'S HAT: LIBERIAN LEGACY. By Cori Thomas. THE BIG GIRLS. By Ann Marie Healy. THE GARDEN VARIETY. By Lloyd Suh. THE LAKE. By Frank D. Gilroy. CREATIVE WRITING. By J. Holtham. NATURAL SELECTION. By Leslie Lyles. FLORA GARDNER. By Graeme Gillis.

RIDDLELIKELOVE (WITH A SIDE OF KETCHUP). By Julie Fitzpatrick and Douglas Anderson. January 8, 2007. Directed by Mr. Anderson. With Ms. Fitzpatrick.

SERENDIB. By David Zellnik. April 4, 2007. Directed by Carlos Armesto; scenery, Ryan Kravetz; costumes, Jennifer Caprio; lighting, Evan Purcell; sound, Graham Johnson; music, Katie Down. With Joseph Adams, Geeta Citygirl, Linda Powell, James Rana, PJ Sosko, Richard B. Watson, Nitya Vidyasagar.

FIRST LIGHT FESTIVAL READINGS 2007. April 2–9, 2007.

EVER MORE INTELLIGENT. By Alex Timbers. THE GREAT DISMAL. By Gwydian Suilebhan. LEAVE A LIGHT ON. By Ann Marie Healy. CHANCE AND NECESSITY. By Jon Klein. DOCTORS JANE AND ALEXANDER. By Edward Einhorn. PERFECT AND CONSTANT. By Rob Askins.

FIRST LIGHT FESTIVAL WORKSHOPS 2007. April 13–27, 2007.

THE TALLEST BUILDING IN THE WORLD. By Matt Schatz. BY PROXY. By Amy Fox. GALOIS. By Sung Rno. ME AND MARIE CURIE. By Alec Duffy.

SHATTER: FOUR ONE-ACT PLAYS. May 16, 2007.

THE LAST DAY. By Justin Quinn Pelegano; adapted from Richard Matheson. Directed by Mr. Pelegano. ANTIGONE NOIR. By Destiny Lilly; adapted from Sophocles. Directed by Ms. Lilly. EYEZ WATCHIN'. By André Ford. Directed by Mr. Ford. MALI AND THE ARC OF THE COVENANT. By Andrew Bergh. Directed by Mr. Bergh.

MARATHON 2007 (SERIES A). May 31–June 20, 2007.

THE NEWS. By Billy Aronson. Directed by Jamie Richards. With Diana Ruppe, Geneva Carr, Thomas Lyons, Grant Shaud.

MY DOG HEART. By Edith Freni. Directed by John Gould Rubin. With Brian Avers, Pepper Binkley, Brian Fenkart.

FIRST TREE IN ANTARCTICA. By Julia Cho. Directed by Kate Whoriskey. With Michi Barall, Jon Norman Schneider.

THE PROBABILITIES. By Wendy MacLeod. Directed by Karen Kohlhaas. With Bruce MacVittie.

THINGS WE SAID TODAY. By Neil LaBute. Directed by Andrew McCarthy. With Dana Delaney and Victor Slezak.

The Flea Theater. Formed to present distinctive, cutting-edge work that raises the standards of Off Off Broadway. Jim Simpson artistic director, Carol Ostrow producing director.

POST MORTEM. By A.R. Gurney. November 2, 2006. Directed by Jim Simpson; scenery, Mimi Lien; costumes, Claudia Brown; lighting, Brian Aldous; sound, Jill BC DuBoff; stage manager, Jennifer Noterman. With Tina Benko, Shannon Burkett, Christopher Kromer.

TWO SEPTEMBER. By Mac Wellman. December 5, 2006. Directed by Loy Arcenas; scenery, Mr. Arcenas; costumes, Oana Botez-Ban; lighting, Ben Stanton; sound, Leah Gelpe; dramaturg, Roweena Mackay; stage manager, Lindsay Stares. With Arthur Acuña, Claro Austria, Christian Baskous, Jayne Haynes, Drew Hildebrand, Annie Scott, Sarah Sirota, Sarah Silk.

'TWAS THE NIGHT BEFORE. Ten-minute works. December 21, 2006.
NOT A CREATURE WAS STIRRING. By Christopher Durang. Directed by Kip Fagan. AWAY IN THE MANGER. By Roger Rosenblatt. Directed by Jason Podplesky. BEFORE THE BEFORE AND BEFORE THAT. By Mac Wellman. Directed by Amanda Wright. CHRISTMAS SONG. By Len Jenkin. Directed by Mr. Jenkin. HOLIDAY MOVES. By Elizabeth Swados. Directed by Ms. Swados. Choreography, Mimi Quillin; scenery, Kyle Chepulis; costumes, Erin Elizabeth Murphy and Sarah Beers; sound, Jill BC DuBoff; stage manager, Lauren Levitt. With Ben Beckley, Elizabeth Hoyt, Leslie Meisel, John Fico, David Skeist, Tanya Fischer, Evan Enderle, Pernell Walker, Katherine Creel, Jonathan Ledoux, Barnett Cohen, Bobby Hodgson, Emily Hyberger, Joseph McLaughlin, Liz Wisan, Ben Horner, Jocelyn Kuritsky, Wil Petre, Mary Schwartz, James Stover, Maiken Wiese, Rob Yang, Cooper Daniels, Brian Morvant, Kendall Rileigh, Julie Ferrell, Megan Raye Manzi, Vadim Newquist, Theresa Ngo, Alexis Macnab, Donal Brophy, Catherine Gowl, David Marcus, James Blanshard, J. Julian Christopher, Dan Cozzens, Emily Firth, Cara Francis, Carson Hinners, Max Jenkins, Rachel Rusch. Presented in association with the Chelsea Art Museum.

THE DIRECTOR. By Barbara Cassidy. March 1, 2007. Directed by Jessica Davis-Irons; choreography, Mimi Quillin; scenery, Neal Wilkinson; costumes, Chloe Chapin; lighting, Peter Ksander; sound, Jill BC DuBoff; video, Dustin O'Neill; stage manager, Lauren Levitt. With Lauren Shannon, Catherine Gowl, Donal Brophy, Barnett Cohen, Jackie Chung, Pernell Walker, Havilah Brewster, Leslie Meisel, Gamze Ceylan, Kristen Ryan, Alexis Macnab, Liz Wisan, Drew Hildebrand, Dalton Wiles.

LOS ANGELES. By Julian Sheppard. March 3, 2007. Directed by Adam Rapp; scenery, David Korins; costumes, Erika Munro; lighting, Miranda Hardy; sound, Eric Shim; music, Mr. Shim, Ray Rizzo and Amelia Zirin-Brown; lyrics, Mr. Sheppard; stage manager, Jess Johnston. With Ben Beckley, Dan Cozzens, Cooper Daniels, Roy Edroso, Evan Enderle, Tanya Fischer, Meredith Holzman, Emily Hyberger, David Skeist, Katherine Waterston, Rob Yang.

Intar. Identifies, develops and presents the talents of gifted Hispanic-American theater artists and mulitcultural visual artists. Eduardo Machado artistic director.

WINDOWS. By Sylvia Bofill. October 18, 2006. Directed by Ms. Bofill; scenery, Jian Jung; costumes, Oana Botez-Ban; lighting, Lucas Krech; sound, David Lawson. With Mercedes Herrero, Carmen de Lavallade, Milena Pérez Joglar.

DAUGHTER OF A CUBAN REVOLUTIONARY. Solo performance piece by Marissa Chibas. May 13, 2007. Directed by Mira Kingsley; scenery, Dan Evans; costumes, Karen Murk;

lighting, Rebecca M.K. Makus; sound, Colbert S. Davis IV; video, Adam Flemming. With Ms. Chibas.

Irish Repertory Theatre. Brings works by Irish and Irish-American playwrights to a wider audience and develops new works focusing on a wide range of cultural experience. Charlotte Moore artistic director, Ciarán O'Reilly producing director.

THE FIELD. By John B. Keane. June 1, 2006. Directed by Ciarán O'Reilly; scenery, Charles Corcoran; costumes, Martha Hally; lighting, Jason Lyons; sound, Zachary Williamson; fight direction, Rick Sordelet; stage manager, Elis C. Arroyo. With Craig Baldwin, Orlagh Cassidy, Malachy Cleary, Paddy Croft, Karen Lynn Gorney, Chandler Williams, Ken Jennings, Laurence Lowry, Marty Maguire, Paul Nugent, John O'Creagh, Tim Ruddy.

THE HAIRY APE. By Eugene O'Neill. October 5, 2006. Directed by Ciarán O'Reilly; scenery, Eugene Lee; costumes, Linda Fisher; lighting, Brian Nelson; sound, Zachary Williamson and Gabe Wood; fight direction, Rick Sordelet; stage manager, Janice M. Brandine. With Kerry Bishé, Jason Denuszek, Greg Derelian, Gerald Finnegan, Delphi Harrington, David Lansbury, Jon Levenson, Allen McCullough, Michael Mellamphy, Kevin O'Donnell.

AN EVENING OF IRISH ONE-ACTS. October 11, 2006–November 5, 2006.

GREAT WHITE AMERICAN TEETH. By Fiona Walsh. Directed by Virginia Scott. With Ms. Walsh.

SWANSONG. By Conor McDermottroe. Directed by David Sullivan. With Tim Ruddy.

MEET ME IN ST. LOUIS. Musical with book by Hugh Wheeler; music and lyrics by Hugh Martin and Ralph Blane. December 14, 2006. Directed by Charlotte Moore; choreography, Barry McNabb; scenery, Tony Straiges; costumes, Tracy Christensen; lighting, Brian Nason; music direction, John Bell; stage manager, Elis C. Arroyo. With George S. Irving, John Hickok, Sarah Pfisterer, Becky Barta, Danielle Piacentile, Gabrielle Piacentile, Doug Boes, Merideth Kaye Clark, Kerry Conte, Ashley Robinson, Bonnie Fraser, Colin Donnell.

DEFENDER OF THE FAITH. By Stuart Carolan. March 8, 2007. Directed by Ciarán O'Reilly; scenery, Charles Corcoran; costumes, Martha Hally; lighting, Brian Nason; sound, Zachary Williamson. With Matt Ball, Marc Aden Gray, Luke Kirby, David Lansbury, Anto Nolan, Peter Rogan.

La MaMa Experimental Theatre Club (ETC). A workshop for experimental theater of all kinds. Ellen Stewart founder and director.

Schedule included:

KING LEAR. Revival of the play by William Shakespeare. June 18, 2006. Directed by Patrick Swanson; scenery and costumes, David R. Gammons; lighting, Mark O'Maley; sound and music, Bill Barclay; fight direction, Robert Walsh; stage manager, Adele Nadine Traub. With Mr. Barclay, Allyn Burrows, Ken Cheeseman, Dan Domingues, Alvin Epstein, Benjamin Evett, William Gardiner, Jennie Israel, Colin Lane, Paula Langton, Gabriel Levey, Doug Lockwood, Sarah Newhouse, Michael Forden Walker. Presented in association with Actors' Shakespeare Project, Boston.

THE TOOTH OF CRIME. By Sam Shepard. October 5, 2006. Directed by George Ferencz; scenery, Bill Stabile; costumes, Sally Lesser, lighting, Jeff Tapper; sound, Tim Schellenbaum; music direction, Bob Jewett; stage manager, Elyzabeth Gorman. With Ray Wise, Arthur Adair, Raul Aranas, Gideon Charles Davis, Nick Denning, Cary Gant, John Andrew Morrison, Jenne Vath, Tass Filipos, Marc Jaffee, Jeff LaMarre, Kevin Joy, Denny McCormick.

MODERN LIVING. By Richard Sheinmel. October 13, 2006. Directed by Michael Barron; scenery, John McDermott; costumes, Jennifer Caprio; lighting, Jay Scott; sound, Tim Schellenbaum; music, Clay Zambo. With Meg Anderson, Christopher Borg, Mick Hilgers, Mr. Sheinmel, Nomi Tichman.

THE WHORE FROM OHIO. By Hanoch Levin; translated by Sandra Silverston. November 30, 2006. Directed by Geula Jeffet Attar and Victor Attar; scenery and costumes, Rob Eggers; lighting, Chaim Gitter and Sebastian Adamo; music, Yuval Mesner. With Mr. Attar, Udi Razzin, Zishan Ugurlu.

A CRAZY SOUND. By Dario D'Ambrosi. December 21, 2006. Directed by Mr. D'Ambrosi; scenery and costumes, Vittorio Terracina; lighting, Danilo Facco; sound, Stefano Zazzera; music direction, John La Barbera. With Lucy Alibar, Sheila Dabney, Celeste Moratti, Meredith Summers, Emma Lynn Worth, Kat Yew.

PARTY TIME. By Paul Zimet. January 10, 2007. Directed by Mr. Zimet; scenery, Lino Fiorito; lighting, Lenore Doxsee; music, Peter Gordon; video, Kit Fitzgerald. With William Badgett, Joe Roseto. Presented in association with the Talking Band.

THE BURIAL AT THEBES. By Seamus Heaney; based on Sophocles's *Antigone*. January 25, 2007. Directed by Alexander Harrington; choreography, Claire Pavlich; music; Carman Moore. With Frank Anderson, Janice Bishop, Jessica Crandall, Louise Flory, Liz Frost, John McCarthy, Jason Adamo, Rebecca Austin, Judith F. Bradshaw, Maija Lisa Currie, Sarah Ecton-Luttrell, Erik Gratton, Carrie Anne James, Christopher Keogh, Liz Sanders, Randi Sobol, Jason Weiss. Presented in association with Eleventh Hour Theatre Company.

LA VIE NOIR. By Jim Neu. February 15, 2007. Directed by Keith McDermott; scenery and costumes, Meg Zeder; lighting, Carol Mullins; sound, Jacob Burckhardt; music, Harry Mann and Neal Kirkwood. With Deborah Auer, John Costelloe, Agosto Machado, Chris Maresca, Mr. Neu, Tony Nunziata, Paco, Mary Schultz, Black-Eyed Susan.

REPUBLIC OF DREAMS. By Stacy Klein, Carlos Uriona and Matthew Glassman; based on the work of Bruno Schulz. March 8, 2007. Directed by Ms. Klein; design, Mira Zelechower Aleksiun; music, Jacek Ostaszewski; dramaturg, Ilan Stavans. Presented in association with Double Edge Theatre and the Polish Cultural Institute.

THE EXILES. By Theodora Skipitares; adapted from Euripides's *Orestes*. March 22, 2007. Direction and design, Ms. Skipitares; lighting, Pat Dignan, puppets, Cecilia Schiller and Ms. Skipitares; music, Tim Schellenbaum; video, Kay Hines. With Sheila Dabney, Chris Maresca, Alissa Mello, Nicky Paraiso, Sonja Perryman, Aneesh Sheth, Amanda Villalobos.

WAXING WEST. By Saviana Stanescu. April 5, 2007. Directed by Benjamin Mosse; scenery, Kanae Heike; costumes, Alixandra Gage; sound, Sharath Patel; music, Lucian Ban; stage manager, Adam Ganderson. With Elizabeth Atkeson, Kathryn Kates, Jason Lawergren, Alexis McGuinness, Tony Naumovski, Grant Neale, Dan Shaked, Marnye Young. Presented in association with East Coast Artists.

TROPHY WIFE. Musical with book by Mary Fulham; music by Terry Waldo; lyrics by Paul Foglino; based on Anton Chekhov's "Anna on the Neck." April 12, 2007. Directed by Ms. Fulham; choreography, Heidi Latsky; scenery, Gregory John Mercurio; costumes, Ramona Ponce; lighting, Federico Restrepo; sound, Tim Schellenbaum; video, Ray Roy and Eva Mantell. With Hal Blankenship, Sharon Ann Farrell, Brian P. Glover, Joan Jaffe, Jacqueline Kroschell, Max Lodge, Lisa Passero, Michael Rader, William Ryall, Jack Slattery. Presented in association with Watson Arts.

ROMEO AND JULIET. Revival of the play by William Shakespeare; adapted by Ellen Stewart. May 27, 2007. Directed by Ms. Stewart; choreography, Renouard Gee and H.T. Chen; scenery, Mark Tambella, Jun Maeda and Ms. Stewart; costumes, Radu, Miruna Boruezescu and Kanako Hiyama; lighting, Federico Restrepo; music, Ms. Stewart, Genji Ito, Michael Sirotta; music direction, Mr. Sirotta. With Noshir Dalal, George Drance, Brian P. Glover, Malaika Queano, Steven Ryan, Shigeko Suga, Ronny Wasserstrom, Meredith Wright. Presented in association with the Great Jones Repertory Company.

Lincoln Center Festival 2006. An annual international summer arts festival offering classic and contemporary work. Nigel Redden director.

DRUIDSYNGE: THE COMPLETE PLAYS OF JOHN MILLINGTON SYNGE. *Riders to the Sea, The Playboy of the Western World, Deirdre of the Sorrows, The Shadow of the Glen, The Well of the Saints, The Tinker's Wedding.* By John Millington Synge. July 10, 2006. Directed by Garry Hynes; choreography, David Bolger; scenery, Francis O'Connor; costumes, Kathy Strachan; lighting, Davy Cunningham; sound, John Leonard; music, Sam Jackson; stage manager, Tim Smith. With Sarah-Jane Drummey, Richard Flood, Simone Kirby, Mick Lally, Marcus Lamb, Nick Lee, Louise Lewis, Eoin Lynch, Hannah McCabe, Charlie McCarthy, Aaron Monaghan, Eamon Morrissey, Marie Mullen, Derry Power, Peg Power, Gemma Reeves,

Catherine Walsh, John Gaughan, Joseph Gaughan. Presented in association with Druid Theatre of Galway.

GRENDEL. By Elliot Goldenthal, Julie Taymor and J.D. McClatchy; based on the novel by John Gardner and *Beowulf.* July 11, 2006. Directed by Ms. Taymor; choreography, Angelin Preljocaj; scenery, George Tsypin; costumes, Constance Hoffman; lighting, Donald Holder; puppets and masks, Ms. Taymor and Michael Curry. With Eric Owens, Denyce Graves, Desmond Richardson, Laura Claycomb, Jay Hunter Morris, Richard Croft, Raymond Aceto, David Gagnon, Jonathan Hays, Charles Temkey, Hanan Alattar, Maureen Francis, Sarah Coburn. Presented in association with Los Angeles Opera.

ERARITJARITJAKA: MUSÉE DES PHRASES. By Heiner Goebbels; based on texts by Elias Canetti. July 27, 2006. Directed by Mr. Goebbels; scenery and lighting, Klaus Grünberg; costumes, Florence von Gerkan; sound, Willi Bopp; video, Bruno Deville. With André Wilms and the Mondriaan Quartet. Presented in association with Théâtre Vidy-Lausanne.

GEISHA. By Ong Keng Sen; text by Robin Loon. July 27, 2006. Directed by Mr. Sen; costumes, Mitsuishi Yanaihara; lighting, Scott Zielinski; sound, Toru Yamanaka. With Karen Kandel, Gojo Masanosuke, Kineya Katsumatsu. Presented in association with TheatreWorks, Singapore.

MCC Theater. Dedicated to the promotion of emerging writers, actors, directors and theatrical designers. Robert LuPone, Bernard Telsey, William Cantler artistic directors, John G. Schultz executive director.

NIXON'S NIXON. By Russell Lees. October 4, 2006. Directed by Jim Simpson; scenery, Kyle Chepulis; costumes, Claudia Brown; lighting, Brian Aldous; sound, Jill BC DuBoff; projections, Brian H. Kim; stage manager, Elizabeth Wiesener Page. With Gerry Bamman, Steve Mellor. Presented in association with the Lucille Lortel Theatre Foundation.

A VERY COMMON PROCEDURE. By Courtney Baron. February 14, 2007. Directed by Michael Greif; scenery, Robin Vest; costumes, Miranda Hoffman; lighting, Tyler Micoleau; sound and music, Fabian Obispo; stage manager, Amy McCraney. With Amir Arison, Lynn Collins, Stephen Kunken. Presented in association with the Lucille Lortel Theatre Foundation.

Mint Theater Company. Committed to bringing new vitality to worthy but neglected plays. Jonathan Bank artistic director.

SUSAN AND GOD. By Rachel Crothers. June 18, 2006. Directed by Jonathan Bank; scenery, Nathan Heverin; costumes, Clint Ramos; lighting, Josh Bradford; sound, Jane Shaw; dramaturg, Heather J. Violanti; stage manager, Jennifer Grutza. With Opal Alladin, Al Sapienza, Katie Firth, Anthony Newfield, Jordan Simmons, Alex Cranmer, Leslie Hendrix, Timothy Deenihan, Jennifer Blood, Matthieu Cornillon.

JOHN FERGUSON. By St. John Ervine. September 25, 2006. Directed by Martin Platt; scenery, Bill Clarke; costumes, Mattie Ullrich; lighting, Jeff Nellis; sound, Lindsay Jones; stage manager, Heather Prince. With Adam Branson, Robertson Carricart, Joyce Cohen, John Keating, Terrence Markovich, Mark Saturno, Justin Schultz, Greg Thornton, Marion Wood.

THE MADRAS HOUSE. By Harley Granville Barker. February 15, 2007. Directed by Gus Kaikkonen; scenery, Charles Morgan; costumes, Clint Ramos; lighting, William Armstrong; sound, Ellen Mandel; dramaturg, Amy Stoller; stage manager, Allison Deutsch. With Mary Bacon, Ross Bickell, Lisa Bostnar, Thomas M. Hammond, Jonathan Hogan, Laurie Kennedy, Roberta Maxwell, Allison McLemore, Pamela McVeagh, Mark L. Montgomery, George Morfogen, Angela Reed, Scott Romstadt, Kraig Swartz.

New Dramatists. An organization devoted to playwrights. Members may use the facilities for projects ranging from private readings of their material to public scripts-in-hand readings. Listed below are readings open to the public during the season under review. Todd London artistic director, Joel K. Ruark executive director.

HIP HOP HAMLET. By Marcus Gardley. June 5, 2006. Directed by Wes Grantom. With Andre Holland, Chad Goodridge, Kelly McCreary, Nick Mills, Hubert Point-Du Jour, Amanda Mills, DJ Blade.

NUTHIN' MASKS A VILLAGE. By Sung Rno. June 5, 2006. Directed by Abigail Marateck. With Cristofer Jean, Alfredo Narciso, Kristen Harlow, Sam Younis, Michi Barall, Maha Chehlaoui.

ADVERSE POSSESSION. By Herman Daniel Farrell III. June 6, 2006. Directed by John Steber. With Rochelle Hogue, Danyon Davis, Linda Marie Larson, Bill Camp, Daniel Talbott, Kelly McCreary.

ROBINSON AWAKE. By Barbara Wiechmann. June 12, 2006. With T. Ryder Smith.

. . . ," SAID SAÏD. By Ken Lin. June 14, 2006. Directed by Jackson Gay. With Matthew Lewis, Rita Wolf, Bridget Flanery, Victor Slezak, Greg Derelian.

NEW PLAYWRIGHT WELCOME. September 11, 2006. THE DRUNKEN CITY. By Adam Bock. Directed by Trip Cullman. With Mary Bacon, Samantha Soule, Emily Morse. RUST. By Kirsten Greenidge. Directed by Annie Dorsen. With Kibibi Dillon, Dion Graham, Keith Randolph Smith, Nedra McClyde. THE APPEAL AND SONGS OF THE DRAGON FLYING TO HEAVEN. By Young Jean Lee. With Ms. Lee. LEAVING EDEN. By Chiori Miyagawa. Directed by Stephanie Gilman. With Andrew McGinn, Veronica Cruz, Pamela Nyberg. BLUE DOOR. By Tanya Barfield. With Ms. Barfield. WE ARE NOT THESE HANDS. By Sheila Callaghan. Directed by Kip Fagan. With Lula Graves, Bess Rous, Greg McFadden. THIS STORM IS WHAT WE CALL PROGESS. By Jason Grote. Directed by Katie Pearl. With Jan Leslie Harding, Jeff Biehl, Kate Benson. FLESH AND THE DESERT (monologues). By Carson Kreitzer. With Ms. Kreitzer.

HALF-LIGHT. By Julie Hebert. September 15, 2006. Directed by Gordon Dahlquist. With Michael Potts, Vinie Burrows, Kristina Valada-Viars, Deborah Hazlett.

A WONDERFUL NOISE. By Michael Hollinger and Vance Lehmkuhl. September 29, 2006. Directed by Harriet Power. With Jeremiah Miller, Christopher Kale Jones, Doug Shapiro, Tracie Higgins, Julie Ellis, Mallory Hawks, Faith Sandberg, Natalie Moore, Benjamin Dibble, Robert McClure.

THE WAR PARTY. By Leslie Lee. October 3, 2006. Directed by Ms. Lee. With Victor Dickerson, Timothy Douglas, Larry Floyd, Michael Leonard James, Heather Massie, Pamela Monroe, Nina Murano, Marcus Naylor, Sandra Mills Scott, Adrian Washington.

THE LABYRINTH OF DESIRE. By Caridad Svich. October 5, 2006. Directed by Jean Randich. With Michael Tisdale, Jeffrey Carlson, Mia Katigbak, Polly Lee, Florencia Lozano, Simon Kendall, Andres Munar, Carlos Valencia, Eunice Wong.

GRADUATION FESTIVAL. October 12–30, 2006. HIDE TOWN. By Lisa D'Amour. Directed by Brooke O'Harra. With Neil Austin, Eric Dyer, Jim Frangione, Linda Marie Larson, Matt Maher, Maggie Mariolis, Heidi Schreck, Andrew Zimmerman. THE SCHOOLMASTER. By Mark Bazzone. Directed by Mr. Bazzone. With Nikos Brisco, Brienin Nequa Bryant, Lynn Cohen, Craig Alan Edwards, Linda Jones, Brian Keane, Ron Riley, Yuri Skujins. GOLIATH. By Karen Hartman. Directed by Chay Yew. With J. Ed Araiza, Jeremy Rishe, Stacey Sargeant, Lori Wilner, Laura Flanagan. UP. By Bridget Carpenter. Directed by Anne Kauffman. With Joanna Adler, Jeff Biehl, Gary Brownlee, Maria Dizzia, Molly Powell, Rufus Tureen. HAWKING. By Lonnie Carter. Directed by Gordon Dahlquist. With Lynn Cohen, Danyon Davis, Joseph Anthony Foronda, David Grimm, Oni Faida Lampley, Forrest McClendon, Honor Molloy, Jennifer R. Morris, Tanya Selvaratnam. BY THE WAY, MEET VERA STARK. By Lynn Nottage. Directed by Liesl Tommy. With Phyllis Johnson, Jordan Mahome, Jennifer Mudge, Nicolle Rochelle, Stacey Sargeant.

A VIEW FROM THE HARBOR. By Richard Dresser. October 16, 2006. Directed by Kevin O'Rourke. With Betsy Aidem, Larry Bryggman, Brian Hutchison, Maggie Lacey.

CASTLE OF BLOOD. By Alejandro Morales. October 30, 2006. Directed by Scott Ebersold. With David Grimm, Polly Lee, Frank Liotti, Patrick Melville, Susan Louise O'Connor, Chris Wells, Travis York.

AUX COPS. By Quincy Long. October 31, 2006. Directed by Ethan McSweeny. With Quincy Tyler Bernstine, Maria Dizzia, Chris McMann, John Pankow, Armando Riesco.

26 MILES. By Quiara Alegría Hudes. November 1, 2006. Directed by Davis McCallum. With Mateo Gomez, Zabryna Guevara, Jon Krupp, Susan Louise O'Connor.

LEAF. By Chiori Miyagawa. November 14, 2006. Directed by Carolyn Cantor. With Betsy Aidem, Tina Benko, John McAdams.

ARE YOU NOW OR HAVE YOU EVER BEEN . . . By Carlyle Brown. November 21, 2006. With Mr. Brown.

TRIPPIN'. By Marcus Gardley, Germono T. Bryant and Daniel Beaty. November 27–December 1, 2006. Directed by Mr. Beaty. With Giovanni Adams, Pilin Broden, Kimberly Gregory, Paul J. Medford, John Rankin, Kecia Lewis Evans, Stephen Conrad Moore.

PLAYTIME. December 4–16, 2006. AN OPENING FOR MURDER. By Joseph Goodrich. Directed by Nick Faust. With Ned Eisenberg, Erik Lieberman, Leslie Lyles, John MacAdams, Molly Powell. VOICES FROM HARPER'S FERRY. By Dominic Taylor. Directed by Clinton Turner Davis and Helga Davis. With Brandon Dirden, Craig Alan Edwards, Erik Laray Harvey, John Rankin, Sonja Perryman, Keith Randolph Smith. GALOIS. By Sung Rno and Jeremy Bass. Directed by Debbie Saivetz. With Erik Laray Harvey, Polly Lee, Erik Lieberman, Leslie Lyles, Andres Munar, Andy Pang, Keith Randolph Smith. PHOENIX FABRIK. By Daniel Alexander Jones. With Vinie Burrows, Julia Knight, John Rankin, Sonja Perryman. GREEDY. By Karl Gajdusek. Directed by Pam MacKinnon. With Joanna Adler, Ned Eisenberg, Michael J.X. Gladis, Nina Hellman, Ana Reeder.

CASUS BELLI. By Herman Daniel Farrell III. January 4, 2007. Directed by Nancy Jones. With Catherine Curtin, Derek Lucci, David Margulies, Laura Ruth Marks, Joseph Urla.

PLAYGROUND CTC. (In association with the Children's Theatre Company, Minneapolis). January 8–January 12, 2007. THE BOOK AND THE BUCCANEER. By Liz Duffy Adams and Ellen Maddow. Directed by Martha Banta. With Carlo Alban, Kelly McCreary, Rheaume Crenshaw, Julie Ellis, Jack Ferver, David Grimm, Timothy Huang, Jon Krupp, Sarah Lord, Isaac Maddow-Zimet, April Matthis, Natalie McKnight, Natalie Moore, Molly Powell, Ann Rooney, Lawrence Stallings. THE PEOPLE COULD FLY. By Zakiyyah Alexander. Directed by Victor Maog. With Abena Asamoah, Kibibi Dillon, Zabryna Guevara, Taifa Harris, Keith Randolph Smith, Albert Lee Jones. SONS AND MOTHER. By Oni Faida Lampley. Directed by Leah Gardiner. With Armando Batista, Chad Goodridge, Forrest McClendon, Nedra McClyde.

STRIKE-SLIP. By Naomi Iizuka. January 17–January 20, 2007. Directed by Chay Yew. With Ali Ahn, Tim Altmeyer, Heather Lea Anderson, Romi Dias, J. Salome Martinez Jr., Thom Sesma, Keith Randolph Smith, Hanson Tse.

THE BLACK MONK. By Wendy Kesselman. January 18–January 19, 2007. Directed by Michael Barakiva and Vadim Feichtner. With Adam Berry, Shawn Nacol, Austin Pendleton, Maria Thayer, Peter Van Wagner.

JOVE'S WIFE. By Joel Wyman. January 23, 2007. Directed by Lynn Thomson. With Polly Adams, Buzz Bovshow, Jim DeMarse, Dawn Evans, Kristin Griffith, Michael Leonard James, Marjorie Johnson, Yuri Skujins.

CONSTANCE DRINKWATER AND THE FINAL DAYS OF SOMERSET. By Stephen Carleton. January 25, 2007. Directed by Ken Rus Schmoll. With Kibibi Dillon, Kristin Griffith, Robert Emmet Lunney, James Saito, Hanson Tse, Joseph Urla.

ASTRONOMICAL QUITCLAIM DEEDS. By Julia Jordan. January 29, 2007. Directed by Erica Schmidt. With Len Cariou, Michael Chernus, Roberta Maxwell.

POST OFFICE. February 13–20, 2007. By Melissa James Gibson and J. Michael Friedman. Directed by Kris Kukul. With Aysan Celik, Gibson Fraizer, Kelly McCreary, Olivia Oguma, Stephen Plunkett.

KEY LIGHT. By Mark Druck. February 22, 2007. Directed by Mr. Druck. With Blanche Baker, H. Daniel Harkins, Mark Irish.

THAT PRETTY PRETTY. By Sheila Callaghan. March 1, 2007. Directed by Kip Fagan. With Lula Graves, Rebecca Hart, Jennifer R. Morris, David Brooks, Travis York, Daniel Manley.

1001. By Jason Grote. March 9, 2007. Directed by Ethan McSweeny. With Drew Cortese, Daoud Heidami, Lanna Joffrey, John Livingstone Rolle, Jeanine Serralles, Sara Thurston, Josh Philip Weinstein.

POST OFFICE. By Melissa James Gibson and J. Michael Friedman. March 15, 2007. With Aysan Celik, Gibson Frazier, Kelly McCreary.

CHURCH. By Young Jean Lee. April 10–14, 2007. With Katie Workum, Karinne Keithley, Weena Pauly.

CHERRY SMOKE. By James McManus. April 18, 2007. Directed by Matt August. With Sarah Lord, LeRoy McClain, James McMenamin, Jess Weixler.

KILLING HILDA. By David Grimm and Peter Golub. April 19–21, 2007. Directed by Mr. Golub. With Emily Albrink, Tim McDevitt, Matthew Morris.

O DARK HUNDRED. By Honor Molloy. May 10, 2007. With Ms. Molloy, David Grimm, Caroline Winterson, Jarlath Conroy.

BELIEVER. By Lee Kalcheim. May 22, 2007. Directed by Michael Lembeck. With Boyd Gaines, Malik Hammond, Erica Huang, Samantha Lucier, Kathy McNenny, Zach Mills, Miriam Shor, Michael Tucker, Lee Wilkof.

New Federal Theatre. Dedicated to integrating minorities into the mainstream of American theater through the training of artists and the presentation of plays by minorities and women. Woodie King Jr. producing director.

NTOZAKE SHANGE: A RETROSPECTIVE. February 7–March 4, 2007.

Schedule included:

BOOGIE WOOGIE LANDSCAPE. By Ntozake Shange. A PHOTOGRAPH: LOVERS IN MOTION. By Ntozake Shange. FROM OKRA TO GREENS/A DIFFERENT KIND OF LOVE STORY. By Ntozake Shange. LAILA'S DREAM. By Ntozake Shange. MOTHER COURAGE. By Bertolt Brecht; adapted by Ntozake Shange. Presented in association with Abrons Arts Center.

IT HASN'T ALWAYS BEEN THIS WAY. By Ntozake Shange. February 21, 2007. Directed by Dianne McIntyre. With Ms. Shange, Shireen Dickson, Nina Domingue, Petronia Paley, Charles E. Wallace, Olu Dara. Presented in association with the Castillo Theatre.

THE TAKING OF MISS JANIE. By Ed Bullins. December 3, 2006. Directed by Shauneille Perry; choreography, Chiquita Ross. With Alia Chapman, Lee Gundersheimer, Garrett Lee Hendricks, Royce Johnson, Kate Russell.

The New Group. Provides an artistic home for fresh acting, writing and design talent. Committed to cultivating a young and diverse theatergoing audience. Scott Elliott artistic director, Geoffrey Rich executive director.

EVERYTHINGS TURNING INTO BEAUTIFUL. By Seth Zvi Rosenfeld. August 3, 2006. Directed by Carl Forsman; scenery, Beowulf Boritt; costumes, Theresa Squire; lighting, Josh Bradford; sound, Daniel Baker; music, Jimmie James; stage manager, Erin Grenier. With Daphne Rubin-Vega, Malik Yoba.

THE PRIME OF MISS JEAN BRODIE. By Jay Presson Allen; adapted from Muriel Spark's novel. October 9, 2006. Directed by Scott Elliott; scenery, Derek McLane; costumes, Eric Becker; lighting, Jason Lyons; sound, Daniel Baker; music, Tom Kochan; stage manager, Valerie A. Peterson. With Cynthia Nixon, Emily Bicks, Ritchie Coster, Lisa Emery, Halley Wegryn Gross, Betsy Hogg, Zoe Kazan, Caroline Lagerfelt, John Pankow, Caity Quinn, Matthew Rauch, Sarah Steele.

THE ACCOMPLICES. By Bernard Weinraub. April 9, 2007. Directed by Ian Morgan; scenery, Beowulf Boritt; costumes, Theresa Squire; lighting, Jeff Croiter; sound and music, Matt Sherwin; stage manager, Valerie A. Peterson. With Daniel Sauli, David Margulies, Zoe Lister-Jones, Robert Hogan, Mark Zimmerman, Andrew Polk, Catherine Curtin, Jon DeVries, Mark Zeisler.

THE NEW GROUP (naked). Productions presented on a modest scale.

JAYSON WITH A Y. By Darci Picoult. June 13, 2006. Directed by Sheryl Kaller; scenery, Adrian W. Jones; costumes, Amy Clark; lighting, Russell H. Champa and Justin Partier;

sound, Shane Rettig; stage manager, Andrea Hayward. With Kevin Geer, Marin Hinkle, Daniel Oreskes, Maryann Plunkett, Miles Purinton, Alysia Reiner.

STRANGERS KNOCKING. By Robert Tenges. May 14, 2007. Directed by Marie Masters; sound, Bart Fasbender. With Talia Balsam, Mercer Boffey, Julie Halston, Stella Maeve, Michael Stahl-David, Jonathan Walker.

EXPATS. By Heather Lynn MacDonald. May 18, 2007. Directed by Ari Edelson; scenery, Peter R. Feuchtwanger; costumes, Kristine Koury; lighting, Nicole Pearce; sound, Travis Walker. With Reiko Aylesworth, James Badge Dale, Jesse Hooker, Jay Klaitz, Matthew Rauch, Taylor Wilcox, Natalia Zvereva.

New York Theatre Workshop. Dedicated to nurturing artists at all stages of their careers and to developing provocative new works. James C. Nicola artistic director, Lynn Moffat managing director.

Schedule included:

A VERY MERRY UNAUTHORIZED CHILDREN'S SCIENTOLOGY PAGENT. Musical with book, music and lyrics by Kyle Jarrow. December 10, 2006. Directed and choreographed by Alex Timbers; scenery, David Evans Morris; costumes, Jennifer Rogien; lighting, Juliet Chia; music direction, Gabriel Kahane; stage manager, Alaina Taylor. With Dahlia Chacon, Hudson Cianni, Lauren Kelly, Jolie Libert, Steven Lobman, Elizabeth Lynn, Sean Moran, Kat Peters, Alex Swift, William Wiggins. Presented in association with Les Freres Corbusier.

Pan Asian Repertory Theatre. Introducing Asian-American theater to the general public with the aim of deepening appreciation and understanding of Asian-American cultural heritage. Tisa Chang artistic producing director.

YOHEN. By Philip Kan Gotanda. October 18, 2006. Directed by Seret Scott; scenery, Charles Corcoran; costumes, Carol Pelletier; lighting, Kazuko Oguma; sound, Cliff Caruthers; stage manager, T. Rick Jones. With David Fonteno, Dian Kobayashi.

TEA. By Velina Hasu Houston. May 30, 2007. Directed by Tina Chen; scenery, Charles Corcoran; costumes, Carol Pelletier; lighting, Victor En Yu Tan; sound, Genevieve-Marie C. Nicolas; stage manager, Elis C. Arroyo. With Ako, Akiko Hiroshima, Karen Tsen Lee, Jo Shui, Momo Yashima.

Performance Space 122. Provides artists of a wide range of experience a chance to develop work and find an audience. Vallejo Gantner artistic director, Anne Dennin executive director.

Schedule included:

ORANGE LEMON EGG CANARY. By Rinne Groff. July 12, 2006. Directed by Michael Sexton; scenery, Andromache Chalfant; costumes, Oana Botez-Ban; lighting, Ben Stanton; sound, Eric Shim; fight direction, Jeff Barry; stage manager, Christine Lemme. With Laura Kai Chen, Steve Cuiffo, Aubrey Dollar, Emily Swallow.

INVISIBLE MESSAGES. By Peter S. Petralia. October 12, 2006. Directed by Mr. Petralia; lighting, Rebecca M.K. Makus; music, Max Giteck Duykers; dramaturg, Glenn Kessler; stage manager, Ashley Kosier. With Mandy Caughey, Alessandro Magania, Meredith Smart.

TALE OF 2CITIES: PART I, GRIFTERS, DRIFTERS AND DODGERS and PART II, MEGA MIXICANA WALTZ. By Heather Woodbury. October 12, 2006. Directed by Dudley Saunders. With Winsome Brown, Michael Ray Escamilla, Tracey A. Leigh, Leo Marks, Diane Rodriguez, Ed Vassallo, Ms. Woodbury.

PANIC. By Rafael Spregelburd. November 5, 2006. Directed by Brooke O'Harra; scenery, Peter Ksander; costumes, Anka Lupes; lighting, Justin Townsend; stage manager, Kevin Gay. With Jess Barbagallo, David Brooks, Laryssa Husiak, Scott Lyons, Nadia Mahdi, Maggie Mariolis, Tatiana Pavela, Rosemary Quinn, Heidi Schreck, Tina Shepard.

CARRIE. By Erik Jackson. December 9, 2006. Directed by Josh Rosenzweig; scenery, Tobin Ost; costumes, David Moyer; lighting, Paul Hackenmueller; sound and music, Robert

Kaplowitz; visual effects, Basil Twist; stage manager, Molly Minor Eustis. With Kate Goehring, David Ilku, Keri Meoni, Kathy Searle, Rafi Silver, Danielle Skraastad, Sherry Vine, Matt Wilkas, Marnye Young.

PURITY. By Thomas Bradshaw. January 4, 2007. Directed by Yehuda Duenyas; scenery, Clint Ramos; costumes, Jessica Gaffney; lighting, Ben Kato; sound, Mr. Duenyas and Jody Elff; stage manager, Michelle Leigh Chang. With Kate Benson, Spencer Scott Barros, Albert Christmas, Alexa Scott-Flaherty, Daniel Manley, James Scruggs, Jenny Seastone Stern.

YOU BELONG TO ME: DEATH OF NATIONS, PART V. By Josh Fox. January 4, 2007. Directed by Mr. Fox; scenery and costumes, Petra Maria Wirth, Judith Kästner, Julien Renard and Tara Shamskho; lighting, Charles Foster and Scott Needham; dramaturg, Frank M. Raddatz. With Beau Allulli, Harold Kennedy German, Carrie Getman, Irene Christ, Beth Griffith, Okwui Okpokwasili, Robert Saietta, Angelika Sautter, Rory Sheridan.

PARTICULARLY IN THE HEARTLAND. By the TEAM. February 26, 2007. Directed by Rachel Chavkin; scenery, Nicholas Vaughan; costumes, Kristen Sieh; lighting, Jake Heinrichs; sound, Matt Hubbs; dramaturgs, Stephanie Douglass and Chantal Pavageaux; stage manager, Rebecca Spinac. With Jessica Almasy, Frank Boyd, Jill Frutkin, Libby King, Jake Margolin, Ms. Sieh.

GOODNESS. By Michael Redhill. March 1, 2007. Directed by Ross Manson; costumes, Teresa Przybylski; lighting, Rebecca Picherack; sound, John Gzowksi; music direction, Brenna MacCrimmon. With Victor Ertmanis, Lili Francks, Tara Hughes, Jack Nicholsen, Gord Rand, Amy Rutherford. Presented in association with the Carol Tambor Theatrical Foundation and Volcano Theatre.

Savage WASPs: Charles Socarides and Jeremy Blackman in Indian Blood. *Photo: James Leynse*

1001 BEDS. Solo performance piece by Tim Miller. March 8, 2007. With Mr. Miller.

CHURCH. By Young Jean Lee. April 26, 2007. Directed by Ms. Lee; choreography, Faye Driscoll; scenery, Eric Dyer; costumes, Normandy Sherwood; lights, Mark Barton; sound, Matthew Tierney; stage manager, Sam Seymour. With Greg Hildreth, Karinne Keithley, Weena Pauly, Katie Workum.

Primary Stages. Dedicated to new American plays. Casey Childs executive producer, Andrew Leynse artistic director.

INDIAN BLOOD. By A.R. Gurney. August 9, 2006. Directed by Mark Lamos; scenery, John Arnone; costumes, Ann Hould-Ward; lighting, Howell Binkley; sound and music, John Gromada; projections, Leah Gelpe; fight direction, B.H. Barry; stage manager, Frederic H. Orner. With Matthew Arkin, Jeremy Blackman, Jack Gilpin, Rebecca Luker, Katherine McGrath, John McMartin, Pamela Payton-Wright, Charles Socarides. Presented in association with Jamie deRoy.

SOUTHERN COMFORTS. By Kathleen Clark. October 18, 2006. Directed by Judith Ivey; scenery, Thomas Lynch; costumes, Joseph G. Aulisi; lighting, Brian Nason; sound, T. Richard Fitzgerald; music, Paul Schwartz; fight direction, B.H. Barry; stage manager, Misha Siegel-Rivers. With Penny Fuller, Larry Keith.

EXITS AND ENTRANCES. By Athol Fugard. April 4, 2007. Directed by Stephen Sachs; scenery, Charles Corcoran; costumes, Shon Le Blanc; lighting, Brian Nason; sound, David B. Marling; stage manager, Samone B. Weissman. With Morlan Higgins, William Dennis Hurley. Presented in association with Dasha Epstein and Jamie deRoy.

The Public Theater. Schedule of special projects, in addition to its regular Off Broadway productions. Oskar Eustis artistic director, Mara Manus executive director.

NEW WORK NOW! FESTIVAL OF NEW PLAY READINGS.

THINGS WE WANT. By Jonathan Marc Sherman. October 23, 2006. Directed by Ethan Hawke.

IN THE RED AND BROWN WATER. By Tarell McCraney. October 25, 2006. Directed by Tina Landau.

THE GOOD NEGRO. By Tracey Scott Wilson. October 29, 2006. Directed by Leisl Tommy.

CELEBRITY ROW. By Itamar Moses. November 2, 2006. Directed by Oskar Eustis.

UNTITLED DARFUR PLAY. By Winter Miller. November 3, 2006. Directed by Joanna Settle.

ARAB-ISRAELI FESTIVAL. Staged readings of plays by Israeli, Arab and American writers responding to Middle Eastern turmoil.

IWITNESS. By Joshua Sobol; adapted by Barry Edelstein. October 24, 2006. Directed by Mr. Edelstein.

WHEN THE BULBUL STOPPED SINGING. By David Greig; adapted from the diaries of Raja Shenhadeh. October 26, 2006. Directed by JoAnne Akalaitis.

UNTITLED. By Najla Said. BETWEEN OUR LIPS. By Nathalie Handal. Directed by Shana Gold. POWER LUNCH. By Kia Corthron. October 27, 2006.

UNTITLED. By Leila Buck. LA COSA DEI SOGNI. By Nathalie Handal. LEBANON. By Nibras. October 28, 2006.

THE MURDER OF ISAAC. By Motti Lerner; translated from the Hebrew by Anthony Berris. October 30, 2006. Directed by Irene Lewis.

AGAIN AND AGAINST–THE ART OF HOPING INDEFINITELY. By Betty Shamieh. November 4, 2006. Directed by Robert O'Hara.

O JERUSALEM. By A.R. Gurney. November 6, 2006. Directed by Jim Simpson.

UNDER THE RADAR. January 12–27, 2007.

A BEAUTIFUL VIEW (Canada). By Daniel MacIvor. Directed by Mr. MacIvor.

ANOTHER YOU (Seattle). By Allen Johnson. Directed by Sean Ryan. With Mr. Johnson.

EPISTLE TO YOUNG ACTORS (France). By Olivier Py. Directed by Mr. Py.

INVINCIBLE SUMMER (New York; Seattle). By Mike Daisey. Directed by Jean-Michele Gregory. With Mr. Daisey.

RADIO MACBETH (New York). By the SITI Company; based on the play by William Shakespeare. Directed by Anne Bogart and Darron L. West. With the SITI Company.

THE BE(A)ST OF TAYLOR MAC (New York). By Taylor Mac. Directed by David Drake. With Mr. Mac.

THE BROTHERS SIZE (New York). By Tarell McCraney. Directed by Tea Alagic.

TWO SONGS (San Francisco). By John O'Keefe. With Mr. O'Keefe.

Puerto Rican Traveling Theatre. Professional company presenting English and Spanish productions of Puerto Rican and Hispanic playwrights, emphasizing subjects of relevance today. Miriam Colón Valle founder and producer.

BAD BLOOD (MALASANGRE). By Roberto Ramos-Perea; English translation by Charles Philip Thomas. May 3, 2007. Directed by Miriam Colón Valle; scenery, Randall Parsons; costumes, Marion Talan; lighting, Scott Andrew Cally. With Francis Mateo, Jazmin Caratini, Felipe Javier Gorostiza, Gladys Perez, German Nande.

Signature Theatre Company. Dedicated to the exploration of one playwright's body of work over the course of a single season. James Houghton artistic director.

TWO TRAINS RUNNING. By August Wilson. December 3, 2006. Directed by Lou Bellamy; scenery, Derek McLane; costumes, Mathew J. Lefebvre; lighting, Robert Wierzel; sound, Brett R. Jarvis; fight direction, Rick Sordelet; stage manager, Babette Roberts. With Leon Addison Brown, Chad L. Coleman, Frankie Faison, Arthur French, Ron Cephas Jones, January LaVoy, Ed Wheeler.

Soho Rep. Dedicated to the development and production of exuberant, unconventional new plays. Sarah Benson artistic director, Alexandra Conley executive director.

THE THUGS. By Adam Bock. October 7, 2006. Directed by Anne Kauffman; scenery, David Korins; costumes, Michelle R. Phillips; lighting, Ben Stanton; sound, Robert Kaplowitz and Jeremy J. Lee; stage manager, Sarah Bishop-Stone. With Saidah Arrika Ekulona, Brad Heberlee, Carmen M. Herlihy, Chris Heuisler, Keira Keeley, Lynne McCullough, Maria Elena Ramirez, Mary Shultz.

Theater for the New City. Developmental theater and new experimental works. Crystal Field artistic director.

THE FUNNIEST SHOW IN THE WORLD. By Danny Bacher and Josh Bacher. September 10, 2006. Directed by Dom J. Buccafusco; choreography, Meg'een Corcoran and Moina Sidwell; scenery, Robert Monaco; costumes, Mama Jean; lighting, Randy Glickman; video, Messrs. Bacher, Elliot Passantino and Lorraine Mulrane; stage manager, Christian Curtis. With Messrs. Bacher.

GREATER BUFFALO. By Robyn Burland. October 7, 2006. Directed by Jessica Davis-Irons; scenery, Meganne George; lighting, Drew Florida. With Shira Gregory, Michael Kohn.

NEW SCIENCE. By Jessica Slote. November 16, 2006. Directed by Martin Reckhaus; scenery, costumes and lighting, Gary Brackett and Pamela Mayo; music, Patrick Grant; stage manager, Victoria Barbiana. With Johnson Anthony, Adela María Bolet, Sheila Dabney, Carlos Fernandez, Claire Lebowitz, Pamela Mayo, Thomas S. Walker, Naisha Walton, Debra Wassum.

WODEN. By Gene Ruffini. December 14, 2006. Directed by Mr. Ruffini; scenery and lighting, Jason Sturm. With Bob Armstrong, Elizabeth Burke, William Greville, Deborah Johnstone, Bryan Luethy, Carol Ann Palmaro, Dorian Shorts, Jessica Tate.

ANGRY YOUNG WOMEN IN LOW-RISE JEANS WITH HIGH-CLASS ISSUES. By Matt Morillo. January 4, 2007. Directed by Mr. Morillo; scenery, Jana Mattioli; lighting, Amith A.

Chandrashaker. With Nicholas J. Coleman, Martin Friedrichs, Angelique Letizia, Rachel Nau, Thomas J. Pilutik, Devon Pipars, JessAnn Smith.

SLEEP OVER. By Maria Micheles. March 8, 2007. Directed by Kitt Lavoie; scenery, Mr. Lavoie; costumes, Jennifer Reichert; lighting, Justin Partier; projections, Russell Hankin; stage manager, Jenny Kirlin. With Lucy Alibar, Jennifer Curfman, Chris Stack.

MY INNER MARK BERMAN. Musical by Evan Laurence. May 3, 2007. Directed by Richard Mazda; choreography, Tana Leigh Pierce; lighting, Mi Sun Choi. With Mr. Laurence, Richard C. Lurie, Christopher Noffke, David F. Slone, Danny Smith.

IN THE SCHOOLYARD. Musical with book and lyrics by Paulanne Simmons; music by Margaret Hetherman. May 4, 2007. Directed by Ms. Simmons; choreography, James Martinelli; scenery, Bill Wood; lighting, Ken Kruk. With Jody Bell, Dave Benger, Arthur Brown, Richard Bryson, Mickey Corporon, Lizzie Czerner, Mr. Martinelli, Theresa Martinelli, Heather Meagher, Jimmy Moon, Jackie Savage.

Theatre for a New Audience. Founded in 1979, the company's mission is to energize the performance and study of Shakespeare and classic drama. Jeffrey Horowitz founding artistic director, Dorothy Ryan managing director.

THE JEW OF MALTA. Revival of the play by Christopher Marlowe. February 4, 2007. Directed by David Herskovits; scenery, John Lee Beatty; costumes, David Zinn; sound, Jane Shaw; fight direction, J. Steven White; dramaturg, Michael Feingold; stage managers, Renee Lutz and Jamie Rose Thoma. With F. Murray Abraham, Kenajuan Bentley, Arnie Burton, Cameron Folmar, Kate Forbes, Ezra Knight, John Lavelle, Nicole Lowrance, Vince Nappo, Tom Nelis, Saxon Palmer, Matthew Schneck, Christen Simon, Marc Vietor. Presented in repertory with *The Merchant of Venice.*

THE MERCHANT OF VENICE. Revival of the play by William Shakespeare. February 4, 2007. Directed by Darko Tresnjak; scenery, John Lee Beatty; costumes, Linda Cho; lighting, David Weiner; sound, Jane Shaw; video, Matthew Myhrum; dramaturg, Michael Feingold; stage managers, Renee Lutz and Jamie Rose Thoma. With F. Murray Abraham, Kenajuan Bentley, Arnie Burton, Cameron Folmar, Kate Forbes, Ezra Knight, John Lavelle, Nicole Lowrance, Vince Nappo, Tom Nelis, Saxon Palmer, Matthew Schneck, Christen Simon, Marc Vietor. Presented in repertory with *The Jew of Malta.*

OLIVER TWIST. By Charles Dickens; adapted by Neil Bartlett. April 1, 2007. Directed by Mr. Bartlett; scenery and costumes, Rae Smith; lighting, Scott Zielinski; sound, David Remedios; music, Gerard McBurney; music direction, Simon Deacon; stage manager, Chris De Camillis. With Remo Airaldi, Steven Boyer, Greg Derelian, Thomas Derrah, Ned Eisenberg, Carson Elrod, Jennifer Ikeda, Elizabeth Jasicki, Will LeBow, Karen MacDonald, Craig Pattison, Lucas Steele, Michael Wartella.

Vineyard Theatre. The company is committed to nurturing the work of developing playwrights and composers, while providing established artists with a supportive environment in which to experiment, take risks, and grow. Douglas Aibel artistic director, Jennifer Garvey-Blackwell executive director.

STOPPING TRAFFIC. By Mary Pat Gleason. June 7, 2006. Directed by Lonny Price; scenery, Neil Patel; costumes, Tracy Christensen; lighting, David Weiner; sound, Obadiah Eaves; stage manager, Kate Hefel. With Ms. Gleason.

THE INTERNATIONALIST. By Anne Washburn. November 7, 2006. Directed by Ken Rus Schmoll; scenery, Andromache Chalfant; costumes, Michelle R. Phillips; lighting, Jeff Croiter; sound, Robert Kaplowitz; stage manager, Megan Smith. With Liam Craig, Nina Hellman, Gibson Frazier, Ken Marks, Zak Orth, Annie Parisse.

MARY ROSE. By J.M. Barrie. February 20, 2007. Directed by Tina Landau; scenery, James Schuette; costumes, Michael Krass; lighting, Kevin Adams; sound and music, Obadiah Eaves; stage manager, Megan Smith. With Betsy Aidem, Susan Blommaert, Ian Brennan, Michael Countryman, Keir Dullea, Tom Riis Farrell, Darren Goldstein, Paige Howard, Richard Short.

AMERICAN FIESTA. By Steven Tomlinson. April 26, 2007. Directed by Mark Brokaw; scenery, Neil Patel; lighting, David Lander; sound, David Van Tieghem and Jill BC DuBoff; music, Mr. Van Tieghem; projections, Jan Hartley, S. Katy Tucker; stage manager, Megan Smith. With Mr. Tomlinson.

LAB PRODUCTION SERIES.

THE AGONY AND THE AGONY. By Nicky Silver. December 9, 2006; Directed by Terry Kinney; scenery, Andromache Chalfant; costumes, Mattie Ullrich; lighting, Jeff Croiter; sound and music, Obadiah Eaves; stage manager, Christine Lemme. With Victoria Clark, Michael Esper, Harry van Gorkum, Cheyenne Jackson, Mr. Silver, Marilyn Torres.

Women's Project. Nurtures, develops and produces plays written and directed by women. Julie Crosby producing artistic director.

TEN CENTURIES OF WOMEN PLAYWRIGHTS. Staged reading series.

THE HROTSVITA PLAYS. By Deborah Stein; adapted from the work of Hrotsvita of Gandersheim (Hrosvitha). October 23, 2006. Directed by Lear deBessonet. Presented in association with Allison Prouty (Stillpoint Productions).

THE FEIGN'D COURTESANS. By Aphra Behn; adapted by Rebecca Patterson. November 13, 2006. Directed by Ms. Patterson.

VICTORIA MARTIN: MATH TEAM QUEEN. By Kathryn Walat. January 21, 2007. Directed by Loretta Greco; scenery, Robert Brill; costumes, Valerie Marcus Ramshur; lighting, Sarah Sidman; sound, Daniel Baker; music, Broken Chord Collective; stage manager, Brian Meister. With Zachary Booth, Jessi Campbell, Adam Farabee, Tobias Segal, Matthew Stadelmann.

TRANSFIGURES. By Lear deBessonet; with text by Bathsheba Doran, Charles L. Mee, Erin Sax Seymour, Russell Shorto, Joan of Arc and Henrik Ibsen. April 16, 2007. Directed by Ms. deBessonet; choreography, Andrea Haenggi; scenery, Jenny Sawyer; costumes, Clint Ramos; lighting, Ryan Mueller; sound, Mark Huang; dramaturgy, Megan E. Carter; stage manager, Jack Gianino. With David Adkins, Dylan Dawson, Juliana Francis, Nate Schenkkan, T. Ryder Smith, Marguerite Stimpson.

GIRLS JUST WANNA HAVE FUNDS. Festival of short plays. May 16–19, 2007.

KEEP THE CHANGE. By Joy Tomasko and Christina Gorman. Directed by May Adrales. I WANT WHAT YOU HAVE. By Saviana Stanescu. Directed by Gia Forakis. DIME SHOW. By Molly Rice. Directed by May Adrales. REMEMBRANCE. By Katori Hall. Directed by Jyana Gregory. A PEDDLER'S TALE: BUTTONS, GUTS, AND BLUETOOTH. By Andrea Lepcio. Directed by Kim Weild. SONG. By Addie Brownlee.

The York Theatre Company. Dedicated to the development of small-scale musicals, to the rediscovery of underappreciated musicals from the past and to serving the community through educational initiatives. James Morgan producing artistic director.

DEVELOPMENTAL READING SERIES. June 7–27, 2006.

MRS. LINCOLN. Musical with book by June Bingham; music and lyrics by Carmel Owen. June 7, 2006. FRIENDS LIKE THESE. Musical with book by Jay Jeffries and John McMahon; music by Mr. McMahon; lyrics by Mr. Jeffries. June 21, 2006. THE LEGEND OF SLEEPY HOLLOW. Musical with book by Robert L. Stempin; music and lyrics by James Crowley. June 27, 2006.

CHRIS AND ADELMO. By Mike Wills. August 24, 2006. Directed by Mr. Wills; music direction, Bruce Staysna. With Christopher Cain, Adelmo Guidarelli.

ASYLUM: THE STRANGE CASE OF MARY LINCOLN. Musical with book by June Bingham; music and lyrics by Carmel Owen. September 14, 2006. Directed by Fabrizio Melano; scenery, James Morgan; costumes, Terese Wadden; lighting, Chris Robinson; music direction and arrangements, Bob Goldstone; stage manager, Scott Dela Cruz. With Bertilla Baker, Edwin Cahill, Ansel Elgort, John Jellison, Joy Lynn Matthews, Carolann Page, Daniel Spiotta.

MUSICALS IN MUFTI. October 13–29, 2006.

TAKE ME ALONG. Musical with book by Joseph Stein and Robert Russell; music and lyrics by Bob Merrill; based on the play *Ah, Wilderness!* by Eugene O'Neill. October 13, 2006.

Directed by Michael Montel. With Susan Bigelow, Melissa Bohon, Ken Cavett, Matthew Crowle, Ryan Driscoll, Jay Aubrey Jones, Jacob Levy, Lorinda Lisitza, Robyne Parrish, Andrew Rasmussen, David Schramm, Deborah Jean Templin, Nick Wyman.

CARMELINA. Musical with book by Alan Jay Lerner and Joseph Stein; music by Burton Lane; lyrics by Mr. Lerner; additional lyrics by Barry Herman; based on the film *Buona Sera, Mrs. Campbell* by Melvin Frank, Sheldon Keller and Dennis Norden. October 20, 2006. Directed by Michael Leeds. With Marla Schaffel, Nat Chandler, Joseph Kolinski, Daniel Marcus, Camille Saviola, Alison Walla, Ray Wills, Eli Zoller.

PLAIN AND FANCY. Musical with book by Joseph Stein and Will Glickman; music by Albert Hague; lyrics by Arnold B. Horwitt. October 27, 2006. Directed by David Glenn Armstrong. With Nancy Anderson, Ward Billeisen, Sara DeLaney, Erick Devine, Rick Hilsabeck, Cady Huffman, Beth Kirkpatrick, Adam Laird, Jordan Leeds, Jack Noseworthy, Charlotte Rae, Dan Sharkey, Jim Sorenson.

BLIND LEMON BLUES. Musical by Alan Governar and Akin Babatunde. February 15, 2007. Directed and choreographed by Mr. Babatunde; scenery, Russell Parkman; costumes, Tommy Bourgeois; lighting, Steve Woods. With Benita Arterberry, Mr. Babatunde, Timothy Parham, Sam Swank, Lillias White, Cavin Yarborough, Alisa Peoples Yarbrough.

MISCELLANEOUS

ABINGDON THEATRE COMPANY. *Elvis and Juliet* by Mary Willard. June 2, 2006. Directed by Yvonne Conybeare; with Bridget Clark, Lori Gardner, Warren Kelley, Haskell King, Christy McIntosh, Carole Monferdini, Pamela Paul, David Rasche, Justin Schultz, Fred Willard. *Cherish* by Ken Duncum. June 8, 2006. Directed by June Stein; with Rebecca Challis, Jeffrey Danneman, Jessica Lions, Alvaro Sena. *Krankenhaus Blues* by Sam Forman. October 8, 2006. Directed by Donna Mitchell; with Christine Bruno, Angela DeMatteo, Bill Green, Joe Sims. *My Deah* by John Epperson. October 25, 2006. Directed by Mark Waldrop; with Peter Brouwer, Lori Gardner, Michael Hunsaker, Geoffrey Molloy, Nancy Opel, Jay Rogers, Kevin Townley. *The Frugal Repast* by Ron Hirsen. February 7, 2007. Directed by Joe Grifasi; with Julie Boyd, Roberto DeFelice, Kyrian Friedenberg, Frank Liotti, Dawn Luebbe, Lizbeth MacKay, Kathleen McElfresh, Harold Todd, David Wohl. *Straight to Hell* by Stephen Stahl. March 14, 2007. Directed by Mr. Stahl; with John Dalmon, David Goldshteyn, Jules Hartley, Annette Hillary, Paul Hufker, Patrick Knighton, Carolin Haydée López. *Dreams of Friendly Aliens* by Daniel Damiano. March 18, 2007. Directed by Kim T. Sharp; with Gene Gallerano, Maureen Griffin, Brandon Jones, Lenore Loveman, Jamie Ward. *The President and Her Mistress* by Jan Buttram. April 13, 2007. Directed by Rob Urbinati; with Jeremy Beck, Constance Boardman, Ms. Buttram, Lori Gardner, Susanna Guzman, Sherry Skinker, Danton Stone.

THE ACTORS COMPANY THEATRE (TACT). *Home* by David Storey. December 7, 2006. Directed by Scott Alan Evans; with Cynthia Darlow, Cynthia Harris, Simon Jones, Larry Keith, Ron McClary. *The Sea* by Edward Bond. April 21, 2007. Directed by Scott Alan Evans; with Jamie Bennett, Lauren Bloom, Nora Chester, Ruth Eglsaer, Richard Ferrone, Rachel Fowler, Delphi Harrington, Timothy McCracken, Christopher McCutchen, Greg McFadden, Allen Read, Gregory Salata, Caroline Tamas.

THE ACTORS TEMPLE THEATRE. *The Big Voice: God or Merman?* by Jim Brochu and Steve Schalchlin. November 30, 2006. Directed by Anthony Barnao; with Messrs. Brochu, Schalchlin. *The J.A.P. Show* by Cory Kahaney. April 4, 2007. Directed by Dan Fields; with Jackie Hoffman, Ms. Kahaney, Jessica Kirson, Cathy Ladman.

ALTERED STAGES. *The Porch* By Kari Floren. June 4, 2006. Directed by Michael Berry; with Don Harvey, Lauren Mufson, Javier Munoz, Shirley Roeca. *The View From K Street Steak* by Walt Stepp. April 12, 2007. Directed by Tom Herman; with Rachel Darden Bennett, Kwaku Driskell, Bill Green, Christopher Hurt, Brian Patrick Mooney, Bill Tatum, Brad Thomason, Samantha Wynn. *Mommies' Boys* by Jack Dowd. May 9, 2007. Directed by John Capo; with Carol Brooks, Ryan Coyle, Jason Gotay, Jordan Kaplan, Andrea Marshall-Money, Diana Prano. *North of Providence* by Edward Allan Baker. May 24, 2007. Directed by Glory Sims Bowen; with Chad Meador, Yvonne Roen.

AMAS MUSICAL THEATRE. *Magpie.* Musical with book by Steven M. Jacobson; music by Gary William Friedman; lyrics by Edward Gallardo. March 9, 2007. Directed by Rajendra Ramoon Maharaj; with J. Cameron Barnett, Kimberly Reid Dunbar, Jessica Fields, Jene Hernandez, Dennis Holland, Gary Lindemann, Joseph Melendez, Ronny Mercedes, Michael Murnoch, Julian Rebolledo, Natalie Toro.

AMERICAN THEATRE OF ACTORS. *Miles to Babylon* by Ann Harson. October 12, 2006. Directed by Tom Thornton; with Angela Della Ventura, Denise Fiore, Karen Gibson, James Nugent, Rachel Schwartz. *The Maids* by Jean Genet. July 26, 2006. Directed by Laura Parker; with Jessica Hester, Lisette Hazan, Amy Matthews. *Side Show.* Musical with book by Bill Russell; music by Henry Krieger; lyrics by Mr. Russell. August 31, 2006. Directed by Ryan Mekenian; with Dane Agostinis, Kevin Bradley Jr., Nathan Brisby, Jordan Kai Burnett, Josh Isaacs, Carey McCray. *The Mammy Project* by Michelle Matlock. January 16, 2007. Directed by Amy Gordon; with Ms. Matlock. *Silence* by Moira Buffini. January 16, 2007. Directed by Suzanne Agins; with Helen Piper Coxe, Greg Hildreth, Kelly Hutchinson, Chris Kipiniak, Joe Plummer, Makela Spielman. *Girl* by Megan Mostyn-Brown. February 11, 2007. Directed by Josh Hecht; with Susan Hunt, Florencia Lozano, Rachel Mewbron, Thom Rivera, Maggie Siff. *The Naked Eye Planets* by Rebecca Tourino. March 9, 2007. Directed by Magdalena Zira; with Maria Cellario, Brandon Collinsworth, Glenn Kalison, Jeanne LaSala, Quinn Mander, Emily Rogge, Amanda Sayle, Sean Tarrant, Heidi Tokheim, Diane Tyler. *Let's Speak Tango* by Carlo Magaletti. April 20, 2007. Directed by Mr. Magaletti; with Diego Blanco, Hernan Brizuela, Heather Gehring, Miwa Kaneko, Katja Lechthaler, Fausto Lombardi, Mr. Magaletti, Ana Padron, Walter Perez, Valeria Solomonoff.

ARCLIGHT. *Jitter* by Richard Sheinmel. June 15, 2006. Directed by Clyde Baldo; with Dan Almekinder, Camille Burford, Zach McCoy, Colette McGuire, Sara Van Beckum. *Machiavelli* by Richard Vetere. September 24, 2006. Directed by Evan Bergman; with Jason Howard, Stephanie Janssen, Chip Phillips, Liza Vann, James Wetzel, Lex Woutas. *The Germans in Paris* by Jonathan Leaf. January 8, 2008. Directed by James Milton; with Angelica Torn, Bruce Barton, Ross Beschler, Alexander Bilu, Jon Krupp, Kathryn Elisabeth Lawson, David Lamberton, Brian Wallace, Claire Winters. *Uncle* by Dean Gray. February 10, 2007. Directed by Wayne Maugans; with Richard Bowden, James Heatherly, Darren Lougée, Nancy McDoniel, Brian Patacca. *La Magnani* by Theresa Gambacorta. March 29, 2007. Directed by Elizabeth Kemp; with Ms. Gambacorta.

ATLANTIC STAGE 2. *Facing East* by Carol Lynn Pearson. May 29, 2007. Directed by Jerry Rapier; with Charles Lynn Frost, Jayne Luke, Jay Perry.

AXIS THEATRE COMPANY. *Levittown* by Marc Palmieri. June 26, 2006. Directed by George Demas; with Brian Barnhart, Joe Fuer, Michael Laurence, Margo Passalaqua, Cecelia Riddett, Ian Tooley, Joe Viviani. *Hospital 2006* by Axis Theatre Company. September 29, 2006. Directed by Randy Sharp; with Paul Marc Barnes, Brian Barnhart, David Crabb, George Demas, Joe Fuer, Laurie Kilmartin, Lynn Mancinelli, Sue Ann Molinell, Matt Neely, Edgar Oliver, Marc Palmieri, Margo Passalaqua, Tom Pennacchini, Randy Spence, Jim Sterling, Ian Tooley. *Seven in One Blow, Or The Brave Little Kid* by Randy Sharp. December 1, 2006. Directed by Mr. Sharp; with Brian Barnhart, David Crabb, George Demas, Deborah Harry, Kate Hettesheimer, Laurie Kilmartin, Sue Ann Molinell, Edgar Oliver, Marc Palmieri, Margo Passalaqua, Jim Sterling. *Confidence, Women!* by Robert Cucuzza. March 1, 2007. Directed by Mr. Cucuzza; with Kelsey Bacon, Regina Betancourt, Ella Bole, Britt Genelin, Gina Guarnieri, Hagar Moor, Kelly Sharp.

BANK STREET THEATRE. *The Architect of Destiny* by Michael Gianakos. June 1, 2006. Directed by Luke Hancock; with Mr. Gianakos, Martha Cary, Mr. Hancock, Joe Lattanzi, Jamie Milward, Greg Wands. *Nickel and Dimed* by Joan Holden; based on *Nickel and Dimed, on (Not) Getting By in America* by Barbara Ehrenreich. October 5, 2006. Directed by Dave Dalton; with Dorothy Abrahams, Margot Avery, Suzanne Barbetta, Jeremy Beck, Kathleen Bishop, Elizabeth Bunnell, Cherelle Cargill, Richard Ferrone, Annie McGovern, Chelsea Silverman, Nancy Wu. *Neglect* by Sharyn Rothstein. October 5, 2006. Directed by Catherine Ward. *Count Down* by Dominique Cieri. November 8, 2006. Directed by Elyse Knight; with Valerie Blazek, Sandi Carroll, Reina Cedeno, Major Dodge, Megan Ferguson, Kasey Lockwood, Shawand McKenzie, Adepero Oduye, Dania Ramos. *Arrivals* by David Gow. February 8, 2007. Directed by Dan Wackerman; with D. Michael Berkowitz, Michael Gabriel Goodfriend, Susan Jeffries, Laurence Lau, Lanie MacEwan, Sal Mistretta, Brigitte Viellieu-Davis.

THE BARROW GROUP (TBG). *The Legend of Pearl Hart*. Musical with book and lyrics by Cathy Chamberlain; music by Rich Look. June 9, 2006. Directed by Lea Orth; with Michael Shane Ellis, Laurie Gamache, Catherine Hesse, Keith Krutchkoff, Trip Plymale, George Riddle, Dax Valdes. *'night Mother* by Marsha Norman. July 6, 2006. Directed by Shannon Patterson; with Lucy Avery Brooke, Amy Loughead. *Chekhov and Maria* by Jovanka Bach. July 7, 2006. Directed by John Stark; with Ron Bottitta and Gillian Brashear. *Evensong* by Mary Gage. August 11, 2006. Directed by Lewis Magruder; with Mary Ellen Ashley, Arthur French, Sarah Lambert, Pat Nesbit, Lucille Patton. *The Timekeepers* by Dan Clancy. October 18, 2006. Directed by Lee Brock; with Seth Barrish, Chris Cantwell, Eric Paeper. *Makeout Session* by Kenan Minkoff. October 20, 2006. Directed by Matt Cowart; with Andrew Pastides, Adrian Wyatt. *Glass Jaw* by Jane Shepard. December 1, 2006. Directed by Donna Jean Fogel; with Ms. Shepard. *Scituate* by Martin Casella. March 23, 2007. Directed by David Hilder; with Holly Barron, Constance Boardman, Damian Buzzerio, Curran Connor, Missy Hargraves, Chad Hoeppner, Laurence Lau, Matthew Mabe, Stefanie Zadravec. *Signs of Life* by Deborah Brevoort. May 4, 2007. Directed by Donald Kimmel; with Marcia DeBonis, Dan da Silva. *Myth America* by Stephen Wargo. April 14, 2007. Directed by Nicholas Cotz and Adam Fitzgerald; with Frank Anderson, Sean-Michael Bowles, Darian Dauchan, Vivia Font, Rich Fromm, Ann Hu, Ken Maharaj, Rob Maitner, Margo Brooke Pellmar, Lori Prince, James Saito. *A Kiss From Alexander*. Musical with book and lyrics by Stephan De Ghelder, music by Brad Simmons. May 26, 2007. Directed by DJ Salisbury; with Gavin Esham, Jeremiah James, Charles Logan, Matthew Marks, Eddie Rabon, Craig Ramsey, Brendt Reil, "Knuckles" Simmons, Jamison Stern, Justin Wilcox.

BOOMERANG THEATRE COMPANY. *Anna Christie* by Eugene O'Neill. September 7, 2006. Directed by Cailin Heffernan; with Steven M. Bari, Dunsten J. Cormack, Jennifer Larkin, Linda S. Nelson, Aidan Redmond, Christopher Yeatts. *Love in the Insecurity Zone* by Mike Folie. September 9, 2006. Directed by Rachel Wood; with Trevor Davis, Jodi Dick, Catherine Dowling, John C. Fitzmaurice, Justin R.G. Holcomb, Alisha R. Spielmann. *The Ugly Man* by Brad Fraser. September 14, 2006. Directed by Christopher Thomasson; with Paul Caiola, Bret Jaspers, Jennifer Lyn Sullivan, Jaime West, Joe Whelski. *Fenway: Last of the Bohemians* by Kelly McAllister and Lisa Margaret Holub. November 3, 2006. Directed by Tim Errickson; with Carrie Brewer, Reyna de Courcy, Margaret A. Flanagan, Jack Halpin, James David Jackson, Tom Knutson, Paul Navarra.

BRICK THEATRE. SELLOUT FESTIVAL. June 3–July 2, 2006. Schedule included: *Bad Girls Good Writers* by Sibyl Kempson. Directed by Shoshone Currier. *Bonbons for Breakfast* by Lisa Ferber. Directed by Ivanna Cullinan. *Greed: A Musical Love Story* by Robert Honeywell, Whitney Gardner and Meighan Stoopers. Directed by Mr. Honeywell. *The Impotent General* by Gary Winter. Directed by Meredith McDonough. *The Kung Fu Importance of Being Earnest* by Timothy Haskell; adapted by Michael Gardner. Directed by Mr. Gardner. *The Nigerian Spam Scam Scam* by Dean Cameron. Directed by Paul Provenza; with Mr. Cameron, Victor Isaac. *Stars in Her Eyes* by Clay McLeod Chapman. Directed by Moritz von Stuelpnagel. *That's What We're Here for* by Ian W. Hill. Directed by Mr. Hill. *Men of Steel* by Qui Nguyen. October 17, 2006. Directed by Robert Ross Parker. *Strom Thurmond Is Not A Racist* and *Cleansed* by Thomas Bradshaw. February 8, 2007. Directed by Jose Zayas.

CAP 21 THEATER. *The Classics Professor* by John Pielmeier. June 1, 2006. Directed by Clayton Phillips; with Elaine Anderson, Peggy Cosgrave, Bram Heidinger, Steve Liebman, Christina Morrell, Mr. Pielmeier. Barbara Wolff Monday Night Reading Series. October 16–November 20, 2006. *My Bernhardt Summer* by Mark St. Germain. Directed by Steve Ramshur; with Joanna Merline, Eliza Ventura. *Little Heart* by Irene O'Garden. Directed by Lisa Rothe; with Rebecca DuMaine. *Carousel*. Musical with book and lyrics by Oscar Hammerstein II; music by Richard Rodgers. Directed by Paul Johnson; with Larry Arancio, Randy Blair, Maria Brinkman, Susan Cameron, Nick Cianfrogna, Holly Davis, Peter Van Derek, Robbie Eicher, J. Austin Eyer, Mary Kate Law, Carey McCray, Michael Miller, Ryan Murray, Chris Norwood, Kiera O'Neil, Jonathan Todd Ross, Martha Sullivan. DOROTHY STRELSIN NEW WORKS MONDAY NIGHT READING SERIES. February 12–April 2, 2007. *The Cosmopolitan* by Lance Horne, Lorin Latarro and Josh Rhodes. Directed by Peter Flynn; with Rick Hilsabeck, Karen Mason, Sal Viviano. *Upfronts and Personal* by Ken Levine. Directed by Janet Brenner. *A Womb With a View* by Debra Barsha. *Cabaret*. Musical with book by Joe Masteroff; music by John Kander; lyrics by Fred Ebb. February 15, 2007. Directed by Aimée Francis. BARBARA WOLFF MONDAY NIGHT READING SERIES. February 26–March 26, 2007. *South Pacific*. Musical with book by Oscar Hammerstein II and Joshua Logan; music by Richard Rodgers; lyrics by Mr. Hammerstein; adapted by Eliza Ventura.

CASTILLO THEATRE. *Outing Wittgenstein* by Fred Newman. October 20, 2006. Directed by Dan Friedman; with James Arden, Natasha Danielian, Drummond Doroski, Athena Freedlander, Emily Gerstell, Luis Gomez, Daniel Gurian, Kenneth Hughes, Paul C. Newport, Michael Padilla, Gary Patent, Morgan Scott, Christine Tracy-Garrison, Serge Velez.

CENTER STAGE, NY. *The Dirty Talk* by Michael Puzzo. January 11, 2007. Directed by Padraic Lillis; with Kevin Cristaldi, Sidney Williams. *Not Waving* by Ellen Melaver. March 26, 2007. Directed by Douglas Mercer; with Heidi Armbuster, Josh Barrett, Eleanor Handley, Greg Keller, Kristine Nielsen, Tim Spears. *An Octopus Love Story* by Delaney Britt Brewer. May 2, 2007. Directed by Mike Klar; with Michael Cyril Creighton, Andrew Dawson, Jenny Greer, Kelli Holsopple, Eric Kuehnemann, Krista Sutton, Josh Tyson.

CHASHAMA. *Miss Julie* by August Strindberg. September 7, 2006. Directed by Tara Matkosky; with Sandi Carroll, Louis Ozawa Changchien, Elizabeth Lee Malone. *To Be Loved* by Alex DeFazio. November 30, 2006. Directed by Jody P. Person; with Bobby Abid, Albert Aeed, Kelly Markus, Brady Niederer, Jesse Soursourian, Elizabeth Sugarman, Brian Sufalko. *Mr. A's Amazing Maze Plays* by Alan Ayckbourn. May 25, 2007. Directed by Carlton Ward; with Charley Layton, Madeleine Maby, Sara Montgomery, Elizabeth Neptune, Ben Wood.

CHERRY LANE THEATRE. *Drug Buddy* by David Folwell. September 30, 2006. Directed by Alex Kilgore; with Jesse Hooker, Carrie Shaltz, Jake M. Smith, Matthew Stadelmann. *Bhutan* by Daisy Foote. October 29, 2006. Directed by Evan Yionoulis; with Tasha Lawrence, Sarah Lord, Amy Redford, Jedadiah Schultz. *Dutchman* by Amiri Baraka. January 16, 2007. Directed by Bill Duke; with Dulé Hill and Jennifer Mudge. *Fugue* by Lee Thuna. March 13, 2007. Directed by Judith Ivey; with Charlotte Booker, Ari Butler, Lily Corvo, Liam Craig, Deirdre O'Connell, Danielle Skraastad, Rick Stear, Catherine Wolf. *The Memory of Water* by Shelagh Stephenson. May 17, 2007. Directed by Ellen Lichtensteiger; with Victoria Bundonis, Zoe Frazer, Borden Hallowes, Abby Overton, Todd Reichart, Karen Sternberg. MENTOR PROJECT 2007. March 20–May 12, 2007. *100 Saints You Should Know* by Kate Fodor (Jules Feiffer, mentor). *The Secret Agenda of Trees* by Colin McKenna (Lynn Nottage, mentor). *Topsy Turvy Mouse* by Peter Gil-Sheridan (Michael Weller, mentor). *Training Wisteria* by Molly Smith Metzler (Jules Feiffer, mentor).

CLASSICAL THEATRE OF HARLEM. *Waiting for Godot* by Samuel Beckett. June 1, 2006. Directed by Christopher McElroen; with Billy Eugene Jones, J. Kyle Manzay, Chris McKinney, Wendell Pierce, Tanner Rich. *King Lear* by William Shakespeare. September 29, 2006. Directed by Alfred Preisser; with Duane Allen, Jerome Preston Bates, Jaime Carrillo, Noshir Dalal, André De Shields, George C. Hosmer, Zainab Jah, Ty Jones, Shayshahn MacPherson, Sean Patrick Reilly, Christina Sajous, Ken Schatz, Alex Sovronsky, John Douglas Thompson, Robyn Landiss Walker. *Marat/Sade* by Peter Weiss. February 2, 2007. Directed by Christopher McElroen; with Danny Camiel, Andrew Guilarte, Nathan Hinton, Thomas Layman, John Andrew Morrison, Jonathan Payne, Ron Simons, David Ryan Smith, T. Ryder Smith, Daniel Talbott, Eric Walton, Dana Watkins. *Electra* by Sophocles; adapted by Alfred Preisser. May 24, 2007. Directed by Mr. Preisser; with Samuel Ray Gates, Khadeejah Gray, Tracy Jack, Zainab Jah, Trisha Jeffrey, Sandra Miller, Petronia Paley, Christina Sajous.

CLEMENTE SOTO VELEZ CULTURAL CENTER (CSV). *The Metamorphosis* by Franz Kafka. September 15, 2006. Directed by Rene Migliaccio; with Eric Pettigrew, Jieun Lee, Juliette Morel. *The Trial* by Franz Kafka. September 24, 2006. Directed by Rene Migliaccio; with Yasser Akhtar, Brenda Cooney, Yvette Feuer, Steve Howe, John Maurice, Leah Rudick, Deven Sisler, Lori M. Vincent, Gabriel Williams. *King of Dominoes* by Bill Vargas. November 8, 2006. Directed by Michael J. Narvaez; with Michael Philip Del Rio, Jason Flores, Indio Melendez, Teresa Yenque. *All Fall Down* by David Ledoux and Allison Smith. December 3, 2006. Directed by Mr. Ledoux; with Samantha Anderson, Sal Bardo, Michael Bordwell, Kate Braden, Dave Collins, Candice Goodman, Vincent Ingrisano, Jesse Irwin, James Poling, Erin Leigh Schmoyer, Alley Scott, Julia Susman, Timothy Thurston, Jenna Weinberg.

CLUBBED THUMB. SUMMERWORKS 2006. June 4–24, 2006. Schedule included: *I Have Loved Strangers* by Anne Washburn. June 4, 2006. Directed by Johanna McKeon; with Jeff Biehl, Elliotte Crowell, Laura Flanagan, Jennifer R. Morris, Jay Smith, T. Ryder Smith, James Stanley. *Alice the*

Magnet by Erin Courtney. Directed by Pam MacKinnon; with Cohlie Brocato, Maria Dizzia, Sheri Graubert, Quentin Maré. *Quail* by Rachel Hoeffel. Directed by Kip Fagan; with Gerry Bamman, Zuleyma Guevara, Elizabeth Meriwether, Benjamin Pelteson, Everett Quinton.

COLLECTIVE: UNCONSCIOUS. *Turning Tables* by Michael Ferrell, Ishah Janssen-Faith, Jack McGowan, Hemmendy Nelson, Phil Vos. September 29, 2006. Directed by Gita Reddy; with Messrs. Ferrell, Janssen-Faith, McGowan, Nelson, Vos. *Exposed: Experiments in Love, Sex, Death and Art* by Annie Sprinkle and Elizabeth Stephens. April 26, 2007. Directed by Neon Weiss; with Mses. Sprinkle and Stephens.

CONNELLY THEATRE. *In the Matter of J. Robert Oppenheimer* by Heinar Kipphardt. June 7, 2006. Directed by Carl Forsman; with Dan Daily, Peter Davies, Matt Fischel, Wilbur Henry, Jonathan Hogan, DJ Mendel, Matthew Rauch, Steve Routman, Thomas J. Ryan, Rocco Sisto, Ian Stuart. *Angel Mountain* by John-Richard Thompson. July 6, 2006. Directed by Jessica Davis-Irons; with Arthur Aulisi, Danny Deferrari, Jessica Dickey, Rachel Peters, Abby Royle, Noah Trepanier. *Fools and Lovers* by Gregory Sherman and Gregory Wolfe. September 28, 2006. Directed by Mr. Wolfe; with Djola Branner, David DelGrosso, Kate Greer, Lynn Lobban, Rhonda S. Musak, David Pixley, Yvonne Roen, Jonathan Todd Ross, Emily Shoolin, James Wolfe. *All the Way Home* by Tad Mosel; based on the novel *A Death in the Family* by James Agee. November 5, 2006. Directed by Jack Cummings III; with Barbara Andres, Patrick Boll, John Braden, Alice Cannon, Corinne Edgerly, Chandler Frantz, Patrick Gilbert, Joseph Kolinski, Michael Lewis, Tom Ligon, Ben Masur, Joanna Parson, Monica Russell, Irma St. Paule, Letty Serra. *The Dark at the Top of the Stairs* by William Inge. March 30, 2007. Directed by Jack Cummings III; with Patrick Boll, Donna Lynne Champlin, Paul Iacano, Liz Mamana, Colby Minifie, Michele Pawk, Jay Potter, Jack Tartaglia, Matt Yeager.

THE CULTURE PROJECT. *Cloud Tectonics* by Jose Rivera. July 18, 2006. Directed by James Phillip Gates; with Frederique Nahmani, Julio Rivera, Luis Vega. *The Treatment* by Eve Ensler. September 12, 2006. Directed by Leigh Silverman; with Dylan McDermott, Portia. *Port Authority Throw Down* by Mike Batistick. October 26, 2006. Directed by Connie Grappo; with Edwin Lee Gibson, Annie McNamara, Debargo Sanyal, Aladdin Ullah. *Dai (Enough)* by Iris Bahr. January 14, 2007. Directed by Will Pomerantz; with Ms. Bahr. *My Trip to Al-Qaeda* by Lawrence Wright. March 1, 2007. Directed by Gregory Mosher; with Mr. Wright.

DR2. *Esoterica*. Solo performance piece by Eric Walton. September 19, 2006. Directed by Elysa Marden; with Mr. Walton. *BFF* by Anna Ziegler. February 24, 2007. Directed by Josh Hecht; with Sasha Eden, Laura Heisler, Jeremy Webb.

THE DUKE ON 42ND STREET. *The Bluest Eye* by Lydia Diamond; adapted from the novel by Toni Morrison. November 3, 2006. Directed by Hallie Gordon; with Alana Arenas, Victor J. Cole, Monifa M. Days, Noelle Hardy, James Vincent Meredith, TaRon Patton, Libya V. Pugh, Chavez Ravine.

EAST 13TH STREET THEATRE. *Arabian Night* by Roland Schimmelpfennig. June 12, 2006. Directed by Trip Cullman; with Roxanna Hope, Piter Marek, Brandon Miller, Stelio Savante, Jicky Schnee. *The Milliner* by Suzanne Glass. November 1, 2006. Directed by Mark Clements; with Michel Gill, Julia Haubner, Caralyn Kozlowski, Maria Cellario, Donna Davis, Steven Hauck, Glenn Kalison.

EMERGING ARTISTS THEATRE COMPANY. EATFEST 2006. October 31–November 19, 2006. Schedule included: *Can't You See We're Acting* by Carl L. Williams. Directed by Glenn Schudel; with Peter Byrne, Peter Levine, Hershey Miller, Jennifer Pawlitschek, Jacqueline Sydney. *Customer Disservice* by Gregg Pasternack. Directed by Kelly Haydon; with William Reinking, Amol Tripathi. *Five Minutes* by Allan Baker. Directed by Kevin Brofsky; with Brian Duguay, Hunter Gilmore, Brian Louis Hoffman, Scott Katzman, Sandra Mills Scott, Gameela Wright. *Fit for Love* by Rich Orloff. Directed by Christopher Maring; with Marc Castle, Brian Louis Hoffman, Allyson Morgan. *Forgetting to Remember* by Greg Kalleres. Directed by Ian Streicher; with Michael Cuomo, Greg Homison, Rebecca Hoodwin. *Help Thyself* by Greg Kalleres. Directed by Derek Jamison; with Matt Boethin, Glory Gallo. *Must the Show Go On?* by Carl L. Williams. Directed by Deb Guston; with Paul Adams, Tracee Chimo, Wayne Henry, Lee Kaplan. *Neverland* by Kim Kelly. Directed by Rebecca Nyahay; with Michael Batelli, Helen Green, Shannon Marie Kerr. *Our Lady of the Sea* by Aoise Stratford. Directed by Troy Miller; with Scott Klavan, Tim Seib, Matt Stapleton. *Recoil* by Karen Schiff. Directed by Jonathan Warman; with Ron Bopst, Blanche Cholet. *Room at the Inn* by Barbara Lindsay. Directed by Roberto Cambeiro; with Damon Boggess, Daniel Carlton, Karen Stanion. *Sick* by Bekah Brunstetter. Directed by Tzipora Kaplan; with Enid Cortes, Matthew A.J.

Gregory, William Jackson Harper, Stacy Mayer, Jeffrey Parrillo, Jess Phillips. *Triple Play* by Marc Castle. Directed by Carter Inskeep; with Erik Baker, Jeannie Dalton, Erin Hadley. *(mis)Understanding Mammy: The Hattie McDaniel Story* by Joan Ross Sorkin. February 10, 2007. Directed by David Glenn Armstrong; with Capathia Jenkins.

59E59 THEATERS. *Sisters* by Declan Hassett. September 17, 2006. Directed by Michael Scott; with Anna Manahan. *The Death in the Juniper Grove* by Le Wilhelm. August 19, 2006. Directed by Mr. Wilhelm; with Kristin Carter, Vito Cottone, Nancy McDoniel, Paul A. Nicosia, Jon Oak, Joanie Schumacher, Jaclyn Sokol. *Trousers* by David Parnell and Paul Meade. October 12, 2006. Directed by Mr. Meade; with Gary Gregg, Daniel Stewart. *The Cleric* by Tim Marks. October 25, 2006. Directed by Paula D'Alessandris; with Armand DesHarnais, Daniel Haughey, Sean Heeney, James Kloiber, Richard T. Lester. *The Sunset Limited* by Cormac McCarthy. October 29, 2996. Directed by Sheldon Patinkin; with Freeman Coffey, Austin Pendleton. ROMANIA, KISS ME! November 19–December 3, 2006. *Bus* by Cristian Panaite. Directed by Liesl Tommy. *Red Bull* by Vera Ion. Directed by Marcy Arlin. *Diagnosis* by Iona Moldovan. Directed by Tom Caruso. *Romania, Kiss Me!* by Bogdan Georgescu. Directed by Kaipo Schwab. *Fuck You, Eu.ro.Pa!* by Nicoleta Esinencu. Directed by Jackson Gay. *Our Children* by Cristian Panaite. Directed by Liesl Tommy. *Get Your War on* by Kirk Lynn and the Rude Mechanicals; adapted from the work of David Rees. January 11, 2007. Directed by Shawn Sides; with Ron Berry, Jason Liebrecht, Lana Lesley, Mr. Lynn, Sarah E. Richardson. *Gone* by Charles L. Mee. Febuary 2, 2007. Directed by Kenn Watt; with Jennifer Wright Cook, Pam Diem, Signe Harriday, Clark Huggins, Peter Richards. *The Attic* by Yoji Sakate; translated by Leon Ingulsrud and Keiko Tsuneda. February 21, 2007. Directed by Ari Edelson; with Michi Barall, Fiona Gallagher, Trey Lyford, Brandon Miller, Jesse J. Perez, Caesar Samayoa, Ed Vassallo. *Rearview Mirror* by Eric Winick. March 31, 2007. Directed by Carl Forsman; with Mark Alhadeff, Sarah Nina Hayon, Audrey Lynn Weston.

45TH STREET THEATRE. *The Happy Idea* by Adé Adémola. June 8, 2006. Directed by Shela Xoregos; with Marilyn Bernard, Lino Delcore, Lawrence Merritt, Stephanie Stone. *A First Class Man* by David Freeman. October 7, 2006. Directed by Kareem Fahmy; with Bobby Abid, Chriselle Almeida, Amir Arison, Kelly Eubanks, Steve French, Davis Hall, Timothy Roselle, Doug Simpson, Vikram Somaya, Radhika Vaz. *My Secret Garden* by Nancy Friday; adapted by Ms. Friday and Christopher Scott. February 14, 2007. Directed by Mr. Scott; with Jane Blass, McKenzie Frye, Lyn Philistine, Mimi Quillin. *The Waiting Room* by Samm-Art Williams. March 16, 2007. Directed by Charles Weldon; with Elain Graham, Ebony Jo-Ann, Ron Millkie, Ed Wheeler.

14TH STREET Y. *Nerve* by Adam Szymkowicz. June 12, 2006. Directed by Scott Ebersold; with Susan Louise O'Connor, Travis York. *Two Destinies* by Guile Branco. July 9, 2006. Directed by Emanuelle Villorini; with Mr. Branco, Robert Haufrecht. *Me, My Guitar and Don Henley* by Krista Vernoff. October 7, 2006. Directed by Peter Paige; with SuEllen Estey, Tara Franklin, Mary Elaine Monti, Stephanie Nasteff, Kaili Vernoff, Jennifer Dorr White. *Volume of Smoke* by Clay McLeod Chapman. March 22, 2007. Directed by Isaac Butler; with Katie Dietz, Abe Goldfarb, Daryl Lathon, Ronica Reddick, Brian Silliman, Molly Wright Stuart.

GENE FRANKEL THEATRE. *Heart's Desire* by Caryl Churchill. June 21, 2006. Directed by Max Seide; with Allison Abrams, Janice Bishop, Jay Horton, Mimi Jefferson, Cash Tilton. *Jesus Hector Christ* by Ian Schoen. June 21, 2006. Directed by Mr. Schoen; with Eric Brown, Brenda Cooney, Chris Norwood. *Pvt. Wars* by James McLure. January 25, 2007. Directed by Max Montel; with Ethan Baum, Jeffry Denman, Chapin Springer.

HARLEM REPERTORY THEATRE. *Dreamgirls.* Musical with book and lyrics by Tom Eyen; music by Henry Krieger. June 23, 2006. Directed and choreographed by Keith Lee Grant; with Alexandra Bernard, Christina Burnette, Natalia Peguero, Danhy Clermont, Isis Kenney, Danyel Fulton, Mabel Gomez, Jean-Pierre Barthelemy, Donovan Thompson, Jose Altidor, Nabil Vinas, Greer Samuels, Monica Delgado, Marcus Dargan, Alex Boucher, Dimitry, Nicholas Betito, Alfredo Millan, Yaritza Pizarro, Edward Corcino, Roderick Warner, Marcel Torres, Lynette Braxton. *Bye Bye Birdie.* Musical with book and lyrics by Michael Stewart; music by Charles Strouse and Lee Adams. August 4, 2006. Directed and choreographed by Keith Lee Grant; with Jose Altidor, Alexandra Bernard, Nicholas Betito, Barbara Blair, Alex Boucher, Lynette Braxton, Krissi Burnette, Danhy Clermont, Marcus Degan, Monica Delgado, Dimitry, Danyel Fulton, Mabel Gomez, Ashley Hatcher, Isis Kenney, Alfredo Millan, Heriberto Oquendo, Yaritza Pizarro, Greer Samuels, Pamela Tabb, Donovan Thompson, Marcel Torres, Nabil Vinas, Roderick Warner.

HERE ARTS CENTER. *Her Majesty the King* by Sarah Overman. June 12, 2006. Directed by Patrick McNulty; with Justin Adams, Mimi Cozzens, Antonia Fairchild, Michael Keyloun, Jason Kolotouros, Baylen Thomas. AMERICAN LIVING ROOM. July 28–August 30, 2006. Schedule included: *Between the Shadows* by Rania Khalil. Directed by Ms. Khalil; with Beth Phillips, Nellie Perrara, Jolyn Hope Arisman. *The Joy of Lex* by Alexia Vernon. Directed by Jon Stancato; with Ms. Vernon, Jon Campbell. *Mrs. Hodges Was Struck by a Meteorite* by Michael Bodel. With Mr. Bodel, Christopher Kaminstein, Lily Skove. *Songs of the Dragons Flying to Heaven* by Young Jean Lee. September 25, 2006. Directed by Ms. Lee; with Brian Bickerstaff, Juliana Frances, Haerry Kim, Jennifer Lim, Becky Yamamoto. *Heresy* by Sabina Berman; translated by Adam Versenyi. December 7, 2006. Directed by Marcy Arlin; with Manny Alfaro, Anitra Brooks, Bill Cohen, Daniel Damiano, Andrew Eisenman, Rahti Gorfien, Jim Himelsbach, Susan Hyon, Kathryn Kates, Mauricio Leyton, Aubrey Levy, Tony Naumovski, Jelena Stupljanin, Daniel Talbott, Morteza Tavakoli, Elizabeth West. *Progress* by Matel Visniec; translated by Joyce Nettles. December 7, 2006. Directed by Ian Morgan; with Manny Alfaro, Anitra Brooks, Bill Cohen, Daniel Damiano, Andrew Eisenman, Rahti Gorfien, Jim Himelsbach, Susan Hyon, Kathryn Kates, Mauricio Leyton, Aubrey Levy, Tony Naumovski, Jelena Stupljanin, Daniel Talbott, Morteza Tavakoli, Elizabeth West. *Orestes 2.0* by Charles L. Mee. March 29, 2007. Directed by Jose Zayas; with Julia Arazi, Joseph Carusone, Jessamyn Conrad, Neil Donahue, Barrett Doss, Paula Ehrenberg, Robert Fuller, Jessica Kaye, Daniel Manley, David Myers, Bobby Moreno, Hugh Sinclair, Peter Schuyler, DJ Thacker, Carleigh Welsh. *Giants* by Laura von Holt. April 9, 2007. Directed by Jen Wineman; with Lisa Barnes, Autumn Hurlbert, Evan Lubeck, Michael Markham.

HUDSON GUILD THEATRE. *Trouble in Paradise* by David Simpatico. June 20, 2006. Directed by Elyse Singer; with Carolyn Baeumler, Geoffrey Cantor, Cynthia Darlow, Nina Hellman. *Scenes From an Execution* by Howard Barker. May 25, 2007. Directed by Zander Teller; with Angela Jewell Arnold, Micah Freedman, Charles Hendricks, Elena McGhee, Matt McIver, Julia Beardsley O'Brien, Mick O'Brien, Christian Pedersen, Corey Tazmania.

IRISH ARTS CENTER. *The Gold Standard* by Daniel Roberts. June 3, 3006. Directed by Alex Lippard; with Alie Carey, Jordan Charney, Sabine Singh, Yasu Suzuki, Daniel Talbott.

KRAINE THEATER. *Food for Fish* by Adam Szymkowicz. July 8, 2006. Directed by Alexis Poledouris; with Katie Honaker, Anna Hopkins, Luis Moreno, Ana Luis Perera, Caroline Tamas, Orion Taraban. *The Boys* by Gordon Graham. September 8, 2006. Directed by Craig Baldwin; with Sarah-Jane Casey, Kimberly Cooper, Angela Ledgerwood, Nick Stevenson, Nico Evers-Swindell, Fiana Toibin, Jeremy Waters. *Dirty Girl* by Ronnie Koenig. January 6, 2007. Directed by Robert W. McMaster; with Corrie Beula, Bridget Harvey, Ms. Koenig, Michael Littner, Jesse Teeters. *Apocalypse Neo* by Rob Neill. February 2, 2007. Directed by Jacquelyn Landgraf; with Jorge Cordova, Ryan Good, Eevin Hartsough, Leslie Korein. *Your Face Is a Mess* by Marc Spitz. February 15, 2007. Directed by Carlo Vogel; with Camille Habacker, Ivan Martin.

LABYRINTH THEATER COMPANY. *Intringulis* by Carlo Alban. March 26, 2007. Directed by David Anzuelo; with Mr. Alban. *Pretty Chin Up* by Andrea Ciannavei. May 15, 2007. Directed by Michele Chivu; with Ms. Ciannavei, Bronwen Coleman, Cusi Cram, Salvatore Inzerillo, Trevor Long, Sidney Williams.

LARK PLAY DEVELOPMENT CENTER. PLAYWRIGHTS' WEEK 2006. September 13–18, 2006. *The Bridegroom of Blowing Rock* by Catherine Trieschmann. Directed by Victor Maog; with Jason Asprey, Jennifer Dundas, Adriana Gaviria, Deirdre O'Connell, Laura Heisler, John Douglas Thompson, Marty Zentz. *Hand, Foot, Arm and Face* by Mat Smart. Directed by Jeremy Cohen; with Francois Battiste, Alyssa Bresnahan, Susan Hunt, Ariel Shafir, Rutina Wesley. *Layla and Majnun* by Nastaran Ahmadi. Directed by Susanna Gellert; with Erin Buckley, Peter Macklin, Najla Said, David Sajadi. *Love Person* by Aditi Brennan Kapil. Directed by John Clinton Eisner; with Eileen Dulen, Alok Tewari, Alexandria Wailes, Jennifer Dorr White. *Neighbourhood Upside Down* by Nina Mitrovic. Directed by Michael Johnson-Chase; with Fred Burrell, Walter Brandes, Maggie Burke, William Franke, Erik Jensen, Robert Lavelle, Natasha Piletich, Nathan Ramos, Wayne Schroder, Jessica Warner. *Vaidehi* by Gautam Raja. Directed by Gia Forakis; with Purva Bedi, Rajesh Bose, Sean Krishnan, Debargo Sanyal. *Wild Men of the Woods* by Elisabeth Karlin. Directed by Sturgis Warner; with Rodney Gardiner, Jesse Hooker, Bryant Mason, Nancy Rodriquez, Anne Thibault. *Bucharest Calling* by Peca Stefan. November 2, 2006. Directed by Victor Maog. *Polaroid* by Jeroen Van Den Berg. November 16, 2006. Directed by John Clinton Eisner. THURSDAYS

AT THE LARK. Schedule included: *Yellow Face* by David Henry Hwang. November 30, 2006. *Danger of Bleeding Brown* by Enrique Ureuta. December 7, 2006. *Bengal Tiger at the Baghdad Zoo* by Rajiv Joseph. April 13, 2007. Directed by Giovanna Sardelli; with Hend Ayoub, Joseph Kamal, Ryan King, Tom Ligon, LeRoy McClain, Sharone Sayegh, Alok Tewari.

THE LIVING THEATRE. *The Brig* by Kenneth H. Brown. April 26, 2007. Directed by Judith Malina; with Johnson Anthony, Gene Ardor, Kesh Baggan, Steven Scot Bono, Brent Bradley, Brad Burgess, John Kohan, Albert Lamont, Jeff Nash, Bradford Rosenbloom, Jade Rothman, Isaac Scranton, Joshua Striker-Roberts, Morteza Tavakoli, Evan True, Antwan Ward, Louis Williams.

MANHATTAN REPERTORY THEATRE. FALL ONE-ACT PLAY FESTIVAL. September 28–October 14, 2006. Schedule included: *Always* by Angel Dillemuth. *Comfort* by Keith Glass. *Customer Service* by Marlene Rhein and Jennifer Ostrega. *Eating Mimi* by Liza Lentini. *Muse* by William Andrew Horn. *Wristbands* by Maureen McSherry. *Pinata* by Zach Messner. *Platonic* by Rudy Cecera. *Realer Than That* by Kitt Lavoie. *There's Always a Band* by Isaac Rathbone.

MANHATTAN THEATRE SOURCE. *Burn This* by Lanford Wilson. March 14. 2007. Directed by Laura Standley; with Kevin Connell, Anna Fitzwater, Michael Schantz, Victor Verhaeghe. *A Lie of the Mind* by Sam Shepard. April 4, 2007. Directed by Daryl Boling; with Todd D'Amour, Hank Davies, Campbell Echols, Cindy Keiter, Emily Mitchell, Ridley Parson, Laura Schwenninger, Jeff Wills. *A Coupla White Chicks Sitting Around Talking* by John Ford Noonan. May 9, 2007. Directed by Steven Bloom; with Monica Russell, Nancy Sirianni.

MA-YI THEATRE COMPANY. *The Romance of Magno Rubio* by Lonnie Carter. May 27, 2007. Directed by Loy Arcenas; with Arthur Acuña, Bernardo Bernardo, Jojo Gonzalez, Paolo Montalban, Ramon De Ocampo.

MCGINN/CAZALE THEATRE. *Getting Home* by Anton Dudley. June 14, 2006. Directed by David Schweizer; with Marcy Harriell, Brian Henderson, Manu Narayan. *Shinbone Alley*. Musical with book by Joe Darion and Mel Brooks; music by George Leinsinger; lyrics by Mr. Darion. November 7, 2007. Directed by Thomas Mills; with Kim Brownell, Erik McEwen, Thursday Farrar, Elena Gutierrez, Gene Jones, Trent Armand Kendall, Lisa Marie Morabito, Val Moranto, Kwame Michael Remy, Leajato Amara Robinson, Justin Sayre, Allyson Tucker, Lee Zarrett. *My New York*. Musical with book by Carla Jablonski; music and lyrics by Rick Hip-Flores. November 18, 2006. Directed by Linda Ames Key; with Barrett Doss, Sarah Levine, Paul Pino, Dilhya Ross, Dax Valdes, EJ Zimmerman. VITAL SIGNS. FESTIVAL OF NEW WORKS. November 30–December 17, 2006. Schedule included: *Antarctica* by Anton Dudley. *The Bloomingdale Road* by Mark Loewenstern. *Breaking Routine* by Robin Rothstein. *Bright Apple Crush* by Steven Yockey. *Crimes Against Humanity* by Ross Maxwell. *Discovering Columbus* by Kim Rosenstock. *Double Fantasy* by David Ben-Arie. *Five Wishes* by Thomas H. Diggs. *How I Won the War* by Andrea Lepcio. *It's Giuliani Time* by Aurin Squire. *The Remote* by Mark Harvey Levine. *Souvenirs* by Michael John Garcés. *The Country Wife* by William Wycherly. January 8, 2007. Directed by John Ficarra; with Maurice Edwards, Richard Haratine, Linda Jones, Dolores Kenan, Steve Kuhel, Janna Kefelas, Robert Lehrer, Brian Linden, Laura LeBleu, Kristin Price, Ray Rodriguez, Joan Slavin, Bridgette Shaw, Mike Yahn. *The Happy Time* by N. Richard Nash. March 6, 2007. Directed by Thomas Mills; with Larry Daggett, Annie Edgerton, David Geinosky, George S. Irving, Andy Jobe, Michael Masters, Lauren Mufson, Rachel Alexa Norman, Charly Seamon, Sarah Solie, Timothy Warmen, Michael Wolland. *The Game Boy* by Robin Rothstein. March 10, 2007. Directed by Mary Catherine Burke; with Julia Arazi, Kally Duling, Lance Marshall, Andy McKissick, Kristina Wilson, Tim Woods. *Irene*. Musical with book by Hugh Wheeler and Joseph Stein; music by Harry Tierney, Charles Gaynor and Otis Clements; lyrics by Joseph McCarthy, Messrs. Gaynor and Clements. April 17, 2007. Directed by Thomas Mills; with Richard Barth, Selby Brown, Marnie Buckner, Jacque Carnahan, Janet Carroll, Jody Cook, Kellie Drinkhahn, Jillian Louis, Michael Jennings Mahoney, Katherine McClain, Laura Pavell, Patrick Porter, Justin Sayre, Micah Sheppard, Jendi Tarde.

MEDICINE SHOW THEATRE. *All This Intimacy* by Rajiv Joseph. July 27, 2006. Directed by Giovanna Sardelli; with Gretchen Egolf, Adam Green, Amy Landecker, Kate Nowlin, Krysten Ritter, Thomas Sadoski. *Lemkin's House* by Catherine Filloux. September 17, 2006. Directed by Jean Randich; with John Daggett, Christopher Edwards, Laura Flanagan, Christopher McHale, Connie Winston. *Twenty Years of Agnes* by Juan Riquelme; translated by Camilo Fontecilla. September 29, 2006. Directed by Mr. Fontecilla; with Debra Kay Anderson, Jacquelyn Poplar, Atticus Rowe. *The Happiest*

Girl in the World. Musical with book and lyrics by E.Y. Harburg; music by Jacques Offenbach. November 26, 2006. Directed by Barbara Vann; with Ray Bendana, Rachel Black, Mark J. Dempsey, Sarah Engelke, Ilona Farkas, Mark Gering, Nique Haggerty, Amanda Hargrove, Mary Ellen Hickey, Cedric Jones, Samuel H. Perwin, Andrea Pinyan, Kip Potharas, Jonathan Roufaeal, Sven Salumaa, Sky Seals. *Horowitz: The Acrobat at Rest* by Stellios Manolakakis. February 9, 2007. Directed by Elias Kasman; with Mr. Manolakakis, Alyssa Simon. *The Balcony* by Jean Genet; translated by Barbara Vann. March 29, 2007. Directed by Ms. Vann; with Karen Amatrading, Sara Copeland, Mark J. Dempsey, Sean Dill, Ron Dreyer, Ilona Farkas, Mark Gering, Felix Gadron, Lauren LoGiudice, Louise Martin, Tassos Pappas, Charles J. Roy, Jose Ramon, Jonathan Roufaeal, Mr. Schmitz, Ms. Vann.

METROPOLITAN PLAYHOUSE. *The Octoroon* by Dion Boucicault. September 2, 2006. Directed by Alex Roe; with Arthur Acuña, Alia Chapman, Andrew Clateman, Lee Dobson, Mike Durkin, Sarah Hankins, Michael Hardart, David Lamb, Ray McDavitt, Wendy Merritt, John Rengstorff, Margaret Loesser Robinson, Justin Stevens, Alex Ubokudom, Tryphena Wade. *The Truth* by Clyde Fitch. November 18, 2006. Directed by Yvonne Conybeare; with Rene Becker, Shanara Gabrielle, Christy McIntosh, Evan Palazzo, Jeff Pucillo, Peter Reznikoff, Rob Skolits, Amy L. Smith. *André* by William Dunlap. March 2, 2007. Directed by Elfin Frederick Vogel; with Sebastian Conybeare, Lee Dobson, Kathleen Dobbs, Chris Harcum, Ron Johnson, Joseph C. Mirer, Shane Colt Jerome, Nicholas Richberg, Suzanne Savoy, Joseph Yeargain.

MIDTOWN INTERNATIONAL THEATRE FESTIVAL. July 17–August 6, 2006. Schedule included: *The Answer Is Horse* by Julia Holleman. Directed by Joya Scott; with Katie Naka, Elizabeth Days, Russell Feder, Cody Lindquist, Katie Naka, Albert Sanchez Jr. *LOL* by Tony Sportiello. Directed by Jerry Less; with CK Allen, Jean Tawfik Bookner, Kari Swenson Reilly, Michael Reilly, Greg Skura, Nicole Taylor, Debra Whitfield. *The Maternal Instinct* by Monica Bauer. Directed by Melissa J. Wentworth; with Rena Baskin, Stephen Cooper, Alisha Jansky, Elise Audrey Manning, Karen Woodward Massey. *Motion and Location* by Lorna Littleway. Directed by Sue Lawless; with Susan Froix, Tamara Green, Geany Masai. *Surgery* by Karin Diann Williams. Directed by Stuart Hynson Culpepper; with Debra Kay Anderson, David Crommett, David McDaniel, Melissa Miller, Katherine Puma, Laura L.C. Smith, Kira Sternbach, Joe Wachowski. *Where Three Roads Meet* by John Carter. Directed by Will Warren; with Morgan Baker, Emily Fink, Andrew Firda, Robb Hurst, Kathryn Merry, Elena McGhee, Curtis Neilsen. *Countdown* by Vincent Caruso. Directed by Jerry Mond; with Peter J. Coriaty, Angela Della Ventura, Allison Lane, John Leone, Jordana Oberman. *Props* by Michael Roderick. Directed by Moira K. Costigan; with Jennifer Boehm, Corey Haydu, Amy Lerner, Leigh Poulos, Ben Sumrall. *The Quiet Model* by L.A. Mitchell. Directed by Chelsea Miller; with Michelle Brown, Megan Ferguson, Marguerite French, Cary Hite, Sam Masotto, Chelsea Miller, Scott Price, Emily Tuckman. *Remuda* by William Donnelly. Directed by Tzipora Kaplan; with Luciana Magnoli, Chris Mazza, Bradley Wells. *Shoot the Dog* by Brittany Rostron. Directed by Dennis X. Tseng; with Garrett Lee Hendricks, Yashvinee Narechania, Matt Wise. *Sticky Girls: The Anti-Reality Show* by Linda Evans. Directed by Constance George; David Copeland, Robin Jones, Jennifer Loryn, Mark Mitchell, Sharon O'Connell. *The Wastes of Time* by Duncan Pflaster. Directed by David Gautschy; with Andrew Rothkin, Susan Barnes Walker, Jess Cassidy White. *Das Brat* by Eric Bland. Directed by Mr. Bland; with Noah Burger, Bibiane Choi, Scott Eckert, Cara Marsh Sheffler. *Fleeing Katrina* by Rob Florence. Directed by Mary Lee Kellerman; with David Wayne Britton, Corey Gibson, Deborah Johnstone, Ronnie Khalil, Heather Massie, Rudy Rasmussen. *In a Bucket of Blood* by John Kearns. Directed by Michael Mellamphy; with Patrick J. Barnett, Jamie Carroll, Gary Gregg, Mr. Mellamphy, John Skocik.

NATIONAL ASIAN AMERICAN THEATER COMPANY (NAATCO). *The Dispute* by Pierre Marivaux; translated by Neil Bartlett. August 8, 2006. Directed by Jean Randich; with Alexis Camins, Jennifer Chang, Claro de los Reyes, Mel Duane Gionson, Lanny Joon, Jennifer Ikeda, Mia Katigbak, Annabel LaLonde, Alfredo Narciso, Olivia Oguma.

NEW GEORGES. *Dead City* by Sheila Callaghan. June 1, 2006. Directed by Daniella Topol; with Shannon Burkett, Rebecca Hart, Dan Illian, April Matthis, Alfredo Narciso, Elizabeth Norment, Peter Rini. *Rainbow Skin* by Desi Moreno-Penson. March 22, 2007. Directed by Jose Zayas. *God's Ear* by Jenny Schwartz. May 7, 2007. Directed by Anne Kauffman; with Christina Kirk, Gibson Frazier, Judith Greentree, Raymond McAnally, Annie McNamara, Matthew Montelongo, Monique Vukovic.

NEW YORK INTERNATIONAL FRINGE FESTIVAL. August 11–27, 2006. Schedule included: *Absolute Flight: A Reality Show With Wings* by Barbara Blumenthal-Ehrlich. Directed by Rosemary Andress; with Keith Eric Chappelle, Cameron Hughes, Effie Johnson, Amy Landon, Garth T. Mark, Marishka Phillips, Jay Riedl. *Big Doolie* by Richard Thompson. Directed by Jenn Thompson; with Tim Artz, Todd Gearhart, James Hyland, Marty Futch, Jack Mungo, Evan Thompson, Peterson Townsend, Adina Verson, David Christopher Wells. *Blue Balls* by Michael Tester. Directed by Rye Mullis; with Alexandra Bosquet, C.J. Dion, Vincent Ortega III, Mr. Tester. *The Deepest Play Ever: The Catharsis of Pathos* by Geoffrey Decas; music and lyrics by Michael Wells. Directed by Ryan Purcell; with Mr. Decas, Boo Killebrew, Chinasa Ogbuagu, Christopher Ouellette, Phillip Taratula, TJ Witham. *The Fan Tan King.* Musical with book by C.Y. Lee; music by Douglas Lackey and Gene Kauer; lyrics by Hy Silver. Directed and choreographed by Tisa Chang; with Arthur Acuña, Sandia Ang, John Baray, Bonnie Black, Richard Chang, John Chou, Ming Lee. *Hermanas* by Monica Yudovich. Directed by Claudia Zelevansky; with Paolo Andino, Ryan Duncan, Adriana Gaviria, Kathryn Kates, Bridget Moloney, Denise Quiñones, Ms. Yudovich. *I Was Tom Cruise* by Alexander Poe. Directed by Mr. Poe and Joseph Varca; with Jeff Addiss, Gideon Banner, Jeff Berg, Teddy Bergman, Cormac Blueston, Natasha David, Colby Disarro, Amy Flanagan, Victoria Haynes, Laura Perloe. *The Infliction of Cruelty* by Andrew Unterberg and Sean McManus. Directed by Joel Froomkin; with Justin Barrett, Aimee DeShayes, Holter Graham, Elizabeth Van Meter, Pawel Szajda. *Light and Love* by S.P. Riordan. Directed by Mr. Riordan; with Dan Domingues, James Huffman, Jessica Ripton. *Moral Values: A Grand Farce or Me No Likey the Homo Touch-Touch* by Ian McWethy. Directed by Jeffrey Glaser; with Richardson Rob Jones, Josh La Casse, Roger Lirtsman, Carrie McCrossen, Maria McConville, Isaac Oliver, Graham Skipper. *Never Swim Alone* by Daniel MacIvor. Directed by Mr. MacIvor; with Craig Garcia, Tim O'Brien, John Pinckard. *Open House* by Ross Maxwell. Directed by Josh Hecht; with Bill Dawes, Cynthia Silver. *Perfect* by Tanya Klein. Directed by Ms. Klein; with Ali Baynes, Natasha Graf, Karen Green, Michael Jalbert, Mateo Moreno, Laurie Ann Orr. *Perfect Harmony* by Andrew Grosso. Directed by Mr. Grosso; with David Barlow, Jeff Binder, Autumn Dornfeld, Scott Janes, Maria Elena Ramirez, Jeanine Serralles, Marina Squerciati, Vayu O'Donnell, Margie Stokley, Noah Weinberg, Blake Whyte. *Permanent Whole Life* by Zayd Dohrn. Directed by Wesley Savick; with Ken Baltin, Stacy Fischer, Robert Kropf, Lisa Morse. *The Pool With Five Porches* by Peter Zablotsky. Directed by John Ahlers; with Kent Jackman, Scott Whitehurst. *Return of the Wayward Son* by Brian D. Fraley. Directed by Mr. Fraley; with Benna Douglas, John Fenzl, Max Ferguson, Scot Hamlin, Alex Haselbeck, Brandon Lappie, Howard Mears, Tim Moore, Andrew Said Thomas. *A Show of Force* by Donnie Mather. Directed by Leon Ingulsrud; with Mr. Mather. *Something More Pleasant: An Anti-Fairy Tale* by Joshua William Gelb. Directed by Brittany O'Neill; with Ashley Bell, Rusty Buehler, Craig Jorczak, James Malley, Ally Rachel, Steve Smith, Lindsay Wolf. *A Time to Be Born: A 1940s New York Musical* by Tajlei Levis; music by John Mercurio; based on the novel by Dawn Powell. Directed by Marlo Hunter; with Maria Couch, Christy Morton. *Walmartopia.* Musical with book by Catherine Capellaro; music and lyrics by Andrew Rohn. Directed by Ms. Capellaro; with Anna Jayne Marquardt.

NEW YORK MUSICAL THEATRE FESTIVAL. September 10–October 1, 2006. Schedule included: *Alive in the World* by Paul Scott Goodman. Directed by Kurt Deutsch; with Marcy Harriell, Aaron Lohr, Greg Naughton, Kelli O'Hara. *Behind the Limelight* by Christopher Curtis. Directed by Peter Unger; with Scott Barnhardt, Randy Blair, Luther Creek, Molly Curry, Sarah Darling, Michael J. Farina, Danny Hallowell, Tommy Hallowell, Joel Hurt Jones, Kristin Knutson, Garrett Long, Andrea McArdle, Janet Metz, Brooke Sunny Moriber, Sean Palmer, Rob Rokicki. *Desperate Measures.* Musical with book and lyrics by Peter Kellogg; music by David Friedman. Directed by Eleanor Reissa; with Merwin Foard, Patrick Garner, Ginifer King, Jenny Powers, Max Von Essen, Nick Wyman. *Emerald Man.* Musical with book and lyrics by Janet Cole Veldez; music by Marc Bosserman and Tom Valdez. Directed and choreographed by Josh Prince; with John Ashley Brown, LaDonna Burns, Christian Kaneko Carter, Sincee Daniels, Stephen Graybill, Elena Gutierrez, Jaygee Macapugay, Kathleen McCann, Jessie Novotny, Ben Rauch, Christian Whelan, Dashaun Young. *Flight of the Lawnchair Man.* Musical with book by Peter Ullian; music and lyrics by Robert Lindsey-Nassif. Directed by Lynne Taylor-Corbett; with Donna Lynne Champlin, Christopher Sutton. *Have a Nice Life.* Musical with book by Matthew Hurt and Conor Mitchell; music and lyrics by Mr. Mitchell. Directed by Pip Pickering; with Michael Berry, Michelle Blakely, Kevin Carolan, Charles Hagerty, Jacquelyn Piro, Emily Skinner, Nikki Snelson. *Hot and Sweet.* Musical with book, music and lyrics by Barbara Schottenfeld. Directed by Casey Hushion; with Anastasia Barzee, Amy Eschman, Liz Larsen, Stefanie Morse, Wendy Perelman. *Journey to the West.* Musical with book and lyrics by Robert Taylor and Richard Oberacker; music by Mr. Oberacker. With Angela Ai, Steven Booth, David Girolmo, Christine Hudman, Nicholas Kohn, Ann Burnette Mathews, Kevyn Morrow, AJ Ocampo, Philip Solomon, Shannon Stoeke, Daniel Therrien, W. Wong. *Kingdom.* Musical with book, music and lyrics by Ian Williams and Aaron Jafferis. Directed by Louis Moreno; with Marisa Echeverria, Michael Improta, Ronny Mercedes, Andres Munar, Flaco Navaja, Gio Perez, Gerardo Rodriguez. *The Night of the Hunter.* Musical with book and lyrics by Stephen Cole; music by Claibe Richardson. Directed by Matthew Ward; with Sy Adamowsky, Matt Bailey, Allison Fischer, Beth Fowler, Ellen Harvey, Lois Hart, Dee Hoty, Tina Johnson, Brian Noonan, Doug R. Paulson, Morgan Reilly, Michael Turay, Gerry Vichi, Gordon Weiss. *Party Come Here.* Musical with book by Daniel Goldfarb; music and lyrics by David Kirshenbaum. Directed by Will Frears; with Randy Aaron, Cathryn Basile, Kerry Butler, Fyvush Finkel, Hunter Foster, Kaitlin Hopkins, Katie Klaus, Terrence Mann, Karen Olivo. *River's End.* Musical with book and lyrics by Cheryl Coons; music by Chuck Larkin. Directed by Rick DesRochers; with Evan Casey, Colby Foytik, Dani Marcus, Phyllis Somerville, Tempe Thomas. *The Unauthorized Musicology of Ben Folds.* Musical revue with music and lyrics by Ben Folds. Directed by Jess McLeod; with Michael Arden, Stephen Bogardus, Kevin Cahoon, Manoel Felciano, Alison Fraser, John Gallagher Jr., Liz McCartney, Brendan Milburn, Kevyn Morrow, Anthony Rapp, Daphne Rubin-Vega, J. Robert Spencer, Valerie Vigoda, Michael Winther, Chip Zien. *Wallenberg.* Musical with book and lyrics by Laurence Holzman and Felicia Needleman; music by Benjamin Rosenbluth. Directed by Annette Jolles; with Lauren Adler, Darrel Blackburn, Heather Braverman, Andrea Burns, Maria Couch, Max Damashek, Nicole DeBace, Matthew Deming, George Dvorsky, Alice Evans, Kathryn Feeney, Colby Foytik, Alan Gillespie, Deborah Grausman, Gregory Lee Harrell, Dennis Holland, Michael Iannucci, A.J. Irvin, Tommy Labanaris, Lauren Lebowitz, Kristin McLaughlin, Robin Manning, Lauren Mufson, Laura Patinkin, Guy Paul, Trip Pettigrew, Tedman Rapp, Roger Rifkin, Staci Rudnitsky, James Sasser, Doug Shapiro, Gordon Stanley, Nick Verina, Thom Christopher Warren, Brent Watkins, Jennifer Zimmerman. *Warrior.* Musical with book, music and lyrics by Marcus Hummon. Directed by Michael Bush; with Sherrie Austin, Eric Bergen, Cole Burden, Aaron Capps, Trisha Jeffrey, Deven May, Erick Pinnick, Brian Charles Rooney, Maria Schaffel, Nancy Slusser, Louis Tucci.

OHIO THEATER. *Fizz* by Rogelio Martinez. September 17, 2006. Directed by Sam Gold; with Cheryl Lynn Bowers, Matt D'Amico, Sam Forman, Bryant Mason, Keira Naughton, Mary Rasmussen, Reginald Veneziano. THE IGNITE FESTIVAL. October 4–22, 2006. Schedule included: *Advice to Iraqi Women* by Martin Crimp. *Beautiful Radiant Things* by Jane Ray. *Clarisse and Larmon* by Deb Margolin. *The Club* by James Christy. *Displaced* by Isabelle Bruno. *The Doorman's Double Duty* by Robert Lyons. *The Drill* by Trish Harnetiaux. *The Elephant* by Henry Meyerson. *God and Country: A Vaudeville* by Clay McLeod Chapman. *Grand Marshal* by Clay McLeod Chapman. *Me and Shirley* by Henry Meyerson. *A Modest Adjustment* by Daniel Rebellato. *Stretch: A Fantasia* by Susan Bernfield. *The Sniper* by Yussef El Guindi. *Sounds of Silence* by Eliza Jane Schneider and Jon Daach. *Wabenzi* by Richard Bean. *The Dreamer Examines His Pillow* by John Patrick Shanley. November 30, 2006. Directed by Rusty Owen; with Joe Petcka, David Ditto Tawil, Eleni Tzimas. *As Yet Thou Art Young and Rash*; adapted from Euripides's *The Suppliant Women.* January 9, 2007. Directed by David Herskovits; with Satya Bhabha, Mia Katigbak, May Neufeld, Tina Shepard, Stephanie Weeks. *The Women of Trachis* by Sophocles; adapted by Kate E. Ryan. January 18, 2007. Directed by Alice Reagan; with Sara Buffamanti, Todd D'Amour, Birgit Huppuch, Joel Lin, Rebecca Lingafelter, Debargo Sanyal, Heidi Schreck, Indika Senanayake. *The Jaded Assassin* by Michael Voyer. February 8, 2007. Directed by Timothy Haskell; choreography, Rod Kintner; with Nick Arens, Laine D'Souza, Marius Hanford, Aaron Haskell, Jo-anne Lee, Maggie MacDonald, Judi Ockler, Jason Schumacher, Tony Tirado.

ONTOLOGICAL-HYSTERIC THEATRE. *Wake Up Mr. Sleepy! Your Unconscious Mind is Dead!* by Richard Foreman. January 25, 2007. Directed by Mr. Foreman; with Joel Israel, Chris Mirto, Stefanie Neukirch, Stephanie Silver, James Peterson.

PEARL THEATRE COMPANY. AMERICA: THE READING SERIES. June 26–September 11, 2006. Schedule included: *André* by William Dunlap. *The Octoroon* by Dion Boucicault. *Rip Van Winkle* as played by Joseph Jefferson. *The Great Divide* by William Vaughn Moody. *Home of the Brave* by Arthur Laurents. *Arms and the Man* by George Bernard Shaw. October 8, 2006. Directed by Gus Kaikkonen; with Richard Bolster, Rachel Botchan, Robin Leslie Brown, Bradford Cover, TJ Edwards, Dominic Cuskern, Noel Velez, Hana Moon. *School for Wives* by Molière; translated by Earle Edgerton. November 19, 2006. Directed by Shepard Sobel; with Rachel Botchan, Bradford Cover, Dominic

Cuskern, Dan Daily, TJ Edwards, Hana Moon, Noel Velez. *Toys in the Attic* by Lillian Hellman. January 14, 2007. Directed by Austin Pendleton; with Rachel Botchan, Robin Leslie Brown, Joanne Camp, Sean McNall, Robert Colston, RJ Foster, Jon Froehlich, Marcus Naylor, Ivy Vahanian, William White. *The Cave Dwellers* by William Saroyan. March 4, 2007. Directed by Shepard Sobel; with Francile Albright, Barthelemy Atsin, Collin Batten, Dominic Cuskern, RJ Foster, Robert Hock, Mahira Kakkar, Sarah Lemp, Sean McNall, Marcus Naylor, Carol Schultz.

PERRY STREET THEATRE. *Treason* by Sallie Bingham. June 15, 2006. Directed by Martin Platt; with Philip Pleasants, Jennifer Sternberg, Nicole Orth-Pallavicini, Damon Gupton, Rachel Fowler, Peter Van Wagner, Kathleen Early, David B. Heuvelman, Mary Bacon.

PETER JAY SHARP THEATER. *Single Black Female* by Lisa Thompson. June 17, 2006. Directed by Colman Domingo; with Soara-Joye Ross, Riddick Marie. *Asking For It* by Joanna Rush. July 10, 2006. Directed by Lynne Taylor-Corbett; with Ms. Rush.

PHOENIX THEATRE ENSEMBLE. *The Sneeze* by Michael Frayn; adapted from plays and stories by Anton Chekhov. *Two* by Jim Cartwright. October 14, 2006. Directed by John Giampetro. *Antigone* by Jean Anouilh. November 28, 2006. Directed by Eve Adamson. *The Lesson* by Eugene Ionesco. December 7, 2006. Directed by Amy Wagner; with Jennifer Curfman, Sarah Hartman, John Lenartz, Angela Madden, Laura Piquado, Craig Smith. *The Painting* by Eugene Ionesco. December 9, 2006. Directed by Kevin Confoy; with Jennifer Curfman, Sarah Hartman, John Lenartz, Angela Madden, Laura Piquado, Craig Smith. *On the Verge, or the Geography of Yearning* by Eric Overmyer. April 28, 2007. Directed by Karen Chase Cook; with Angela Madden, Elise Stone, Michael Surabian, Angela Vitale.

THE PLAYERS THEATRE. *Fate's Imagination* by Randall David Cook. May 31, 2006. Directed by Hayley Finn; with Donna Mitchell, Elizabeth Norment, Jed Orlemann.

PRODUCERS CLUB. *Beer for Breakfast* by Robert Scott Sullivan. June 21, 2006. Directed by Jenn Bornstein; with Meg Bartholomay, Nathan Bock, Justine Campbell-Elliot, Kenneth Hatlee, Topher Mikels, Richardo Maldonado, Tom Olori. *A Family's Play* by Shawn Luckey. July 13, 2006. Directed by Mr. Luckey; with Steve Jean-Baptiste, Sean Eddy, Mariah Freda, Gurlaine Jean-Mary, April Lisbeth, Mr. Luckey, Gwen Majette, Mark Thaddeus Mallek, Patrick Mitchell, Farah Snipes, Nia D. Spaulding, C. Truth, Dwight Ali Williams, McGregor Wright. *My Life as You* by Laura Rohrman. September 14, 2006. Directed by Fritz Brekeller; with Jeff Branson, Ashley Wren Collins, Stuart Lopoten, Kelli Porterfield. *Macdeath* by John Martin and Dudley Stone. October 11, 2006. Directed by Brian Nelson; with David Berent, Charles Karel, Ben Killberg, Ellen Mittenthal, Cyrus Newitt, Christine Rendel, Stephanie Stone. *Geology of the Mind* by Shahan Stepanian. September 22, 2006. Directed by Stacee Mandeville; with Josephine Cashman, Anne Connolly, Matt Scott, Robert Rivera, Stephanie Taylor, Maxwell Zener. *Men Are Dogs* by Joe Simonelli. October 26, 2006. Directed by Donna Stiles; with Carol Brooks, John Hill, Donna Jeanne, Tim Kelsey, Heather Lynn Milner, Rachel Marcus, Steph Van Vlack, Leslie Wheeler. *Snake in Fridge* by Brad Fraser. October 26, 2006. Directed by Blake Bradford; with Molly Church, Jim de Prophetis, Alicia Green, David Law, Charlie Mengine, Vallen Pilgrim, Peggy Queener, Ted Sangalis, Will Strong. *Unwrap Your Candy* by Doug Wright. October 26, 2006. Directed by Wayne Yeager; with Casey Duncan, Matthew Gologor, Richard Handy-Kroft, Jeffy Michaels, Lizzie Schwarz, Christine Vinh, Brandon Yeager. *Bridal Terrorism* by Bill Rosenfield. November 8, 2006. Directed by Bill Barry; with Mr. Barry, Val Balaj, Amy Boeding, Nina Capone, Lorraine Condos, Laurence Waltman. *The Madonna Whore: Confessons of a Dirty Mind* by Tim Douglas. November 29, 2006. Directed by Eric Thal; with Simcha Boranstein, Mr. Douglas, Laura Faulkner, Randy Jones, Leah Thomas, Larry Weeks. *Random Particles of Matter Floating in Space* by Michael Allen. April 11, 2007. Directed by Denyse Owens; with Jonathan Albert, Aaron Haskell, Elba Sette-Camara.

PROSPECT THEATER COMPANY. *Tock Tick*. Musical with book and lyrics by Tim Nevits; music by Gihieh Lee. February 3, 2007. Directed by Jackson Gay; with David Abeles, Maria Couch, David Foley Jr., Christopher Graves, Melissa Hart, Joshua Landay, Mark Mozingo, Robby Sharpe, Laura Beth Wells. *West Moon Street* by Rob Urbinati; based on "Lord Arthur Savile's Crime" by Oscar Wilde. April 21, 2007. Directed by Davis McCallum; with Michael Crane, Avi Glickstein, Jocelyn Greene, Judith Hawking, Melissa Miller, Glenn Peters, Alex Webb, David Ruffin.

RATTLESTICK PLAYWRIGHTS THEATER. *It Goes Without Saying* by Bill Bowers. September 7, 2006. Directed by Martha Banta; with Mr. Bowers. *Dark Matters* by Roberto Aquirre-Sacasa.

November 21, 2006. Directed by Trip Cullman; with Reed Birney, Justin Chatwin, Michael Cullen, Elizabeth Marvel. *Stay* by Lucy Thurber. March 15, 2006. Directed by Jackson Gay; with Jenny Maguire, Sam Rosen, Thomas Sadoski, Maggie Siff, Jess Weixler.

RED ROOM. *Kansas City or Along the Way* by Robert Attenweiler. October 5, 2006. Directed by Seth Duerr; with Becky Benhayon, Adam Groves. *The Turn of the Screw* by Jeffrey Hatcher; adapted from the novella by Henry James. October 27, 2006. Directed by Marc Silberschatz; with Erin Cunningham, Tim Scott. *Kill Me Like You Mean It* by Kiran Rikhye. January 5, 2007. Directed by Jon Stancato; with Tommy Dickie, Sam Dingman, Cameron J. Oro, Alexia Vernon, Liza Wade White.

RICHMOND SHEPARD THEATRE. *Moby Dick: Rehearsed* by Orson Welles. March 7, 2007. Directed by Marc Silberschatz; with Philip Bartolf, Justin Birdsong, Pauly Burke, Ned Cray, Seth Duerr, John Ivy, Shawn Renfro, Mickey Ryan, Tony Scheinman, Tim Scott, David Skigen.

SANFORD MEISNER THEATRE. *The Ledge* by Jack Hanley. December 1, 2006. Directed by Christopher Eaves; with Mike Houston. *The Bald Soprano* by Eugene Ionesco. May 10, 2007. Directed by Joe Benenati; with Teri Black, Michael Edmund, Phil Garfinkel, Martha Lopez Gilpin, Jay Aubrey Jones, Donna Lee Michaels. *The Lesson* by Eugene Ionesco. May 10, 2007. Directed by Christopher Bellis; with Michael Gilpin, Judy Jerome, Joan Valentina.

78TH STREET THEATRE LAB. *The Beginning of the and* by Daniel Roberts. September 5, 2006. Directed by Brian Ziv; with Will Brunson, Alie Carey, Davis Hall, John Kaisner, Kevin Perri, Romany Reagan, Arleigh Richards, Scott Sortman, Daniel Talbott. *Language of Angels* by Naomi Iizuka. October 12, 2006. Directed by Garrett Ayers; with Brian Frank, Erin Gorski, Joe Jung, Emily Moulton, Ben Rosenblatt, Jenny Schutzman, Sarah Stockton, Brit Whittle. *Two Rooms* by Lee Blessing. November 30, 2006. Directed by Melanie Moyer Williams; with Jennifer Lucas, David Mason, Emilie E. Miller, Brian Patacca. *Strings* by Carole Bugge. December 16, 2006. Directed by Marvin Kaye; with Mia Dillon, Keir Dullea, Drew Dix, Kurt Elftmann, Andrea Gallo, Warren Kelley. *Still Life* by Emily Mann. February 16, 2007. Directed by Ric Sechrest; with Heather E. Cunningham, Erik Potempa, Kristen Vaughan.

SOHO PLAYHOUSE. *A Stone Carver* by William Mastrosimone. July 27, 2006. Directed by Robert Kalfin; with Jim Iorio, Dan Lauria, Elizabeth Rossa. *Cherry's Patch* by Ron Scott Stevens. September 7, 2006. Directed by Richard Caliban; with Angelo Angrisani, Scott Griffith, John Mondin, Jim Moody, Joe Petcka, Drew Platner, Harvey Ross, Maren Uecker. *The Voyage of the Carcass* by Dan O'Brien. October 16, 2006. Directed by Randy Baruh; with Noah Bean, Dan Fogler, Kelly Hutchinson.

ST. ANN'S WAREHOUSE. *Hell House* by Les Freres Corbusier; text by Pastor Keenan Roberts. October 10, 2006. Directed by Alex Timbers; with Teddy Bergman, Jeff Biehl, David Flaherty, Pat Inglis, Julie Klausner, Julie Lake, Rob O'Hare, Wil Petre, Jared Reinmuth, Amanda Sayle, Katie Vagnino, Mike Walker. *Woyzeck* by Georg Buchner; adapted by Daniel Kramer. November 16, 2006. Directed by Mr. Kramer; choreographed by Ann Yee; with Myriam Acharki, Roger Evans, David Harewood, Edward Hogg. *Must Don't Whip 'Um* by Cynthia Hopkins; in collaboration with Jim Findlay and Jeff Sugg. January 17, 2007. With Steve Cuiffo, Aleta Claire Findlay, Jim Findlay, Ms. Hopkins, Susan Oetgen, Jony Perez, Scott Shepherd, James Sugg, Jeff Sugg, Gary Wilmes, Willow the Cat, Ben Holmes, Kristin Mueller, Reut Regev, Josh Stark, Philippa Thompson, Karen Waltuch.

STUDIO DANTE. *The Given* by Francine Volpe. October 21, 2006. Directed by Michael Imperioli and Zetna Fuentes; with Sharon Angela, Remy Auberjonois, Jason C. Brown, Elzbieta Czyzewska, Anthony De Sando, Laura Heisler. *Chicken* by Mike Batistick. February 28, 2007. Directed by Nick Sandow; with Sharon Angela, Raul Aranas, Quincy Tyler Bernstine, EJ Carroll, Michael Imperioli, Lazaro Perez.

THEATER BY THE BLIND (TBTB). *A Midsummer Night's Dream* by William Shakespeare. January 27, 2007. Directed by Ike Schambelan; with George Ashiotis, Jon Levenson, Ann Marie Morelli, Erin O'Leary, Andrew Rein, Nicholas Viselli.

THEATRE 54. *In Between the Sheets* by Ian McEwan; adapted by Seth Duerr. June 4, 2006. Directed by Mr. Duerr; with Mac Brydon, Martin Ewens, David Garry, Nicole Maggi, Paul Rubin, Timothy Smallwood, Kymberly Tuttle, Billy Wheelan, Paulette Williams. *Tales of the Lost Formicans* by Constance Congdon. March 28, 2007. Directed by Brett Maughan; with Celia Bressak, Rebecca

Challis, Jovinna Chan, Brian J. Coffey, Lindsay Goranson, Michael Hartney, Nico Phillips, Rien Schlecht, Dirk Smile, Russell Waldman. *The Sanitation Chronicles* by Paul Brno and Mary Humphrey Baldridge. April 18, 2007. Directed by Peter De Maio; with Richard Bey, Danny Cleary, Mr. De Maio, Christina George, Joe Albert Lima, Michael Locascio, Vivian Neuwirth, Aidan O'Shea, Bryan Pugh.

THEATRE ROW THEATRES. SUMMER PLAY FESTIVAL 2006. July 5–30, 2006. Schedule included: *The Butcherhouse Chronicles* by Michael P. Hidalgo. Directed by Thomas Caruso. *Father Joy* by Sheri Wilner. Directed by Pam MacKinnon. *The Fearless* by Elan Frankel. Directed by Scott Schwartz. *Gardening Leave* by Joanna Pinto. Directed by Michael Goldfried. *Hardball* by Victoria Stewart. Directed by Lou Jacob. *Hitting the Wall* by Barbara Blumenthal-Ehrlich. Directed by Drew Barr. *Marge* by Peter Morris. Directed by Alex Timbers. *Millicent Scowlworthy* by Rob Handel. Directed by Ken Rus Schmoll. *A Wive's Tale* by Christina Ham. Directed by Rosemary Andress. *Spain* by Jim Knable. Directed by Jeremy Dobrish. *Training Wisteria* by Molly Smith Metzler. Directed by Evan Cabnet. *Swansong* by Patrick Page. Directed by David Muse. *Sonia Flew* by Melinda Lopez. Directed by Justin Waldman. THE ACORN. *The Accomplices* by Bernard Weinraub. March 20, 2007. Directed by Ian Morgan; with Catherine Curtin, Jon DeVries, Robert Hogan, Zoe Lister-Jones, David Margulies, Andrew Polk, Daniel Sauli, Mark Zeisler, Mark Zimmerman. THE BECKETT. *Anais Nin: One of Her Lives* by Wendy Beckett. August 5, 2006. Directed by Ms. Beckett; with David Bishins, Angela Christian, Alysia Reiner, Rocco Sisto. *The Imaginary Invalid* by Molière. November 3, 2006. Directed by Rebecca Patterson; with Virginia Baeta, Amy Driesler, Valentina McKenzie, Gisele Richardson, Samarra, Carey Urban, Kari Washington. *The Mail Order Bride* by Charles L. Mee. November 4, 2006. Directed by Eric Parness; with John Henry Cox, Booth Daniels, Susan Ferrara, Vivia Font, Sue Jean Kim, Sam Kitchin, Peter McCain, Lori McNally, Melissa Miller, Susan Louise O'Connor. *Tall Grass* by Brian Harris. March 3, 2007. Directed by Nick Corley; with Mark H. Dold, Edward O'Blenis, Maria Schaffel. *Lipstick on a Pig* by Linda Evans. May 23, 2007. Directed by David Epstein; with Alexis Croucher, John Farrell, Dennis Hearn, Christa Kimlico Jones. THE CLURMAN. THE EQUALITY PLAY FESTIVAL. August 11–August 26, 2006. Schedule included: *Clean Living* by Robert Askins. Directed by Steven Ditmyer. *Cold Flesh* by Jorshinelle Taleon-Sonza. Directed by Adam Fitzgerald. *Veils* by Joe Byers. Directed by Gregory Simmons. *Onna Field* by Stuart Harris. Directed by Carlos Armesto. *Theophilus North* by Matthew Burnett; based on the work of Thornton Wilder. September 14, 2006. Directed by Carl Forsman; with Margaret Daly, Joe Delafield, Brian Hutchison, Virginia Kull, Giorgio Litt, Geddeth Smith, Regan Thompson. *Becoming Adele*. Solo performance piece by Eric Houston. December 20, 2006. Directed by Victor Maog; with Kimberly Stern. *The Vietnamization of New Jersey* by Christopher Durang. January 16, 2007. Directed by Robert Saxner; with Blanche Baker, Michael Cyril Creighton, Frank Deal, Susan Gross, James Duane Polk, Corey Sullivan, Nick Westrate. *Tea and Sympathy* by Robert Anderson. March 6, 2007. Directed by Jonathan Silverstein; with Heidi Armbruster, Dan McCabe, Dan Cordle, Randy Danson, Brandon Espinoza, Ben Hollandsworth, Jake Levy, Craig Mathers, Cal Robertson, Mark Setlock. *Beauty on the Vine* by Zak Berkman. May 2, 2007. Directed by David Schweizer; with Helen Piper Coxe, Barbara Garrick, Howard Overshown, Jessica Richardson, Victor Slezak, Olivia Wilde. THE KIRK. *Nami* by Chad Beckim. September 14, 2006. Directed by John Gould Rubin; with Quincy Tyler Bernstine, Michael J.X. Gladis, Eva Kaminsky, Mark Rosenthal, Alfredo Narciso. *The Great Conjurer* by Christine Simpson. October 25, 2006. Directed by Kevin Bartlett; with Michael Jerome Johnson, Roseanne Medina, Tzahi Moskovitz, Brian Nishii, Kelly Paredes, Andy Place, Sara Thigpen, Paula Wilson. *Lebensraum* by Israel Horovitz. December 17, 2006. Directed by Jonathan Rest; with Suli Holum, T. Ryder Smith, Ryan Young. *Blackout* by Michael I. Walker. January 11, 2007. Directed by Kira Simring; with Ryan Patrick Bachand, Teddy Bergman, Almeria Campbell, Kate Goehring, Kevin Mambo, Darnell Williams. *The Secret of Mme. Bonnard's Bath* by Israel Horovitz. February 8, 2007. Directed by Mr. Horovitz; with Michael Bakkensen, Stephanie Janssen, John Shea. *Widowers' Houses* by George Bernard Shaw; adapted by Ron Russell and Godfrey L. Simmons Jr. March 14, 2007. Directed by Mr. Russell; with Peter Jay Fernandez, Rachael Holmes, Jessica Richardson, Mr. Simmons, Jacob Ming Trent, James Wallert. *Jump* by Lisa McGee. *Realism* by Anthony Neilson. April 15, 2007. Directed by Ari Edelson; with Bree Elrod, Jordan Gelber, Ali Marsh, Stephen Plunkett, Kathryn Rossetter, Herbert Rubens, Tim Spears, Daniel Talbott, Sarah Grace Wilson, Meredith Zinner. *Don Juan in Chicago* by David Ives. May 30, 2007. Directed by Owen M. Smith; with Stephen Balantzian, Greg Barresi, Mike Cinquino, Doug Nyman, Shayna Padovano, Dayle Pivetta, Virginia Stringel, Vincent Vigilante. THE LION. *Marco Millions (based on lies)* by Waterwell; adapted from the play by Eugene O'Neill. August 12, 2006. Directed by Tom Ridgely; with Hanna Cheek, Rodney Gardiner, Arian Moayed, Tom Ridgely, Kevin Townley, Lauren Cregor, Gunter Gruner, Jenny Hill, Adam Levine, Joe Morse. *Nelson* by Sam Marks. February 14, 2007. Directed by Kip Fagan; with Alexander Alioto, Frank Harts, Jordan Mahome. *Lunch Hour* by Jean Kerr. April 26, 2007. Directed by Maura Farver; with Morgan Baker, Laura Faith, Jeff Pagliano, J.T. Michael Taylor, Mary Willis White.

THEATRE 3. *The Servant of Two Masters* by Carlo Goldoni. January 3, 2007. Directed by Stuart Vaughan; with Steve Campbell, Nick Fleming, John Hart, Rich Hollman, Grant Kretchik, Ronald Rand, Craig Rising, Gray Stevenson, Alok Tewari, Alessandra Ziviani.

37 ARTS THEATER. *Love's Labour's Lost* by William Shakespeare. August 23, 2006. Directed by Daniel Spector; with Teddy Alvaro, Michael Bartelle, Dawn Cantwell, Patrick Carlyle, Erica Diamond, Richard Douglass, Marc LeVasseur, Beth Lopes, Grace McLean, Hubert Point-Du Jour, Randy Thompson, Lauren Sowa, Stephen Stout, Gillian Wiggin.

3LD ART AND TECHNOLOGY CENTER. *Losing Something* by Kevin Cunningham. April 3, 2007. Directed by Mr. Cunningham; with Michael Bell, Victoria Chamberlin, Livia De Paolis, Aldo Perez, Catherine Yeager.

TRIAD THEATRE. *Bush Is Bad: Impeachment Edition.* Musical revue by Joshua Rosenblum. September 28, 2006. Directed and choreographed by Gary Slavin; with Janet Dickinson, Neal Mayer, Michael McCoy. *When the Lights Go on Again.* Musical revue by Bill Daugherty. October 28, 2006. Directed by Mr. Daugherty; with Mr. Daugherty, Paul Kropfl, Christina Morrell, Connie Pachl. *Piano Bar.* Musical revue by Stephen Cole. November 15, 2006. Directed by Mr. Cole and Diane Pulzello; with Viola Harris, David Hibbard, Susan J. Jacks, Joy Lynn Matthews, Cathy Trien, Matthew Ward; and special guests Tommy Femia, Marni Nixon, Barbara Minkus.

UNDER ST. MARKS. *The Bad Bruise of Billy MacBean* by Eric Brand. January 2, 2007. Directed by Noah Burger; with Charlie Hewson, Katie Morris. *The Gringo of the Deli Acapulco* by Eric Brand. January 2, 2007. Directed by Noah Burger; with Scott Eckert, Reema Zaman. *The Big Funk* by John Patrick Shanley. May 13, 2007. Directed by Dana Panepinto; with Colleen Britt, Ellen Hauck, Toby Knops, Deanna McGovern, Michael Schantz, Jesse Soursourian. *The Most Beautiful Lullaby You've Ever Heard* by Greg Romero. May 24, 2007. May24, 2007. Directed by Andrew Merkel; with John Conor Brooke, Dianna Marino, Lucy Walters.

URBAN STAGES. *Clean* by Bob Epstein. June 19, 2006. Directed by Christopher Maring; with Albert Insinnia, Karl Jacob, John Kudan, Nancy Rodriguez, Cherene Snow, Bjorn Thorstad, Sarah Viccellio. *Brutality of Fact* by Keith Reddin. August 17, 2006. Directed by Stephanie Yankwitt; with Bronwen Coleman, Marshall Correro; Amy da Luz, Joy Franz, D.H. Johnson, Donna Robinson. *Live Girls* by Victoria Stewart. October 25, 2006. Directed by Lou Jacob; with Christina Brucato, Pamela Hart, Jenny Maguire. *The Magical Forest of Baba Yaga* by Eugene Schwartz; translated by Stanton Wood. December 14, 2006. Directed by Aleksey Burago. *Apostasy* by Gino Dilorio. March 24, 2007. Directed by Frances Hill; with Susan Greenhill, Susan Louise O'Connor, Harold Surratt. *Of Mice and Men* by John Steinbeck. May 10, 2007. Directed by Pat Diamond; with Douglas Taurel, Vincent Allocca, Erik Gislason, Elizabeth A. Davis, Paul Barry, James Broderick, Matthew Floyd Miller, Jason L. Grossman, General Fermon Judd Jr., Justin Swain.

THE VACLAV HAVEL FESTIVAL. October 5–December 4, 2006. Schedule included: *An Evening With the Family*; translated by Carol Rocamora and Tomas Rychetsky. Directed by Glory Sims Bowen; with Jassica Baily, Brenda Crawley, Noemy Hernandez, Eric Christopher Hoelle, Amy Liszka, David Nash, Iracel Rivero, Isaac Scranton, Medina Senghore, David Skigen, Anthony Stevenson, Jonathan Weirich. *Audience*; translated by Jan Novak. Directed by Edward Einhorn; with Dan Leventritt, Scott Simpson. *The Garden Party*; translated by Jan Novak. Directed by Andrea Boccanfuso; with James Bentley, Sergei Burbank, John Kohan, Michael Marion, David Nelson, Steve Russo, Alley Scott, Laura Stockton, Kristine Waters. *The Beggar's Opera*; translated by Paul Wilson. Directed by Amy Trompetter and Sergei Zemtsov. *A Butterfly on the Antenna*; translated by Carol Rocamora and Tomas Rychetsky. Directed by Henry Akona; with Dawn Jamieson, Richard Renner, Philip Emeott. *The Conspirators*; translated by Carol Rocamora and Tomas Rychetsky. Directed by Kay Matschullat. *The Increased Difficulty of Concentration*; translated by Stepan Simek. Directed by Yolanda Hawkins; with John Hagan, Brad Holbrook, Shira Kobren, Meret Oppenheim, David Ott, Matthew Park, Amy Quint, Kate Reilly. *Largo Desolato*; translated by Tom Stoppard. Directed by Eva Burgess; with Jennifer Boutell, Joshua Briggs, Jon Okahayashi, Nancy Nagrant, Brian Quirk, Erik Kever Ryle, Greg Skura, Skyler Sullivan, Janet Ward. *The Memo*; translated by Paul Wilson. Directed by Edward Einhorn; with Peter Bean, V. Orion Delwaterman, Ryan Dutcher, Talaura Harms, Uma Incrocci, Alice Starr McFarland, Skid Maher, Tom McCarten, Josh Mertz, Shelly Ray, Leah Reddy, Andrew Rothkin, Josh Silverman, Ken Simon, Maxwell Zener. *Mistake*; translated by Carol Rocamora and Tomas Rychetsky. Directed by Isaac Rathbone and Jennifer Rathbone; with Joe Beaudin, Daryl Brown, David Nelson, Laura Stockton, Alley Scott, Kristine Waters. *Mountain Hotel*; translated by Jitka Martinova. Directed by Michael Gardner; with Gyda Arber, Fred Backus, Bryan Enk, Robert Honeywell, Heath Kelts, Devon Hawkes Ludlow, Alanna Medlock, R. David Robinson, Alyssa Simon, Moira Stone, Art Wallace. *Protest*; translated by Jan Novak. Directed by Robert Lyons; with Andy Paris, Richard Toth.

WALKERSPACE. *Mark Smith* by Kate E. Ryan. June 5, 2006. Directed by Ken Rus Schmoll; with Hannah Cabell, Andrew Dinwiddie, Alissa Ford, Kristen Kosmas, Melissa Miller, Eric Dean Scott. *Cleansed* by Thomas Bradshaw. July 7, 2006. directed by Elize Day Hittman; with Kaaron Briscoe, Albert Christmas, Nancy Franklin, Aimee McCormack, Bobby Monero, Di Quon. *Blood Wedding* by Federico Garcia Lorca; translated by Lillian Groag. July 25, 2006. Directed by Stephen Squibb and Gabriel Hainer Evansohn. *The Polish Play* by Alfred Jarry. January 19, 2007. Directed by Henry Wishcamper; with James Bentley, Jeff Biehl, Jordan Gelber, Torsten Hillhouse, Jacob H. Knoll, Lucas Caleb Rooney, Ryan Ward, Eunice Wong. *Hotel Oracle* by Bixby Elliot. March 8, 2007. Directed by Stephen Brackett; with Tessa Gibbons, Raymond Hill, Katie Honaker, Jim Kane, Paul Keany, Deb Martin. *Mud Blossom* by Ashlin Halfnight. April 12, 2007. Directed by Kate Pines; with Corinne Edgerly, Jennifer McCabe, Liz Myers. *Kraken* by Len Jenkin. May 11, 2007. Directed by Michael Kimmel; with Tom Escovar, Marc Geller, Richardson Jones, Tracy Liz Miller, Heidi Niedermeyer, Eva Patton, Augustus Truhn.

WINGS THEATRE COMPANY. *Autumn Moon*. Musical with book, music and lyrics by David Velarde. August 11, 2006. Directed by Jonathan Cerullo; with Dana Barathy, William Broyles, Jesse Easley, Mishaela Faucher, Sara Fetgatter, Scott Richard Foster, Jeremy Jonet, Marissa Lupp, Rebecca Riker, Amber Shirley, David Weitzer. BEYOND CHRISTOPHER STREET. November 19– December 16, 2006. *Better Now* by Mark Finley. Directed by Steven McElroy; with Chad Austin, Amy Bizjak, Desmond Dutcher. *Work Wife* by David Pumo. Directed by Antonio Merenda; with Moe Bertran, Nick Mathews, Karen Stanion. *Ramble* by A.B. Lugo. Directed by K. Lorrel Manning; with Michael Cuomo, Carol Nelson. *A Kiss Is Just a Kiss* by Jonathan Kronenberger. Directed by Glenn Schudel; with Jason Alan Griffin, Zach McCoy, Andrew Shoffner. *The Jocker* by Clint Jeffries. May 11, 2007. Directed by Jeffrey Corrick; with Stephen Cabral, Jason Alan Griffin, Michael Lazar, Nick Matthews, Stephen Tyrone Williams.

WORKSHOP THEATER COMPANY. *Intellectuals* by Scott C. Sickles. September 11, 2006. Directed by David Gautschy; with Bill Blechingberg, Ellen Dolan, Patricia O'Connell, Kari Swenson Riely, Bill Tatum, Kim Weston-Moran, Jess Cassidy White. *Liberty*. Musical with book and lyrics by Dana Leslie Goldstein; music and lyrics by Jonathan Goldstein. October 18, 2006. Directed by Robert Bruce McIntosh; with Paul Aguirre, Alexandra Devin, Cheryl Dowling, Peter Farrell, Richard Kent Green, Victoria Malvagno, Nedra McClyde, Robert Bruce McIntosh, Kevin McKelvy, Joanie Schumacher, Mark L. Smith.

THE SEASON AROUND
THE UNITED STATES

STEINBERG/AMERICAN THEATRE CRITICS NEW PLAY AWARD AND CITATIONS

○ ○ ○ ○ ○

A DIRECTORY OF NEW UNITED STATES PRODUCTIONS

T HE AMERICAN THEATRE CRITICS ASSOCIATION (ATCA) is the organization of drama critics in all media throughout the United States. One of the group's stated purposes is "To increase public awareness of the theater as a national resource." To this end, ATCA has annually cited outstanding new plays produced around the US, which were excerpted in our series beginning with the 1976–77 volume. As we continue our policy of celebrating playwrights and playwriting in *Best Plays*, we offer essays on the recipients of the 2007 Harold and Mimi Steinberg/ATCA New Play Award and Citations. The Steinberg/ATCA New Play Award of $25,000 was given to Peter Sinn Nachtrieb for his play *Hunter Gatherers*. The Steinberg/ATCA New Play Citations were given to Jeff Daniels for *Guest Artist*—which was also named a Best Play during its Off Broadway run—and Michael Hollinger for *Opus*. Citation honorees receive prizes of $7,500 each.

The ATCA awards are funded by the Harold and Mimi Steinberg Charitable Trust, which supports theater throughout the United States with its charitable giving. The awards were renamed this year, putting the Steinberg family name first, to honor the trust's renewed (and enhanced) commitment to the honors. The Steinberg/ATCA New Play Award and Citations are given in a ceremony at Actors Theatre of Louisville. Essays in the next section—by Robert Hurwitt (*San Francisco Chronicle*), Martin F. Kohn (*Detroit Free Press*) and George Hatza (*Reading Eagle*)—celebrate the Steinberg/ATCA Citation honorees.

ATCA's 14th annual M. Elizabeth Osborn Award for a new playwright was voted to Ken LaZebnik for *Vestibular Sense*, which was produced in 2006 by Mixed Blood Theatre in Minneapolis, Minnesota.

The process of selecting these outstanding plays is as follows: any American Theatre Critics Association member may nominate the first full professional production of a finished play (not a reading or an airing as a play-in-progress) that premieres outside New York City during the calendar year under consideration.

Nominated 2006 scripts were studied and discussed by the New Plays Committee chaired by Bill Hirschman (*South Florida Sun-Sentinel*). The committee included ATCA members Misha Berson (*The Seattle Times*), Judith Egerton (*Louisville Courier Journal*), Michael Elkin (*Jewish Exponent, Philadelphia*), Jay Handelman (*Sarasota Herald Tribune*), Claudia W. Harris (freelance, Orem, Utah), George Hatza (*Reading Eagle*), Chad Jones (*The Oakland Tribune*), Elizabeth Maupin (*The Orlando Sentinel*), Wendy Parker (*Village Mill*, Virginia), Michael Sander (*Back Stage*) and Herbert Simpson (TotalTheater.com, Rochester).

Committee members made their choices on the basis of script rather than production. If the timing of nominations and openings prevents some works from being considered in any given year, they may be eligible for consideration the following year if they have not since moved to New York City.

2007 Steinberg/ATCA New Play Award

HUNTER GATHERERS

By Peter Sinn Nachtrieb

○ ○ ○ ○ ○

Essay by Robert Hurwitt

RICHARD: I listen to my body. It tells me what to do, not the other way around. Put me on a soccer field, and I want to be the best player on the grass. Show me meat and I want to make the most delicious dinner ever. Show me an attractive hole and I want to fill it and fill it and fill it till I shoot. And I will.

A N ALPHA MALE for the metrosexual Gen-X age, Richard isn't really the hero of Peter Sinn Nachtrieb's *Hunter Gatherers*. But you'd never convince him of that. Richard dominates everyone else onstage. He has more to say than anyone else. His appetites—he knows no distinction between his hunger for food, sex and what he considers his art—drive the action of the annual mutual-wedding anniversary that he and his wife Pam celebrate with their best friends, Wendy and Tom. But if Wendy is Richard's earth-mother counterpart in rampant egoism, and Tom his chosen whipping boy, it is the quiet, self-effacing, naively altruistic Pam who emerges as the play's hero—and sole survivor.

A large part of Nachtrieb's success in his first professionally produced full-length play lies in its firm grounding. *Hunter Gatherers* is a savage satire, graced with a Monty Pythonesque sense of the ridiculous, about sophisticated urbanites in a city much like San Francisco. In many respects it is a *Killer Joe* come home to roost, not in a low-rent trailer park but in a chic converted-loft condo. Nachtrieb's slapstick comedy is no less lethal than Tracy Letts's in *Killer Joe*, and it is nearly as transgressive. The sex and violence in *Hunter Gatherers*, however, derive not from the stunted intelligence of ne'er-do-wells hiring a rogue-cop hit man but from trends in gourmet cooking, new age self-actualization ideas, back-to-nature longings and skewed notions of male and female sexual empowerment.

It is a promising first step for the playwright and for the production company, as well as something of a testament to the play's development process. Nachtrieb wrote the play under a New Works Fund grant from

Alpha cook: Jon Wolanske and Alexis Lezin in Hunter Gatherers. *Photo: Daniel Brennan*

Theatre Bay Area—a San Francisco-based service organization—and developed the script with the Playwrights Foundation at the 2005 Bay Area Playwrights Festival. It was picked up by Killing My Lobster, an improv comedy company that had begun producing annual programs of scripted one-acts two years earlier and wanted to take the plunge into staging full-length works. Nachtrieb had worked with Lobster as an actor and director, and contributed one of the more successful scripts in its first one-act festival. *Hunter* opened early in June 2006, at San Francisco's Thick House, produced by Lobster and directed by Tracy Ward. It proved a popular and critical success, enjoying a sold-out, extended run through most of the summer. It received the Will Glickman Playwright Award, given annually to the best play to have its world premiere in the Bay Area, as selected by a jury of five local newspaper theater critics (of which I am a member), about a month before it received the Steinberg/American Theatre Critics New Play Award.

At this writing, *Hunter* is in rehearsal for its East Coast premiere, directed by Gip Hoppe at the Wellfleet Harbor Actors Theatre on Cape Cod. This and other future productions will test how well the play's San

Francisco setting and point of view translate to other regions. It shouldn't prove much of a stretch. Except for a very few specific geographic references (which could easily be replaced with places that carry similar connotations in each region), the mindsets of Nachtrieb's characters and the culture from which they spring should be instantly recognizable to the inhabitants of any American urban area who take the usual pride in their unique level of sophistication.

The action is character-driven, as established from the opening interaction between Richard and Pam. Erik Flatmo's converted-loft set nicely telegraphed the couple's economic status and cultural pretensions: metal

---

The comic violence builds by carefully calculated degrees.

---

sculptures on a corrugated metal wall, a large abstract painting, tasteful but generically upscale furnishings. We first meet Pam, her arms laden with grocery bags, staring in shock at Richard who's kneeling above a large cardboard box, wielding a big butcher's knife. The knife, of course, is Chekhov's "gun on the wall" destined for a central role in the final moments, as reflected in the reds of Flatmo's color scheme. The shuffling sounds and occasional bleats from inside the box and Richard's raised knife set the course of the action to come, along with Pam's opening line: Was the butcher closed?

RICHARD, WHO CONSIDERS himself an artist, isn't just an alpha male but an alpha cook. Each year, when the Fab Four gather to celebrate their joint wedding anniversary, Richard outdoes himself. As Wendy says when she arrives: "Every year, he raises the bar. Last year, my god. Who knew a chicken would fit in a duck, and then fit in a turkey?" This time, Richard is fixing lamb, from a recipe cited in comically poetic detail that calls for freshly, lovingly slaughtered and butchered meat. Fresh blood is mother's milk to Richard, who revels in his physical strength and macho sense of fulfilling his true nature by giving free rein to every conceivable natural urge.

> PAM: Every morning, when I'm in bed and don't really want to get out because of all the scariness, I think, "At least there are three people in this world that I can love unconditionally, that

unconditionally love me, that I know will always be there, care for me, tell me the truth."

By the time Pam utters these words, we know that her trust in each of the others is completely misplaced. Played with wide-eyed innocence by Melanie Case in the Lobster premiere, she's the lamb, the apparent sacrificial victim gainfully employed but still trying to find herself: timid but willing to go along on all sorts of dubious enterprises and ridiculously, then fatally blind to the ulterior motives of her best friends since high school. If she is unfulfilled, on almost every level, she thinks it is no one's fault but her own and she just has to try harder, perhaps by pleasing others. She is also the assistant chef, a role that covers everything from calming the lamb and holding it for slaughter to baking brownies for dessert.

Richard is interested in nothing but his appetites and bodily functions. Though he professes love for Pam, he sees his mission as propagating his genes as widely as possible ("Gotta lot of wombs to fill") and filling every other hole he can as well. Seeing Tom is, for Richard, a natural occasion to wrestle the other man to the ground, assert his dominance and, if time permits, rape him. As embodied by Jon Wolanske, with intimidating

Raging testosterone: Jon Wolanske, Alexis Lezin and John Kovacevich in Hunter Gatherers. *Photo: Daniel Brennan*

self-assurance and a bare-fanged lupine grin, he is a force of nature, rampaging energy barely contained within the social necessities of the moment—if at all. He's an archetype, even to himself. When he feels most aroused, hurt or inspired, Richard speaks of himself in the third person.

Wendy has always looked down upon Pam and resented her. Played by Alexis Lezin with a complete indulgence in her own appetites to match Richard's, she has always seen herself as Richard's natural mate, if she hadn't been cheated by a terrible twist of fate at spin-the-bottle long ago. She inhales the aromas of Richard's cooking with a sensual intensity verging on orgasmic, openly despises her less-than-macho, barren husband Tom and finds any excuse to get alone with Richard for a quick grope or hard sex. Like Richard, she is half-frozen in the glories of their teen years, including magical memories of her first period. Self-fulfillment for her means having a baby, preferably Richard's. Pam remains unaware of this, no matter how obvious Wendy tries to make it.

> WENDY: I am a lonely field horse, Pam. Sadly nibbling on hay. Dreaming that one day I might meet a kind, generous mare who happens to be horse-married to a prime, hoofing thoroughbred. And perhaps that generous mare doesn't want to be a mother herself and wouldn't mind unlocking the stable door and taking a long long trot to the mall, looking the other way so all the field horse's dreams can come true.

Tom (rigid and congenitally unhappy as played by John Kovacevich) is more than aware of what Wendy and Richard are up to. The fact that he is the most successful of the group in conventional terms—he's a doctor, respected among his peers—makes him no less the butt of Richard's machismo (Richard calls him "my best bitch"). He is the eternal outsider, suffering humiliation in search of acceptance and beginning to realize his resentment. "Oh why, why, why didn't I listen to my mom?" he erupts. "'They're very mean to you,' she said. 'Friends don't treat friends that way.'"

As Richard and Wendy become absorbed in an ever more blatantly lascivious mating dance, Tom manages to convince Pam not only of the obvious infidelity of their spouses but of the appropriateness of taking revenge in kind. The result is at first a very funny, inept sex scene:

> TOM: Pam.
>
> PAM: Yes, Tom.
>
> TOM: Am I, uh, am I, oh . . .
>
> PAM: In?
>
> TOM: Yes.

(*Pause.*)

PAM: You're in the general area.

The sex gets better and the comedy darker as Tom realizes what Richard has always known, that he's really a bottom. Pam finds her inner beast as a top, a pleasure she's never experienced in her marriage. She explodes with her finest (possibly first) orgasm in a slyly outrageous *In the Realm of the Senses* (1976) moment. Tom does not survive her sexual epiphany.

NACHTRIEB BUILDS THE play's comic violence by carefully calculated degrees. It starts with a pratfall, then Richard's bullish wrestling of Tom to the floor followed by an offstage coital mishap in the kitchen that results in Tom having to stitch up Richard's head. That's just the beginning. The bloodshed is never as shocking as that in *Killer Joe,* but it is as effective in its own right. As in Letts's play, Nachtrieb has created characters that are cartoon exaggerations, on the one hand, but so fully drawn that they exist as individualized humans on another level. The violence finds a level between slapstick and drama that enables us to revel in its comic poetic justice as well as to empathize with the plight of the survivor. Once the characters start to die, the stakes are raised, but the surreal turns of events keep us at a necessary distance. There is death by that menacing knife, of course, but also death by leg of lamb. A climactic struggle over a bag of sperm destroys much of the set and, with it, the architecture of a civilization that confines the characters as much as it was designed to protect them.

The ending, with bodies strewn all over the floor, is neither comic nor tragic but sweetly poignant and ambiguously hopeful. "We'll just do our best to be ready for anything that happens. Won't we, Pam? Won't we?" the lone survivor says as she surveys the carnage and destruction of her former home. Armed with only that knife, a leg of lamb and all the brownies she can carry, Pam exits into the lush green forest that magically appears beyond the apartment's walls.

2007 Steinberg/ATCA New Play Citation

GUEST ARTIST
By Jeff Daniels

○ ○ ○ ○ ○

Essay by Martin F. Kohn

KENNETH: Y'know how they say all the great playwrights are dead? It's not true. Some of the best playwrights ever to grace the stage are alive and well and off in a room somewhere slaving over a Second Act. That's one of them. Right before my very eyes.

FOR ALL OF THE TALK about theater as a collaborative art, it could not exist without the solitary and lonely act of putting pen to paper or hand to keyboard. To Jeff Daniels, actor, playwright and founder of the Purple Rose Theatre Company in his hometown of Chelsea, Michigan, no sight was more forlorn than playwright Lanford Wilson getting off a train in Toledo, Ohio, one morning around six.

The two had first worked together at the beginning of Daniels's career at New York's Circle Rep in the 1970s. Decades later, Daniels commissioned Wilson to write a play for his theater and had driven to meet him. Wilson won't fly, and when you travel by rail from New York, Toledo is as close as you can get to Chelsea on the trunk line to Chicago.

"So there I was at the Toledo train station," Daniels said in an interview, "and here comes a Pulitzer Prize-winning playwright, disheveled, unshaven, coming off this train—and I'll never forget it—I'm looking at this Pulitzer Prize winner, one of our greatest American playwrights, and this is what it's come to. I got angry about that, and that's been in me for a long time."

A long time, indeed: eight years elapsed between the train station welcome in 1998 and the Purple Rose premiere of *Guest Artist* in 2006.

Wilson's arrival at the train station led to something of a departure for Daniels as a playwright. Of Daniels's eleven produced plays, nearly all have been comedies. The comedies are deftly constructed, indulge in physical humor—fart jokes, a food fight, a man handcuffed to a living room recliner—and generally express some variation on the theme: it's too bad you can't choose your relatives but your friends aren't so hot either.

Good host: Patrick Michael Kenney and Randall Godwin in Guest Artist. *Photo: Danna Segrest*

GUEST ARTIST ISN'T SET in the Toledo railroad station but in the analogous desolation of a bus station in Steubenville, Ohio, on a similar dark night of the soul. The place is the epitome of the ordinary. The stage directions are a litany of the commonplace: "Some chairs, benches. Two vending machines[. . . .]" As are the opening words, spoken by Ticket Man behind his cage: "Now arriving, 1156 out of Wheeling, Barnesville, Cambridge, Zanesville, Columbus, Cincinnati and Nashville."

Kenneth Waters, a young apprentice with the local professional theater, the Dean Martin Repertory Company—named for Steubenville's celebrated native son—awakens in his chair. The Dean Martin Rep has commissioned Pulitzer Prize-winning playwright Joseph Harris's next play and Kenneth has been waiting for Harris to arrive from New York.

Paying no attention to the only other person in the waiting room, an older man fast asleep, an agitated Kenneth asks Ticket Man what happened to 4465, the bus from New York.

> TICKET MAN: There is no 4465 out of New York. There's the 4465 out of Weirton, Pittsburgh, Monroeville—

The bus, of course, originated in New York but Ticket Man's provincial purview doesn't extend quite that far.

Nor is Kenneth's vision all that expansive. The bus arrived on time, more than an hour earlier—the apprentice must have slept through it. Although he carries a well-worn paperback of Harris's plays, with the playwright's photo on the back cover, Kenneth doesn't realize that the man sleeping in a rumpled, ill-fitting suit is Joseph Harris in the flesh.

Mr. Harris—Kenneth and the script always call him Mr. Harris—is brilliant, alcoholic, eccentric, cantankerous, at once a delight and an irritant,

Art is about standing alone and telling the truth.

reveling in the belief that wherever he happens to be he is the smartest guy in the room but also understanding that few people seem to care.

Sleep-deprived and a bit disoriented, Mr. Harris offers a quick critique of the town. "This feels," he says, "like one of those places you go only if you have to." Kenneth is the nearest target and Mr. Harris pokes fun at being in "Stupidville," home to "the Jerry Lewis Repertory Company." Then he starts in on "The masses."

> KENNETH: The who?
>
> MR. HARRIS: The ones who no longer go to the theater because they're too busy watching *American Idol*. O'Neill was so lucky to have written when he did. (*re: TICKET MAN*) Look at him in there. Trapped in a cage. Of your own making, I might add. (*to KENNETH*) Ignore the symbolism. Go.

The obstinate Mr. Harris won't leave the station, however, until Kenneth tells him a joke. The best Kenneth can manage is a story about a drunken actor who, playing the doctor in *The Miracle Worker* ruins the first scene, the play and his career by informing Mr. and Mrs. Keller that their daughter has died.

Mr. Harris responds (we're not sure how truthfully) with the name of the actor, the identity of the theater and the astonishing fact that he happened to be in the audience that very night.

> MR. HARRIS: And for the record, that was not a joke, but an anecdote. And hardly comedic. Tragic, to be sure, in the classical sense. You're aware of the Greeks?

But enough of showing off for the kid. What Mr. Harris really wants is a drink. Kenneth demurs. Under orders from his boss and from Mr. Harris's agent, he's to keep the playwright away from alcohol, and vice versa. If that's how it is, Harris says, he'll just take the next bus back to New York.

Panic-stricken, Kenneth tries flattery, which in his case happens to be genuine. He's an aspiring playwright and starts quoting Mr. Harris's own published words about the state of American theater, which prompts a few more from the man himself.

> MR. HARRIS: [. . .] No one writes for the theater anymore, unless they have to, Mr. Waters. It's all about screenplays and six figure development deals and getting a place at the table with twelve other ex-playwrights, hoping in this week's episode one of your jokes makes it into the mouth of your own, personal sitcom star. [. . .]

Kenneth persists, praising Mr. Harris for having never abandoned the theater, whereupon Mr. Harris urges him to stop. He hands Kenneth a check. He is returning the commission, he says. There is no play.

This would seem like a natural place to end Act I but Mr. Harris is not the sort of fellow you can just stop, even if you're the one who created

Stand and deliver: Patrick Michael Kenney and Grant R. Krause in Guest Artist. *Photo: Danna Segrest*

him. Looking for money to buy a ticket back to New York Mr. Harris rummages through Kenneth's knapsack, finding a few dollars and the manuscript of Kenneth's play. Mr. Harris offers to read it while he waits for the bus and engages Kenneth in a conversation about theater and writing. To encourage Kenneth to believe in himself Mr. Harris stands on a chair and proclaims "I am an artist and this is my art!," urging Kenneth to join him.

Ticket Man grabs his microphone and cites the regulations against such behavior. Mr. Harris quotes William Blake and carries on, eventually removing his jacket and shirt. Ultimately, he calms down and whispers to Kenneth, "That . . . was theater."

Using Kenneth's money, Mr. Harris prevails on the by-the-book Ticket Man to sell him a bottle of whiskey from behind the counter and talks to Kenneth about September 11, 2001. Mr. Harris was in Manhattan that day.

> MR. HARRIS: The helplessness remains, of course. Humankind's defining characteristic. But what happened to all of our sadness and anger and rage? Where did all of that get to?
>
> KENNETH: I don't know.
>
> MR. HARRIS: I do. I know exactly where it went.

Mr. Harris takes Kenneth's play and the bottle of whiskey as Act I ends.

ACT II BEGINS WITH Kenneth waking and Mr. Harris still asleep, presumably having read Kenneth's play. Ticket Man confirms this for the young writer and, after paying Ticket Man $20 for a cup of real coffee from his thermos, Kenneth hands him another $10 to describe Harris's reaction to the play.

"Kafka-esque," says Ticket Man, astonishing Kenneth. "Look at him. [. . .] He's trying to escape. But he can't. He's trapped. Forever." Ticket Man compares Harris's state to the condition of humankind as a whole, concluding his jaw-dropping existential analysis with an offhanded "More coffee?"

If Mr. Harris, then, symbolizes theater's past and Kenneth its future, who or what does Ticket Man represent?

The answer would seem to be: the audience, the masses Mr. Harris so derides. Dull and unimaginative on the surface, unable to say anything that hasn't been written by the bus company, Ticket Man is capable of surprising depths. He understands: assumptions must be reworked. And the assumption that Kenneth represents the future of American theater is about to go out the window, too. Harris, now awake, hated Kenneth's play.

MR. HARRIS: I cannot hear you in your play.

Here he pointedly delivers the kind of message he tried to communicate when he removed his shirt and climbed on the chair: that art is about standing alone and telling the truth, but also about connecting with other human beings.

MR. HARRIS: The truth. About me. Through you. Through your play. In order to do that I have to hear you. If I hear you, if as I read your words I can hear your voice, I will in turn hear mine. [. . .]

And now it's Kenneth's turn to be an advocate for truth.

KENNETH: Why haven't you written anything in ten years?

It takes a while, but Mr. Harris finally says that he is so desperately tired of telling people truths that they really don't want to hear.

KENNETH: You came all this way hoping for once in your life you were wrong.

KENNETH ACCUSES HARRIS of being afraid to admit that he is still able to think, to write and to care. An ardent student of Harris's words—not just in his plays and essays but in conversation—Kenneth has a hunch. He opens Harris's suitcase, rummages through books and clothing and takes out a manuscript: "*Untitled New Play* by Joseph Harris."

MR. HARRIS: [. . .] When did you know?

KENNETH: When you got on the bus to come here. You said it yourself. "No one comes to a place like this unless they have to."

Kenneth begins reading from Harris's play, a page or two where a man talks about stepping out of a Greenwich Village bar on the morning of September 11, 2001, and seeing an airplane crash into the World Trade Center. Eventually, Harris takes over the recitation, from memory, thus explaining his statement in Act I about knowing what happened to all the sadness, anger and rage of September 11. It went into his play.

Away goes the premise that Mr. Harris symbolizes the theater's past. He may yet represent its present and its future. By giving the veteran playwright courage enough to offer his work to the public again, by bringing out in Mr. Harris what has been bottled up by a kind of disability, a disability of the spirit, Kenneth Waters, theater apprentice and aspiring playwright, may also be a miracle worker.

2007 Steinberg/ATCA New Play Citation

OPUS

By Michael Hollinger

○ ○ ○ ○ ○

Essay by George Hatza

> DORIAN: Music is ephemeral. Like us[. . . .] That's the beauty of it;
> that's the tragedy. That's why a resonant hall is so poignant—the
> notes last a half-second longer, giving the brief illusion of immortality.

A RELATIONSHIP IS SIMILAR to art: It takes practice. You have to work at it every day until the effort vanishes into rote behavior, when the subtle psychological shifts and self-conscious maneuvers no longer are noticeable—until it feels rather like breathing.

The characteristics that combine to form the artistic personality are not dissimilar from the millions of genetic codes that compose a human being. The artist—painter, musician, actor, poet—discovers he has a talent that ultimately defines him. Intrinsic to that discovery is the essence of identity, the source of individuality, as powerful as any inherited physical or mental attribute. To be a member of a string quartet, one must possess individual talent. The nature of a string-quartet performance rests, however, on the harmony of its parts. One's peculiar qualities, the quirks that make one unique, must be suppressed and homage paid to the demands of the composition. The performance is at once a denial of self and an act of creation that approaches the divine. That, finally, is what art can do: welcome heaven to earth for a moment and allow us to peer into the eyes of God before it retreats, out of reach.

At the core of Michael Hollinger's mesmerizing *Opus*—a play in which a string quartet struggles to reconcile human failures with artistic genius—lies an inescapable conflict. To make great art, each member silences, for a time, his or her inherent eccentricities. Ironically, a superb string-quartet musician—someone with the ability to direct emotion toward the work being performed—also partially disables the source from which passion derives. With that in mind, it is not much of a stretch to discern what Hollinger, a trained violist himself, creates in *Opus*. The play is much more than a clichéd life-imitates-art versus art-imitates-life debate. It is the search

Fab four: Patrick McNulty, Greg Wood, Douglas Rees, David Whalen in Opus. *Photo: Mark Garvin*

for a perfect blend of music, musicians, co-workers, friends. More specifically, this quest leads to the choice every artist inevitably confronts: art or a conventional life?

THE PERSONAL LIVES of the characters in *Opus* are in shambles, which has led them to the point where they must re-create their professional lives as well. Hollinger's first clue is that there are five characters, and *Opus* is a play about a quartet.

The four men in the play—the original members of the Lazara Quartet (the biblical connotation is not a coincidence, as the quartet attempts to rise from the dead)—are all in their 40s: Elliot, first violin; Alan, second violin; Dorian, viola; and Carl, cello. Dorian has vanished under mysterious circumstances; we later learn that he and Elliot had a volatile romantic relationship. In Dorian's absence, the other members have agreed to audition a new violist—the aptly named Grace, who is 25, beautiful and an extraordinarily skilled musician. In music, "grace notes" embellish an existing score, are short-lived and can be removed at the will of the conductor—or, in this case, by vote of the quartet members. We are led instantly to believe that Grace will be the source of division among the remaining quartet members. It is the long-absent Dorian, however, whose reappearance alters the chemistry of the quartet.

Alan's marriage is finished, and he has eyes for Grace. Elliot finds their dalliance distracting, one can surmise, because his own affair with Dorian eventually resulted in the latter's sudden departure. Carl, a family man, is dying of cancer. And there's the surprise return of Dorian, who, late in the play, meets Grace at an audition for the Pittsburgh Symphony. It is clear that at least one character is in big trouble; at times the play has the edge-of-your-seat pull of a suspense tale. To the playwright's credit, *Opus*—a

---

This quest leads to the choice every artist inevitably confronts.

---

serious work with dark undertones—has comic moments whose repercussions are more ominous.

In the play's opening sequence, a series of interviews—conducted by an unseen documentary filmmaker—are spliced together after the individual sessions. We hear them in succession, but the characters do not. The musicians are captured individually under pin spots and speak directly to the audience. Asked to define a string quartet, Alan jokes:

> ALAN: Okay, how 'bout this: a string quartet is like a marriage, only with more fidelity[. . . .] Actually, don't tell my wife I said that.

Carl, not comfortable with humor, responds:

> CARL: One good violinist, one bad violinist, one former violinist, and someone who doesn't even like the violin[. . . .] No, it's just a joke[. . . .] Some of my best friends are violinists.

Dorian, however, takes the question seriously:

> DORIAN: At its best . . . when everything's working right, when everyone's open to it, it's . . . lovemaking. Elliot starts a phrase, maybe just a bit softer than usual, so we come in under, Alan and I, like we're . . . coddling it, like more than a breath would kill it. Then Carl lands on the bottom, terra firma, and the whole thing rises, floats, together, falls back, arches upward, no one leading, no one following, it's just . . . pulsating, like it's alive, like some living, pulsing organism. . . . Copulating with itself.

Underscoring Dorian's answer we hear the Cavatina movement of Beethoven's Opus 130. The music desists abruptly after the phrase, "pulsating organism."

In this sequence, containing some of the play's most poetic language, we understand why musicians of a certain level do what they do. Hollinger also establishes the play's unique structure: Language will unfold in the manner of a musical composition and music will serve as a different kind of language. Music becomes dramatic subtext and when the characters are simply playing their instruments, the actors' body language and the sound of the music combine to create a means of direct communication with the audience.

The effect is spellbinding not only because beautiful music affects our consciousness in inexplicable ways, but because in our heads it actually sounds like emotion. It is as if the characters are speaking their innermost thoughts. That level of accomplishment is possible only when the director, actors, visual artists and musicians connect intuitively with the playwright's dramatic vision, as they unquestionably did in *Opus*'s world premiere at Philadelphia's Arden Theatre Company (in a co-production with the City Theatre Company of Pittsburgh).

The fragility of the relationships in *Opus* matches a similar vulnerability in the nature of music as well. The experiences of playing music and listening

Grace under pressure: Patrick McNulty and Erika Cuenca in Opus. *Photo: Mark Garvin*

to it are fleeting. Elliot, who will eventually pay a price for his prickly intolerance, inflexibility and lack of warmth, nonetheless surpasses his colleagues in his intellectual understanding of the process of making music.

> ELLIOT: I would like to finish our Beethoven cycle—all sixteen quartets. That might feel like an opus. Something . . . tangible.
>
> GRACE: How many do you have left to record?
>
> ELLIOT: Just this one. (*Beat.*) Otherwise, our work disappears as soon as it's born. That's why we say a note "decays." (*He plays the first eight notes of the Gavotte from Bach's Partita No. 3 in E major for solo violin, then listens as the last note disappears.*) There, it's gone. (*Beat.*) And if you had carpeting, it would have disappeared even faster.

It is significant that the opus of Elliot's dreams will be completed without him. Just like the notes, professional and personal relationships "decay." They run their course. All that's left is the memory of the sound and the feeling of being part of something.

WHY DOES HOLLINGER choose Beethoven's difficult Opus 131 in C sharp minor? Written near the end of his life, it is generally believed that the composer considered it his best work—though he never heard it performed. Most music historians agree that it remains an anomaly in his *oeuvre*, particularly among his string quartets. What sets it apart is the unexpected recurrence of its motifs in which themes emerge, are completed and then return later. For its time, this was a groundbreaking, even shocking technique.

Its adherence to the formal conventions of the early 19th century works in opposition to the composer's melodic (and aesthetic) statement. The merriment suggested by Opus 131's opening fugue structure exists in counterpoint to the heartbreaking solemnity of the music. To a layman's ear, it is a work of emotional foreboding set in opposition to the physical placement of the notes. It is as if a painter were to use somber, morbid hues to capture a cheerful day in the park. A daunting creation, Opus 131 effectively mirrors the events, mood and thematic framework of Hollinger's play—for example, the play's opening interview sequence is performed in the style of a fugue.

Before *Opus* can cascade to its moribund finale, all hell breaks loose. After the Lazara's triumphant performance at the White House, Dorian's premeditated appearance backstage leads to catastrophe and the quartet's ultimate reconfiguration. Dorian means to return to the quartet, named after the man who crafted the group's centuries-old, priceless viola and violin. He sets his strategy in motion, and as he does all of *Opus*'s facets converge: the narrative suspense, the theatrical dissection of art, the profundity of the music, the paradox that is the artist's life, and the sacrifice—especially the sacrifice.

When Carl, given a death sentence by his oncologist, smashes the Lazara violin over the back of a chair, the explosion of the instrument resonates more painfully than anything the quartet has played, even the 131. In that instant, the quartet—and the lives of its artists, past and present—is transformed. There is no repair for what has been destroyed, literally and metaphorically.

Hollinger does not rely on contrivances. The situations that unfold in *Opus* and lead to what can be considered inevitable, in retrospect do not, as Elliot says earlier about a musical note, deteriorate due to a lack of authenticity—at least not structurally. The thematic and narrative acoustics are pitch-perfect and distinctly in harmony. Certainly the relationships collapse. With Carl's cancer, Alan's philandering, Dorian's mental instability, Elliot's emotional rigidity and Grace's callow indecisiveness it seems miraculous—yet nonetheless plausible—that these artists make music that might seduce the gods.

In a telling moment Dorian explains the rationale for his actions in the climactic scene:

> DORIAN: (*Looking at GRACE.*) When I heard her in Pittsburgh, I started to imagine a sound, a vibrant, muscular sound—not a *blend*, not a four-way compromise, but something greater than the sum of its parts. (*To ALAN.*) It's a wonderful sound; I can hear it.

To our amazement, so can we.

A DIRECTORY OF NEW
UNITED STATES PRODUCTIONS
○ ○ ○ ○ ○
Compiled by Rue E. Canvin

THIS LISTING INCLUDES professional productions that opened during the June 1, 2006–May 31, 2007 season. Its focus is on new plays—and other productions of note—by a variety of resident companies around the United States. Production information listed here in alphabetical order, by state, was supplied by the 62 producing organizations included. Resident theaters producing new plays and operating under contracts with Actors' Equity Association were queried for this comprehensive directory. Active US theater companies not included in this list may not have presented new (or newly revised) scripts during the year under review or had not responded to our query by July 1, 2007. Productions listed below are world premieres, US premieres, regional premieres, substantial revisions or otherwise worthy of note. Relatively new plays that have received widespread production are not listed here due to space and other considerations. Theaters in the US are encouraged to submit proposed listings of new works, new adaptations and other productions of significant concept or cast to the editor of *The Best Plays Theater Yearbook* series.

ARIZONA

Arizona Theatre Company, Tucson
David Ira Goldstein artistic director, Jessica L. Andrews executive director

ELLA. Musical with book by Jeffrey Hatcher; music by various artists; based on a play by Dyke Garrison. December 1, 2006. Direction, Rob Ruggiero; scenery, Michael Schweikardt; lighting, John Lasiter; costumes, Alejo Vietti; sound, Michael Miceli; musical direction, Danny Holgate; stage mangement, Bruno Ingram. Presented in association with Asolo Repertory Theatre, the Cleveland Play House and San Jose Repertory Theatre.

Ella Fitzgerald .... Tina Fabrique   Norman Granz .... Harold Dixon
    Musicians: George Caldwell piano, Brian Sledge trumpet, Rodney Harper drums, Clifton Kellem bass.

    Musical numbers included: "How High the Moon," "It Don't Mean a Thing (If It Ain't Got That Swing,") "Love and Kisses," "Judy," "Cow Cow Boogie," "I'll Never Be the Same," " Mr. Paganini," "The Nearness Of You," "They Can't Take That Away From Me," "Our Love Is Here to Stay," "A-Tisket, A-Tasket," "Flying Home,""Night and Day," "That Old Black Magic," "Lullaby of Birdland,"

"'S Wonderful," "Cheek to Cheek," "Let's Call the Whole Thing Off," "My Buddy, "The Man I Love," "Something to Live For," "Blue Skies, "How High the Moon," "Lady Be Good."
Time: 1966. Place: Nice, France. Presented in two parts.

ARKANSAS

Arkansas Repertory Theatre, Little Rock
Robert Hupp producing artistic director

BERTRAND PRIEST. By Ian Cohen. April 27, 2007 (world premiere). Direction, Brad Mooy; scenery, Mike Nichols; costumes, Olivia Koach; lighting, Matthew Webb; sound, M. Jason Pruzin; stage management, Stephen Horton.

Al Steinberg	Matt Walker	Katrina Chernov	Josie DiVincenzo
Dennis Kennedy	Eric Martin Brown	Anchorperson	Molly Collier-Rawn
Bertrand Priest	Mark Fisher		

Presented without intermission.

CALIFORNIA

American Conservatory Theater, San Francisco
Carey Perloff artistic director, Heather Kitchen executive director

HAPPY END. Musical with book by Elisabeth Hauptmann and Bertolt Brecht; music by Kurt Weill; lyrics by Mr. Brecht; adapted by Michael Feingold. June 14, 2006. Direction, Carey Perloff; choreography, John Carrafa; scenery, Walt Spangler; costumes, Candice Donnelly; lighting, Robert Wierzel; sound, Jeff Curtis; music direction, Constantine Kitsopoulos; dramaturgy, Michael Paller; stage management, Kimberly Mark Webb.

Bill Cracker	Peter Macon	Miriam	Celia Shuman
Sam "Mammy" Wurlitzer	Jack Willis	Maj. Stone	Joan Harris-Gelb
The Governor	Sab Shimono	Capt. Jackson	Steven Anthony Jones
The Reverend	Charles Dean	Lt. Lillian Holiday	Charlotte Cohn
The Professor	Rod Gnapp	Sister Mary	Rene Augesen
Baby Face	Justin Leath	Sister Jane	Lianne Marie Dobbs
The Fly	Linda Mugleston	Brother Ben	Jud Williford

Ensemble: Jackson Davis, Dan Hiatt, Drew Kirschfield, Wendy James, Stephanie Saunders, Colin Thomson.

Musical numbers included: "The Bilbao Song," "Ballad of the Pirates," "Lieutenant of the Lord," "March Ahead," "The Sailor's Tango," "Brother, Give Yourself a Shove," "Song of the Big Shot," "Don't Be Afraid," "In Our Childhood's Bright Endeavor," "The Liquor Dealer's Dream," "The Mandalay Song," "Surabaya Johnny," "Ballad of the Lily of Hell.

Time: December 1919. Place: Chicago. Presented in three parts.

The First Look New Plays Festival. January 16–27, 2007.

THE TOSCA PROJECT. By Carey Perloff and Val Caniparoli. January 16, 2007. Direction, Ms. Perloff.

BRAINPEOPLE. By José Rivera. January 19, 2007. Direction, Erica Gould.

THE IMAGINARY INVALID. By Molière; adapted by Constance Congdon. January 26, 2007. Direction, Ron Lagomarsino.

HEDDA GABLER. By Henrik Ibsen; translated by Paul Walsh. February 14, 2007. Direction, Richard E.T. White; scenery, Kent Dorsey; costumes, Sandra Woodall; lighting, Alexander V. Nichols; sound and music, John Gromada; dramaturgy, Michael Paller; stage management, Elisa Guthertz.

Hedda Gabler .... Rene Augesen	Ms. Elvsted .... Finnerty Steeves
George Tesman .... Anthony Fusco	Eilert Lovborg .... Stephen Barker Turner
Juliane Tesman .... Sharon Lockwood	Commissioner Brack .... Jack Willis
Berte .... Barbara Oliver	

Presented in two parts.

AFTER THE WAR. By Philip Kan Gotanda. March 28, 2007 (world premiere). Direction, Carey Perloff; choreography, Julia Adam; scenery, Donald Eastman; costumes, Lydia Tanji, lighting, James F. Ingalls and Nancy Schertler; sound, Jake Rodriguez; dramaturgy, Michael Paller; stage management, Kimberly Mark Webb.

Chester Monkawa .... Hiro Kanagawa	Leona Hitchings .... Harriett D. Foy
Earl T. Worthing .... Steven Anthony Jones	Olga Mikhoels .... Delia MacDougall
Lillian Okamura .... Sala Iwamatsu	Benji Tucker .... Ted Welch
Mary-Louise Tucker .... Carrie Paff	Mr. Goto .... Sab Shimono
Mr. Oji .... Francis Jue	

Time: 1948. Place: Japanese Town, San Francisco. Presented in two parts.

Berkeley Repertory Theatre
Tony Taccone artistic director, Susan Medak managing director

MOTHER COURAGE AND HER CHILDREN. By Bertolt Brecht; translated by David Hare. September 13, 2006. Direction, Lisa Peterson; scenery, Rachel Hauck; costumes, David Zinn; lighting, Alexander V. Nichols, sound, Jill BC DuBoff; music, Gina Leishman; dramaturgy, Shirley Fishman; stage management, Michael Suenkel. Presented in association with La Jolla Playhouse.

Recruiting Officer .... Marc Damon Johnson	Eilif .... Justin Leath
Sergeant .... Brent Hinkley	Cook .... Jarion Monroe
Mother Courage .... Ivonne Coll	Yvette Pottier .... Katie Barrett
Kattrin .... Katie Huard	Chaplain .... Patrick Kerr
Swiss Cheese .... Drew Hirshfield	

Musicians: David W. Collins, Mark Danisovszky, Ara Anderson.

Presented in two parts.

PASSING STRANGE. Musical with book and lyrics by Stew; music by Heidi Rodewald. October 25, 2006 (world premiere). Direction, Annie Dorsen; choreography, Karole Armitage; scenery, David Korins; costumes, Annie Smart; lighting, Kevin Adams; sound, Jake Rodriguez; music direction, Ms. Rodewald and Jon Spurney; dramaturgy, Madeleine Oldham; stage management, Cynthia Cahill. Presented in association with the Public Theater, New York.

Edwina; others .... de'Adre Aziza	Hugo; others .... Chad Goodridge
Youth .... Daniel Breaker	Sherry; others .... Rebecca Naomi Jones
Mother .... Eisa Davis	Narrator .... Stew
Franklin; others .... Colman Domingo	

Musicians: Marc Doten, Russ Kleiner, Stew, Ms. Rodewald, Mr. Spurney.

Musical numbers included: "Blues Scales," "Baptist Fashion Show," "Gospel Jam," "Freight Train," "Just As I Am," "Arlington Hill," "Punk Rock Sole Brother," "Must Have Been High," "A Living Thing," "Merci beaucoup M. Godard," "Amsterdam," "Keys," "We Just Had Sex," "L.A. Was in My Mind," "Stoned/Mom Song," "Surface," "Damage," "Mom vs. James Brown," "Identity," "The Black One," "Voice of America," "Come Down Now," "Work the Wound," "Love Like That," "Drinking Song."

Presented in two parts.

ALL WEAR BOWLERS. By Geoff Sobelle and Trey Lyford. November 29, 2006. Direction, Aleksandra Wolska; scenery, Edward E. Haynes Jr.; costumes, Tara Webb; lighting, Randy "Igleu" Glickman; sound, James Sugg; music, Michael Friedman; film, Michael Glass; stage management, Michelle Blair. Presented in association with Rainpan43.

Earnest .... Geoff Sobelle   Wyatt .... Trey Lyford
Presented without intermission.

TO THE LIGHTHOUSE. By Adele Edling Shank; based on the novel by Virginia Woolf. February 28, 2007 (world premiere). Direction, Les Waters; scenery, Annie Smart; costumes, Christal Weatherly; lighting, Matt Frey; sound, Darron L. West; music, Paul Dresher; video, Jedediah Ike; dramaturgy, Madeleine Oldham; stage management, Elizabeth Moreau.

William Bankes .... Jarion Monroe   Charles Tansley .... David Mendelsohn
Lily Briscoe .... Rebecca Watson   Prue; Adult Cam .... Whitney Bashor
Mrs. Ramsay .... Monique Fowler   Minta Doyle; Mrs McNabb .... Lauren Grace
Mr. Ramsay .... Edmond Genest   Paul Rayley .... Noah James Butler
Andrew; Adult James .... Clifton Guterman
Presented in two parts.

BLUE DOOR. By Tanya Barfield. April 11, 2007. Direction, Delroy Lindo; scenery, Kate Edmunds; costumes, Emilio Sosa; lighting, Kathy A. Perkins; sound and music, Andre Pluess; stage management, Michael Suenkel.

Simon; others .... Teagle F. Bougere   Lewis .... David Fonteno
Presented without intermission.

OLIVER TWIST. By Charles Dickens; adapted by Neil Bartlett. May 16, 2007. Direction, Mr. Bartlett; scenery and costumes, Rae Smith; lighting, Scott Zielinski; sound, David Remedios; music, Gerard McBurney; music direction, Simon Deacon; stage management, Chris De Camillis. Presented in association with American Repertory Theatre and Theatre for a New Audience.

Mr. Bumble .... Remo Airaldi   Nancy .... Jennifer Ikeda
Noah; Tom .... Steven Boyer   Rose; Charlotte .... Elizabeth Jasicki
Mr. Sowerberry .... Thomas Derrah   Mr. Brownlow .... Will LeBow
Bill Sykes .... Gregory Derelian   Mrs. Bumble .... Karen MacDonald
Fagin .... Ned Eisenberg   Charley Bates .... Craig Pattison
John Dawkins;   Toby Crackit .... Lucas Steele
   Artful Dodger .... Carson Elrod   Oliver Twist .... Michael Wartella
Presented in two parts.

Center Theatre Group, Los Angeles
Michael Ritchie artistic director, Charles Dillingham managing director

CURTAINS. Musical with book by Rupert Holmes; music by John Kander, lyrics by Fred Ebb; original book by Peter Stone; additional lyrics by Messrs. Kander and Holmes. August 9, 2006 (world premiere). Direction, Scott Ellis; choreography, Rob Ashford; scenery, Anna Louizos; costumes, William Ivey Long; lighting, Peter Kaczorowski; sound,

Brian Ronan; music direction, David Loud; fight direction, Rick Sordelet; in the Ahamanson Theatre. Presented in association with Roger Berlind, Roger Horchow and Daryl Roth.

Lt. Frank Cioffi	David Hyde Pierce	Daryl Grady	John Bolton
Carmen Bernstein	Debra Monk	Johnny Harmon	Michael X. Martin
Georgia Hendricks	Karen Ziemba	Oscar Shapiro	Michael McCormick
Aaron Fox	Jason Danieley	Bobby Pepper	Noah Racey
Niki Harris	Jill Paice	Bambi Bernstein	Megan Sikora
Christopher Belling	Edward Hibbert	Sidney Bernstein	Robert Walden

Ensemble: Nili Bassman, Ward Billeisen, Jennifer Dunne, David Eggers, J. Austin Eyer, Matt Farnsworth, Patty Goble, Mary Ann Lamb, Brittany Marcin, Jim Newman, Jessica Lea Patty, Joe Aaron Reid, Darcie Roberts, Christopher Spaulding.

Musical numbers included: "Wide Open Spaces," "What Kind of Man?," "Thinking of Him," "The Woman's Dead," "Show People," Coffee Shop Nights," "In the Same Boat 1," "I Miss the Music," "Thataway!," "He Did It," "Kansasland," "It's a Business," "In the Same Boat 2," "A Tough Act to Follow," "In the Same Boat 3," "In the Same Boat."

Time: 1959. Place: The Colonial Theatre in Boston. Presented in two parts.

WATER AND POWER. By Richard Montoya and Culture Clash. August 6, 2006 (world premiere). Direction, Lisa Peterson; choreography, Jennifer Sanchez; scenery, Rachel Hauck; costumes, Christopher Acebo; lighting, Alexander V. Nichols; sound and music, Paul James Prendergast; dramaturgy, John Glore; stage management, James T. McDermott; in the Mark Taper Forum.

Norte; Sur	Ric Salinas	Deer Dancer; Gibby; Gabby	Moises Arias
Water (Gilbert Garcia)	Richard Montoya	El Musico; Vendor	Emilio Rivera
Power (Gabriel Garcia)	Herbert Sigüenza	The Fixer	Dakin Matthews
Asunción Garcia	Winston J. Rocha		

Time: Before and after. Place: Los Angeles. Presented without intermission.

NIGHTHAWKS. By Douglas Steinberg. September 6, 2006 (world premiere). Direction, Stefan Novinski; scenery, Donna Marquet; costumes, A. Jeffrey Schoenberg, lighting, Rand Ryan; music, Michael Roth; stage management, Scott Harrison; in the Kirk Douglas Theatre.

Quig	Dan Castellaneta	Lucy	Kelly Karbacz
Jimmy Nickels	Dennis Cockrum	Mae	Colette Kilroy
Sam	Brian T. Finney	Customer	Morgan Rusler
Clive	Joe Fria		

Presented in two parts.

NIGHTINGALE. Solo performance piece by Lynn Redgrave. October 15, 2006. Direction, Joseph Hardy; scenery, Tobin Ost; costumes, Candice Cain; lighting, Rui Rita; sound, Cricket S. Myers; stage management, David S. Franklin; in the Mark Taper Forum.

Mildred Asher	Lynn Redgrave

Presented without intermission.

13. Musical with book by Dan Elish; music and lyrics by Jason Robert Brown. January 7, 2007 (world premiere). Direction, Todd Graff; choreography, Michele Lynch; scenery, David Gallo; costumes, Candice Cain; lighting, Mike Baldassari; sound, Duncan Robert Edwards, projections, Zachary Borovay; music direction, David O., stage management, William Coiner; in the Mark Taper Forum. Presented in association with Bob Boyett.

Evan	Ricky Ashley	Charlotte	Jenae Burrows
Lucy	Caitlin Baunoch	Kendra	Emma Degerstedt

Cassie .... Tinashe Kachingwe
Archie .... Tyler Mann
Patrice .... Sara Niemietz
Ritchie .... Ryan Ogburn
Brett .... J.D. Phillips

Simon .... Ellington Ratliff
Molly .... Chloe Smith
Eddie .... Christian Vandal
Malcolm .... Seth Zibalese

Musicians: David O. keyboards, Charlie Rosen keyboards, Chris Raymond guitar 1, Molly Bernstein guitar 2, Nehemiah Williams bass, Jamie Eblen percussion.

Musical numbers included: "Thirteen!", "All the Cool Kids," "Get Me What I Need," "What It Means To Be A Friend," "Getting Ready," "The Bloodmaster," "Being a Geek," "Angry Boy," "Tell Her," "It Can't Be True," "Getting Over It," "My Name is Archie," "Brand New You."

Place: Appleton, Indiana. Presented without intermission.

DISTRACTED. By Lisa Loomer. March 25, 2007 (world premiere). Direction, Leonard Foglia; scenery and projections, Elaine J. McCarthy; costumes, Robert Blackman; lighting, Russell H. Champa; sound, Jon Gottlieb; stage management, David S. Franklin; in the Mark Taper Forum.

Mama .... Rita Wilson
Jesse .... Hudson Thames
Dad .... Ray Porter
Mrs. Holly .... Stephanie Berry

Dr. Broder .... Bronson Pinchot
Sherry .... Marita Geraghty
Vera .... Johanna Day
Natalie .... Emma Hunton

Presented in two parts.

SLEEPING BEAUTY WAKES. Musical with book by Rachel Sheinkin; music and lyrics by Brendan Milburn and Valerie Vigoda. April 7, 2007 (world premiere). Direction and choreography, Jeff Calhoun; scenery, Tobin Ost; costumes, Maggie Morgan; lighting, Michael Gilliam; sound, Eric Snodgrass; stage management, William Coiner; in the Kirk Douglas Theatre. Presented in association with Deaf West Theatre.

Beauty; Princess Rose .... Alexandria Wailes
Groundskeeper's Son .... Russell Harvard
King .... Clinton Derricks-Carroll

Queen .... Christia Mantzke
Bad Fairy .... Deanne Bray

Ensemble: Erika Amato, Kevin Earley, Shannon Ford, Troy Kotsur, Brendan Milburn, Valerie Vigoda.

Musical numbers included: "Everything Changes but You," "Wake Up Call for Love," "Can You Cure Me?" "Only a King," "Dream With Me," "It's a Girl," "Uninvited," "Gift Giving Sequence," "Lullaby"/"Dream With Me" (Reprise), "Out of Harm's Way," "Trouble," "Drifting," "Out of Harm's Way (Reprise)," "Bring It On," "Wheel Goes Round," "She's Awake," "Eyes Wide Open," "Can You Cure Me? (Reprise)," "You Make Me Feel Awake," "Still Small Hours," "Only a King" (Reprise)," "Ordinary Magic," "Quintet," "Lullaby" (Reprise), "Take It Back"/"Bring It On" (Reprise)/"Beauty's Dream," "Everything Changes but You" (Reprise).

YELLOW FACE. By David Henry Hwang. May 20, 2007 (world premiere). Direction, Leigh Sillverman; scenery, David Korins; costumes, Myung Hee Cho; lighting, Donald Holder; sound, Darron L. West; stage management, James T. McDermott; in the Mark Taper Forum. Presented in association with the Public Theater, New York, and East West Players.

DHH .... Hoon Lee
HYH; others .... Tzi Ma
Marcus Gee .... Peter Scanavino
Leah; others .... Julienne Hanzelka Kim

Jane; others .... Kathryn A. Layng
Stuart; others .... Lucas Caleb Rooney
Announcer .... Tony Torn

Presented in two parts.

Geffen Playhouse, Los Angeles
Gilbert Cates producing director, Randall Arney artistic director,
Stephen Eich managing director

HEROES. By Gerald Sibleyras; translated by Tom Stoppard. April 18, 2007. Direction, Thea Sharrock; scenery and costumes, Robert Jones; lighting, Howard Harrison; sound, Jonathan Burke; stage management, Mary Michele Miner. Presented in association with David Pugh, Dafydd Rogers and the Shubert Organization.

Philippe	Richard Benjamin	Gustave	George Segal
Henri	Len Cariou		

Presented without intermission.

Laguna Playhouse, Laguna Beach
Andrew Barnicle artistic director, Richard Stein executive director

AND THE WINNER IS. By Mitch Albom. Opened June 3, 2006. Direction, Andrew Barnicle; scenery, John Berger; costumes, Julie Keen; lighting, Paulie Jenkins; sound, David Edwards; stage management, Julie Haber.

Tyler Johnes	Kelly Boulware	Teddy	Jeff Marlow
Seamus	Nicolas Coster	Kyle Morgan	Brent Schindele
Sheri	Ann Marie Lee	Serenity	Annie Abrams

Presented in two parts.

SONIA FLEW. By Melinda Lopez. September 16, 2006. Direction, Juliette Carrillo; scenery, Myung Hee Cho; costumes, Joyce Kim Lee; lighting, Lonnie Rafael Alcaraz; sound, David Edwards; music, Chris Webb; stage management, Vernon Willet.

Pilar; Nina	Marissa Chibas	Zak; Jose	Christian Barillas
Sonia; Marta	Judith Delgado	Daniel; Tito	Matt Gottlieb
Jen; Young Sonia	Tanya Perez	Sam; Orfeo	Geno Silva

Time: 2001; 1961. Place: Minneapolis; Havana. Presented in two parts.

A MARVELOUS PARTY: THE NOËL COWARD CELEBRATION. Musical revue by David Ira Goldstein, Carl Danielsen, Mark Anders, Patricia Wilcox, Anna Lauris; adapted from the work of Noël Coward. November 18, 2006. Direction, Mr. Goldstein; choreography, Ms. Wilcox; scenery, Bill Forrester; costumes, David Kay Mickelsen; lighting, Todd Hensley; sound, David Edwards; music direction, Mr. Danielsen; stage management, Vernon Willet.

Performed by Mark Anders, Carl Danielsen, Anna Lauris.

Presented in two parts.

Musical numbers included: "Together With Music," "London Is a Little Bit of Alright," "London Pride," "Any Little Fish," "Chase Me Charlie," "What Ho! Mrs. Brisket," "Would You Like to Stick a Pin in My Balloon?," "Has Anybody Seen Our Ship," "Matelot," "I Like America," "Mad Dogs and Englishmen," "Mrs. Wentworth-Brewster," "Welcome to Pootzie Van Doyle," "The Coconut Girl," "Paddy Macneil and His Automobile," "Swing Song," "Lilies of the Valley," "The Walla Walla Boola," "Mrs. Worthington," "Mad About the Boy," "I've Been to a Marvelous Party," "Why Do the Wrong People Travel," "Sail Away," "There Are Bad Times," "Just Around the Corner," "A Room With a View"/"Dance Little Lady," "Someday I'll Find You," "I'll Follow My Secret Heart," "If Love Were All," "Nina," "Let's Do It," "The Party's Over Now"/"I'll See You Again."

THE PURSUIT OF HAPPINESS. By Richard Dresser. January 6, 2007 (world premiere). Direction, Andrew Barnicle; scenery, Tom Buderwitz; costumes, Julie Keen; lighting, Paulie Jenkins; sound, David Edwards; stage management, Nancy Staiger.

Annie .... DeeDee Rescher	Spud .... Preston Maybank
Jodi .... Joanna Strapp	Tucker .... Tim Cummings
Neil .... Matt Reidy	

Time: The present. Place: United States of America. Presented in two parts.

THE ICE-BREAKER. By David Rambo. February 17, 2007. Direction, Art Manke; scenery, Tom Buderwitz; costumes, Angela Balogh Calin; lighting, Paulie Jenkins; sound and music, Steven Cahill; stage management, Rebecca M. Green.

Sonia Milan .... Monette Magrath	Lawrence Blanchard .... Andrew Barnicle

Presented in two parts.

THE MASTER OF THE HOUSE. By Shmuel Hasfari; translated from Hebrew by Anthony Berris. March 31, 2007. Direction, Richard Stein; scenery, Narelle Sissons; costumes, Julie Keen; lighting, Tom Ruzika; sound, David Edwards; stage management, Rebecca M. Green.

Zippa Ben Ephraim .... Bryna Weiss	Motti Ben Ephraim .... Barry Alan Levine
Shayeh Ben Ephraim .... Joseph Cardinale	Yigal Kadosh .... Andrew Ross Wynn
Naomi Ben Ephraim .... Elizabeth Tobias	Yuval Ben Ephraim .... Tyler Logan
Yoel Ben Ephraim .... Jonathan Goldstein	Ro'i Kadosh .... Brett Ryback
Nava Ben Ephraim .... Stacie Chaiken	

Time: Spring 2001. Place: Tel Aviv. Presented in two parts.

La Jolla Playhouse

Des McAnuff artistic director, Steven B. Libman managing director

ZORRO IN HELL. By Culture Clash (Richard Montoya, Ric Salinas and Herbert Sigüenza). October 4, 2006. Direction, Tony Taccone; scenery, Christopher Acebo; costumes, Christal Weatherly; lighting and video, Alexander V. Nichols; sound, Robbin E. Broad; fight direction, Dave Maier; dramaturgy, Shirley Fishman; stage management, Kimberly Mark Webb.

Clasher .... Richard Montoya	Diego; Zorro .... Joseph Kamal
Kyle the Bear .... Ric Salinas	200-Year-Old Woman .... Sharon Lockwood
Don Ringo .... Herbert Sigüenza	El Musico .... Vincent Christopher Montoya

Presented in two parts.

THE WIZ. October 11, 2006. Musical with book by William F. Brown; music and lyrics by Charlie Smalls; based on *The Wonderful Wizard of Oz* by L. Frank Baum; "Everybody Rejoice" by Luther Vandross. Directed by Des McAnuff; choreography, Sergio Trujillo; scenery, Robert Brill; costumes, Paul Tazewell; lighting, Howell Binkley; sound, Peter Fitzgerald; projections, Michael Clark; music direction, Ron Melrose; orchestrations, Harold Wheeler; stage management, Frank Hartenstein.

Dorothy .... Nikki M. James	Evillene .... E. Faye Butler
The Wiz .... David Alan Grier	Addaperle .... Heather Lee
Lion .... Tituss Burgess	Aunt Em .... Valarie Pettiford
Tinman .... Michael Benjamin Washington	Uncle Henry .... Orville Mendoza
Scarecrow .... Rashad Naylor	Toto .... Albert Blaise Cattafi

Ensemble: Charl Brown, Courtney Corey, Mark Emerson, Dionne D. Figgins, Demond Green, Albert Guerzon, Dominique Kelly, Ron Kellum, Alan Mingo Jr., Anisha Nagarajan, NRaca, Karine Plantadit, Tera-Lee Pollin, Liz Ramos, Keiana Richard, Liz Ramos, Marcos Santana, Jonathan Taylor.

Musical numbers included: "The Feeling We Once Had," 'He's the Wizard," "Ease on Down the Road #1," "Soon As I Get Home," "I Was Born on the Day Before Yesterday," "Ease on Down the Road #2," "Slide Some Oil to Me," "Ease on Down the Road #3," "Mean Ole Lion," "Ease on Down the Road #4," "So You Wanted to Meet the Wizard," "What Would I Do?," "No Bad News," "Everybody Rejoice (Brand New Day)," "Y'all Got It," :"If You Believe," "Home."

Magic Theatre, San Francisco
Chris Smith artistic director, David Jobin managing director

GOD OF HELL. By Sam Shepard. September 30, 2006. Direction, Amy Glazer; scenery, Erik Flatmo; costumes, Fumiko Bielefeldt; lighting, Kurt Landisman; sound, Don Seaver; stage management, Angela Nostrand.

Emma	Anne Darragh	Welch	Michael Santo
Frank	John Flanagan	Mr. Haynes	Jackson Davis

MOVING RIGHT ALONG. By Elaine May (*On the Way* and *George Is Dead*) and Jan Mirochek (*Killing Trotsky*). October 28, 2006 (world premiere). Direction, Elaine May (*Killing Trotsky* and *George Is Dead*) and Jeannie Berlin (*On the Way*); scenery, James Mulligan; costumes, Christine Dougherty and Mark Zunino; lighting, Kurt Landisman and David Robinson; sound, Lindsay Jones and Norman Kern; stage management, Karen Runk.

Killing Trotsky (Jan Mirochek; translated by Herbert Kotik)

Otto	Reed Martin	Anna	Julia Brothers
Max	Mark Rydell	Mrs. Hager	Wanda McCaddon

On the Way (Elaine May)

George	Mark Rydell	Freddie	Daveed Diggs

George Is Dead (Elaine May)

Doreen	Marlo Thomas	Old Woman	Wanda McCaddon
Carla	Julia Brothers	Funeral Director	Maxon Davis
Michael	Reed Martin		

Presented in two parts.

PLEASURE + PAIN. By Chantal Bilodeau. February 10, 2007 (world premiere). Direction, Jessica Heidt; scenery, Matt McAddon; costumes, Leah Marthinsen; lighting, Michael Palumbo; sound, Dynamite Schultz; stage management, Karen Runk.

Peggy	Jennifer Clare	Ruth	Catherine Smitko
Boyfriend	Max Moore	Man	Andrew Utter
Dean	Robert Parsons		

Presented without intermission.

RUST. By Kirsten Greenidge. February 24, 2007 (world premiere). Direction, Raelle Myrick-Hodges; scenery, Matt McAddon; costumes, Cassandra Carpenter; lighting, Michael Palumbo; sound, Tyson Fechter; stage management, Karen Runk.

Jeannie	April Matthis	Ella Mae Walker	Cathleen Riddley
Randall Mifflin	Mikaal Sulaiman	Gin George	L. Peter Callender
Chunk-Chunk Adams	Donald Lett	Andrew	Lance Gardner
LaDonna Adams	Nicole C. Julien	Bill	Eric Fraisher Hayes

Presented without intermission.

'BOT. By C. Michèle Kaplan. March 10, 2007 (world premiere). Direction, Chris Smith; scenery, Robert Broadfoot; costumes, Victoria Livington-Hall; lighting, Mike Oesch; sound, Richard Scholwin; stage management, Nicole Dickerson.

Ian	Dan Hiatt	Janey	Julia Brothers
Clara	Juliet Tanner	Mella	Karen Aldridge
Charlie	Jonathan Rosen	Stephan	Steve Irish

Presented without intermission.

The Old Globe, San Diego
Jack O'Brien artistic director, Jerry Patch resident artistic director,
Louis G. Spisto executive director

LINCOLNESQUE. By John Strand. August 10, 2006 (world premiere). Direction, Joe Calarco; scenery, Michael Fagin; costumes, Anne Kennedy; lighting, Chris Rynne; sound, Lindsay Jones; stage management, Monica A. Cuoco.

Francis	T. Ryder Smith	Secretary of War; Daly	James Sutorius
Leo	Leo Marks	Carla	Magaly Colimon

Time: The present. Place: Washington, DC. Presented in two parts.

PIG FARM. By Greg Kotis. September 28, 2006. Direction, Matt August; scenery, Takeshi Kata; costumes, Jenny Mannis; lighting, Chris Rynne; sound, Paul Peterson; fight direction, Steve Rankin; stage management, Esther Emery. Presented in association with Roundabout Theatre Company, New York.

Tom	Ted Koch	Tina	Colleen Quinlan
Tim	Ian White	Teddy	Ken Land

Time: The present. Place: A pig farm somewhere in the US. Presented in two parts.

ACE. Musical with book and lyrics by Robert Taylor and Richard Oberacker; music by Mr. Oberacker. January 18, 2007. Direction, Stafford Arima; choreography, Andrew Palermo; scenery, David Korins; costumes, Marie Anne Chiment; lighting, Christopher Akerlind; sound, John H. Shivers and David Patridge; orchestrations, Greg Anthony; stage management, Andrea L. Shell.

Billy	Noah Galvin	Ruth	Heather Ayers
Mrs. Crandall	Traci Lyn Thomas	Emily	Gabrielle Boyadjian
Elizabeth	Lisa Datz	Anique	Gabrielle Stravelli
Louise	Betsy Wolfe	Teacher	Susan Kokot Stokes
Edward	Duke Lafoon	Nurse	Kelli Barrett
Ace	Darren Ritchie	Toy Store Owner	James Judy
John Robert	Michael Arden	Lt. Sanders	Richard Barth
School Bully	Ian Brininstool	Cooper	Danny Rothman
Sidekick	Maddie Shea Baldwin	Tennaman	Kevin Reed

Time: 1952. Place: St. Louis. Presented in two parts.

THE FOUR OF US. By Itamar Moses. February 8, 2007 (world premiere). Direction, Pam MacKinnon; scenery, Kris Stone; costumes, Markas Henry; lighting, Russell H. Champa; sound, Paul Peterson; stage management, Tracy Skoczelas.

David	Sean Dugan	Benjamin	Gideon Banner

Presented without intermission.

Pasadena Playhouse
Sheldon Epps artistic director, Lyla White executive director

FENCES. By August Wilson. September 1, 2006. Direction, Sheldon Epps; scenery, Gary L. Wissmann; lighting, Paulie Jenkins; costumes, Dana Rebecca Woods; sound, Pierre Dupree; stage management, Conwell S. Worthington III.

Troy Maxson	Laurence Fishburne	Gabriel	Orlando Jones
Jim Bono	Wendell Pierce	Cory	Bryan Clark
Rose	Angela Bassett	Raynell	Victoria Matthews
Lyons	Kadeem Hardison		

Presented in two parts.

SISTER ACT. Musical with book by Cheri Steinkellner and Bill Steinkellner; music by Alan Menken; lyrics by Glenn Slater; based on the Touchstone Pictures film. November 3, 2006 (world premiere). Direction, Peter Schneider; choreography, Marguerite Derricks; scenery, David Potts, costumes, Garry Lennon; lighting, Donald Holder; sound, Carl Casella and Domonic Sack; music direction, Brent-Alan Huffman; orchestrations, Doug Besterman; fight direction, Tim Weske; stage management, Eileen F. Haggerty. Presented in association with Alliance Theatre Company, Atlanta.

Mother Superior	Elizabeth Ward Land	Sgt. Eddie Souther	David Jennings
Kay-T	Pátina Renea Milller	Sister Mary Patrick	Amy K. Murray
Larosa	Badia Farha	Sister Mary Robert	Beth Malone
Deloris Van Cartier	Dawnn Lewis	Sister Mary Lazarus	Audrie Neenan
Curtis Shank	Harrison White	Sister Mary Hope	Andi Gibson
TJ	Melvin Abston	Sister Mary Bertrand	Roberta B. Wall
Bones	Danny Stiles	Sister Mary Edward	Lisa Robinson
Dinero	Dan Domenech	Sister Mary Dominique	Claci Miller
Willard	Henry Polic II	Sister Mary Gabriel	Wendy Melkonian

Ensemble: Wilkie Ferguson, Wendy James.

Presented in two parts.

South Coast Repertory, Costa Mesa
David Emmes producing artistic director, Martin Benson artistic director

RIDICULOUS FRAUD. By Beth Henley. October 21, 2006. Direction, Sharon Ott; scenery, Hugh Landwehr; costumes, Joyce Kim Lee; lighting, Peter Maradudin; sound, Stephen LeGrand; fight direction, Martin Noyes; dramaturgy, John Glore; stage management, Randall K. Lum.

Lafcad Clay	Ian Fraser	Uncle Baites	Randy Oglesby
Andrew Clay	Matt McGrath	Georgia	Eliza Pryor
Willow Clay	Betsy Brandt	Maude Chrystal	Nike Doukas
Kap Clay	Matt Letscher	Ed Chrystal	Paul Vincent O'Connor

Time: One year. Place: New Orleans; Louisiana back country. Presented in two parts.

THE PIANO TEACHER. By Julia Cho. March 16, 2007 (world premiere). Direction, Kate Whoriskey; scenery and costumes, Myung Hee Cho; lighting, Jason Lyons; sound, Tom Cavnar; dramaturgy, Megan Monaghan; stage management, Jamie A. Tucker.

Mrs. K	Linda Gehringer	Michael	Kevin Carroll
Mary Fields	Toi Perkins		

Time: The present. Place: Mrs. K's living room. Presented in two parts.

MY WANDERING BOY. By Julie Marie Myatt. April 7, 2007 (world premiere). Direction, Bill Rauch; scenery, Christopher Acebo; costumes, Shigeru Yaji; lighting, Lonnie Rafael Alcaraz; sound, Paul James Prendergast; dramaturgy, Megan Monaghan; stage management, Randall K. Lum.

John	Brent Hinkley	Sally Wright	Purva Bedi
Liza Boudin	Elizabeth Ruscio	Rooster Forbes	John Cabrera
Wesley Boudin	Richard Doyle	Miranda Stevens	Veralyn Jones
Detective Howard	Charlie Robinson		

    Time: The present. Place: United States of America. Presented in two parts.

SYSTEM WONDERLAND. By David Wiener. April 28, 2007 (world premiere). Direction, David Emmes; scenery and costumes, Myung Hee Cho; lighting, Lap-Chi Chu; sound, Tom Cavnar; dramaturgy, John Glore; stage management, Erin Nelson.

Jerry	Robert Desiderio	Aaron	John Sloan
Evelyn	Shannon Cochran		

    Time: The present. Place: A house on the coast of Los Angeles county. Presented in two parts.

Pacific Playwrights Festival. May 4–6, 2007.

BOLEROS FOR THE DISENCHANTED. By José Rivera. Direction, Octavio Solis; dramaturgy, Lenora Inez Brown. Performed by Jonathan Nichols, Gary Perez, Isabelle Ortega, Joe Quintero, Adriana Sevan, Sona Tatoyan.

SHIPWRECKED! AN ENTERTAINMENT: THE AMAZING ADVENTURES OF LOUIS DE ROUGEMONT (AS TOLD BY HIMSELF). By Donald Margulies. Direction, Bart DeLorenzo; dramaturgy, John Glore. Performed by Michael Daniel Cassady, Gregory Itzin, Charlayne Woodard.

PO' BOY TANGO. By Kenneth Lin. Direction, Chay Yew; dramaturgy, Megan Monaghan. Performed by Nelson Mashita, Jeanne Sakata, Kimberly Scott.

OUR MOTHER'S BRIEF AFFAIR. By Richard Greenberg. Direction, Pam MacKinnon; dramaturgy, John Glore. Performed by Adam Arkin, Jill Clayburgh, Arye Gross, Valerie Mahaffey.

AN ITALIAN STRAW HAT. Musical with book and lyrics by John Strand; music by Dennis McCarthy. Direction, Stefan Novinski. Performed by Daniel Blinkoff, Dan Butler, Michelle Duffy, Patrick Kerr, Katrina Lenk, Matt McGrath, Daniel T. Parker, Melissa van der Schyff, John Vickery.

TheatreWorks, Palo Alto
Robert Kelley artistic director, Phil Santora managing director

VANITIES. Musical with book by Jack Heifner; music and lyrics by David Kirshenbaum; based on the play by Mr. Heifner. June 24, 2006 (world premiere). Direction, Gordon Greenberg; choreography, Dan Knechtges; scenery, John Arnone; costumes, Cathleen Edwards; lighting, Jeff Croiter; sound, Cliff Caruthers; music direction, Carmel Dean; dramaturgy, Vickie Rozell; stage management, Rebecca Muench.

Kathy	Leslie Kritzer	Joanne	Sarah Stiles
Mary	Megan Hilty		

    Musical numbers included: "Hey There, Beautiful," "Nothing Like a Friend," "An Organized Life," "All the Brendas of the World," "I Can't Imagine," "I Don't Wanna Hear About It," "Fly Into the Future," "Feelin' Sunny," "Open Up Your Mind," "In the Same Place," "Friendship Isn't What It Used to Be," "Lookin' Good."

Time: Fall 1963; spring 1968; summer 1974. Place: A gymnasium; a sorority house; a penthouse terrace. Presented in two parts.

COLORADO

Denver Center Theatre Company
Kent Thompson artistic director

1001. By Jason Grote. January 26, 2007 (world premiere). Direction, Ethan McSweeny; scenery, Rachel Hauck; costumes, Murell Horton; lighting, Charles R. MacLeod; sound, Matthew C. Swartz; stage management, Christopher C. Ewing.

Performed by Drew Cortese, Daoud Heidami; Lanna Joffrey, John Livingstone Rolle, Jeanine Serralles, Josh Philip Weinstein.

Presented without intermission.

PURE CONFIDENCE. By Carlyle Brown. March 29, 2007. Direction, Kent Gash; scenery, Emily Beck; costumes, Austin K. Sanderson; lighting, Liz Lee; sound, Eric Stahlhammer; stage management, Lyle Raper.

Simon Cato	Gavin Lawrence	Caroline	Heather Alicia Simms
Col. Wiley Johnson	Philip Pleasants	George DeWitt; Clerk	Mike Hartman
Mattie Johnson	Maureen Silliman	Auctioneer; Reporter	David Ivers

Time: 1860–77. Place: Kentucky; Saratoga, New York. Presented in two parts.

THE SWEETEST SWING IN BASEBALL. By Rebecca Gilman. April 12, 2007. Direction, Wendy C. Goldberg; scenery, Alexander Dodge; costumes, Anne Kennedy; lighting, Charles R. MacLeod; sound, Iaeden Hovorka; stage management, Mister Erock.

Dana	Kathleen McCall	Rhonda; Dr. Gilbert	Megan Byrne
Roy; Gary	Sam Gregory	Brian; Michael	Brad Heberlee
Erica; Dr. Stanton	Caitlin O'Connell		

Time: The present. Place: A gallery and a mental hospital in and near a large city. Presented in two parts.

CONNECTICUT

Eugene O'Neill Theater Center, Waterford
Amy Sullivan and Preston Whiteway executive directors

O'Neill Playwrights' Conference. Wendy C. Goldberg, artistic director.

BIRD IN THE HAND. By Jorge Ignacio Cortiñas. July 5, 2006. Direction, Louis Tyrrell. Performed by Michael Ray Escamilla, Abe Cruz, Kate Guyton, Marin Ireland, Tasha Gordon-Solmon.

AIR CONDITIONING. By Tommy Smith. July 6, 2006. Direction, Steve Cosson. Performed by Caitlin O'Connell, Kevin Geer, Lillian Meredith, Kate Buddeke, Stephen Schnetzer, Drew Schad.

1001. By Jason Grote. July 12, 2006. Direction, Kent Thompson. Performed by Aysan Celik, Daoud Heidami, Stephen Kunken, Makela Spielman, Cyrus Farmer, Abe Cruz.

THE RECEPTIONIST. By Adam Bock. July 13, 2006. Direction, Jeremy B. Cohen. Performed by Stephen Schnetzer, Jayne Houdyshell, Romi Dias, Chris Kipiniak.

THE TALE. By Tommy Smith and Michael McQuilken. July 16, 2006. Direction, Sarah Rasmussen. Performed by Cathy Cawthon, Bradley Cherna, Claire Cook, Tasha Gordon-Solmon, Jake Jeppson, Julia Leist, Brian Mummert, Drew Schad, Kate Stahl, Alessandra Zsiba.

THE K OF D. By Laura Schellhardt. July 19, 2006. Direction, Melissa Kievman. Performed by Susan Pourfar.

FALSE CREEDS. By Darren Canady. July 20, 2006. Direction, Wendy C. Goldberg. Performed by Stephen Conrad Moore, Tymberlee Chanel, Rachel Nicks, Eisa Davis, Colman Domingo, Rachel Leslie.

THE EXCHANGE. By Ursula Rani Sarma. July 28, 2006. Direction, Michael Barakiva. Performed by John Jellison, Ross Bickell, Amanda Cobb, Ryan King, Makela Spielman, Maggie Lacey, Annie O'Sullivan, Jenny Sterlin.

O'Neill Music Theater Conference. Paulette Haupt, artistic director.

KIKI BABY. Musical with book by Lonny Price; music by Grant Sturiale, lyrics by Ellen Fitzhugh. July 15, 2006. Direction, Matt Cowart; music direction and piano, Stan Tucker. Performed by Jenn Colella, William Parry, Allison Briner, Dan Sharkey, Colby Foytik, David Pittu, Mary Pat Gleason, Veanne Cox, Adam Heller, Phyllis Somerville, Anne L. Nathan.

TRIANGLE. Musical with book by Joshua V. Scher; music by Curtis Moore; lyrics by Thomas Mizer. July 22, 2006. Direction, Robert Longbottom; music direction and piano, Dale Rieling. Performed by Colin Hanlon, Stephen Bienskie, Heather Ayers, Jodie Langel, Rich Affannato, Megan McGinnis, Alicia Irving, David Brummel, Eleanor Reissa.

Goodspeed Musicals, East Haddam

Michael P. Price executive director

PIRATES OF PENZANCE. Musical with book and lyrics by William S. Gilbert; music by Arthur S. Sullivan; additional book and lyrics by Nell Benjamin. November 1, 2006. Direction, Gordon Greenberg; choreography, Warren Carlyle; scenery, Bob Bissinger, costumes, David C. Woolard; lighting, Jeff Croiter; arrangements and music supervision, John McDaniel; orchestrations, Dan DeLange; music direction, Michael O'Flaherty; fight direction, Rick Sordelet; stage management, Donna Cooper Hilton. Presented in association with Paper Mill Playhouse, Milburn, New Jersey.

Pirate King	Andrew Varela	Frederic	Jason Michael Snow
Major General	Ed Dixon	Samuel	John O'Creagh
Mabel	Farah Alvin	Sergeant	Gerry McIntyre
Ruth	Joanna Glushak	Edith	Julia Osborne

Ensemble: Matt Baker, Ryan Bauer-Walsh, Matthew Scott Campbell, Kyle Fichtman, Michael Scott Harris, Robyn Kramer, Nick Mannix, Lindsay K. Northen, Tory Ross, Michael Rossmy, Roger Preston Smith, Leah Sprecher, Rebecca Strimaitis, Leonard E. Sullivan.

Musical numbers included: "Pour, O Pour the Pirate Sherry," "Apprenticed To a Pirate," "The Pirate Curse," "The Pirate King," "Oh, False One," "Into the Jungle," "Stop, Ladies, Pray," "Oh, Is There Not One Maiden?," "Poor Wandering One," "The Weather," "A Modern Major-General," "An Orphan Boy," "Away, Away," "The Nightmare," "Tarantara," "A Paradox," "Away, Away" (Reprise), "Stay, Frederic, Stay," "A Policeman's Lot," "Cat-Like Tread," "A Noise," "Finale."

MEET JOHN DOE. Musical with book by Andrew Gerle and Eddie Sugarman; music by Mr. Gerle; lyrics by Mr. Sugarman; additional story by Matt August. November 9, 2006 (world premiere). Direction, Michael Baron; choreography, Karma Kamp; scenery, Court Watson; costumes, Alejo Vietti; lighting, Jennifer Kiser; sound, Jay Hilton; music direction, Albin Konopka; stage management, Jess W. Speaker III.

Ann Mitchell	Donna Lynne Champlin	John Doe	James Moye
Mother	Melanie Vaughan	Colonel	Joel Blum
Beany	Keegan Michael Brown	D.B. Norton	Patrick Ryan Sullivan
Connell	Guy Paul		

Ensemble: David Andrew Anderson, Ronald L. Brown, Rachel Clark, Monique French, Victoria Huston-Elem, Aaron Lee Lambert, Nicole Mangi, Mark Sanders, Jaron Vesely.

Musical numbers included: "Can't Read the Paper Anymore," "I'm Your Man," "Page Eight, at the Top," "I'll Know Him When I See Him," "Perfect Days," "Money Talks," "This Other Guy," "Be More," "What Man," "He Speaks To Me," "The John Doe," "Thank You," "Bigger Than Baseball," "What Could Be The Harm?," "Who the Hell?," "Lighthouses," "Here's to America," "Before You."

Presented in two parts.

Hartford Stage
Michael Wilson artistic director, Michael Stotts managing director

BREAKFAST, LUNCH AND DINNER. By Luis Alfaro. March 9, 2007. Direction, Lisa Peterson; scenery, Rachel Hauck; costumes, Christopher Acebo; lighting, Christopher Akerlind; sound and music, Paul James Prendergast; stage management, Jennifer Sturch.

Minerva	Elisa Bocanegra	Al	Felix Solis
Alice	Yetta Gottesman	Officer Martinez	James Martinez

Time: Now. Place: A working-class suburb in America. Presented in two parts.

TheaterWorks, Hartford
Steve Campo executive and artistic director

MAKE ME A SONG: THE MUSIC OF WILLIAM FINN. Musical revue with music and lyrics by Mr. Finn. August 18, 2006. Direction, Rob Ruggiero; scenery, Luke Hegel-Cantarella; costumes, Alejo Vietti; lighting, John Lasiter; music direction, Michael Morris; stage management, Sharon Lynn Miner.

Performed by Sandy Binion, Joe Cassidy, Adam Heller, Sally Wilfert and pianist John DiPinto.

Musical numbers included: "Mister, Make Me a Song," "Heart and Music," "Hitchhiking Across America," "How Marvin Eats His Breakfast," "I Have Found," "Change," "Republicans," "(Billy's) Law of Genetics," "Passover," "Only One," "I'd Rather Be Sailing," "Dear Reader," "Why We Like Spelling," "Four Jews in a Room Bitching," "A Tight-Knit Family," "Trina's Song," "March of the Falsettos," "The Games I Play," "The Baseball Game," "Something Bad," "Holding to the Ground," "Unlikely Lovers," "All Fall Down," "Stupid Things I Won't Do," "That's Enough For Me," "I Went Fishing With My Dad," "When the Earth Stopped Turning," "Anytime (I Am There)," "Innocence and Experience," "Finale."

Presented in two parts.

COMPOSITION. By Timothy McCracken. February 2, 2007 (world premiere). Direction, Steve Campo; scenery, Adrian W. Jones; costumes, Camille Assaf; lighting, Marcus Doshi; sound, Daniel Baker; music, Randy Redd; stage management, Sharon Lynn Miner.

Henry	Timothy McCracken	Alexandra	Tara Falk
Curtis	Tommy Schrider		

Presented in two parts.

NIGHTINGALE. By Lynn Redgrave. May 31, 2007. Direction, Joseph Hardy; scenery, Tobin Ost; costumes, Alejo Vietti; lighting, Rui Rita and Jeff Nellis; sound and music, John Gromada; stage management, C.A. Clark.

Mildred Asher .... Lynn Redgrave

Presented without intermission.

Westport Country Playhouse

Tazewell Thompson artistic director

THE ARCHBISHOP'S CEILING. By Arthur Miller. August 26, 2006. Direction, Gregory Mosher; scenery, Alexander Dodge; costumes, Jane Greenwood; lighting, Clifton Taylor; sound, John Gromada; stage management, Christine Catti.

Adrian	Bruce McCarty	Irina	Heather Kenzie
Maya	Sara Surrey	Sigmund	Thomas G. Waites
Marcus	David Rasche		

Presented in two parts.

ALL ABOUT US. Musical with book by Joseph Stein; music by John Kander; lyrics by Fred Ebb; based on Thornton Wilder's *The Skin of Our Teeth*. April 14, 2007. Direction, Gabriel Barre; choreography, Christopher Gattelli; scenery, James Youmans; costumes, Ann Hould-Ward; lighting, Ken Billington; sound, Brian Ronan; music direction, Patrick Vaccariello; orchestrations, William David Brohn and Michael Gibson; stage management, Bess Marie Glorioso. Presented in association with Jacki Barlia-Florin.

George Antrobus	Shuler Hensley	Telegram Boy	David Standish
Maggie Antrobus	Yvette Freeman	Socrates; Announcer	Daniel Marcus
Sabina Fairweather	Cady Huffman	Plato	Michael Thomas Holmes
Esmeralda	Eartha Kitt	Homer	Frank Vlastnik
Henry	Carlo Alban	Moses	Michael James Leslie
Gladys	Samantha Futerman	Cleopatra	J. Elaine Marcos
Stage Manager	Tony Freeman	Helen	Sally Ann Tumas
Mammoth No. 1	Eric Michael Gillett	Joan	Rachelle Rak
Mammoth No. 2	Drew Taylor		

Musical numbers included: "Eat the Ice Cream," "Sabina!," "A Telegram," "We're Home," "The Wheel," "Warm," "A Whole Lot of Lovin'!," "When Pops Comes Home," "Save the Human Race," "A Discussion, Rain," "Beauty Pageant," "World Peace," "He Always Comes to Me," "You Owe It To Yourself," "Nice People," "Military Man," "Lullaby," "Another Telegram," "The Skin of Our Teeth," "At the Rialto."

Presented without intermission.

Yale Repertory Theatre, New Haven

James Bundy artistic director, Victoria Nolan managing director

EURYDICE. By Sarah Ruhl. September 28, 2007. Direction, Les Waters; choreography, John Carrafa; scenery, Scott Bradley; costumes, Meg Neville; lighting, Russell H. Champa; sound, Bray Poor; dramaturgy, Amy Boraiko; stage management, James Mountcastle.

Eurydice	Maria Dizzia	Orpheus	Joseph Parks
Loud Stone	Gian-Murray Gianino	Father	Charles Shaw Robinson
Little Stone	Carla Harting	Nasty Interesting Man	Mark Zeisler
Big Stone	Ramiz Monsef		

Presented without intermission.

BLACK SNOW. By Keith Reddin; adapted from the novel by Mikhail Bulgakov. December 7, 2006. Direction, Evan Yionoulis; scenery, Dustin Eshenroder; costumes, Rachel Myers; lighting, Stephen Strawbridge; sound, David Budries; stage management, Derek DiGregorio.

Sergei .... Adam Stein   Ivan Vasilievich .... Alvin Epstein

Ensemble: Brian Hutchison, Matthew Boston, Charles Semine, Anthony Manna, Steve Routman, Katie Barrett, Amir Arison, Susan Blommaert, Tamilla Woodard, David Lapkin.

Presented in two parts.

LULU. By Frank Wedekind; adapted by Mark Lamos and Drew Lichtenberg from a translation by Carl R. Mueller. April 5, 2007. Direction, Mr. Lamos; choreography, Seán Curran; scenery, Rumiko Ishii; costumes, Christina Bullard; lighting, Burke Brown; sound, David Thomas; stage management, Katrina Lynn Olson.

Lulu .... Brienin Bryant	Animal Trainer .... Michael Braun
Rodrigo .... Jesse J. Perez	Escherich; Hugenberg .... Joseph Gallagher
Countess Geschwitz .... Felicity Jones	Ferdinand .... Alexander Beard
Dr. Ludwig; Schon .... John Bedford Lloyd	Ludmilla .... Sarita Covington
Walter Schwarz .... Louis Cancelmi	Kadidja .... Brianna Hill
Alwa Schon .... Charles Socarides	Magelone .... Erica Sullivan
Schigolch .... Jordan Charney	Henriette .... Laura Esposito
Dr. Goll .... Joe Vincent	

Presented without intermission.

THE UNMENTIONABLES. By Bruce Norris. May 10, 2007. Direction, Anna D. Shapiro; scenery, Todd Rosenthal; costumes, James Schuette; lighting, Ann G. Wrightson; sound, Amy Altadonna; stage management, Ryan C. Durham.

Etienne .... Jon Hill	Don .... Paul Vincent O'Connor
Dave .... Brian Hutchison	Aunt Mimi .... Ora Jones
Jane .... Kelly Hutchinson	Soldier 1 .... Chike Johnson
The Doctor .... Kenn E. Head	Soldier 2 .... Sam Gordon
Nancy .... Lisa Emery	

Presented in two parts.

DISTRICT OF COLUMBIA

Arena Stage

Molly Smith artistic director, Stephen Richard executive director

9 PARTS OF DESIRE. By Heather Raffo. October 5, 2006. Direction, Joanna Settle; choreography, David Neumann; scenery, Antje Ellermann; costumes, Kasia Walicka Maimone; lighting, Peter West; sound, Obadiah Eaves; dramaturgy, Michelle T. Hall; stage management, Martha Knight.

Performed by Heather Raffo.

Presented without intermission.

Downstairs Readings in the Old Vat Room.

BOLERO. By Nilo Cruz. November 6, 2006. Direction, Molly Smith.

THE BIOGRAPHY OF A CONSTELLATION. By Lila Rose Kaplan. December 11, 2006. Direction, Gregg Henry.

WILLING. By Amy Herzog. February 12, 2007. Direction, Stephen Fried.

MARY T. AND LIZZIE K. By Tazewell Thompson. March 12, 2007. Direction, Rebecca Bayla Taichman.

SANTA ANA. By Eric Overmyer. April 16, 2007. Direction, Howard Shalwitz.

EMILIE AND VOLTAIRE . . . WERE HERE. By Karen Zacarias. May 14, 2007. Direction, Molly Smith.

GEM OF THE OCEAN. By August Wilson. February 1, 2007. Direction, Paulette Randall; scenery, Scott Bradley; costumes, Ilona Somogyi; lighting, Allen Lee Hughes; sound, Timothy M. Thompson; fight direction, Cliff Williams; dramaturgy, Mark Bly; stage management, Lloyd Davis Jr.

Eli	Clayton LeBouef	Rutherford Selig	Timmy Ray James
Citizen Barlow	Jimonn Cole	Solly Two Kings	Joseph Marcell
Aunt Ester	Lynnie Godfrey	Caesar	Leland Gantt
Black Mary	Pascale Armand		

Time: 1904. Place: 1839 Wylie Street, Pittsburgh.

The Kennedy Center

CARNIVAL! Musical with book by Michael Stewart; music and lyrics by Bob Merrill; based on material by Helen Deutsch; book revisions by Francine Pascal. February 24, 2007. Direction and choreography, Robert Longbottom; scenery, Andrew Jackness; costumes, Paul Tazewell; lighting, Ken Billington; sound, Kurt Fischer; music direction, David Chase; stage management, Shari Silberglitt.

Jacquot	Michael Arnold	Pony Dancers	Sarah Lin Johnson
Rosalie	Natascia Diaz		Amanda Kloots
Carnival Singer	Jazmin Gorsline		Lauren Pastorek
Schlegel	Jonathan Lee Iverson		Krista Saab
Marco	Sebastian La Cause	Roustabouts	Adam Laird
Olga	Nanette Michele		Denis Lambert
Grobert	Mike Mosallam		Chad L. Schiro
Lili	Ereni Sevasti		Steven Wenslawski
Paul	Jim Stanek	Tricksters	Matt Baker
Greta	Rebecca Young		Sean McKnight
Dancing Bear	Alan Bennett		Lance Olds
Carnival Puppeteer	Ed Christie		Christopher Sergeeff
Aerialists	Elisabeth Page Carpenter		Tara Siesener
	Laura Anne Carpenter		

Musical numbers included: "Direct From Vienna," "Mira," "I've Got to Find a Reason," "A Sword and a Rose and a Cape," "Humming," "Yes, My Heart," "Magic, Magic," "Love Makes the World Go Round," "Everybody Likes You," "Yum Ticky Ticky Tum Tum," "We're Rich," "Beautiful Candy," "Her Face," "Grand Imperial Cirque de Paris," "I Hate Him," "Always, Always You," "She's My Love," "Finale Ultimo."

Place: A boardwalk in the South of France. Presented without intermission.

The Shakespeare Theatre
Michael Kahn artistic director, Nicholas T. Goldsborough managing director

AN ENEMY OF THE PEOPLE. By Henrik Ibsen; translated by Rick Davis and Brian Johnston. August 29, 2006. Direction, Kjetil Bang-Hansen; scenery and costumes, Timian Alsaker; lighting, Charlie Morrison; sound, Martin Desjardins; stage management, Amber Wedin.

Dr. Thomas Stockman .... Joseph Urla
Mrs. Stockmann .... Caitlin O'Connell
Petra .... Samantha Soule
Eilif .... Ben Schiffbauer,
Sean McCoy (alt.)
Morten .... Connor Aikin,
Sam Zarcone (alt.)

Peter Stockmann .... Philip Goodwin
Morten Kiil .... Robin Gammell
Hovstad .... Derek Lucci
Billing .... Tyrone Mitchell Henderson
Captain Horster .... Peter Rini
Aslaksen .... Rick Foucheux
Ensemble .... Nick Vienna

Presented in two parts.

THE BEAUX' STRATAGEM. By George Farquhar; adapted by Thornton Wilder and Ken Ludwig. November 7, 2006. Direction, Michael Kahn; choreography, Peter Pucci; scenery, James Kronzer; costumes, Robert Perdziola; lighting, Joel Moritz; sound and music, Martin Desjardins; fight direction, Paul Dennhardt; stage management, M. William Shiner.

Jack Archer .... Christopher Innvar
Tom Aimwell .... Christian Conn
Sullen .... Ian Bedford
Scrub .... Hugh Nees
Boniface .... Drew Eshelman
Gloss .... Rick Foucheux
Lady Bountiful .... Nancy Robinette
Dorinda .... Julia Coffey
Mrs. Kate Sullen .... Veanne Cox
Cherry .... Colleen Delany

Hounslow .... Dan Crane
Bagshot .... Nick Vienna
Country Woman .... Anne Stone
Daniel .... Matthew Stucky
A Lady .... Diane Ligon
Foigard .... Floyd King
Servant .... Maria Kelly
Sir Charles .... Daniel Harray
Ensemble .... David Murgittroyd

Presented in two parts.

TITUS ANDRONICUS. By William Shakespeare. April 3, 2007. Direction, Gale Edwards; scenery, Peter England; costumes, Murell Horton; lighting, Mark McCullough; sound and music, Martin Desjardins; fight direction, Rick Sordelet; stage management, M. William Shiner.

Romans
Titus Andronicus .... Sam Tsoutsouvas
Marcus Andronicus .... William Langan
Lucius .... Chris Genebach
Quintus .... Christopher Scheeren
Martius .... David Murgittroyd
Mutius .... Danny Binstock
Lavinia .... Colleen Delany
Saturnius .... Alex Podulke
Bassianus .... Michael Brusasco
Emilius .... Bill Hamlin

Young Lucius .... James Chatham
Publius .... Nick Vienna
Nurse .... Julie-Ann Elliott

Goths
Tamora .... Valerie Leonard
Aaron .... Peter Macon
Demetrius .... Ryan Farley
Chiron .... David L. Townsend
Alarbus .... Matthew Stucky

Ensemble: C. Travis Atkinson, Bob Barr, Andy English, Maria Kelly, Kyle Magley, Robert Rector, Ben Rosenblatt.

Presented in two parts.

Theater Alliance

Paul Douglas Michnewicz, interim artistic director

3/4 OF A MASS FOR ST. VIVIAN. By Phoebe Rusch. August 10, 2006. Direction, Paul Douglas Michnewicz; scenery, Dan Conway; costumes, Kathleen Geldard; lighting, Dan Covey; sound, Mark K. Anduss; stage management, Lindsay Miller.

Performed by Marybeth Fritzky and Nora Woolley.

Presented without intermission.

THE BLUEST EYE. By Toni Morrison; adapted by Lydia Diamond. October 12, 2006. Direction, David Muse; scenery, Tony Cisek; costumes, Reggie Ray; lighting, John Burkland; sound, Ryan Rumery; music direction, Tracy Lynn Olivera, stage mangement, Jenn Carlson.

Performed by Lynn Chavis, Jessica Frances Dukes, Aakhu TuahNera Freeman, Alfred Kemp, Lia LaCour, Erica Rose, Carleen Troy, Jeorge Watson.

Time: 1941. Place: Lorain, Ohio. Presented without intermission.

INSURRECTION: HOLDING HISTORY. By Robert O'Hara. March 1, 2007. Direction, Timothy Douglas; scenery, Tony Cisek; costumes, Kate Turner-Walker; lighting, Dan Covey; sound, Vincent Olivieri; stage management, Vivian Woodland.

Performed by Frank Britton, Jeremy Brown, MaConnia Chesser, Jessica Frances Dukes, Aakhu TuahNera Freeman, Cleo House, Cedric Mays, Maya Lynne Robinson, KenYatta Rogers.

Presented in two parts.

IN ON IT. By Daniel MacIvor. April 27, 2007. Direction, Colin Hovde; costumes, Erin Nugent; lighting, Andrew Cissna; sound, Mark K. Anduss; stage management, Lisa Blythe.

Performed by Jason Lott and Jason Stiles.

Presented without intermission.

Theater J
Ari Roth artistic director

PICASSO'S CLOSET. By Ariel Dorfman. June 25, 2006. Direction, John Dillon; scenery, Lewis Folden; costumes, Kate Turner-Walker; lighting, Martha Mountain; sound, Ryan Rumery; stage management, David Elias.

Picasso	Mitchell Hebert	Max Jacob	Bill Hamlin
Dora Maar	Katherine Clarvoe	Jaime Sabartes	Lawrence Redmond
Albert Lucht	Saxon Palmer	Michel Leiris	Jim Jorgensen
Charlene Petrossian	Kathleen Coons		

Presented in three parts.

SCHLEMIEL THE FIRST. Musical with book by Isaac Bashevis Singer and Robert Brustein; music by Hankus Netsky; lyrics by Arnold Weinstein; additional music by Zalmen Mlotek; based on the play by Mr. Singer. October 8, 2006. Direction, Nick Olcott; costumes, Franklin Labovitz; music direction, Mr. Mlotek; stage management, David Elias.

Schlemiel	Thomas Howley	Tryna Rytza	Amy McWilliams
Yenta Pesha	Donna Migliaccio	Gronam Ox	Dan Manning

Ensemble: Peter Gil, Rob McQuay, Dwayne Nitz, Howard Stregack, Max Talisman, Isabel Thompson.

Musicans: David Julian Gray, Daniel Hoffman, Alex Tang.

Presented in two parts.

SPRING FORWARD, FALL BACK. By Robert Brustein. October 25, 2006. Direction, Wesley Savick; scenery, Lewis Folden; costumes, Kathleen Geldard; lighting, Colin K. Bills; sound, Matt Rowe; stage management, Rebecca Berlin.

Old Richard	Bill Hamlin	Minnie; Naomi	Susan Rome
Young Richard; David	Sean Dugan	Christine	Anne Petersen
Abe; Richard	Mitchell Greenberg	Sean	Joe Baker

Presented without intermission.

SLEEPING ARRANGEMENTS. By Laura Shaine Cunningham. January 9, 2007 (world premiere). Direction, Delia Taylor; scenery, Kathleen Runey; costumes, Melanie Clark; lighting, Colin K. Bills; sound, Mark K. Anduss; projections, Michael Skinner; stage management, Lindsay Miller.

Lily	Tessa Klein	Susan	Lindsay Haynes
Etka	Halo Wines	Manny	Thomas Howley
Uncle Len	Paul Morella	Mrs. Aventuro	Cam Magee
Uncle Gabe	David Elias	Mrs. Hassan	Susan Moses
Diana	Tiffany Fillmore	Rosie	Becky Peters

Presented in two parts.

EITHER OR. By Thomas Keneally. May 6, 2007. Direction, Daniel De Raey; scenery, James Kronzer; costumes, Misha Kachman; lighting, Martha Mountain; sound, Ryan Rumery; stage management, Kate Kilbane.

Kurt Gerstein	Paul Morella	Bertha Gerstein	Meghan Grady
Ludwig Gerstein	Ralph Cosham	Ludwig Dewitz	John-Michael MacDonald
Franz Gerstein	John Lescault	Capt. Haught	Parker Dixon
Elfriede Bensch	Elizabeth H. Richards	Ernst Zerrer	Conrad Feininger
Pastor Niemoller	John Dow	Maj. Evans	Clay Steakley

Presented in two parts.

Woolly Mammoth Theatre Company
Howard Shalwitz artistic director, Kevin Moore managing director

THE FACULTY ROOM. By Bridget Carpenter. June 11, 2006. Direction, Howard Shalwitz; scenery, Robin Stapley; costumes, Melanie Clark; lighting, Jay A. Herzog; sound, Michael Kraskin; fight direction, John Gurski; stage management, William V. Carlton.

Zoe	Megan Anderson	Bill	Michael Willis
Adam	Ethan T. Bowen	Student	Miles Butler
Carver	Michael Russotto		

Presented in two parts.

MARTHA, JOSIE AND THE CHINESE ELVIS. By Charlotte Jones. November 12, 2006. Direction, John Vreeke; scenery, Dan Conway; costumes, Kate Turner-Walker; lighting, Colin K. Bills; sound, Matthew M. Nielson; stage management, William V. Carlton.

Martha	Sarah Marshall	Lionel	David Bryan Jackson
Brenda-Marie	Kimberly Gilbert	Timothy Wong	Tony Nam
Josie	Beth Hylton	Shelley-Louise	Tiffany Fillmore

Presented in two parts.

VIGILS. By Noah Haidle. January 29, 2007. Direction, Colette Searls; choreography, Michael J. Bobbit; scenery, Daniel Ettinger; costumes, Kate Turner-Walker; lighting, Colin K. Bills; sound and music, Ryan Rumery; flying, Foy; stage management, Laura Smith.

Widow	Naomi Jacobson	Body	Matthew Montelongo
Soul	Michael Russotto	Child	Connor Aikin
Wooer	J. Fred Shiffman		

Presented without intermission.

GEORGIA

Alliance Theatre, Atlanta
Susan V. Booth artistic director, Thomas Pechar managing director

ELLIOT, A SOLDIER'S FUGUE. By Quiara Alegría Hudes. September 13, 2006. Direction, Kent Gash; scenery, Emily Beck; costumes, English Benning; lighting, William H. Grant III; sound, Clay Benning.

Grandpop	Gilbert Cruz	Ginny	Mary Lynn Owen
Pop	Matthew Montelongo	Elliot	Ivan Quintanilla

Presented without intermission.

FALSE CREEDS. By Darren Canady. February 14, 2007 (world premiere). Direction, Wendy C. Goldberg; choreography, Karma Camp; scenery, Todd Rosenthal; costumes, Anne Kennedy; lighting, Joshua Epstein; sound, Clay Benning; music, Kendall Simpson; dramaturgy, Celise Kalke; stage management, lark hackshaw.

Fannie	Joniece Abbott-Pratt	Janie	Alecia Robinson
Lydia	Joy C. Hooper	Amelia	chandra thomas
Jason	Warner Miller	Marcus	Geoffrey D. Williams

Time: 1921; 1995. Place: Tulsa.

ILLINOIS

Chicago Shakespeare Theater
Barbara Gaines artistic director, Criss Henderson executive director

HAMLET. By William Shakespeare. September 10, 2006. Direction and lighting, Terry Hands; scenery and costumes, Mark Bailey; sound, James Savage; music, Colin Towns; fight direction, Robin H. McFarquhar; stage management, Jennifer Matheson Collins.

Francisco	Bill Bannon	Ophelia	Lindsay Gould
Barnardo	Braden Moran	Osric	Kevin Rich
Horatio	Timothy Edward Kane	Hamlet	Ben Carlson
Gravedigger #1	Roderick Peeples	Rosencrantz	Matt Schwader
Claudius; Ghost	Bruce A. Young	Guildenstern	Ben Viccellio
Gertrude	Barbara Robertson	First Player	James Harms
Laertes	Andrew Ahrens	Player King	Aaron Alpern
Polonius	Mike Nussbaum	Player Queen	Wendy Robie

Presented in two parts.

THE THREE MUSKETEERS. Musical with book by Peter Raby; music by George Stiles; lyrics by Paul Leigh; based on the novel by Alexandre Dumas. January 3, 2007. Direction and choreography, David H. Bell; scenery, Tom Burch; costumes, Mariann Verheyen; lighting, Donald Holder; sound, Cecil Averett; music direction, Dale Rieling; music supervision, George Stiles; orchestrations, David Shrubsole; fight direction, Kevin Asselin; stage management, Deborah Acker and Jennifer Matheson Collins.

D'Artagnan	Kevin Massey	Milady	Blythe Wilson
Athos	Juan Chioran	Constance	Abby Mueller
Aramis	Aaron Ramey	Rochefort	Jeff Parker
Porthos	Steven Jeffrey Ross	Bonacieux	Greg Vinkler

Planchet .... Brian Sills	King Louis .... Terry Hamilton
Buckingham .... Kevin Asselin	Cardinal Richelieu .... Jeffrey Baumgartner
Queen Anne .... Johanna McKenzie Miller	Treville .... Neil Friedman

Ensemble: Rebecca Finnegan, George Keating, Brianna Borger, Devin DeSantis, Constantine Germanacos, Karl Sean Hamilton, John Hickman, Scott Alan Jones, Meg Miller, Jessie Mueller.

Musical numbers included: "Riding to Paris," "Thrust With the Point," "The Challenges," "Count Me In," "Any Day," "Paris by Night," "Doing Very Well Without You," "The Life of a Musketeer," "Ride On! "Gentlemen, Time"/"Ghosts," "A Good Old-Fashioned War," "Who Could Have Dreamed of You?," "Take a Little Wine," "No Gentlemen (The Kidnap)," "All That I Am," "Pour la France," "Beyond the Walls."

Presented in two parts.

MARIONETTE MACBETH. By Eugenio Monti Colla and Kate Buckley; adapted for marionettes from the Scottish play by William Shakespeare. March 14, 2007. Puppetry direction, Mr. Colla; spoken-word direction, Ms. Buckley; scenery, Carlo III Colla; lighting, Franco Citterio; sound, Lindsay Jones; music, Fabio Vacchi; stage management, Jennifer Matheson Collins. Presented in association with Compagnia Marionettistica Carlo Colla e Figli of Milan, Italy.

Witch 1; others .... Martin Yurek	Macduff; others .... Matt Penn
Witch 2; others .... Christopher Kelly	Macbeth .... Jim Mezon
Witch 3; Lady Macbeth .... Lisa Dodson	Banquo; Soldier .... Neil Friedman
Duncan; Gerolamo .... Joe Foust	

Puppeteers: Carlo III Colla, Eugenio Monti Colla, Justin Arienti, Franco Citterio, Mariagrazia Citterio, Piero Corbella, Debora Coviello, Cecilia di Marco, Tommaso Franchin, Egon Gorghetto, Mariapia Lanino, Tiziano Marcolegio, Sheila Perego, Giovanni Schiavolin.

Presented in two parts.

Court Theatre, Chicago
Charles Newell artistic director

HOTEL CASSIOPEIA. By Charles L. Mee. November 18, 2006. Direction, Anne Bogart; scenery, Neil Patel; costumes, James Schuette; lighting, Brian H. Scott; sound, Darron L. West; projections, Greg King; dramaturgy, Adrien-Alice Hansel; stage management, Elizabeth Moreau. Presented in association with SITI Company.

Joseph .... Barney O'Hanlon	Pharmacist .... J. Ed Araiza
Waitress .... Michi Barall	Ballerina .... Ellen Lauren
Astronomer .... Stephen Webber	Mother .... Akiko Aizawa
Herbalist .... Leon Ingulsrud	

Presented without intermission.

UNCLE VANYA. By Anton Chekhov; translated by Paul Schmidt. January 20, 2007. Direction, Charles Newell; scenery, Leigh Breslau; costumes, Miranda Hoffman; lighting, John Culbert; sound, Andre Pluess and Ben Sussman; stage management, Kimberly Osgood.

Serebriakov .... James Harms	Astrov .... Timothy Edward Kane
Yelena .... Chaon Cross	Telegin .... Matthew Krause
Sonya .... Elizabeth Ledo	Marina .... Penny Slusher
Mrs. Voinitsky .... Peggy Roeder	Hired Man .... Dave Belden
Vanya .... Kevin Gudahl	

Presented without intermission.

The Goodman Theatre, Chicago

Robert Falls artistic director, Roche Schulfer executive director

THE DREAMS OF SARAH BREEDLOVE. By Regina Taylor. June 27, 2006. Direction, Ms. Taylor; choreography, Hope Clarke; scenery, Scott Bradley; costumes, Jacqueline Firkins; lighting, Scott Zielinski; sound, Richard Woodbury; music, Daryl Waters; dramaturgy, Tanya Palmer; stage management, Alden Vasquez.

Sarah Breedlove	L. Scott Caldwell	Leila	Nikki E. Walker
Nola	Cheryl Lynn Bruce	Mae	Libya Pugh
Freeman	Roland Boyce Sr.	C.J. Walker	Keith Randolph Smith

Presented in two parts.

KING LEAR. By William Shakespeare. September 19, 2006. Direction, Robert Falls; scenery, Walt Spangler; costumes, Ana Kuzmanic; lighting, Michael Philippi; sound, Richard Woodbury; fight direction, Rick Sordelet; dramaturgy, Tom Creamer; stage management, Joseph Drummond.

Kent	Steve Pickering	Albany	Kevin Gudahl
Gloucester	Edward Gero	Cornwall	Chris Genebach
Edmund	Jonno Roberts	Burgundy	Andrew Navarro
Lear	Stacy Keach	France	Brian J. Gill
Goneril	Kim Martin-Cotten	Edgar	Joaquin Torres
Regan	Kate Arrington	Oswald	Dieterich Gray
Cordelia	Laura Odeh	Fool	Howard Witt

Ensemble: Kareem K. Bandealy, Jeffrey Baumgartner, David Blixt, Patrick Clear, Carolyn Defrin, Hans Fleischmann, Jose Antonio Garcia, Michael F. Goldberg, Ann James, Christopher Johnson, Elise Kauzlaric, Ronald Keaton, Kyle Lemieux, Steve Schine, Matthew Lon Walker.

Presented in two parts.

New Stages Series. September 25–30, 2006.

THE BROTHERS SIZE. By Tarell Alvin McCraney. Direction, Henry Godinez. September 25, 2006.

OUR LADY OF THE UNDERPASS. By Tanya Saracho. Direction, Andrea J. Dymond. September 26, 2006.

MASSACRE (SING TO YOUR CHILDREN). By José Rivera. Direction, Chuck Smith. September 27, 2006.

TILL. By Ifa Bayeza. Direction, Derrick Sanders. September 28, 2006.

AMERIVILLE. By Universes (Steven Sapp, Mildred Ruiz, Gamal Chasten, Ninja). Direction, Chay Yew. September 29, 2006.

VIGILS. By Noah Haidle. October 24, 2006 (world premiere). Direction, Kate Whoriskey; choreography, Randy Duncan; scenery and costumes, Walt Spangler; lighting, Jason Lyons; sound and music, Rob Milburn and Michael Bodeen; projections, John Boesche; dramaturgy, Tanya Palmer; stage management, Kimberly Osgood.

Widow	Johanna Day	Body	Steve Key
Wooer	Coburn Goss	Child	Lillian Almaguer
Soul	Marc Grapey		

Presented without intermission.

FRANK'S HOME. By Richard Nelson. December 5, 2006 (world premiere). Direction, Robert Falls; scenery, Thomas Lynch; costumes, Susan Hilferty; lighting, Michael Philippi;

sound, Richard Woodbury, dramaturgy, Tom Creamer; stage management, T. Paul Lynch. Presented in association with Playwrights Horizons.

Frank Lloyd Wright	Peter Weller	Louis Sullivan	Harris Yulin
Catherine	Maggie Siff	Miriam Noel	Mary Beth Fisher
Helen Girvin	Holley Fain	Lloyd	Jay Whitaker
William	Jeremy Strong	Kenneth	Chris Henry Coffey

Presented without intermission.

RADIO GOLF. By August Wilson. January 23, 2007. Direction, Kenny Leon; scenery, David Gallo; costumes, Susan Hilferty; lighting, Donald Holder; sound, Dan Moses Schreier; music, Kathryn Bostic; dramaturgy, Todd Kreidler; stage management, Joseph Drummond.

Elder Joseph Barlow	Anthony Chisholm	Roosevelt Hicks	James A. Williams
Sterling Johnson	John Earl Jelks	Harmond Wilks	Hassan El-Amin
Mame Wilks	Michole Briana White		

Presented in two parts.

RABBIT HOLE. By David Lindsay-Abaire. March 20, 2007. Direction, Steve Scott; scenery, Scott Bradley; costumes, Birgit Rattenborg Wise; lighting, Robert Christen; sound and music, Richard Woodbury; stage management, Alden Vasquez.

Howie	Daniel Cantor	Nat	Mary Ann Thebus
Izzy	Amy Warren	Jason	Jürgen Hooper
Becca	Lia D. Mortensen		

Time: The present. Place: Larchmont, New York. Presented in two parts.

MASSACRE (SING TO YOUR CHILDREN). By José Rivera. April 2, 2007 (world premiere). Direction, Chuck Smith; scenery, Brian Sidney Bembridge; costumes, Christine Pascual; lighting, Mary MacDonald Badger; sound, Mikhail Fiksel. Presented in association with Teatro Vista.

Panama	Henry Godinez	Vivy	Sandra Marquez
Erik	Joe Minoso	Eliseo	Juan F. Villa
Hector	Edward F. Torres	Lila	Sona Tatoyan
Janis	Sandra Delgado	Joe	Anthony Moseley

Presented in two parts.

OEDIPUS COMPLEX. By Frank Galati; adapted from Sophocles's *Oedipus the King*, translated by Stephen Berg and Diskin Clay; and Sigmund Freud's *The Interpretation of Dreams* and *Letters to Wilhelm Fliess*, translated by A.A. Brill, Eric Mosbacher and James Strachey. May 8, 2007. Direction, Mr. Galati; choreography, Christina Ernst; scenery, James Schuette; costumes, Mara Blumenfeld; lighting, Michael Chybowski; sound and music, Todd Barton; dramaturgy, Tom Creamer; stage management, Joseph Drummond.

Freud; Priest of Zeus	Nick Sandys	Jocasta	Susan Hart
Oedipus	Ben Viccellio	Messenger	Patrick Clear
Kreon	Roderick Peeples	Shepherd	Bradley Armacost
Teiresias	Jeffrey Baumgartner		

Ensemble: Kevin Asselin, Phillip James Brannon, Cliff Chamberlin, Sean Fortunato, Jose Antonio Garcia, Stephen Louis Grush, Derek Hasenstab, Joel Hatch, Timothy W. Hull, John Phillips, Craig Spidle, Edward Stevens, Safia Hannin, Laney Kraus-Taddeo.

Presented without intermission.

Lookingglass Theatre Company, Chicago
David Catlin artistic director, Rachel E. Kraft executive director

ARGONAUTIKA. By Mary Zimmerman; based on texts by Gaius Valerius Flaccus, translated by David R. Slavitt; and Appolonius Rhodius, translated by Peter Green. October 29, 2006. Direction, Ms. Zimmerman; scenery, Daniel S. Ostling; costumes, Ana Kuzmanic; lighting, John Culbert; sound and music design, Andre Pluess and Ben Sussman; puppets, Michael Montenegro; stage management, Jonathan Templeton.

Jason	Ryan Artzberger	Pollux	Tony Hernandez
Hera	Lisa Tejero	Hercules; Aeetes	Glenn Fleshler
Athena	Mariann Mayberry	Hylas	Jarrett Sleeper
Pelias	Allen Gilmore	Andromeda	Victoria Caciopoli
Idmon	Jesse J. Perez	Amycas	David Catlin
Meleager	Dan Kenney	Aphrodite	Angela Walsh
Castor	Larry DiStasi	Medea	Atley Loughridge

Presented in two parts.

Marriott Theatre, Lincolnshire
Andy Hite and Aaron Thielen artistic directors, Terry James executive producer

ONCE UPON A TIME IN NEW JERSEY. Musical with book and lyrics by Susan DiLallo; music by Stephen Weiner. July 12, 2006. Direction and choreography, Marc Robin; scenery, Thomas M. Ryan; costumes, Nancy Missimi; lighting, Diane Ferry Williams; sound, Cecile Averett; music direction, Richard Carsey; orchestrations, Dimitri Nakhamkin and David Siegel; stage management, Rita Vreeland.

Vinnie LoBianco	Jim Weitzer	Buddy	Scott Aiello
Angie Moscato	Kathy Voytko	Tony	Norm Boucher
Rocco Fabrizio	Will Swenson	Ed Vendetta	Michael Accardo
Celeste Castiglione	Christine Sherill	Loretta	Cheryl Avery
Billy Castiglione	Matt Orlando	Conchetta	Lara Filip
Millie LoBianco	Paula Scrofano	Etta	Liz Baltes

Ensemble: Cory Goodrich, Abby Mueller, Stephen Schellhardt.

Musical numbers included: "Once Upon a Time in New Jersey," "What'll Be Today," "Girl Like Her," "Rocco," "Quiet Little Dinner," " Someone That I Hate," "How'd You Like to Be Me," "God Knows, Mrs. LoBianco," "One of a Kind," "Little Girl, Beware," "Quando Scungilli," "Quiet Little Dinner Tango," "Mama, Mama," "A Good Job," "I Always Knew It Was You," "Sandwiches to Make," "In the Deli," "Billy."

Presented in two parts.

Royal George Theatre, Chicago

HATS! Musical revue with book by Marcia Milgrom Dodge and Anthony Dodge; music and lyrics by Doug Besterman, Susan Birkenhead, Michele Brourman, Pat Bunch, Gretchen Cryer, Mr. Dodge, Ms. Dodge, Beth Falcone, David Friedman, Kathie Lee Gifford, David Goldsmith, Carol Hall, Henry Krieger, Stephen Lawrence, Melissa Manchester, Amanda McBroom, Pam Tillis, Sharon Vaughn; based on the experiences of the Red Hat Society. April 29, 2007. Direction and choreography, Lynne Taylor-Corbett; scenery, Narelle Sissons; costumes, Judanna Lynn; lighting, Jason Kantrowitz; sound, Ben Neafus; puppets, Eric Wright and Emily DeCola; music direction, Steven M. Alper and Jeremy Ramey; orchestrations, Larry Blank and Peter Myers; arrangements, Messrs. Besterman and Alper; stage management, Shawn Pryby. Presented by Sibling Theatricals in association with BG Prods. and Hats Holdings.

Dame .... Rosalyn Rahn Kerins	Princess .... Kate Young
Baroness................................. Vickie Daignault	Duchess.. Laura Walls
Contessa .... Nora Mae Lyng	Lady .... Marilyn Bogetich
MaryAnne .... Melissa Manchester	

Musical numbers included: "Fifty," "I Don't Want," "Cinco Pasos de la Vida," "The Older the Fiddle, the Sweeter the Tune," "Celebrate," "My Empty Nest," "Just Like Me," "My Oven's Still Hot," "Yes We Can," "The Older the Fiddle, the Sweeter the Tune" (Reprise), "Invisible," "Fifty" (Reprise), "A Big Red Hat," "Put Your Red Hat On."

Presented without intermission.

Steppenwolf Theatre Company, Chicago
Martha Lavey artistic director, David Hawkanson executive director

THE UNMENTIONABLES. By Bruce Norris. July 9, 2006. Direction, Anna D. Shapiro; scenery, Todd Rosenthal; costumes, James Schuette; lighting, J.R. Lederle; sound, Rob Milburn and Michael Bodeen; fight direction, Joe Dempsey; dramaturgy, Edward Sobel; stage management, Robert H. Satterlee.

Etienne .... Jon Hill	Don .... Rick Snyder
Dave .... Lea Coco	Aunty Mimi .... Ora Jones
Jane...................................... Shannon Cochran	Soldier 1 .... Chike Johnson
The Doctor .... Kenn E. Head	Soldier 2 .... Adeoye
Nancy .... Amy Morton	

Time: The present. Place: An African country. Presented in two parts.

100 SAINTS YOU SHOULD KNOW. By Kate Fodor. July 20, 2006. Direction, BJ Jones; scenery, Jack Magaw; costumes, Tatjana Radisic; lighting, J.R. Lederle; sound, Martha Wegener; dramaturgy, Rosie Forrest; stage management, Deb Styer. Presented in the First Look Festival.

Theresa .... K.K. Dodds	Garrett .... Bryce Pegelow
Matthew .... John Hoogenakker	Colleen .... Mary Ann Thebus
Abby .... Kelly O'Sullivan	

Presented in two parts.

SPARE CHANGE. By Mia McCullough. July 21, 2006. Direction, Lisa Portes; scenery, Jack Magaw; costumes, Tatjana Radisic; lighting, J.R. Lederle; sound, Martha Wegener; dramaturgy, Ann Filmer. Presented in the First Look Festival.

Brad .... Paul Noble	Michael Ann; Mikki .... Yetide Badaki
Claire .... Janelle Snow	Ensemble .... Alana Arenas

Presented in two parts.

THE BUTCHER OF BARABOO. By Marisa Wegrzyn. July 22, 2006. Direction, Dexter Bullard; scenery, Jack Magaw; costumes, Tatjana Radisic; sound, Martha Wegener; dramaturgy, Sarah Gubbins; stage management, Lauren V. Hickman. Presented in the First Look Festival.

Valerie .... Annabel Armour	Midge.. Rebecca Sohn
Sevenly .... Danica Ivancevic	Gail .... Natalie West
Donal.. John Judd	

Presented in two parts.

SONIA FLEW. By Melinda Lopez. December 9, 2006. Direction, Jessica Thebus; scenery, Stephanie Nelson; costumes, Janice Pytel; lighting, J.R. Lederle; sound, Andre Pluess and Ben Sussman; stage management, Malcolm Ewen.

Nina; Pilar	Vilma Silva	Zak; José	Andrew Perez
Sonia; Marta	Sandra Marquez	Daniel; Tito	Jeff Still
Jen; Young Sonia	Sandra Delgado	Sam; Orfeo	Alan Wilder

Time: December 2001; April 1961. Place: Minneapolis; Havana.

Presented in two parts.

THE DIARY OF ANNE FRANK. By Frances Goodrich and Albert Hackett; adapted by Wendy Kesselman. April 5, 2007. Direction, Tina Landau; scenery, Richard Hoover; costumes, James Schuette; lighting, Scott Zielinski; sound, Rob Milburn and Michael Bodeen; dramaturgy, Rosie Forrest; stage management, Malcolm Ewen.

Anne Frank	Claire Elizabeth Saxe	Mrs. Van Daan	Kathy Scambiaterra
Otto Frank	Yasen Peyankov	Mr. Van Daan	Francis Guinan
Edith Frank	Gail Shapiro	Mr. Dussel	Alan Wilder
Margot Frank	Carolyn Faye Kramer	First Man	Kirk Anderson
Miep Gies	Mariann Mayberry	Second Man	Jason Bradley
Peter Van Daan	Mark Buenning	Third Man	Christopher McLinden
Mr. Kraler	Robert Breuler		

Presented in two parts.

Victory Gardens Theater, Chicago

Dennis Zacek artistic director, Marcelle McVay managing director

DENMARK. By Charles Smith. October 15, 2006 (world premiere). Direction, Dennis Zacek; scenery, Mary Griswold; costumes, Judith Lundberg; lighting, Robert Shook; sound, Andre Pluess; stage management, Tina M. Jach.

Beck Monroe	Velma Austin	Reverend Canker	Gregory Lush
Denmark Vesey	Anthony Fleming III	Reverend Brown	A.C. Smith
Omar Sewell	Kenn E. Head	Colonel Monroe	Joe Van Slyke
Captain Vesey	Raoul Johnson		

Time: Early 1800s. Place: The feverish mind of an imprisoned Denmark Vesey.

THE SNOW QUEEN. Musical with book by Michael Smith and Frank Galati; music and lyrics by Mr. Smith; based on the story by Hans Christian Andersen. December 11, 2006 (world premiere). Direction, Mr. Galati; scenery, Blair Thomas; costumes, Tatjana Radisic; lighting, Jenna McDanold; sound, Joe Cerqua; puppets, Blair Thomas and Meredith Miller; puppet direction, Ben T. Matchstick; stage management, Tina M. Jach.

Storyteller	Cheryl Lynn Bruce	Kai	Andrew Keltz
Gerda	Mattie Hawkinson		

Puppeteers: Jayson Rackley, Erik Weltz, Barbara Whitney.

Ensemble: Barbara Barrow, Kat Eggleston, Anthony Shepherdstone, Linda M. Smith, Michael Smith, Chris Walz.

Musical numbers included: "The Snow Queen's Palace," "Summertime Kids," "Now Old Winter," "The White Bees," "I'm Cold," "Hitchin'," "Red Shoes," "Wooden Soldiers," "Golden Comb," "House of Ice," "Rose Bush Song," "November Already," "Ravenheart," "The Princess and Memory," "Jenny Lind," "Robber Girl," "Lapland," "Love Letter on a Fish," "Finn Woman," "Snow Queen Soldiers," "Blood Red Roses," "Warm Bright Beautiful Summer."

Presented in two parts.

COURT-MARTIAL AT FORT DEVENS. By Jeffrey Sweet. February 12, 2007 (world premiere). Direction, Andrea J. Dymond; scenery, Mary Griswold; costumes, Birgit Rattenborg Wise; lighting, Charles Cooper; sound, Victoria Delorio; stage management, Rita Vreeland.

Tenola Stoney .... Velma Austin	Mr. Steele; others .... Morocco Omari
Gertrude; Ruby .... Lili-Anne Brown	Virginia Boyd .... Ericka Ratcliff
Victoria Lawson;	Johnnie Mae; others .... Samantha D. Tanner
Eleanor Roosevelt .... Cameron Feagin	Julian Rainey;
Kimball; others .... James Krag	Virginia's father .... Philip Edward Van Lear

Presented without intermission.

CYNICAL WEATHERS. By Douglas Post. April 16, 2007 (world premiere). Direction, Dennis Zacek; scenery, Samuel Ball; costumes, Judith Lundberg; lighting, Patrick Chan; sound, Andre Pluess; stage management, Tina M. Jach.

Cat McDaniels .... Bethanny Alexander	Lee Gelman .... Ben Brooks Cohen
Dixon McDaniels .... Tom Amandes	Andrea Brady .... Lindsay Gould
Manny Hernandez .... Tony Castillo	

Presented in two parts.

KENTUCKY

Actors Theatre of Louisville
Marc Masterson artistic director, Jennifer Bielstein managing director

31st Annual Humana Festival of New American Plays. March 2–April 1, 2007

DARK PLAY OR STORIES FOR BOYS. By Carlos Murillo March 2, 2007. Direction, Michael John Garcés; scenery, Michael B. Raiford; costumes, Lorraine Venberg; lighting, Brian J. Lilienthal; sound, Matt Callahan; fight direction, Drew Fracher; dramaturgy, Mary Resing; stage management, Megan Schwarz.

Nick .... Matthew Stadelmann	Male Netizen .... Lou Sumrall
Molly; Rachel .... Liz Morton	Female Netizen .... Jennifer Mendenhall
Adam .... Will Rogers	

Time: Now. Place: A college dorm room; an affluent town along the Southern coast; cyberspace. Presented without intermission.

STRIKE-SLIP. By Naomi Iizuka. March 8, 2007. Direction, Chay Yew; scenery, Paul Owen; costumes, Christal Weatherly; lighting, Deb Sullivan; sound, Andre Pluess; fight direction, Lee Look; dramaturgy, Julie Felise Dubiner; stage management, Debra Anne Gasper.

Lee Sung Cho .... Nelson Mashita	Viviana Ramos .... Romi Dias
Frank Richmond .... Keith Randolph Smith	Rachel Morse .... Heather Lea Anderson
Rafael Guttierez .... Justin Huen	Dan Morse .... Tim Altmeyer
Angie Lee .... Ali Ahn	Vince Lee .... Hanson Tse

Time: The present. Place: Los Angeles. Presented in two parts.

WHEN SOMETHING WONDERFUL ENDS. Solo performance piece by Sherry Kramer. March 10, 2007. Direction by Tom Moore; scenery, Paul Owen; costumes, Lorraine Venberg; lighting, Brian J. Lilienthal; sound, Matt Callahan; dramaturgy, Carrie Hughes; stage management, Michele Traub. Produced in association with InterAct Theatre Company, Philadelphia.

Sherry .... Lori Wilner

Time: The present. Place: Sherry's childhood home in Springfield, Missouri. Presented without intermission.

THE AS IF BODY LOOP. By Ken Weitzman. March 15, 2007. Direction, Susan V. Booth; scenery, Paul Owen; costumes, Christal Weatherly; lighting, Deb Sullivan; sound, Benjamin Marcum; fight direction, Lee Look; dramaturgy, Julie Felise Dubiner; stage management, Paul Mills Holmes.

Aaron	Marc Grapey	Attic Lady	Jana Robbins
Sarah	Kristen Fiorella	Martin	Keith Randolph Smith
Glenn	Josh Lefkowitz		

Time: Christmas 2002. Place: Philadelphia; Queens; Manhattan. Presented in two parts.

BATCH: AN AMERICAN BACHELOR/ETTE PARTY SPECTACLE. By Whit MacLaughlin, Alice Tuan and New Paradise Laboratories. March 20, 2007. Direction, Mr. MacLaughlin; scenery, Matt Saunders; costumes, Rosemarie McKelvey; lighting, Brian J. Lilienthal; sound, Mr. MacLaughlin; video, Jorge Cousineau; dramaturgy, Adrien-Alice Hansel; stage management, Nancy Pittelman.

Round 1 and Beyond		Round 2 and Beyond	
Betsy Competitive	McKenna Kerrigan	Taggis	Aaron Mumaw
Matty Jay	Jeb Kreager	Chet	Matt Saunders
Betty Lee	Lee Ann Etzold	Smoak	Jeb Kreager
Becky Steem	Matt Saunders	Lars	Lee Ann Etzold
Mara Faye	Aaron Mumaw	Mike	Mary McCool
Mary Bette	Mary McCool	Wesley	McKenna Kerrigan

Presented without intermission.

THE OPEN ROAD ANTHOLOGY. By Constance Congdon, Kia Corthron, Michael John Garcés, Rolin Jones, A. Rey Pamatmat and Kathryn Walat. March 23, 2007. Direction, Will MacAdams; scenery, Paul Owen; costumes, Susan Neason; lighting, Nick Dent; sound, Benjamin Marcum; music, GrooveLily; music supervision, Brigid Kaelin; dramaturgy, Adrien-Alice Hansel and Julie Felise Dubiner; stage management, Melissa Miller.

Performed by Timo Aker, Sean Andries, Katie Barton, Loren Bidner, Eleanor Caudill, Maurine Evans, Emily Tate Frank, Kristen B. Jackson, Rafael Jordan, Jane Lee, Nicole Marquez, Jake Millgard, Michael Judson Pace, Zachary Palamara, Phil Pickens, Zarina Shea, Zdenko Slobodnik, Jeff Snodgrass, Ashley B. Spearman, Angela Sperazza, Mark Stringham, Biz Wells.

Presented without intermission.

Ten-Minute Plays. March 31–April 1, 2007.

I AM NOT BATMAN. By Marco Ramirez. Direction, Ian Frank; scenery, Paul Owen; costumes, Susan Neason; lighting, Paul Werner; sound, Benjamin Marcum; fight direction, Lee Look; dramaturgy, Joanna K. Donehower; stage management, Michael D. Domue and Debra Anne Gasper.

A Boy	Phil Pickens	A Drummer	Zdenko Slobodnik

Time: Middle of the night. Place: A city.

CLARISSE AND LARMON. By Deb Margolin. Direction, Jessica Burgess; scenery, Paul Owen; costumes, Susan Neason; lighting, Paul Werner; sound, Benjamin Marcum; fight direction, Lee Look; dramaturgy, Joanna K. Donehower; stage management, Michael D. Domue and Debra Anne Gasper.

Clarisse	Romi Dias	Soldier	Timo Aker
Larmon	Keith Randolph Smith		

Place: At work.

MR. AND MRS. By Julie Marie Myatt. Direction, Jessica Burgess; scenery, Paul Owen; costumes, Susan Neason; lighting, Paul Werner; sound, Benjamin Marcum; fight direction, Lee Look; dramaturgy, Joanna K. Donehower; stage management, Michael D. Domue and Debra Anne Gasper.

Debra .... Maurine Evans   Steven .... Mark Stringham
    Place: A wedding reception.

365 DAYS/365 PLAYS. By Suzan-Lori Parks. March 30–April 1, 2007. Direction, Sean Daniels; scenery, Paul Owen; costumes, Susan Neason; lighting, Paul Werner; sound, Paul L. Doyle; dramaturgy, Kyle J. Schmidt; stage management, Michael D. Domue, Debra Anne Gasper.

FATHER COMES HOME FROM THE WARS (PART 1). (Written for November 14, 2006.) Performed by Lou Sumrall and Jennifer Mendenhall.

THE GREAT ARMY IN DISGRACE. (Written for December 18, 2006.) Performed by Tim Altmeyer and Rafael Jordan.

2 MARYS. (Written for January 3, 2007.) Performed by Jana Robbins, Heather Lea Andersen and Marc Grapey.

THE BIRTH OF TRAGEDY. (Written for January 6, 2007.) Performed by Loren Bidner, Rafael Jordan, Jane Lee, Zarina Shea, Samuel Blackerby Weible.

IF I HAD TO MURDER ME SOMEBODY. (Written for January 31, 2007.) Performed by Justin Huen.

(AGAIN) THE BUTCHER'S DAUGHTER (FOR BONNIE). (Written for February 13, 2007.) Performed by Lou Sumrall and Angela Sperazza.

A PLAY FOR THE FIRST DAY OF SPRING ENTITLED *HOW DO YOU LIKE THE WAR?* (Written for March 21, 2007.) Performed by the ensemble (Tim Altmeyer, Heather Lea Anderson, Loren Bidner, Emily Tate Frank, Marc Grapey, Justin Huen, Kristen B. Jackson, Rafael Jordan, Jane Lee, Jennifer Mendenhall, Jana Robbins, Zarina Shea, Jeff Snodgrass, Angela Sperazza, Matthew Stadelmann, Lou Sumrall, Samuel Blackerby Weible).

GEORGE BUSH VISITS THE CHEESE AND OLIVE. (Written for April 1, 2007.) Performed by Emily Tate Frank, Kristen B. Jackson, Zarina Shea, Matthew Stadelmann.

MAINE

Portland Stage Company
Anita Stewart artistic director

IRON KISSES. By James Still. March 2, 2007. Direction, Risa Brainin; scenery and costumes, Anita Stewart; lighting, Michael Klaers; music, Hans Indigo Spencer; stage management, Marjorie Gallant.

Billy .... Tom Ford   Barbara .... Janice O'Rourke
    Time: Now. Place: A small town in the Midwest and San Francisco. Presented without intermission.

AUGUSTA. By Richard Dresser. May 4, 2007. Direction, Michael Rafkin; scenery, Anita Stewart; costumes, Susan Picinich; lighting, Gregg Carville; sound, Stephen Swift; stage management, Marjorie Gallant.

Jimmy	Charlie Kevin	Molly	Rae C. Wright
Claire	Sally Wood		

Time: The present. Place: An office in Maine; a summer home; a diner; a hotel room. Presented in two parts.

MARYLAND

Center Stage, Baltimore
Irene Lewis artistic director, Michael Ross managing director

TROUBLE IN MIND. By Alice Childress. February 7, 2007. Direction, Irene Lewis; scenery, David Korins; costumes, Catherine Zuber; lighting, Rui Rita; sound, David Budries; dramaturgy, Catherine Sheehy; stage management, Mike Schleifer.

Willetta Mayer	E. Faye Butler	Judy Sears	Maria Dizzia
Henry	Laurence O'Dwyer	Bill O'Wray	Daren Kelly
John Nevins	LeRoy McClain	Al Manners	Craig Wroe
Millie Davis	Starla Benford	Eddie Fenton	Garrett Neergaard
Sheldon Forrester	Thomas Jefferson Byrd	Stagehand	B. Thomas Rinaldi

Time: 1957. Place: A Broadway theater. Presented in two parts.

THINGS OF DRY HOURS. By Naomi Wallace. May 2, 2007. Direction, Kwame Kwei-Armah; scenery, Riccardo Hernández; costumes, David Burdick; lighting, Michelle Habeck; sound, Shane Rettig; fight direction, J. Allen Suddeth; dramaturgy, Gavin Witt; stage management, Mike Schleifer.

Corbin Teel	Steven Cole Hughes	Tice Hogan	Roger Robinson
Cali Hogan	Erika LaVonn		

Time: Early 1930s. Place: Small cabin near railroad in Birmingham, Alabama. Presented in two parts.

Round House Theatre, Bethesda
Blake Robison producing artistic director

CRIME AND PUNISHMENT. By Fyodor Dostoyevsky; adapted by Marilyn Campbell and Curt Columbus. April 4, 2007. Direction, Blake Robison; scenery, Robin Stapley; costumes, Bill Black; lighting, Kenton Yeager; sound, Matthew M. Nielson; stage management, Jennifer Woodham.

Raskolnikov	Aubrey Deeker	Porfiry	Mitchell Hébert
Sonia	Tonya Beckman Ross		

Presented without intermission.

THE DIRECTOR: THE THIRD ACT OF ELIA KAZAN. Solo performance piece by Leslie A. Kobylinski. April 20, 2007 (world premiere). Direction, Ms. Kobylinski, scenery, Grant Kevin Lane; lighting, Justin Thomas; sound, Matthew M. Nielson; music, Steve McWilliams; dramaturgy, Suzanne Maloney; stage management, Maribeth Chaprnka.

Elia Kazan	Rick Foucheux

Presented without intermission.

MASSACHUSETTS

American Repertory Theatre, Cambridge
Robert Woodruff artistic director

WINGS OF DESIRE. By Gideon Lester and Dirkje Houtman; adapted from the film (*Der Himmel über Berlin*) by Wim Wenders, Peter Handke and Richard Reitinger; translated by Gideon Lester and Ko van den Bosch. November 29, 2006 (world premiere). Direction, Ola Mafaalani; scenery and lighting, André Joosten; costumes, Regine Standfuss; sound and music, Andy Moor; aerial choreography, Mam Smith; dramaturgy, Messrs. Lester and Houtman; stage management, Chris De Camillis. Presented in association with Toneelgroep Amsterdam.

Damiel	Bernard White	Dying man	Fred Goessens
Casssiel	Mark Rosenthal	Child	Andris Freimanis
Marion	Mam Smith	The Suicide	Daniel Robert Pecci
Former angel	Stephen Payne	Thoughts; live music	Jesse Lenat,
Homer	Frieda Pittoors		Hadewych Minis
Newsreader	Robin Young		

Ensemble: W. Kirk Avery, Jerome Quinn, Greta Merchant, Betty Milhendler.

Presented without intermission.

THE ONION CELLAR. By Amanda Palmer, Jonathan Marc Sherman, Marcus Stern, Christine Jones, Anthony Martignetti and the company. December 13, 2006 (world premiere). Direction, Mr. Stern; scenery, Ms. Jones; costumes, Clint Ramos; lighting, Justin Townsend; sound, David Remedios; dramaturgy, Ryan McKittrick and Neena Arndt; stage management, Jennifer Sturch.

Performed by the Dresden Dolls (Amanda Palmer and Brian Viglione), Remo Airaldi, Claire Elizabeth Davies, Thomas Derrah, Brian Farish, Kristen Frazier, Jeremy Geidt, Merritt Janson, Karen MacDonald, Neil Stewart.

Presented without intermission.

OLIVER TWIST. By Charles Dickens; adapted by Neil Bartlett. February 2, 2007. Direction, Mr. Bartlett; scenery and costumes, Rae Smith; lighting, Scott Zielinski; sound, David Remedios; music, Gerard McBurney; music direction, Simon Deavon; stage management, Chris De Camillis. Presented in association with Theatre for a New Audience, New York, and Berkeley Repertory Theatre.

John Dawkins;		Nancy	Jennifer Ikeda
Artful Dodger	Carson Elrod	Fagin	Ned Eisenberg
Oliver Twist	Michael Wartella	Noah Claypole	Steven Boyer
Mr. Bumble	Remo Airaldi	Charley Bates	Craig Pattison
Mrs. Bumble	Karen MacDonald	Toby Crackit	Lucas Steele
Mr. Sowerberry	Thomas Derrah	Mr. Brownlow	Will LeBow
Bill Sykes	Greg Derelian	Rose Brownlow	Elizabeth Jasicki

Presented in two parts.

Berkshire Theatre Festival, Stockbridge
Kate Maguire artistic director

AMADEUS. By Peter Shaffer. June 23, 2006. Direction, Eric Hill; scenery, Karl Eigsti; costumes, Olivera Gajic; lighting, Matthew E. Adelson; sound, Nathan Leigh; stage management, Jason Hindelang.

Salieri .... Jonathan Epstein
Mozart .... Randy Harrison
Constanze Weber .... Tara Franklin
Joseph II .... Walter Hudson
Baron van Swieten .... Ron Bagden
Ct. von Strack .... Bob Jaffe
Ct. Orsini-Rosenberg .... Stephen Temperley
Venticelli One .... Tom Story
Venticelli Two .... James Barry
   Presented in two parts.

THE PILGRIM PAPERS. By Stephen Temperley. August 2, 2006 (world premiere). Direction, Vivian Matalon; scenery, R. Michael Miller; costumes, Tracy Christensen; lighting, Ann G. Wrightson; sound, Craig Kaufmann; stage management, Barbara Janice Kielhofer.

Jones; Billington .... Martin Askin
Narrator .... Austin Durant
Standish .... Joshua Davis
Robinson; Winslow .... Brent Michael Eroy
Bradford .... Phil Sletteland
Dorothy .... Arnica Skulstad-Brown
Peter .... Justin Stoney
   Time: The 1620s to the present. Setting: William Bradford's house in Plymouth, Massachusetts; other locations around the settlement. Presented in two parts.

THE NIGHT OF THE IGUANA. By Tennessee Williams. August 4, 2006. Direction, Anders Cato; scenery, Carl Sprague; costumes, Murell Horton; lighting, Jeff Davis; sound and music, Scott Killian; stage management, Jason Hindelang.

Lawrence Shannon .... Garret Dillahunt
Hannah Jelkes .... Amelia Campbell
Maxine Faulk .... Linda Hamilton
Miss Judith Fellows .... Charlotte Maier
Nonno .... William Swan
Charlotte Goodall .... Lauren Orkus
Jake Latta .... Sam Kitchin
Hank .... Aaron Costa Ganis
Pedro .... Joshua Gunn
Pancho .... Ricky Fromeyer
   Presented in two parts.

Huntington Theatre Company, Boston

Nicholas Martin artistic director

MAURITIUS. By Theresa Rebeck. October 18, 2006 (world premiere). Direction, Rebecca Bayla Taichman; scenery, Eugene Lee; costumes, Miranda Hoffman; lighting, Paul Whitaker; sound and music, Martin Desjardins; fight direction, Rick Sordelet; stage management, Stephen M. Kaus.

Dennis .... Michael Aronov
Philip .... Robert Dorfman
Jackie .... Marin Ireland
Mary .... Laura Latreille
Sterling .... James Gale
   Presented in two parts.

THE CHERRY ORCHARD. By Anton Chekhov; translated by Richard Nelson. January 10, 2007. Direction, Nicholas Martin; scenery, Ralph Funicello; costumes, Robert Morgan; lighting, Donald Holder; sound, Drew Levy; music, Michael Friedman; stage management, Stephen M. Kaus.

Ranevskaya .... Kate Burton
Lopakin .... Will LeBow
Dunyasha .... Jessica Dickey
Yephikhodov .... Jeremy Beck
Anya .... Jessica Rothenberg
Gaev .... Mark Blum
Varya .... Sarah Hudnut
Pishchik .... Jeremiah Kissel
Charlotta .... Joyce Van Patten
Yasha .... Gene Farber
Firs .... Dick Latessa
Trofimov .... Enver Gjokaj
Tramp .... Robert Bonotto
Station Master .... Patrick Lynch
   Ensemble: Colin Blattel, Julia Coe, Jessica Grant, Julie Kilpatrick, Julie Kun, Dan Lovley, Alex Wyse.

PERSEPHONE. By Noah Haidle. April 11, 2007 (world premiere). Direction, Nicholas Martin; scenery, David Korins; costumes, Jenny Mannis; lighting, Ben Stanton; sound and music, Mark Bennett; stage management, David H. Lurie.

Demeter	Melinda Lopez	Celia	Mimi Lieber
Giuseppe	Seth Fisher	Alfonso	Jeremiah Kissel

Time: 1507; 2007. Place: Florence, Italy; a city park. Presented in two parts.

PRESENT LAUGHTER. By Noël Coward. May 23, 2007. Direction, Nicholas Martin; scenery, Alexander Dodge; costumes, Mariann Verheyen; lighting, Rui Rita; sound, Drew Levy; stage management, Stephen M. Kaus.

Garry Essendine	Victor Garber	Miss Erikson	Nancy E. Carroll
Liz Essendine	Lisa Banes	Fred	James Joseph O'Neill
Roland Maule	Brooks Ashmanskas	Henry Lyppiatt	Richard Snee
Monica Reed	Sarah Hudnut	Morris Dixon	Marc Vietor
Joanne Lyppiatt	Pamela J. Gray	Lady Saltburn	Alice Duffy
Daphne Stillington	Holley Fain		

Presented in three parts.

Williamstown Theatre Festival
Roger Rees artistic director

THE OPPOSITE OF SEX. Musical with book by Robert Jess Roth and Douglas J. Cohen; music and lyrics by Mr. Cohen; based on the screenplay by Don Roos. August 10, 2006. Direction, Mr. Roth; scenery, Derek McLane; costumes, Sarah Laux; lighting, Norm Schwab; sound, Nick Borisjuk; music direction and arrangements, Lynne Shankel; stage management, B.J. Forman.

Dedee Truitt	Kerry Butler	Matt Matteo	David Burtka
Randy Cates	Ian Scott McGregor	Lucia Dalury	Kaitlin Hopkins
Bill Truitt	Gregg Edelman	Carl Tippett	Herndon Lackey
Jason Bock	Lance Rubin		

Musical numbers included: "I've Got News for You," "Rub a Little Lotion," "It Just Happened," "A Normal Life," "Better Days," "I Think You Know What I Want," "I Think You Know What I Want" (Reprise), "L.A.," "Destiny," "You Are Going Back to Indiana," "A Normal Life" (Reprise), "Grateful," "End of the Line," "Dead Ex-Lover," "It's Not Enough," "Lucia (Heaven and Hell)," "I've Got News for You" (Reprise), "Not Tom," "Labor of Love," "Look for Me First," "The Opposite of Sex," "I've Got News for You" (Reprise).

Presented in two parts.

MICHIGAN

Purple Rose Theatre Company, Chelsea
Guy Sanville artistic director, Jeff Daniels executive director,
Alan Ribant managing director

ESCANABA IN LOVE. By Jeff Daniels. October 7, 2006 (world premiere). Direction, Guy Sanville; scenery, Daniel C. Walker; costumes, Ivan Ingermann; lighting, Reid G. Johnson; sound, Quintessa Gallinat; stage management, Katie M. Doral.

Alphonse Soady	Will David Young	Albert Soady Jr.	Jake Christensen
Albet Soady, Sr.	Paul Hopper	Big Betty Balou	Charlyn Swarthout
Jim Negamanee	Wayne David Parker		

Time: November 14, 1944. Place: Soady Deer Camp northwest of Escanaba, Michigan. Presented in two parts.

WHEN THE LIGHTS COME ON. By Brian Letscher. April 13, 2007 (world premiere). Direction, Guy Sanville; scenery, Dennis G. Crawley; costumes, Vikte Jankus Moss; lighting, Dana White; sound, Quintessa Gallinat; stage management, Stefanie Din.

Jamie Jones-Leonard	Rhiannon R. Ragland	Don Gephardt	Grant R. Krause
Tommy Leonard	Brian Letscher	Tina Harley	Michelle Mountain
Rolly Jones	Jim Porterfield	Tulie Barnes	Kathryn Ruth Mayer
Frank Harley	Wayne David Parker	Joe Haverstick	Nicaolas J. Smith
Marty Wick	Phil Powers		

Time: The present, Place: Western State University, in the Midwest.

MINNESOTA

Guthrie Theater, Minneapolis
Joe Dowling artistic director, Thomas C. Proehl managing director

THE GREAT GATSBY. By F. Scott Fitzgerald; adapted by Simon Levy from the novel. July 21, 2006 (world premiere). Direction, David Esbjornson; scenery, Thomas Lynch; costumes, Jane Greenwood; lighting, Michael Philippi; sound, Scott Edwards; music, Wayne Barker; dramaturgy, Amy Wegener; stage management, Chris A. Code.

Jay Gatsby	Lorenzo Pisoni	George Wilson	Mark Rhein
Nick Carraway	Matthew Amendt	Myrtle Wilson	Christina Baldwin
Daisy Buchanan	Heidi Armbruster	Lucille McKee	Kate Eifrig
Jordan Baker	Cheyenne Casebier	Chester McKee	Bob Davis
Tom Buchanan	Erik Heger	Meyer Wolfshiem	Raye Birk
Saxman	Dean Brewington		

Ensemble: Caroline Cooney, Jennifer Cragg, Ali Dachis, Matt Franta, Karl Meyer, Ben Rosenbaum, Andrew Rotchadi, Laura Lynne Tapper.

Time: Summer 1922. Place: Long Island, New York. Presented in two parts.

EDGARDO MINE. By Alfred Uhry; based on the book *The Kidnapping of Edgardo Mortara* by David I. Kertzer. November 10, 2006. Direction, Mark Lamos; scenery, Riccardo Hernández; costumes, Candice Donnelly, lighting, Mimi Jordan Sherin; sound, Reid Rejsa; music, Robert Waldman; fight direction, Peter Moore; dramaturgy, Jo Holcomb; stage management, Chris A. Code.

Marianna Mortara	Jennifer Regan	Il Dottore	J.C. Cutler
Pope Pius IX (Nono)	Brian Murray	Lucidi	Tyson Forbes
Momolo Mortara	Ron Menzel	Fr. Giovanni	Sasha Andreev
Cardinal Antonelli	Stephen D'Ambrose	Boy	Tucker Garborg,
Nina Morisi	Nancy Rodriguez		Mykola Rieland

BOATS ON A RIVER. By Julie Marie Myatt. May 23, 2007 (world premiere). Direction, Michael Bigelow Dixon; scenery, Victor A. Becker; costumes, Lynda K. Myers; lighting, Matthew Reinert; sound, Reid Rejsa; video, Heidi Edwards; dramaturgy, Amy Wegener; stage management, Jody Gavin.

Sidney Webb	Nathaniel Fuller	Jonathan Black	Kris L. Nelson
Tam Webb	Yoko Fumoto	Lida	Mayano Ochi
Ted Thompson	Peter Hansen	Yen	Jeany Park
Sister Margaret	Dale Hodges	Max	Randy Reyes

Kolab .... Rebecca J. Wall

Cambodian Girl .... Aeola Lu

Cambodian Girl .... Megan K. Mecklenburg

Cambodian Girl .... Anna Northenscold

Cambodian Girl .... Isabelle Yang

Presented in two parts.

MISSOURI

Kansas City Repertory Theatre

Peter Altman producing artistic director, William Prenevost managing director

UNDER MIDWESTERN STARS. By Esther Blumenfeld. May 16, 2007 (world premiere). Direction, Stephen Rothman; scenery, David Potts; costumes, Antonia Ford-Roberts; lighting, Victor En Yu Tan; sound and music, Joe Cerqua.

Joseph .... Mark Mineart

Rachel .... Autumn Dornfeld

Lena .... Crista Moore

The Repertory Theatre of St. Louis

Steven Woolf artistic director, Mark Bernstein managing director

ACE. Musical with book and lyrics by Robert Taylor and Richard Oberackcr; music by Mr. Oberacker. September 6, 2006 (world premiere). Direction, Stafford Arima; choreography, Andrew Palermo; scenery, David Korins; costumes, Marie Anne Chiment; lighting, Christopher Akerlind; sound, David Patridge and John H. Shivers; music direction, David Kreppel; stage management, Glenn Dunn. Presented in association with Cincinnati Playhouse in the Park and the Old Globe in San Diego.

Billy .... Noah Galvin	Ruth .... Heather Ayers
Mrs. Crandall .... Traci Lyn Thomas	Emily .... Gabrielle Boyadjian
Elizabeth .... Jessica Boevers	Anique .... Gabrielle Stravelli
Louise .... Amy Bodnar	Teacher .... Susan Kokot Stokes
Edward .... Duke Lafoon	Nurse .... Kelli Barrett
Ace .... Matt Bogart	Toy Store Owner .... James Judy
John Robert .... Chris Peluso	Lt. Sanders .... Richard Barth
School Bully .... Jimmy McEvoy	Cooper .... Danny Rothman
Sidekick .... Ariane Rinehart	Tennaman .... Kevin Reed

Time: 1952. Place: St. Louis, Missouri. Presented in two parts.

Musical numbers included: "It's Better This Way," "Fill in the Blank," "In These Skies," "Life Can Be Cruel," "It Took This Moment," "Now I'm On Your Case," "Make It From Scratch," "Be My Bride," "Letter From the Front," "Joie de Vivre," "The Dogfight," "Call Me Ace," "Soaring Again," "It's Just a Matter of Time," "I Know," "It Can Be Done," "Missing Pieces," "Sooner or Later," "We're the Only Ones," "Seeing Things in a Different Light," "That's What It Should Say," "Choose To Fly."

Presented in two parts.

ORDINARY NATION. By Carter W. Lewis. October 25, 2006 (world premiere). Direction, Andrea Urice; scenery, Robert Mark Morgan; costumes, Dorothy Marshall Englis; lighting, John Wylie; sound, Tori Meyer; stage management, Shannon B. Sturgis.

G. J. Jones .... George Bartenieff	Allison Jones .... Angela Reed
Frankie Jones .... Dana Acheson	Gibb Aston .... Curt Hostetter
Nation Jones .... Gregory Northrop	

Time: The present in autumn. Place: A Midwestern city. Presented in two parts.

NEW JERSEY

Centenary Stage Company, Hackettstown
Carl Wallnau artistic director

THE DEW POINT. By Neena Beber. November 4, 2006 (world premiere). Direction, Margo Whitcomb, scenery and lighting, Ed Matthews; costumes, Julia Sharp; sound, Matthew Given; stage management, Kevin Brophy.

Greta	Jennifer Graven	Jack	Peter Ludwig
Kai	Jim Ireland	Phyllis	Liz McConahay
Mimi	Helen Coxe		

Women Playwrights' Series.

LUNA PARK. By Caridad Svich. April 4, 2007.

DAPHNE DOES DIM SUM. By Eugenie Chan. April 10, 2007.

BLACKWATER DEPARTURE. By Therese Kunz. April 18, 2007.

THE TEDIOUS SCANDAL OF SIR ROBERT KINGWOOD. By Megan E. Lindsay. April 25, 2007.

Luna Stage, Montclair
Jane Mandel artistic director, Charlotte McKim managing director

THE KREUTZER SONATA. By Leo Tolstoy; adapted by Margaret Pine and Larry Pine. October 7, 2006. Direction and sound, Ms. Pine; scenery, Fred Kinney; costumes, Kristine Koury; lighting, Jill Nagle; stage management, Patrick Starega.

Pozdnyshev	Larry Pine	Violinist	Gil Morgenstern
Pianist	Priya Mayadas		

Time: 1890. Place: A train compartment.

HONOR AND THE RIVER. By Anton Dudley. February 1, 2007 (world premiere). Direction, Nancy Robillard; scenery, Robert Monaco; costumes, Colleen Kesterson; lighting, Dave Feldman; sound, Andy Cohen; stage management, Paul Whelihan.

Mr. Roberts	Reathel Bean	Eliot	Andy Phelan
Honor	David Michael Holmes	Wawa	Carolyn Popp

Time: The present. Place: New England. Presented in two parts.

LITTLE BEASTS. By Jeanne Marshall. April 26, 2007 (world premiere). Direction, Jane Mandel; scenery, Fred Kinney; costumes, Colleen Kesterson; lighting, Jill Nagle; sound, Andy Cohen; stage management, Patrick Starega.

Ella	Mona Hennessy	Natalie Barney	Nancy Shaheen
Beatrice	Rebecca Lingafelter	Henri	Lawrence E. Street
Romaine Brooks	Kathleen Marsh		

Time: Late 1920s. Place: Paris.

The Shakespeare Theatre of New Jersey, Madison
Bonnie J. Monte artistic director

PRIDE AND PREJUDICE. By Jane Austen; adapted by Bonnie J. Monte. October 21, 2006. Direction, Ms. Monte; choreography, Cheryl E. Clark; scenery, Michael Schweikardt;

costumes, Kim Gill; lighting, Brenda Gray; sound, Steven L. Beckel; stage management, Christine Whalen.

Mr. Bennet	Edmond Genest	Mr. Darcy	Marcus Dean Fuller
Mrs. Bennet	Monique Fowler	Charlotte Lucas	Jessica Ires Morris
Elizabeth	Victoria Mack	Maria Lucas	Elizabeth G. Wilson
Kitty	Katelin Wilcox	Harriet Long	Kersti Bryan
Jane	Nisi Sturgis	Col. Forster	Phil Brown
Mary	Saluda Camp	Col. Fitzwilliam	Josh Carpenter
Lydia	Gardner Reed	Mr. Blake	Jake O'Connor
Lady Lucas	Hanna Hayes	Servant	Michael Striano
Sir William	Ashton Crosby	Mr. Collins	Michael Stewart Allen
Mr. Bingley	Sean Mahan	Mr. Wickham	David Andrew Macdonald
Miss Bingley	Alison Ostergaard	Lady Catherine	Elizabeth Shepherd
Mrs. Hurst	Megan Irene Davis	Mrs. Gardiner	Kathleen Rosamond Kelly
Mr. Hurst	Paul Reisman	Mr. Gardiner	Joseph Costa

Presented in two parts.

McCarter Theatre Center, Princeton
Emily Mann artistic director, Jeffrey Woodward managing director

MRS. PACKARD. By Emily Mann. May 11, 2007 (world premiere). Direction, Ms. Mann; scenery, Eugene Lee; costumes, Jennifer von Mayrhauser; lighting, Jeff Croiter; sound and music, Rob Milburn and Michael Bodeen; fight direction, Rick Sordelet; dramaturgy, Douglas Langworthy; stage management, Cheryl Mintz.

Elizabeth Packard	Kathryn Meisle	Mrs. Chapman	Molly Regan
Dr. McFarland	Dennis Parlato	Mrs. Stockton	Georgine Hall
Theophilus Packard	John C. Vennema	Dr. Brown	Jeff Brooks
Mrs. Vonner	Fiana Toibin	Mr. Smith	Robin Chadwick
Mrs. Tenney; Mrs. Dole	Julie Boyd		

Ensemble: Karen Christie-Ward, Beth Dzuricky, Mitchell Michaliszyn, Quinn Warren, Ray Wiederhold.

Time: 1861. Place: Illinois. Presented in two parts.

NEW YORK

Bay Street Theatre, Sag Harbor
Sybil Christopher and Murphy Davis artistic directors, Stephen Hamilton executive director

VIVA LA VIDA! By Diane Shaffer. July 18, 2006 (world premiere). Direction, Susana Tubert; scenery, Narelle Sissons; costumes, Toni-Leslie James; lighting, Stephen Strawbridge; sound, Tony Melfa; stage management, Brian Meister.

Frida Kahlo	Mercedes Ruehl	Rosita	Liza Colón-Zayas
Diego Rivera	Rene Pereyra		

Mariachis: Jamie Robert Carillo, Andres De La Fuente, Chuck Novatka.

Time: April 1953–July 1954. Place: Frida Kahlo's Blue House and other locations in Coyoacán.

OHIO

Cincinnati Playhouse in the Park
Edward Stern, producing artistic director; Buzz Ward executive director

1:23. By Carson Kreitzer. February 8, 2007 (world premiere). Direction, Mark Wing-Davey; scenery, Douglas Stein and Peter Ksander; costumes, Kaye Voyce; lighting, David Weiner; sound and music, Marc Gwinn; video, Ruppert Bohle; fight direction, Jenny Jones; stage management, Jenifer Morrow.

McManus	Josh Shirley	Stevens	Robert Elliott
Susan	Deborah Knox	Carjacker	Rege Lewis
Andrea	Eva Kaminsky	Juana; La Llorona	Shirley Roeca

MURDERERS. By Jeffrey Hatcher. March 29, 2007. Direction, Sarah Gioia; scenery, Joseph P. Tilford; costumes, Gordon DeVinney; lighting, Betsy Adams; stage management, Wendy J. Dorn.

Gerald	Steve Hendrickson	Minka	Carolyn Swift
Lucy	Rita Gardner		

Time: The present. Place: Riddle Key, Florida.
Presented without intermission.

The Cleveland Play House
Michael Bloom artistic director

RABBIT HOLE. By David Lindsay-Abaire. September 20, 3006. Direction, Michael Bloom; scenery, Russell Parkman; costumes, Beth Novak; lighting, Michael Lincoln; sound, James C. Swonger; stage management, John Godbout.

Jason	Troy Deutsch	Nat	Kate Skinner
Izzy	Genevieve Elam	Howie	Danton Stone
Becca	Angela Reed		

RFK. By Jack Holmes. November 1, 2007. Direction, Seth Gordon; scenery, Neil Patel; lighting, David Weiner; sound, Phillip Lojo and James C. Swonger; stage management, John Godbout. Presented in association with Winship Cook, Arleen Sorkin, Martin Davich.

Robert F. Kennedy .... Jack Holmes

Time: 1964–68. Place: Various locations.

CUTTIN' UP. By Charles Randolph-Wright; based on the book by Craig Marberry. February 7, 2007. Direction, Israel Hicks; scenery, Michael Carnahan; costumes, David Kay Mickelsen; sound, James C. Swonger; lighting, Philip Monat; stage management, Melissa L.F. Turner.

Rudy	Dorian Logan	Rev. Jenkins	Bill Grimmette
Andre	Darryl Alan Reed	Karen	Iona Morris
Howard	Adolphus Ward	John	Maceo Oliver
Kenny	Harvy Blanks	Howard Jr.	Jacques C. Smith

Presented in two parts.

THE CLEAN HOUSE. By Sarah Ruhl. March 7, 2007. Direction, Davis McCallum; scenery, Andromache Chalfant; costumes, Murell Horton; lighting, Matthew Richards; sound, James C. Swonger; music, Michael Friedman; stage management, John Godbout.

Matilde	Ursula Cataan	Lane	Patricia Hodges
Ana	Janis Dardaris	Charles	Terry Layman
Virginia	Beth Dixon		

Presented in two parts.

LINCOLNESQUE. By John Strand. May 2, 2007. Direction, Michael Bloom; scenery, Todd Rosenthal; costumes, Catherine Norgren; lighting, Robert Wierzel; sound, James C. Swonger, stage management, John Godbout.

Francis	Donald Carrier	Carla; Doctor	Tracey Conyer Lee
Leo	Brian J. Carter	Secretary of War; Daly	Walter Charles

    Time: The present. Place: Washington, DC. Presented in two parts.

2007 FusionFest. May 2–13, 2007.

LUNACY. By Sandra Perlman. May 3, 2007. Direction, Mark Alan Gordon. Performed by Bernadette Clemens, Dan Hammond, Michael Regnier.

TRUMBO: RED, WHITE AND BLACKLISTED. By Christopher Trumbo. May 4, 2007. Direction, Michael Bloom. Performed by Robert Vaughn and Charles Kartali.

EMERGENCE-SEE! By Daniel Beaty. May 8, 2007. Direction, Kenny Leon. Performed by Mr. Beaty.

FOR YOU. By Iona Morris. May 11, 2007. Performed by Ms. Morris.

The Next Stage at FusionFest. May 4–10, 2007.

WADE IN THE WATER. By Nina Dominque.

THE FREE AND THE BRAVE. By Richard Brooks.

FOR BETTER. By Eric Coble.

THE ALICE SEED. By Michael Sepesy.

SOLOMON'S BLADE. By Lisa Beth Allen.

PENNSYLVANIA

Arden Theatre Company, Philadelphia
Terrence J. Nolen artistic director

DEX AND JULIE SITTIN' IN A TREE. By Bruce Graham. January 11, 2007 (world premiere). Direction, James J. Christy; scenery, James Wolk; costumes, Janus Stefanowicz; lighting, Jerold R. Forsyth; sound, Jorge Cousineau; dramaturgy, Michele Volansky; stage management, Patricia G. Sabato.

Michael "Dex" Dexter	John Lumia	Dr. Julie Chernitsky	Jennifer Childs

Philadelphia Theatre Company
Sara Garonzik producing artistic director

MURDERERS. By Jeffrey Hatcher. October 11, 2006. Direction, Michael Bush; scenery, James Noone; costumes, Karen Ann Ledger; lighting, Traci Klainer; sound and music, Ryan Rumery; dramaturgy, Warren Hoffman; stage management, Victoria L. Hein.

Gerald	Brent Langdon	Minka	Kristine Nielsen
Lucy	Marylouise Burke		

    Time: The present. Place: Riddle Key, Florida. Presented in two parts.

NERDS://A MUSICAL SOFTWARE SATIRE. Musical with book and lyrics by Jordan Allen-Dutton and Erik Weiner; music by Hal Goldberg. January 31, 2007. Direction, Philip Wm. McKinley; choreography, Joey McKneely; scenery, David Gallo; costumes, Alejo Vietti; lighting, Michael Baldassari; sound, Fitz Patton; projections, Zachary Borovay; music direction, Matt Doebler; orchestrations, Dave Pierce; dramaturgy, Warren Hoffman; stage management, Phyllis Schray.

Sally	Chandra Lee Schwartz	Allen	Andrew Cassese
Dustin	Michael Parrish DuDell	Jobs	Charlie Pollock
Herbert	Brian M. Golub	Woz	David Rossmer
Myrtle	Emily Shoolin	Watson	Joseph Dellger
Gates	Jim Poulos		

Musical numbers included: "Homebrew Computer Club," "I Am Just a Nerd," "Revolution Starts With One," "Dim the Lights," "Whatever It Takes ," "Stroll Through the PARC," "Macintosh," "Nerd Action," "I Always Thought The Last One Would Be You," "Secrets," "Windows," "Down and Out in Silicon Valley," "Let's Merge," "Think Different," "I Gotta Love Money."

Presented in two parts.

Pig Iron Theatre, Philadelphia

Gabriel Quinn Bauriedel, Dito van Reigersberg and Dan Rothenberg artistic directors

LOVE UNPUNISHED. By the company. June 3, 2006 (world premiere). Direction, Dan Rothenberg; choreography, David Brick; scenery, Mimi Lien; costumes, Oana Botez-Ban; lighting, Tyler Micoleau; sound, Troy Herion and Sean Mattio; stage management, Carol Laratonda.

Performed by Gabriel Quinn Bauriedel, Dito van Reigersberg, James Sugg, Sarah Sanford, Mikaal Sulaiman, Jaamil Kosoto, Hinako Arao, Wendy Staton, Makoto Hirano.

Presented without intermission.

Pittsburgh Public Theater

Ted Pappas producing artistic director, Mark R. Power managing director

THE SECRET LETTERS OF JACKIE AND MARILYN. By Mark Hampton and Michael Sharp; based on *The Secret Letters of Marilyn Monroe and Jacqueline Kennedy* by Wendy Leigh. November 17, 2006 (world premiere). Direction, Leonard Foglia; scenery, Michael McGarty; costumes, David C. Woolard; lighting, Howell Binkley; sound, Zach Moore, stage management, Fred Noel.

Jacqueline Kennedy	Gretchen Egolf	Marilyn Monroe	Heather Tom
Patty, Marilyn's stylist	Carole Shelley		

Presented in two parts.

THE GLORIOUS ONES. Musical with book and lyrics by Lynn Ahrens; music by Stephen Flaherty; based on the novel by Francine Prose. April 27, 2007 (world premiere). Direction and choreography, Graciela Daniele; scenery, Daniel S. Ostling; costumes, Mara Blumenfeld; lighting, Stephen Strawbridge; sound, Zach Moore; music direction, Thomas Murray; stage management, Nevin Hedley.

Columbina	Natalie Venetia Belcon	Flaminio Scala	Paul Schoeffler
Dottore	John Kassir	Armanda Ragusa	Julyana Soelistyo
Pantalone	David Patrick Kelly	Francesco Andreini	Jeremy Webb
Isabella Andreini	Jenny Powers		

Musical numbers included: "The Glorious Ones," "Angels," "Making Love," "Pantalone Alone," "The Comedy of Love," "The Madness of Columbina," "Angels"/"The Glorious Ones" (Reprise),

"Absalom," "The Invitation to France," "Flaminio Scala's Historical Journey to France," "Armanda's Tarantella," "So Be It," "The World She Writes," "Opposite You," "The Elopement," "My Body Wasn't Why," "The Madness of Isabella," "Flaminio's Dream," "The World She Writes" (Reprise), "Rise and Fall," "The Moon Woman," "Angels" (Reprise), "I Was Here," "Armanda's Sack," "The Comedy of Love."

Presented without intermission.

VIRGINIA

Signature Theatre, Arlington

Eric Schaeffer artistic director, Sam Sweet managing director

CRAVE. By Sarah Kane. February 4, 2007. Direction, Jeremy Skidmore; scenery, Tony Cisek; costumes, Kate Turner-Walker; lighting, Dan Covey; sound, Mark K. Anduss; stage management, Roy A. Gross.

A	John Lescault	C	Kathleen Coons
B	Joe Isenberg	M	Deborah Hazlett

SAVING AIMEE. Musical with book and lyrics by Kathie Lee Gifford; music by David Pomeranz and David Friedman. April 22, 2006 (world premiere). Direction, Eric Schaeffer; choreography, Christopher d'Amboise; scenery, Walt Spangler; costumes, Anne Kennedy; lighting, Chris Lee; sound, Robert Kaplowitz; projections, Michael Clark; music direction, Michael Rice; orchestrations, Michael Coughlin; stage management, Kerry Epstein. Presented in association with Lambchop Productions.

Asa Keyes	Andrew Long	Robert Semple	Steve Wilson
Aimee S. McPherson	Carolee Carmello	Dr. Samuels	Harry A. Winter
Emma Jo Schaeffer	E. Faye Butler	Mac McPherson	Adam Monley
Minnie Kennedy	Florence Lacey	Rolph	Michael Bannigan
James Kennedy	Ed Dixon	Roberta	Corrieanne Stein

Ensemble: Doug Bowles, Priscilla Cuellar, James Gardiner, Evan Hoffmann, Jennifer Irons, Carrie A. Johnson, Diego Prieto, Tammy Roberts, Margo Seibert.

Musical numbers included: "Stand Up!," "For Such a Time as This," "Why Can't I?," "He Will Be My Home," "That Sweet Lassie From Cork," "Come Whatever May," "I Will Love You That Way," "Follow Me!," "A Girl's Gotta Do What a Girl's Gotta Do," "Why Can't I Just Be a Woman?," "God Will Provide," "Adam and Eve," "Sampson and Delilah," "Let My People Go!," "Saving Aimee," "The Silent, Sorrowful Shadows," "Demon in a Dress," "Emma Jo's Lament," "Lost or Found," "Paying the Price," "I Had a Fire."

Presented in two parts.

NEST. By Bathsheba Doran. April 29, 2007 (world premiere). Direction, Joe Calarco; scenery, James Kronzer; costumes, Kate Turner-Walker; lighting, Chris Lee; sound, Matthew M. Nielson; stage management, Katherine C. Mielke.

Joe	Michael Grew	Daniel Boone	Richard Pelzman
Elizabeth	Vanessa Lock	Drumble	James Slaughter
Chaplain	Stephen Patrick Martin	Suzanna Cox	Anne Veal
Jacob	Charlie Matthes		

Presented without intermission.

WASHINGTON

ACT Theatre, Seattle
Kurt Beattie artistic director, Susan Trapnell managing director

MITZI'S ABORTION. By Elizabeth Heffron. July 27, 2006 (world premiere). Direction, Kurt Beattie; scenery, Narelle Sissons; costumes, Sarah Nash Gates; lighting, Chris Reay; sound, Dominic CodyKramers; stage management, JR Welden.

Thomas Aquinas	Eric Ray Anderson	Mitzi	Sharia Pierce
Chuck	Sean Cook	Nita	Shelley Reynolds
Vera	Kit Harris	Rudolfo	Richard Ziman
Reckless Mary	Leslie Law		

Intiman Theatre, Seattle
Bartlett Sher artistic director, Laura L. Penn managing director

NATIVE SON. By Richard Wright and Paul Green; adapted by Kent Gash. October 27, 2006. Direction, Mr. Gash; scenery, Edward E. Haynes Jr.; costumes, Frances Kenny; lighting, William H. Grant III; sound, Joseph Swartz; music, Chic Street Man; fight direction, Geoffrey Alm; stage management, Wendiana Walker.

Bigger Thomas	Ato Essandoh	Newsreel Narrator; Max	Richard Kline
Mrs. Thomas; Ernie	Myra Lucretia Taylor	Mr. Dalton	Ken Grantham
Buddy Thomas	Lukas Shadair	Mrs. Dalton	Kimberly King
Vera Thomas; Bessie	Felicia V. Loud	Mary Dalton	Carol Roscoe
Gus; Reverend	Earl Alexander	Jan Erlone; Britten	MJ Sieber

Time: The late 1930s. Place: Various locations in Chicago. Presented without intermission.

Seattle Repertory Theatre
David Esbjornson artistic director, Benjamin Moore managing director

THE GREAT GATSBY. By F. Scott Fitzgerald; adapted by Simon Levy. November 8, 2006. Direction, David Esbjornson; choreography, Seán Curran; scenery, Thomas Lynch; costumes, Jane Greenwood; lighting, Scott Zielinski; sound, Scott Edwards; music, Wayne Barker; fight direction, Geoffrey Alm; stage management, James Latus.

Nick Carraway	Matthew Amendt	Tom Buchanan	Erik Heger
Daisy Buchanan	Heidi Armbruster	Mrs. McKee	Gretchen Krich
Jordan Baker	Cheyenne Casebier	Myrtle Wilson	Kathryn Van Meter
George Wilson	Bradford Farwell	Jay Gatsby	Lorenzo Pisoni
Wolfsheim	Seán G. Griffin	Saxman	David J. Wright III

Ensemble: Justin Alley, Anna-Lisa Carlson, Sabrina Prada, Doug Fahl, Pamela Mijatov, Trick Danneker.

THE LADY FROM DUBUQUE. By Edward Albee. January 17, 2007. Direction, David Esbjornson; scenery, John Arnone; costumes, Elizabeth Hope Clancy; lighting, James F. Ingalls; stage management, Elisabeth Farwell.

Fred	Hans Altwies	Sam	Charlie Matthes
Elizabeth	Myra Carter	Carol	Chelsey Rives
Lucinda	Kristen Flanders	Edgar	Paul Morgan Stetler
Jo	Carla Harting	Oscar	Frank X

MY NAME IS RACHEL CORRIE. By Alan Rickman and Katharine Viner; based on the writings of Rachel Corrie. March 21, 2007. Direction, Braden Abraham; scenery, Jennifer Zeyl; costumes, Harmony J.K. Arnold; lighting, L.B. Morse; sound, Obadiah Eaves; video, Nick Schwartz-Hall; dramaturgy, Kati Sweaney; stage management, Erica Schwartz and Jessica Bomball.

Rachel Corrie .... Marya Sea Kaminiski

Presented without intermission.

FACTS AND
FIGURES

LONG RUNS ON BROADWAY

○ ○ ○ ○ ○

THE FOLLOWING SHOWS have run 500 or more continuous performances in a single production, usually the first, not including previews or extra nonprofit performances, allowing for vacation layoffs and special one-booking engagements, but not including return engagements after a show has gone on tour. In all cases, the numbers were obtained directly from the show's production offices. Where there are title similarities, the production is identified as follows: (p) straight play version, (m) musical version, (r) revival, (tr) transfer.

THROUGH MAY 31, 2007

PLAYS MARKED WITH ASTERISK WERE STILL PLAYING JUNE 1, 2007

Plays	Performances
*The Phantom of the Opera	8,065
Cats	7,485
Les Misérables	6,680
A Chorus Line	6,137
Oh! Calcutta! (r)	5,959
*Beauty and the Beast	5,393
*Rent	4,612
*Chicago (m)(r)	4,390
Miss Saigon	4,097
*The Lion King	3,974
42nd Street	3,486
Grease	3,388
Fiddler on the Roof	3,242
Life With Father	3,224
Tobacco Road	3,182
Hello, Dolly!	2,844
My Fair Lady	2,717
The Producers	2,502
Annie	2,377
Cabaret (r)	2,377
*Mamma Mia!	2,337
Man of La Mancha	2,328
Abie's Irish Rose	2,327
Oklahoma!	2,212
Smokey Joe's Cafe	2,036
*Hairspray	1,996
Pippin	1,944
South Pacific	1,925
The Magic Show	1,920
Aida	1,852
Deathtrap	1,793
Gemini	1,788
Harvey	1,775

Plays	Performances
Dancin'	1,774
La Cage aux Folles	1,761
Hair	1,750
The Wiz	1,672
Born Yesterday	1,642
The Best Little Whorehouse in Texas	1,639
Crazy for You	1,622
Ain't Misbehavin'	1,604
*Avenue Q	1,599
Mary, Mary	1,572
Evita	1,567
The Voice of the Turtle	1,557
Jekyll & Hyde	1,543
Barefoot in the Park	1,530
Brighton Beach Memoirs	1,530
42nd Street (r)	1,524
Dreamgirls	1,522
Mame (m)	1,508
Grease (r)	1,503
*Wicked	1,496
Same Time, Next Year	1,453
Arsenic and Old Lace	1,444
The Sound of Music	1,443
Me and My Girl	1,420
How to Succeed in Business Without Really Trying	1,417
Hellzapoppin'	1,404
The Music Man	1,375
Funny Girl	1,348
Mummenschanz	1,326
Movin' Out	1,303
Angel Street	1,295
Lightnin'	1,291

Plays	Performances
Promises, Promises	1,281
The King and I	1,246
Cactus Flower	1,234
Sleuth	1,222
Torch Song Trilogy	1,222
1776	1,217
Equus	1,209
Sugar Babies	1,208
Guys and Dolls	1,200
Amadeus	1,181
Cabaret	1,165
Mister Roberts	1,157
Annie Get Your Gun	1,147
Guys and Dolls (r)	1,144
The Seven Year Itch	1,141
Bring in 'da Noise, Bring in 'da Funk	1,130
Butterflies Are Free	1,128
Pins and Needles	1,108
Plaza Suite	1,097
Fosse	1,092
They're Playing Our Song	1,082
Grand Hotel (m)	1,077
Kiss Me, Kate	1,070
Don't Bother Me, I Can't Cope	1,065
The Pajama Game	1,063
Shenandoah	1,050
Annie Get Your Gun (r)	1,046
The Teahouse of the August Moon	1,027
Damn Yankees	1,019
Contact	1,010
Never Too Late	1,007
Big River	1,005
The Will Rogers Follies	983
Any Wednesday	982
Sunset Boulevard	977
The Odd Couple	966
Urinetown	965
A Funny Thing Happened on the Way to the Forum	964
Anna Lucasta	957
Kiss and Tell	956
Show Boat (r)	949
Dracula (r)	925
Bells Are Ringing	924
The Moon Is Blue	924
Beatlemania	920
*Spamalot	920
Proof	917
The Elephant Man	916
Kiss of the Spider Woman	906
Thoroughly Modern Millie	903
Luv	901
The Who's Tommy	900
Chicago (m)	898
Applause	896
Can-Can	892
Carousel	890

Plays	Performances
I'm Not Rappaport	890
Hats Off to Ice	889
Fanny	888
Children of a Lesser God	887
Follow the Girls	882
Kiss Me, Kate (m)(r)	881
City of Angels	878
Camelot	873
I Love My Wife	872
The Bat	867
My Sister Eileen	864
No, No, Nanette (r)	861
Ragtime	861
Song of Norway	860
Chapter Two	857
A Streetcar Named Desire	855
Barnum	854
Comedy in Music	849
Raisin	847
Blood Brothers	839
You Can't Take It With You	837
La Plume de Ma Tante	835
Three Men on a Horse	835
The Subject Was Roses	832
Black and Blue	824
The King and I (r)	807
Inherit the Wind	806
Anything Goes (r)	804
Titanic	804
No Time for Sergeants	796
Fiorello!	795
Where's Charley?	792
The Ladder	789
Fiddler on the Roof (r, 4)	781
Forty Carats	780
Lost in Yonkers	780
The Prisoner of Second Avenue	780
M. Butterfly	777
The Tale of the Allergist's Wife	777
Oliver!	774
The Pirates of Penzance (1980 r)	772
The Full Monty	770
Woman of the Year	770
My One and Only	767
Sophisticated Ladies	767
Bubbling Brown Sugar	766
Into the Woods	765
State of the Union	765
Starlight Express	761
The First Year	760
Broadway Bound	756
You Know I Can't Hear You When the Water's Running	755
Two for the Seesaw	750
Joseph and the Amazing Technicolor Dreamcoat (r)	747
Death of a Salesman	742

Plays	Performances
For Colored Girls . . .	742
Sons o' Fun	742
Candide (m, r)	740
Gentlemen Prefer Blondes	740
The Man Who Came to Dinner	739
Nine	739
Call Me Mister	734
Victor/Victoria	734
West Side Story	732
High Button Shoes	727
Finian's Rainbow	725
Claudia	722
The Gold Diggers	720
Jesus Christ Superstar	720
Carnival	719
The Diary of Anne Frank	717
A Funny Thing Happened on the Way to the Forum (r)	715
I Remember Mama	714
Tea and Sympathy	712
Junior Miss	710
Footloose	708
Last of the Red Hot Lovers	706
The Secret Garden	706
Company	705
Seventh Heaven	704
Gypsy (m)	702
The Miracle Worker	700
That Championship Season	700
The Music Man (m)(r)	698
Da	697
Cat on a Hot Tin Roof	694
Li'l Abner	693
The Children's Hour	691
Purlie	688
Dead End	687
The Lion and the Mouse	686
White Cargo	686
Dear Ruth	683
East Is West	680
Come Blow Your Horn	677
The Most Happy Fella	676
Defending the Caveman	671
The Doughgirls	671
The Impossible Years	670
Irene	670
Boy Meets Girl	669
The Tap Dance Kid	669
Beyond the Fringe	667
Who's Afraid of Virginia Woolf?	664
Blithe Spirit	657
A Trip to Chinatown	657
The Women	657
Bloomer Girl	654
The Fifth Season	654
*Jersey Boys	653
Rain	648

Plays	Performances
Witness for the Prosecution	645
Call Me Madam	644
Janie	642
The Green Pastures	640
Auntie Mame (p)	639
A Man for All Seasons	637
Jerome Robbins' Broadway	634
The Fourposter	632
Dirty Rotten Scoundrels	627
The Music Master	627
*The Color Purple	623
The Tenth Man	623
The Heidi Chronicles	621
Is Zat So?	618
Anniversary Waltz	615
The Happy Time (p)	614
Two Gentlemen of Verona (m)	614
Separate Rooms	613
Affairs of State	610
Oh! Calcutta! (tr)	610
Star and Garter	609
The Mystery of Edwin Drood	608
The Student Prince	608
Sweet Charity	608
Bye Bye Birdie	607
Riverdance on Broadway	605
Irene (r)	604
Sunday in the Park With George	604
Adonis	603
Broadway	603
Peg o' My Heart	603
Master Class	601
Street Scene (p)	601
Flower Drum Song	600
Kiki	600
A Little Night Music	600
Art	600
Agnes of God	599
Don't Drink the Water	598
Wish You Were Here	598
Sarafina!	597
A Society Circus	596
Absurd Person Singular	591
A Day in Hollywood/ A Night in the Ukraine	588
The Me Nobody Knows	586
The Two Mrs. Carrolls	585
Kismet (m)	583
Gypsy (m, r)	582
Brigadoon	581
Detective Story	581
No Strings	580
Brother Rat	577
Blossom Time	576
Pump Boys and Dinettes	573
Show Boat	572
The Show-Off	571

Plays	*Performances*
Sally	570
Jelly's Last Jam	569
Golden Boy (m)	568
One Touch of Venus	567
The Real Thing	566
Happy Birthday	564
Look Homeward, Angel	564
Morning's at Seven (r)	564
The Glass Menagerie	563
I Do! I Do!	560
Wonderful Town	559
The Last Night of Ballyhoo	557
Rose Marie	557
Strictly Dishonorable	557
Sweeney Todd	557
The Great White Hope	556
A Majority of One	556
The Sisters Rosensweig	556
Sunrise at Campobello	556
Toys in the Attic	556
Jamaica	555
Stop the World—I Want to Get Off	555
Florodora	553
Noises Off	553
Ziegfeld Follies (1943)	553
Dial "M" for Murder	552
Good News	551
Peter Pan (r)	551
How to Succeed in Business Without Really Trying (r)	548
Let's Face It	547
Milk and Honey	543
Within the Law	541
Pal Joey (r)	540
The Sound of Music (r)	540
What Makes Sammy Run?	540
The Sunshine Boys	538
What a Life	538
Crimes of the Heart	535
Damn Yankees (r)	533

Plays	*Performances*
The Unsinkable Molly Brown	532
The Red Mill (r)	531
Rumors	531
A Raisin in the Sun	530
Godspell (tr)	527
Fences	526
The Solid Gold Cadillac	526
Doubt, a Parable	525
Biloxi Blues	524
Irma La Douce	524
The Boomerang	522
Follies	522
Rosalinda	521
The Best Man	520
Chauve-Souris	520
Blackbirds of 1928	518
The Gin Game	517
Side Man	517
Sunny	517
Victoria Regina	517
Fifth of July	511
Half a Sixpence	511
The Vagabond King	511
The New Moon	509
The World of Suzie Wong	508
The Rothschilds	507
On Your Toes (r)	505
Sugar	505
The Light in the Piazza	504
Shuffle Along	504
Up in Central Park	504
Carmen Jones	503
Saturday Night Fever	502
The Member of the Wedding	501
Panama Hattie	501
Personal Appearance	501
Bird in Hand	500
Room Service	500
Sailor, Beware!	500
Tomorrow the World	500

LONG RUNS OFF BROADWAY

Plays	Performances
The Fantasticks	17,162
*Tubes	8,241
*Perfect Crime	8,191
*Stomp	5,579
Tony 'n' Tina's Wedding	4,914
*I Love You, You're Perfect, Now Change	4,517
Nunsense	3,672
The Threepenny Opera	2,611
*Naked Boys Singing!	2,554
De La Guarda	2,473
Forbidden Broadway 1982–87	2,332
Little Shop of Horrors	2,209
Godspell	2,124
Vampire Lesbians of Sodom	2,024
Jacques Brel	1,847
Forever Plaid	1,811
Vanities	1,785
Menopause: The Musical	1,724
You're a Good Man, Charlie Brown	1,597
The Donkey Show	1,488
The Blacks	1,408
The Vagina Monologues	1,381
One Mo' Time	1,372
Grandma Sylvia's Funeral	1,360
Let My People Come	1,327
Late Nite Catechism	1,268
Driving Miss Daisy	1,195
The Hot l Baltimore	1,166
I'm Getting My Act Together and Taking It on the Road	1,165
Little Mary Sunshine	1,143
Steel Magnolias	1,126
El Grande de Coca-Cola	1,114
The Proposition	1,109
Our Sinatra	1,096
Beau Jest	1,069
Jewtopia	1,052
Tamara	1,036
One Flew Over the Cuckoo's Nest (r)	1,025
Slava's Snowshow	1,004
The Boys in the Band	1,000
Fool for Love	1,000
Other People's Money	990
Forbidden Broadway: 20th Anniversary Celebration	983
Cloud 9	971
Secrets Every Smart Traveler Should Know	953
Sister Mary Ignatius Explains It All for You & The Actor's Nightmare	947
*Altar Boyz	939
Your Own Thing	933
Curley McDimple	931

Plays	Performances
Leave It to Jane (r)	928
Hedwig and the Angry Inch	857
Forbidden Broadway Strikes Back	850
When Pigs Fly	840
The Mad Show	871
Scrambled Feet	831
The Effect of Gamma Rays on Man-in-the-Moon Marigolds	819
Forbidden Broadway: Special Victims Unit	816
Over the River and Through the Woods	800
A View From the Bridge (r)	780
The Boy Friend (r)	763
True West	762
Forbidden Broadway Cleans Up Its Act!	754
Isn't It Romantic	733
Dime a Dozen	728
The Pocket Watch	725
The Connection	722
The Passion of Dracula	714
Love, Janis	713
Adaptation & Next	707
Oh! Calcutta!	704
Scuba Duba	692
The Foreigner	686
The Knack	685
Fully Committed	675
The Club	674
The Balcony	672
Penn & Teller	666
Dinner With Friends	654
America Hurrah	634
Cookin'	632
Oil City Symphony	626
The Countess	618
The Exonerated	608
Drumstruck	607
Hogan's Goat	607
Beehive	600
Criss Angel Mindfreak	600
The Trojan Women	600
The Syringa Tree	586
The Dining Room	583
Krapp's Last Tape & The Zoo Story	582
Three Tall Women	582
The Dumbwaiter & The Collection	578
Forbidden Broadway 1990	576
Dames at Sea	575
The Crucible (r)	571
The Iceman Cometh (r)	565
Forbidden Broadway 2001: A Spoof Odyssey	552

NEW YORK DRAMA CRITICS' CIRCLE
1935–1936 TO 2006–2007

○ ○ ○ ○ ○

L ISTED BELOW ARE the New York Drama Critics' Circle Awards from 1935–1936 through 2006–2007 classified as follows: (1) Best American Play, (2) Best Foreign Play, (3) Best Musical, (4) Best, Regardless of Category (this category was established by new voting rules in 1962–63 and did not exist prior to that year).

1935–36 (1) *Winterset*

1936–37 (1) *High Tor*

1937–38 (1) *Of Mice and Men*, (2) *Shadow and Substance*

1938–39 (1) No award, (2) *The White Steed*

1939–40 (1) *The Time of Your Life*

1940–41 (1) *Watch on the Rhine*, (2) *The Corn Is Green*

1941–42 (1) No award, (2) *Blithe Spirit*

1942–43 (1) *The Patriots*

1943–44 (2) *Jacobowsky and the Colonel*

1944–45 (1) *The Glass Menagerie*

1945–46 (3) *Carousel*

1946–47 (1) *All My Sons*, (2) *No Exit*, (3) *Brigadoon*

1947–48 (1) *A Streetcar Named Desire*, (2) *The Winslow Boy*

1948–49 (1) *Death of a Salesman*, (2) *The Madwoman of Chaillot*, (3) *South Pacific*

1949–50 (1) *The Member of the Wedding*, (2) *The Cocktail Party*, (3) *The Consul*

1950–51 (1) *Darkness at Noon*, (2) *The Lady's Not for Burning*, (3) *Guys and Dolls*

1951–52 (1) *I Am a Camera*, (2) *Venus Observed*, (3) *Pal Joey* (Special citation to *Don Juan in Hell*)

1952–53 (1) *Picnic*, (2) *The Love of Four Colonels*, (3) *Wonderful Town*

1953–54 (1) *The Teahouse of the August Moon*, (2) *Ondine*, (3) *The Golden Apple*

1954–55 (1) *Cat on a Hot Tin Roof*, (2) *Witness for the Prosecution*, (3) *The Saint of Bleecker Street*

1955–56 (1) *The Diary of Anne Frank*, (2) *Tiger at the Gates*, (3) *My Fair Lady*

1956–57 (1) *Long Day's Journey Into Night*, (2) *The Waltz of the Toreadors*, (3) *The Most Happy Fella*

1957–58 (1) *Look Homeward, Angel*, (2) *Look Back in Anger*, (3) *The Music Man*

1958–59 (1) *A Raisin in the Sun*, (2) *The Visit*, (3) *La Plume de Ma Tante*

1959–60 (1) *Toys in the Attic*, (2) *Five Finger Exercise*, (3) *Fiorello!*

1960–61 (1) *All the Way Home*, (2) *A Taste of Honey*, (3) *Carnival*

1961–62 (1) *The Night of the Iguana*, (2) *A Man for All Seasons*, (3) *How to Succeed in Business Without Really Trying*

1962–63 (4) *Who's Afraid of Virginia Woolf?* (Special citation to *Beyond the Fringe*)

1963–64 (4) *Luther*, (3) *Hello, Dolly!* (Special citation to *The Trojan Women*)

1964–65 (4) *The Subject Was Roses*, (3) *Fiddler on the Roof*

1965–66 (4) *The Persecution and Assassination of Marat as Performed by the Inmates of the Asylum of Charenton Under the Direction of the Marquis de Sade*, (3) *Man of La Mancha*

1966–67 (4) *The Homecoming*, (3) *Cabaret*

1967–68 (4) *Rosencrantz and Guildenstern Are Dead*, (3) *Your Own Thing*

1968–69 (4) *The Great White Hope*, (3) *1776*

1969–70 (4) *Borstal Boy*, (1) *The Effect of Gamma Rays on Man-in-the-Moon Marigolds*, (3) *Company*

1970–71 (4) *Home*, (1) *The House of Blue Leaves*, (3) *Follies*

1971–72 (4) *That Championship Season*, (2) *The Screens* (3) *Two Gentlemen of Verona* (Special citations to *Sticks and Bones* and *Old Times*)

1972–73 (4) *The Changing Room*, (1) *The Hot l Baltimore*, (3) *A Little Night Music*

1973–74 (4) *The Contractor*, (1) *Short Eyes*, (3) *Candide*

1974–75 (4) *Equus* (1) *The Taking of Miss Janie*, (3) *A Chorus Line*

1975–76 (4) *Travesties*, (1) *Streamers*, (3) *Pacific Overtures*

1976–77 (4) *Otherwise Engaged*, (1) *American Buffalo*, (3) *Annie*

1977–78 (4) *Da*, (3) *Ain't Misbehavin'*

1978–79 (4) *The Elephant Man*, (3) *Sweeney Todd, the Demon Barber of Fleet Street*

1979–80 (4) *Talley's Folly*, (2) *Betrayal*, (3) *Evita* (Special citation to Peter Brook's Le Centre International de Créations Théâtrales for its repertory)

1980–81 (4) *A Lesson From Aloes*, (1) *Crimes of the Heart* (Special citations to *Lena Horne: The Lady and Her Music* and the New York Shakespeare Festival production of *The Pirates of Penzance*)

1981–82 (4) *The Life & Adventures of Nicholas Nickleby*, (1) *A Soldier's Play*

1982–83 (4) *Brighton Beach Memoirs*, (2) *Plenty*, (3) *Little Shop of Horrors* (Special citation to Young Playwrights Festival)

1983–84 (4) *The Real Thing*, (1) *Glengarry Glen Ross*, (3) *Sunday in the Park With George* (Special citation to Samuel Beckett for the body of his work)

1984–85 (4) *Ma Rainey's Black Bottom*

1985–86 (4) *A Lie of the Mind*, (2) *Benefactors* (Special citation to *The Search for Signs of Intelligent Life in the Universe*)

1986–87 (4) *Fences*, (2) *Les Liaisons Dangereuses*, (3) *Les Misérables*

1987–88 (4) *Joe Turner's Come and Gone*, (2) *The Road to Mecca*, (3) *Into the Woods*

1988–89 (4) *The Heidi Chronicles*, (2) *Aristocrats* (Special citation to Bill Irwin for *Largely New York*)

1989–90 (4) *The Piano Lesson*, (2) *Privates on Parade*, (3) *City of Angels*

1990–91 (4) *Six Degrees of Separation*, (2) *Our Country's Good*, (3) *The Will Rogers Follies* (Special citation to Eileen Atkins for her portrayal of Virginia Woolf in *A Room of One's Own*)

1991–92 (4) *Dancing at Lughnasa*, (1) *Two Trains Running*

1992–93 (4) *Angels in America: Millennium Approaches*, (2) *Someone Who'll Watch Over Me*, (3) *Kiss of the Spider Woman*

1993–94 (4) *Three Tall Women* (Special citation to Anna Deavere Smith for her unique contribution to theatrical form)

1994–95 (4) *Arcadia*, (1) *Love! Valour! Compassion!* (Special citation to Signature Theatre Company for outstanding artistic achievement)

1995–96 (4) *Seven Guitars*, (2) *Molly Sweeney*, (3) *Rent*

1996–97 (4) *How I Learned to Drive*, (2) *Skylight*, (3) *Violet* (Special citation to *Chicago*)

1997–98 (4) *Art*, (1) *Pride's Crossing*, (3) *The Lion King* (Special citation to the revival production of *Cabaret*)

1998–99 (4) *Wit*, (3) *Parade*, (2) *Closer* (Special citation to David Hare for his contributions to the 1998–99 theater season: *Amy's View*, *Via Dolorosa* and *The Blue Room*)

1999–00 (4) *Jitney*, (3) *James Joyce's The Dead*, (2) *Copenhagen*

2000–01 (4) *The Invention of Love*, (1) *Proof*, (3) *The Producers*

2001–02 (4) *Edward Albee's The Goat, or Who is Sylvia?* (Special citation to Elaine Stritch for *Elaine Stritch at Liberty*)

2002–03 (4) *Take Me Out*, (2) *Talking Heads*, (3) *Hairspray*

2003–04 (4) *Intimate Apparel* (Special citation to Barbara Cook for her contribution to the musical theater)

2004–05 (4) *Doubt, a Parable*, (2) *The Pillowman*

2005–06 (4) *The History Boys*, (3) *The Drowsy Chaperone*

2006–07 (4) *The Coast of Utopia*, (1) *Radio Golf* (3) *Spring Awakening* (Special citation to the Broadway revival of *Journey's End*)

NEW YORK DRAMA CRITICS' CIRCLE VOTING 2006–2007

Adam Feldman (*Time Out New York*), President

AT ITS MAY 7, 2007, meeting the New York Drama Critics' Circle chose honorees for best play, best American play, best musical and a special citation. The first ballot saw five works receive votes for best play: Tom Stoppard's *The Coast of*

Utopia, August Wilson's *Radio Golf*, David Harrower's *Blackbird*, Peter Morgan's *Frost/Nixon* and Adam Bock's *The Thugs*. Stoppard's play missed a majority on the first ballot by one vote when *The Coast of Utopia* received only 10 of the 20 votes cast. The first play-ballot resulted in the tallies that follow: *The Coast of Utopia* 10 (Clive Barnes, *New York Post*; Melissa Rose Bernardo, *Entertainment Weekly*; Joe Dziemianowicz, *Daily News*; Adam Feldman, *Time Out New York*; Elysa Gardner, *USA Today*; Michael Kuchwara, The Associated Press; David Rooney, *Variety*; David Sheward, *Back Stage*; Terry Teachout, *The Wall Street Journal*; Linda Winer, *Newsday*), *Blackbird* 3 (David Cote, *Time Out New York*; Robert Feldberg, *The Bergen Record*; Frank Scheck, *New York Post*) *Frost/Nixon* 3 (Jacques le Sourd, Gannett Newspapers; John Simon, Bloomberg News; Michael Sommers, Newhouse Newspapers), *Radio Golf* 3 (Michael Feingold, *The Village Voice*; John Heilpern, *The New York Observer*; Jeremy McCarter, *New York*), *The Thugs* 1 (Eric Grode, *New York Sun*). A procedural second ballot determined that an award should be given, so a third, weighted ballot was undertaken.

The third ballot saw more plays added to the mix as second and third choices were included by the voting critics. The 10 who voted for *Coast of Utopia* on the first ballot were joined by Feldberg whose second-place ranking of *Coast of Utopia* helped insure that it would receive enough points to move into the honored position. On that third ballot *Radio Golf* placed second and *Frost/Nixon* third. As a result of the ranked ballot, 11 additional plays were added to the mix: Sarah Ruhl's *The Clean House*, Julia Cho's *Durango*, Christopher Shinn's *Dying City*, Keith Bunin's *The Busy World Is Hushed*, David Hare's *The Vertical Hour*, A.R. Gurney's *Indian Blood*, Nilaja Sun's *No Child . . .*, Daniel Beaty's *Emergence-See*, David Greig's *The American Pilot*, Bruce Norris's *The Pain and the Itch* and Bob Glaudini's *Jack Goes Boating*.

Despite the abstentions of Feldberg, Scheck and Teachout on the first ballot of the best American play category, *Radio Golf* managed to amass 9 votes. By the third ballot, Feldberg and Teachout ranked *Radio Golf* first, Scheck ranked it second and the Wilson play finally won the day. Due to the ranked ballot, four plays not mentioned above were also considered: Neil LaBute's *Wrecks* and *Some Girl(s)*, Theresa Rebeck's *The Scene* and Oren Safdie's *The Last Word*.

In the best musical category, Steven Sater and Duncan Sheik's *Spring Awakening* swamped the competition receiving 17 of 20 votes. The other musical contenders were *LoveMusik* 2 (Simon and Teachout) and *In the Heights* 1 (Feingold).

A special citation was voted to the Broadway revival of R.C. Sherriff's World War I drama, *Journey's End*.

Honorees received their accolades at an Algonquin cocktail party May 14, 2007.

PULITZER PRIZE WINNERS
1916–1917 TO 2006–2007

1916–17 No award
1917–18 *Why Marry?* by Jesse Lynch Williams
1918–19 No award
1919–20 *Beyond the Horizon* by Eugene O'Neill
1920–21 *Miss Lulu Bett* by Zona Gale
1921–22 *Anna Christie* by Eugene O'Neill
1922–23 *Icebound* by Owen Davis
1923–24 *Hell-Bent fer Heaven* by Hatcher Hughes
1924–25 *They Knew What They Wanted* by Sidney Howard
1925–26 *Craig's Wife* by George Kelly
1926–27 *In Abraham's Bosom* by Paul Green
1927–28 *Strange Interlude* by Eugene O'Neill
1928–29 *Street Scene* by Elmer Rice
1929–30 *The Green Pastures* by Marc Connelly
1930–31 *Alison's House* by Susan Glaspell
1931–32 *Of Thee I Sing* by George S. Kaufman, Morrie Ryskind, Ira and George Gershwin
1932–33 *Both Your Houses* by Maxwell Anderson
1933–34 *Men in White* by Sidney Kingsley
1934–35 *The Old Maid* by Zoe Akins
1935–36 *Idiot's Delight* by Robert E. Sherwood
1936–37 *You Can't Take It With You* by Moss Hart and George S. Kaufman
1937–38 *Our Town* by Thornton Wilder
1938–39 *Abe Lincoln in Illinois* by Robert E. Sherwood
1939–40 *The Time of Your Life* by William Saroyan
1940–41 *There Shall Be No Night* by Robert E. Sherwood
1941–42 No award
1942–43 *The Skin of Our Teeth* by Thornton Wilder
1943–44 No award
1944–45 *Harvey* by Mary Chase
1945–46 *State of the Union* by Howard Lindsay and Russel Crouse
1946–47 No award
1947–48 *A Streetcar Named Desire* by Tennessee Williams
1948–49 *Death of a Salesman* by Arthur Miller
1949–50 *South Pacific* by Richard Rodgers, Oscar Hammerstein II and Joshua Logan
1950–51 No award
1951–52 *The Shrike* by Joseph Kramm
1952–53 *Picnic* by William Inge

1953–54 *The Teahouse of the August Moon* by John Patrick
1954–55 *Cat on a Hot Tin Roof* by Tennessee Williams
1955–56 *The Diary of Anne Frank* by Frances Goodrich and Albert Hackett
1956–57 *Long Day's Journey Into Night* by Eugene O'Neill
1957–58 *Look Homeward, Angel* by Ketti Frings
1958–59 *J.B.* by Archibald MacLeish
1959–60 *Fiorello!* by Jerome Weidman, George Abbott, Sheldon Harnick and Jerry Bock
1960–61 *All the Way Home* by Tad Mosel
1961–62 *How to Succeed in Business Without Really Trying* by Abe Burrows, Willie Gilbert, Jack Weinstock and Frank Loesser
1962–63 No award
1963–64 No award
1964–65 *The Subject Was Roses* by Frank D. Gilroy
1965–66 No award
1966–67 *A Delicate Balance* by Edward Albee
1967–68 No award
1968–69 *The Great White Hope* by Howard Sackler
1969–70 *No Place To Be Somebody* by Charles Gordone
1970–71 *The Effect of Gamma Rays on Man-in-the-Moon Marigolds* by Paul Zindel
1971–72 No award
1972–73 *That Championship Season* by Jason Miller
1973–74 No award
1974–75 *Seascape* by Edward Albee
1975–76 *A Chorus Line* by Michael Bennett, James Kirkwood, Nicholas Dante, Marvin Hamlisch and Edward Kleban
1976–77 *The Shadow Box* by Michael Cristofer
1977–78 *The Gin Game* by D.L. Coburn
1978–79 *Buried Child* by Sam Shepard
1979–80 *Talley's Folly* by Lanford Wilson
1980–81 *Crimes of the Heart* by Beth Henley
1981–82 *A Soldier's Play* by Charles Fuller
1982–83 *'night, Mother* by Marsha Norman
1983–84 *Glengarry Glen Ross* by David Mamet
1984–85 *Sunday in the Park With George* by James Lapine and Stephen Sondheim
1985–86 No award

1986–87   *Fences* by August Wilson
1987–88   *Driving Miss Daisy* by Alfred Uhry
1988–89   *The Heidi Chronicles* by Wendy Wasserstein
1989–90   *The Piano Lesson* by August Wilson
1990–91   *Lost in Yonkers* by Neil Simon
1991–92   *The Kentucky Cycle* by Robert Schenkkan
1992–93   *Angels in America: Millennium Approaches* by Tony Kushner
1993–94   *Three Tall Women* by Edward Albee
1994–95   *The Young Man From Atlanta* by Horton Foote
1995–96   *Rent* by Jonathan Larson
1996–97   No award

1997–98   *How I Learned to Drive* by Paula Vogel
1998–99   *Wit* by Margaret Edson
1999–00   *Dinner With Friends* by Donald Margulies
2000–01   *Proof* by David Auburn
2001–02   *Topdog/Underdog* by Suzan-Lori Parks
2002–03   *Anna in the Tropics* by Nilo Cruz
2003–04   *I Am My Own Wife* by Doug Wright
2004–05   *Doubt, a Parable* by John Patrick Shanley
2005–06   No Award
2006–07   *Rabbit Hole* by David Lindsay-Abaire

2007 TONY AWARDS

○ ○ ○ ○ ○

THE AMERICAN THEATRE WING'S 61st annual Tony Awards, named for Antoinette Perry, are presented in recognition of distinguished achievement in the Broadway theater. The League of American Theatres and Producers (Gerald Schoenfeld, chairman; Charlotte St. Martin, executive director) and the American Theatre Wing (Sondra Gilman, chairman; Doug Leeds, president; Howard Sherman, executive director) present these awards, founded by the Wing in 1947. Legitimate theater productions opening in 39 eligible Broadway theaters during the present Tony season—May 11, 2006 to May 9, 2007—were considered by the Tony Awards Nominating Committee (appointed by the Tony Awards Administration Committee) for the awards in 25 competitive categories. The 2006–2007 Nominating Committee consisted of Victoria Bailey, Joe Benincasa, Susan Birkenhead, Stephen Bogardus, Edward Burbridge, Robert Callely, Ben Cameron, Betty Corwin, John Dias, Mercedes Ellington, Sue Frost, Joanna Gleason, Andrew Jackness, Betty Jacobs, Robert Kamlot, Todd London, Jon Nakagawa, Lynn Nottage, Gilbert Parker, Jonathan Reynolds, Steven Suskin, Jac Venza, Tom Viola and Franklin Weissberg.

The Tony Awards are voted from the list of nominees by members of the theater and journalism professions: the governing boards of the five theater artists' organizations (Actors' Equity Association, the Dramatists' Guild, the Society of Stage Directors and Choreographers, United Scenic Artists and the Casting Society of America), members of the designated first night theater press, the board of directors of the American Theatre Wing and the membership of the League of American Theatres and Producers. Because of fluctuation in these groups, the size of the Tony electorate varies from year to year. For the 2006–2007 season there were 785 qualified Tony voters.

The 2006–2007 nominees follow, with winners in each category listed in **bold face type**.

PLAY (award goes to both author and producer). *The Coast of Utopia* **by Tom Stoppard, produced by Lincoln Center Theater, André Bishop, Bernard Gersten, Bob Boyett**. *Frost/Nixon* by Peter Morgan, produced by Arielle Tepper Madover, Matthew Byam Shaw, Robert Fox, Act Productions, David Binder, Debra Black, Annette Niemtzow, Harlene Freezer, the Weinstein Company, the Donmar Warehouse. *The Little Dog Laughed* by Douglas Carter Beane, produced by Roy Gabay, Susan Dietz, Morris Berchard, Steve Bozeman, Ted Snowdon, Jerry Frankel, Doug Nevin, Jennifer Manocherian, Ina Meibach, Second Stage Theatre, Carole Rothman, Ellen Richard. *Radio Golf* by August Wilson, produced by Jujamcyn Theaters, Margo Lion, Jeffrey Richards, Jerry Frankel, Tamara Tunie, Wendell Pierce, Fran Kirmser, Bunting Management Group, Georgia Frontiere and Open Pictures, Lauren Doll, Steven Greil and the August Wilson Group, Jack Viertel, Gordon Davidson.

MUSICAL (award goes to the producer). *Curtains* produced by Roger Berlind, Roger Horchow, Daryl Roth, Jane Bergère, Ted Hartley, Center Theatre Group. *Grey Gardens* produced by East of Doheny, Staunch Entertainment, Randall L. Wreghitt, Morton Swinsky, Michael Alden, Edwin W. Schloss, Playwrights Horizons. *Mary Poppins* produced by Disney, Cameron Mackintosh. *Spring Awakening* **produced by Ira Pittelman, Tom Hulce, Jeffrey Richards, Jerry Frankel, Atlantic Theater Company, Jeffrey Sine, Freddy DeMann, Max Cooper, Morton Swinsky, Cindy and Jay Gutterman, Joe McGinnis, Judith Ann Abrams, ZenDog Productions, CarJac Prods., Aron Bergson Prods., Jennifer Manocherian, Ted Snowdon, Harold Thau, Terry Schnuck, Cold Spring Productions, Amanda Dubois, Elizabeth Eynon Wetherell, Jennifer Maloney, Tamara Tunie, Joe Cilibrasi, StyleFour Productions**.

BOOK OF A MUSICAL. Rupert Holmes and Peter Stone for *Curtains*. Doug Wright for

Grey Gardens. Heather Hach for *Legally Blonde*. **Steven Sater** for *Spring Awakening*.

ORIGINAL SCORE (music and/or lyrics). John Kander (music) and Fred Ebb, John Kander and Rupert Holmes (lyrics) for *Curtains*. Scott Frankel (music) and Michael Korie (lyrics) for *Grey Gardens*. Laurence O'Keefe and Nell Benjamin (music and lyrics) for *Legally Blonde*. **Duncan Sheik (music)** and **Steven Sater (lyrics)** for *Spring Awakening*.

REVIVAL OF A PLAY (award goes to the producer). *Inherit the Wind* produced by Boyett Ostar Productions, the Shubert Organization, Lawrence Horowitz, Jon Avnet, Ralph Guild, Roy Furman, Debra Black, Daryl Roth, Bill Rollnick, Nancy Ellison Rollnick, Stephanie P. McClelland. *Journey's End* **produced by Boyett Ostar Productions, Stephanie P. McClelland, Bill Rollnick, James D'Orta, Philip Geier**. *Talk Radio* produced by Jeffrey Richards, Jerry Frankel, Jam Theatricals, Francis Finlay, Ronald Frankel, James Fuld Jr., Steve Green, Judith Hansen, Patty Ann Lacerte, James Riley, Mary Lu Roffe, Morton Swinsky, Sheldon Stein, Terri and Timothy Childs, StyleFour Productions, Irving Welzer, Herb Blodgett. *Translations* produced by Manhattan Theatre Club, McCarter Theatre Center, Lynne Meadow, Barry Grove, Emily Mann, Jeffrey Woodward.

REVIVAL OF A MUSICAL. *The Apple Tree* produced by Roundabout Theatre Company, Todd Haimes, Harold Wolpert, Julia C. Levy. *A Chorus Line* produced by Vienna Waits Productions. *Company* **produced by Marc Routh, Richard Frankel, Tom Viertel, Steven Baruch, Ambassador Theatre Group, Tulchin Bartner Productions, Darren Bagert, Cincinnati Playhouse in the Park**. *110 in the Shade* produced by Roundabout Theatre Company, Todd Haimes, Harold Wolpert, Julia C. Levy.

LEADING ACTOR IN A PLAY. Boyd Gaines in *Journey's End*, **Frank Langella** in

Frost/Nixon, Brían F. O'Byrne in *The Coast of Utopia*, Christopher Plummer in *Inherit the Wind*, Liev Schreiber in *Talk Radio*.

LEADING ACTRESS IN A PLAY. Eve Best in *A Moon for the Misbegotten*, Swoosie Kurtz in *Heartbreak House*, Angela Lansbury in *Deuce*, Vanessa Redgrave in *The Year of Magical Thinking*, **Julie White** in *The Little Dog Laughed*.

LEADING ACTOR IN A MUSICAL. Michael Cerveris in *LoveMusik*, Raúl Esparza in *Company*, Jonathan Groff in *Spring Awakening*, Gavin Lee in *Mary Poppins*, **David Hyde Pierce** in *Curtains*.

LEADING ACTRESS IN A MUSICAL. Laura Bell Bundy in *Legally Blonde*, **Christine Ebersole** in *Grey Gardens*, Audra McDonald in *110 in the Shade*, Debra Monk in *Curtains*, Donna Murphy in *LoveMusik*.

FEATURED ACTOR IN A PLAY. Anthony Chisholm in *Radio Golf*, **Billy Crudup** in *The Coast of Utopia*, Ethan Hawke in *The Coast of Utopia*, John Earl Jelks in *Radio Golf*, Stark Sands in *Journey's End*.

FEATURED ACTRESS IN A PLAY. **Jennifer Ehle** in *The Coast of Utopia*, Xanthe Elbrick in *Coram Boy*, Dana Ivey in *Butley*, Jan Maxwell in *Coram Boy*, Martha Plimpton in *The Coast of Utopia*.

FEATURED ACTOR IN A MUSICAL. Brooks Ashmanskas in *Martin Short: Fame Becomes Me*, Christian Borle in *Legally Blonde*, John Cullum in *110 in the Shade*, **John Gallagher Jr.** in *Spring Awakening*, David Pittu in *LoveMusik*.

FEATURED ACTRESS IN A MUSICAL. Charlotte d'Amboise in *A Chorus Line*, Rebecca Luker in *Mary Poppins*, Orfeh in *Legally Blonde*, **Mary Louise Wilson** in *Grey Gardens*, Karen Ziemba in *Curtains*.

SCENIC DESIGN OF A PLAY. **Bob Crowley** and **Scott Pask** for *The Coast of Utopia*, Jonathan Fensom for *Journey's End*, David Gallo for *Radio Golf*, Ti Green and Melly Still for *Coram Boy*.

SCENIC DESIGN OF A MUSICAL. **Bob Crowley** for *Mary Poppins*, Christine Jones for *Spring Awakening*, Anna Louizos for *High Fidelity*, Allen Moyer for *Grey Gardens*.

COSTUME DESIGN OF A PLAY. Ti Green and Melly Still for *Coram Boy*, Jane Greenwood for *Heartbreak House*, Santo Loquasto for *Inherit the Wind*, **Catherine Zuber** for *The Coast of Utopia*.

COSTUME DESIGN OF A MUSICAL. Gregg Barnes for *Legally Blonde*, Bob Crowley for *Mary Poppins*, Susan Hilferty for *Spring Awakening*, **William Ivey Long** for *Grey Gardens*.

LIGHTING DESIGN OF A PLAY. Paule Constable for *Coram Boy*, Brian MacDevitt for *Inherit the Wind*, **Brian MacDevitt**, **Kenneth Posner** and **Natasha Katz** for *The Coast of Utopia*, Jason Taylor for *Journey's End*.

LIGHTING DESIGN OF A MUSICAL. **Kevin Adams** for *Spring Awakening*, Christopher Akerlind for *110 in the Shade*, Howard Harrison for *Mary Poppins*, Peter Kaczorowski for *Grey Gardens*.

DIRECTION OF A PLAY. Michael Grandage for *Frost/Nixon*, David Grindley for *Journey's End*, **Jack O'Brien** for *The Coast of Utopia*, Melly Still for *Coram Boy*.

DIRECTION OF A MUSICAL. John Doyle for *Company*, Scott Ellis for *Curtains*, Michael Greif for *Grey Gardens*, **Michael Mayer** for *Spring Awakening*.

CHOREOGRAPHY. Rob Ashford for *Curtains*, Matthew Bourne and Stephen Mear for *Mary Poppins*, **Bill T. Jones** for *Spring Awakening*, Jerry Mitchell for *Legally Blonde*.

ORCHESTRATIONS. Bruce Coughlin for *Grey Gardens*, **Duncan Sheik** for *Spring Awakening*, Jonathan Tunick for *LoveMusik*, Jonathan Tunick for *110 in the Shade*.

SPECIAL THEATRICAL EVENT. *Jay Johnson: The Two and Only!* **produced** by **Roger Alan Gindi, Stewart F. Lane and Bonnie Comley, Dan Whitten, Herbert Goldsmith Productions, Ken Grossman, Bob and Rhonda Silver, Michael A. Jenkins Dallas Summer Musicals, Inc., Wetrock Entertainment**. *Kiki and Herb: Alive on Broadway* produced by David J. Foster, Jared Geller, Ruth Hendel, Jonathan Reinis, Inc., Billy Zavelson, Jamie Cesa, Anne Strickland Squadron, Jennifer Manocherian, Gary Allen, Melvin Honowitz.

REGIONAL THEATRE. **Alliance Theatre**, Atlanta, Georgia.

TONY AWARD WINNERS, 1947–2007

LISTED BELOW ARE the Antoinette Perry (Tony) Award winners in the catgories of Best Play and Best Musical from the time these awards were established in 1947 until the present.

1947—No play or musical award
1948—*Mister Roberts*; no musical award
1949—*Death of a Salesman*; *Kiss Me, Kate*
1950—*The Cocktail Party*; *South Pacific*
1951—*The Rose Tattoo*; *Guys and Dolls*
1952—*The Fourposter*; *The King and I*
1953—*The Crucible*; *Wonderful Town*
1954—*The Teahouse of the August Moon*; *Kismet*
1955—*The Desperate Hours*; *The Pajama Game*
1956—*The Diary of Anne Frank*; *Damn Yankees*
1957—*Long Day's Journey Into Night*; *My Fair Lady*
1958—*Sunrise at Campobello*; *The Music Man*
1959—*J.B.*; *Redhead*
1960—*The Miracle Worker*; *Fiorello!* and *The Sound of Music* (tie)
1961—*Becket*; *Bye Bye Birdie*
1962—*A Man for All Seasons*; *How to Succeed in Business Without Really Trying*
1963—*Who's Afraid of Virginia Woolf?*; *A Funny Thing Happened on the Way to the Forum*
1964—*Luther*; *Hello, Dolly!*
1965—*The Subject Was Roses*; *Fiddler on the Roof*
1966—*The Persecution and Assassination of Marat as Performed by the Inmates of the Asylum of Charenton Under the Direction of the Marquis de Sade*; *Man of La Mancha*
1967—*The Homecoming*; *Cabaret*
1968—*Rosencrantz and Guildenstern Are Dead*; *Hallelujah, Baby!*

1969—*The Great White Hope*; *1776*
1970—*Borstal Boy*; *Applause*
1971—*Sleuth*; *Company*
1972—*Sticks and Bones*; *Two Gentlemen of Verona*
1973—*That Championship Season*; *A Little Night Music*
1974—*The River Niger*; *Raisin*
1975—*Equus*; *The Wiz*
1976—*Travesties*; *A Chorus Line*
1977—*The Shadow Box*; *Annie*
1978—*Da*; *Ain't Misbehavin'*
1979—*The Elephant Man*; *Sweeney Todd, the Demon Barber of Fleet Street*
1980—*Children of a Lesser God*; *Evita*
1981—*Amadeus*; *42nd Street*
1982—*The Life & Adventures of Nicholas Nickleby*; *Nine*
1983—*Torch Song Trilogy*; *Cats*
1984—*The Real Thing*; *La Cage aux Folles*
1985—*Biloxi Blues*; *Big River*
1986—*I'm Not Rappaport*; *The Mystery of Edwin Drood*
1987—*Fences*; *Les Misérables*
1988—*M. Butterfly*; *The Phantom of the Opera*
1989—*The Heidi Chronicles*; *Jerome Robbins' Broadway*
1990—*The Grapes of Wrath*; *City of Angels*
1991—*Lost in Yonkers*; *The Will Rogers Follies*
1992—*Dancing at Lughnasa*; *Crazy for You*
1993—*Angels in America, Part I: Millennium Approaches*; *Kiss of the Spider Woman*

1994—*Angels in America, Part II: Perestroika*; *Passion*
1995—*Love! Valour! Compassion!*; *Sunset Boulevard*
1996—*Master Class*; *Rent*
1997—*The Last Night of Ballyhoo*; *Titanic*
1998—*Art*; *The Lion King*
1999—*Side Man*; *Fosse*
2000—*Copenhagen*; *Contact*

2001—*Proof*; *The Producers*
2002—*The Goat, or Who is Sylvia*; *Thoroughly Modern Millie*
2003—*Take Me Out*; *Hairspray*
2004—*I Am My Own Wife*; *Avenue Q*
2005—*Doubt, a Parable*; *Monty Python's Spamalot*
2006—*The History Boys*; *Jersey Boys*
2007—*The Coast of Utopia*; *Spring Awakening*

2007 LUCILLE LORTEL AWARDS

○ ○ ○ ○ ○

THE LUCILLE LORTEL AWARDS for outstanding Off Broadway achievement were established in 1985 by a resolution of the League of Off Broadway Theatres and Producers, which administers them and has presented them annually since 1986. Eligible for the 22nd annual awards in 2007 were Off Broadway productions that opened between April 1, 2006 and March 31, 2007.

PLAY. **Stuff Happens** by David Hare.

MUSICAL (tie). **In the Heights**. Book by Quiara Alegría Hudes, music and lyrics by Lin-Manuel Miranda. **Spring Awakening**. Book and lyrics by Steven Sater, music by Duncan Sheik.

SOLO. **No Child . . .** by Nilaja Sun.

REVIVAL. **Two Trains Running** by August Wilson, produced by Signature Theatre Company.

ACTOR. **Peter Francis James** in *Stuff Happens*.

ACTRESS. **Gloria Reuben** in *Stuff Happens*.

FEATURED ACTOR. **Arthur French** in *Two Trains Running*.

FEATURED ACTRESS. **Sherie Rene Scott** in *Landscape of the Body*.

DIRECTION. **Daniel Sullivan** for *Stuff Happens*.

CHOREOGRAPHY. **Andy Blankenbuehler** for *In the Heights*.

SCENERY. **Derek McLane** for *The Voysey Inheritance*.

COSTUMES. **Gregory Gale** for *The Voysey Inheritance*.

LIGHTING. **Kevin Adams** for *Spring Awakening*.

SOUND. **Martin Desjardins** for *columbinus*.

BODY OF WORK. **Classical Theatre of Harlem**.

EDITH OLIVER AWARD. **Rick Sordelet**.

LIFETIME ACHIEVEMENT. **Kevin Kline**.

PLAYWRIGHTS' SIDEWALK INDUCTEE. **Christopher Durang**.

SPECIAL AWARD. **Actors Fund of America**.

LORTEL AWARD WINNERS 1986–2007

LISTED BELOW ARE the Lucille Lortel Award winners in the categories of Outstanding Play and Outstanding Musical from the time these awards were established until the present.

1986—*Woza Africa!*; no musical award

1987—*The Common Pursuit*; no musical award

1988—No play or musical award

1989—*The Cocktail Hour*; no musical award

1990—No play or musical award

1991—*Aristocrats*; *Falsettoland*

1992—*Lips Together, Teeth Apart*; *And the World Goes 'Round*

1993—*The Destiny of Me*; *Forbidden Broadway*

1994—*Three Tall Women*; *Wings*

1995—*Camping With Henry & Tom*; *Jelly Roll!*

1996—*Molly Sweeney*; *Floyd Collins*

1997—*How I Learned to Drive*; *Violet*

1998—*Gross Indecency*, and *The Beauty Queen of Leenane* (tie); no musical award

1999—*Wit*; no musical award

2000—*Dinner With Friends*; *James Joyce's The Dead*

2001—*Proof*; *Bat Boy: The Musical*

2002—*Metamorphoses*; *Urinetown*

2003—*Take Me Out*; *Avenue Q*

2004—*Bug*; *Caroline, or Change*

2005—*Doubt, a Parable*; *The 25th Annual Putnam County Spelling Bee*

2006—*The Lieutenant of Inishmore*; *The Seven*

2007—*Stuff Happens*; *In the Heights, Spring Awakening.*

HAROLD AND MIMI STEINBERG
NEW PLAY AWARD AND CITATIONS

PRINCIPAL CITATIONS AND AMERICAN THEATRE CRITICS
ASSOCIATION NEW PLAY AWARD WINNERS, 1977–2007

○ ○ ○ ○ ○

The American Theatre Critics Association (ATCA) has cited one or more outstanding new plays in United States theater since the 1976–1977 season. The principal honorees have been honored in *The Best Plays Theater Yearbook* since the first year. In 1986 the ATCA New Play Award was given for the first time, along with a $1,000 prize. The award and citations were renamed the American Theatre Critics/Steinberg New Play Award and Citations in 2000 when the Harold and Mimi Steinberg Charitable Trust committed $25,000 per year to the honors. Beginning with the 2006 honors, the awards were renamed the **Harold and Mimi Steinberg/American Theatre Critics Association New Play Award and Citations** to reflect an increased financial commitment of $40,000 per year from the Trust. (See essays on the 2007 Steinberg/ATCA honorees in the Season Around the United States section of this volume.) The award dates were renumbered beginning with the 2000–2001 *Best Plays* volume to correctly reflect the year in which ATCA conferred the honor.

New Play Citations (1977–1985)

1977—*And the Soul Shall Dance* by Wakako Yamauchi
1978—*Getting Out* by Marsha Norman
1979—*Loose Ends* by Michael Weller
1980—*Custer* by Robert E. Ingham
1981—*Chekhov in Yalta* by John Driver and Jeffrey Haddow
1982—*Talking With* by Jane Martin
1983—*Closely Related* by Bruce MacDonald
1984—*Wasted* by Fred Gamel
1985—*Scheherazade* by Marisha Chamberlain

New Play Award (1986–1999)

1986—*Fences* by August Wilson
1987—*A Walk in the Woods* by Lee Blessing
1988—*Heathen Valley* by Romulus Linney
1989—*The Piano Lesson* by August Wilson
1990—*2* by Romulus Linney
1991—*Two Trains Running* by August Wilson
1992—*Could I Have This Dance?* by Doug Haverty
1993—*Children of Paradise: Shooting a Dream* by Steven Epp, Felicity Jones,
    Dominique Serrand and Paul Walsh
1994—*Keely and Du* by Jane Martin
1995—*The Nanjing Race* by Reggie Cheong-Leen
1996—*Amazing Grace* by Michael Cristofer
1997—*Jack and Jill* by Jane Martin
1998—*The Cider House Rules, Part II* by Peter Parnell
1999—*Book of Days* by Lanford Wilson.

ATCA/Steinberg New Play Award and Citations

2000—*Oo-Bla-Dee* by Regina Taylor
    Citation: *Compleat Female Stage Beauty* by Jeffrey Hatcher
    Citation: *Syncopation* by Allan Knee

2001—*Anton in Show Business* by Jane Martin
    Citation: *Big Love* by Charles L. Mee
    Citation: *King Hedley II* by August Wilson

2002—*The Carpetbagger's Children* by Horton Foote
    Citation: *The Action Against Sol Schumann* by Jeffrey Sweet
    Citation: *Joe and Betty* by Murray Mednick

2003—*Anna in the Tropics* by Nilo Cruz
    Citation: *Recent Tragic Events* by Craig Wright
    Citation: *Resurrection Blues* by Arthur Miller

2004—*Intimate Apparel* by Lynn Nottage
    Citation: *Gem of the Ocean* by August Wilson
    Citation: *The Love Song of J. Robert Oppenheimer* by Carson Kreitzer

2005—*Singing Forest* by Craig Lucas
    Citation: *After Ashley* by Gina Gionfriddo
    Citation: *The Clean House* by Sarah Ruhl

2006—*A Body of Water* by Lee Blessing
    Citation: *Radio Golf* by August Wilson
    Citation: *Red Light Winter* by Adam Rapp
2007—*Hunter Gatherers* by Peter Sinn Nachtrieb
    Citation: *Guest Artist* by Jeff Daniels
    Citation: *Opus* by Michael Hollinger

ADDITIONAL PRIZES AND AWARDS 2006–2007

THE FOLLOWING IS a list of major awards for achievement in the theater this season. The names of honorees appear in **bold type**.

2005–2006 GEORGE JEAN NATHAN AWARD. For dramatic criticism. **Charles Isherwood**.

26TH ANNUAL WILLIAM INGE THEATRE FESTIVAL AWARD. For distinguished achievement in American theater. **Jerry Bock** and **Sheldon Harnick**. Otis Guernsey New Voices Award: **J.T. Rogers**. Jerome Lawrence Award: **Jackson R. Bryer**. Peter Stone Award: **Joseph Stein**.

2007 M. ELIZABETH OSBORN AWARD. Presented by the American Theatre Critics Association to an emerging playwright. **Ken LaZebnik** for *Vestibular Sense*.

29TH ANNUAL KENNEDY CENTER HONORS. For distinguished achievement by individuals who have made significant contributions to American culture through the arts. **Andrew Lloyd Webber, Zubin Mehta, Dolly Parton, William "Smokey" Robinson, Steven Spielberg**.

2006 NATIONAL MEDALS OF THE ARTS. For individuals and organizations who have made outstanding contributions to the excellence, growth, support and availability of the arts in the United States, selected by the President from nominees presented by the National Endowment. **William Bolcom, Cyd Charisse, Roy R. DeCarava, Wilhelmina Holladay, Interlochen Center for the Arts, Erich Kunzel, Preservation Hall Jazz Band,** **Gregory Rabassa, Viktor Schreckengost, Ralph Stanley**.

2007 DRAMATISTS' GUILD AWARDS. Elizabeth Hull–Kate Warriner Award: **Steven Sater** and **Duncan Sheik** for *Spring Awakening*. Frederick Loewe Award for Dramatic Composition: **Scott Frankel**. Flora Roberts Award: **Ed Bullins**. Wendy Wasserstein Award: **Linda Ramsey**. Lifetime Achievement: **Horton Foote**.

2007 HENRY HEWES DESIGN AWARDS. For design originating in the US, selected by a committee comprising Jeffrey Eric Jenkins (chairman), David Barbour, Tish Dace, Michael Feingold, Glenda Frank, Mario Fratti, and Joan Ungaro. Scenery: **David Gallo** for *Radio Golf*. Costumes: **Clint Ramos** for *The Madras House*. Lighting: **Kevin Adams** for *Spring Awakening*. Notable effects: **Kevin Cunningham** for the production design of *Losing Something*. Special Achievement Award to the design team of *The Coast of Utopia*: **Angelina Avallone** (makeup), **Mark Bennett** (sound), **Bob Crowley** (scenery), **William Cusick** (projections), **Paul Huntley** (hair and wigs), **Natasha Katz** (lighting), **Brian MacDevitt** (lighting), **Scott Pask** (scenery), **Kenneth Posner** (lighting), **Tom Watson** (hair and wigs), **Catherine Zuber** (costumes).

29TH ANNUAL SUSAN SMITH BLACKBURN PRIZE. For women who have written works of outstanding quality for the English-speaking theater. Special awards: **Lucy Caldwell** for *Leaves*, **Sheila Callaghan** for *Dead City*, **Stella Feehily** for *O Go My Man* and **Abbie Spallen** for *Pumpgirl*.

2006 GEORGE FREEDLEY MEMORIAL AWARD. Recognizing the year's outstanding book in the area of live performance, given by the Theatre Library Association. *The Masks of Anthony and Cleopatra* by **Marvin Rosenberg**. Special jury prizes: *Lady in the Dark: Biography of a Musical* by **Bruce D. McClung** and *Wagner and the Art of Theatre* by **Patrick Carnegy**.

63RD ANNUAL CLARENCE DERWENT AWARDS. Given to a female and a male performer by Actors' Equity Association based on New York work that demonstrates promise. **Leslie Kritzer** and **Lin-Manuel Miranda**.

2007 RICHARD RODGERS AWARDS. For productions and staged readings of musicals in nonprofit theaters, administered by the American Academy of Arts and Letters and selected by a jury including Stephen Sondheim (chairman), Lynn Ahrens, John Guare, Sheldon Harnick, Jeanine Tesori and John Weidman. Staged reading awards: *Calvin Berger* by **Barry Wyner** and *Main-Travelled Roads* by **Paul Libman** and **Dave Hudson**.

73rd ANNUAL DRAMA LEAGUE AWARDS. For distinguished achievement in the American theater. Play: *The Coast of Utopia*. Musical: *Spring Awakening*. Revival of a play: *Journey's End*. Revival of a musical: *Company*. Performance: **Liev Schreiber** in *Talk Radio*. Achievement in musical theater: **John Kander** and **Fred Ebb**. Julia Hansen Award: **Michael Mayer**. Unique contribution to the theater: **Broadway Cares/Equity Fights AIDS**.

2007 NEW DRAMATISTS LIFETIME ACHIEVEMENT AWARD. To an individual who has made an outstanding artistic contribution to the American theater. **Edward Albee**.

2007 *THEATRE WORLD* AWARDS. For outstanding debut performers in Broadway or Off Broadway theater during the 2006–2007 season, selected by a committee including Peter Filichia, Harry Haun, Frank Scheck, Matthew Murray, Michael Sommers, Douglas Watt and Linda Winer. **Fantasia Barrino** for *The Color Purple*, **Eve Best** for *A Moon for the Misbegotten*, **Mary Birdsong** for *Martin Short: Fame Becomes Me*, **Erin Davie** for *Grey Gardens*, **Xanthe Elbrick** for *Coram Boy*, **Johnny Galecki** for *The Little Dog Laughed*, **Jonathan Groff** for *Spring Awakening*, **Gavin Lee** for *Mary Poppins*, **Lin-Manuel Miranda** for *In the Heights*, **Bill Nighy** for *The Vertical Hour*, **Stark Sands** for *Journey's End*, **Nilaja Sun** for *No Child*.

52nd ANNUAL DRAMA DESK AWARDS. For outstanding achievement in the 2006–2007 season, voted by an association of New York drama reporters, editors and critics from nominations made by a committee. New play: *The Coast of Utopia*. New musical: *Spring Awakening*. Revival of a play: *Journey's End*. Revival of a musical: *Company*. Book of a musical: **Rupert Holmes** and **Peter Stone** for *Curtains*. Music: **Duncan Sheik** for *Spring Awakening*. Lyrics: **Steven Sater** for *Spring Awakening*. Music for a play: **Mark Bennett** for *The Coast of Utopia*. Actor in a play: **Frank Langella** in *Frost/Nixon*. Actress in a play: **Eve Best** in *A Moon for the Misbegotten*. Featured actor in a play: **Boyd Gaines** in *Journey's End*. Featured actress in a play: **Martha Plimpton** in *The Coast of Utopia*. Actor in a musical: **Raúl Esparza** in *Company*. Actress in a musical (tie): **Audra McDonald** in *110 in the Shade* and **Donna Murphy** in *LoveMusik*. Featured actor in a musical: **Gavin Lee** in *Mary Poppins*. Featured actress in a musical: **Debra Monk** in *Curtains*. Solo performance: **Vanessa Redgrave** in *The Year of Magical Thinking*. Director of a play: **Jack O'Brien** for *The Coast of Utopia*. Director of a musical: **Michael Mayer** for *Spring Awakening*. Choreography: **Andy Blankenbuehler** for *In the Heights*. Orchestrations (tie): **Mary Mitchell Campbell** for *Company* and **Jonathan Tunick** for *LoveMusik*. Scenery (play): **Bob Crowley** and **Scott Pask** for *The Coast of Utopia*. Scenery (musical): **Bob Crowley** for *Mary Poppins*. Costumes: **Catherine Zuber** for *The Coast of Utopia*. Lighting: **Brian MacDevitt**, **Kenneth Posner** and **Natasha Katz** for *The Coast of Utopia*. Sound: **Gregory Clarke** for *Journey's End*. Unique Theatrical Experience: *Edward Scissorhands*. Career achievement: **John Kander** and **Fred Ebb**. Ensemble performance: The casts of *In the Heights* and *Lebensraum*. Special awards: **Austin Pendleton, Transport Group** and **National Yiddish Theatre Folksbiene**.

57TH ANNUAL OUTER CRITICS' CIRCLE AWARDS. For outstanding achievement in the 2006–2007 season, voted by critics on out-of-town periodicals and media. Broadway play: *The Coast of Utopia*. Off Broadway play: *Indian Blood*. Revival of a play: *Journey's End*. Actor in a play: **Frank Langella** in *Frost/Nixon*. Actress in a play: **Eve Best** in *A Moon for the Misbegotten*. Featured actor in a play: **Boyd Gaines** in *Journey's End*. Featured actress in a play: **Martha Plimpton** in *The Coast of Utopia*. Director of a play: **Jack O'Brien** for *The Coast of Utopia*. Broadway musical: *Spring Awakening*. Score: **Steven Sater** and **Duncan Sheik** for *Spring Awakening*. Off-Broadway musical: *In the Heights*. Revival of a musical: *Company*. Actor in a musical: **Raúl Esparza** in *Company*. Actress in a musical: **Donna Murphy** in *LoveMusik*. Featured actor in a musical: **David Pittu** in *LoveMusik*. Featured actress in a musical: **Karen Ziemba** in *Curtains*. Director of a musical: **Michael Mayer** for *Spring Awakening*. Choreography: **Andy Blankenbuehler** for *In the Heights*. Scenery: **Bob Crowley** and **Scott Pask** for *The Coast of Utopia*. Costumes: **Catherine Zuber** for *The Coast of Utopia*. Lighting:

Brian MacDevitt, **Kenneth Posner** and **Natasha Katz** for *The Coast of Utopia*. Solo performance: **Nilaja Sun** in *No Child*. John Gassner Playwriting Award: **Nilaja Sun** for *No Child*. Special achievement: **Angela Lansbury** and **Marian Seldes**.

52nd ANNUAL *VILLAGE VOICE* OBIE AWARDS. For outstanding achievement in Off and Off Off Broadway theater. Performance: **Donna Lynne Champlin** for *The Dark at the Top of the Stairs*, **Ain Gordon** for *Stories Left to Tell*, **David Greenspan** for *Faust* and *Some Men*, **Nina Hellman** for *Trouble in Paradise*, **Nancy Opel** for *My Deah*, **Roslyn Ruff** for *Seven Guitars*, **James Saito** for *Durango*, **Michael Stuhlbarg** for *The Voysey Inheritance*, **Nilaja Sun** for *No Child*, **Harris Yulin** for *Frank's Home*. Performance (sustained excellence): **Betsy Aidem, Andre De Shields** and **Ron Cephas Jones**. Performance (ensemble): *Tale of 2Cities* (**Winsome Brown, Michael Ray Escamilla, Tracey A. Leigh, Leo Marks, Diane Rodriguez, Ed Vassallo, Heather Woodbury**). Direction: **Lou Bellamy** for *Two Trains Running*, **Anne Kauffman** for *The Thugs*, **Matthew Maguire** for *Abandon*, **Eirik Stubo** for *The Wild Duck*, **Chay Yew** for *Durango*. Playwriting: **Adam Bock** for *The Thugs*. Music (sustained excellence): **Michael Friedman**. Choreography: **Bill T. Jones** for *Spring Awakening*. Music and lyrics: **Lin-Manuel Miranda** for *In the Heights*. Design (sustained excellence): **Beowulf Boritt** (scenery) and **Robert Kaplowitz** (sound). Design (scenery and costumes): **Rae Smith** for *Oliver Twist*.

Special Citations: **Daniel Beaty** for *Emergence-SEE*, **Tim Crouch** for *An Oak Tree*, **Edward Hall** and **Propeller** for *Taming of the Shrew*, **The Living Theatre, Judith Malina** and **Steve Ben Israel** for *The Brig* (**Johnson Anthony, Gene Ardor, Kesh Baggan, Steven Scot Bono, Gary Brackett, Brent Bradley, Brad Burgess, John Kohan, Albert Lamont, Peter Lester, Jeff Nash, Josh Roberts, Bradford Rosenbloom, Jade Rothman, Isaac Scranton, Morteza Tavakoli, Evan**

True, **Antwan Ward**, **Louis Williams**. Ross Wetzsteon Award: **Rattlestick Theater**. Lifetime Achievement: **Alvin Epstein**. Grants: **Peculiar Works Project**, **The Play Company**, **Synapse Productions**, **Transport Group**. Emerging Playwright Grant: **Young Jean Lee**.

17TH ANNUAL CONNECTICUT CRITICS' CIRCLE AWARDS. For outstanding achievement in Connecticut theater during the 2006–2007 season. Production of a play: **Long Wharf Theatre** for *Uncle Vanya*. Production of a musical: **Goodspeed Musicals** for *Singin' in the Rain*. Actress in a play: **Donna Wandrey** in *Murderers*, TheaterWorks. Actor in a play (tie): **Marco Barricelli** in *Uncle Vanya*, Long Wharf Theatre and **James Lecesne** in *I Am My Own Wife*, Hartford Stage. Actress in a musical: **Hollis Resnik** in *Man of La Mancha*, Long Wharf Theatre. Actor in a musical: **Jon Peterson** in *George M. Cohan Tonight!*, Seven Angels Theatre. Direction of a play: **Gordon Edelstein** for *Uncle Vanya*, Long Wharf Theatre. Direction of a musical: **Rob Ruggiero** for *Make Me a Song*, TheaterWorks. Choreography: **Warren Carlyle** for *Pirates of Penzance*, Goodspeed Musicals. Scenery: **Scott Bradley** for *Eurydice*, Yale Repertory Theatre. Costumes: **Angela Wendt** for *Singin' in the Rain*, Goodspeed Musicals. Lighting: **Russell H. Champa** for *Eurydice*, Yale Repertory Theatre. Sound: **David Remedios** for *No Exit*, Hartford Stage. Ensemble performance: **Jackie Burns**, **Amy D. Forbes**, **Billy Johnstone**, **Erin Sousa Stanley** and **Eric Strong** in *A Grand Night for Singing*, Ivoryton Playhouse.

Roadshow: **The Bushnell** for *Spamalot*. Debut award: **Vanessa Kai** in *Far East*, Stamford Theatre Works. Tom Killen Memorial Award: **James Bundy**, Yale Repertory Theatre and Yale School of Drama.

25th ANNUAL ELLIOT NORTON AWARDS. For outstanding contribution to the theater in Boston, voted by a Boston Theater Critics Association Selection Committee comprising Terry Byrne, Carolyn Clay, Iris Fanger, Louise Kennedy, Joyce Kulhawik, Robert Nesti, Ed Siegel and Caldwell Titcomb. Sustained Excellence: **Eugene Lee**. Musical production: *Caroline, or Change*, SpeakEasy Stage Company. Visiting production: *Doubt*, Jon B. Platt. Large resident production: *Mauritius*, Huntington Theatre Company. Midsize resident production: *Miss Witherspoon*, Lyric Stage Company; Small resident production: *A Midsummer Night's Dream*, Boston Theatre Works. Local fringe production: *Stuff Happens*, Zeitgeist Stage Company. Solo performance: **Stan Strickland** in *Coming Up for Air: An AutoJAZZography*, Alliger Arts. Actor (large company): **Michael Aronov** in *Mauritius*, Huntington Theatre Company. Actor (small or midsize company): **Larry Coen** in *The Plexiglass Menagerie*, *Silent Night of the Lambs*, the Gold Dust Orphans; *Miss Witherspoon*, Lyric Stage Company; *The Taming of the Shrew*, Commonwealth Shakespeare Company; *Samurai 7.0: Under Construction*, Beau Jest Moving Theatre. Actress (large company): **Joan MacIntosh** in *Britannicus*, American Repertory Theatre. Actress (small or midsize company): **Paula Plum** in *A Midsummer Night's Dream*, Boston Theatre Works; *Miss Witherspoon*, Lyric Stage Company. Musical performance: **Leigh Barrett** in *Ragtime*, New Repertory Theatre; *Souvenir*, Lyric Stage Company. Director (large company): **Nicholas Martin** for *Love's Labour's Lost*, Huntington Theatre Company. Director (midsize company): **David R. Gammons** for *Titus Andronicus*, Actors' Shakespeare Project. Director (small or fringe company): **Jon Lipsky** for *Coming Up for Air: An AutoJAZZography*, Alliger Arts; *King of the Jews*, Boston Playwrights' Theatre. Design (large company): **Christine Jones** for scenery and **Justin Townsend** for lighting in *The Onion Cellar*, American Repertory Theatre. Design (small or midsize company): **Dewey Dellay** for sound in *Miss Witherspoon*, *9 Parts of Desire*, Lyric Stage

Company; *The Women*, SpeakEasy Stage Company. Twenty-fifth anniversary awards: **Mayor Thomas Menino**, **Robert Woodruff**, **Jon Platt**, **Jon Kimbell**. Special citation: **Harvard Theatre Collection** for its preservation of performing arts memorabilia.

23RD ANNUAL HELEN HAYES AWARDS. In recognition of excellence in Washington, DC, theater, presented by the Washington Theatre Awards Society.

Resident productions—Play: *Measure for Measure*, Folger Theatre. Musical: *Caroline, or Change*, the Studio Theatre. Lead actress, musical: **Julia Nixon** in *Caroline, or Change*, the Studio Theatre. Lead actor, musical: **Will Gartshore** in *Assassins*, Signature Theatre (Virginia). Lead actress, play: **Johanna Day** in *The Rainmaker*, Arena Stage. Lead actor, play: **Andrew Long** in *Frozen*, the Studio Theatre Secondstage. Supporting actress, musical: **Donna Migliaccio** in *Assassins*, Signature Theatre (Virginia). Supporting actor, musical: **Andy Brownstein** in *Assassins*, Signature Theatre (Virginia). Supporting actress, play: **Kate Eastwood Norris** in *A Midsummer Night's Dream*, Folger Theatre. Supporting actor, play: **Philip Goodwin** in *An Enemy of the People*, Shakespeare Theatre Company. Director, play (tie): **Michael Kahn** for *Love's Labour's Lost*, Shakespeare Theatre Company; **Aaron Posner**, *Measure for Measure*, Folger Theatre. Director, musical: **Joe Calarco** for *Assassins*, Signature Theatre (Virginia). Scenery: **James Kronzer** for *The Beaux' Stratagem*, Shakespeare Theatre Company. Costumes: **Catherine Zuber** for *Love's Labour's Lost*, Shakespeare Theatre Company. Lighting: **Charlie Morrison** for *The Elephant Man*, Olney Theatre Center. Sound: **Matthew M. Nielson** for *A Prayer for Owen Meany*, Round House Theatre. Choreography: **Irina Tsikurishvili** for *Frankenstein*, Synetic Theater. Musical direction: **George Fulginiti-Shakar** for *Cabaret*, Arena Stage. Ensemble: *The Resistible Rise of Arturo Ui*, Catalyst Theater Company.

Non-resident productions—Production: *In the Continuum* produced by Woolly Mammoth Theatre Company. Lead actress: **Danai Gurira** in *In the Continuum*, Woolly Mammoth Theatre Company. Lead actor: **David Burnham** in *The Light in the Piazza*, the Kennedy Center. Supporting performer: **Jeff Dumas** in *Spamalot*, the National Theatre.

Charles MacArthur Award for outstanding new play: *Short Order Stories* by **Renee Calarco**, Charter Theatre Company.

38TH ANNUAL JOSEPH JEFFERSON AWARDS. For achievement in Chicago theater during the 2005–2006 season, given by the Jefferson Awards Committee in 28 competitive categories. Of the 51 producing organizations considered during the season under review, 14 companies were honored. Court Theatre led all companies with 10 awards, six of which went to the company's version of *Man of La Mancha*. The awards ceremony was held November 6, 2006 in DePaul University's Meryl Reskin Theatre.

Resident productions—New work (play): *Voyeurs de Venus* by **Lydia R. Diamond**, Chicago Dramatists. New work (musical): *Loving Repeating: A Musical of Gertrude Stein* by and **Frank Galati**, About Face Theatre and the Museum of Contemporary Art. New Adaptation (tie): *The Old Curiosity Shop* by **Raymond Fox**, **Heidi Stillman** and **Laura Eason**, Lookingglass Theatre Company; *A Flea in Her Ear* by **David Ives**, Chicago Shakespeare Theater. Play: *Fences*, Court Theatre. Musical: *Man of La Mancha*, Court Theatre. Revue: *A Marvelous Party: The Noël Coward Celebration*, Northlight Theatre and Geva Theatre Center. Director, play: **Ron OJ Parson** for *Fences*, Court Theatre. Director, musical: **Charles Newell** for *Man of La Mancha*, Court Theatre. Ensemble: *Man of La Mancha*, Court Theatre. Director, revue: **David Ira Goldstein**, *A Marvelous Party: The Noël Coward Celebration*, Northlight Theatre and Geva Theatre Center. Actor in a principal role, play: **A.C. Smith** in *Fences*, Court Theatre. Actress in a principal role, play (tie): **Kirsten Fitzgerald** in *The Sea Horse*, A Red Orchid Theatre; **Jacqueline Williams**, *Fences*, Court Theatre. Actor in a supporting role, play: **Rick Boynton** in *A Flea in Her Ear*, Chicago Shakespeare Theater. Actress in a supporting role, play: **Ella Joyce** in *Crumbs From the Table of Joy*, the Goodman Theatre. Actor in a principal role, musical: **Michael Buchanan** in *Urinetown*, Blue Dog Entertainment LLC. Actress in a principal role, musical: **Cindy Gold** in *Loving Repeating: A Musical of Gertrude Stein*, About Face Theatre and the Museum of Contemporary Art. Actor in a supporting role, musical: **Jeff Kuhl** in *Grand Hotel: The Musical*, Drury Lane Theatre Water Tower Place. Actress in a supporting role, musical: **Barbara Robertson** in *Grand Hotel: The Musical*, Drury Lane Theatre Water Tower Place. Actor in a revue: **Carl Danielsen** in *A Marvelous Party: The Noël Coward Celebration*, Northlight Theatre and Geva Theatre Center. Actress in a revue: **Anna Lauris** in *A Marvelous Party: The Noël Coward Celebration*, Northlight Theatre and Geva Theatre Center. Solo: **Michael Patrick Thornton** in *The Good Thief*, the Gift Theatre. Scenery: **John Culbert** for *Man of La Mancha*, Court Theatre. Costumes: **Mara Blumenfeld** for *A Flea in Her Ear*, Chicago Shakespeare Theater. Lighting: **Mark McCullough** for *Man of La Mancha*, Court Theatre. Sound: **Mikhail Fiksel** and **Andre Pluess** for *Blind Mouth Singing*, Teatro Vista. Choreography: **Brian Loeffler** for *Urinetown*, Blue Dog Entertainment LLC. Musical direction: **Doug Peck** for *Man of La Mancha*, Court Theatre. Original incidental music: **Alaric Jans** and **Lindsay Jones** for *Henry IV, Parts 1 and 2*, Chicago Shakespeare Theater; **Andre Pluess** and **Ben Sussman**, *after the quake*, Steppenwolf Theatre Company. Special award: **Robert Falls** and **Roche Schulfer** honoring their 20-year collaboration at the Goodman Theatre.

34TH ANNUAL JOSEPH JEFFERSON CITATIONS. For outstanding achievement in professional productions during the 2006–2007 season of Chicago-area theaters not operating under union contracts. Production, play (tie): ***Blues for an Alabama Sky***, Eclipse Theatre Company; ***The Sparrow***, House Theatre of Chicago. Production, musical (tie): ***Fiorello!***, TimeLine Theatre Company; ***Side Show***, Bohemian Theatre Ensemble. Ensemble (tie): ***Marathon '33***, Strawdog Theatre Company; *The Sparrow*, House Theatre of Chicago. Director, play (tie): **Nathan Allen** for *The Sparrow*, House Theatre of Chicago; **Steven Fedoruk** for *Blues for an Alabama Sky*, Eclipse Theatre Company. Director, musical or revue (tie): **Nick Bowling** for *Fiorello!*, TimeLine Theatre Company; **Stephen M. Genovese** for *Side Show*, Bohemian Theatre Ensemble. New work (tie): **Chris Mathews**, **Jake Minton** and **Nathan Allen** for *The Sparrow*, House Theatre of Chicago; **David Alan Moore** for *In Times of War*, Stage Left Theatre. New adaptation: **Frances Limoncelli** for *Gaudy Night*, Lifeline Theatre. Actress in a principal role, play (tie): **Michelle Courvais** in *Boy Gets Girl*, Eclipse Theatre Company; **Deborah Hearst** in *Fat Pig*, Profiles Theatre. Actress in a principal role, musical (tie): **Cat Davis** in *Mack and Mabel*, Circle Theatre; **Vanessa Panerosa** and **Andrea Prestinario** for *Side Show*, Bohemian Theatre Ensemble. Actor in a principal role, play: **Peter Oyloe** in *Equus*, Actors Workshop Theatre. Actor in a principal role, musical: **Michael Mahler** in *My Favorite Year*, Bailiwick Repertory Theatre. Actress in a supporting role, play (tie): **Danica Ivancevic** in *Faith Healer*, Uma Productions; **Charlette Speigner** in *Blues for an Alabama Sky*, Eclipse Theatre Company; **Lindsay Weisberg** in *One Fine Day*, Stage Left Theatre. Actress in a supporting role, musical or revue: **Danielle Brothers** in *Flora, the Red Menace*, Theo Ubique Theatre Company and Michael James. Actor in a supporting role, play: **Alfred Kemp** in *Blues for an Alabama Sky*, Eclipse Theatre Company. Actor in a supporting role, musical (tie): **Terry Hamilton** in *Fiorello!*, TimeLine Theatre Company; **Eric Lindahl** in *Side*

Show, Bohemian Theatre Ensemble. Scenery: **Courtney O'Neill** for *Mud*, the Hypocrites. Costumes: **Jesus Perez** for *Mack and Mabel*, Circle Theatre. Lighting: **Jared Moore** for *Angels in America, Part Two: Perestroika*, the Hypocrites and Bailiwick Repertory Theatre. Sound: **Michael Griggs** and **Mikhail Fiksel** for *Angels in America, Part Two: Perestroika*, The Hypocrites and Bailiwick Repertory Theatre. Projections: **Lucas Merino** for *The Sparrow*, the House Theatre of Chicago. Choreography: **Tommy Rapley** for *The Sparrow*, the House Theatre of Chicago. Fight direction: **Matt Hawkins** for *Hatfield and McCoy*, the House Theatre of Chicago. Original incidental music: **Kevin O'Donnell** for *The Sparrow*, the House Theatre of Chicago. Musical direction: **Doug Peck** for *Fiorello!*, TimeLine Theatre Company. Object design: **Object Design Team** for *The Golden Truffle*, Redmoon Theater. Puppet design: **Kass Copeland** for *Once Upon a Time (or the Secret Language of Birds)*, Redmoon Theater.

THE THEATER HALL OF FAME

○ ○ ○ ○ ○

THE THEATER HALL OF FAME was created in 1971 to honor those who have made outstanding contributions to the American theater in a career spanning at least 25 years. Honorees are elected annually by members of the American Theatre Critics Association, members of the Theater Hall of Fame and theater historians. Names of those elected in 2006 and inducted January 29, 2007 appear in **_bold italics_**.

GEORGE ABBOTT	ETHEL BARRYMORE	PETER BROOK
MAUDE ADAMS	JOHN BARRYMORE	JOHN MASON BROWN
VIOLA ADAMS	LIONEL BARRYMORE	ROBERT BRUSTEIN
JACOB ADLER	HOWARD BAY	BILLIE BURKE
STELLA ADLER	NORA BAYES	ABE BURROWS
EDWARD ALBEE	JOHN LEE BEATTY	RICHARD BURTON
THEONI V. ALDREDGE	JULIAN BECK	MRS. PATRICK CAMPBELL
IRA ALDRIDGE	SAMUEL BECKETT	ZOE CALDWELL
JANE ALEXANDER	BRIAN BEDFORD	EDDIE CANTOR
MARY ALICE	S.N. BEHRMAN	LEN CARIOU
WINTHROP AMES	BARBARA BEL GEDDES	MORRIS CARNOVSKY
JUDITH ANDERSON	NORMAN BEL GEDDES	MRS. LESLIE CARTER
MAXWELL ANDERSON	DAVID BELASCO	GOWER CHAMPION
ROBERT ANDERSON	MICHAEL BENNETT	FRANK CHANFRAU
JULIE ANDREWS	RICHARD BENNETT	CAROL CHANNING
MARGARET ANGLIN	ROBERT RUSSELL BENNETT	STOCKARD CHANNING
JEAN ANOUILH	ERIC BENTLEY	RUTH CHATTERTON
HAROLD ARLEN	IRVING BERLIN	PADDY CHAYEFSKY
GEORGE ARLISS	SARAH BERNHARDT	ANTON CHEKHOV
BORIS ARONSON	LEONARD BERNSTEIN	INA CLAIRE
ADELE ASTAIRE	EARL BLACKWELL	BOBBY CLARK
FRED ASTAIRE	KERMIT BLOOMGARDEN	HAROLD CLURMAN
EILEEN ATKINS	JERRY BOCK	LEE J. COBB
BROOKS ATKINSON	RAY BOLGER	RICHARD L. COE
LAUREN BACALL	EDWIN BOOTH	GEORGE M. COHAN
PEARL BAILEY	JUNIUS BRUTUS BOOTH	ALEXANDER H. COHEN
GEORGE BALANCHINE	SHIRLEY BOOTH	JACK COLE
WILLIAM BALL	PHILIP BOSCO	CY COLEMAN
ANNE BANCROFT	DION BOUCICAULT	CONSTANCE COLLIER
TALLULAH BANKHEAD	ALICE BRADY	ALVIN COLT
RICHARD BARR	BERTOLT BRECHT	BETTY COMDEN
PHILIP BARRY	FANNY BRICE	MARC CONNELLY

BARBARA COOK

THOMAS ABTHORPE COOPER

KATHARINE CORNELL

NOEL COWARD

JANE COWL

LOTTA CRABTREE

CHERYL CRAWFORD

HUME CRONYN

RACHEL CROTHERS

RUSSEL CROUSE

CHARLOTTE CUSHMAN

JEAN DALRYMPLE

AUGUSTIN DALY

GRACIELA DANIELE

E.L. DAVENPORT

GORDON DAVIDSON

OSSIE DAVIS

OWEN DAVIS

RUBY DEE

ALFRED DE LIAGRE JR.

AGNES DE MILLE

COLLEEN DEWHURST

HOWARD DIETZ

DUDLEY DIGGES

MELVYN DOUGLAS

EDDIE DOWLING

ALFRED DRAKE

MARIE DRESSLER

JOHN DREW

MRS. JOHN DREW

WILLIAM DUNLAP

MILDRED DUNNOCK

CHARLES DURNING

ELEANORA DUSE

JEANNE EAGELS

FRED EBB

BEN EDWARDS

FLORENCE ELDRIDGE

LEHMAN ENGEL

MAURICE EVANS

ABE FEDER

JOSE FERRER

CY FEUER

ZELDA FICHANDLER

DOROTHY FIELDS

HERBERT FIELDS

LEWIS FIELDS

W.C. FIELDS

JULES FISHER

MINNIE MADDERN FISKE

CLYDE FITCH

GERALDINE FITZGERALD

HENRY FONDA

LYNN FONTANNE

HORTON FOOTE

EDWIN FORREST

BOB FOSSE

BRIAN FRIEL

RUDOLF FRIML

CHARLES FROHMAN

DANIEL FROHMAN

ROBERT FRYER

ATHOL FUGARD

JOHN GASSNER

LARRY GELBART

PETER GENNARO

GRACE GEORGE

GEORGE GERSHWIN

IRA GERSHWIN

BERNARD GERSTEN

WILLIAM GIBSON

JOHN GIELGUD

W.S. GILBERT

JACK GILFORD

WILLIAM GILLETTE

CHARLES GILPIN

LILLIAN GISH

SUSAN GLASPELL

JOHN GOLDEN

MAX GORDON

RUTH GORDON

ADOLPH GREEN

PAUL GREEN

CHARLOTTE GREENWOOD

JANE GREENWOOD

JOEL GREY

TAMMY GRIMES

GEORGE GRIZZARD

JOHN GUARE

OTIS L. GUERNSEY JR.

A.R. GURNEY

TYRONE GUTHRIE

UTA HAGEN

PETER HALL

LEWIS HALLAM

T. EDWARD HAMBLETON

OSCAR HAMMERSTEIN II

WALTER HAMPDEN

OTTO HARBACH

E.Y. HARBURG

SHELDON HARNICK

EDWARD HARRIGAN

JED HARRIS

JULIE HARRIS

ROSEMARY HARRIS

SAM H. HARRIS

REX HARRISON

KITTY CARLISLE HART

LORENZ HART

MOSS HART

TONY HART

JUNE HAVOC

HELEN HAYES

LELAND HAYWARD

GEORGE HEARN

BEN HECHT

EILEEN HECKART

THERESA HELBURN

LILLIAN HELLMAN

KATHARINE HEPBURN

VICTOR HERBERT

JERRY HERMAN

JAMES A. HERNE

Henry Hewes

Gregory Hines

Al Hirschfeld

Raymond Hitchcock

Hal Holbrook

Celeste Holm

Hanya Holm

Arthur Hopkins

De Wolf Hopper

John Houseman

Eugene Howard

Leslie Howard

Sidney Howard

Willie Howard

Barnard Hughes

Henry Hull

Josephine Hull

Walter Huston

Earle Hyman

Henrik Ibsen

William Inge

Bernard B. Jacobs

Elsie Janis

Joseph Jefferson

Al Jolson

James Earl Jones

Margo Jones

Robert Edmond Jones

Tom Jones

Jon Jory

Raul Julia

Madeline Kahn

John Kander

Garson Kanin

George S. Kaufman

Danny Kaye

Elia Kazan

Gene Kelly

George Kelly

Fanny Kemble

Jerome Kern

Walter Kerr

Michael Kidd

Richard Kiley

Willa Kim

Sidney Kingsley

Kevin Kline

Florence Klotz

Joseph Wood Krutch

Bert Lahr

Burton Lane

Frank Langella

Lawrence Langner

Lillie Langtry

Angela Lansbury

Charles Laughton

Arthur Laurents

Gertrude Lawrence

Jerome Lawrence

Eva Le Gallienne

Canada Lee

Eugene Lee

Ming Cho Lee

Robert E. Lee

Lotte Lenya

Alan Jay Lerner

Sam Levene

Robert Lewis

Beatrice Lillie

Howard Lindsay

John Lithgow

Frank Loesser

Frederick Loewe

Joshua Logan

William Ivey Long

Santo Loquasto

Pauline Lord

Lucille Lortel

Dorothy Loudon

Alfred Lunt

Patti LuPone

Charles MacArthur

Steele MacKaye

Judith Malina

David Mamet

Rouben Mamoulian

Richard Mansfield

Robert B. Mantell

Fredric March

Nancy Marchand

Julia Marlowe

Ernest H. Martin

Mary Martin

Raymond Massey

Elizabeth Ireland McCann

Ian McKellen

Siobhan McKenna

Terrence McNally

Sanford Meisner

Helen Menken

Burgess Meredith

Ethel Merman

David Merrick

Jo Mielziner

Arthur Miller

Marilyn Miller

Liza Minnelli

Helena Modjeska

Ferenc Molnar

Lola Montez

Victor Moore

Robert Morse

Zero Mostel

Anna Cora Mowatt

Paul Muni

Brian Murray

Tharon Musser

George Jean Nathan

Mildred Natwick

Alla Nazimova

Patricia Neal

James M. Nederlander

Mike Nichols

Elliot Norton	Diana Sands	Margaret Sullavan
Sean O'Casey	William Saroyan	Arthur Sullivan
Clifford Odets	Joseph Schildkraut	Jessica Tandy
Donald Oenslager	Harvey Schmidt	Laurette Taylor
Laurence Olivier	Alan Schneider	Ellen Terry
Eugene O'Neill	Gerald Schoenfeld	Sada Thompson
Jerry Orbach	Arthur Schwartz	Cleon Throckmorton
Geraldine Page	Maurice Schwartz	Tommy Tune
Joseph Papp	George C. Scott	Gwen Verdon
Estelle Parsons	Marian Seldes	Robin Wagner
Osgood Perkins	Irene Sharaff	Nancy Walker
Bernadette Peters	George Bernard Shaw	Eli Wallach
Molly Picon	Sam Shepard	James Wallack
Harold Pinter	Robert E. Sherwood	Lester Wallack
Luigi Pirandello	J.J. Shubert	Tony Walton
Christopher Plummer	Lee Shubert	Douglas Turner Ward
Cole Porter	Herman Shumlin	David Warfield
Robert Preston	Neil Simon	***Wendy Wasserstein***
Harold Prince	Lee Simonson	Ethel Waters
Jose Quintero	Edmund Simpson	Clifton Webb
Ellis Rabb	Otis Skinner	Joseph Weber
John Raitt	Maggie Smith	Margaret Webster
Tony Randall	Oliver Smith	Kurt Weill
Michael Redgrave	Stephen Sondheim	Orson Welles
Vanessa Redgrave	E.H. Sothern	Mae West
Ada Rehan	Kim Stanley	Robert Whitehead
Elmer Rice	Jean Stapleton	Richard Wilbur
Lloyd Richards	Maureen Stapleton	Oscar Wilde
Ralph Richardson	Frances Sternhagen	Thornton Wilder
Chita Rivera	Roger L. Stevens	Bert Williams
Jason Robards	Isabelle Stevenson	Tennessee Williams
Jerome Robbins	Ellen Stewart	***August Wilson***
Paul Robeson	Dorothy Stickney	***Elizabeth Wilson***
Richard Rodgers	Fred Stone	Lanford Wilson
Will Rogers	Peter Stone	P.G. Wodehouse
Sigmund Romberg	Tom Stoppard	Peggy Wood
Harold Rome	Lee Strasberg	Alexander Woollcott
Billy Rose	August Strindberg	Irene Worth
Lillian Russell	Elaine Stritch	Teresa Wright
Donald Saddler	Charles Strouse	Ed Wynn
Gene Saks	Jule Styne	Vincent Youmans

STARK YOUNG   FLORENZ ZIEGFELD   PATRICIA ZIPPRODT

THE THEATER HALL OF FAME
FOUNDERS AWARD
○ ○ ○ ○ ○

ESTABLISHED IN 1993 in honor of Earl Blackwell, James M. Nederlander, Gerard Oestreicher and Arnold Weissberger, The Theater Hall of Fame Founders Award is voted by the Hall's board of directors to an individual for his or her outstanding contribution to the theater.

1993 JAMES M. NEDERLANDER	1998 EDWARD COLTON	2002 NO AWARD
1994 KITTY CARLISLE HART	1999 NO AWARD	2003 PRICE BERKLEY
1995 HARVEY SABINSON	2000 GERARD OESTREICHER	2004 NO AWARD
1996 HENRY HEWES	2000 ARNOLD WEISSBERGER	2005 DONALD SEAWELL
1997 OTIS L. GUERNSEY JR.	2001 TOM DILLON	2006 NO AWARD

MARGO JONES
CITIZEN OF THE THEATER MEDAL

PRESENTED ANNUALLY TO a citizen of the theater who has made a lifetime commitment to theater in the United States and has demonstrated an understanding and affirmation of the craft of playwriting.

1961 LUCILLE LORTEL

1962 MICHAEL ELLIS

1963 JUDITH R. MARECHAL
GEORGE SAVAGE

1964 RICHARD BARR,
EDWARD ALBEE
CLINTON WILDER
RICHARD A. DUPREY

1965 WYNN HANDMAN
MARSTON BALCH

1966 JON JORY
ARTHUR BALLET

1967 PAUL BAKER
GEORGE C. WHITE

1968 DAVEY MARLIN-JONES

1968 ELLEN STEWART

1969 ADRIAN HALL
EDWARD PARONE

1969 GORDON DAVIDSON

1970 JOSEPH PAPP

1971 ZELDA FICHANDLER

1972 JULES IRVING

1973 DOUGLAS TURNER
WARD

1974 PAUL WEIDNER

1975 ROBERT KALFIN

1976 GORDON DAVIDSON

1977 MARSHALL W. MASON

1978 JON JORY

1979 ELLEN STEWART

1980 JOHN CLARK DONAHUE

1981 LYNNE MEADOW

1982 ANDRE BISHOP

1983 BILL BUSHNELL

1984 GREGORY MOSHER

1985 JOHN LION

1986 LLOYD RICHARDS

1987 GERALD CHAPMAN

1988 NO AWARD

1989 MARGARET GOHEEN

1990 RICHARD COE

1991 OTIS L. GUERNSEY JR.

1992 ABBOT VAN NOSTRAND

1993 HENRY HEWES

1994 JANE ALEXANDER

1995 ROBERT WHITEHEAD

1996 AL HIRSCHFELD

1997 GEORGE C. WHITE

1998 JAMES HOUGHTON

1999 GEORGE KEATHLEY

2000 EILEEN HECKART

2001 MEL GUSSOW

2002 EMILIE S. KILGORE

2003 NO AWARD

2004 CHRISTOPHER DURANG
MARSHA NORMAN

2005 NO AWARD

2006 JEROME LAWRENCE
ROBERT E. LEE

MUSICAL THEATRE HALL OF FAME

THIS ORGANIZATION WAS established at New York University on November 10, 1993.

HAROLD ARLEN

IRVING BERLIN

LEONARD BERNSTEIN

EUBIE BLAKE

ABE BURROWS

GEORGE M. COHAN

DOROTHY FIELDS

GEORGE GERSHWIN

IRA GERSHWIN

OSCAR HAMMERSTEIN II

E.Y. HARBURG

LARRY HART

JEROME KERN

BURTON LANE

ALAN JAY LERNER

FRANK LOESSER

FREDERICK LOEWE

COLE PORTER

ETHEL MERMAN

JEROME ROBBINS

RICHARD RODGERS

HAROLD ROME

IN MEMORIAM
JUNE 2006–MAY 2007

○ ○ ○ ○ ○

PERFORMERS

Albert, Edward (55) – September 22, 2006
Albrecht, Tim (41) – December 9, 2006
Allen, Elizabeth (77) – September 19, 2006
Allyson, June (88) – July 8, 2006
Andrews, Tige (86) – January 27, 2007
Bergere, Lee (88) – January 31, 2007
Bigley, Isabel (80) – September 30, 2006
Blair, Janet (85) – February 19, 2007
Blair, Joyce (73) – August 19, 2006
Boyle, Peter (71) – December 12, 2006
Brown, Ruth (78) – November 17, 2006
Browne, Roscoe Lee (81) – April 11, 2007
Campanella, Frank (87) – December 30, 2006
Carey, Ron (71) – January 16, 2007
Conte, John (90) – September 4, 2006
Conway, Shirl (90) – May 7, 2007
Corley, Pat (76) – September 11, 2006
Cornthwaite, Robert (89) – July 20, 2006
Curnock, Richard (84) – February 6, 2007
DeCarlo, Yvonne (84) – January 8, 2007
Dommartin, Solveig (45) – January 11, 2007
Ebsen, Vilma (96) – March 12, 2007
Ford, Glenn (90) – August 30, 2006
Ford, Larkin (86) – January 13, 2007
George, Lovette (44) – September 6, 2006
Griffin, Victor (88) – February 3, 2007
Hanley, Ellen (80) – February 12, 2007
Hayden, Melissa (83) – August 9, 2006
Hendrickson, Benjamin (55) – July 3, 2006
Hill, Arthur (84) – October 22, 2006
Hughes, Barnard (90) – July 11, 2006
Hutton, Betty (86) – March 11, 2007
Janson, Gene (72) – October 4, 2006
Jay, Tony (73) – August 13, 2006
Jeni, Richard (49) – March 10, 2007
Jones, Griffith (97) – January 30, 2007
Jones, Robert Earl (96) – September 7, 2006
King, Charmion (81) – January 6, 2007
Kirby, Bruno (57) – August 14, 2006
Kirk, Phyllis (79) – October 19, 2006
Kreuger, Kurt (89) – July 12, 2006

Lockhart, Calvin (72) – March 29, 2007
Ludwig, Salem (91) – April 1, 2007
Mako (72) – July 21, 2006
Martin, Alan (62) – April 22, 2007
McDonald, Daniel (46) – February 15, 2007
McNair, Barbara (73) – February 4, 2007
Nelson, Barry (86) – April 7, 2007
Nye, Carrie (69) – July 12, 2006
Owens, Edwin C. (64) – September 16, 2006
Palance, Jack (87) – November 10, 2006
Pinsent, Charmion King (81) – January 6, 2007
Pitoniak, Anne (85) – April 22, 2007
Poston, Tom (85) – April 30, 2007
Pownall, Leon (63) – June 2, 2006
Pugh, Richard Warren (55) – June 9, 2006
Ramos, Richard (65) – October 30, 2006
Raymond, Sid (97) – December 1, 2006
Red Buttons (87) – July 13, 2006
Reilly, Charles Nelson (76) – May 25, 2007
Richardson, Ian (73) – February 9, 2007
Ryder, Mark (85) – July 13, 2006
Saunders, Lanna (65) – March 10, 2007
Sheets, J.C. (53) – February 4, 2007
Shelly, Adrienne (40) – November 1, 2006
Snell, Don (57) – December 2, 2006
St. Paule, Irma (80) – January 9, 2007
Timberlake, Craig (86) – December 31, 2006
Warden, Jack (85) – July 19, 2006
Weston, Eddie (81) – September 6, 2006
Wyatt, Jane (96) – October 20, 2006
Wyler, Gretchen (75) – May 27, 2007

DESIGNERS

Jenkins, George (98) – April 6, 2007
Klotz, Florence (86) – November 1, 2006
Mitchell, Robert D. (77) – August 18, 2006
Murray, Rupert (55) – August 17, 2006
Parry, Chris (54) – January 16, 2007
Stern, Rudi (69) – August 15, 2006

PRODUCERS, DIRECTORS, CHOREOGRAPHERS

Adamson, Eve (67) – October 9, 2006
Altman, Robert (81) – November 21, 2006
Baitzel, Edgar (51) – March 11, 2007
Bolender, Todd (92) – October 12, 2006
Boris, Ruthanna (88) – January 5, 2007
Brolly, Brian (70) – October 28, 2006
Cooperman, Alvin (83) – August 11, 2006
Davis, Montgomery (67) – May 20, 2007
Dempster, Curt (71) – January 19, 2007
Drummond, John (71) – September 6, 2006
Gaines, Leonard (84) – February 15, 2007
Gannon, Ben (54) – January 4, 2007
Hazzard, Robert T. (74) – February 9, 2007
Krantz, Milton (94) – October 11, 2006
LeTang, Henry (91) – April 26, 2007
Lewis, Arthur (89) – June 30, 2006
Nykvist, Sven (83) – September 20, 2006
Pimlott, Steven (52) – February 14, 2007
Richards, Lloyd (87) – June 29, 2006
Sacharow, Lawrence J. (68) – August 14, 2006
Scott, Harold (70) – July 16, 2006
Simonson, Susan Raab (37) – November 27, 2006
Smuin, Michael (68) – April 23, 2007
Spelling, Aaron (83) – June 23, 2006
Wilson, Darlene (45) – March 2, 2007

COMPOSERS, LYRICISTS, SONGWRITERS

Arnold, Malcolm (84) – September 23, 2006
Comden, Betty (89) – November 23, 2006
Daniels, Stan (72) – April 6, 2007
Evans, Ray (92) – February 15, 2007
Grand, Murray (87) – March 7, 2007
Gray, Timothy (79) – March 17, 2007
Grudeff, Marian (79) – November 4, 2006
Svoboda, Karel (68) – January 28, 2007
Prince, Robert (78) – March 4, 2007
Slade, Julian (76) – June 17, 2006

PLAYWRIGHTS

Balzer, George (91) – September 28, 2006
Bishop, John (77) – December 20, 2006
Farrell, Marty (78) – July 19, 2006
Hayes, Joseph (88) – September 11, 2006
Sheldon, Sidney (89) – January 30, 2007
Sundgaard, Arnold (96) – October 22, 2006

MUSICIANS

Barrett, Syd (60) – July 7, 2006
Brown, James (73) – December 25, 2006
Fender, Freddy (69) – October 14, 2006
Laine, Frankie (93) – February 6, 2007
McNair, Barbara (72) – February 4, 2007
Preston, Billy (59) – June 6, 2006

OTHER NOTABLES

Adams, Bret (76) – July 25, 2006
Literary agent
Buchwald, Art (81) – January 17, 2007
Journalist
Colbin, Rod (83) – February 4, 2007
Fencing instructor
Cooperman, Alvin (83) – August 13, 2006
Shuberts' booker and producer
Crane, Aviva (76) – December 12, 2006
Actor, co-founder of Jeff Awards
Douglas, Mike (81) – August 11, 2006
Talk show host and singer
Fennell, Bob (48) – November 12, 2006
Press agent
Froese, Dieter (68) – June 30, 2006
Video artist and editor of *Theatre Talk*
Garfield, Kim (72) – October 31, 2006
Press agent
Gilman, Richard (83) – October 29, 2006
Theater critic and teacher
Harnick, Jay (78) – February 27, 2007
Founder of TheatreWorks/USA
Hart, Kitty Carlisle (96) – April 17, 2007
Actor and arts advocate
Hewes, Henry (89) – July 18, 2006
Theater critic and advocate
Johnson, Judith (69) – October 2, 2006
Australian theater publicist
Kareman, Fred (77) – February 25, 2007
Acting teacher
Mead, Gilbert (76) – May 29, 2007
Philanthropist
Morley, Sheridan (65) – February 16, 2007
Theater critic
Muratalla, G. Eric (35) – September 24, 2006
Broadway company manager
Perry, Margaret (94) – April 8, 2007
Actor, director, daughter of Antoinette Perry

Pietersen, Taliep (56) – December 16, 2006
South African producer and writer
Pincus, Warren (68) – December 31, 2006
Goodspeed casting director
Quinn, Patrick (55) – September 24, 2006
Actors' Equity executive director and
actor
Rosenberg, Ruth (46) – March 2, 2007
Theatrical advertising executive
Rosenstone, Howard (68) – June 7, 2006
Literary agent

Sardi Jr., Vincent (91) – January 4, 2007
Restaurant owner
Shurtleff, Michael (86) – January 28, 2007
Casting director and author
Stanton, Frank (98) – December 24, 2006
Former president of CBS
Webb, Ruth (88) – December 4, 2006
Talent agent
Young, Edgar B. (98) – April 6, 2007
Lincoln Center executive

THE BEST PLAYS AND MAJOR PRIZEWINNERS
1894–2007

○ ○ ○ ○ ○

LISTED IN ALPHABETICAL order below are all works selected as Best Plays in previous volumes of the *Best Plays Theater Yearbook* series, except for the seasons of 1996–1997 through 1999–2000. During those excluded seasons, *Best Plays* honored only major prizewinners and those who received special *Best Plays* citations. Opposite each title is given the volume in which the play is honored, its opening date and its total number of performances. Two separate opening-date and performance-number entries signify two separate engagements when the original production transferred. Plays marked with an asterisk (*) were still playing June 1, 2007 and their numbers of performances were figured through May 31, 2007. Adaptors and translators are indicated by (ad) and (tr), the symbols (b), (m) and (l) stand for the author of the book, music and lyrics in the case of musicals and (c) signifies the credit for the show's conception, (i) for its inspiration. Entries identified as 94–99, 99–09 and 09–19 are late–19th and early–20th century plays from one of the retrospective volumes. 94–95, 95–96, 96–97, 97–98, 98–99 and 99–00 are late–20th century plays.

PLAY	VOLUME	OPENED	PERFS
ABE LINCOLN IN ILLINOIS—Robert E. Sherwood	38–39	Oct. 15, 1938	472
ABRAHAM LINCOLN—John Drinkwater	19–20	Dec. 15, 1919	193
ACCENT ON YOUTH—Samson Raphaelson	34–35	Dec. 25, 1934	229
ADAM AND EVA—Guy Bolton, George Middleton	19–20	Sept. 13, 1919	312
ADAPTATION—Elaine May; and			
NEXT—Terrence McNally	68–69	Feb. 10, 1969	707
AFFAIRS OF STATE—Louis Verneuil	50–51	Sept. 25, 1950	610
AFTER ASHLEY—Gina Gionfriddo	04–05	Feb. 28, 2005	35
AFTER THE FALL—Arthur Miller	63–64	Jan. 23, 1964	208
AFTER THE RAIN—John Bowen	67–68	Oct. 9, 1967	64
AFTER-PLAY—Anne Meara	94–95	Jan. 31, 1995	400
AGNES OF GOD—John Pielmeier	81–82	Mar. 30, 1982	599
AH, WILDERNESS!—Eugene O'Neill	33–34	Oct. 2, 1933	289
AIN'T SUPPOSED TO DIE A NATURAL DEATH—(b, m, l)			
Melvin Van Peebles	71–72	Oct. 20, 1971	325
ALIEN CORN—Sidney Howard	32–33	Feb. 20, 1933	98
Alison's House—Susan Glaspell	30–31	Dec. 1, 1930	41
ALL MY SONS—Arthur Miller	46–47	Jan. 29, 1947	328
ALL IN THE TIMING—David Ives	93–94	Feb. 17, 1994	526
ALL OVER TOWN—Murray Schisgal	74–75	Dec. 29, 1974	233
ALL THE WAY HOME—Tad Mosel, based on			
James Agee's novel *A Death in the Family*	60–61	Nov. 30, 1960	333
ALLEGRO—(b, l) Oscar Hammerstein II,			
(m) Richard Rodgers	47–48	Oct. 10, 1947	315

CONTRIBUTORS TO *BEST PLAYS*

○ ○ ○ ○ ○

Sheryl Arluck worked in healthcare administration, serving as director of continuing medical-education at New York University for more than 10 years, before becoming vice president of a special-events company. After September 11, 2001, she spent a year working with the New York recovery effort. In addition to her duties for *The Best Plays Theater Yearbook*, Arluck is a freelance event planner.

Rue E. Canvin worked at the *New York Herald Tribune*, first as a secretary in the advertising department and then as an editorial assistant in the drama department for 15 years where she worked with the editors and the arts critics until the demise of the newspaper in 1966. She also worked at the *World Journal Tribune* until it closed in 1967. Canvin has served as an assistant editor of *The Best Plays Theater Yearbook* series since 1963. She has also transcribed taped interviews for the Dramatists Guild and Authors League.

David Cote is the theater editor and chief drama critic of *Time Out New York*. He is also a contributing critic on NY1's *On Stage* and has written for *The New York Times, Opera News* and *The Times* of London. Cote blogs at histriomastix.typepad.com. He has written popular companion books to the Broadway shows *Wicked, Jersey Boys* and *Spring Awakening*. A member of the New York Drama Critics' Circle, he is also a librettist and playwright. The short opera, *Fade,* for which he wrote the text, will have its London premiere in fall 2008. Cote also has a play in development commissioned by Gingold Theatrical Group. He received his BA from Bard College in 1992.

Garrett Eisler has written essays and criticism for *The Village Voice, The Journal of American Drama and Theatre, Time Out New York* and *Studies in Musical Theatre*. Since May 2005, he has also been writing The Playgoer, a theater news and commentary blog at playgoer.blogspot.com. Formerly literary manager of Syracuse Stage, Eisler holds an MFA in directing from Boston University and is completing a PhD in theater history at the Graduate Center of the City University of New York. He has taught at New York University, Boston University, Syracuse University and at the Dalton School in Manhattan.

Michael Feingold is chief theater critic of *The Village Voice*, chairman of the Obie Awards committee, and literary advisor to New York's Theatre for a New Audience (TFANA), for which he curates an annual reading series, the Literary Supplement. His numerous translations include the standard versions of Bertolt Brecht and Kurt Weill's works *Happy End, The Threepenny Opera* and *Rise and Fall of the City of Mahagonny*, the last of which was recently broadcast on PBS in a production by the Los Angeles Opera, starring Patti LuPone and Audra MacDonald, directed by John Doyle.

Paul Hardt of Stuart Howard Associates works in casting for theatre, television and film. His casting credits include the national tours of *LEGENDS!* starring Joan Collins and Linda Evans, *On Golden Pond* starring Tom Bosley and Michael Learned, *The Who's Tommy* and *Leader of the Pack*. Stuart Howard Associates cast *I Love You, You're Perfect, Now Change, On Golden Pond* starring James Earl Jones and Leslie Uggams, *The Caine Mutiny Court-Martial, Hot Feet* and the American casting for *A Moon for the Misbegotten*.

George Hatza has been the entertainment editor for the *Reading Eagle* since 1985 and the paper's principal theater critic since 1981. He holds a bachelor's degree in English from Bucknell University and an MFA in theater directing from Boston University. Hatza has been a member of the American Theatre Critics Association since 1989, now serving as vice-chair of its New Play Awards committee, which annually selects the Steinberg/ATCA New Play Awards. He is a member of the New York Drama Desk and has taught at Pennsylvania universities in disciplines that include theater, criticism and fine-arts writing.

Robert Hurwitt is the theater critic for the *San Francisco Chronicle*. He was the theater critic and arts editor for the *East Bay Express* from 1979 until 1992, when he became chief theater critic for the *San Francisco Examiner*, moving to the *Chronicle* in 2000. He was editor of the new-play anthology series *West Coast Plays*, volumes 15–22, and has been awarded the George Jean Nathan Award for Dramatic Criticism.

Charles Isherwood is a theater critic for *The New York Times*. He served as chief theater critic for *Variety* from 1998 to 2004, and worked as a Los Angeles-based critic and editor for the publication beginning in 1993. He has also written about theater for *The Times* of London and contributed arts writing to other publications including the *Advocate* magazine.

John Istel has edited and contributed to a variety of performing arts, general interest and reference publications over the last 20 years including *American Theatre*, *The Atlantic*, *Back Stage*, *Contemporary Playwrights*, *Elle*, *Mother Jones*, *Newsday*, *New York*, *Stagebill* and *The Village Voice*. He has taught at New York University, Medgar Evers College and and currently teaches at New Design High School on Manhattan's Lower East Side.

Jeffrey Eric Jenkins became editor of *The Best Plays Theater Yearbook* series in 2001. Before joining *Best Plays* he served as theater critic, contributor and editor for a wide variety of publications. For most of the past 20 years, he has taught history, literature and performance at New York University, Carnegie Mellon University, the University of Washington and SUNY–Stony Brook. Jenkins received degrees in drama and theater arts from Carnegie Mellon University and San Francisco State University, and has directed more than two dozen productions in professional and educational theaters across the United States. He is a former chairman of the American Theatre Critics Association and now serves on the boards of the Theater Hall of Fame and the American Theatre Wing. He also chairs the Henry Hewes Design Awards, which is supported by the late critic's family and the American Theatre Wing.

Vivian Cary Jenkins spent more than twenty years as a healthcare executive and teacher before becoming an assistant editor for *The Best Plays Theater Yearbook* series. Prior to her career in healthcare, she was a dancer and a Peace Corps volunteer in Honduras.

Chris Jones is the chief theater critic of the *Chicago Tribune*. For many years, he reviewed and reported on the Broadway road for *Variety*. Over the past two decades, his articles on theater and culture have also appeared in *The New York Times*, *American Theatre*, The Washington Post and the *Los Angeles Times*, along with many other newspapers, journals and magazines. He holds a PhD in theater from Ohio State University.

Robert Kamp is the owner of I Can Do That Productions, Inc., a graphic design company in New York City. Prior to starting his own business, Kamp worked for several arts and entertainment publications including *Stagebill* and *City Guide Magazine*. Kamp designed the *Best Plays* logo, and has worked on the book's photos and graphic images since the 2000–2001 edition.

Martin F. Kohn, chief theater critic at the *Detroit Free Press* for nine years, took a buyout in December 2007, just before this edition went to press. He now teaches at Michigan State University and is a freelance writer. Kohn's work has appeared in *American Theatre, Back Stage, Entertainment Weekly, Parents* magazine and *USA Today*. He received the ASCAP-Deems Taylor Award for excellence in music journalism and once won an award for writing about bowling.

Charles McNulty is the chief theater critic of the *Los Angeles Times*. Before joining the *Times*, he was the theater editor of *The Village Voice*, chairman of the Obie Awards and head of Brooklyn College's program in graduate dramaturgy and theater criticism. A long time theater critic for the *Voice*, he was a member of the Obie Award panel for a decade. His writing has appeared in *The New York Times, Variety, Modern Drama, American Theatre* and *Theater*. He serves on the advisory board of Literary Managers and Dramaturgs of the Americas (LMDA). He received his DFA in dramaturgy and dramatic criticism from the Yale School of Drama. He lives in West Hollywood with his partner, Alex Press, their two cats and one dog.

Christopher Rawson has been theater critic and theater editor at the *Pittsburgh Post-Gazette* since 1983. Along with writing local reviews, features, news and columns, he reviews regularly in New York, London and Canada. His BA came from Harvard, his PhD from the University of Washington and his love of theater from his father, actor Richard Hart. Since 1968, he has taught English literature at the University of Pittsburgh, where his subjects include Shakespeare and August Wilson. He coordinates the selection process for the Theater Hall of Fame and is currently chairman of the American Theatre Critics Association.

Alisa Solomon teaches at Columbia University's Graduate School of Journalism, where she directs the MA concentration in Arts and Culture. A longtime theater critic and political and cultural journalist, she has written for *The New York Times*, GuardianAmerica.com, WNYC radio, *The Forward, American Theatre*, nextbook.org, and *The Village Voice*, where she was on the staff for 21 years. Solomon is the author of *Re-Dressing the Canon: Essays on Theater and Gender*, winner of the George Jean Nathan Award for Dramatic Criticism, and co-editor (with Tony Kushner) of *Wrestling With Zion: Progressive Jewish-American Responses to the Israeli-Palestinian Conflict*.

Jennifer Ashley Tepper, originally from Florida, is a graduate of New York University's Tisch School of the Arts. She has worked for the Rodgers and Hammerstein Organization and the York Theatre Company. Tepper was also a research assistant on *The South Pacific Companion* (Fireside, 2008) and *Make 'Em Laugh*, a documentary miniseries for public broadcasting. Tepper created and directed a musical theater showcase at NYU to benefit Broadway Cares/Equity Fights AIDS. She currently assists the creative team of the musical *[title of show]*.

Anne Marie Welsh has been theater critic for the *San Diego Union-Tribune* since 1997. Welsh earned her MA and PhD degrees in English and drama from the University of Rochester. In 1976, she joined the staff of the *Washington Star* where she was dance critic and backup theater critic until the paper's demise. Welsh came to the *San Diego Union* in 1983 serving as the paper's dance critic, second-chair theater critic and arts reporter before assuming her current post. She co-edited *The Longman Anthology of Modern and Contemporary Drama: A Global Perspective* and co-authored *Shakespeare: Script, Stage and Screen*. She has served on the jury for the Pulitzer Prize in drama and is a member of the *Best Plays* editorial board. She is also the proud mother of three sons.

Charles Wright has contributed essays to seven editions of *The Best Plays Theater Yearbook*. His writing has appeared in *Biography Magazine* (for which he was a columnist), *The New Yorker, Stagebill* and TheaterMania.com, among other publications. As a business affairs executive at A&E Television Networks, Wright has been involved in hundreds of hours of nonfiction programming, including *Jesus Camp*, produced by A&E IndieFilms, released by Magnolia Pictures, and nominated for a 2007 Academy Award as Best Documentary Feature. A native of Tennessee and longtime resident of New York City, Wright holds degrees from Vanderbilt, Oxford, and the University of Pennsylvania.

Index

Play titles appear in bold. Asterisks (*) mark titles shortened for the index.
Page numbers in italic indicate essay citations.
Page numbers in bold italic indicate Broadway and Off Broadway listings.
Nouns or numbers in parentheses delineate different entities with similar names.